U0525837

中国特色汉英分类词典系列

中国风土民俗汉英词典

主编 章宜华

图书在版编目(CIP)数据

中国风土民俗汉英词典/章宜华主编；王倩倩等编写.
—北京：商务印书馆，2023
（中国特色汉英分类词典系列）
ISBN 978-7-100-22989-0

Ⅰ.①中… Ⅱ.①章…②王… Ⅲ.①风俗习惯—中国—词典—汉、英　Ⅳ.①K892-61

中国国家版本馆CIP数据核字（2023）第175931号

权利保留，侵权必究。

中国特色汉英分类词典系列
中国风土民俗汉英词典
章宜华　主编
王倩倩　等　编写

商 务 印 书 馆 出 版
（北京王府井大街36号　邮政编码100710）
商 务 印 书 馆 发 行
北京市十月印刷有限公司印刷
ISBN 978-7-100-22989-0

2023年11月第1版	开本 880×1230　1/32
2023年11月北京第1次印刷	印张 17 3/8

定价：110.00元

主　　　编：章宜华

主 要 编 写：章宜华

编 写 人 员：王倩倩　　　唐舒航　　　何宇艳

部 分 参 编：张凯文　　　吴舒莹　　　陈　珊　　　崔仲爻

特色词整理：廖彩宴　　　徐　浩　　　张　弦　　　范宝仪　　　翟佳慧
　　　　　　廖承敏　　　吴慧敏　　　张梦雨　　　王浩东　　　王欢欢
　　　　　　禹　婷　　　何　贝　　　陈　静　　　谢莉颖　　　胡　博
　　　　　　田盛凯　　　高冠鹏　　　胡　惠　　　刘　思　　　罗丽沙
　　　　　　苏海霞

特色词提取：黎思敏　　　阳豆豆　　　杨雅艺　　　李　玲　　　余文涛
　　　　　　张　慧　　　郑　飞　　　邹婷婷　　　刘　燕　　　朱　垚
　　　　　　程佳琳　　　王彬聪　　　蔡佳良　　　王　丽　　　戴　琴
　　　　　　刘　燕　　　李惠贤　　　贺志桢　　　赵天凤　　　于珊珊
　　　　　　车振卿　　　万芳吁　　　李梅梅　　　宁　萍

语料整理：吴婷婷　　　葛小帅　　　张红岩　　　吴　澄　　　盛　蔚
　　　　　　卢念春　　　王　燕　　　成莉铭　　　何　帆　　　潘良发
　　　　　　刘燕菲　　　葛南南　　　刘梦露　　　吉伟琴　　　翟朗维
　　　　　　蒋佩洁　　　熊　怡　　　刘小芹

英 语 审 校：Fraser Sutherland

序

2017年仲秋,商务印书馆英语室主任马浩岚女士来广外调研,在参观词典学研究中心主持的国家社科重点项目"涉华英语语言知识库及应用平台建设研究"的成果时,对涉华英语语料库以及从语料库中提取的中国特色文化词很感兴趣,于是提议在该项目成果的基础上编写《中国特色汉英分类词典》系列。由于我们的前期研究比较扎实,积累的相关语言资源多,很快便得到商务印书馆立项,并纳入了中国出版集团的重点出版规划。

当时之所以申报"涉华英语语言知识库",是因为我们作为高校的外语教师强烈地感受到"涉华英语"或"中国英语"在英语教学、教材编写和词典编纂中的缺位。我国英语学习者众多,仅高校在校学生就有4 000余万人,他们大多学习英语,而英语教学却缺乏原创教材,要么是国外引进,要么是用国外的语言素材编写而成,更缺乏面向中国EFL学习者编写的词典。因此,英语学习主要是域外语言文化的单向输入,即教材、词典和教学内容都来自英美等国家,语言描述的对象和语境都是西方的,教师强调让学生学习地道的英美英语,而学生学到的大多是用英语表达外国事物的技能。然而,绝大多数学生毕业后是立足国内工作的,但却不善于用英语表达本国事物,这直接限制了他们英语能力的发挥。因此,我们想结合"中国英语"(China English)的研究,从语言资源上入手改变目前的这种情况。于是便申报了国家社科基金重点课题,建成了涉华英语语料库和中国特色词英语表达库,以期为英语教学以及教材和词典的编写提供规范的中国特色英语(normative China English),让学生既能较轻松地学会地道的英语,又能够用英语表达国内的事件或事物。同时,这也有利于中国文化的对外传播,向世界阐释中国的作为及其对世界"人类共同体"建设和发展的积极意义,塑造中国的形象。

目前,国内辞书市场上只有几本"汉英新特色词汇(词典)",收词2 000—5 000条,仅提供英语对等词或表达,尚无法满足现实需要。本词典是基于大规模涉华语料库而编写,从中国风土民俗、中国社会生活、中国文史艺术、中国政经法商等四类80多个方面全面收录反映中国文化历史、发展和现实特色词汇,并从其发展历史、使用语域、英语表达、文化内涵和发生地等多方面进行注释和解释。

由于语料库取自多种渠道,因此一个中国特色词,甚至是专名往往都会有多种表达方式。例如,经典汉语特色词汇由于起源较早,英译形式有拉丁字母拼写、威妥玛式和汉语拼音拼写等,还夹杂着港澳的特殊拼写形式;现代的文化特色词也有音译、直译、意译,以及简译、全译等,构成十分复杂。同一个汉语词在不同时期、不同语料来源往往有不同的表述方法,造成"一对多"的现象普遍存在。这给统一和"规范"带来很大的难度。为此,主持人利用英美访学的机会,对特色词的各种英语表达方法进行了问卷调查,又就前期样稿及中国经典特色词部分书面征求了美国汉学家夏洛特·孙(Charlotte Sun)和教育学专家米汉甫的意见,并请加拿大词典专家弗雷泽·萨瑟兰(Fraser Sutherland)审校了全部的前期词条。在综合各方意见的基础上确定以"尊重历史、立足现实、面向未来,描写为主、适当规范"为总原则进行词典的收词和释义,既要重视历史存在,又考虑了当前的语言现实和今后国际语言传播的趋势。在这个总原则下较好地处理了中国特色词多样化英语表达的问题。

当前,无论是国际文化传播和交流,还是"一带一路"之"五通"(政策沟通、设施联通、贸易畅通、资金融通、民心相通),其关键都是语言交流的畅通;而语言的畅通,主要是要消除中国特色词表达和理解的障碍。但从目前的研究来看,我们外宣中特色词的表达仍比较混乱,有些译法经常会出现错误,造成误解和交流障碍,期望这部系列词典的出版有助于解决这些问题。

  该系列词典收词量大(达 4 万余条),涉及的语料来源多,同一汉语词所对应的英语表达多种多样,如何取舍和编排,在处理的系统性和规范性等方面仍有较大的改进空间。这当然也涉及一些需要学术探索的内容,也需要辞书学界同仁来共同探讨和研究。

章宜华

广东外语外贸大学词典学研究中心

外国语言学及应用语言研究中心

2021 年 12 月

前　言

《中国特色汉英分类词典》系列主要是基于大型"涉华英语语料库"编写而成的。首先通过专门的分词和提取软件从语料库中提取中国特色词汇的英语表达,然后人工干预识别,确定英语词表;最后由英语翻译成"地道"的汉语,并把汉语确定为词目词。这种方法与先确立汉语词表然后进行翻译的传统做法有很大的不同。"涉华英语语料库"分为两个子库和一个专题库,子库-I为英语母语者书写或翻译的涉华语料,子库-II是中国媒体和出版社出版的中国人用英语写成或翻译的涉华语料。每一子库又分为在线媒体和纸质媒体两部分。在线部分取自具有广泛影响的报纸和刊物,纸质部分取自有关中国历史、文化、经典,以及社会、政治、经济等书籍。这些资料都出自国内外著名出版社,语言质量可信度比较高。专题库的英语语料主要来源于《中国丛报》(Chinese Repository),是由美部会的传教士裨治文和卫三畏创办和主持编辑,共出版220期1 300余篇文章,其中90%涉及中国当时的语言、地理、自然、风土人情、宗教、文化和社会生活等内容,主要目的一是向西方介绍中国国情,二是做实时报道和评论,故有很多反映中国文化特色的英语表达。

三个子库的总文本数为176 605,字符数为5.829亿,单词数为1.18亿词。这种语料库对于提取普通中国特色英语词(China English for general use)是足够了,但对于编写有关多民族的风土民俗、文化遗产、文史艺术和社会文化等方面的词典则显得有些不足。于是,我们便利用人工关键词索引的方法,对词典所涉及各个领域的英语资料进行了广泛的搜集、梳理、筛选和整理,以补充涉华英语语料库的不足。

由于语料库取自多种渠道、收词的时间跨度长,语料所反映的特色词英语对应表达多而杂乱。针对这种情况,我们编制了详尽的《中国特色汉英分类词典》编写方案。为了解决好中国特色词中的"一对多"的现象,给读者提供客观、准确和"规范"的英语表达,编写组在英美相关大学就特色词翻译方法进行了问卷调查,又把相关稿子交给美国爱达荷大学从事中国儒学研究的夏洛特·孙(Charlotte Sun)教授和伊利诺伊大学华裔教授米汉甫先生审校,在综合各方意见的基础上确定以"尊重历史、立足现实、面向未来,描写为主、适当规范"为词典编纂的总原则。在此基础上又根据各类特色词的特点拟定了约万字的翻译原则,对各种专用名称、旅游景区和景点、国家物质和非物质文化遗产、政府和组织机构名称和中国菜肴等做了具体规定。

为了确保汉语词目的地道性和"习语性"、英语译文的正确性和易解性,我们首先对从英语翻译过来的汉语词目词进行逐条审核,然后从原文语境中弄清其真实含义后进行审定。在实际操作层面上,取自"涉华英语语料库"的英语表达质量上大多比较可靠,只需稍作调整即可;但后面通过网络在相关网站上收集的专题语料质量上不太可靠,特别是一些旅游景区、文化遗产、传统习俗、风土人情方面的词,大多是汉语拼音组成,或是按字面意思逐字翻译而成,大多不能直接采用,需要通过网络逐条查阅其命名的来源和含义后重新翻译。例如,一些地名或景点的名称含有"山""河""湾""湖""潭""滩""沟""峡""岭""龙""凤"等,对确实与指称相关联的要译出其含义,因为它们反映了地名或景点的基本特征;如果仅是个地名,就按其字面音译。对于一些根据典故和经典诗词名篇命名的景点,要考证其诗文的原文含义,归纳其核心寓意,然后进行翻译,例如承德避暑山庄的72景等分别是康熙和乾隆皇帝命名的,其名如诗,其意如画,要译出其精髓绝非易事,都需要逐条考证其命名过程。对于其他特色词,通常会对一些特色鲜明的词采用音译加注释,或音译/直译加意译的方法。为了考察编写的质量,我们把前期初步编好的两万多词条全部交给英语母语词典专家,加拿大的弗雷泽·萨瑟兰(Fraser Sutherland)进行了审核,最后又请了广外高翻学院的余东、张保红和欧阳俊峰教授对部分经典特色词和国家物质/非物质文化遗产的译名等进行复审。在此基础上,确定了我们整个特色词翻译的质量标准。

《中国特色汉英分类词典》系列共收词4万余条,分为中国风土民俗、中国社会生活、中国文史艺术、中国政经法商四部,每部收词1万左右。具体内容如下:

1)中国风土民俗包括:人文地理(含旅游景区)、动植物,节气、节日、节庆,民族生活(含特有茶、酒、饮食等)、民族乐器、民族音乐/戏曲,体育、运动、风俗、习俗(婚丧嫁娶)等。

2)中国社会生活包括:茶、酒、饮食、炊具、陶瓷、布料、服饰、中医、中药、货币、度量;社会展示、社会教育、社会现象、社会关系、社会生活、社会职业、社会团体以及新兴事物等。

3)中国文史艺术包括:历史朝代、历史人物、历史事件、文化遗产,宗教哲学、理论学说、经典名篇、传统文化、传统习惯表达、语言文学史实,书法艺术、乐器音乐、电影戏曲等。

4)中国政经法商包括:国家体制、社会制度,政治、经济、司法、商业、科技、金融;革命运动、社会变革、武器战争,国家机构团体(政府、事业和服务机构)、政治人物及职业等。

每部词典的内容又分两大部分。普通词条放在词典的正文中,提供语域(使用场合)或性质状态、应用范围信息,特色词的英语表达及其文化、百科、语义和属地等解释,以及必要的参见标注等;系统的、"成建制"条目按不同的类别组织在一起,作为词典的附录。两部分内容均按汉语拼音次序编排。

本词典所依据的涉华英语语料库和知识库的建设始于2013年,广外词典学研究中心研究生自2011级到2021级都不同程度地参与了有关语料搜集和特色词提取等工作,特别是2014级、2016级、2017级、2018级研究生作出了比较突出的贡献。值此词典出版之际对他们的工作表示最诚挚的感谢。本系列词典收词多,语言现象十分复杂,尽管制定了详细的编纂体例和翻译原则,也只是挂一漏万,难以周全;词条种类繁多,统一难度大。况且,学无止境,特色词的文化蕴含深邃博奥,需要不断地追寻探索,不能浅尝辄止。切望广大用户帮助发现问题,以利改进与提高。

章宜华

广东外语外贸大学词典学研究中心

外国语言学及应用语言学研究中心

2021 年 12 月

目 录

凡 例		1
正 文		1—355
附录一	国家 AAAA 级旅游景区	356
附录二	国家 AAAAA 级旅游景区	414
附录三	中国国家森林公园	431
附录四	中国国家地质公园、中国国家矿山公园	466
附录五	国家级自然保护区	474
附录六	中国国家湿地公园	489

凡 例

一、词目

1. 选词立目

参照语料库频率统计,结合具体需要进行选词。同一概念有多种表达方式时,选取使用最多、最广泛的为词目词;如果有多个变体都常用的,则分别立目;术语、短语、组织机构名一般收其全称,十分常用的简称可收为副条。对于部分搭配能力强、可生成多种短语的表达结构,酌情抽象出核心句式立为词目。

2. 词目词处理

对于典籍等名称保留书名号,对词目词构成成分有特殊含义的按源文保留引号。对于词目的变体或结构相近的词,如果只是局部变化,则用"[ ]"注释,表示内容替换,不另立条目,如"浪费公共资产[资金]"等。对于词目词的缩写形式或非局部变化的变体,则另立条目。

3. 排序

词目的排列顺序,以词目词的拼音、声调为主,笔画为辅;同音异调的,按声调顺序排列;同音同调而异形的,按笔画数排列;笔画数相同时,按起笔横、竖、撇、点、折顺序排列。词目词首字相同时,则按第二个字排序,以此类推。词目中的字母、数字或省略号也参加排序;书名号和引号不参加排序。

二、语域标签

1. 词典不设置门类词,而是按汉语词目的语言属性和特色词提取的语境设置统一的"域"标注,说明使用范围。

2. 标注内容包括:来源域(不同的民族)、语域(使用场合或领域)、时域(使用的时期)、地域(特定地方或方言),社会域(不同社会团体/阶层用词)、专业领域(各专业门类用词)等。

3. 域标注用尖括号"〈 〉"表示。如果涉及两个及以上的域名时,均放在同一个括号内,中间用逗号","分隔。

4. 时域的划分只分为两类:〈旧〉〈古〉。

三、英语释义

1. 由于本词典是基于涉华英美语言语料库编写的,英语对等表达只需反映语言现实,不刻意区分英语和美语拼写方式。

2. 所提供的英语表达(含短语、句式和小句)一律作抽象的词汇单位来处理,除专名和构词本身需要外,一般不加定冠词,起始字母一般不大写,尾部不加句号。

3. 对于"山""河"之类专名,若确与实物相关联则需译出其含义,但对于"单音节专名+通名"构成的专名,需保留其全部专名拼音再加意译通名,如"珠江/Zhujiang River"等。

4. 为了提高词典的参考性和丰富性,适当保留从语料库提取出来的"一对多"英语表达,但一般不超过三个。

5. 在多个英语近义表达中,若只有个别词汇的差异,且形式较长的话,用斜杠"/"并列书写变体,表示可视使用语境相互替代。

6. 对于重要的党政和组织机构的名称,原则优先提供正式文件中使用或约定俗成的英语表达,若有推荐表达则排列在后面。

7. 英语对等词为专名者按语言规则首字母大写,其他如中药名、中医处方名、中餐菜名等,其所有构成成分的实词首字母大写。

8. 景区或景点作为唯一专名者首字母一律大写,但多地都有的景点则当作普通名称处理。

9. 普通名词(如公路、市县、村镇、山川河流等)只有充当某个地方专名的一部分时,才将其首字母大写。当它们单独出现或与专名无关(不指称唯一)时,不大写。

10. 对于带连字符(-)的词,如果两个词都是实词则首字母均需大写,如果前面是词缀或虚词,后面的词小写;姓名的名字中间有连字符的,后面的也小写。

四、英语注释

1. 英语注释分为前注和后注两种,用圆括号"( )"标记。前注说明被释义词英语表达的具体使用场景或适用范围,后注主要提供语义、文化、百科和属地信息等。

2. 前注以"(of …)"形式标注,后注直接放在圆括号内。对于专属景点和景区,注明其所在省的名称(名称中出现省名者不重复加注);大景区内的景点不再加属地注释。

3. 带书名号的词目词,英语表达前注属性(如有必要),后注其作者和年代／年份等。

4. 在英语表达中,音译词后有些会提供括注,说明其指称意义。

五、参见

1. 对于有某种关联的词目词之间提供参见注释,以汉语形式表达,放在整个词条的结尾处。

2. 对于常用的简称,一般另立词条,提供简称的对等词,并参见全称。

3. 对于同一事物、事件和概念有几种汉语表达,且都十分常用的,可以分立词目,并相互参见,如有主次之分的则只设单向参见。

A

阿波罗绢蝶	〈动〉*Parnassius apollo*; apollo butterfly
阿昌族	Achang ethnic group; Achang
阿昌族水酒	Achang watery wine
阿尔山	A'ershan; Arxan (Inner Mongolia)
阿尔山森林公园	Arxan/A'ershan Forest Park (Inner Mongolia)
阿尔泰山(脉)	Altai Mountains (Inner Mongolia)
阿克多帕	〈维吾尔族〉Akduopar (a kind of cap) (Xinjiang)
阿克萨依湖	Aksay Lake (Xinjiang)
阿克苏河	Aksu River (Xinjiang)
阿肯对唱会	〈哈萨克族〉Akens antiphonal singing assembly
阿拉套山	Alataw Mountain (Xinjiang)
阿里山景区	Alishan Mountain Scenic Area/Spot (Taiwan)
阿里山脉	Ali Mountain Range; Ali Mountains (Taiwan)
阿里山小鲵	〈动〉*Hynobius arisanensis*; Alisan's salamander
阿里山姊妹潭	Alishan Sisters' Ponds (Taiwan)
阿庐古洞	Alu Ancient Cave/Cavern (Yunnan)
阿妹节	〈瑶族〉A'mei Festival (on the 8th day of the 4th lunar month)
阿咪东索	Ami Dongsuo Mountain (Qinghai)
阿那律	〈佛〉Aniruddha (one of the ten disciples of the Buddha, best-known for his divyacaksus [heavenly eyes])
阿难陀	〈佛〉Ananda (one of the ten disciples of the Buddha, best-known for his well-informedness)
阿尼玛卿山	Amne Machin Mountain (Qinghai)
阿尼桥湍蛙	〈动〉*Amolops aniqiaoensis*; Aniqiao torrent frog

阿涅节	〈达斡尔族〉New Year's Day of Daur (from the 1st day to the 15th day of the 1st lunar month)
阿帕克霍加墓	Abakh Hoja Tomb (Xinjiang) →香妃墓
阿琼[安穹]南宗寺	Aqiong Nanzong Temple (Qinghai)
阿诗玛	〈彝族〉(of folk literature) Ashima
阿述拉节	〈回族〉Ashura Festival (on the 10th January in Islamic calendar)
阿斯哈图石林	Arshihaty/Asihatu Stone Forest (Inner Mongolia)
阿斯塔那古墓群	Astana Ancient Tombs; Ancient Tombs at Astana (Xinjiang)
阿斯塔纳洞古墓群	Astana Ancient Tombs; Ancient Astana Tomb Complex (Xinjiang)
阿斯塔纳-哈拉和卓古墓群	Astana-Hara Hozuo Tomb Complex; Tombs of Astana and Karakhoja (underground museum) (Xinjiang)
阿佤山	Mount Awa; Awa Mountain (Yunnan)
阿文绶贝	〈动〉*Mauritia arabica*; Arabian cowry
阿细跳月	〈彝族〉(of folk dance) Axi Jumping to the Moon
阿雅格库里湖	Ayakkum/Ayarkkol Lake (Xinjiang)
阿育王山	King Asoka Mountain (Zhejiang)
阿育王寺	King Asoka Temple (Zhejiang)
阿育王柱	King Asoka's Pillar (known as the first stone pillar of China) (Jiangsu)
哀牢蟾蜍	〈动〉*Bufo ailaoanus*; Ailao toad
哀牢山	Ailao Mountain (Yunnan)
哀乐	〈丧〉funeral music
矮灵祭	〈赛夏人〉Pastaai; Dwarf Spirit Ceremony (held every two years)
矮岩羊	〈动〉*Pseudois schaeferi*; dwarf blue sheep
艾比湖沙拐枣	〈植〉*Calligonum ebi-nuricum*
艾德莱斯绸	Atlas Silk (Xinjiang)
艾丁湖	Aydingkol Lake; Moonlight Lake (Xinjiang)
艾捷克	〈乐〉Gijak (a bowed-stringed instrument of Xinjiang)

艾提尕尔清真寺	Etigar Mosque; Id Kah Mosque (Xinjiang)
艾西曼湖	Aiximan Lake (Xinjiang)
爱河	Aihe River; Love River (Taiwan)
爱猴节	〈壮族〉Love-for-Monkey Festival (on the 5th day of the 5th lunar month)
爱尼人	Aini people; Aini (a branch of the Hani)
爱晚亭	Aiwan Pavilion; Loving Dusk Pavilion (Hu'nan)
爱玉冻[冰]	〈烹饪〉Vegetarian Gelatin (a famous local snack in Taiwan)
爱秩序湾公园	Aldrich Bay Park (Hong Kong)
安床	〈风水〉bedding ritual; to place bridal bed or relocate the old bed
安丰塘	Anfeng Pond (one of the four water conservancy projects in ancient China) (Anhui)
安徽第一名人藏馆	The First Celebrities' Museum of Anhui
安徽名人馆	Anhui Museum of Historical Notables; Anhui's Celebrities Museum
安徽瑶螈	〈动〉*Tylototriton anhuiensis*; Anhui knobby newt
安吉小鲵	〈动〉*Hynobius amjiensis*; Amji's salamander
安吉竹子博览园	Anji Bamboo Expo Garden (Zhejiang)
安澜(索)桥	Anlan Suspension/Rope Bridge (Sichuan)
安乐寺	anle temple
安宁河	Anning River (Sichuan)
安平[平安]古堡	Anping/Pingan Old Fort; Fort Zeelandia (Taiwan)
安平桥	Anping Bridge (Fujian)
安期炼丹洞	Anqi Alchemy Cave (Zhejiang)
安穹南宗寺	→阿琼[安穹]南宗寺
安山湿地公园	Anshan Wetland Park (Hubei)
安顺文庙	Anshun Confucius Temple (Guizhou)
安亭老街	Anting Old Street (Shanghai)
安西都护府	〈古〉Anxi Frontier Command (the administrative organ of Xinjiang during the Tang Dynasty)
安阳三熏	〈烹饪〉Anyang San Xun; Anyang Three Smoked Meats (a famous dish in Anyang, He'nan)

安义古村	Anyi Ancient Village (a typical village of Gan Shang culture in Jiangxi)
安源路矿工人俱乐部旧址	Former Site of the Anyuan Railway and Mineworkers' Club (Jiangxi)
安远庙	Anyuan Temple (one of the eight temples outside Chengde Summer Resort in Hebei)
暗八仙	dharma-vessel/dharma-treasure of the Eight Immortals (their magic instruments)
暗香疏影楼	(of Lion Grove Garden) Scented Shadow Tower; Faint Fragrance and Dim Shadow Hall
昂昂溪古文化遗址	Angangxi Ancient Cultural Relics (Heilongjiang)
昂船洲大桥	Angchuan Zhou Bridge; Stonecutters Bridge (Hong Kong)
昂坪 360	Ngong Ping 360 (Hong Kong)
昂坪广场	Ngong Ping Plaza/Square (Hong Kong)
昂坪市集	Ngong Ping Village (Hong Kong)
凹叶木兰	〈植〉*Magnolia sargentiana*
敖包	〈蒙古族〉Aobao; a pile of stones, earth, or wood (used by Mongolians originally as a road or boundary sign, and then as a sacrificial symbol for bumper harvest and people's safety)
敖包节	〈蒙古族〉Aobao Festival (from the 5th to 7th month of the lunar calendar, for sacrifices to the heaven, earth, sun, moon and nature)
敖包盛会	Aobao Worship Ceremony →敖包
敖伦布拉格大峡谷	Aolunbulage Grand Canyon (Inner Mongolia)
敖伦苏木城遗址	Site of Aolunsumu City (Inner Mongolia)
鳌鱼峰	(of Mount Huangshan) Dragon Fish Peak
鳌园	Turtle Garden; Kah Kee Park (Fujian)
澳凼大桥	Macau-Taipa Bridge (Ponte Governador Nobre de Carvalho) (Macao)
澳门奥林匹克体育中心	Macao Olympic Sports Center
澳门半岛	Peninsula of Macao (Península de Macau)
澳门博物馆	Museum of Macao (Museu de Macau)

澳门赌场	Macao casino
澳门二龙喉公园	Macao Double Dragonmaw Park (Jardim da Flora of Macau)
澳门疯堂斜巷	Macao Crazy Hall Inclined Lane
澳门福隆新街	Macao Fulong (great fortune) Street (Rua da Felicidade de Macau)
澳门关闸	Macao Border Gate (Portas do Cerco)
澳门观音庙	Macao Guanyin Temple; Goddess of Mercy Temple in Macao (the place where the Wangxia Treaty was signed)
澳门观音岩	Macao Guanyin Rock
澳门黑沙海滩	Praia de Hac Sá
澳门金光大道度假区	Macao Cotai Strip Resorts
澳门九澳水库郊野公园	Macao Jiu'ao Reservoir Country Park (Parque de Merendas da Barragem de Ká-Hó)
澳门旧城墙遗址	Section of the Old City Walls in Macao; Macao Old City Wall Ruins
澳门烂鬼楼巷	Macao Ghost House Lane (Travessa do Armazém Velho)
澳门历史城区	Historic Centre of Macao
澳门旅游塔	Macao Tower
澳门妈祖像	A-Ma Statue; Statue of Mazu in Macao
澳门民政总署大楼	Leal Senado Building of Macao
澳门赛马会	Macao Jockey Club
澳门沙梨头土地庙	Sha Li Tau Land Temple of Macao
澳门十六浦 3D 奇幻世界	Macao Shiliupu 3D Fantasy World; Pier 16 Macau 3D World
澳门十月初五日街	Macao October Fifth Street (Rua de Cinco de Outubro) →澳门泗孟街
澳门市政厅	Macao City Hall; Municipal Council of Macau
澳门水塘	Macao Reservoir
澳门四面佛	Macao Four-Faced Buddha
澳门泗孟街	Si Meng Street of Macao →澳门十月初五日街
澳门天后宫	Macao Tin Hau Temple; Tianhou Palace of Macao

澳门望海观音像	Macao Seaside Guanyin Statues
澳门威尼斯人国际娱乐场	Venetian International Casino in Macao
澳门文化中心广场	Macao Cultural Center Plaza (Praca do Centro Cultural de Macau)
澳门叶挺故居	General Ye Ting's Former Residence in Macao
澳门一号广场	Macao No. 1 Plaza
澳门医灵庙	Macao Medical Temple
澳门邮政总局大楼	General Post Office Building in Macao
澳门渔人码头	Macao Fisherman's Wharf
澳门运动场	Macao Stadium
澳门竹林寺	Macao Zhulin Temple; Macao Bamboo Forest Temple
澳门总督府	〈旧〉Macao Government House

B

八宝景区	Babao Scenic Area (Yunnan)
八达岭长城	Badaling Great Wall; Great Wall at Badaling (Beijing)
八达岭野生动物世界	Badaling Wildlife World (Beijing)
八大山人故居	former residence of Badashanren (the surname of the painter Zhu Da in the late Ming and early Qing Dynasties) (Jiangxi)
八大山人纪念馆	Badashanren Hall; Badashanren Memorial Hall (Jiangxi)
八斗子渔港	Badouzi Fishing/Fishery Harbour (Taiwan)
八峰森林公园	Bafeng (Eight-Peak) Forest Park (Hubei)
八峰崖	Eight Peak Cliff (Gansu)
八公山	Bagong Mountain (Anhui)
八公山景区	Bagong Mountain Scenic Area (Anhui)
八卦基本八掌	Bagua basic eight palms
八卦山自然保护区	Bagua Mountain Nature Reserve (Hubei)
八卦亭	Eight Diagram Pavilion
八卦掌	〈武术〉Bagua palm; Eight-Diagram palm
八卦掌趟泥步	〈武术〉Bagua mud-wading step
八极拳	〈武术〉Baji Quan; Baji Boxing; Octupole Boxing
八角鼓	〈满族〉octagonal drum
八角街	→八廓[角]街
八角莲	〈植〉*Dysosma versipellis*
八角楼	Bajiao Lou; Eight-Square Pavilion (Jiangxi)
八节斋	〈道〉Fasts of the Eight Seasons; Fasts of the Eight Solar Terms

八廓[角]街	Barkhor Street (Tibet)
八里沟景区	Baligou Scenic Area; Bali Valley Scenic Area (He'nan)
八岭山古墓群	Ancient Tombs at Baling Mountain (Hubei)
八路军重庆办事处旧址	Site of Chongqing Office of the Eighth Route Army
八路军桂林办事处旧址	Site of Guilin Office of the Eighth Route Army (Guangxi)
八路军前方总部旧址	Site of the General Front Headquarters of the Eighth Route Army (Shanxi)
八路军西安办事处纪念馆	Memorial Hall of Xi'an Office of the Eighth Route Army; Eighth Route Army Memorial (Shaanxi)
八路军西安办事处旧址	Site of Xi'an Office of the Eighth Route Army (Shaanxi)
八路军一二九师司令部旧址	Site of the Headquarters of the 129th Division of the Eighth Route Army (Hebei)
八路军一一五师司令部旧址	Site of the Headquarters of the 115th Division of the Eighth Route Army (Shandong)
八路军总司令部旧址	Site of the General Headquarters/Command of the Eighth Route Army (Shanxi)
八七会议旧址	Site of August 7th Meeting/Conference (Hubei)
八台山	Baitai Mountain (Sichuan) →川东峨眉
八仙	〈道〉(of legend) Eight Immortals
八仙庵	〈道〉Ba Xian Nunnery; Temple of the Eight Immortals (Shaanxi) →万寿八仙宫
八仙洞	(of Mount Taishan) Eight Immortals Cave
八仙观	(of Mount Wudang) Temple of Eight Immortals
八仙过海	Eight Immortals crossing the sea (a Chinese fairy story that means each one showing his or her special feats)
八仙山	Baxian Mountain (Tianjin)
八一广场	August 1st Square (Jiangxi)
八一建军节	→中国建军节

八一起义	August 1st Uprising (the armed uprising launched by the Communist Party of China in 1927)
"八一起义"指挥部旧址	Site of August 1st Uprising Headquarters (Jiangxi)
八月节	〈仡佬族〉August Day (from the 15th to the 20th day of the 8th lunar month)
八字桥	Bazi Bridge (Zhejiang)
巴丹吉林庙	Badain Jaran Temple (Inner Mongolia)
巴丹吉林沙漠	Badain Jaran Desert (Inner Mongolia)
巴东长江大桥	Badong Yangtze River Bridge (Hubei)
巴戟天	〈植〉*Morinda officinalis*; morinda
巴克图口岸	Baketu/Baktu Port (Xinjiang)
巴拉特节	〈维吾尔族〉Bharat Festival (in the middle of August in Muslim Calendar)
巴里坤草原	Barkol Grassland (Xinjiang)
巴里坤湖	Barkol Lake (Xinjiang) →蒲类海
巴林石	Bairin/Balin Stone (one of the four famous stones in China)
巴罗提节	〈塔吉克族〉Parot Festival (in the August in Muslim Calendar) →灯节
巴塘河	Batang River (Qinghai)
巴桃园景区	Bataoyuan Scenic Area (Hubei)
巴[把]乌	〈乐〉Bawu (a reed pipe musical instrument)
巴雾峡	Bawu Gorge (the second gorge of the Lesser Three Gorges) (Chongqing)
巴颜喀拉山	Bayankara Mountain; Bayan Har Mountain (Qinghai)
巴颜喀拉山脉	Bayankara Mountain range; Bayan Har Mountain chain (Qinghai)
巴音布鲁克草原	Bayinbuluke Grassland; Bayanbulak Grassland (Xinjiang)
巴音塔拉宫	Bayintala Palace; Bayintara Palace (Inner Mongolia)

巴音西乐生态旅游区	Bayin Xile Eco-tourism Area (Inner Mongolia)
拔草祭	〈高山族〉Weed-Pulling Up Ceremony (held in the 2nd or 3rd lunar month)
拔丝地瓜	〈烹饪〉Hot Candied Sweet Potatoes
把乌	→巴[把]乌
霸王岭森林公园	Bawang Ridge Forest Park (Hai'nan)
霸王岭自然保护区	Bawang Ridge Nature Reserve (Hai'nan)
灞陵河景区	Baling River Scenic Area (Guizhou)
灞陵桥景区	Baling Bridge Scenic Area (He'nan)
灞桥遗址	Site of Baqiao Bridge; Baqiao Bridge Ruins (Shaanxi)
白草寺	Baicao Temple; White Grass Temple (Shaanxi)
白城沙滩	Baicheng Beach (Fujian)
白齿唇兰	〈植〉*Anoectochilus candidus*
白唇鹿	〈动〉*Przewalskium albirostris*; white-lipped deer
白瓷莲瓣座灯台	(of Tang Dynasty ceramic kiln) white glazed lamppost with design of lotus petals; white porcelain lampstand with lotus petal base
白刺湍蛙	〈动〉*Amolops albispinus*
白(沙)堤	(of West Lake) Bai Causeway
白帝城	Baidi City; White Emperor City (the west entrance of the Three Gorges) (Chongqing)
白豆杉	〈植〉*Pseudotaxus chienii*
白鹅岭	(of Mount Huangshan) White Goose Ridge
白腹巨鼠	〈动〉*Leopoldamys edwardsi*; Chinese white-bellied rat
白鸽巢公园	White Dove Nest Park (Macao)
白鸽巢前地	Camoes Grotto and Gardens (Macao)
白冠长尾雉	〈动〉*Syrmaticus reevesii*; white-crowned long-tailed pheasant
白鹤亮翅	〈武术〉(of Tai Chi) White crane spreading its wings
白鹤灵芝	〈植〉*Rhinacanthus nasutus*; bignose rhinacanthus branchlet and leaf
白鹤山景区	White Crane Mountain Scenic Area (Guangxi)
白鹤亭	White Crane Pavilion (Shanghai)

白虎洞自然景区	White Tiger Stream Natural Scenic Area →北京后花园景区
白鸡腰森林公园	Baijiyao Forest Park (Jilin)
白祭	〈蒙古族〉white sacrifice; sacrifice to heaven with dairy products →红祭
白节	〈蒙古族〉Baijie; White Festival (Mongolian Lunar New Year)
白金宝遗址	Site of Bai Jinbao; Bai Jinbao Ruins (Heilongjiang)
白金婚	platinum wedding (the 70th anniversary of marriage)
白颈长尾雉	〈动〉*Syrmaticus ellioti*; white-necked long-tailed pheasant
白酒酿造遗址	sites for liquor making in China
白居寺	Baiju Lamasery; Palkor Chode; Sku-Vbumchenmo (Tibet)
白兰瓜	〈植〉bailan melon; honey dew melon
白莲	〈植〉white lotus
白莲河湿地公园	Bailianhe Wetland Park (Hubei)
白莲河水利景区	Bailianhe Water Conservancy Scenic Area (Hubei)
白灵菇扣鸭掌	〈烹饪〉Mushrooms with Duck Feet
白龙池	(of Mount Taishan) White Dragon Pond
白龙洞	white dragon cave
白龙江	Bailong (White Dragon) River (a tributary of Jialing River)
白龙江流域	Bailong (White Dragon) River basin
白龙泉	Bailong Spring; White Dragon Spring (Yunnan)
白鹿洞书院	〈古〉(of Mount Lushan) Bailudong Academy; White Deer Cave Academy
白鹭洲公园	Bailuzhou Park (Jiangsu)
白露	〈节气〉White Dew (the 15th solar term)
白马大峡谷	(of Tiantang Zhai) White Horse Valley

白马大峡谷景区	Baima (White Horse) Grand Canyon Scenic Area (Anhui)
白马洞	White Horse Cave (Hubei)
白马峰	(of Tiantang Zhai) White Horse Peak
白马鸡	〈动〉*Crossoptilon crossoptilon*; white eared pheasant
白马寺	Baima Temple; White Horse Temple (China's oldest Buddhist temple) (He'nan)
白马潭景区	Baimatan Scenic Area; White Horse Pond Scenic Area (Anhui)
白马峡谷瀑布	Baima (White Horse) Valley Waterfall (Fujian)
白马雪山自然保护区	Baima Snow Mountain Nature Reserve (Yunnan)
白马岩绝壁	White Horse Rock Cliff (Guizhou)
白毛卷瓣兰	〈植〉*Bulbophyllum albociliatum*
白牡丹	〈植〉white peony
白娘子	Lady White (a protagonist in Legend of the White Snake)
白鳍豚	〈动〉*Lipotes vexillifer*; white-flag dolphin; Yangtze River dolphin
白切肉	〈烹饪〉Boiled Pork Sliced
白雀寺	baique temple
白鹊山民宿	Baique Mountain Homestay; Homestay at Baique Mountain (Hubei)
白沙壁画	Baisha Mural; Baisha Fresco (Yunnan)
白沙古镇	Baisha Ancient Town (Yunnan)
白沙农具会	〈纳西族〉Baisha Farm Implements Fair (on the 20th day of the 1st lunar month)
白蛇传	Legend of the White Snake; Madame White Snake; Tale of the White Serpent (one of the four Chinese folk love legends)
白石山	Baishi Mountain; White Stone Mountain (Hebei)
白石山森林公园	Baishi Mountain Forest Park (Hebei)
白石轩	(of Garden of Harmony) Pavilion of Wonder Stone Worship
白事对联	funeral couplets

白术	〈植〉*Atractylodes macrocephala*; white atractylodes rhizome
白水江自然保护区	Baishui River Nature Reserve (Gansu)
白穗花	〈植〉*Speirantha gardenii*
白塔	white pagoda
白塔公园	White Pagoda Park (Zhejiang)
白塔山公园	Baita Mountain Park; White Pagoda Mountain Park (Gansu)
白塔寺	White Pagoda Temple (Beijing) →妙应寺
白藤湖	Baiteng Lake (Guangdong)
白薇	〈植〉*Cynanchum atratum*; blackend swallowwort
白鹇	〈动〉*Lophura nycthemera*; silver pheasant
白心	〈民俗〉pure heart (an old Chinese occupational custom: young laborers and apprentices must kneel and swear to their boss on New Year's Eve)
白雪节	〈维吾尔族〉Snow Day; White Snow Festival (held on the 1st day of snowfall)
白鲟	〈动〉*Psephurus gladius*; Chinese paddlefish
白崖山	Baiya (White Cliff) Mountain (Anhui)
白杨沟	Baiyang Valley; White Poplar Valley (Xinjiang)
白羊峪长城	Baiyangyu Great Wall; Great Wall at Baiyangyu (Hebei)
白洋淀	Baiyangdian Lake; Baiyang Lake (Hebei)
白洋淀千里堤	Qianli Dike in Baiyangdian (Hebei)
白音乌拉游牧文化区	Baiyinwula Nomadic Culture Zone (Inner Mongolia)
白音锡勒草原自然保护区	Baiyinxile Grassland Nature Reserve (Inner Mongolia)
白鱼口公园	Baiyukou Park (Yunnan)
白玉河	White Jade River (Qinghai) →玉龙喀什河
白玉寺	White Jade Temple; Palyul Monastery (Sichuan)
白云洞军事旅游景区	Baiyun (White Cloud) Cave Military Tourism Scenic Area (Hubei)
白云峰	(of Mount Changbai) Baiyun Peak; White Cloud Peak

白云古寺	White Cloud Ancient Temple (Guangdong)
白云观	〈道〉Baiyun Temple; White Cloud Temple (Beijing, Shaanxi)
白云群洞	(of Mount Qingcheng) White Cloud Caves
白云山馆	(of Mount Mogan) White Cloud Mountain House
白云山景区	Baiyun Mountain Scenic Area; White Cloud Mountain Scenic Area (Guangdong)
白云寺	Baiyun Temple (He'nan)
白云溪	(of Mount Huangshan) White Cloud Stream
白云岩	(of Mount Wuyi) White Cloud Rock
白竹园寺国家森林公园	National Forest Park of Baizhu Yuan Temple
白族	Bai ethnic group; Bai
百宝寨景区	Baibao Valley Scenic Area (Hubei)
百宝寨岩屋群	Baibao Valley Rock House Group (Hubei)
百草园	Baicao (Hundred Grass) Garden (Zhejiang)
百尺峡	(of Mount Huashan) Baichi Valley; Hundred-Foot Valley (one of the Three Major Risks Mount Huashan)
百福廊	One-Hundred Fu (Happiness) Gallery (Guangdong)
百花山国家级自然保护区	Baihuashan National Nature Reserve; Baihua Mountain National Nature Reserve (Beijing)
百家宴	〈民俗〉hundred-family reunion banquets; new China delight
百家衣	〈民俗〉patchwork clothes (made of different pieces of cloth from various families with the hope of the healthy growth of children)
百里荒草原	Alpine Grassland of Baili Huang (Hubei)
百里荒水利景区	Water Conservancy Scenic Area at Baili Huang (Hubei)
百灵节	〈壮族〉Bailing's Day (on the 9th day of the 9th lunar month, in memory of the young warrior Bailing, who killed the evil dragon for people)
百鸟乐园	(of Zhangjiajie) Birds Paradise

百泉景区	Baiquan Scenic Area (He'nan)
百日	1〈丧〉the hundredth day after one's death 2〈民俗〉the hundredth day after a child's birth
百日宴[酒]	〈民俗〉one-hundred-day banquet; hundred-day feast →百天, 百日
百色起义纪念公园	Baise Uprising Memorial Park; Baise Revolt Monument Park (Guangxi)
百色起义纪念馆	Baise Uprising Museum
百色起义纪念园	Baise Uprising Memorial Park
百山祖冷杉	〈植〉*Abies beshanzuensis*; beshanzufir
百天	〈民俗〉one-hundred-day celebration →百日宴[酒], 百日
百溪河湿地公园	Baixi River Wetland Park (Hubei)
百丈飞瀑	Baizhang Waterfall; Thousand Feet Waterfall (Zhejiang)
百丈瀑	(of Mount Huangshan) Thousand Feet Waterfall
百丈峡	(of Zhangjiajie) Baizhang Valley; Thousand Feet Valley
百丈崖	Baizhang Cliff; Thousand Feet Cliff (Anhui)
柏林禅寺	Bailin Temple (Hebei)
柏乡汉牡丹园	Baixiang Han Peony Garden (Hebei)
柏孜克里克千佛洞	Bezeklik Thousand-Buddha Caves (Xinjiang)
柏孜克里克石窟	Bezeklik Grottos (Xinjiang)
摆莲	〈武术〉(Flying) Lotus kick
拜贺礼	congratulation ceremony
拜庙	〈民俗〉to go to the temple to worship the gods
拜年	to pay a New Year visit; to pay a new year call (expressing good wishes at the end of the old year and the beginning of the New Year)
拜亲访友	to visit friends and relatives
拜请月神节	〈壮族〉Moon God Worship Festival (on the 15th day of the 8th lunar month) →中秋节
拜日望会	〈白族〉Bairiwang Fair (from the 13th to 19th day of the 2nd lunar month)

拜堂	〈婚〉to perform the formal wedding ceremony; to perform three formal bows
拜土地神	〈民俗〉to worship the local god of land
拜瓦哈山	〈纳西族〉Waha Mountain Worship (on the 15th day of the 7th lunar month)
班禅新宫	Panchen Summer Palace; New Palace of Panchen Lama (Tibet)
班果土林	Banguo Soil Forest (Yunnan)
班智达葛根庙	Banzhida Gegen Temple (Inner Mongolia) → 贝子庙
般若寺	prajna temple; bore temple
般若相	(of Chengde Mountain Resort) Temple of Ultimate Wisdom
颁金节	〈满族〉Banjin Festival (Manchu "birthday") (on the 13th day of the 10th lunar month)
斑翅山鹑	〈动〉*Perdix dauurica*; daurian partridge
斑喙丽金龟	〈动〉*Adoretus tenuimaculatus*; Chinese rose beetle
斑铜	variegated copperware (a specially traditional handicraft in Yunnan)
斑头雁	〈动〉*Anser indicus*; bar-headed goose
斑尾榛鸡	〈动〉*Tetrastes sewerzowi*; Chinese grouse
斑叶兰	〈植〉*Goodyera schlechtendaliana*
斑竹	〈植〉*Phyllostachys bambusoides*; mottled bamboo
斑子麻黄	〈植〉*Ephedra rhytidosperma*
板壁岩	(of Shennongjia) Banbi Rock
板栗红烧肉	〈烹饪〉Braised Pork with Chestnuts
板栗节	Chinese chestnut festival
板桥女儿湖	Banqiao Girl Lake (Hubei)
板约瀑布	Banyue Waterfall (Guangxi)
半枫荷	〈植〉*Semiliquidambar cathayensis*
半马步	Half horse stance
半年节	Half-a-year Festival (on the 1st day of the 6th lunar month)
半坡(村)遗址	Banpo Villige Ruins/Remains; Banpo Neolithic Village Site (Shaanxi)

半日花	〈植〉*Helianthemum songaricum*; half-day flower
半山寺	(of Mount Huangshan) Mid-mountain Temple; Mountainside Temple
半月沉江	〈烹饪〉Black Mushrooms and Wheat Gluten Soup
伴夜	〈丧〉(of funeral) to accompany the deceased in the night
邦马山	Bangma mountain (Yunnan)
梆子腔	〈戏〉Bangzi Tune (one of the four major tunes of Han traditional opera)
梆子戏	Bangzi Opera
棒棒会	〈纳西族〉Farm Tool Fair (on the 15th day of the 1st lunar month)
棒槌峰森林公园	Bangchui Mountain Forest Park (Hebei) →棒槌山
棒槌山	Bangchui Mountain; Hammering Stick Mountain (Hebei) →棒槌峰森林公园
棒距无柱兰	〈植〉*Amitostigma bifoliatum*
包公庙	Baogong temple
包公园	Baogong Garden (Anhui)
包谷烧	baogu liquor (made of corn with ancient methods by Tujia or Miao people)
包河公园	Baohe Park (Anhui) →包公园
包头石门景区	Shimen Tourist Site of Baotou (Inner Mongolia)
苞藜	〈植〉*Baolia bracteata*
苞叶大黄	〈植〉*Rheum alexandrae*
饱食罐	〈旧〉(of funeral) satiety jar (with food placed in the coffin)
宝成奇石园	Baocheng Alpine Garden; Wonder-Stone Garden (Tianjin)
宝德尔石林	Baodel Stone Forest (Inner Mongolia)
宝顶山经目塔	Catalog Stupa on Baoding Mountain (Chongqing)
宝顶山摩崖造像	Cliffside Sculptures on Baoding Mountain (Chongqing)
宝顶山牧牛图	carvings of Buffaloes and Herdsmen on Baoding Mountain (Chongqing)

宝顶山千手观音	thousand-armed Avalokitesvara on Baoding Mountain (on the south cliff at the big Buddha Crescent) (Chongqing)
宝顶山圣寿寺	Shengshou Temple on Baoding Mountain (Chongqing)
宝顶山圆觉洞	Cave of Full Enlightenment on Baoding Mountain (Chongqing)
宝鼎瀑布	Baoding Waterfall (Guangxi)
宝鼎[顶]山	Baoding Mountain (Chongqing)
宝峰湖	(of Zhangjiajie) Baofeng Lake
宝公塔	→宝志[公]塔
宝镜崖	(of Jiuzhai Valley) Magic Mirror Cliff
宝莲禅寺	Po Lin (Precious Lotus) Monastery (Hong Kong)
宝莲灯	(of a legend) Lotus Lantern; Precious Lotus Lantern →劈山救母
宝轮寺	Baolun Temple (Chongqing)
宝轮寺塔	Baolun Temple Pagoda (He'nan)
宝瓶口	Treasure Bottle Inlet (referring to the river month which acts as a "check gate" and can automatically control the inflow of water into the inland river)
宝瓶塔	Baoping (Treasure Vase) Pagoda
宝山国际民间艺术节	Baoshan International Folk Arts/Art Festival (Shanghai)
宝山牌坊	Baoshan Archway (Guangxi)
宝山寺	Baoshan Temple (Shanghai)
宝石流霞	(of West Lake) Gem Bathed in Flowing Rosy Clouds; Precious Stone Hill Floating in Rosy Cloud
宝石山	Precious Stone Hill; Gem Mountain (Zhejiang)
宝天曼生物圈保护区	Baotianman Biosphere Reserve (He'nan) →宝天曼自然保护区
宝天曼自然保护区	Baotianman Natural Reserve (He'nan) →宝天曼生物圈保护区

宝相寺	Baoxiang Temple (Shandong, Yunnan, Jiangsu)
宝兴齿蟾	〈动〉*Oreolalax popei*; Baoxing toothed toad
宝云阁	(of Summer Palace) Baoyun Pavilion; Treasure Cloud Pavilion
宝云塔	Baoyun Pagoda; Baoyun Tower; Treasure Cloud Pagoda/Tower (Hebei)
宝志[公]塔	Baozhi Pagoda (Jiangsu)
宝座	throne (a seat for an emperor to show the majesty of the ruler)
保安族	Bon'an ethnic group; Bon'an
保定桥	Baoding Bridge (Tianjin)
保国寺	Baoguo Temple (Zhejiang)
保和殿	(of Imperial Palace) Baohe Palace; Hall of Preserving Harmony
保护母亲河日	Mother River Protection Day (March 9th)
保圣寺罗汉塑像	Sculptures of Arhats at Baosheng Temple; Arhat Statues of Baosheng Temple (Jiangsu)
保亭热带植物园	Baoting Tropical Botanical Garden (Hai'nan)
保卫和平坊	(of Zhongshan Park) Defending Peace Archway
报恩寺	bao'en temple
报恩塔	Thanksgiving Tower (Sichuan)
报国寺	(of Mount Emei) Baoguo Temple; Temple Dedicated to the Nation
报丧	〈丧〉to give an obituary notice
报丧炮	firecracker for reporting one's death
报丧帖	obituary notice
报喜	〈民俗〉annunciation of new birth
抱犊寨	Baodu Village (Hebei)
抱茎叶无柱兰	〈植〉*Amitostigma amplexifolium*
抱拳礼	〈武术〉Palm and fist salute; Fist-palm salute
抱月亭	Baoyue (Moon Holding) Pavilion (Jiangxi)
抱掌	〈武术〉Embracing palm
趵突泉	Baotu Spring (Shandong)
趵突泉公园	Baotu Spring Park (Shandong)

爆发力	〈武术〉explosive power
爆竹	firecracker
碑坊	memorial archway
碑林	beilin museum; forest of steles
碑文	stone tablet script; inscription on a tablet; monumental writing
背篓会	〈高山族〉Packbasket Ceremony (in the evening of the 15th day of the 8th lunar month)
北部湾	Beibu Gulf (South China Sea)
北部湾广场	Beibu Gulf Square (Guangxi)
北朝墓群	Northern Dynasties tombs (Hebei)
北辰山	Beichen Mountain (Fujian)
北大湖滑雪场	Beidahu Ski Resort/Area (Jilin)
北大山石海森林公园	Stone Sea Forest Park in Beida Mountain (Hebei)
北大屿郊野公园	Lantau North Country Park (Hong Kong)
北戴河景区	Beidaihe Scenic Area (Hebei)
北戴河秦行宫遗址	Beidahe Qin Dynasty Palace Ruins; Site of Imperial Temporary-Dwelling Palace of Qin at Beidaihe (Hebei)
北帝古庙	Beidi Ancient Temple (worship for the god of the north in Macao and Hong Kong)
北方丝绸之路	Northern Silk Road
北风	(of Mahjong) North Wind
北峰	(of Mount Huashan) North Peak →云台峰
北峰山	North Peak Mountain (Guangdong)
北宫森林公园	Beigong Forest Park (Beijing)
北国笔乡	Writing Brush Land of North China (referring to both Linquan county in Anhui and Houdian village of Hengshui in Hebei)
北海公园	Beihai Park (Beijing)
北海龟石景区	Beihai Turtle Rock Scenic Area (Guangxi)
北海及团城	Beihai Park and Round Castle (imperial gardens of the Ming and Qing dynasties) (Beijing)
北海景区	(of Mount Huangshan) North Sea area

北海静心斋	Beihai Heart-East Study (Beijing)
北海银滩	Beihai Silver Beach (Guangxi)
北回归线标志塔	tropic of cancer symbol/sign tower
北霍布逊盐湖	North Hobson Salt Lake (Qinghai)
北街梦寻	(of West Lake) Chasing Dreams at Beishan Street
北京798艺术区	Beijing 798 Art District
北京奥林匹克公园	Beijing Olympics Park
北京奥林匹克森林公园	Beijing Olympics Forest Park
北京奥运村	Beijing Olympic Village
北京奥运会吉祥物	mascot of Beijing Olympics
北京城东南角楼	Southeasten Watchtower of Beijing City; Southeastern Corner Tower of Beijing City
北京大兴西瓜节	Beijing Daxing Watermelon Festival (on the 28th May)
北京大学红楼	Red Building of Peking University (one of the important places of May 4th Movement) (Beijing)
北京大学生电影节	Beijing College Student Film Festival
北京东岳庙	〈道〉Beijing Dongyue Temple
北京冬奥会	→北京冬季奥运比赛
北京冬季奥运比赛	Beijing Winter Olympic Games (in 2022)
北京动物园	Beijing Zoo
北京工人体育馆	Beijing Workers' Stadium
北京古代建筑博物馆	Beijing Ancient Architecture Museum
北京古观象台	Beijing Ancient Observatory
北京古玩城	Beijing Curio/Antique City
北京鼓楼	Beijing Drum Tower
北京国际电影节	Beijing International Film Festival
北京国际青年戏剧节	Beijing International Youth Theater Festival
北京哈巴狗	Pekingese; Pekinese
北京海洋馆	Beijing Aquarium; Beijing Ocean Hall
北京红楼文化艺术博物馆	Beijing Red Mansion Culture and Art Museum
北京后花园景区	Beijing Back Garden Scenic Area →白虎涧自然景区
北京欢乐谷	Beijing Happy Valley

北京京剧院	Jingju Theater Company of Beijing
北京孔庙	Beijing Confucius Temple; Beijing Temple of Confucius
北京历史博物馆	Beijing History Museum
北京民俗博物馆	Beijing Folk Custom Museum; Beijing Folklore Museum
北京人民艺术剧院	Beijing People's Art Theater
北京人艺	→北京人民艺术剧院
北京石花洞	Beijing Shihua Cave
北京石刻艺术博物馆	Beijing Stone Carving Art Museum; Beijing Art Museum of Stone Carvings →真觉寺
北京世界公园	Beijing World Park
北京西(客)站	Beijing West Railway Station
北京戏曲博物馆	Beijing Traditional Opera Museum
北京鸭	Peking duck; Beijing duck (special local product of Beijing)
北京野生动物园	Beijing Wildlife Park
北京艺术博物馆	Beijing Art Museum
北京猿人	*Homo erectus pekinensis*; Peking man
北京植物园	Beijing Botanical Garden
北京钟楼	Beijing Bell Tower
北盘江	Beipan River (Yunnan)
北盘江大桥	〈旧〉Beipan River Bridge (Yunnan, Guizhou) →北盘江第一桥
北盘江第一桥	The First Beipan River Bridge (Yunnan, Guizhou) →北盘江大桥
北平(府)	Peking; Peking Government (set to have jurisdiction over Daxing of Beijing in 1368 and renamed Shuntian Government in 1402)
北埔乡	Beipu Township (Taiwan)
北普陀寺	North Putuo Temple (Beijing)
北琴海	〈古〉Beiqin Sea (the name for Khanka Lake in the Jin Dynasty) (Heilongjiang) →兴凯湖

北沙参	〈中药〉Glehnia littoralis; Radix Glehniae; Coastal Glehnia Root
北山公园	Beishan Park; North Mountain Park (Jilin)
北山国家森林公园	Beishan Mountain National Forest Park (Qinghai)
北山龙潭	Dragon Pond on North Mountain (Fujian)
北山数珠手观音	Rosary Avalokitesvara on North Hill (Chongqing)
北山转轮经藏窟	Zhuanlun Jing Grotto on North Hill; Dharma-Wheel Scripture Grotto on North Hill (Chongqing)
北石窟寺	North Grotto Temple (Gansu)
北寺宋塔	Song Pagoda at North Temple; North Temple Pagoda of the Song Dynasty (Shaanxi)
北寺塔	North Temple Pagoda (Shanxi, Jiangsu)
北宋东京城遗址	Eastern Capital City Site of the Northern Song Dynasty (He'nan)
北塔山	Baytik Mountain; Beita Mountain (Xinjiang)
北塘古镇	Beitang Ancient Town (Tianjin)
北庭故城遗址	Ancient City Site of Beiting Headquarters (Xinjiang)
北武当山	Mount Beiwudang; Beiwudang Mountain (Shanxi)
北武当生态旅游区	Beiwudang Ecotourism Area (Ningxia)
北武当寺	Beiwudang Temple (Ningxia)
北洋水师［舰队］	〈旧〉Northern Fleet; North-Ocean Navy (in the late Qing Dynasty)
北饮泉	Beiyin Spring (Heilongjiang)
北岳恒山	Northern Mount Hengshan; Northern Hengshan Mountain (as the North One of the Five Sacred Mountains in China) (Shanxi)
北岳庙	Beiyue Temple (Hebei)
北运河郊野公园	North Canal Country Park (Tianjin)
北枕双峰	(of Chengde Mountain Resort) North Pavilion between Two Peaks
北镇庙	Beizhen Temple (Liaoning)

北庄遗址	Site of Beizhuang; Beizhuang Prehistoric Site (Shandong)
北宗曲阜孔庙	Confucius Temple of North Sect; Confucius Temple at Qufu (Shandong)
贝壳馆	shell house; museum of sea shell
贝子庙	Beizi Temple (Inner Mongolia)
背牛顶景区	Beiniuding (Back Cow Top) Scenic Area (Hebei)
背蛇生	〈植〉Aristolochia tuberosa
本命年	year of fate; animal year
本仁堂	(of Imperial Palace) Hall of Original Benevolence
本溪地质博物馆	Benxi Geological Museum (Liaoning)
本溪枫叶节	Benxi Maple Leaf Festival (Liaoning)
本溪水洞	Benxi Water Cave (Liaoning)
本主会	〈白族〉Local Guardian Festival
崩尖子自然保护区	Bengjianzi Nature Reserve (Hubei)
鼻烟壶	snuff bottle
比干庙	Bigan Temple (He'nan)
笔架山	Bijia Mountain; Pen-Rack-Mountain (Liaoning)
笔架山岛	Bijia Mountain Island (Liaoning)
笔架山景区	Bijia Mountain Scenic Spot (Liaoning)
笔砚	brush and inkstone
毕升湖水利景区	Bishenghu Water Conservancy Scenic Area (Hubei)
筚篥	〈乐〉bili (an ancient wind instrument)
碧峰峡	Bifeng Valley (Sichuan)
碧海金沙水上乐园	Bihai Golden Sand Water Park (Shanghai)
碧海浴场	Bihai Bathing Beach (Hebei)
碧罗雪山	Biluo Snow Mountain (Yunnan)
碧石岩	(of Mount Wuyi) Green Rock
碧梧栖凤	(of Garden of Harmony) Pavilion Chinese parasol and phoenix-tail bamboo
碧霞元君	〈道〉(of Mount Taishan) Primordial Lady of Emerald Clouds →天仙玉女
碧玉洞	Green Jade Cave (Guangdong)

碧玉瀑	Green Jade Waterfall (Jiangxi)
碧玉潭	Green Jade Pond (Jiangxi)
碧云寺	Biyun Temple; Azure Cloud Temple (Beijing)
篦子三尖杉	〈植〉*Cephalotaxus oliveri*; oliver's plum yew
壁画临摹本	duplicate version of murals
臂戴黑纱	〈丧〉to wear black veils
璧水桥	Bridges of Jade River (Shandong)
边境经济合作区	border economic cooperation zone
边民互市点	border dwellers' trading zones
编磬	〈乐〉bianqing; stone-chime (ancient percussion instrument of the Han ethnic group)
鞭炮	firecracker; a string of small crackers
鞭拳	〈武术〉Spinning horizontal back fist/boxing
鞭腿	→侧弹腿［鞭腿］
扁担舞	〈壮族〉biandan dance; shoulder-pole dance
卞万年旧居	Bian Wannian's Former Residence (Tianjin)
变脸	〈戏〉bianlian; fast mask-changing (a special effect of Sichuan traditional opera performance)
变色湖大观	Great Spectacle of Color-Changing Lake (Qinghai)
别有洞天	1 (of Yuanming Garden) Place of Unique Beauty 2(of Humble Administrator's Garden) Moon Gate
宾川角蟾	〈动〉*Megophrys binchuanensis*; Binchuan horned toad
宾礼	〈古〉etiquette of receiving guests; etiquette for entertaining guests (one of the Five Rites/Etiquettes of the Western Zhou Dynasty)
宾阳洞	Binyang Cave (He'nan) →灵岩寺
宾阳三洞	(of Longmen Grottoes) Three Binyang Caves
彬县大佛寺石窟	Dafo Temple Grottoes of Binxian County (Shaanxi)
滨海观赏鱼科技园区	Binhai Aquarium Fish Science and Technology Park (Tianjin)
滨海航母主题公园	Binhai Aircraft Carrier Theme Park (Tianjin)

滨海新区	Binhai New Area (Tianjin)
滨江道	Binjiang Road (a commercial street in Tianjin)
滨江森林公园	Riverside Forest Park (Shanghai)
冰灯展	ice-lantern exhibition
冰雕	ice carving
冰壶洞	Ice-Pot Cave (Zhejiang)
冰雪节	ice and snow festival
冰峪沟	Bingyu Valley; Ice Valley (Liaoning)
兵马俑	terracotta soldiers and horses; wooden or clay figures of warriors and horses buried with the dead
兵马俑博物馆	Museum of Terracotta Warriors and Horses (Shaanxi)
兵书宝剑峡	(of Three Gorges) Bingshu Baojian Gorge; Gorge of Military Books and Swords
秉志齿蟾	〈动〉*Oreolalax pingii*; ping's toothed toad
秉志肥螈	〈动〉*Pachytriton granulosus*; ping's fat newt
炳灵寺	Bingling Temple (Gansu)
炳灵寺石窟	Bingling Temple Grottoes; Grottoes at Bingling Temple (Gansu)
炳灵异角蟾	〈动〉*Xenophrys binlingensis*
拨浪鼓	drum-shaped rattle; rattle-drum; shaking drum (an old and traditional folk instrument and toy which was first used in the Warring States period)
波拉拉山	Polala Mountain (Tibet)
波密卷瓣兰	〈植〉*Bulbophyllum bomiense*
波普拟髭蟾	〈动〉*Leptobrachium bompu*
波月洞	Waving Moon Cave (Hu'nan)
播种节	sowing festival; seed sowing festival
伯多禄五世剧院	Dom Pedro V Theater (China's first western theater) (Macao) →岗顶剧院
伯乐树	〈植〉*Bretschneidera sinensis*
泊头清真寺	Botou Mosque (Hebei)
博爱牌坊	(of Mausoleum of Sun Yat-sen) Memorial Archway of Universal Fraternity

博鳌亚洲论坛	Bo'ao Forum for Asia; BFA
博尔济吉特氏族	〈古〉Borjigin clan (Genghis Khan's family name)
博格达峰	Mount Bogda (the highest peak in the eastern part of the Tianshan Mountain) (Xinjiang)
博格达[多]山	Bogda Mountain (Xinjiang)
博寮洲	→南丫岛
博南山	Bonan Mountain (Yunnan)
博斯腾湖	Bosten Lake (Xinjiang)
渤海	Bohai Sea
渤海大楼	Bohai Building (Tianjin)
渤海经济圈	Bohai Sea economic circle
渤海上京龙泉府遗址	Site of the Upper Capital of Bohai State (Heilongjiang)
渤海湾	Bohai Gulf; Bohai Bay
渤海湾盆地	Bohai Bay Basin
渤海中京城遗址	Zhongjing Ruins of Bohai State; Site of the Middle Capital of Bohai State (Jilin)
搏拊	〈乐〉bofu; bofu drum
薄扶林郊野公园	Pok Fu Lam Country Park (Hong Kong)
薄荷	〈植〉*Mentha canadensis*; field mint
薄山湖景区	Boshan Lake Scenic Area (He'nan)
卜奎清真寺	Bukui Mosque; Pukui Muslim Temple (Heilongjiang)
卜公花园	Blake Garden (Hong Kong)
补秋山房	(of Mountain Villa with Embracing Beauty) Make-up Autumn Gallery
补山亭	Bushan Pavilion (Guangdong)
捕鱼祭	〈阿美人〉Fishing Day (held in autumn)
捕鱼节	〈蒙古族〉Fishing Festival (in mid June)
堡子里古建筑群	Buzili ancient architectural/building complex (Hebei)
不倒翁	Chinese tumbler (an ancient toy, the earliest record appears in the Tang Dynasty)
不肯去观音院	(of Mount Putuo) Unwilling-to-go Kwan-yin Temple

布达拉宫	Potala Palace (Tibet)
布朗族	Bulang ethnic group; Bulang
布伦托海	Buluntuo Lake (Xinjiang) →乌伦古湖
布洛阿特峰	Buluote Peak (Xinjiang)
布依族	Buyi/Bouyei ethnic group; Buyi/Bouyei
步高里	Cite Bourbobne; Bugao Lane (a typical old-style residential complex) (Shanghai)

C

猜灯谜	to guess lantern riddle
猜点令	to guess the dots (an entertaining game at the banquet)
猜拳	finger-guessing game; finger guessing (an entertaining game at the banquet)
财神山景区	Caishen (God of Wealth) Mountain Scenic Area (Shandong) →凤凰城堡
采草节	〈景颇族〉Grass-Picking Festival (in the 9th or 10th lunar month)
采花节	〈藏族〉Flower-Picking Day (on the 5th day of the 5th lunar month)
采菱渡	(of Chengde Mountain Resort) Ferry for Picking up Water Caltrops
采桑节	〈侗族〉Mulberry-Picking Day (on the 4th day of the 4th lunar month)
彩虹瀑	Rainbow Waterfall (Jiangxi) →水口瀑布
彩绘泥俑	colored clay figurine; clay figurine with colored drawing
彩陶	colored pottery
踩高跷	to walk on stilts; stilt-walking; stilt walk
踩鼓节	〈苗族〉Stepping on Drum Festival
蔡侯祠	Memorial Hall of Marquis Cai (Hu'nan)
仓姑寺	Canggu Temple (a Gelug Sect Temple of Tibetan Buddhism and the only nun temple in Lhasa) (Tibet)
苍峰园	Cangfeng Garden (Tianjin)
苍龙岭	(of Mount Huashan) Canglong Ridge

苍山	Cangshan Mountain (Yunnan)
苍头燕雀	〈动〉*Fringilla coelebs*; common chaffinch
苍岩山景区	Cangyan Mountain Scenic Area (Hebei)
苍鹰	〈动〉*Accipiter gentilis*; northern goshawk
沧浪海旅游港	Canglang Hai Tourism Port (Hubei)
沧浪亭	Canglang Pavilion; Pavilion of Surging Wave (Jiangsu)
沧浪屿	(of Chengde Mountain Resort) Islet in Rippling Wave
沧源崖画	Cangyuan Rock Paintings (Yunnan)
沧州铁狮子	Cangzhou Iron Lion (Hebei)
藏经阁[楼]	Buddhist scripture garret; depository of Buddhist texts
藏龙岛湿地公园	Canglong Island Wetland Park (Hubei)
曹操墓	Cao Cao's Tomb; Tomb of Cao Cao (He'nan)
曹国舅	Ts'ao Kuo-chiu; Royal Uncle Cao (one of the Eight Immortals)
曹家大院	Cao Family Courtyard (Shanxi)
草地短柄草	〈植〉*Brachypodium pratense*
草岭古道	Caoling Historic Trail (Taiwan)
草庐亭	Caolu (Hut) Pavilion (Hubei)
草堂寺	Caotang Temple; Straw Cottage Temple (Shaanxi)
草原石人	stone figures on grassland (Xinjiang)
侧柏	〈植〉*Platycladus orientalis*; Chinese arborvitae; oriental arborvitae
侧蹬腿	〈武术〉Side kick with heel
侧空翻	〈武术〉Aerial cartwheel; Side somersault; Side airspring
侧手翻	〈武术〉Cartwheel
侧摔	〈武术〉Side slam; Side fall; Throw sideways
侧弹腿[鞭腿]	〈武术〉Side spring kick
侧踢	〈武术〉Side kick; Side piercing kick
侧踢腿	〈武术〉Sideway kick to front; Side front kick
侧压腿	〈武术〉Side stretching of the leg

插艾叶	〈民俗〉to hang moxa leaf in house (before and after the Dragon Boat Festival)
插花节	〈彝族〉Flower Arrangement Festival (on the 8th day of the 2nd lunar month)
插柳戴花	〈丧〉to plant willow and wear flowers (a custom of Tomb-Sweeping Day)
插茱萸	〈民俗〉to pin the leaves of cornus on clothes; to carry a spray of dogwood; to wear dogwood (a custom of Tomb-Sweeping Day)
茶荷	〈茶〉tea holder (a utensil for making tea)
茶卡盐湖	Chaka/Caka Salt Lake (Qinghai)
茶马古道	Ancient Tea-Horse Road (the trade channel in Southwest China)
茶马古道路线	routes of the Ancient Tea-Horse Road
茶叶蛋	〈烹饪〉Tea Egg (eggs stewed in tea and soy sauce)
茶子树	→油茶
查干敖包庙	Chagan Aobao Temple (Inner Mongolia)
查干浩特旅游度假区	Chagan Haote Tourism Resort (Jilin)
查干湖	Chagan Lake (Jilin)
查干湖自然保护区	Chagan Lake Nature Reserve (Jilin)
察尔汗盐湖	Qarhan/Chaerhan Salt Lake (Qinghai)
察尔森森林公园	Qarsan Forest Park (Inner Mongolia)
察尔森水库景区	Qarsan Reservoir Scenic Area (Inner Mongolia)
察砂	〈风水〉to inspect the landforms; to inspect locations among mountains
察隅棘蛙	〈动〉*Maculopaa chayuensis*; Chayu paa/sping frog
察隅湍蛙	〈动〉*Amolops chayuensis*; Chayu torrent/sucker frog
檫木	〈植〉*Sassafras tzumu*; Chinese sassafras
柴达木盆地	Qaidam Basin (Qinghai)
柴达木沙拐枣	〈植〉*Calligonum zaidamense*
禅林寺古银杏风景园	Ancient Ginkgo Landscape Garden of Chanlin Temple (Hebei)
蝉虾	Norway lobster

昌江河	Changjiang River (Hu'nan)
昌黎黄金海岸	Changli Golden Coast (Hebei)
昌陵	(of the Palace Museum) Changling Mausoleum
昌瑞山	Changrui Mountain (Hebei)
昌珠寺	Changzhu Temple; Trandruk Monastery; Trandruk Temple (Tibet)
菖蒲	〈植〉*Acorus calamus*; sweet sedge; calamus
长安城	〈古〉Chang'an City (ancient Chinese capital, presently Xi'an)
长白瀑布	Changbai Waterfall (Jilin)
长白山	Mount Changbai; Changbai Mountain (Jilin)
长白山北坡景区	North Slope Scenic Area of Changbai Mountain (Jilin)
长白山大瀑布	Grand Waterfall of Changbai Mountain (Jilin)
长白山迷宫	Changbai Mountain Maze (Jilin)
长白山南坡景区	South Slope Scenic Area of Changbai Mountain (Jilin)
长白山天池	Tianchi Lake of Changbai Mountain; Heavenly Lake of Changbai Mountain (Jilin)
长白山温泉度假村	Changbai Mountain Hot Spring Resort (Jilin)
长白山自然保护区	Changbai Mountain Nature Reserve (Jilin)
长白松	〈植〉*Pinus syluestriformis*; Changpai scotch pine
长苞铁杉	〈植〉*Tsuga longibracteata*
长柄新月蕨	〈植〉*Pronephrium longipetiolatum*
长城	Great Wall
长城倒挂胜景	A Scenery of Overhanging Great Wall (Hebei)
长城红葡萄酒	Great Wall red wine
长城狩猎场	Great Wall Hunting Ground (Hebei)
长城音乐节	Great Wall Music Festival
长春电影主题公园	Changchun Film Theme Park (Jilin)
长春宫	(of Imperial Palace) Palace of Eternal Spring
长春宫戏台	(of Imperial Palace) Stage at the Palace of Eternal Spring
长春观	Changchun Taoism Temple (Hubei)

长春世界雕塑公园	Changchun World Sculpture Park (Jilin)
长风公园	Changfeng Park (Shanghai)
长冠苣苔	〈植〉*Rhabdothamnopsis sinensis*
长海	(of Jiuzhai Valley) Long Lake
长虹饮练	(of Chengde Mountain Resort) Long Dragon Sipping at Silky Water
长江	Changjiang River; Yangtze/Yangtse River
长江第一湾	The First Bend of Yangtze River (Yunnan)
长江江豚	〈动〉*Neophocaena asiaeorientalis*; Yangtze finless porpoise; narrow-ridged finless porpoise
长江流域	Changjiang River basin; Yangtze River valley
长江三角洲	Yangtze River Delta
长江三峡	Yangtze Three Gorges (Hubei)
长江三峡水利枢纽工程	Three Gorges Hydroelectric Power Station (Hubei) →三峡工程
长江武汉关	Wuhan Customs of Yangtze River (Hubei)
长江中下游地区	mid-low reaches of Yangtze River
长空栈道	(of Mount Huashan) Chang Kong Plank Road
长廊	(of Summer Palace) Long Gallery; Long Corridor
长陵	Changling Mausoleum (Shaanxi, He'nan)
长隆飞鸟乐园	Chime-Long Birds Park →广州鳄鱼公园
长隆海洋王国	Chime-Long Ocean Kingdom (Guangdong)
长隆欢乐世界	Changlong Paradise; Chime-Long Paradise (Guangdong)
长隆水上乐园	Chime-Long Water Park (Guangdong)
长隆野生动物世界	Chime-Long Safari Park (Guangdong)
长明灯	〈习俗〉eternal fire; altar lamp (which is lit day and night)
长桥海	Changqiao Lake (Yunnan)
长桥饮马	Watering Horses at Long-Bridge (Xinjiang)
长拳	〈武术〉Chang Quan; Long-Style Boxing; Long-Range Punching
长拳自选套路	〈武术〉optional routine of Long-Style Boxing; optional routine of Long-Range Punching

长山列岛	Changshan Islands; Changshan Archipelago (Shandong)
长寿酒	longevity wine
长寿桥	(of Mount Taishan) Longevity Bridge
长寿山	longevity mountain
长寿鱼	〈动〉*Hoplostethus atlanticus*; long-live fish
长尾鼩鼹	〈动〉*Scaptonyx fusicaudus*; long-tailed mole
长信门	(of Imperial Palace) Gate of Eternal Faith
长兴岛	Changxing Island (Shanghai)
长阳清江古城	Qingjiang Ancient City of Changyang (Hubei)
长阳人	Changyang Man (human in the middle Paleolithic Age in Central China, belonging to the early homo sapiens) (Hubei)
长阳人化石洞	Changyang Man Fossil Cave (Hubei)
长阳人遗址	Site of Ancient Changyang Man (Hubei)
长阳中武当道观	Wudang Taoist Temple in Changyang (Hubei)
长叶榧	〈植〉*Torreya jackii*
长叶蜻蜓兰	→台湾[长叶]蜻蜓兰
长叶蹄盖蕨	〈植〉*Athyrium elongatum*
长揖	〈礼〉deep bow (a salute in which hands were held high and then dropped down)
长揖不拜	〈成〉to make a deep bow but do not kneel down
长影世纪城	Changchun Movie Wonderland; Changying Century City (Jilin)
长征胜利景园	Long March Victory Garden (Gansu)
长洲关公忠义亭	Kwan Kung Pavilion of Cheung Chau (Hong Kong)
长洲玉虚宫	Yuk Hui Temple of Cheung Chau (Hong Kong)
尝[吃]新节	Tasting Festival (on the 7th day of the 7th lunar month)
常山战鼓	〈乐〉Changshan war drum
常熟沙家浜旅游节	Shajia Bang Tourism Festival in Changshu
常熟虞山风筝节	Yushan Mountain Kite Festival in Changshu (Jiangsu)

嫦娥	Chang'e (goddess of the moon)
嫦娥奔月	(of legend) Goddess Chang'e Flying to the Moon
畅音阁	(of Imperial Palace) Belvedere of Pleasant Sound; Studio of Unimpeded Sound (an theatre pavilion)
畅远台	(of Chengde Mountain Resort) Hathpace with Broad Vision
巢湖湿地	Chaohu Lake wetland (Anhui)
朝鸡节	〈白族〉Pilgrimage-to-Jizu Mountain Day (from the 1st to 15th day of the 1st lunar month)
朝山会	mountain worship day; Buddhist temple worship festival; mountain pilgrimage festival
朝[转]山节	〈摩梭人〉Mountain Worship Festival (celebrated by the Mosuo people living by Lugu Lake on the 25th day of the 7th lunar month)
朝山习俗	a custom of the pilgrimage to the mountain
朝天门广场	Chaotianmen Square (Chongqing)
朝鲜族	Korean ethnic group; Korean
朝阳洞	sun-facing cave
朝阳峰	(of Mount Huashan) Sunrise Peak; Sun-Facing Peak (East Peak)
朝阳楼	Chaoyang Gate Arch; Gate Arch Facing the Sun (which is named "small Tian An Men") (Yunnan)
朝阳三慧洞	(of Qianling Mountain) Chaoyang Sanhui (Three-Wisdom) Caves
朝云峰	(of Three Gorges) Chaoyun Peak; Cloud-Facing Peak
潮汕平原	Chaoshan Plain (Guangdong)
潮汕蝾螈	〈动〉*Cynops orphicus*; dayang newt
潮州八景	Eight Views of Chaozhou (Guangdong)
潮州滨江长廊	Chaozhou Riverside Promenade (Guangdong)
潮州瓷器	Chaozhou ceramics; Chaozhou porcelain
潮州西湖	Chaozhou West Lake (Guangdong)
炒豆胡同	Chaodou hutong (Beijing)

车尔臣河	Qarqan River (Xinjiang)
车前草	〈植〉*Plantago depressa*; plantain herb
车前紫草	〈植〉*Sinojohnstonia plantaginea*
沉香阁	Chenxiang Pavilion (Shanghai) →慈云禅寺
沉香木	chenxiang wood; aloewood; agalloch
沉香亭	Chenxiang Pavilion (Shaanxi)
陈家祠(堂)	Ancestral Temple of the Chen Family (Guangdong)
陈氏异角蟾	〈动〉*Xenophrys cheni*
陈毅广场	Chen Yi Square (Shanghai)
陈祝龄旧居	Chen Zhuling's Former Residence (Tianjin)
陈棕	→琼[陈]棕
撑红伞	〈婚〉(of wedding) to put up a red umbrella; to hold a red umbrella
成都非物质文化遗产节	Chengdu Intangible Cultural Heritage Festival
成都平原	Chengdu Plain (Sichuan)
成服	(of funeral) mourning apparel
成吉思汗陵	Mausoleum of Genghis Khan; Genghis Khan's Mausoleum (Inner Mongolia)
成吉思汗庙	Genghis Khan Temple (Inner Mongolia)
成年礼	coming-of-age ceremony; initiation rite
成山卫天鹅湖	Swan Lake at Chengshan Guarding Post (Shandong)
成语典故之都	Hometown of Idioms and Allusions (referring to Handan, Hebei)
呈贡蝾螈	〈动〉*Cynops chenggongensis*; Chenggong fire salamanders
诚肃殿	(of Imperial Palace) Hall of Sincere Solemnity
承德避暑山庄	Chengde Imperial Summer Resort; Chengde Mountain Resort; Chengde Summer Resort (Hebei) →热河行宫
承乾宫	(of Imperial Palace) Palace of Heavenly Providence
承志堂	Chengzhi Hall (Anhui)

城陛庙	Town God Temple (Shanxi)
城高岩	(of Mount Wuyi) Chenggao Rock; City-Like Cliff
城隍庙	chenghuang temple; town God's temple
城隍台遗址	Ruins of Chenghuang Tai (ancient city defense facilities) (Hubei)
城门谷公园	Shing Mun Valley Park (Hong Kong)
城门郊野公园	Shing Mun Country Park (Hong Kong)
城墙岩	city wall rock
城曲草堂	(of Couple's Retreat Garden) Chengqu Thatched Cottage; Thatched Cottage in City Corner
程海	Chenghai Lake (Yunnan)
程阳风雨桥	Chengyang Wind and Rain Bridge (Guangxi)
澄碧河	Chengbi River (Guangxi)
澄波叠翠	(of Chengde Mountain Resort) Lucid Ripples and Superposed Green
澄观斋	(of Chengde Mountain Resort) Study of Lucid Mind for Peaceful Meditation
澄泥砚	Chengni ink-stone (one of the four famous ink-stones in China, which is produced in He'nan and Shanxi)
澄泉绕石	(of Chengde Mountain Resort) Limpid Stream Running around White Stone
澄瑞亭	(of Imperial Palace) Pavilion of Auspicious Clarity
澄虚道院	Chengxu Taoist Temple (Jiangsu)
橙脊瘰螈	〈动〉*Paramesotriton aurantius*; orange-spined warty newts
吃虫节	〈仫佬族〉Insect-Eating Festival (on the 2nd day of the 6th lunar month)
吃立节	〈壮族〉Chili Festival; Triumph Celebration Festival (on the 30th day of the 1st lunar month)
吃三朝	〈民俗〉to join in a baby's third day of birth celebration
吃山酒	〈彝族〉drinking on the mountain (a love activity of young men and women of Yi ethnic group)

吃新节	→尝[吃]新节，新禾节
吃信节	〈苗族〉Chixin Festival; New Grain Tasting Festival (in Wu Day of the 7th lunar month)
蚩尤部落	Chiyou tribe (Hai'nan)
摛藻堂	(of Imperial Palace) Hall of Culture Promotion
篪	〈乐〉chi (an ancient bamboo wind instrument)
齿缘石山苣苔	〈植〉*Petrocodon dealbatus*
赤壁丹崖	red cliff and rock
赤峰红山文化节	Hongshan Cultural Festival in Chifeng (Inner Mongolia)
赤峰旅游节	tourism festivals in Chifeng (Inner Mongolia)
赤峰桥	Chifeng Bridge (Tianjin)
赤狐	〈动〉*Vulpes vulpes*; red fox
赤崁楼	Fort Provintia (Taiwan)
赤龙湖湿地公园	Chilong Lake Wetland Park (Hubei)
赤石山	Red Rock Mountain (Xinjiang)
赤水丹霞	Chishui Danxia (Guizhou)
翅果油树	〈植〉*Elaeagnus mollis*
冲泡盅	〈茶〉brewing vessel
冲拳	〈武术〉Punching fist; Thrust punching
冲虚庵	(of Mount Wudang) Chongxu Nunnery
虫王节	〈满族〉Insect King Festival (on the 6th day of the 6th lunar month)
重九节	Double Ninth Festival →重阳节
重庆博物馆	Chongqing Museum →重庆中国三峡博物馆
重庆湖广会馆	Hu-Guang Guild Hall in Chongqing
重庆南山	Chongqing Nanshan Mountain
重庆人民广场	Chongqing People's Square
重庆中国三峡博物馆	Chongqing China Three Gorges Museum →重庆博物馆
重阳糕	Chongyang cake; Double Ninth cake
重阳节	Chung Yeung; Chongyang Festival; Double Ninth Festival (on the 9th day of the 9th lunar month) →老人节，重九节

重阳酒	〈习俗〉Chongyang wine
崇安湍蛙	〈动〉*Amolops chunganensis*; Chong'an torrent frog
崇安髭蟾	〈动〉*Leptobrachium liui*; Chongan moustache toad
崇福寺	chongfu temple; lofty happiness temple
崇湖湿地公园	Chonghu Lake Wetland Park (Hubei)
崇敬殿	(of Imperial Palace) Hall of Esteem
崇觉寺铁塔	Iron Pagoda of Chongjue Temple (Shandong)
崇礼住宅	Chongli Quadrangle; Residence of Scholar Chongli (Beijing)
崇陵	Chongling Mausoleum (Hebei)
崇明岛	Chongming Island (Shanghai)
崇明东滩湿地	Chongming Dongtan Wetland; East Chongming Wetland (Shanghai)
崇庆寺	Chongqing Temple (Shanxi)
崇山沟谷	Chongshan Valley (Tianjin)
崇善寺	Chongshan Temple (Shanxi)
崇圣寺	Chongsheng Temple (Yunnan)
崇圣寺三塔	Three Pagodas of Chongsheng Temple (Yunnan) →大理三塔
崇武城墙	Chongwu City Wall (Fujian)
丑角	〈戏〉(of Beijing Opera) Chou; a role of Chou (comic role)
臭椿	〈植〉*Ailanthus altissima*; tree of heaven; Chinese sumac
出殡	〈表〉to carry a coffin to the cemetery/burial place; to hold a funeral procession
出门告	〈表〉to paste up the obituary on the door
出洼节	〈阿昌族〉Chuwa Festival; Sending-Buddha Day (on the 15th December in Dai calendar)
出夏节	→开门[出夏]节
出纸	to parade and show the paper works (a part of northern customs in funeral)
初祖庵	Chuzu Monastery; The First Patriarch Temple (He'nan)

除夕（夜）	Eve of Chinese New Year; Chinese New Year's Eve; Eve of the Spring Festival (on the 30th day of the 12th lunar month)
除夕晚会	Chinese New Year's Eve party
处暑	〈节气〉End/Limit of the Heat (the 14th solar term)
储秀宫	(of Imperial Palace) Palace of Concentrated Beauty/Elegance
楚布寺	Tsupu Monastery (Tibet)
楚河汉界	(of chess) border between the states of Chu and Han; border of two opposing powers
楚南小鲵	〈动〉*Hynobius sonani*
楚普跳神	〈藏族〉Cham (Lama Dancing) in Tshurpu Monastery
楚天台	Chutian Tower; Tower of the State Chu (Hubei)
楚庄王墓	Tomb of King Zhuang of the Chu State (Hubei)
川北齿蟾	〈动〉*Oreolalax chuanbeiensis*; Chuanbei toothed toad
川贝母	〈植〉*Fritillaria cirrhosa*; bulbus fritillariae
川东灯台报春	〈植〉*Primula mallophylla*
川东第一牌坊	The First Memorial Arch of Eastern Sichuan (Chongqing) →滩口牌坊
川东峨眉	Emei Mountain in Eastern Sichuan →八台山
川金丝猴	〈动〉*Rhinopithecus roxellanae*; golden snub-nosed monkey; Sichuan snub-nosed monkey
川剧	〈戏〉Chuan Opera; Sichuan Opera
川南短腿蟾	〈动〉*Brachytarsophrys chuannanensis*; southern Sichuan short-legged toad
川南疣螈	〈动〉*Tylototriton pseudoverrucosus*; southern Sichuan crocodile newt
川柿	〈植〉*Diospyros sutchuensis*; Sichuan persimmon
川西凤仙花	〈植〉*Impatiens apsotis*; western Sichuan jewelweed
川藏线	Sichuan-Tibet route
川藻	〈植〉*Dalzellia sessilis*; Sichuan algae

穿洞人	〈古〉Chuandong man (late homo sapien of China)
穿洞遗址	(of late Paleolithic) Site of Chuandong; Chuandong Ruins (Guizhou)
穿心莲	〈植〉*Andrographis paniculate*; green chiretta
穿掌	〈武术〉Penetrating palm
穿掌下势	〈武术〉(of Tai Chi) Penetrating palm pushing down
传话游戏	Chinese whispers; passing words
传统满族礼仪	traditional Manchu rite
传统民间艺术	traditional folk art
传统戏剧表演	traditional opera performance; to perform traditional opera
传统戏曲	traditional drama and opera
传统中国节日	traditional Chinese festival
传统中国乐器	traditional Chinese musical instrument
传统中式婚礼	traditional Chinese wedding
传昭大法会	〈藏族〉Monlam Great Prayer Festival (from the 4th to the 25th day of January in Tibetan calendar)
船祭	〈高山族〉Ship Sacrifice (held for ten days in the 7th or 8th lunar month)
串果藤	〈植〉*Sinofranchetia chinensis*
窗花	paper-cut for window decoration; paper-cutting pasted on panes (used in the Spring Festival and ceremonies like wedding)
床前茶	early morning tea
闯王陵	Chuangwang's Tomb; Tomb of King Chuangwang (Hubei)
吹箫引凤	(of Mount Huashan) Blowing the Flute to Attract the Phoenix
垂花门	festooned gate/door; floral-pendant gate/door
垂柳	〈植〉*Salix babylonica*; weeping willow
锤峰落照	(of Chengde Mountain Resort) Sunset View on Qingchui Peak
春城	Spring City; City of Perpetual Spring (referring to Kunming)

春分	〈节气〉Spring Equinox; Vernal Equinox (the 4th solar term)
春耕节	Ploughing Ceremony; Spring Ploughing Day (on the 2nd day of the 2nd lunar month) →龙抬头
春剑	〈植〉*Cymbidium tortisepalum*
春节	Spring Festival; Chinese New Year; Chinese Lunar New Year (on the 1st day of the 1st lunar month) →过年
春节联欢晚会	Spring Festival Gala; Spring Festival Gala Evening
春节旅游高峰	Spring Festival travel peak
春节庙会	Spring Festival temple fair
春节晚会	→春节联欢晚会
春联	chunlian; Spring Festival couplets (pasted on each side of a doorway for good wishes)
春龙节	Spring Dragon Festival (on the 2nd day of the 2nd lunar month) →龙抬头, 春耕节
春秋阁	Spring and Autumn Pavilion (Hubei)
春晚	→春节联欢晚会
春晓园	Chunxiao Garden (Shaanxi)
纯色万代兰	〈植〉*Vanda subconcolor*
纯阳殿	(of Mount Emei) Chunyang Hall (for the worship of Lü Dongbin, one of the Eight Immortals)
茈碧湖	Cibi Lake (Yunnan)
瓷婚	china wedding (the 20th anniversary of marriage)
辞旧岁	to bid farewell to the old year
辞旧迎新	to ring out the old year and ring in the new; to bid farewell to the old and usher in the new
辞灵	〈丧〉(of funeral) to bow to the coffin before leaving
辞青	〈民俗〉to have an outing at the Double Ninth Festival
慈禅寺石窟	Cichan Temple Grottoes (Shaanxi)

慈光阁	(of Mount Huangshan) Mercy Light Temple
慈宁宫	(of Imperial Palace) Palace of Amiability and Tranquility
慈宁宫花园	(of Imperial Palace) Garden of Amiability and Tranquility
慈宁门	(of Imperial Palace) Gate of Amiability and Tranquility
慈云禅寺	Ciyun Temple (Shanghai) →沉香阁
慈云阁	Ciyun Pavilion (Hebei)
磁山(文化)遗址	Site of Cishan; Cishan Ancient Cultural Relics (Hebei)
磁县北朝墓群	Northern Dynasties Tombs in Cixian County (Hebei)
磁州窑	Cizhou Kiln (Hebei)
磁州窑遗址	Site of Cizhou Kiln (Hebei)
雌雄飞瀑	Twin (Female and Male) Waterfalls (Yunnan)
雌雄银杏	(of Hongluo Temple) Male and Female Maidenhairtree
刺萼参	〈植〉*Echinocodon lobophyllus*
刺儿菜	〈植〉*Cirsium arvense*
刺胸齿突蟾	〈动〉*Scutiger mammatus*
刺绣	embroidery (an outstanding traditional national craft in China); to embroid
刺绣缎面鞋	embroidered satin shoes
刺绣鸳鸯	embroidered mandarin duck
苁蓉	〈植〉*Cistanche salsa*; desert cistanche
丛台公园	Congtai Park (Hebei)
蹴鞠	〈古〉cuju (an ancient Chinese football game)
催妆	〈婚〉cuizhuang; bridegroom's gift of cosmetic (given to the bride on the day before the weeding)
脆皮大头蛙	〈动〉*Limnonectes fragilis*; fragile large-headed frog
脆虾白菜心	〈烹饪〉Chinese Cabbage with Fried Shrimps
翠菊	〈植〉*Callistephus chinensis*; China aster

翠玲珑	(of Surging Waves Pavilion) Exquisite Bamboo Pavilion
翠屏峰	cuiping peak
翠屏山	Cuiping Mountain (Sichuan, Tianjin)
翠屏书院	Cuiping Academy (Sichuan)
翠岩峰	(of Mount Wutai) Peak of Green Rock; Green Rock Peak
翠云馆	(of Imperial Palace) Hall of Emerald Clouds
翠云岩	(of Chengde Mountain Resort) Crags in Green Jade Cloud
措吉颇章(宫)	(of Norbulingka) Tsokyil Potrang (Palace)
错金博山炉	Boshan Incense Burner Inlaid with Gold Decorations
错那棘蛙	〈动〉*Maculopaa conaensis*; cona spiny frog

D

达布逊盐湖	Dabsun Salt Lake (Qinghai)
达旦明久颇章(宫)	(of Norbulingka) Takten Migyur Potrang; New Summer Palace
达呼尔鼠兔	〈动〉*Ochotona daurica*
达克雅鲁斯夏雷寺院遗址	Yalusxialey Remains of Monastery (Xinjiang)
达里诺尔湖	Dali Nuoer Lake; Dali Lake (Inner Mongolia)
达玛节	〈藏族〉Dama Festival (from the 10th to the 28th day of April in Tibetan calendar)
达摩洞	Bodhidharma Cave; Dharma Cave (Jiangsu)
达摩十八景	Eighteen Sights of Bodhidharma (Fujian)
达摩堂	Dharma Hall
达瓦孜表演	〈维吾尔族〉dawaz performance (walking with a pole in hands on a tight-rope)
达旺大法会	〈门巴族〉Dawang Dharma Assembly (on the 29th day of November in Tibetan calendar)
达斡尔奶酒	〈达斡尔族〉Daur/Tahur milk wine
达斡尔族	Daur/Tahur ethnic group; Daur/Tahur
打邦[帮]河	Dabang River (Guizhou)
打歌会	〈彝族〉Dage Singing and Dancing Festival (a self-entertainment gathering)
打躬作揖	to make a bow with hands folded in front; to bow and raise one's clasped hands in salute
打谷场	threshing ground; threshing floor
打虎亭汉墓	Han Tombs at Dahuting; Han Dynasty Tombs at Tiger Hunting Pavilion (He'nan)

打酒印	〈苗族〉(of wedding banquet) to stamp a liquor seal (to put a mark on the face of the guest for each cup he drinks)
打马印	〈蒙古族〉to mark horse with a brand
打马印节	〈蒙古族〉Horse Branding Day (around Tomb-Sweeping Day or Dragon Boat Festival) →打马印
打泥巴仗节	〈侗族〉Mud Fighting Day (around the 9th solar term: Grain in Ear)
打三朝	〈民俗〉Da San Zhao; Ceremony of the Third Day after Childbirth (celebration between the 3rd to the 7th day after giving a birth)
打铁节	〈基诺族〉Forging-Iron Festival (from 6th to 8th day of February)
大澳杨侯古庙	Tai O Yanghou Temple (Hong Kong)
大坝森林公园	Daba Forest Park (Sichuan)
大霸尖山	Tapachien Mountain; Dabajian Mountain (Taiwan)
大报恩寺琉璃宝塔	Glazed Pagoda of Dabao'en Temple; Porcelain Tower of Dabao'en Temple (Jiangsu)
大报恩寺遗址	Dabao'en Temple Ruins (Jiangsu)
大悲殿	hall of great mercy; palace of great sorrow
大悲寺	dabei temple; temple of great mercy/sorrow
大别勒滩盐湖	Dabieletan Salt Lake (Qinghai)
大别山(脉)	Dabie Mountain; Dabie Mountain Range
大别山彩虹瀑布	Rainbow Waterfall at Dabie Mountain (Anhui)
大别山地质博物馆	(of Tiantang Zhai) Dabie Mountain Geological Museum
大别山区	Dabie Mountain area/region
大别瑶螈	〈动〉*Yaotriton dabienicus*; dabie salamander
大钹[镲]	〈乐〉dabo; dacha; large cymbal
大布苏-狼牙坝自然保护区	Dabusu-Langyaba National Nature Reserve (Jilin)
大布苏自然保护区	Dabusu Nature Reserve (Jilin)

大仓鼠	〈动〉*Tscherskia triton*; greater long-tailed hamster
大藏峰	(of Mount Wuyi) Dacang Peak; Big-Treasure Peak
大曹溶洞	Dacao Karst Cave (Guangxi)
大成殿	dacheng hall; hall of great accomplishment; main hall of the Confucius temple
大城山公园	Dacheng Mountain Park (Hebei)
大乘庵	(of Mount Putuo) Mahayana Buddhist Nunnery
大乘禅院	(of Mount Putuo) Mahayana Buddhist Monastery
大乘寺	Mahayana temple
大齿蟾	〈动〉*Oreolalax major*; large toothed toad
大慈恩寺	Grand Ci'en Temple (Shaanxi)
大嶝岛	Dadeng Island (Fujian) →女人岛
大地湾文化	〈古〉Dadiwan culture (4800-8000 B.C., an ancient civilization created by Chinese ancestors in the Yellow River basin)
大地湾遗址	Site of Dadiwan; Dadiwan Prehistoric Site (Gansu)
大甸子遗址	Site of Dadianzi; Dadianzi Bronze Age Site (Inner Mongolia)
大殿	grand hall
大东海景区	Dadong Sea Scenic Spot (Hai'nan)
大都	grand capital; grand capital of the Yuan Dynasty (referring to Beijing at present) →元大都
大杜鹃	〈动〉*Cuculus canorus*; common cuckoo
大渡河	Dadu River (the main source or largest tributary of Minjiang River)
大渡河大峡谷	Dadu River Grand Gorge (Sichuan)
大渡桥	→泸定[大渡]桥
大佛殿	Great Buddha Hall (He'nan) →大雄宝殿
大佛洞	Great Buddha Cave (Shaanxi)
大佛阁	great Buddha pavilion
大佛寺	Great Buddha Temple

大佛寺景区	Great Buddha Temple Scenic Area (Zhejiang)
大佛岩	Great Buddha Rock (Zhejiang)
大夫第	mansion of senior official (private homes of senior officials in ancient times)
大高玄殿	Grand Gaoxuan Palace (ancient architecture of royal Taoist temple of Ming and Qing Dynasties) (Beijing)
大功	〈丧〉gown of processed flax (one of five funeral garments) →五服
大沽炮台	Dagu Fort (Tianjin)
大孤山	dagu mountain; grand gu mountain
大鼓	〈乐〉bass drum
大观楼	Daguan Pavilion; Grand View Pavilion (Yunnan)
大观园	daguan park; grand view garden (a showplace in Dream of the Red Chamber)
大海子湿地	dahaizi wetland
大寒	〈节气〉Great Cold; Major Cold (the 24th solar term)
大汉阳峰	Great Hanyang Peak (the highest peak of Lushan Mountain) (Jiangxi)
大汗行宫	Khan Temporary Palace (Hebei)
大好河山休闲旅游区	Dahao Heshan Leisure Tourism Area (Hubei)
大河北原始森林	Grand Hebei Primeval Forest (Liaoning)
大红灯笼	large/big red lantern
大红袍景区	(of Mount Wuyi) Dahongpao Scenic Area
大花无耳蟾	〈动〉*Atympanophrys gigantica*
大花无叶兰	〈植〉*Aphyllorchis gollanii*; huge leafless orchid
大黄	〈植〉*Rheum palmatum*; Chinese rhubarb
大蓟	〈中药〉*Cirsii Japonici Herba Carbonisata*; Japanese Thistle Herb/Root
大金瓦寺	(of Ta'er Monastery) Dajinwa Temple; Daikin Tile Temple; Greater Hall of the Golden Roof
大经堂	main assembly hall; sutra chanting hall
大觉山	Mount Dajue; Dajue Mountain (Jiangxi)

大觉寺	Dajue Temple; Temple of Enlightenment (Beijing, Jiangsu)
大浪湾石刻	Rock Carving at Big Wave Bay (Hong Kong)
大理古城	Dali Ancient/Old City (Yunnan)
大理三塔	Three Pagodas of Dali (Yunnan) →崇圣寺三塔
大殓	〈丧〉dalian (the funeral process of moving the deceased from the bed into the coffin)
大凉疣螈	〈动〉*Tylototriton taliangensis*; taliang knobby newt
大梁自然保护区	Daliang Nature Reserve (Hubei)
大亮子河漂流	Daliangzi River rafting (Heilongjiang)
大亮子河森林公园	Daliangzi River Forest Park (Heilongjiang)
大龙宫寺	Dalonggong Temple (Liaoning)
大龙湫	(of Mount Yandang) Dalong Waterfall; Big Dragon Waterfall
大龙潭金丝猴研究中心	Dalongtan Golden Monkey Research Center (Hubei)
大龙潭景区	Dalongtan (Grand Dragon Pond) Scenic Area (Guangxi)
大龙湾景区	Dalongwan (Grand Dragon Bay) Scenic Area (Zhejiang)
大茂山森林公园	Damao Mountain Forest Park (Hebei)
大庙湾刻石	Rock Inscription/Carving at Joss House Bay (a declared monument of Hong Kong)
大明宫遗址	Daming Palace Ruins (Shaanxi)
大明宫遗址公园	Daming Palace Heritage Park (Shaanxi)
大明湖	Daming Lake (Shandong)
大明寺	Daming Temple (Jiangsu)
大明孝陵神功圣德碑	Tablet of the Divine Power and Virtue of Xiaoling Tomb of Ming Dynasty (Jiangsu)
大鲵	〈动〉*Andrias davidianus* →娃娃鱼
大年	New Year (generally from the last day of the last lunar month to the 15th day of the first lunar month)

大年初一	Lunar New Year's Day; the first day of Chinese Lunar New Year
大宁河	Daning River
大宁灵石公园	Daning Lingshi Park (Shanghai)
大鹏湾	Dapeng Bay; Mirs Bay
大埔海滨公园	Tai Po Waterfront Park (Hong Kong)
大埔滘自然护理区	Tai Po Kau Nature Reserve (Hong Kong)
大埔瞭望台	Tai Po Lookout (Hong Kong)
大埔碗窑窑址	Site of Tai Po Bowl Kiln (Hong Kong)
大蹼铃蟾	〈动〉*Bombina maxima*; Yunnan firebelly toad; large-webbed bell toad
大青沟生态区	Daqing Valley Eco-Zone (Inner Mongolia)
大青山	Daqing Mountain (Zhejiang)
大清真寺	Great Mosque (Shaanxi)
大日如来佛	Buddha Mahāvairocana
大三巴牌坊	Ruins of St. Paul's (Macau)
大散关	Sanguan Pass (Shaanxi)
大扫除	〈民俗〉general cleaning; thorough cleanup (for welcoming the new year)
大圣南岩宫	(of Mount Wudang) South Peak Palace of Grand Sage
大十五节	〈普米族〉Fifteenth Day Festival (on the 15th day of the 12th lunar month)
大石围天坑群	Dashiwei Tiankeng Group; Dashiwei Karst Dolines (Guangxi)
大士阁	Dashi Pavilion (Guangxi, Anhui)
大暑	〈节气〉Great Heat; Major Heat (the 12th solar term)
大水井古建筑群	Dashuijing Ancient Architectural Group; Ancient Building Complex of Grand Well (Hubei)
大蒜果树	〈植〉*Dysoxylum Hai'nanense*; garlic fruit trees
大台北地区	Greater Taipei area →台北都会区
大潭山郊野公园	Tai Tam Country Park (Parque Natural da Taipa Grande) (Macao)
大唐芙蓉园	Datang Hibiscus Garden; Tang Paradise; Lotus Palace of the Tang Dynasty (Shaanxi)

大天池	(of Mount Lushan) Greater Heaven Pond
大天后宫	Grand Matsu Temple (Taiwan)
大同火山群	Datong Volcano Group/Cluster (Shanxi)
大同九龙壁	Nine-Dragon Wall of Datong (Shanxi)
大屯火山群	Datun Volcano Group (Taiwan)
大屯山	Datun Mountain (Taiwan)
大屯土司庄园	Datun Headman's Manor; Datun Chieftain's Manor (Guizhou)
大万伍佛洞	(of Longmen Grottoes) Dawanwu Buddha Cave
大王峰	(of Mount Wuyi) Great King Peak
大围山森林公园	Dawei Mountain Forest Park (Hu'nan)
大围异角蟾	〈动〉*Xenophrys daweimontis*
大汶口文化遗址	Dawenkou Cultural Relics (Shandong)
大雾梁歌会	〈侗族〉Dawuliang Singing Festival (held for three days in April)
大西沟景区	Daxigou Scenic Area (Hubei)
大溪神牛观光区	Daxi Shenniu (God Ox) Tourist Area (Taiwan)
大溪湿地公园	Daxi Wetland Park (Hubei)
大峡谷温泉	Great Canyon Hot Spring (Yunnan)
大相国寺	Daxiangguo Temple; Grand Xiangguo Monastery (He'nan) →建国寺
大象山	Daxiang Mountain; Elephant Mountain (Gansu)
大兴安岭	Greater Khingan Range; Greater Khingan Mountains (Heilongjiang)
大兴善寺	Da Xingshan Temple (Shaanxi)
大雄宝殿	〈佛〉precious hall of the great hero; main shrine hall; great Buddha's hall; Mahavira hall (main hall of a Buddhist temple)
大熊猫	〈动〉*Ailuropoda melanoleuca*; giant panda
大熊猫国家公园	Giant Panda National Park
大圩古镇	Daxu Ancient/Old Town (Guangxi)
大雪	〈节气〉Great Snow; Major Snow (the 21st solar term)
大雪锅山	Grand Snow Pot Mountain (the highest peak of Ailao Mountain, Yunnan)

大雪山景区	Grand Snow Mountain Scenic Area (Yunnan)
大崖头飞瀑	Dayatou Waterfall (Hubei)
大研古镇	Dayan Ancient Town (Yunnan)
大雁塔	Dayan Pagoda; Big Wild Goose Pagoda (Shaanxi)
大洋海底世界	Ocean Underwater World; Ocean Aquarium World (Shanghai)
大窑龙泉窑遗址	Site of Longquan Kiln at Dayao; Longquan Kilin Ruins at Dayao (Zhejiang)
大窑文化遗址	Dayao Cultural Relics (stone implement workshop) (Inner Mongolia)
大叶蒟	〈中药〉*Piper laetispicum*
大叶榉树	〈植〉*Zelkova schneideriana*; schneider zelkova
大叶杓兰	〈植〉*Cypripedium fasciolatum*
大邑刘氏庄园博物馆	Liushi Manorial Museum in Dayi; Manorial Museum of the Liu Family in Dayi (Sichuan)
大英死海	Daying Dead Sea (Sichuan) →中国死海
大盈江旅游区	Daying River Tourism Area (Yunnan)
大屿山(岛)	Lantau Island (Hong Kong)
大禹陵	Great Yu Mausoleum (Zhejiang)
大禹神话园	Da Yu Mythology Park (Hubei)
大禹治水	(of legend) Da Yu flood control
大云寺	dayun temple
大运河	〈古〉Grand Canal (a man-made canal built in ancient times)
大枣	〈植〉*Ziziphus jujuba*; (Chinese) red date
大栅栏	Dashilan (a famous commercial street) (Beijing)
大昭寺	Dazhao Temple; Jokhang Temple (Tibet)
大政殿	(of Shenyang Imperial Palace) Dazheng Hall
大智禅寺	Dazhi Temple (Zhejiang)
大中华(地)区	Greater China; Greater China region/area
大钟寺	Great Bell Temple (Beijing)
大洲岛	Dazhou Island (Hai'nan)
大足石刻	Dazu Rock Carvings; Dazu Stone Sculptures (Chongqing)

傣族	Dai ethnic group; Dai
傣族村寨	Dai village; village of Dai ethnic group (Yunnan)
岱庙	(of Mount Taishan) Dai Temple
岱王山	Daiwang Mountain; King Dai Mountain (Shandong)
岱宗牌坊	Daizong Archway (Shandong)
戴红	〈民俗〉to wear red clothes (for exorcising evil spirits)
戴孝帽	〈丧〉(of funeral) to wear mourning hat
戴云湍蛙	〈动〉*Amolops daiyunensis*; Daiyun torrent/sucker frog
丹陛	danbi (referring to palace steps)
丹陛桥	(of Temple of Heaven) Danbi Bridge; Red Stairway Bridge; Red Walkway Bridge
丹陛石雕	Danbi Stone Carving (Beijing) →祈年殿
丹顶鹤	〈动〉*Grus japonensis*; red-crowned crane
丹江口市烈士陵园	Martyrs Cemetery of Danjiangkou City (Hubei)
丹江口水库景区	Danjiangkou Reservoir Scenic Area (Hubei)
丹江漂流	Danjiang River Rafting (Shaanxi)
丹麻戏	〈土族〉Danma Opera (performed from the 11th to the 15th day of the 6th lunar month, for protecting young crops)
丹参	〈植〉*Salvia miltiorrhiza*; red salvia
丹梯铁索	(of Danxia Mountain) Dan Iron Chain Ladder
丹土遗址	Site of Dantu; Dantu Cultural Ruins (a late Neolithic cultural site, Shandong)
丹霞地貌	danxia landform
丹霞地质公园	Danxia Geopark (Gansu)
丹霞谷	Danxia Valley (Guizhou)
丹霞山	Mount Danxia; Danxia Mountain (Guangdong)
丹霞山景区	Danxia Mountain Scenic Area (Guangdong)
丹霞十二景	twelve sceneries in Danxia Mountain (Guangdong)
丹霞梧桐	〈植〉*Firmiana danxiaensis*; Danxia phoenix tree
丹崖山	Danya Mountain; Red Cliff Mountain (Shandong)

丹云峡	(of Huanglong Valley) Red Cloud Gorge
丹云峡景区	Red Cloud Gorge Scenic Area (Sichuan)
丹洲景区	Danzhou Scenic Area (Guangxi)
单鞭下势	(of Tai Chi) Single whip and pushing down
单唇无叶兰	〈植〉*Aphyllorchis simplex*
单拍脚	Single slap kick
单叶鞭叶蕨	〈植〉*Cynomidiciyum basipinnnaium*
疍家	danjia (fishermen who live on a boat in Guangdong, Guangxi, Fujian and Hai'nan)
淡菜	ried mussel meat
淡肩异角蟾	〈动〉*Xxenophrys boettgeri*; pale-shouldered horned toad
淡竹叶	〈植〉*Lophatherum gracile*; lophatherum gracile
蛋茶	egg tea (a folk snack served as hospitality custom in Ningde, Fujian)
当代漆画	contemporary lacquer painting
当归	〈植〉*Angelica sinensis*; Chinese angelica
当惹雍措	Dangreyong Lake; Lake Tangra Yumco (the 4th largest lake in Tibet)
珰奈湿地	Dangnai Wetland (Heilongjiang)
党参	〈植〉*Codonopsis pilosula*; tangshen
党项(族)	〈古〉Tangut ethnic group; Dangxiang (a branch of the west Qiang ethnic group and one of the oldest tribes in northwest China)
氹仔岛	Taipa Island (Macao)
氹仔市政公园	Taichai Municipal Park (Macao) →嘉模公园
氹仔市政花园	Taipa Municipal Garden (Macao)
氹仔中央公园	Dangzai Central Park (Macao)
荡秋千	to play on a swing
刀杆节	〈傈僳族〉Knife-Pole Festival; Sword Pole Festival; Knifeladder Climbing Festival (a traditional sport game held on the 8th day of the 2nd lunar month)

刀郎木卡姆	Dolan Muqam; Dolan Mukam (a variety of art shows with song, dance and music in Daolang region of Xinjiang)
刀郎人	Uyghur Dolans (descendants of ancient nomads)
刀郎舞	Doran/Daolang dance (representing the hunting process of Daolang people in Xinjiang)
刀术	〈武术〉broadsword play; Sabreplay
倒稿节	〈瑶族〉Daogao Festival (on the 16th day of the 10th lunar month for celebrating the harvest)
倒卷肱	(of Tai Chi) stepping back and whirling arms on both sides; forearm rolling on both sides
倒毛跟斗	backward somersault
倒踢	reverse arch kick
道德经幢	Tao Te Jing Peristele; Scripture-of-Ethic Stele (a stone pillar inscribed with the Classic of the Virtue) (Hebei)
道风山	Tao Fong Mountain (Hong Kong)
道孚塔遗址	Ruins of Daofu Pagoda (Beijing)
道福山祠	Daofu Mountain Temple (Hong Kong)
道光廿五酒	Daoguang 25th year spirit (the only liquid relic in China, which was made during the Daoguang reign of the Qing Dynasty)
道教圣地	site for Taoist pilgrimage; Taoist holy places
道县野桔	〈植〉*Citrus daoxianensis*
稻城亚丁自然保护区	Daocheng Aden Nature Reserve (Sichuan)
得胜花园	Victory Garden (Macao)
得月楼	Deyue Pavilion (a boite which is famous for Subang Cuisine, Jiangsu)
得真亭	(of Humble Administrator's Garden) Reality Reflection Pavilion
德昂族	De'ang ethnic group; De'ang
德碑夕照	Debei Afterglow (one of the eight old sights of Jilin)
德格印经院	Dege Sutra-Printing House (Sichuan)

德和园	(of Summer Palace) Garden of Virtue and Harmony
德庆学宫	Deqing Confucius Temple (Guangdong)
德天瀑布	Detian Waterfall (Guangxi)
德义堂	Deyi Hall (a typical Hui-style courtyard dwelling, Anhui)
灯杆节	〈仡佬族〉Light Pole Festival (from the 1st to the 15th day of the 1st lunar month)
灯会	lantern show (large lighting exhibition organized by the government with various folk activities)
灯节	Lamp Festival →巴罗提节
灯笼	Chinese lantern
灯笼草	〈植〉*Clinopodium polycephalum*; physalis peruviana; downy groundcherry fruit or herb
灯笼洲灯塔	Lighthouse at Tang Lung Chau (Hong Kong)
灯谜	(of Lantern Festival) lantern riddle; riddles written on lanterns
灯影峡	Dengying Gorge; Lantern Shadow Gorge (Hubei)
登高节	Height Ascending Festival →重阳节
登龙峰	Denglong Peak (one of the twelve peaks of Wushan Mountain, Chongqing)
蹬腿	Heel kick
滴翠峡	Dicui Gorge (the longest and deepest one of the Lesser Three Gorges) (Chongqing)
滴水湖	Dripping Lake (Shanghai)
滴水滩瀑布	Dishuitan Waterfall (Guizhou)
地堡街	Bunker Street (Macao)
地缸	large pottery vat
地构叶	〈植〉*Speranskia tuberculata*
地炉	sunken hearth (a pit in the indoor ground used for making a fire to keep warm with the bricks and stones laid around)

地母祭	〈阿昌族〉Earth Mother Ceremony (which is held three times every year, respectively on the 21st Day of the 2nd lunar month, the 28th day of the 5th lunar month and the 25th day of the 6th lunar month)
地热谷	Geothermal Valley; Thermal Valley (Taiwan)
地坛公园	Temple of Earth (Beijing)
地戏	〈布依族〉Dixi Opera (the ancient mask dance)
地下大峡谷	Underground Grand Canyon (Guizhou)
地下宫殿	underground palace
地下河	underground river
地下迷宫	underground labyrinth
地下森林	Underground Forest (Jilin)
地榆	〈植〉*Sanguisorba officinalis*; great burnet; garden burnet
地藏节	Ksitigarbha Festival (on the 30th day of the 7th lunar month)
地藏寺	Ksitigahba temple
滇池	Dianchi Lake (Yunnan)
滇池蝾螈	〈动〉*Cynops wolterstorffi*; Yunnan Lake Newt
滇东高原	Eastern Yunnan Plateau (Yunnan)
滇金丝猴	〈动〉*Rhinopithecus bieti*; Yunnan/black snub-nosed monkey
滇南桫椤	〈植〉*Alsophila austroyunnanensis*
滇南疣螈	〈动〉*Tylototriton yangi*
滇楠	〈植〉*Phoebe nanmu*
滇润楠	〈植〉*Machilus yunnanensis*
滇蜀无柱兰	〈植〉*Amitostigma tetralobum*
滇蛙	〈动〉*Nidirana pleuraden*; Yunnan pond frog
滇螈	〈动〉*Hypselotriron wolterstorffi*; Yunnan lake newt
滇藏线	Yunnan-Tibet route
滇中粮仓	granary in central Yunnan (referring to Yiliang county of Kunming, Yunnan)
点斑齿蟾	〈动〉*Oreolalax multipunctatus*; spotted toothed toad

点苍山	Diancang Mountain; Cangshan Mountain (Yunnan) →苍山
点桃虾球	〈烹饪〉Walnut Shrimp
店子坪当代红色教育基地	Contemporary Red Education Base at Dianziping (Hubei)
淀山湖	Dianshan Lake (the source of Huangpu River) (Shanghai)
奠济宫	Dianji Temple (Taiwan)
殿春簃	(of Master-of-Nets Garden) Late Spring Study
叼羊	scrambling for a sheep (a folk sport in Xingjiang in which players ride horses to scramble a sheep)
雕龙碑遗址	Diaolongbei Neolithic Site; Neolithic Site at Carved Dragon Stele (Hubei)
雕梅	〈烹饪〉Carved Plum (a traditional and special food of Bai ethnic group)
吊(脚)楼	stilted building; pile dwelling; suspended (wooden) building
吊罗山	Diaoluo Mountain (one of the rarest primeval tropical rain forest areas in China, Hai'nan)
吊丧	〈丧〉(of funeral) to visit the bereaved to offer one's condolences; to pay a condolence call
钓鱼岛	Diaoyu Island (East China Sea)
钓鱼岛及其附属岛屿	Diaoyu Island and its affiliated islands
钓鱼台国宾馆	Diaoyutai State Guesthouse (Beijing)
钓鱼湾	Anglers' Beach (Hong Kong)
叠彩山	Diecai Hill; Piled Silk Hill; Folded Brocade Hill (Guangxi)
丁香	〈植〉*Syzygium aromaticum*; flos caryophyllata; lilac
丁忧守制	〈古〉to be in mourning for a parent; officials' bereavement of parents

顶碗	pagoda of bowls; balancing a stack of bowls on the head (a traditional Chinese acrobatic show where the actor perches on his head a pile of porcelain bowls and performs extremely difficult acrobatic elements)
鼎	〈古〉ding (one of the most important species of ancient bronzes, which was used to cook meat or as meat storage utensil in ancient times)
鼎湖峰	Dinghu Peak (Zhejiang)
鼎湖山	Dinghu Mountain (Guangdong)
订婚	to become engaged or betrothed
订婚酒	engagement banquet
定安八景	Eight Views of Dingan (Hai'nan)
定东陵	Dingdong Mausoleum (Hebei)
定海神针	(of Zhangjiajie) Magic Sea Needle; Magic Golden Cudgel →如意金箍棒
定慧寺	dinghui temple
定亲	to become engaged or betrothed
定窑	〈古〉Ding Kiln (one of the five famous kilns in ancient China)
定窑瓷器	〈古〉Ding-Ware; Ding Porcelain (one of the five famous chinawares in ancient China)
定州塔	Dingzhou Tower (Hebei)
东安门	Dong'an Gate (one of the four gates of the imperial city, Beijing)
东澳岛	Dong'ao Island (Guangdong)
东巴宫壁画	Mural/Fresco in Dongba Palace (Yunnan)
东巴教	〈纳西族〉Dongba Religion
东巴文化博物馆	Museum of Dongba Culture (Yunnan)
东宝仙人岩	Dongbao Xianren (Immortal) Rock (Hubei)
东北[远东]刺猬	〈动〉*Erinaceus amurensis*; Manchurian hedgehog
东北[西伯利亚]虎	〈动〉*Panthera tigris*; Siberian tiger; Amur tiger
东北虎林园	Siberian Tiger Park (Heilongjiang)
东北虎野生动物园	Siberian Tiger Wild Animal Park

东北黄山	Huangshan Mountain in Northeast (referring to the Fenghuang/Phoenix Mountain of Dandong) (Liaoning)
东北角[宜兰]海岸国家景区	Northeast Coast National Scenic Area (Taiwan)
东北平原	Northeast China Plain; Northeast Plain
东北小鲵	〈动〉*Hynobius leechii*; Northeastern China salamander
东部线柱兰	〈植〉*Zeuxine tabiyahanensis*
东川红土地	Dongchuan Red Land; Lateritic Land in Dongchuan (Yunnan)
东川尾凤蝶	〈动〉*Bhutanitis thaidina dongchuanensis*
东方佛都	Oriental Buddha Park; Oriental Capital of Buddhism (Sichuan)
东方基金会会址	Casa Garden; headquarters of the Oriental Foundation (Macao)
东方净琉璃世界	〈佛〉Oriental pure glazed world
东方铃蟾	〈动〉*Bombina orientalis*; oriental firebellied toad
东方美人	oriental beauty
东方明珠	Oriental Pearl (Shanghai)
东方蝾螈	〈动〉*Cynops orientalis*; oriental fire-bellied newt
东方三圣	〈佛〉Three Saints of the East
东方水韭	〈植〉*Isoetes orientalis*
东方体育中心	Oriental Sports Center (Shanghai)
东方威尼斯	Oriental Venice (referring to Suzhou) (Jiangsu)
东方夏威夷	Oriental Hawaii (referring to Sanya) (Hai'nan)
东方泽泻	〈植〉*Alisma orientale*; orientale water plantain rhizome
东方之珠	Pearl of East (referring to Hong Kong)
东方侏罗纪	Oriental Jurassic →中华恐龙园
东风航天城	Dongfeng Aviation City (Gansu) →酒泉卫星发射中心
东宫门	(of Summer Palace) East Palace Gate; East Gate of the Palace

东关清真大寺	Dongguan Grand Mosque (Qinghai)
东海	East China Sea
东海大桥	East Sea Bridge (which connects Shanghai and Zhejiang)
东海第一胜境	No.1 Fairyland in the East China Sea (referring to Lianyungang) (Jiangsu)
东胡	donghu (an ancient nomadic people of northeast China)
东华门	(of Imperial Palace) Donghua Gate; East Prosperity Gate
东江	Dongjiang River (a tributary of Pearl River)
东江豆腐煲	〈烹饪〉Tofu in Clay Pot; Dongjiang Tofu en Casserole
东江湖	Dongjiang Lake (Hu'nan)
东江流域	Dongjiang River basin
东疆湾人造黄金海岸	Dongjiang Bay Artificial Golden Coast (Tianjin)
东郊椰林	Dongjiao Coconut Forest; Eastern Suburb Coconut Grove (Hai'nan)
东焦得布山	East Jiaodebu Mountain (Heilongjiang)
东丽湖景区	Dongli Lake Scenic Area (Tianjin)
东林寺	(of Mount Lushan) Donglin Temple; East Forest Temple
东六宫	(of Imperial Palace) East Six Palaces
东龙门山	East Longmen Mountain (Heilongjiang)
东龙洲	Tung Lung Chau (Hong Kong) →南堂岛
东平森林公园	Dongping Forest Park (Shanghai)
东平洲	Tung Ping Chau (Hong Kong)
东坡井	Dongpo well
东坡书院	Dongpo Academy (Jiangsu, Hai'nan)
东普陀讲寺	Tung Po Tor Monastery (Hong Kong)
东沙群岛	Dongsha Islands (South China Sea)
东山岭	Dongshan Ridge (Hai'nan) →笔架山
东望洋灯塔	Guia Lighthouse (Macao)
东西配殿	(of palace) eastern and western wings; east and west side halls

东乡族	Dongxiang ethnic group; Dongxiang
东涌炮台	Tung Chung Fort (Hong Kong)
东岳大帝	East Mountain Emperor; God of Mount Tai (one of the Chinese folk religious beliefs)
东岳宫	Dongyue Palace (Hu'nan)
东岳泰山	Mount Taishan; Taishan Mountain (as the Eastern One of the Five Sacred Mountains in China) (Shandong)
东寨港自然保护区	East Harbour Reserve (Hai'nan)
冬不拉	〈乐〉Dombra (a traditional plucked string instrument of the Kazakh in Xinjiang)
冬瓜	〈植〉*Benincasa hispida*; Chinese watermelon
冬红花	〈植〉*Holmskioldia sanguinea*; Chinese-hat plant
冬季大法会	〈藏族〉GreatPrayer Festival in Winter
冬笋	winter bamboo shoot
冬至	〈节气〉Winter Solstice (the 22nd solar term)
董家口长城	Dongjiakou Great Wall (Hebei)
董志原[塬]	Dongzhi Plain (Loess Plateau) (Gansu)
董棕壶	dong brown pot (a kind of wine set used by the Drung ethnic group living in western Yunnan)
动蕊花	〈植〉*Kinostemon ornatum*
动物缓冲区	zoological buffer area
侗寨	Dong stronghold; stockaded villages of Dong people (Guangxi)
侗寨鼓楼	drum tower of Dong village (Guizhou)
侗族	Dong ethnic group; Dong
侗族大歌	Dong chorus; grand songs of Dong ethnic group
洞房	〈婚〉(of wedding) bridal chamber
洞房花烛夜	wedding festivities night
洞沟古墓群	Donggou Ancient Tombs (Jilin)
洞景佛寺	Dongjing Buddhist Temple (Yunnan)
洞阔尔独贡殿	(of Wudang Lamasery) Dongkuo'er Dugong Hall
洞生耳蕨	〈植〉*Polystichum cavernicola*
洞庭湖	(of Yangtze River basin) Dongting Lake (Hu'nan)

斗	dou (a container for measuring grain)
斗鸡山	Douji Mountain; Cockfighting Mountain (one of the ten wonders of the Lijiang River, Guangxi)
斗母宫	(of Mount Taishan) Palace to Goddess Dou Mu
斗南花市	Dounan Flower Market (Yunnan)
斗鸟会	〈侗族〉Bird-Fighting Gathering
斗牛节	〈侗族〉Bullfighting Festival (on the 8th day of the 4th lunar month)
豆蔻	〈植〉*Amomum kravanh*; whitefruit amomum
都江堰	Dujiang Weir; Dujiangyan Irrigation System (Sichuan)
都江堰熊猫基地	Dujiangyan Panda Base (Sichuan)
都拉塔口岸	Dulata Port (Xinjiang)
都兰古墓	Dulan Ancient Tombs (Qinghai)
都兰国际狩猎场	Dulan International Hunting Ground (Qinghai)
都龙边境集市	Dulong Border Fair (on Sundays in Yunnan)
都塔尔	〈乐〉Dutar (a traditional plucked string instrument in Xinjiang)
都瓦节	〈维吾尔族〉Duwa Festival (for sacrifice to ancestors around the 5th day of 4th lunar month)
独根草	〈植〉*Orestitrophe rupifraga*
独贵龙运动	〈旧〉Duguilong movement (an organizational form of the Mongolian people's struggle against imperialism and feudalism in modern times)
独花兰	〈植〉*Changnienia amoena*
独乐寺	Dule Temple; Temple of Solitary Joy (one of the three remaining Liao monasteries, Tianjin) →大佛寺
独立打虎	〈武术〉(of Tai Chi) Beating tiger on single leg; Stepping back to hit the tiger
独立托掌	〈武术〉(of Tai Chi) Standing on one leg and holding palm
独龙江	Dulong River (Yunnan)
独龙江峡谷	Dulong River Gorge (Yunnan)

独龙族	Dulong ethnic group; Dulong/Derung
独秀峰景区	Solitary Beauty Peak Scenic Area (Guangxi)
杜甫草堂	Du Fu Thatched Cottage (Sichuan)
杜公湖湿地公园	Dugong Lake Wetland Park (Hubei)
杜鹃	1 〈动〉*Cuculus*; cuckoo 2 〈植〉*Rhododendron simsii*; azalea
杜鹃红山茶	〈植〉*Camellia azalea*
杜鹃峡	(of Kangding Love Song Scenic Area) Cuckoo Gorge
杜康造酒说	Du Kang Inventing Wine (a folklore)
杜陵	Duling Mausoleum (Shaanxi)
杜仲	〈植〉*Eucommia ulmoides*; eucommia ulmoides
肚兜	〈服〉dudou (an undergarment covering the chest and abdomen); bellyband; stomacher
渡江战役总前委旧址	Site of the General Front Committee of the Crossing-the-Yangtze-River Campaign (Anhui)
端节	〈水族〉Duanjie Festival (held to celebrate the harvest and ring out the Old Year and ring in the New Year)
端午节	Duanwu Festival; Chinese Dragon Boat Festival (on the 5th day of the 5th lunar month) →龙舟节
端砚	Duanzhou ink-stone; Duan ink-stone (one of the four famous ink-stones in China, which is produced in Zhaoqing, Guangdong)
短柄乌头	〈植〉*Aconitum brachypodum*
短毛美冠兰	〈植〉*Eulophia hirsuta*
短序石豆兰	〈植〉*Bulbophyllum brevispicatum*
短肢角蟾	〈动〉*Megophrys brachykolos*
断七	〈丧〉to finish the Sevenths (the Buddhist Service on each the 7th day within 49 days after one's death)
断桥	(of West Lake) Broken Bridge
断桥残雪	(of West Lake) Melting Snow at Broken Bridge

堆秀山	(of Imperial Palace) Mountain of Accumulated Elegance
堆绣	barbola (a special Tibetan art that employs the techniques of embossed decoration to the object of portray)
对歌	antiphony (a popular culture in Leqing, Zhejiang)
对歌节	〈壮族、侗族、布依族〉Antiphony Festival (on the 3rd day of the 3rd lunar month)
对话石	(of Temple of Heaven) Dialogue-Stone
对联	antithetical couplets; poetic couplets; couplets
敦煌壁画	Dunhuang Mural; Dunhuang Fresco (Gansu)
敦煌莫高窟	Dunhuang Mogao Grottoes (Gansu)
敦煌千佛洞	Dunhuang Thousand-Buddha Cave (Gansu)
炖排骨	〈烹饪〉Braised Pork Ribs; Braised Short Ribs
盾果草	〈中药〉*Thyrocarpus sampsonii*; Root of Sampsonii Hance
盾叶薯蓣	〈植〉*Dioscorea zingiberensis*
顿首	〈古〉to make a ceremonious nod (one of the nine ways of kowtow); kowtow
多疣狭口蛙	〈动〉*Kaloula verrucosa*; verrucous digging frog
躲猫猫	hide-and-seek game →捉迷藏

E

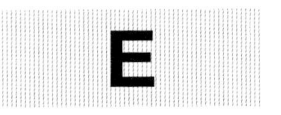

阿房宫遗址	E-pang Palace Ruins/Remains; Site of the Epang Palace (Shaanxi)
俄罗斯族	Russian ethnic group; Russian
俄喜节	〈藏族〉E'xi Festival (on the 7th day of the 12th lunar month)
莪术	〈植〉*Curcuma phaeocaulis*; curcuma zedoary
峨眉齿蟾	〈动〉*Oreolalax omeimontis*
峨眉耳蕨	〈植〉*Polystichum omeiense*
峨眉角蟾	〈动〉*Megophrys omeimontis*
峨眉(山)金顶	〈佛〉Mount Emei Jinding (Golden Summit) (Sichuan) →金顶华藏寺
峨眉金线兰	〈植〉*Anoectochilus emeiensis*
峨眉冷杉	〈植〉*Abies fabri*
峨眉拳	Emei Quan; Emei Boxing
峨眉山	Mount Emei; Emei Mountain (one of the four famous Buddhist mountains) (Sichuan)
峨眉山报国寺	Baoguo Temple at Emei Mountain (Sichuan)
峨眉山博物馆	(of Mount Emei) Mount Emei Museum
峨眉山圣寿万年寺铜铁佛像	Bronze and Iron Buddha Statue in Shengshou Wannian Temple at Mount Emei (Sichuan)
峨眉山游人中心	(of Mount Emei) Tourist Center of Mount Emei
峨眉山自然生态猴区	Natural Eco-Zone of Monkeys in Emei Mountain (Sichuan)
峨眉无柱兰	〈植〉*Amitostigma faberi*
峨眉虾脊兰	〈植〉*Calanthe emeishanica*
峨眉竹茎兰	〈植〉*Tropidia emeishanica*

峨眉髭蟾	〈动〉*Leptobrachium boringii*; Emei moustache toad
峨热竹	〈植〉*Bashania spanostachya*
峨山掌突蟾	〈动〉*Paramegophrys oshanensis*; Oshan metacarpal-tubercled toad
鹅池亭	Goose Pond Pavilion (in memory of Wang Xizhi) (Zhejiang)
鹅掌楸	〈植〉*Liriodendron chinense*; Chinese tulip tree
额尔齐斯河	Ertix Rivers; Irtysh River (Xinjiang)
额敏塔	Emin Minaret (Xinjiang) →苏公塔
额什丁墓	Eshiding Mausoleum (Xinjiang)
鄂尔多斯文化艺术中心	Ordos Culture and Art Center (Inner Mongolia)
鄂陵湖	Ngoring Lake (Qinghai)
鄂伦春族	Oroqen ethnic group; Oroqen
鄂温克族	Ewenki ethnic group; Ewenki
鄂豫边区革命烈士陵园	Cemetery of Revolutionary Martyrs in Hubei-He'nan Border Region (Hubei)
鄂州贺龙军部旧址	Former Site of Helong Military Headquarters at Ezhou (Hubei)
鳄蜥	〈动〉*Shinisaurus crocodilurus*; Chinese crocodile lizard
鳄鱼山景区	Crocodile Mountain Scenic Area (Guangxi)
恩格贝生态区	Engebei Eco-Zone (Inner Mongolia)
恩施大峡谷	Enshi Grand Canyon (Hubei)
恩施观音峡	Enshi Guanyin Gorge; Goddess of Mercy Gorge in Enshi (Hubei)
恩施龙鳞宫	Enshi Dragon Scale Palace (Hubei)
恩施清江风景旅游区	Enshi Qingjiang River Scenic Area (Hubei)
恩施清江蝴蝶崖景区	Enshi Qingjiang Butterfly Cliff Scenic Area (Hubei)
耳闸公园	Er'zha Park (Tianjin)
洱海	Erhai Lake (Yunnan)
二道海	Erdao Lake (Sichuan)

二胡	〈乐〉erhu; two-stringed Chinese fiddle
二黄	〈戏〉erhuang (a music for voice in traditional Chinese opera)
二黄调	〈戏〉erhuang tune
二郎剑景区	Erlang Jian Scenic Area (Qinghai)
二郎山	Erlang Mountain (Sichuan)
二郎山景区	Erlang Mountain Scenic Spot (He'nan)
二里头遗址	Site of Erlitou Ancient Culture; Erlitou Ancient Cultural Relics (He'nan)
二七纪念塔	Erqi Memorial Tower; February 7th Memorial Hall; Zhengzhou Memorial Tower for Feb. 7th Strike (He'nan)
二起脚	Jump flying kick
二人转	erren zhuan; a song-and-dance duet (popular in the northeast of China)
二色卷瓣兰	〈植〉*Bulbophyllum bicolor*
二十四节气	twenty-four solar terms
二十四孝	twenty-four filial exemplars
二十四孝铜雕群	(of Wanfo Garden) Copper sculpture group of Twenty-Four Filial Exemplars
二梳百年好合	(of wedding) the second combing, harmony throughout your marriage
二天门	(of Mount Wudang) The Second Gate of Heavenly Palace
二王庙	Two Kings Temple (Sichuan)
二仙岩湿地自然保护区	Erxianyan Wetland Nature Reserve (Hubei)
二月二	Eryueer Festival (on the 2nd day of the 2nd lunar month) →龙抬头
二祖庵	(of Shaolin Temple) The Second Patriarch Temple

F

发菜	〈植〉*Nostoc flagelliforme*; hair weeds; black moss
发红包	〈民俗〉to give/offer a red envelope (containing money as a gift, bribe or kickback)
发压岁钱	〈民俗〉to give new year lucky money (for celebrating Chinese New Year)
法定节假日	national statutory holiday
法海寺	Fahai Temple; Dharma-samudra Vihāra (Beijing)
法门寺	Famen Temple (Shaanxi)
法门寺文化景区	Famen Temple Cultural Scenic Area (Shaanxi)
法器	Buddhist ritual instrument (used in a Buddhist or Taoist mass)
法泉寺	Faquan Temple (Gansu)
法堂	1 hall for preaching the Buddhist doctrine; hall for expounding the dharma in a temple 2 〈旧〉court of law
法王寺	(of Shaolin Temple) Fawang Temple
法王寺景区	Fawang Temple Scenic Area (He'nan)
法兴寺	Faxing Temple (Shanxi, Beijing)
法雨寺	(of Mount Putuo) Fayu Temple
法源寺	Fayuan Temple (Beijing)
法云阁	〈旧〉Fayun Pavilion (Yunnan) →五凤楼
翻白叶树	〈植〉*Pterospermum heterophyllum*
反对	couplets antithetical in meaning
饭含	〈丧〉(of funeral) fanhan (some bead, jade, grain or money are put into the mouth of the deceased)

梵净山自然保护区	Fanjing Mountain Nature Reserve (Guizhou)
梵天寺	Fantian Temple (Fujian)
方河	(of Yuanming Garden) Square Lake
方壶胜境	(of Yuanming Garden) Wonderland on Fanghu Island
方塔园	Fangta Garden (Shanghai)
方外观	(of Yuanming Garden) Octagonal Belvedere (Mosque)
方丈殿	hall of Buddhist abbot
坊子白酒酿造工艺	Fangzi spirit brewing and distillation technology/processing
芳草海	(of Jiuzhai Valley) Fragrant Grass Lake
芳渚临流	(of Chengde Mountain Resort) Beautiful Islet with Charming Landscape-View
钫	〈古〉fang (a container for serving wine)
防风	〈植〉*Saposhnikovia divaricata*; anisomeles
房县红军烈士纪念塔	Fangxian Red Army Martyrs Memorial Tower (Hubei)
放鞭炮	〈民俗〉to set/let off firecrackers; to shoot firecrackers
放灯	〈民俗〉to light colorful lanterns (for exorcising evil spirits, and welcoming prosperity and happiness)
放风筝	to fly a kite
放生池	free life pond; life releasing pond (a facility in a Buddhist temple)
飞凤峰	(of Mount Wushan) Feifeng Peak
飞凤瀑	Feifeng Waterfall; Flying Phoenix Waterfall (Jiangxi)
飞凤潭	Feifeng Pond; Flying Phoenix Pond (Jiangxi)
飞虹塔	(of Guangsheng Temple) Feihong Tower; Flying Rainbow Tower
飞鸿山	Feihong Mountain (Jiangxi)
飞狐峪	Feihu Valley; Flying Fox Valley (Hebei)

飞来峰	Feilai Peak; Peak Flown from Afar (Zhejiang)
飞来峰造像	Feilaifeng Cliffside Sculptures; Carved Stone Statues on the Peak Flown from Afar (Zhejiang)
飞来石	(of Mount Huangshan) Stone from Heaven
飞来寺	Feilai Temple (Yunnan)
飞龙洞	Feilong Cave; Flying Dragon Cave (Guizhou)
飞龙瀑	Feilong Waterfall; Flying Dragon Waterfall (Yunnan)
飞龙山	feilong mountain; flying dragon mountain
飞龙铁鼎	Flying Dragon Iron Ding (Sichuan)
飞龙峡景区	Feilong Gorge Scenic Area; Flying Dragon Gorge Scenic Area (Sichuan)
飞瀑涧	(of Qingshan Valley) Flying Waterfall Valley
飞瀑流辉	(of Jiuzhaigou Valley) Rosy Flying Waterfall
飞瀑泻玉	(of Xingtai Canyon group) Flying Waterfall Droping Jades
飞泉沟	Flying Spring Valley (Sichuan)
飞沙堰溢洪道	(of Dujiangyan Irrigation System) Flying Sand Spillway
飞升崖	(of Mount Wudang) Ascension Cliff
飞天凤凰	Flying Phoenix (the orchid which won the Special Gold Award in the 10th Orchid Exposition in Zhejiang)
飞雪泉	(of Mountain Villa with Embracing Beauty) Spring of Flying Snow; Flying Snow Spring
飞云洞	Feiyun Cave; Flying Cloud Cave (Guizhou) →飞云崖
飞云崖	Feiyun Cliff; Flying Cloud Cliff (Guizhou) →飞云洞
翡翠池	(of Mount Huangshan) Jadeite Pond
翡翠岛	Jade/Jadeite Island; Emerald Island (Hebei)
翡翠谷	(of Mount Huangshan) Jadeite Valley; Emerald Valley
翡翠峡	Jade/Jadeite Gorge; Emerald Gorge (Hubei)
费氏刘树蛙	〈动〉*Liuixalus feii*

分流炮台	Fan Lau Fort (Hong Kong)
分龙节	〈瑶族〉Dragon Distribution Festival
分子钱	〈民俗〉money/cash given as a wedding gift
汾河	Fenhe River (a tributary of the Yellow River in Shanxi)
粉背叶人字果	〈植〉*Dichocarpum hypoglaucum*
粉彩瓷	famille rose porcelain
粉蕉	〈植〉*Musa nana*; dwarf banana; Chinese banana
粉岭龙跃头天后宫	Lung Yeuk Tau Tianhou Palace in Fenling Ridge (Hong Kong)
粉岭彭氏宗祠	Ancestral Hall of the Peng Family in Fenling Ridge (Hong Kong)
奋起湖景区	Fenqi Lake Scenic Area (Taiwan)
丰都鬼城	Fengdu Ghost City (Chongqing)
丰镐遗址	Feng and Hao Site; Ruins of Fengjing and Haojing (ancient capital of the Western Zhou Dynasty) (Shaanxi)
丰乐生态园	Fengle Ecological Garden (Anhui)
丰年祭	〈高山族〉Harvest Ceremony (during the autumn harvest for around a week)
丰收祭	→收获[丰收]祭
风景长廊	scenery corridor; long corridor with scenery/landscape
风铃草	〈植〉*Campanula medium*; bellflower; Canterbury bell
风炉	〈古〉wind stove (specially used for making tea in the Tang Dynasty)
风泉清听	(of Chengde Mountain Resort) Garden of Breeze and Stream Echoes
风水理论	fengshui theory; geomantic omen theory
风穴寺	Fengxue Temple (He'nan)
风雨桥	wind-rain bridge; wind-rain proof bridge (for pedestrians taking shelter from the wind and rain)
风筝节	Kite Festival; Festival of Kite

枫泾古镇	Fengjing Ancient Town (Shanghai)
封江口湿地公园	Fengjian River Mouth Wetland Park (Hubei)
封开异角蟾	〈动〉*Xenophrys acuta*
封龙山	Fenglong Mountain (Hebei)
封泥	〈古〉clay impression of seal; mudcap
封山育林区	region closed for afforestation
封氏墓群	Feng's Tomb Group; Tombs of the Feng Family (Hebei)
封穴	〈丧〉(of funeral) to seal the tomb
烽火台	beacon tower (used for lighting fireworks to send messages in ancient times)
凤	(of Chinese legend) feng (the perfect male bird used by ancient priests to sacrifice to the gods) →凰
凤堡钟亭	(of Mount Emei) Bell Pavilion on Phoenix Mound
凤冠霞帔	〈服〉(of wedding) a chaplet and official robe
凤凰	(of Chinese legend) fenghuang (a bird of wonder); phoenix
凤凰城堡	Phoenix Castle (Shandong) →财神山景区
凤凰古城	Fenghuang Ancient Town; Phoenix Ancient Town (Hu'nan) →湘西明珠
凤凰谷鸟园	Fenghuang Valley Bird Park (Taiwan)
凤凰山	fenghuang mountain; phoenix mountain
凤凰山革命旧址	Site of the Phoenix/Fenghuang Mountain Revolution (Former Residence of The CPC Central Committee) (Shaanxi)
凤凰山公园	Phoenix Mountain Park (Sichuan)
凤凰山石豆兰	〈植〉*Bulbophyllum rubrolabellum*
凤凰温泉	Fenghuang Hot Spring; Phoenix Hot Spring (Shaanxi)
凤凰饮泉	(of Three Gorges) Phoenix Fountain
凤栖山	(of Zhangjiajie) Fengqi Mountain; Perching Phoenix Mountain
凤山	Fengshan Mountain (Guangxi)

凤翔彩绘泥塑	Painted Clay Sculpture in Fengxiang (Shaanxi)
凤翔东湖	Fengxiang East Lake (Shaanxi)
凤阳花鼓	〈曲艺〉Flower Drum of Fengyang; Fengyang Flower Drum; Flower Drum Dance
凤仪亭址	Phoenix Kiosk Site (Hu'nan)
奉茶	to serve tea
奉先殿	(of Imperial Palace) Hall of Ancestral Worship
奉先寺	(of Longmen Grottoes) Fengxian Temple
佛本生故事	Jataka Stories; Jataka Tales; Buddhist Stories (one of the most literary pieces of the Buddhist scriptures)
佛诞日	Buddha's birthday (the 8th day of the 4th lunar month)
佛肚竹	〈植〉*Bambusa ventricosa*; Buddha bamboo
佛光	Buddha light; light of Buddha
佛光山	Foguang Mountain; Buddha Light Mountain (Taiwan)
佛光山寺	Foguangshan Monastery (Taiwan)
佛光寺	foguang temple; Buddha light temple (Shanxi)
佛国天堂	Buddhist Paradise (Sichuan)
佛国岩	(of Mount Wuyi) Buddhist Land Rock
佛吉祥日	〈藏族〉Buddha's Lucky Day (the 15th day of the 4th month in Tibetan calendar) →萨嘎达瓦节
佛教圣地	Buddhist sanctuary; holy land of Buddhism
佛教四大丛林	Four Sections of Buddhism (Qixia Temple in Jiangsu, Lingyan Temple in Shandong, Yuquan Temple in Hubei and Guoqing Temple in Zhejiang)
佛教四大名山	Four Buddhist Holy Mountains; Four Famous Mountains of Buddhism (Mount Wutai in Shanxi, Mount Emei in Sichuan, Mount Jiuhua in Anhui and Mount Putuo in Zhejiang)
佛山祖庙	Ancestral Temple in Foshan; Foshan Ancestral Temple (Guangdong)

佛手	〈植〉*Citrus medica*; fingered citron
佛手石	foshou rock; Buddha's hand rock
佛寺	Buddha temple
佛堂	(family) hall for worshiping the Buddha
佛堂门天后古庙	Tin Hau Temple at Joss House Bay (Hong Kong)
佛堂寺	Fotang Temple (Shanxi)
佛跳墙	〈烹饪〉Buddha Jumping over the Wall (a stew of chicken, duck, trotter, and dried seafoods in wine soup stock)
佛陀僧侣	Buddhist monk
佛香阁	(of Summer Palace) Foxiang Ge; Tower of Buddhist Incense
佛岩垂笑	(of Qianling Mountain) Smiling Buddha Hill
佛祖论经	Buddhist Patriarch Preaching Scriptures (Guangxi)
夫妻对拜	〈婚〉(of wedding) couple's bow to each other; bride and groom exchanging bows
夫妻石	couple stone
夫妻岩	(of Zhangjiajie) Couple Peaks
夫为妻纲	〈古〉husband as the guide of wife (one of the three cardinal guides) →三纲五常
夫子峰	(of Mount Huangshan) Fuzi Peak; Scholar Peak
夫子庙	Confucius Temple (Jiangsu)
伏波山	Fubo Mountain (Guangxi)
伏虎寺	(of Mount Emei) Tiger Taming Temple
伏龙观	Fulong Temple; Tamed Dragon Temple (Sichuan)
伏龙山自然景区	Fulong Mountain Natural Scenic Spot; Natural Scenic Area of Recumbent Dragon Mountain (Hubei)
伏龙寨景区	Fulong Zhai Scenic Area (Hubei)
伏牛山	Funiu Mountain; Recumbent Cattle Mountain (He'nan)
伏羲	Fuxi (the ancestor of Chinese nation and one of the Three Sovereigns)

伏羲庙	Fuxi Temple (Gansu)
伏羲台	Fuxi Tai Temple (Hebei)
扶桑	〈植〉*Hibiscus rosa-sinensis*; Chinese hibiscus →朱槿
芙蓉古村	Furong Ancient Village (Zhejiang)
芙蓉谷	(of Mount Huangshan) Furong Valley; Hibiscus Valley
芙蓉江	Furong River (Guizhou, Chongqing)
芙蓉镇	Furong Town; Hibiscus Town (Hu'nan)
服孝	〈丧〉to wear mourning clothes
服装节	→赛衣[服装]节
浮碧亭	(of Imperial Palace) Pavilion of Floating Jade
浮翠阁	(of Humble Administrator's Garden) Floating Green Pavilion
浮来山景区	Fulai Mountain Scenic Spot (Shandong)
浮梁古县衙	Fuliang Ancient County Government (Jiangxi)
浮桥河湿地公园	Fuqiao River Wetland Park (Hubei)
浮粟泉	Fuli Spring (Hai'nan) →海南第一泉
符望阁	(of Imperial Palace) Belvedere of Imperial Viewing
辐射虾脊兰	〈植〉*Calanthe actinomorpha*
福德正神	(of Chinese legend) God Fude →土地公
福地湖	Fudi Lake (Shaanxi)
福鼎蝾螈	〈动〉*Cynops fudingensis*; fuding fire-bellied newt
福国寺	Fuguo Temple (Yunnan)
福建大头蛙	〈动〉*Limnonectes fujianensis*; Fujian large-headed frog
福建土楼	Fujian earth building; Fujian adobe residence
福建掌突蟾	〈动〉*Paramegophrys liui*
福禄寿星	Three God-Stars (God of Luck, God of Official Rank, God of Longevity)
福庆寺	Fuqing Temple (Hebei)
福娃	(of Olympic mascot) fuwa; Five Friendlies
福州森林公园	Fuzhou Forest Park (Fujian) →福州树木园

福州树木园	〈旧〉Fuzhou Arboretum (Fujian) →福州森林公园
福州双塔	Fuzhou Twin Pagodas (Fujian)
福州西湖	Fuzhou West Lake (Fujian)
抚仙湖	Fuxian Lake (Yunnan)
甫田丛樾	(of Chengde Mountain Resort) Mellon Field in the Shade of Trees
府谷老城	Fugu Old Town (Shaanxi)
府谷文庙	Fugu Confucious' Temple (Shaanxi)
府河湿地公园	Fuhe River Wetland Park (Hubei)
府文庙	Government Confucious' Temple (Fujian)
府州城	Fuzhou City (Shaanxi)
俯掌	Downward palm
父母节	〈瑶族〉Parent Festival (on the 8th day of the 4th lunar month)
父为子纲	〈古〉father as the guide of son (one of the three cardinal guides) →三纲五常
附子	〈植〉Aconitum carmichaeli
复齿鼯鼠	〈动〉Trogopterus xanthipes; complex-toothed flying squirrel
复道回廊	(of Heyuan Garden) Double-Path Cloister
复合葬	〈丧〉complex burial (with more than two burial forms successively)
复芒菊	〈植〉Formania mekongensis
复真观	(of Mount Wudang) Fuzhen Temple; Revelation Temple →太子坡
副净	〈戏〉(of Beijing Opera) fujing (a character good at action with less emphasis on singing)
富河文化	〈古〉Fuhe culture (5300 B.C., a Neolithic culture found in the valley of the Urgimullen River, the north of Chifeng)
富楼那	〈佛〉Purna (one of the ten disciples of the Buddha, best-known for his expounding of Dharma/preaching)

富水湖水利景区	Fushui Lake Water Conservancy Scenic Area (Hubei)
富钟瘰螈	〈动〉*Paramesotriton fuzhongensis*; fuzhong warty newt
腹斑倭蛙	〈动〉*Nanorana ventripunctata*; spot-bellied plateau frog
覆盆子	〈植〉*Rubus idaeus*; raspberry

G

嘎仙洞遗址	Site of the Gaxian Cave; Gaxian Cave Remains (Inner Mongolia)
尕布寺	Gabu Temple (Qinghai)
尕海湖景区	Gahai Lake Scenic Area (Gansu)
钙化滩瀑布	Calcified Shoal Waterfall (Guizhou)
盖步	〈武术〉Cross over step
盖碗茶	lidded-cup tea; tea served in a set of cups
甘草	〈植〉*Glycyrrhiza uralensis*; liquorice
甘丹颇章	Ganden Podrang Palace (Tibet)
甘丹寺	Gandan Kloster; Gandan Monastery (Tibet)
甘露寺	Ganlu (Sweet Dew) Temple (Jiangsu)
甘泉宫遗址	Site of Ganquan Palace; Ganquan Palace Ruins (Shaanxi)
甘泉井	(of Temple of Heaven) Sweet Spring Well
甘什岭自然保护区	Ganshiling Natural Reserve; Ganza Ridge Natural Reserve (Hai'nan)
甘肃仓鼠	〈动〉*Cansumys canus*; Gansu hamster
甘肃桃	〈植〉*Amygdalus kansuensis*; Gansu peach
甘肃雪灵芝	〈植〉*Arenaria kansuensis*
甘肃鼹	〈动〉*Scapanulus oweni*; Kansus mole
柑香亭	(of Liuhou Park) Ganxiang Pavilion; Pavilion of Mandarin Orange Fragrance
赶摆	〈傣族〉Ganbai Festival (a gathering to worship Buddha) (in the mid December of Dai calendar or in the 1st lunar month)
赶歌会	〈苗族〉Gathering for Singing Party

赶歌节	〈侗族〉Gathering for Singing Festival (on the 20th day of the 7th lunar month)
赶降节	〈壮族〉Gathering for Frost's Descent Festival (in December)
赶鸟节	〈瑶族〉Ganniao Festival; Bird-Dispelling Day (on the 1st day of the 2nd lunar month)
赶秋节	〈苗族〉Gathering for Autumn Festival (at the beginning of the autumn)
赶社节	〈侗族〉Ganshe Festival (activities for men and women to go out for spring outings and amorism)
赣江	Ganjiang River
赣州古城墙	Ancient City Wall of Ganzhou (Jiangxi)
冈底斯山	Kailas Range (Tibet)
冈仁波齐（峰）	Kangrinboqe; Kailash Mountain (Tibet)
刚毛藤山柳	〈植〉*Clematoclethra scandens*
钢婚	steel wedding (the 11th anniversary of marriage)
钢绿山古铜矿遗址	Site of Ancient Mining and Smelting at Tonglüshan (Hubei)
缸瓦窑遗址	Site of Vitrified Clay Kiln (Inner Mongolia)
岗顶剧院	Gangding Theater (Macao) →伯多禄五世剧院
岗顶前地	Largo de Santo Agostinho (Macao)
皋兰山	Gaolan Mountain (Gansu)
高昌古城	Ancient City of Gaochang; Gaochang Ancient City (Xinjiang)
高句丽古国都城遗址	Site of Capital City of Ancient Koguryeo Kingdom (Jilin)
高句丽王朝	〈古〉Koguryeo Kingdom (an ancient regime across northeast China and the northern part of the Korean Peninsula from the 1st century B.C. to the 7th century A.D.) (Jilin)
高句丽王城	〈古〉Capital City of Ancient Koguryeo Kingdom (Jilin)
高句丽文物古迹景区	Koguryeo Cultural Relics Scenic Area (Jilin)

高寒水韭	〈植〉*Isoetes hypsophila*
高技术农业园	high-tech agricultural park
高家堡古城	Gaojiapu Ancient Town; Ancient Town of Gaojiapu (Shaanxi)
高甲戏	Gaojia Opera (a traditional local opera in Quanzhou, Fujian)
高栏岛	Gaolan Island (Guangdong)
高黎贡山	Gaoligong Mountain (Yunnan)
高良姜	〈植〉*Alpinia officinarum*; galanga galangal
高粱酒	sorghum liquor; kaoliang spirit
高坡苗乡	Gaopo Township of Miao (Guizhou)
高跷秧歌	stilt yangko dance; yangko dance on stilts
高山棘螈	〈动〉*Echinotriton maxiquadratus*
高山舌突蛙	〈动〉*Liurana alpina*
高山松	〈植〉*Pinus densata*; high mountain pine
高山掌突蟾	〈动〉*Paramegophrys alpinus*
高山族	Gaoshan ethnic group (Taiwan)
高探马	(of Tai Chi) High pat on horse
高原山鹑	〈动〉*Perdix hodgsoniae*; Tibetan partridge
高原鼠兔	〈动〉*Ochotona curzoniae*; plateau pika
高原兔	〈动〉*Lepus oiostolus*; woolly hare
高祖	1 father of the great-grandfather 2 Gaozu (a temple name of ancient emperor/monarch)
戈壁短舌菊	〈植〉*Brachanthemum gobicum*
仡佬节	〈仡佬族〉Gelao Festival (on the 3rd day of the 3rd lunar month)
仡佬族	Gelao ethnic group; Gelao
纥升骨城	〈古〉Geshenggu City (the birthplace of Koguryeo civilization, an ethnic group in Northeast China, and the first royal city of koguryo) (Liaoning)
哥窑	〈古〉Ge Kiln (one of the five famous kilns in ancient China)
哥窑瓷器	〈古〉Ge-Ware; Ge Porcelain (one of the five famous chinawares in ancient China)

搁笔亭	(of Yellow Crane Tower) Gebi (Putting Down the Writing Brush) Pavilion
歌和老街公园	Cornwall Street Park (Hong Kong)
歌节	〈壮族〉→对歌节
歌堂节	〈瑶族〉Getang Festival (on the 16th day of the 10th lunar month and lasting for three or nine days every three to five years)
歌舞之乡	land/hometown of song and dance (generally referring to Xinjiang)
歌仔戏	Gezai Opera (a traditional local opera of Zhangzhou, Xiamen and Quanzhou, Fujian)
革命烈士	revolutionary martyr
阁下	Your Excellency
阁院寺	Geyuan Temple (Hebei)
格格府	Gege (Princess of China) Mansion (Beijing)
格[葛]根塔拉草原	Gegentala Grassland (Inner Mongolia)
格[各]拉丹东山	Geladandong Mountain (the highest peak of the Tanggula Range) (Qinghai)
格鲁巴修道院	Gelugpa Monastery; Monastery of Gelugpa (Tibet)
格鲁派寺庙	Gelug Sect Temple; Temple of Gelug Sect (Tibet)
格鲁派寺院	Gelug Sect Monasteries
格萨尔王狮龙宫殿	King Gesar Lion-Dragon Palace (Qinghai)
格桑花草原	Galsang Flower Grassland (Gansu)
格桑嘉措	Kelsang Gyatso (1708-1757, the 7th Dalai Lama)
格桑颇章(宫)	(of Norbulingka) Kelsang Potrang (Palace) (one of the earliest palaces built in Norbulinka)
格桑寺	Kelsang Temple (Tibet)
格言亭	(of Zhongshan Park) Maxim Pavilion
隔河岩水电站	Geheyan Hydropower Station (Hubei)
葛根会	〈白族〉Gegen Fair (on the 5th day of the 1st lunar month)

葛洪献丹	(of Mount Sanqing) Ge Hong Presenting the Elixir Pill
葛洲坝	Gezhou Dam (Hubei) →葛洲坝水电站
葛洲坝水电站	Gezhou Dam Hydropower Station (Hubei) → 葛洲坝
艮	〈易〉(of I-Ching) mountain (one of the Eight Diagrams)
工布年	〈藏族〉Tibetan New Year in Kongbo Area (on the 1st October of the Tibetan calendar)
工[功]夫茶	Kungfu Tea (traditional tea drinking custom in Chaoshan area, Guangdong)
弓斑肥螈	〈动〉*Pachytriton archospotus*
弓步	〈武术〉Bow stance; Bow step
弓步侧冲拳	〈武术〉Punching sideway in bow stance
弓步劈拳	〈武术〉Hammer boxing in bow stance; Chopping fist in bow step
弓冲拳步	Bow step punching fist; Punching fist in bow stance/step
公道杯	〈古〉fair mug; gongdao mug (a porcelain product for drinking)
公格尔峰[山]	Kongur Peak (the highest peak of the Kunlun Mountain) (Xinjiang)
公格尔山–慕士塔格峰山冰川	Kongur-Muztage Glacier (Xinjiang)
公历	solar calendar; Gregorian calendar
功德寺	Gongde Temple (Beijing)
功德堂	gongde hall
功夫	kung fu
宫灯	〈古〉palace lantern (one of the traditional lantern handicrafts of the Han nationality)
宫绣	→京[宫]绣
恭王府	Prince Gong's Mansion (Beijing)
恭喜发财	may you be prosperous; wish you all the best (for phatic communication)

觥	〈古〉gong (drinking vessel)
巩乃斯草原	Kongnaisi Grassland (Xinjiang)
巩县石窟	Gongxian Grottoes (He'nan)
拱北口岸	Gongbei Port (of Entry) (Guangdong)
拱券门	arch gate/door
拱手礼	〈古〉fist and palm salute →作揖
珙桐	〈植〉*Davidia involucrate*; (Chinese) dove tree
贡茶	〈古〉tribute tea (only used by Chinese imperial court)
贡格尔草原	Gongger Grassland (Inner Mongolia)
贡菊	〈植〉*Florists chrysanthemum*; tribute chrysanthemum
贡山齿突蟾	〈动〉*Scutiger gongshanensis*; Gongshan toothed toad
贡水河湿地公园	Gongshui River Wetland Park (Hubei)
供灵	〈丧〉to sacrifice food for the deceased
勾手	〈武术〉Hook hand
勾踢腿	〈武术〉Low hook kick
勾腿平衡	〈武术〉Balance with one leg crossed behind
沟牙鼯鼠	〈动〉*Aeretes melanopterus*; Northern Chinese flying squirrel
岣嵝碑	Goulou Stele (one of the "Eight Heavenly Books of China", and it is said that the stele was the relics in praise of Xia Yu)
狗尾草	〈植〉*Setaria viridis*; (of traditional Chinese medicine) green bristlegrass; green foxtail
枸杞	〈植〉*Lycium chinense*; goji berry; wolfberry
估衣街	Guyi Street (which was the cradle of the commerce of Tianjin)
沽上艺苑	Gushang Art Garden (Tianjin)
姑姑节	Father's Sister Festival (on the 6th day of the 6th lunar month) →天贶节
姑娘节	Maiden's Day (on the 4th day of the 2nd lunar month for Hani people; on the 8th day of the 4th lunar month for Miao and Dong people)

姑娘追	〈哈萨克族〉girl's chase (equestrian sports and entertainment in Xinjiang)
姑婆节	〈侗族〉Grandaunt Day (in the 12th lunar month)
菰雨生凉	(of Garden of Quiet Meditation) Waterside Tower with Lotus View
古哀牢王国	〈旧〉Ancient Ailao Kingdom (the first Dai regime founded in Yunnan)
古安乐城	〈旧〉Ancient Anle Town (Xinjiang)
古北口长城	Gubeikou Section of the Great Wall (Beijing)
古镖局	ancient escort agency
古渤海王朝遗址	Site of Ancient Bohai Kingdom; Ancient Bohai Kingdom Ruins (Jilin)
古刹	ancient temple; old temple
古刹碑刻	tablet inscription of ancient temple
古长城砖窑	Ancient Brick Kiln of the Great Wall (Beijing)
古城墙	ancient city wall
古代帝王庙号	posthumous title of a monarch; temple name of an emperor
古代文明走廊	corridor of ancient civilizations
古尔班通古特沙漠	Gurbantunggut Desert (Xinjiang)
古尔邦节	〈伊斯兰〉Corban Festival (on the 10th December of the Islamic calendar)
古格王国遗址	Ruins of Guge Kingdom (Tibet)
古华轩	(of Imperial Palace) Bower of the Ancient Catalpa
古槐	ancient Chinese scholar tree
古隆中	Ancient Longzhong (where Zhouge Liang lived in seclusion) (Hubei)
古隆中牌坊	Ancient Longzhong Memorial Archway (Hubei)
古梅亭	(of Mount Langya) Ancient Plum Pavilion
古墓博物馆	Museum of Ancient Tombs (He'nan)
古南河湿地公园	Wetland Park of Ancient Nanhe River (Hubei)
古炮台	ancient fort
古琴台	Ancient Lute Pavilion (Hubei) →俞伯牙台
古山龙	〈植〉*Arcangelisia gusanlung*

古塔风涛	(of Jingzhou Tower) Ancient Tower and Wind Music
古陶瓷博物馆	ancient ceramics museum
古五松园	(of Lion Grove Garden) Ancient Five Pines Garden
古崖居遗址	Guyaju Remains; Guyaju Ruins; Ruins of Guyaju (Beijing)
古岩净苑	Koon Ngam Ching Yuen (Hong Kong)
古阳洞	(of Longmen Grottoes) Guyang Cave
古驿道	ancient courier route; ancient post road
古寨遗风	(of Tiantang Zhai) Legacy of Ancient Village
古栈道	ancient plank road (built along the cliffside)
古筝	〈乐〉guzheng; Chinese zither (a plucked stringed instrument)
谷城汉江湿地公园	Hanjiang River Wetland Park of Gucheng (Hubei)
谷底林海	(of Mount Changbai) Valley Floor Forest; Valley-Bottom Forest
谷雨	〈节气〉Grain Rain (the 6th solar term)
牯牛降景区	Guniujiang Scenic Area (Anhui)
鼓浪屿	Gulangyu/Kulangyu; Gulangyu Islet; Gulang Island (Fujian)
鼓楼	drum tower (ancient buildings where giant drums were placed and used for alarm or hourly chime)
鼓山	Gushan Mountain (Fujian)
固阳秦长城遗址	Site of the Great Wall of Qin at Guyang (Inner Mongolia)
故城遗址	Site of Ancient City (Xinjiang)
故宫	Imperial Palace (Beijing) →紫禁城
故宫博物院	Palace Museum; Forbidden City Museum (Beijing)
瓜蒌	〈植〉*Trichosanthes kirilowii*; fructus trichosanthis
卦	trigram (a tool used for divination in ancient times)

卦台山遗址	Relics of Guatai Mountain; Guatai Mountain Ruins (Gansu)
挂榜山小鲵	〈动〉*Hynobius guabangshanensis*
挂墩角蟾	〈动〉*Megophrys kuatunensis*; kuatun horned/spadefoot toad
挂甲寺	Guajia Temple (Tianjin)
挂年画	〈民俗〉to hang out Chinese New Year's painting
挂月峰	(of Mount Wutai) Hanging Moon Peak
挂轴	hanging scroll
怪石滩景区	Guaishi (Strange Stone) Beach Scenic Spot (Liaoning)
怪石峪	Strange Stone Valley (Xingjiang)
关帝庙	Guandi temple; temple of Guandi (to worship Guan Yu)
关公	Military Saint of Guangong (referring to Guan Yu, a famous general of Shu Han during the Three Kingdoms Period)
关林寺	Guanlin Temple (He'nan)
关陵庙	Guanling Temple (Shanxi)
关门节	〈佛〉Close-Door Festival (on the 15th September of the Dai calendar)
关门山森林公园	Guanmen Mountain Forest Park (Liaoning)
关门山水库	Guanmen Mountain Reservoir (Liaoning)
关王庙	temple of Guan Yu
关中平原	Guanzhong Plain; Central Shaanxi Plain (Shaanxi) →渭河平原
关中十大怪	ten strangenesses/oddities in Guanzhong (ten strange folk habits)
观潮	to watch the tide; tidal bore watching
观灯	to enjoy/view lanterns (at the Lantern Festival)
观复博物馆	Guanfu Museum (Beijing)
观光木	〈植〉*Tsoongiodendron odorum*
观光亭	sightseeing pavilion
观海长廊	Sea-Viewing Corridor (Guangdong)

观海亭	sea-viewing pavilion
观莲所	(of Chengde Mountain Resort) Pavilion with Lotus View
观鸟台	bird-watching tower
观瀑阁	waterfall-watching pavilion
观日亭	(of Mount Danxia) Sun-Watching Pavilion
观山地质公园	Guanshan Geopark (He'nan)
观世音	〈佛〉Kwan-yin; Goddess of Mercy
观世音菩萨	〈佛〉Avalokitesvara; Kwan-yin Bodhisattva
观涛塔	wave-watching tower
观雾山椒鱼	〈动〉*Hynobius fuca*
观星台	(of Shaolin Temple) Astronomical Observatory; Star Observation Platform
观音大士殿	palace of the Goddess of Mercy
观音道场	Kwan-yin Dojo; Goddess of Mercy Temple (Zhejiang) (originally referring to the place where Avalokitesvara Bodhisattva attained enlightenment)
观音洞	(of Qianling Mountain) Guanyin Cave; Mother Buddha Cave; Goddess of Mercy Cave
观音阁	Guanyin pavilion; Goddess of Mercy pavilion
观音莲花苑	Lotus Statue (Macao)
观音庙	Kwan-yin temple; Guanyin temple; Goddess of Mercy temple
观音菩萨圣诞法会	Guanyin Bodhisattva Dharma Assembly
观音山	Kwan-yin hill; Guanyin mountain
观音山黄金沙滩	Guanyin Mountain Golden Beach (Fujian)
观音赏曲	(of Mount Sanqing) Goddess of Mercy Enjoying the Music
观音市[街]	〈白族〉Guanyin Street →三月街
观音堂	Kwan-yin hall; Guanyin hall; hall of Goddess of Mercy
观音像	statue of Guanyin; statue of the Goddess of Mercy

观音岩	(of Huanglong Valley) Guanyin Rock; Goddess of Mercy Cliff
观音寨	Guanyin Village (Hebei)
观月祭	〈高山族〉Moon-Watching Ceremony (held in the 9th lunar month)
官话	〈旧〉kwan; kwan-hwa; mandarin (Chinese)
官窑	〈古〉Guan Kiln; Kuan Kiln (one of the five famous kilns in ancient China)
官窑瓷器	〈古〉Guan-Ware; Guan Porcelain (one of the five famous chinawares in ancient China)
官银号	〈旧〉official bank (financial institutions established by the Qing government)
官字款瓷器	official-style porcelain
馆娃宫	Guanwa Palace (Jiangsu)
管涔山森林公园	Guancen Mountain Forest Park (Shanxi)
冠云峰	(of Lingering Garden) Cloud Capped Peak
冠云台	(of Lingering Garden) Cloud Capped Terrace
冠云亭	(of Lingering Garden) Cloud Capped Pavilion
光明顶	(of Mount Huangshan) Bright Summit (one of three main peaks)
光雾山	Guangwu Mountain (Sichuan)
光孝寺	Guangxiao Temple; Bright Filial Piety Temple (Guangdong)
光绪皇帝	Emperor Guangxu (1871–1908, reigning from 1875 to 1908 in the Qing Dynasty)
光绪年间	Guangxu reign (1875–1908)
光叶蕨	〈植〉*Cystoathyrium chinense*
光岳楼	Guangyue Tower (Shandong)
广东珐琅	Canton enamel
广东凤尾蕨	〈植〉*Pteris guangdongensis*
广东隔距兰	〈植〉*Cleisostoma simondii*
广东华南虎(队)	(of a basketball team) Guangdong Southern Tiger
广东会馆	Guangdong guild hall (gathering/meeting places set up by Canton merchants across the country)

广东十虎	Ten Tigers of Canton (ten outstanding Kungfu masters in Guangdong in the late Qing Dynasty)
广东石豆兰	〈植〉*Bulbophyllum kwangtungense*
广东石斛	〈植〉*Dendrobium wilsonii*
广东粤剧艺术中心	Guangdong Opera Art Centre
广化寺	Guanghua Temple (Shaanxi)
广教寺双塔	Twin Pagodas of Guangjiao Temple (Anhui)
广觉寺	→五当召
"广陵王玺"金印	Golden seal of "Guangling King"
广饶关帝庙大殿	Main Hall of Guandi Temple in Guangrao (Shandong)
广仁寺	Guangren Temple; Guangren Lama Temple (Shaanxi)
广润灵雨祠	(of Summer Palace) Shrine for Universal Blessing Rain
广胜寺	Guangsheng Temple (Shanxi)
广武汉墓群	Han Tombs at Guangwu; Tombs of the Han Dynasty at Guangwu (Shanxi)
广西火桐	〈植〉*Erythropsis kwangsiensis*
广西拟髭蟾	〈植〉*Leptobrachium guangxiense*
广元千佛崖摩崖造像	Guangyuan Thousand-Buddha Cliffside Sculptures (Sichuan)
广州大元帅府旧址	Former Site of Generalissimo Sun Yat-sen's Mansion in Guangzhou (Guangdong)
广州鳄鱼公园	〈旧〉Guangzhou Crocodile Park (Guangdong) → 长隆飞鸟乐园
广州公社旧址	Former Site of Guangzhou Commune (Guangdong)
广州沙面建筑群	Shamian Architectural Complex of Guangzhou (Guangdong)
广州十景	Ten Sights of Guangzhou (Guangdong)
广州石室圣心大教堂	Shishi Sacred Heart Cathedral of Guangzhou (Guangdong)
广宗寺	Guangzong Temple (Ningxia, Inner Mongolia)

归德府城墙	City Wall of Guide Prefecture (He'nan)
归宁	(of marriage) guining; to go back to her paternal home for a visit →回门
归元寺	Guiyuan Temple (Hubei)
归葬	〈丧〉to bury in sb's homeland
龟山	Guishan Mountain; Tortoise Mountain (Guangxi, Hubei)
龟山岛	Guishan Island (Taiwan)
龟山汉墓	Han Tomb at Guishan Mountain; Tomb of the Han Dynasty at Tortoise Mountain (Jiangsu)
鬼谷岭森林公园	Guigu Valley Forest Park; Ghost Valley Forest Park (Shaanxi)
鬼节	〈道〉Ghost Festival; Spirit Festival (on the 15th day of the 7th lunar month) →中元节
鬼门关	(of Chinese legend) gate of hell (a pass in the underworld/netherworld)
鬼门天堑	(of Xingtai Grand Canyon) Ghost Gate Moat
鬼戏	→傩[鬼]戏
簋街	Guijie Street (a famous snack street in Beijing)
贵德明清古建筑群	Ancient Architectural Complex of the Ming and Qing Dynasties in Guide (Qinghai)
贵州拟小鲵	〈动〉*Pseudohynobius guizhouensis*
贵州疣螈	〈动〉*Tylototriton kweichowensis*
桂海碑林	Guihai Forest of Steles (Guangxi)
桂花酒	osmanthus wine
桂酒	gui wine; cinnamon wine (generally referring to good wine)
桂林八景	Eight Wonders in Guilin (Guangxi)
桂林漓江景区	Lijiang River Scenic Area in Guilin (Guangxi)
桂林盘龙洞	Panlong Cave of Guilin (Guangxi)
桂林七星公园	Seven-Star Park of Guilin (Guangxi)
桂林山水	Guilin scenery; Guilin scenery with hills and waters; landscape of Guilin

跪拜(礼)	〈旧〉genuflexion; worship on bended knees
棍术	〈武术〉Staff form; Stick form; Cudgel play
郭沫若故居	Former Residence of Guo Moruo (Beijing)
国博	→中国国家博物馆
国父[孙中山]纪念馆	Sun Yat-sen Memorial Hall; Memorial Hall of Sun Yat-sen (Taiwan)
国槐	〈植〉*Styphnolobium japonicum*; Chinese scholar-tree
国际少林武术节	International Shaolin Wushu Festival; International Shaolin Martial Arts Festival
国家大剧院	National Centre for the Performing Arts (Beijing)
国家地质公园	national geopark
国家公祭日	National Memorial Day (the 13th December) →南京大屠杀死难者国家公祭日
国家花卉博览园	national floriculture expo park
国家京剧院	National Peking Opera Company (Beijing)
国家森林公园	national forest park
国家体育场	Beijing National Stadium →鸟巢
国家游泳中心	National Aquatics Center (Beijing) →水立方
国家园林城市	national landscape garden city
国立历史博物馆筹备处	〈旧〉preparatory office of National Museum of History
国贸大酒店	China World Summit Wing (Beijing)
国民党"一大"旧址	Site of the First National Congress of Kuomintang (Guangdong)
国民政府	〈旧〉Nationalist Government (from the 1st July 1925 to the 20th May 1948)
国庆黄金周	National Day golden week; golden week of National Day
国庆节	National Day (on the 1st October)
国殇墓园	National Martyrs Cemetery (in memory of the dead soldiers of the Anti-Japanese Expeditionary Force) (Yunnan)

国语	1 national language; Mandarin Chinese 2〈旧〉Chinese language course (for school students)
虢国墓地	Cemetery of Guo State; Guo State Cemetery; Cemetery of the State of Guo (He'nan)
果子沟	Fruit Valley (Xinjiang)
果子节	〈白族〉Fruit Day (on the 16th day of the 8th lunar month)
果子狸［花面狸］	〈动〉*Paguma larvata*; masked palm civet; masked civet
过大礼	〈婚〉(of engagement) betrothal gift ceremony; presenting betrothal gifts
过门	〈婚〉to get married to a man
过年	to celebrate Chinese New Year →春节
过年节	〈怒族〉Nu's New Year Festival
过文定	(of wedding etiquette) to present betrothal gift and token (usually one month before the wedding)

H

哈达	hada; khatag (traditional ceremonial scarf used as a greeting gift in Tibetan and Mongolia)
哈达山	Hada Mountain (Jilin)
哈尔滨冰雪大世界	Harbin Ice and Snow World (Heilongjiang)
哈拉墩文化遗址	Haladun Cultural Relics (Xinjiang)
哈利津河	Halijin River (Qinghai)
哈密木卡姆	Hami Mucam (a classical music performance with singing, dancing and music of Uygur in Xinjiang)
哈密盆地	Hami Basin; Hami Depression (Xinjiang)
哈密王墓	Tomb of the King of Hami (Xinjiang) →回王陵
哈尼梯田	Hani Terrace (Yunnan)
哈尼族	Hani ethnic group; Hani
哈萨克毡房	Kazak yurt (with round felt tent)
哈萨克族	Kazak ethnic group; Kazak
海宝塔	Haibao Pagoda (Ningxia)
海宝塔寺	Haibao Pagoda Temple (Ningxia)
海滨公园	seashore park; coastal park
海滨旅游度假区	seashore tourist resort
海沧大桥	Haicang Bridge (Fujian)
海沧旅游区	Haicang Tourist Area (Fujian)
海沧野生动物园	Haicang Wildlife Zoo (Fujian)
海产博物馆	Marine Products Museum (Shandong)
海底世界	marine world; undersea world
海底针	(of Tai Chi) Needle at sea bottom

海丰红宫红场旧址	Site of Haifeng Red Palace and Red Square (Guangdong)
海丰红宫红场旧址纪念馆	Memorial Hall of the Site of Haifeng Red Palace and Red Square (Guangdong)
海峰湿地自然保护区	Haifeng Wetland Nature Reserve (Yunnan)
海港城	Harbour City (the largest shopping mall of West Kowloon in Hong Kong)
海光寺	Haiguang Temple (Tianjin)
海河	Haihe River
海河大桥	Haihe River Bridge (Tianjin)
海河故道公园	Old Course Park of Haihe River (Tianjin)
海河喷泉公园	Haihe River Fountain Park (Tianjin)
海河文化广场	Haihe River Cultural Square (Tianjin)
海昏侯墓	Tomb of Marquis Haihun (the tomb of Liuhe of the Western Han Dynasty) (Jiangxi)
海口骑楼老街	Haikou Arcaded Streets (Hai'nan)
海陵珍珠养殖场	Hailing Pearl Farm (Hai'nan)
海龙屯土司遗址	Site of Hailongtun Chieftain's Castle (Guizhou)
海螺峰	(of Zhangjiajie and Mount Danxia) Conch Peak
海螺沟冰川	Hailuo Vally Glacier (one of the remaining low-altitude glaciers in the world) (Sichuan)
海南长臂猿	〈动〉*Nomascus Hainanus*; Hai'nan black crested gibbon
海南臭蛙	〈动〉*Odorrana Hainanensis*
海南岛	Hai'nan Island (South China Sea)
海南第一泉	The Best Spring in Hai'nan →浮粟泉
海南复叶耳蕨	〈植〉*Arachniodes Hainanensis*
海南虎斑鳽	〈动〉*Gorsachius magnificus*; Chinese night heron →海南鳽
海南节毛蕨	〈植〉*Lastreopsis subrecedens*
海南金星蕨	〈植〉*Parathelypteris subimmersa*
海南鳞始蕨	〈植〉*Lindsaea Hainaniana*
海南刘树蛙	〈动〉*Liuixalus Hainanus*
海南拟髭蟾	〈动〉*Leptobrachium Hainanense*

海南䴉	〈动〉*Gorsachius magnificus*; white-eared night heron →海南虎斑䴉
海南琴蛙	〈动〉*Nidirana Hainanensis*
海南热带飞禽世界	Hai'nan Tropical Bird World
海南热带植物园	Hai'nan Tropical Botanical Garden
海南山鹧鸪	〈动〉*Arborophila ardens*; white-eared partridge; Hai'nan hill-partridge
海南石豆兰	〈植〉*Bulbophyllum Hainanense*
海南兔	〈动〉*Lepus Hainanus*; Hai'nan hare
海南湍蛙	〈动〉*Amolops Hainanensis*
海南瓦韦	〈植〉*Lepisorus affinis*
海南溪树蛙	〈动〉*Buergeria oxycephala*
海南小姬蛙	〈动〉*Micryletta immaculata*
海南新毛猬	〈动〉*Neohylomys Hainanensis*; Hai'nan gymnure
海南椰林	coconut forest/grove in Hai'nan
海南疣螈	〈动〉*Tylototriton Hainanensis*; Hai'nan knobby newt
海瑞祠	Hai Rui Temple (Zhejiang)
海瑞墓	Hai Rui Tomb; Tomb of Hai Rui (Hai'nan)
海上森林公园	Marine Forest Park (Hai'nan)
海上丝绸之路	Maritime Silk Road
海师洞	Cave of Master Hai Tong (Sichuan)
海狮吞月	(of Mount Sanqing) Sea Lion Devouring the Moon
海坛岛	Haitan Island (Fujian)
海棠春坞	(of Humble Administrator's Garden) Malus Spring Castle
海棠花	〈植〉*Malus spectabilis*; Chinese flowering apple
海棠门洞	(of Lion Forest Garden) Gate of Chinese Flowering Crabapples
海外中餐	overseas Chinese food; overseas Chinese cuisine
海鲜面	〈烹饪〉Seafood Noodles
海心公园	Hoi Sham Park (Hong Kong)
海晏堂	(of Yuanming Garden) Hall of National Peace
海洋公园	ocean park
海洋科普馆	ocean science popularization hall

海洋摩天塔	Ocean Skyscrapers Tower (Hong Kong)
海云寺	Haiyun Temple (Yunnan)
海藏寺	Haizang Temple (Gansu, Jiangxi and Taiwan)
海之韵广场	Haizhiyun Square (Liaoning)
含鄱口	(of Mount Lushan) Hanpo Kou (the sun-watching spot)
含鄱亭	(of Mount Lushan) Hanpo Pavilion (the best spot for sun-watching)
含笑九泉	to smile under the Jiuquan (a place under the earth where people are believed to go when they die); to smile in the Heaven
涵碧山房	(of Lingering Garden) Hanbi Mountain Villa
涵秋馆	(of Yuanming Garden) Autumn-Embracing Hall
韩城大禹庙	Dayu Temple in Hancheng (Shaanxi)
韩城文庙	Hancheng Confucian Temple; Confucian Temple in Hancheng (Shaanxi)
韩江	Hanjiang River
韩文公祠	Han Wengong Temple (in memory of Han Yu, a great writer of the Tang Dynasty) (Guangdong)
寒碧山庄	〈旧〉Hanbi Mountain Villa (another name for Lingering Garden in the Qing Dynasty) (Jiangsu) →苏州留园
寒葱顶森林公园	Hancongding Forest Park (Jilin)
寒兰	〈植〉*Cymbidium kanran*
寒露	〈节气〉Cold Dew (the 17th solar term)
寒山寺	Hanshan Temple (Jiangsu)
寒食节	Hanshi Festival; Cold Food Festival (the day before Tomb-sweeping Day when people eat cold food only)
汉兵马俑	terracotta warriors and horses of the Han Dynasty (one of Three Wonders of the Han Dynasty) (Jiangsu)
汉长安城遗址	Site of Chang'an City of the Han Dynasty; Chang'an City Ruins of the Han Dynasty (Shaanxi)

汉朝	Han Dynasty (206 B.C.-220 A.D.)
汉朝古遗址	Remains of Ancient City of the Han Dynasty (Fujian)
汉楚王墓群	Mausoleums/Tombs of the Kings of Chu State in the Han Dynasty (Jiangsu)
汉代三绝	Three Wonders of the Han Dynasty (including terracotta warriors and horses, tombs and stone reliefs)
汉鼎	ding of the Han Dynasty
汉广陵王墓	Guangling King's Tomb in the Han Dynasty; Tomb of Guangling King in the Han Dynasty (Jiangsu)
汉画像石	Stone Sculptures/Reliefs of the Han Dynasty (one of Three Wonders of the Han Dynasty) (Jiangsu)
汉画像石馆	Gallery of Stone Sculptures/Reliefs of the Han Dynasty (Jiangsu)
汉江[水]	Hanshui River; Hanjiang River (the longest tributary of Yangtze River)
汉江大桥	Hanjiang River Bridge (Hubei)
汉江江滩	Hanjiang River Beach (Hubei)
汉江旅游码头	Hanjiang River Tourist Wharf (Hubei)
汉口日清洋行大楼	Riqing Yanghang Building in Hankou (Hubei)
汉锣	〈乐〉gong of Wuhan
汉墓	tombs of the Han Dynasty (one of Three Wonders of the Han Dynasty) (Jiangsu)
汉式建筑	Han-style architecture; Han-style building
汉魏洛阳故城	Luoyang City Ruins of the Han and Wei Dynasties (He'nan)
汉魏许都古城遗址	Site of the Ancient Xuchang City of the Han and Wei Dynasties; Ancient City of Xudu in the Han and Wei Dynasties (He'nan)
汉阳公园	Hanyang Park (Hubei)

汉阳陵	Yangling Mausoleum of the Han Dynasty (Shaanxi)
汉阳造艺术区	Hanyang Manufacture Art District (Hubei)
汉正街	Hanzheng Street (a well-known Commodity Market) (Hubei)
汉中三堰	Three Weirs in Hanzhong (ancient Water Conservancy Project in Shaanxi, including Shanhe weir, Wumen weir and Yangtian weir)
汉族	Han ethnic group; Han
汉族文化	Han culture
汗宫大衙门	Grand Yamen of the Han Palace (Liaoning)
旱地行船	(of Hukou Waterfall) Boating on Sand
翰林	〈古〉member of the Hanlin/Imperial Academy
翰林院	〈古〉Hanlin Academy; Imperial Academy
行业联	industry couplets
杭帮菜博物馆	Hangzhou Cuisine Museum (Zhejiang)
杭扇	→杭州扇子
杭州白菊	Hangzhou white chrysanthemum
杭州长乔极地海洋公园	Hangzhou Changqiao Polar Ocean Park (Zhejiang)
杭州刺绣	Hangzhou embroidery
杭州南宋风情街	Hangzhou Southern Song Style Street (Zhejiang)
杭州南宋御街	Hangzhou Southern Song Imperial Street (Zhejiang)
杭州三绝	Three Wonders of Hangzhou (including Longjing, Hangzhou fan and Hangzhou silk)
杭州扇子	Hangzhou fan (one of Three Wonders in Hangzhou)
杭州世界钱币博物馆	Hangzhou World Numismatic Museum (Zhejiang)
杭州丝绸	Hangzhou silk (one of Three Wonders in Hangzhou)
杭州宋城	Song Cheng City of Hangzhou (a theme park that presents the culture of the Song Dynasty) (Zhejiang)

杭州湾	Hangzhou Bay (Zhejiang)
杭州西湖景区	Hangzhou West Lake Scenic Area (Zhejiang)
杭州亚运会	Hangzhou Asian Game (in 2023)
杭州野生动物世界	Hangzhou Wildlife Park (Zhejiang)
杭州植物园	Hangzhou Botanical Garden (Zhejiang)
蚝仔煎	〈烹饪〉Fried Oysters (a famous traditional snack in Fujian)
濠濮间想	(of Chengde Mountain Resort) Leisurely Dream on Waterside
濠濮亭	(of Lingering Garden) Hao-Pu Pavilion
好森沟森林公园	Haosengou Forest Park (Inner Mongolia)
好太王碑	King Haotai's Stele (about the 19th King of the Koguryo) (Jilin)
浩然亭	(of Yuanming Garden) Noble Spirit Pavilion
皓月园	Bright Moon Garden (in memory of Zheng Chenggong) (Fujian)
喝罚酒	to drink as a forfeit; to drink as the result of having lost a bet
喝交杯酒	(of wedding) to drink wedlock wine; to drink cross-cupped wine
禾魂节	〈瑶族〉Hehun Festival (on the 6th day of the 6th lunar month)
合拢酒	〈侗族〉gathering wine (a banquet with the highest standard for entertaining distinguished guests)
合浦汉墓群	Tombs of the Han Dynasty in Hepu (Guangxi)
合征姬蛙	〈动〉*Microhyla mixtura*; mixtured pygmy frog
何家冲何氏祠堂	Ancestral Hall of the He Family at Hejiachong (He'nan) →红二十五军长征出发地
何首乌	〈植〉*Fallopia multiflora*; tuber fleeceflower root
何王庙长江江豚自然保护区	Yangtze River Dolphin Nature Reserve at Hewang Temple (Hubei)
何仙姑	(of Chinese legend) Immortal Woman He (one of the eight immortals)

何园	Heyuan Garden; Ho Family Garden (a typical garden of the late Qing Dynasty in Jiangsu) →寄啸山庄
和平纪念碑	The Cenotaph; Peace Monument (Hong Kong)
和氏璧	jade of the He family
和田河	Hotan/Khotan River (Xinjiang)
河北平原	Hebei Plain
河北区名人故居群	Former Residence Group of Celebrities in Hebei District (Tianjin)
河滨公园	riverside park
河津寺	Hejin Temple (Shaanxi)
河口叉蕨	〈植〉*Tectaria hekouensis*
河口水蛙	〈动〉*Sylvirana hekouensis*
河姆渡遗址	Hemudu Site; Hemudu Ruins (Zhejiang)
河南卷瓣兰	〈植〉*Bulbophyllum henanense*
河西走廊	Hexi Corridor; River-West Aisle; River-West Corridor (Gansu, Inner Mongolia)
河蟹	→中华绒螯蟹
河渚听曲	(of Xixi National Wetland Park) Music Appreciation in Hezhu
荷风四面亭	(of Humble Administrator's Garden) Pavilion in the Lotus Breezes
荷花池公园	Lotus Lake Park (Jiangsu)
荷花灯	lotus lantern
荷花塘	lotus pond
荷花园	lotus garden
荷叶铁线蕨	〈植〉*Adiantum reniforme*
贺家川革命烈士纪念塔	Memorial Tower of Revolutionary Martyrs at Hejiachuan (Shaanxi)
贺兰山	Mount Helan; Helan Mountain (Inner Mongolia, Ningxia)
贺兰山北寺	North Temple of Helan Mountain (Inner Mongolia)
贺兰山南寺	South Temple of Helan Mountain (Ningxia)

贺兰山森林公园	Helan Mountain Forest Park (Ningxia)
贺兰山岩画	Helan Mountain Rock Painting; Rock Painting of Helan Mountain (Ningxia)
贺兰山自然保护区	Helan Mountain Nature Reserve (Ningxia)
贺兰砚	Helan ink stone (traditional handicrafts in Ningxia)
贺龙公园	(of Zhangjiajie) He Long Park; Park of Marshal He Long
赫哲族	Hezhen ethnic group; Hezhen
褐花杓兰	〈植〉*Cypripedium smithii*
褐马鸡	〈动〉*Crossoptilon mantchuricum*; brown eared pheasant
鹤咀灯塔	Cape D'Angilar Lighthouse; Hezu Lighthouse (Hong Kong)
黑斑肥螈	〈动〉*Pachytriton brevipes*; black-spotted pachytrition
黑宝熊乐园	Heibao Bear Paradise (Heilongjiang)
黑柄叉蕨	〈植〉*Tectaria ebenina*
黑长尾雉	〈动〉*Syrmaticus mikado*; Mikado pheasant
黑城遗址旅游区	Heicheng Ruins Tourist Area (Inner Mongolia)
黑枞垴	(of Zhangjiajie) Heicongnao Peak Terrace
黑冠长臂猿	〈动〉*Nomascus nasutus*; black crested gibbon
黑河国家森林公园	Heihe River National Forest Park (Shaanxi)
黑麂	〈动〉*Muntiacus crinifrons*; black fronted muntjac
黑颈鹤	〈动〉*Grus nigricollis*; black-necked crane; Tibetan crane
黑鳞复叶耳蕨	〈植〉*Arachniodes nigrospinosa*
黑龙江将军府	Heilongjiang Martial's Mansion
黑龙山	Heilong Mountain; Black Dragon Mountain (Heilongjiang)
黑龙石	heilong rock; black dragon rock (a kind of granite)
黑龙潭	Heilong Pool; Black Dragon Pool (Beijing, Yunnan)
黑糯米酒	black glutinous rice wine
黑沙海滩	Black Sand Beach (Macao)

黑沙水库郊野公园	Hac-Sa Reservoir Country Park (Macao)
黑石顶异角蟾	〈动〉*Xenophrys obesa*
黑水河	Blackwater River (in Journey to the West)
黑头角	Blackhead Point (Hong Kong) →讯号山
黑雁	〈动〉*Branta bernicla*; brent goose
恒山	Mount Hengshan; Hengshan Mountain (Shanxi) →北岳恒山
横店影视城	Hengdian Movie/TV Base (Zhejiang)
横断山脉	Hengduan Mountains; Hengduan Mountain Range (the longest, widest and most typical north-south mountain chain in China)
横澜(岛)灯塔	Waglan Lighthouse (Hong Kong)
横批	(of a couplet) horizontal scroll (bearing an inscription)
横纹芫菁	〈动〉*Mylabris cichorii*
衡水湖景区	Hengshui Lake Scenic Area (Hebei)
衡水湖自然保护区	Hengshui Lake Nature Reserve (Hebei)
弘义阁	(of Imperial Palace) Pavilion of Righteousness Promotion
红安七里坪革命旧址	Qiliping Revolutionary Site of Hong'an (Hubei)
红白喜事	〈民俗〉white or black affairs; weddings and funerals
红宝石婚	ruby wedding (the 40th anniversary of marriage)
红背甜槠	〈植〉*Castanopsis eyrei*
红灯笼	red lantern
红点齿蟾	〈动〉*Oreolalax rhodostigmatus*; red-spotted toothed toad
红二十五军长征出发地	Long March Departure Spot of the 25th Army of the Red Army (He'nan) →何家冲何氏祠堂
红封包	red envelope; red packet/pocket →利是
红腹角雉	〈动〉*Tragopan temminckii*; crimson-bellied tragopan; temminck's tragopan
红腹锦鸡	〈动〉*Chrysolophus pictus*; golden pheasant

红盖头	〈婚〉(of wedding) red veil; red bridal veil
红歌	red song; revolutionary song
红歌音乐会	concerts of red songs
红宫大殿	Grand Hall of the Red Palace (Tibet)
红光公园	Hongguang Park; Red Light Park (which highlights the Qin culture) (Shaanxi)
红桧	〈植〉*Chamaecyparis formosensis*; Taiwan cypress; formosan cypress
红海草原	Honghai Grassland (Sichuan)
红河	Honghe River (Yunnan)
红河谷国家森林公园	Honghe River Valley National Forest Park (Shaanxi)
红花	〈植〉*Carthamus tinctorius*; red flower
红花草	→紫云英
红花木莲	〈植〉*Manglietia insignis*; red lotus
红花岩黄耆	〈植〉*Hedysarum multijugum*
红祭	〈蒙古族〉red sacrifice; sacrifice to heaven with slaughtered lamb →白祭
红酒烩牛尾	〈烹饪〉Braised Oxtail in Red Wine
红军洞	Red Army Cave (Zhejiang)
红螺山	Mount Hongluo; Hongluo Mountain (Beijing)
红螺寺	(of Mount Hongluo) Hongluo Temple
红毛五加	〈植〉*Eleutherococcus giraldii*; Acanthopanax giraldii
红门宫	(of Mount Taishan) Red Gate Palace
红木	〈植〉*Pterocarpus*; rosewood
红木雕刻	redwood carving; red sandalwood carving; rosewood carving
红坪画廊	Hongping Gallery (Hubei)
红旗渠	Hongqi Canal; Red Flag Canal (He'nan)
红色娘子军雕像	Statue of the Red Detachment of Women (Hai'nan)
红山	Hongshan Mountain; Red Mountain (Inner Mongolia)
红山文化	〈古〉Hongshan culture (neolithic culture, 4000-3000 B.C.)

红山文化遗址	Site of Hongshan Culture; Site of Ancient Cultural Remains in Hongshan Mountain (Inner Mongolia)
红杉	〈植〉*Larix potaninii*; (of Chinese medicine) Chinese larch
红石峡	red rock gorge; red stone gorge
红四方面军总指挥部旧址	Site of the General Headquarters of the 4th Front Red Army (Sichuan)
红星火山地质公园	Hongxing Volcanic Geopark (Heilongjiang)
红崖天书	Hongya Abstruse Writing; Abstruse Writing on Red Cliff (Guizhou)
红腰带	red belt (for good luck)
红衣节	〈瑶族〉Red Clothes Festival (on the 4th day of the 8th lunar month)
红原大草原	Hongyuan Prairie (Sichuan)
红运	good luck
红嘴相思鸟	〈动〉*Leiothrix lutea*; Pekin robin; red-billed leiothrix
虹桥文化之秋艺术节	Hongqiao Autumn Culture Art Festival (Shanghai)
洪椿坪	Hongchun Terrace (Sichuan)
洪格尔岩画群	Hongor Petrograms; Hongor Rock Paintings (Inner Mongolia)
洪河	Honghe River (Gansu)
洪江古商城	Hongjiang Ancient Commercial City (Hu'nan)
洪拳	〈武术〉Hong Quan; Hong Boxing
洪圣古庙	Hung Shing Temple (Guangdong)
洪洞大槐树寻根祭祖园	Ancestor Memorial Garden of Grand Pagoda Tree in Hongtong (Shanxi)
洪洞水神庙	Hongtong Water God Hall (Shanxi)
洪武年间	Hongwu reign; Hongwu years (1368–1398)
洪崖洞	Hongya Cave (Chongqing)
洪泽湖湿地公园	Hongze Lake Wetland Park (Jiangsu)
洪泽湖湿地自然保护区	Hongze Lake Wetlands Nature Reserve (Jiangsu)

洪州窑遗址	Site/Ruins of Hongzhou Kiln; Hongzhou Kiln Ruins (Jiangxi)
鸿门宴遗址	Site of Hongmen Banquet; Hongmen Banquet Ruins (Shaanxi)
鸿雁	〈动〉*Anser cygnoides*; swan goose
鸿运	good luck
侯马蝴蝶杯	〈古〉Houma Butterfly Cup (drinking vessel)
侯马晋国遗址	Site of the State of Jin at Houma; Jin State Ruins at Houma (Shanxi) →新田遗址
猴年	Year of the Monkey
猴爬岩大峡谷	Houpayan Grand Gorge; Monkey-on-Rock Grand Gorge (Yunnan)
猴拳	〈武术〉Monkey Kung Fu; Monkey Boxing
猴王献宝	(of Mount Sanqing) Monkey King Presenting the Treasure
后高扫腿	〈武术〉High back sweep kick
后宫	1〈古〉imperial harem or seraglio (where the emperor's wives and concubines lived) 2〈古〉a general name for imperial wives and concubines
后滚翻	〈武术〉Backward roll
后花园	〈武术〉(of Zhangjiajie) Rear Garden
后金	late Jin Dynasty (1616–1636, the regime established by Jurchen people in northeast China in the late Ming Dynasty)
后金故宫	Imperial Palace of the late Jin Dynasty (Liaoning) →沈阳故宫
后空翻	〈武术〉Back somersault; Back flip
后撩腿	〈武术〉Back arc kick
后扫堂腿	〈武术〉Backward floor sweep kick
后扫腿	〈武术〉Back sweep
后生节	〈仫佬族〉Housheng Festival; Young Generation Festival (on the 15th day of the 8th lunar month)
后手抄拳	〈武术〉Rear fist/boxing upper cut
后手冲拳	〈武术〉Rear fist jab; Rear boxing jab

后手贯拳	〈武术〉Rear fist side hook
呼韩邪单于	Huhanye Chanyu (?-31 B.C. the leader of Huns in the late Western Han Dynasty)
呼伦贝尔草原	Hulun Buir Grassland (Inner Mongolia)
弧形步	Circular walking step
胡葱[火葱]	〈植〉*Allium ascalonicum*; scallion
胡家台战斗遗址	Hujiatai Battle Site; Site of Hujiatai Anti-Japanese War (Hubei)
胡里山炮台	Hulishan Battery; Hulishan Fortress (Fujian)
胡人	1 〈古〉Hu people (a term for ethnic groups in the north and west of China) 2 〈古〉foreigner
胡西它尔	〈乐〉Khushtar (a bowed stringed instrument of Uygur ethnic group)
胡杨林生态旅游区	populus euphratica forest eco-tourism area; diversiform-leaved poplar eco-tourism area
胡杨林生态园	populus euphratica forest ecopark
壶口冰桥	(of Hukou Waterfall) Hukou Ice Bridge
葫芦雕刻	bottle gourd carving; gourd carving; gourd sculpture
葫芦河	Hulu (Gourd) River (Gansu)
葫芦节	〈拉祜族〉Gourd Festival (from the 8th to 10th April)
葫芦丝	〈乐〉hulusi; cucurbit flute (a minority musical instrument in Yunnan)
湖滨晴雨	(of West Lake) Sunny and Rainy Lakeside
湖南菜	Hu'nan cuisine →湘菜
湖田古瓷窑址	Site of Ancient Porcelain Kiln in Hutian (Jiangxi)
湖心亭	mid-lake pavilion; pond-centered pavilion
蝴蝶谷	butterfly valley
蝴蝶馆	butterfly museum
蝴蝶会	〈白族〉Butterfly Festival (around the 15th day of the 4th lunar month)
蝴蝶泉	Butterfly Spring (Yunnan)
糊窗花	to put up window paper-cuts; to put up paper-cuts for window decoration

虎凤蝶	〈动〉Luehdorfia puziloi; tiger swallowtail
虎符	〈古〉tiger tally (tiger-shaped tally issued to generals as imperial authorization for troop movement)
虎节	〈彝族〉Tiger Festival (from the 8th to the 15th day of the 1st lunar month)
虎年	Year of the Tiger
虎跑梦泉	(of West Lake) Dream of Tiger Spring
虎丘山	Huqiu Mountain; Tiger Mountain (Jiangsu)
虎丘塔	Huqiu Pagoda; Huqiu Tower (Jiangsu)
虎山长城	Hushan Great Wall; Great Wall at Hushan Mountain (Liaoning)
虎山景区	Mount Hushan; Hushan Mountain (Hebei)
虎神节	〈彝族〉Tiger God Festival (from the 8th to the 15th day of the 1st lunar month)
虎跳滩土林	Tiger Leaping Beach Soil Forest (Yunnan)
虎跳峡	Hutiao Gorge; Tiger Leaping Gorge (Yunnan)
虎头景区	Hutou Scenic Area (Heilongjiang)
虎头帽	tiger head imitation cap; tiger-head-shaped cap
虎头鞋	〈服〉tiger-head shoes (for babies with the front part like a tiger head)
虎头要塞	Hutou (Tiger Head) Fortress (a military base built by Japanese army on the former Sino-Soviet border in the east of Northeast China) (Heilongjiang)
虎窝寺	Huwo Temple (Hebei)
虎啸山	Huxiao Mountain; Roaring Tiger Mountain (Heilongjiang)
虎啸岩景区	(of Mount Wuyi) Tiger Roaring Rock Scenic Area
虎榛子	〈植〉Ostryopsis davidiana
户部造币总厂旧址	Former Site of Mint/Coinage Factory of the Ministry of Revenue (in feudal China) (Tianjin)
户县农民画	Huxian Farmer Painting (Shaanxi)
护城河	city moat; fosse

护法神殿	Buddhist Guardian Hall (Qinghai) →小金瓦寺
护国宝塔	Huguo Pagoda (Beijing)
护国寺感应塔碑	Tablet of Ganying Pagoda in Huguo Temple (Gansu)
沪剧	〈戏〉Huju; Shanghai Opera
花边婚	lace wedding (the 13th anniversary of marriage)
花朝节	Flower Fairy Festival; Birthday of All Flowers; Flower Festival (on the 2nd, 12th, 15th or 25th day of the 2nd lunar month)
花车巡游	festooned vehicle parade
花齿突蟾	〈动〉*Scutiger maculatus*; piebald alpine toad
花旦	〈戏〉(of Beijing Opera) huadan (a female role)
花灯	Chinese festival lantern (displayed on the Lantern Festival)
花灯节	Chinese Lantern Festival (on the 8th day of the 4th lunar month)
花灯戏	Huadeng Opera
花儿会	〈土族〉Hua'er Festival (a folk song fair)
花港观鱼	(of West Lake) Viewing Fish at Lotus Pond; Viewing Fish at Flower Harbor
花糕	→重阳糕
花鼓灯	〈舞〉Flower Drum Lantern
花鼓戏	〈戏〉Huagu Opera; Flower Drum Opera
花果婚	floral wedding (the 4th anniversary of marriage) →丝婚
花果山	Huaguo Mountain (Jiangsu)
花海乐园	Flower Paradise (Hubei)
花红	〈植〉*Malus asiatica*; Chinese pear-leaved crabapple
花棘蛙	〈动〉*Maculopaa maculosa*
花江大峡谷	Huajiang River Grand Canyon (Guizhou)
花江大峡谷景区	Huajiang Grand Canyon Scenic Spot (Guizhou)
花江铁索桥	Huajiang River Chain Bridge (Guizhou)
花椒	〈植〉*Zanthoxylum bungeanum*; Sichuan pepper; Chinese prickly ash

花轿	〈旧〉(of wedding) bridal sedan chair; bride's sedan
花径	(of Mount Lushan) Flowery Path
花篮厅	(of Lion Forest Garden) Flower Basket Hall
花脸节	〈彝族〉Painted-Face Festival (in the 2nd lunar month)
花面狸	→果子狸[花面狸]
花木兰	Hua Mulan (an ancient Chinese heroine)
花木兰传奇	(of traditional drama) Legend of Hua Mulan
花鸟灯塔	Lighthouse of Huaniao Island; Lighthouse of Flower and Bird Island (Zhejiang)
花炮节	〈侗族、壮族等〉Firecrackers Festival; Fireworks Festival (in the 1st or 2nd lunar month)
花坪自然保护区	Huaping Nature Reserve (Guangxi)
花瓶石	Flower Vase Stone (Hong Kong)
花山节	〈苗族〉Huashan Festival (in the early 5th lunar month)
花山谜窟	Huashan Mysterious Rock Cave (at the side of Xin'an River) (Anhui)
花石子甬路	(of Imperial Palace) Path of Color Pebbles
花叶鹿蹄草	〈植〉*Pyrola alboreticulata*
花枝羹	〈烹饪〉Squid Thick Soup
花烛	〈旧〉wedding candles; candles lit in the bridal chamber at wedding
花子岭烈士墓	Huaziling Martyrs Tomb (Hubei)
划拳	finger-guessing game (a drinking game at a feast)
华北平原	North China Plain
华表	〈旧〉cloud pillar; ornamental column (in front of palaces, tombs, etc.)
华步小筑	(of Lingering Garden) A Scene in the Lingering Garden
华池双塔寺	Twin-Pagoda Temple of Huachi (Gansu)
华福花	〈植〉*Sinadoxa corydalifolia*

华盖殿	(of Nanjing Imperial Palace) Huagai Audience Hall; Hall of Splendid Canopy
华盖木	〈植〉*Pachylarnax sinica*
华南虎	〈动〉*Panthera tigris amoyensis*; South China tiger
华南缺齿鼹	〈动〉*Mogera insularis*
华南兔	〈动〉*Lepus sinensis*; Chinese hare
华南湍蛙	〈动〉*Amolops ricketti*; South Chinese sucker frog
华南沿海地区	South China coastal area
华南雨蛙	〈动〉*Hyla gongshanensis*; South China tree toad
华侨	overseas Chinese
华清池	Huaqing Pool; Huaqing Hot Spring (one of the four royal gardens in China) (Shaanxi)
华清宫遗址	Site/Ruins of Huaqing Palace; Huaqing Palace Ruins (Shaanxi)
华雀麦	〈植〉*Bromus sinensis*
华深拟髭蟾	〈动〉*Leptobrachium huashen*
华石斛	〈植〉*Dendrobium sinense*
华西雨蛙	〈动〉*Hyla annectans*
华夏	Huaxia (the name for the ancient China)
华夏民族	Huaxia nationality (the former name of the Chinese nation)
华夏人民	Huaxia people; Chinese people
华夏文明	Huaxia civilization
华夏西部影视城	China West Film Studio
华夏先祖	Huaxia ancestry; Chinese ancestry
华夏子孙	descendants of the Chinese Nation
华严顶	(of Mount Emei) Huayan Summit; Vatamsaka Summit
华严寺	Huayan Temple; Huayan Monastery (Shanxi)
华裔	ethnic Chinese; foreign citizen of Chinese origin
华蓥山	Huaying Mountain (Chongqing)
华支睾吸虫	→中华肝吸虫
滑稽动物园	(of Wuqiao Acrobatics World) Comic Zoo
化宝	〈丧〉huabao

华山	Mount Huashan; Huashan Mountain (Shaanxi)
华山摩崖石刻	(of Mount Huashan) Mount Huashan Cliffside Carvings
华山三大险	Three Major Adventures of Mount Huashan (Shaanxi)
华山索道	(of Mount Huashan) Huashan Mountain Ropeway
华山天梯	Ladder in the Cloud of Huashan Mountain (Shaanxi)
华山御温泉	Huashan Mountain Royal Spa; Royal Spa at Huashan Mountain (Shaanxi)
画笔菊	〈植〉*Ajaniopsis penicilliformis*
画舫斋	(of Garden of Harmony) Boat-Shaped Studio of Painting
画苑	picture gallery; painting gallery
画中游	(of Summer Palace) Rambling in Picture
桦木工艺品	birch handicraft
淮海战役	Huaihai Campaign (one of the three major battles in the War of Liberation)
淮海战役纪念馆	Memorial Hall of Huaihai Campaign (Jiangsu)
淮海战役烈士纪念碑	Monument to Martyrs of Huaihai Campaign (Jiangsu)
淮海战役战场旧址	Site of the Huaihai Campaign (Jiangsu)
淮河	Huaihe River
淮河风情园	Huaihe River Style Park (Anhui)
淮河流域	Huaihe River basin; Huaihe River valley
淮河源湿地公园	Huaihe River Headwaters Wetland Park (Hubei)
淮剧	〈戏〉Huaiju Opera
淮南王宫	(of Mount Bagong) Palace of Huainan King
淮山药	〈植〉*Dioscorea opposite*; Chinese yam rhizome
淮扬菜	〈烹饪〉Huaiyang Cuisine
槐树	〈植〉*Styphnolobium japonicum*; Chinese scholar tree; locust tree
欢乐谷	Happy Valley

还砚斋	(of Couple's Retreat Garden) Studio of Returning Ink Stone
环渤海	Bohai Sea rim
环江大桥景区	Huanjiang Bridge Scenic Area (Guizhou)
环荆州古城湿地公园	Wetland Park around Jingzhou Ancient City (Hubei)
环颈雉	〈动〉*Phasianus colchicus*; common pheasant; ring-necked pheasant →雉鸡
环秀山庄	Mountain Villa with Embracing Beauty (Jiangsu)
圜丘坛	(of Temple of Heaven) Circular Mound Altar (where the emperors offered sacrifice to Heaven on the winter solstice)
幻城仙境	Magic City Wonderland (Tianjin)
换庚谱	(of marriage etiquette) to exchange the date of birth and the eight characters of a horoscope
换黄单	〈阿昌族〉Yellow Sheet-Changing Day (in the 9th or 10th lunar month)
换丧服	(of funeral) to put on mourning apparel
浣云沼	(of Lingering Garden) Huanyun Pool
荒漠猫	〈动〉*Felis bieti*; Chinese mountain cat
皇城	Imperial City (inner part of Beijing)
皇帝洞景区	Emperor Cave Scenic Area (Fujian)
皇后像广场	Statue Square (Hong Kong)
皇喙凤蝶	〈动〉*Teinopalpus imperialis*
皇极殿	(of Imperial Palace) Hall of Imperial Supremacy
皇极门	(of Imperial Palace) Gate of Imperial Supremacy
皇乾殿	(of Temple of Heaven) Hall of Imperial Heaven
皇穹宇	(of Temple of Heaven) Imperial Vault of Heaven (where the sacrificial plates are kept)
皇太极	Hongtaiji (1592–1643, the founding emperor of the Qing Dynasty)
皇天后土	Heaven and Earth; Sovereign Heaven and Great Earth
黄斑拟小鲵	〈动〉*Pseudohynobius flavomaculatus*; yellow-spotted salamander

黄堡镇耀州窑遗址	Yaozhou Kiln Site at Huangbao Town; Site of Yaozhou Kiln at Huangbao Town (Shaanxi)
黄草梁地质景区	Huangcao Ridge Geo-Zone (Shanxi)
黄唇鱼	〈动〉*Bahaba taipingensis*; Chinese bahaba
黄大仙祠	Wong Tai Sin Temple (Hong Kong)
黄大仙圣境园	Huang Daxian Holy Land Park (Guangdong)
黄帝	Huangdi; Yellow Emperor (2717B.C.-?, known as the initiator of Chinese civilization and a great tribal leader in the final primitive society of ancient China)
黄帝祠	Yellow Emperor Hall (Hong Kong)
黄帝宫	(of Shaolin Temple) Huang Di's Palace; Yellow Emperor Palace
黄帝故里	(of Shaolin Temple) Birthplace of Huang Di; Hometown of the Yellow Emperor
黄帝陵	Huangdi (Yellow Emperor) Mausoleum (Shaanxi)
黄帝陵旅游区	Huangdi/Yellow Emperor Mausoleum Scenic Spot; Mausoleum of Yellow Emperor Scenic Area (Shaanxi)
黄帝庙	Huangdi Temple; Yellow Emperor Temple (Shaanxi) →轩辕庙
黄杜鹃	〈植〉*Rhododendron molle*; Chinese azalea →羊踯躅
黄飞鸿纪念馆	Huang Feihong Memorial Hall; Memorial Hall of Huang Feihong (Guangdong)
黄腹角雉	〈动〉*Tragopan caboti*; yellow-billied tragopan; cabot's tragopan
黄冈大圣寺塔	Dasheng Temple Pagoda in Huanggang (Hubei)
黄瓜肉丁	〈烹饪〉Stir-Fried Diced Pork with Cucumber
黄果	〈植〉*Citurs sinensis*; yellow fruit
黄果树景区	Huangguoshu Waterfalls Scenic Area (Guizhou)
黄果树瀑布	Huangguoshu Waterfall (Guizhou)
黄海	Yellow Sea
黄河	Huanghe River; Yellow River

黄河风景(名胜)区	Huanghe River Scenic Area; Yellow River Scenic Area (He'nan) →黄河游览区
黄河壶口瀑布	Hukou Waterfall of Huanghe/Yellow River; Kettle Spout Waterfall of Huanghe/Yellow River (Shaanxi, Shanxi)
黄河花园口旅游度假区	Huayuankou Tourist and Holiday Resort on Yellow River (Henan)
黄河流域	Huanghe River basin; Yellow River valley
黄河母亲雕塑	Huanghe River Mother Sculpture; Statue of the Yellow River Mother (Gansu)
黄河漂流	Huanghe River drift; Yellow River drift
黄河三角洲	Huanghe River delta; Yellow River delta
黄河三角洲湿地	Huanghe/Yellow River Delta wetland (Shandong)
黄河三角洲自然保护区	Huanghe/Yellow River Delta Nature Reserve (Shandong)
黄河石林	Huanghe/Yellow River Stone Forest (Gansu)
黄河索道	Huanghe River Cableway; Yellow River Cableway (Gansu)
黄河铁桥	Huanghe/Yellow River Iron Bridge (Gansu)
黄河峡谷	Huanghe River Canyon; Yellow River Canyon (Inner Mongolia)
黄河下游流域	lower Huanghe/Yellow River basin/valley
黄河砚	Huanghe River ink-stone; Yellow River ink-stone
黄河游览区	Huanghe/Yellow River Scenic Area (He'nan)
黄河源国际狩猎场	Huangheyuan International Hunting Ground; International Hunting Ground at the Source of the Yellow River (Qinghai)
黄鹤飞天	(of Huangheqiao) Yellow Crane Flying Apsaras
黄鹤归来铜雕	(of Yellow Crane Tower) Bronze Statue of Returning Yellow Crane
黄鹤楼	Yellow Crane Tower (Hubei)
黄鹤楼公园	Yellow Crane Tower Park (Hubei)
黄鹤桥峰林景区	Huangheqiao Peak Forest Scenic Area; Yellow Crane Bridge Peak Forest Scenic Area (Hubei)

黄花岗七十二烈士墓	Tomb/Mausoleum of 72 Revolutionary Martyrs at Huanghua Gang; Huanghua Gang Mausoleum of 72 Martyrs (Guangdong)
黄花梨木[树]	〈植〉*Dalbergia odorifere*; yellow pear wood →降香黄檀
黄花阵	(of Yuanming Garden) Park of Labyrinth
黄淮平原	Huanghuai Plain; Yellow River-Huaihe River Plain
黄继光纪念馆	Huang Jiguang Memorial Hall; Memorial Hall of Huang Jiguang (Sichuan)
黄巾军寨	〈古〉(of Mount Lingxiao) Yellow Turban Military Stronghold
黄金葛	〈植〉*Epipremnum aureum*; scindapsus; Chinese money plant
黄连河自然景区	Huanglian River Natural Scenic Spot (Yunnan)
黄粱美梦	(of idiom) golden millet dream; living in a fool's paradise
黄粱梦吕仙祠	Lüxian Temple at Huangliangmeng Village (Hebei)
黄陵庙	Huangling Temple (Hubei)
黄琉璃瓦屋顶	yellow glazed tile roof
黄龙洞	(of Zhangjiajie) Huanglong Cave; Yellow Dragon Cave
黄龙沟	Huanglong Valley (Sichuan)
黄龙观民俗文化村	Huanglong Guan Folk Culture Village (Hubei)
黄龙景区	Huanglong Scenic Area; Yellow Dragon Scenic Area (Sichuan)
黄龙泉	(of Zhangjiajie) Huanglong Spring; Yellow Dragon Spring
黄龙寺	(of Huanglong Valley) Huanglong Temple; Ancient Yellow Dragon Monastery
黄龙吐翠	(of West Lake) Yellow Dragon Spitting Greenness; Yellow Dragon Cave Dotted with Green
黄猫峡	Huangmao Gorge; Yellow Cat Gorge (Hubei)

黄梅老祖寺	Huangmei Ancestor Temple (Hubei)
黄牛峡景区	Huangniu (Yellow Ox) Gorge Scenic Area (Hubei)
黄皮	〈植〉*Clausena lansium*; wampee
黄埔军校旧址	Site of Former Whampoa/Huangpu Military Academy (Guangdong)
黄浦江	Huangpu River (Shanghai)
黄浦江观光区	Huangpu River Tourist Area (Shanghai)
黄芩	〈植〉*Scutellaria baicalensis*; baical skullcap
黄山	Mount Huangshan; Huangshan Mountain; Yellow Mountain (Anhui)
黄山第四纪冰川遗址	(of Mount Huangshan) Traces of Quaternary Glacier in Mount Huangshan
黄山怪石	grotesque rocks at Mount Huangshan (Anhui)
黄山国际旅游节	Mount Huangshan International Tourism Festival
黄山角蟾	〈动〉*Megophrys huangshanensis*; Huangshan horned toad
黄山温泉景区	Hot Spring Scenic Area of Mount Huangshan (Anhui)
黄鳝	〈动〉*Monopterus albus*; ricefield eel; finless eel
黄石[狮]寨风景线	(of Zhangjiajie) Huangshi Stronghold line; Yellow Lion Stronghold route
黄石[狮]寨景区	(of Zhangjiajie) Huangshi Stronghold Scenic Area; Yellow Lion Stronghold Scenic Area
黄丝桥古城	Huangsiqiao Ancient Town (Hu'nan)
黄松峪地质公园	Huangsongyu Geopark (Beijing)
黄土高原	Loess Plateau
黄兴故居	Former Residence of Huang Xing; Huang Xing's Former Residence (Hu'nan)
黄崖关	Huangya Pass (Tianjin)
黄崖关长城	Great Wall at Huangya Pass (Tianjin)
黄岩岛	(of South China Sea) Huangyan Island
黄砚岭	(of Mount Taishan) Yellow Ink Stone Ridge
黄羊	〈动〉*Procapra gutturosa*; przewalski's gazelle

黄杨山	Huangyang Mountain (Guangdong)
黄洋界	(of Mount Jinggang) Huangyang Border
黄志双盖蕨	〈植〉*Diplazium wangii*
黄竹	〈植〉*Dendrocalamus membranceus*
黄竹坑石刻	Rock Carving at Wong Chuk Hang (Hong Kong)
凰	(of Chinese legend) huang (the perfect female bird used by ancient priests to sacrifice to the gods) →凤
湟水河	Huangshui River (Qinghai, Xinjiang)
灰金丝猴	〈动〉*Rhinopithecus brelichi*; grey golden monkey
灰胸竹鸡	〈动〉*Bambusicola thoracica*; Chinese bamboo partridge
灰熊	〈动〉*Ursus arctos*; brown bear
灰叶猴	〈动〉*Presbytis phayrei*; Phayre's leaf monkey
辉腾锡勒草原	Huitengxile Grassland (Inner Mongolia)
徽(州)菜	〈烹饪〉Hui Cuisine; Huizhou Cuisine
徽派版画	Hui-style wood block
徽派建筑	buildings of Huizhou style; Hui-style building
徽商	Huizhou businessmen; Huizhou merchants
徽商大宅院	garden of Huizhou businessmen/merchants
徽砚	Huizhou ink-stone
徽州府衙	〈古〉Huizhou Ancient Government Office (Anhui)
徽州牌坊群	Huizhou Memorial Archway Group (Anhui)
徽州文化	Huizhou culture
回鹘	〈古〉Huihu (an ethnic minority tribe, known as the predecessor of today's Uyghur)
回婚节	〈朝鲜族〉Sixty Years' Wedding Anniversary
回甲节	〈朝鲜族〉Celebration for Sixty Years Old
回敬	to drink a toast in return; to return a compliment; to return a salute
回门	〈婚〉huimen; bride's return (to her paternal home on the third day after the wedding) →归宁
回门宴	(of marriage) bride's return banquet →回门

回民小吃街	Muslim Snack Street (Shaanxi)
回王陵	Mausoleum of the King of Hui (Xinjiang) →哈密王墓
回心庵	(of Mount Wudang) Huixin Nunnery; Mind Changing Nunnery
回雁峰	Huiyan Peak; Returning Wild Geese Peak (Hu'nan)
回音壁	(of Temple of Heaven) Echo Wall
回族	Hui ethnic group; Hui
汇湾河水利景区	Huiwan River Water Conservancy Scenic Area (Hubei)
会街节	〈阿昌族〉Huijie Festival (on the 10th day of the 9th lunar month and lasting for five days)
会亲节	〈畲族〉Relatives Visit-and-Reunion Festival (on the 2nd day of the 2nd lunar month)
会亲酒	engagement banquet
会师公园	Huishi Park (Tianjin)
会心桥	(of Yuanming Garden) Bridge of Understanding
惠亭湖湿地公园	Huiting Lake Wetland Park (Hubei)
慧济寺	(of Mount Putuo) Huiji Temple
婚嫁乐队	wedding band; marriage band
婚嫁习俗	marriage custom
婚嫁之礼	wedding ceremony
婚宴	wedding banquet
混元珍珠伞	(of a game) Hunyuan Pearl Umbrella
活路节	〈侗族〉Huolu Festival; Subsistence Festival (the first ten-day period of the 1st lunar month)
活人墓	tomb for the living (that is prepared or purchased for people who are still alive)
火把节	Torch Festival (a traditional festival of the Yi, Bai, Naxi, Jino and Lahu ethnic groups on the 24th day of the 6th lunar month)
火葱	→胡葱[火葱]
火花海	(of Jiuzhai Valley) Sparkling Lake

火山口森林公园	Crater Forest Park (Heilongjiang)
火烧山	Huoshao Mountain; Fire-Burning Mountain (Xinjiang)
火烧屿	Fire Island (Fujian)
火神节	Fire God Festival (on the 7th day of the 1st lunar month)
火石寨森林公园	Huoshizhai Forest Park (Ningxia)
火塘酒	〈拉祜族〉huotang liquor (a formal symbol for marriage engagement)
火焰山	Flaming Mountain (Xinjiang)
火葬	cremation
霍林河	Huolin River (Inner Mongolia)
霍州州署大堂	Huozhou Prefecture Administration Hall (Shanxi)

J

击鼓传花	drum and flower game (one is drumming while the others pass round a cloth flower (whoever has the flower in hands loses the game when the drumbeat stops)
击鼓饮酒	〈民俗〉to beat the drum for drinking (a drinking-game where whoever has the passing flower in hands when the drum stops must drink a cup)
矶头山	Mount Jitou; Jitou Mountain (Hubei)
鸡蛋会	〈土族、回族〉Egg Festival
鸡得节	〈壮族〉Cockerel Day; Kid's Day (on the 5th day of the 5th lunar month)
鸡峰山	Mount Jifeng; Jifeng Mountain (Shaanxi)
鸡公山	Mount Jigong; Jigong Mountain (He'nan)
鸡公山遗址	Jigong Mountain ruins (of Old Stone Age); Late Paleolithic Site at Jigong Mountain (Hubei)
鸡公山自然保护区	Jigong Mountain Nature Reserves (He'nan)
鸡冠滇丁香	〈植〉*Luculia yunnanensis*
鸡冠洞	Cockscomb Cave (He'nan)
鸡冠砬子旅游景区	Comb Lazi (Rock) Scenic Spot (Heilongjiang)
鸡冠山	Cockscomb Peak (Sichuan)
鸡脚冻	〈烹饪〉Chicken Feet Galantine
鸡鸣山	Jiming Hill (Hebei)
鸡鸣寺	Jiming Temple; Crowing Rooster Temple (Jiangsu)
鸡鸣驿	Jimingyi Post; Jimingyi Dak (Hebei)
鸡年	Year of the Rooster (one of the 12 Chinese Zodiac)
鸡汤氽海蚌	〈烹饪〉Sea Clams in Chicken Soup

鸡汤云吞	〈烹饪〉Chicken Wonton Soup
鸡足山	Jizu Mountain (Yunnan) (one of the top ten Buddhist mountains in China)
鸡足山朝山节	Festival of the Pilgrimage to Jizu Mountain (from the 15th day of the 12th lunar month to the 15th day of the 1st lunar month)
积木塞渎	accumulated wood blocks the river (for building Guanwa Palace)
积益殿	(of Imperial Palace) Hall of Collected Benefit
姬氏民居	Folk/Taditional Houses of the Ji Family (Shanxi)
基督教坟场[公墓]	Protestant Cemetery (Macao)
基督教武昌堂	Wuchang Christian Church (Hubei)
基酒[酒基]	substratum of spirit; base wine; base liquor
基隆港	Keelung Port; Port of Keelung (Taiwan)
基隆中正公园	Keelung Chiang Kai-Shek Park (Taiwan)
基诺族	Jino ethnic group; Jino
基羽鞭叶耳蕨	〈植〉*Polystichum basipinnatum*
吉拜	〈旧〉worship for lucky thing (one of the nine worships)
吉贝屿	Chipei Tail; Jibei Island (Taiwan)
吉礼	〈古〉etiquette of sacrifice to gods, earth, humans and ghosts; sacrificial rites (one of the five rites of the Western Zhou Dynasty)
吉力湖	Jili Lake (Xinjiang)
吉林市博物馆	Jilin Municipal Museum; Jilin Meteorite Museum
吉林文庙	Jilin Confucius Temple
吉林爪鲵	〈动〉*Onychodactylus zhangyapingi*; Jilin clawed salamander
吉日良辰	auspicious day
吉祥天母节[日]	〈藏族〉Palden Lhamo Festival (on the 15th day of the 10th month in Tibetan calender)
汲水门(大)桥	Kap Shui Mun Bridge; KSMB (Hong Kong)
极地水族馆	Polar Aquarium (Chongqing)
极乐洞	(of Qianling Mountain) Jile (Sukhavati) Cave

棘侧蛙	〈动〉*Quasipaa shini*; spiny-flanked frog
棘腹蛙	〈动〉*Quasipaa boulengeri*; rana boulenger guenther
棘肛蛙	〈动〉*Unculuana unculuanus*
棘皮湍蛙	〈动〉*Amolops granulosus*; spineskinned torrential frog
棘疣齿蟾	〈动〉*Oreolalax granulosus*; spiny warty toothed toad
棘疣异角蟾	〈动〉*Xenophrys tuberogranulatus*; spiny warty horned toad
棘螈	〈动〉*Acanthostega*
棘指角蟾	〈动〉*Megophrys spinata*
集美解放纪念碑	Jimei Liberation Monument (Fujian)
集美旅游区	Jimei Tourist Areas (Fujian)
集美学村	Jimei School Village (Fujian)
集贤祠	Jixian Temple (Hu'nan)
纪晓岚故居	Former Residence of Ji Xiaolan (Beijing) →阅微草堂
济南百里黄河景区	Hundred-Li Yellow River Scenic Area in Jinan (Shandong)
纪山楚墓群	Chu Tombs at Jishan Town; Tombs of the State of Chu at Jishan Town (Hubei)
忌泪洒尸身	Don't shed tears on the deceased body
忌日	anniversary of a death; death anniversaries of someome
济渎(北海)庙	Jidu Temple (He'nan)
济公	Ji Gong (known as living Buddha in ancient China)
济公观海	(of Xingtai Canyon group) Jigong Sea-Watching
祭拜厅	worshiping hall; worship hall
祭成陵	〈蒙古族〉Mausoleum of Genghis Khan Worship Day (on the 21st day of the 3rd lunar month)
祭风节	〈彝族〉Wind Worship Festival; Sacrifice to Wind Festival (on the 3rd day of the 3rd lunar month)

祭风仪式	〈纳西族〉sacrifice ceremony for wind god (Yunnan)
祭鬼节	Spirit Festval; Ghost Festival (on the 15th day of the 7th lunar month) →鬼节
祭龙	dragon worship; sacrifice to the dragon
祭龙节	〈藏族〉Dragon Worship Festival
祭密枝	→密枝节
祭鸟节	〈白族〉Bird Worship Day (on Tomb Sweeping Day)
祭牛神	〈侗族〉sacrifice to Cattle God
祭萨节	〈侗族〉Jisa Festival (sacrifice to ancestors due to maternity worship) (on the 1st Mao day of the 2nd lunar month)
祭塞门	〈阿昌族〉Sacrifice to Saimen Day (on the 21st day of the 7th lunar month)
祭山节	〈藏族〉Memorial Day for Mountain (on the 6th day of the 3rd lunar month)
祭山神	〈藏族〉sacrifice to the God of mountain
祭神	to honor the god, to offer sacrifices to the god; worship the god
祭树节	〈仡佬族〉Tree-Worship Day (on the 3rd day of the 3rd lunar month)
祭祀	to offer sacrifices to gods or ancestors; to sacrifice/worship (to spiritual beings); worship rituals
祭祀节日	day of sacrifice
祭祀厅［堂］	sacrificial hall (usually for official occasion)
祭太阳神节	〈拉祜族〉Sungod Sacrifice (on Beginning of Summer)
祭吴凤	〈高山族〉sacrifice to Wu Feng
祭羊	lamb offered in sacrifice; goats offered for one's condolences
祭尤节	〈苗族〉Sacrifice to Chi You Day (on the 2nd Chou day of the 10th lunar month)
祭月	Sacrifice to Moon God (on the 15th day of the 8th lunar month)

祭祖［宗］	〈民俗〉ancestor worship; to offer sacrifices to ancestors
祭祖魂(节)	〈壮族〉Ancestor Soul Worship (on the 14th day of the 7th lunar month)
祭祖节	ancestor worship festivals (referring to four major festivals such as Tomb Sweeping Day, Ghost Festival, Double Ninth Festival and New Year's Eve)
祭祖仪式	ritual for ancestor worship
寄畅园	Jichang Garden (Jiangsu)
寄名	〈民俗〉to adopt the surname of the adoptive family; to adopt a religious name of monks/nuns so as to ensure his long life
寄名酒	〈民俗〉banquet for celebrating a surname-giving →寄名
寄啸山庄	Jixiao Mountain Villa (Jiangsu) →何园
稷下学宫	〈古〉Jixia Academy (a higher education institution in the Warring States) (Shandong)
鲫鱼脑	〈中药〉Gold Carp Brain; Crucian Carp Brain
加冠礼	〈古〉capping ceremony (a symbol of coming-of-age for males)
加笄礼	〈古〉hair-pinning ceremony (a symbol of coming-of-age females)
加思栏炮台	St. Francisco Barracks (Macao)
佳乐水景区	Jialeshui Scenic Area (Taiwan)
迦叶佛	Kasyapa Buddha
迦旃延	〈佛〉Katyayana (one of the ten disciples of the Buddha, best-known for his argumentation and exegesis)
家常皮冻	〈烹饪〉Pork Skin Aspic
家乡熏蹄	〈烹饪〉Home-Made Smoked Pork Trotters
嘉北郊野公园	Jiabei Country Park (Shanghai)
嘉道理农场暨植物园	Kadoorie Farm and Botanic Garden (Hong Kong)
嘉定孔庙	Jiading Confucius Temple (Shanghai)

嘉靖皇帝	Emperor Jiajing (1507-1567, reigning from 1521 to 1567 in Ming Dynasty)
嘉靖年间	Reign of Emperor Jiajing (1521-1567)
嘉乐庇总督大桥	Ponte Governador Nobre de Carvalho (Macao)
嘉礼	〈古〉(one of Five Etiquettes of Western Zhou Dynasty) etiquette and ceremony for weddings, crowning, and festive activities
嘉陵江	Jialing River
嘉陵江源头景区	Jialing River Source Scenic Area (Shaanxi)
嘉模公园	Jiamo Park (Macao) →氹仔市政公园
嘉树轩	(of Chengde Mountain Resort) House Surrounded with Big Trees
嘉午[五]台	Jiawutai Peak (Shaanxi)
嘉业堂藏书楼	Jiayetang Library (Zhejiang)
嘉峪关	Jiayu Guan; Jiayu Pass (Gansu)
嘉峪关滑翔基地	Jiayuguan Glider Base (Gansu)
夹砬子景区	Jialazi Scenic Area (Liaoning)
夹墙山自然景区	Jiaqiang Mountain Natural Scenic Area (Hebei)
夹山	Jiashan Mountain (Hu'nan)
荚囊蕨	〈植〉*Struthiopteris eburnea*
假山王国	Kingdom of the Rockeries (Jiangsu) →狮子林
假枝雀麦	〈植〉*Bromus pseudoramosus*
驾幸	〈古〉arrival of the honorable people (usually the imperial tour of inspection)
架桥节	〈侗族〉Bridging Day (on the 2nd day of the 2nd lunar month)
假日海滩	Holiday Beach (Hai'nan)
嫁妆	〈婚〉(of wedding) dowry; trousseau
尖椒香芹牛肉丝	〈烹饪〉Sauté Shredded Beef with Hot Pepper and Celery
尖沙咀	Tsim Sha Tsui (Hong Kong)
尖沙咀[九龙]玫瑰堂	Tsim Sha Tsui Rosary Church (Hong Kong)
尖沙咀钟楼	Tsim Sha Tsuis Clock Tower (Hong Kong)
尖叶鸟舌兰	〈植〉*Ascocentrum pumilum*

间颅鼠兔	〈动〉*Ochotona cansus*; Gansu pika
肩倒立	Balance on the shoulder and arms
蒹葭泛月	Boat-Rowing in the Moonlight (Zhejiang)
剪彩	to cut the ribbon (at an opening ceremony); ribbon cutting
剪彩仪式	ribbon cutting ceremony
剪刀峰	scissors peak
剪马鬃节	〈裕固族〉Horse Hair-cutting Festival (within the middle ten-day period of the 4th lunar month)
剪纸	Chinese paper cutting; paper-cut
剪纸艺术	paper-cut art; kirigami
见面礼	a gift given to sb at the first meeting (especially to a relative of a junior generation); present on first meeting
见山楼	(of Humble Administrator's Garden) Mountain-View Tower
饯别酒	bonailie; stirrup-cup
饯行	to give a farewell dinner
建安堡	Jian'an Fort (Shaanxi)
建岱桥	(of Mount Taishan) Jiandai Bridge
建党节	Party's Day; CPC Founding Day (on July, 1st)
建福宫	(of Imperial Palace) Palace of Happiness Establishment
建国寺	Jianguo Temple (He'nan) →大相国寺
建军节	Army Day; PLA (People's Liberation Army) Day (on August 1st)
建水文庙	Jianshui Confucius Temple (Yunnan)
建水燕子洞	Jianshui Swallow Cave (Yunnan)
建水紫陶	Jianshui Purple Pottery
剑池飞瀑	Sword Pond Plunging Waterfall (Zhejiang)
剑河桥	Bridge of Sword River (Hubei)
剑门关	Jianmen Pass (Sichuan)
剑门蜀道	Sichuan Road at Jianmen (Sichuan)
剑术	Swordsmanship; Sword play

剑岩悬泉	(of Jiuzhai Valley) Hanging Spring of Sword Cliff
涧磁村定窑遗址	Ding Kiln Site of Jianci Village (Hebei)
毽子［球］	jianzi (Chinese chicken-feather shuttlecock for kicking)
鉴碧亭	(of Yuanming Garden) Pavilion of Beautiful Scenery Appreciation
鉴湖	→榕［鉴］湖
鉴真	Jian Zhen (an eminent Buddhist monk in Tang Dynasty)
鉴真纪念堂	Jian Zhen Memorial Hall (Jiangsu)
箭扣长城	Jiankou Great Wall (Beijing)
箭括岭	Jiankuo (Arrowhead) Ridge (Shaanxi)
箭楼	Battlement; Embrasured Watchtower (over a city gate) (Beijing)
箭亭	(of Imperial Palace) Archery Pavilion
箭竹海	(of Jiuzhai Valley) Arrow Bamboo Lake
江汉湖区湿地	Jianghan Lake Area Marsh; Jianhan Lake Wetland (Hubei)
江汉路步行街	Jianghan Lu Walkway; Jianghan Road Walking Street (Hubei)
江湖	〈道〉jianghu (word of outlaws); martial world
江湖文化城	(of Wuqiao Acrobatics World) Cultural City of Ancient Itinerant Entertainers
江淮平原	Jianghuai Plains; Yangtze-Huaihe River Plains
江口景区	Jiangkou Scenic Area (Liaoning)
江郎山	Jianglang Mountain (Zhejiang)
江陵碑苑	Jiangling Monument (Hubei)
江南地区	Jiangnan region; Jiangnan area (in the lower Yangtze River basin)
江南贡院	Historical Exhibition Hall of Jiangnan Institute for Imperial Examination; Jiangnan Examination Hall (Jiangsu)
江南明珠	Jiangnan pearl; south Yangtze pearl (good reputation for the cities in Jiangnan region)

江南三大名楼	Three Famous Buildings in South China; Three Historical Buildings in the South of the Yangtze River (Tengwang Pavilion, Yellow Crane Tower and Yueyang Tower)
江南水乡	water towns in southern China; the south of the lower reaches of the Yangtze River
江南丝竹	〈乐〉Jiangnan Sizhu (the silk and bamboo music, which is listed as one of China's intangible cultural heritages); Jiangnan string and pipe music
江南丝竹馆	Jiangnan Silk and Bamboo Museum; Jiangnan Traditional Stringed and Woodwind Instruments Museum (Jiangsu)
江南晚春	late spring in Jiangnan
江南园林	Jiangnan garden; landscape garden on the Yangtze Delta
江南园林经典之作	classical work of gardens on the south of the Yangtze River
江南织绣馆	Jiangnan embroidery museum; Jiangnan silk product hall
江神庙	River God Temple (Shaanxi)
江中浮玉	floating jade in the Yangtze River (referring to Jiaoshan Hill Scenic Area)
江孜宗山抗英遗址	Site of Resistance to British Aggression at Zongshan in Jiangzi; Gyantse Dzong; Gyantse Fortress (Tibet)
将军岭	General Ridge (Hebei)
将军泡子	Jiangjun Lake Wetland (Inner Mongolia)
将军山	General Mountain Scenic Area (Jiangsu)
将军崖岩画	Jiangjun Cliff Petroglyphs; General Cliff Rock Paintings (Jiangsu)
将军岩	Jiangjun Rock; General Rock (Jiangxi)
将死	(of a chess) checkmate
姜家甸草原[场]	Jiangjiadian grassland (Jilin)

姜女祠	Jiangnü Memorial Temple; Tongchuan Jiang Ancestral Temple (Shaanxi)
姜女石遗址	Jiangnü Stone Site (Liaoning)
姜桑拉姆峰	Jiangsang Lamu Peak (Tibet)
姜氏庄[宅]园[院]	Jiang's Manor (Shaanxi)
姜席堰	Jiang-Xi Dam (Zhejiang)
姜寨遗址	Neolithic Site of Jiangzhai Village (Shaanxi)
蒋介石故居	Chiang Kai-shek's Former Residence (Zhejiang)
蒋介石行辕	Chiang Kai-shek's Field Headquarters; Chiang Kai-shek's Barrack (Beijing)
蒋巷村	Jiangxiang Village (a national key village for rural tourism) (Jiangsu)
蒋巷丰收节	Jiangxiang Harvest Festival
降神节	〈藏族〉God Descending Festival (on the 22nd day of the 9th month in Tibetan calender)
降香黄檀	→黄花梨木[树]
《将相和》	*General and Premier Make Up*; *Reconciliation between the General and the Premier* (one of articles in historical records, by Sima Qian in the Western Han Dynasty)
绛雪轩	(of Imperial Palace) Bower of Crimson Snow
酱豆腐(乳)	fermented bean curd
交臂酒	〈壮族〉jiaobi (arms crossing) wine; cross-arm drinking
交河故城	Jiaohe Ruins; Ancient Jiaohe City (Xinjiang)
交际联	communicative couplets
交泰殿	(of Imperial Palace) Jiaotai Palace; Hall of Union and Peace
胶东半岛	Jiaodong Peninsula (Shandong)
胶济铁路	Jiaoji Railway; Jiaozhou-Jinan Railway
焦岗湖	Jiaogang Lake (Anhui)
焦山碑林	Jiaoshan Forest of Steles (Jiangsu)
焦山寺	Jiaoshan Temple (Jiangsu)
焦庄户地道战遗址纪念馆	Jiaozhuanghu Memorial Hall of Tunnel Warfare Remains (Beijing)

角楼	(of Imperial Palace) Arrow Towers
角山	Mount Jiaoshan; Jiaoshan Mountain (the first mountain of the Great Wall) (Hebei)
角山长城	Jiaoshan Great Wall; Great Wall at Mount Jiaoshan (Hebei)
角状耳蕨	〈植〉*Polystichum aloicorhe*
轿子	〈古〉sedan chair
轿子岭	Jiaozi Mountain Ridge (Guizhou)
轿子山	Jiaozi mountain (Yunnan)
教师节	Teachers' Day (on October 10th)
窖酒	cellar wine
窖酿酒	cellar-fermented wine
滘西洲洪圣古庙	Hung Shing Temple at Kau Sai Chau (Hong Kong)
接风(洗尘)	〈民俗〉to give a dinner for a visitor from afar; to give a reception in honor of a guest from afar; to give a reception in honor of sb
接风酒	〈民俗〉welcoming wine; welcome feast
接三[迎三]	〈旧〉ceremony on the third day of a funeral; Monks chant prayers for the deceased in order to send his soul to the Heaven
接笋峰[岩]	(of Mount Wuyi) Rejoined Bamboo Peak/Rock
接亡	〈丧〉to welcome the soul of the dead back home
接新水节	〈拉祜族〉New Water Taking Festival (offering sacrifice to the God of water, from the 28th to 30th day of the 11th lunar month)
接引殿	Terrace Guidance Hall (Sichuan)
接引寺	Jieyin Temple (Shaanxi)
揭红盖头	〈婚〉(of a wedding) to unwrap the red veil
街津口赫哲族旅游度假区	Jiejinkou Hezhe Holiday Resort (Heilongjiang)
节气	solar term (a day marking one of the 24 divisions of the solar year in the traditional Chinese calendar)
节葬	〈古〉(of Mohism) to save on funeral; frugal funeral
结拜节	〈壮族〉Sworn Day (on the 13th day of the 5th lunar month)

结古河	Gyêgu River (Qinghai)
结古赛马节	Gyêgu Horse Racing Festival
结古藏族康巴节	Gyêgu Tibetan Khampa Festival
截拳道	Jeet Kune Do (a hybrid philosophy of martial arts heavily influenced by the personal philosophy and experiences of martial artist Bruce Lee)
碣石山	Jieshi Mountain (Hebei)
解放碑	Monument for Liberation (Chongqing)
解放碑步行街	Jiefangbei Walkway/Walking Street (Chongqing)
解州关帝庙	Temple of Lord Guanyu in Haizhou; Guan Yu Temple in Haizhou (Shanxi)
芥蓝	〈植〉*Brassica alboglabra*; Chinese kale; Chinese broccoli
金斑喙凤蝶	〈动〉*Teinopalpus aureus*; golden-spotted swallowtail butterfly
金宝塔	(of Wanfo Garden) Gold Pagoda
金鞭溪	Golden Whip Stream; Golden Whip Brook (Hu'nan)
金鞭溪风景线	(of Zhangjiajie) Golden Whip Stream route
金鞭岩	(of Zhangjiajie) Golden Whip Peak
金厂滑雪场	Jinchang Ski Resort (Jilin)
金朝	Jin Dynasty (1115–1234)
金翅雀	〈动〉*Chloris sinica*; goldfinch
金刀峡	Jindao (Golden Knife) Gorge (Chongqing)
金殿	(of Mount Wudang) Golden Palace
金顶	(of Mount Emei) Golden Summit
金顶齿突蟾	〈动〉*Scutiger chintingensis*; chinting alpine toad
金顶华藏寺	(of Mount Emei) Huazang Temple at Golden Summit →峨眉(山)金顶
金顶景区	(of Mount Wudang) Golden Summit area
金顶山	Jinding Mountain (He'nan)
金顶寺	Jinding Temple (Yunnan)
金豆	〈植〉*Fortunella venosa*; golden bean kumquat
金发石杉	〈植〉*Huperzia quasipolytrichoides*; blonde huperzia

金佛甘珠尔	Golden Buddhist Ganzhuer
金佛拟小鲵	〈动〉*Pseudohynobius jinfo*
金佛乔答摩	Golden Buddhas Gautama
金刚殿	king kong hall; hall of Buddha's warrior attendant
金刚钻婚	diamond wedding (the 6th anniversary of marriage)
金刚座舍利宝塔	Sarira-Stupas on "Diamond Thrones"; Vajra Relic Pagoda (Inner Mongolia)
金阁山	Jin'ge Mountain (Hebei)
金圭寺	Jingui Temple (Yunnan)
金龟岩	(of Zhangjiajie) Golden Turtle Peak
金河口森林公园	Jinhekou Forest Park (Hebei)
金湖湿地公园	Jinhu Lake Wetland Park (Hubei)
金湖杨森林公园	Jinhuyang Forest Park (Xinjiang)
金花茶	〈植〉*Camellia nitidissima*; golden camellia
金华山	Jinhua Mountain (Zhejiang)
金婚	golden wedding (the 50th anniversary of marriage)
金鸡独立	(of Tai Chi) Golden cock standing on one leg
金鸡岭	Golden Rooster Hill (Guangdong)
金江湍蛙	〈动〉*Amolops jinjiangensis*; Jinjiang torrent frog
金莲	〈道〉(of a halidome) golden lotus
金莲川	Tropaeolum Mountain (Inner Mongolia)
金莲花广场	Golden Lotus Square (Macao)
金莲映日	(of Chengde Mountain Resort) Trollflowers Shining under the Sun
金陵第一明秀山	the first bright and elegant mountain of Jinling
金龙峡	Golden Dragon Gorge (Shaanxi)
金銮殿	Emperor's Audience Hall; Throne Room; Hall of Golden Chimes (Beijing) →太和殿
金缕玉衣	(of funeral clothes) jade clothes sewn with gold wire; a suit of jade pieces tied together with gold wire; jade suit sewn with gold thread

金马电影节	Golden Horse Film Festival
金毛羚牛	〈动〉*Budorcas taxicolor*; golden takins
金茂大厦	Jinmao Tower (Shanghai)
金门慈湖	Jinmenci Lake (Fujian)
金门国家公园	Kinmen National Park (Fujian, Taiwan)
金门民俗文化村	Kinmen Folk Culture Village (Fujian)
金牛岭公园	Jinniuling Park (Hai'nan)
金牛山	Golden Ox Mountain (Hu'nan)
金牛山古人类遗址	Jinniushan Ancient Human Fossil Site (Liaoning)
金平桦	〈植〉*Betula jinpingensis*
金钱豹	1 〈动〉*Panthera pardus*; leopard 2 〈植〉*Campanumoea jauanica*; golden jaguar
金钱草	〈植〉*Lysimachia christinae*; desmodium
金钱槭	〈植〉*Dipteronia sinensis*; Chinese dipteronia
金钱松	〈植〉*Pseudolarix amabilis*; golden larch
金泉禅寺	Jinquan Temple (Hubei)
金人	〈古〉Jurchen; people of the Jin Dynasty
金色颇章(宫)	(of Norbulingka) Golden Linka
金沙湖湿地公园	Jinsha Lake Wetland Park (Hubei)
金沙江	Jinsha River
金沙湾生态旅游区	Jinshawan Ecotourism Resort (Inner Mongolia)
金沙遗址博物馆	Jinsha Site Museum (Sichuan)
金山岛	(of Chengde Summer Resort) Jinshan Island; Gold Hill Isle
金山岭长城	Great Wall at Jinshan Mountain (Hebei)
金山寺	Jinshan Temple (Jiangsu)
金上京会宁府遗址	Huining Prefecture Site at the Upper Capital of the Jin Dynasty (Heilongjiang)
金声玉振坊	Jinsheng Yuzhen Archway; Stone Memorial Archway of Noble Moral Behavior (Shandong)
金石滩	Pebble Beach Resort; Golden Pebble Beach (Liaoning)
金石滩东部景区	Eastern Jinshitan Scenic Spot (Liaoning)
金水河	jinshui (golden water) river

金水桥	(of Imperial Palace) Jinshui Bridg; Golden Water Bridge
金丝猴	〈动〉*Phinopithecus*; golden monkey; snub-nosed monkey
金丝猴自然保护区	Golden Monkey Nature Reserve (Hubei)
金丝李	〈植〉*Garcinia paucinervis*
金丝峡景区	Jinsi Valley Scenic Area (Shaanxi)
金锁关	(of Mount Huashan) Jinsuo Pass; Golden Lock Pass
金锁潭	Jinsuo Pond; Golden Lock Pond (Jiangxi)
金台观	〈道〉Jintai Taoist Temple; Taoist Temple of Golden Terrace (Shaanxi)
金台森林公园	Jintai Forest Park; Forest Park of Golden Terrace (Shaanxi)
金田起义地址［营盘］	Jintian Uprising Site (Guangxi)
金文	〈古〉Chinese bronze inscription; bronzeware script; bell-cauldron inscription (in the Yin and Zhou Dynasty)
金线鲃属	〈动〉*Sinocyclocheilus*
金星山	Jinxing Mountain (Fujian)
金银岗森林公园	Jinyin Hillock Forest Park (Hubei)
金银湖湿地公园	Jinyin Lake Wetland Park (Hubei)
金银滩草原	Jinyintan Grassland (Qinghai)
金银滩浴场	Jinyintan Bathing Beach (Hebei)
金鱼大观园	Goldfish Grand View Garden (Jiangsu)
金鱼街	Tung Choi Street; Goldfish Market (Hong Kong)
金盏苣苔	〈植〉*Isometrum farreri*; marigold moss
金州大黑山	Jinzhou Dahei Mountain (Liaoning)
金竹岭古文化遗址	Jinzhu Ridge Ancient Cultural Site (Hubei)
金紫荆广场	Golden Bauhinia Square (Hong Kong)
津北森林公园	Jinbei Forest Park (Tianjin)
津门故里牌坊	Jinmen Hometown Archway (Tianjin)
津门庄王府	Jinmen Zhuang Lord's Residence (Tianjin) →李纯祠堂

津南农业科技园	Jinnan Agricultural Science and Technology Park (Tianjin)
津湾河畔露天餐吧街	Open Air Bar Street by Jinwan Riverside (Tianjin)
锦江	Jinjiang River
锦江大峡谷	Jinjiang Grand Canyon (Jilin)
锦江乐园	Jinjiang Paradise (Shanghai)
锦鼠观天	(of Zhangjiajie) Golden Mouse Gazing at the Sky
锦绣谷	(of Mount Lushan) Brocade Valley
锦绣中华	Splendid China (Guangdong)
谨身殿	Hall of Practising and Moral Culture (Nanjing)
进步搬拦捶	(of Tai Chi) Forward step parrying and punching
进步栽捶	(of Tai Chi) Forward step punching downward
进士第	〈古〉a rank jinshi (a classification of the candidates in the highest imperial examination according to their grade); Jinshi Mansion
进屋酒	jingwu wine (banquet for moving into a new house)
进香	to offer incense to Buddha; to offer incense in a temple
晋城二仙庙	Two Immortals Temple in Jincheng (Shanxi)
晋祠圣母殿	Hall of Saintly Mother of Jinci Memorial Temple; Goddess Hall of Jin Temple (Shanxi)
晋国	Kingdom Jin; Jin State (1033 –376 B.C.)
禁风节	〈瑶族〉Forbidden Wind Festival; No-wind Festival (on the 20th day of the 1st lunar month)
缙云山	Jinyun Mountain (Chongqing)
缙云卫矛	〈植〉*Euonymus chloranthoides*
觐廷书室	Kun Ting Study Hall (Hong Kong)
京巴	→北京哈巴狗
京包铁路	Jingbao Railway; Beijing-Baotou Railway
京东大峡谷	Jingdong Grand Canyon (Beijing)
京广铁路	Jingguang Railway; Beijing-Guangzhou Railway
京胡	〈乐〉Jinghu (a two-stringed bowed instrument with a high register); Beijing/Peking Opera fiddle

京九铁路	Jingjiu Railway; Beijing-Kowloon Railway
京剧	Jingju; Beijing Opera; Peking Opera
京剧表演	Beijing/Peking Opera performance
京剧大师	Peking Opera master
京剧服装[饰]	Jingju costume; Peking Opera costume; Beijing Opera costume
京剧故事	Peking Opera story; Beijing Opera story
京剧行当	Beijing/Peaking Opera roles (sheng, dan, jing, mo, chou); a character/role type in Beijing Opera
京剧节目	Beijing/Peking Opera show
京剧脸谱	Beijing/Peking Opera mask; facial makeup in Beijing/Peking Opera
京剧男伶	Beijing/Peking Opera actor
京剧女伶	Beijing/Peking Opera actress
京剧票友	Peking Opera fan/amateur; amateur performer of Peking Opera
京剧团	Beijing/Peking Opera troupe
京剧舞台	Beijing/Peking Opera stage
京剧演出	Beijing Opera performance; Peking Opera show
京剧演员	Beijing Opera performer; Peking Opera actor
京剧院	Beijing/Peking Opera theater
京娘湖	Jingniang Lake (Hebei)
京山茶花园	Jingshan Camellia Gardens (Hubei)
京山烈士公园	Jingshan Martyrs Park (Hubei)
京西神泉	Jingxi Castalia (Beijing)
京[宫]绣	Beijing Embroidery; Palace Embroidery
京珠高速	Jingzhu Expressway; Beijing-Zhuhai Expressway
京族	Gin ethnic group; Gin
经石峪	(of Mount Taishan) Sutra Rock Valley
荆门观音岛	Jingmen Guanyin Island (Hubei)
荆涂山	Jingtu Mountain (Anhui)
荆州长江大桥	Jingzhou Yangtze River Bridge (Hubei)
荆州城墙	Jingzhou City Wall (Hubei)
荆州海洋世界	Jingzhou Ocean World Water Park (Hubei)

荆州环城公园	Around-Jinzhou Park; Park around Jingzhou City (Hubei)
旌介遗址	Jingjie Site (of Shang Dynasty culture) (Shanxi)
惊魂峡	Jinhun Gorge (Yunnan)
惊蛰	〈节气〉Awakening from Hibernation; The Waking of Insects; Insects Awaken (3rd solar term)
晶宝温泉农场	Kingbao Hot Spring Farm (Tianjin)
晶帘瀑布	Jinglian (Crystal Curtain) Waterfall (Liaoning)
精武门中华武林园	Jingwu Gate of Chinese Martial Arts Garden (Tianjin)
精武太极	Jingwu Tai Chi
精武体育会	Chin Woo Athletic Federation; Jingwu Sports Association
井冈山	Jinggang Mountain (Jiangxi)
井冈山革命博物馆	Jinggang Mountain Revolutionary Museum (Jiangxi)
井冈山会师纪念碑	Monument of the Joining of Red Army Forces at Jinggang Mountain (Jiangxi)
井冈山异角蟾	〈动〉*Xenophrys jinggangensis*; Jinggangshan horned toad
景德崇圣殿	Jingde chongsheng Hall (for admiring ethics and sages) (Beijing)
景德镇	Jingdezhen (a leading porcelain-manufacturing centre) (Jiangxi)
景德镇四大传统名瓷	four famous traditional porcelains in Jingdezhen (blue and white porcelain, famille-rose porcelain, rice-pattern decorated porcelain and color glaze porcelain)
景德镇陶瓷博物馆	Jingdezhen Ceramics Museum
景东齿蟾	〈动〉*Oreolalax jingdongensis*; Jingdong toothed toad
景东树鼠	〈动〉*Chiropodomys jingdongensis*; pencil-tailed tree mouse
景东异角蟾	〈动〉*Xenophrys jingdongensis*; Jingdong horned toad
景福阁	(of Summer Palace) Pavilion of Great Happiness

景明楼	(of Summer Palace) Tower of Bright Scene
景颇酒	Jingpo liquor
景颇族	Jingpo ethnic group; Jingpo
景祺阁	(of Imperial Palace) Belvedere of Auspicious Fortune
景仁宫	(of Imperial Palace) Palace of Great Benevolence
景山公园	Jingshan Park (Beijing)
景贤里	King Yin Lei (a declared monument of Hong Kong)
景县舍利塔	〈佛〉Jingxian County Dagoba/Stupa; Relic Pagoda of Jingxian County (Hebei) →景州塔
景阳宫	(of Imperial Palace) Palace of Great Brilliance
景运门	(of Imperial Palace) Gate of Good Fortune
景真八角亭	〈佛〉Jingzhen Octagonal Pavilion (Yunnan)
景忠山景区	Jingzhong Mountain Scenic Area (Hebei)
景州塔	〈佛〉Jingzhou Stupa; Sakyamuni Relic Pagoda (Hebei) →景县舍利塔
警钟台	alarm bell tower
净慈寺	Jingci Temple (Zhejiang)
净角	〈戏〉(of a Beijing Opera role) Jing character; Jing role; painted face character
净觉寺	Jingjue Temple (Hebei)
净瓶山	Jingping Mountain (Guangxi)
净坛峰	(of Three Gorges) Jingtan Peak
净月潭冰雪旅游节	Jingyuetan Ice and Snow Tourism Festival (from December 1st to February 26th the next year)
净月潭森林公园	Jingyuetan (Lake) Forest Park (Jilin)
净月潭森林浴场	Forest Bathing Spot of Jingyuetan National Scenic Area (Jilin)
净月潭水库大坝	Jingyuetan Reservoir Dam (Jilin)
净藏禅师塔	Chan Master Jingzang Stupa (He'nan)
敬茶礼仪	tea-serving etiquette; tea ceremony
敬酒	〈礼〉to propose a toast
敬酒不吃吃罚酒	(of idiom) to refuse a toast only to drink a forfeit
敬罗家塾	King Law Ka Shuk (declared monument of Hong Kong)

敬桥节	〈苗族〉Bridge-Respecting Festival (on the 2nd day of the 2nd lunar month)
敬雀节	〈仡佬族〉Dear Condor Day (on the 1st day of the 2nd lunar month)
敬亭山房	Jingting Mountain Cottage (Jiangsu)
敬一亭	Jingyi Pavilion (Jiangsu)
敬祖节	Ancestor Worship Festival (on the 3rd day of the 3rd lunar month)
靖江王府及王陵	Mansion and Mausoleum of Prince Jingjiang (Guangxi)
靖江王陵	Tombs of Prince Jingjiang (Guangxi)
静安别墅	Jing'an Villa (Shanghai)
静安公园	Jing'an Park (Shanghai)
静安寺	Jing'an Temple (Shanghai)
静好堂	(of Chengde Mountain Resort) Hall of Serenity
静湖度假村	Quiet Lake Resort (Inner Mongolia)
镜海	(of Jiuzhai Valley) Mirror Lake
镜水云岑	(of Chengde Mountain Resort) Multicolored Reflections of Clouds and Hills in Mirror-like Water
九澳七苦圣母小堂	Nine Macau Chapel of Our Lady of Seven Sorrows (Macao)
九拜	〈古〉jiubai (nine ways of kowtows, worship on bended knees); nine worships
九成宫生态园	Jiucheng Palace Ecopark (Inner Mongolia)
九重天	(of legend) the ninth sky (the nine layers of the celestial sphere); empyrean; cloud nine
九重仙阁	(of Zhangjiajie) Nine Layers of Fairy Palaces
九顶铁刹山	〈道〉Jiuding Tiecha Mountain (Liaoning)
九鼎	Nine-Tripod Cauldrons (Symbol of Nine Provinces of ancient China and national unity)
九宫山	Jiugong Mountain (Hubei)
九宫山钦天瑞庆宫	Qintian Ruiqing Palace at Jiugong Mountain (Hubei)
九华山	Jiuhua Mountain; Mount Jiuhua (Anhui)

九节鞭	〈武术〉nine-section whip; nine-segmented whip
九老洞	(of Mount Emei) Jiulao Cave; Nine Sages' Cave
九龙柏	(of Temple of Heaven) Nine-dragon Cypress
九龙半岛	Kowloon Peninsula (Hong Kong)
九龙壁	(of Imperial Palace) Nine-Dragon Wall; Nine-Dragon Screen
九龙池	Nine-Dragon Pool (Yunnan)
九龙齿突蟾	〈动〉*Scutiger jiulongensis*; jiulong cat-eyed toad
《九龙灯》	*Nine-Dragon Chandelier* (Qin Hong, 1994)
九龙公园	Kowloon Park (Hong Kong)
九龙灌浴	Nine Dragons Bathing the Baby Buddha (the birth of Sakyamuni) (Jiangsu)
九龙广场区	Nine-Dragon Square District (Zhejiang)
九龙棘蛙	〈动〉*Quasipaa jiulongensis*; Jiulong paa frog; Jiulong spiny frog
九龙窠	(of Mount Wuyi) Nine Dragon Nest; Nine Dragon Lair
九龙玫瑰堂	→尖沙咀[九龙]玫瑰堂
九龙捧珠	nine dragons hold a pearl
九龙屏风	Nine-Dragon Screen (Shanxi)
九龙瀑	(of Mount Huangshan) Nine Dragon Waterfall
九龙瀑布	Jiulong Waterfall; Nine-Dragon Waterfall (Yunnan)
九龙清真寺	〈伊斯兰〉Kowloon Mosque/Masjid & Islamic Centre (Hong Kong)
九龙山	Jiulong Mountain; Nine-Dragon Mountain (Zhejiang)
九龙山汉代摩崖墓群	Cliff Tombs of Han Dynasty in Jiulong (Nine-Dragon) Mountain (Shandong)
九龙山森林公园	Jiulong (Nine-Dragon) Mountain Forest Park (Tianjin, Zhejiang)
九龙潭	nine-dragon pond
九龙仔公园	Kowloon Tsai Park (Hong Kong)
九龙寨城公园	Kowloon Walled City Park (Hong Kong)

九龙佐治五世纪念公园	Kowloon King George V Memorial Park (Hong Kong)
九阡酒	〈水族〉Jiuqian wine (made of pure glutinous rice)
九曲河	Jiuqu River; Nine-Bend River (Jiangsu)
九曲黄河墙	(of Mount Wudang) Jiuqu Huanghe River Wall; Nine-Bend Yellow River Wall
九曲桥	Jiuqu Bridge; Zigzag Bridge; Bridge of Nine Turnings (Shanghai)
九曲溪	(of Mount Wuyi) Jiuqu Stream; Nine-Bend Stream
九曲银河	Jiuqu Galaxy; Nine-Bend Silver River (Guizhou)
九曲栈道	Jiuqu Plank Road; Nine-Bend Walkway (Sichuan)
九日山摩崖石刻	Rock Calligraphy Groups on Jiuri Mountain (Fujian)
九省通衢	(another name for Wuhan of Hubei Province) Thoroughfare of Nine Provinces
九狮峰	(of Lion Forest Garden) Nine-Lion Peak
九十九道拐	(of Mount Emei) Ninety-nine Turns
九天洞	Cave of Nine Skylights (Hu'nan)
九天飞瀑	Jiutian Flying Waterfall (Beijing)
九天峡谷景区	Jiutian Canyon Scenic Area (Fujian)
九头崖	(of Shimantan National Forest Park) Nine-Headed Cliff
九畹溪大桥	Grand Bridge of Jiuwan Stream (Hubei)
九畹溪电站	Power Station of Jiuwan Stream (Hubei)
九溪十八涧	(of West Lake) Nine Brooks and Eighteen Dales (another name of Nine Creeks in Misty Forest) →九溪烟树
九溪烟树	(of West Lake) Nine Creeks in Misty Forest; Nine Creeks Meandering through a Misty Forest; Trees in Mist by the Nine Rivulets →九溪十八涧
九仙阁	Jiuxian Pavilion; Nine Immortals' Pavilion (Fujian)
九仙观	Temple of Nine Immortals

九仙山	Jiuxian Mountain (Fujian)
九乡景区	Jiuxiang Scenic Area (Yunnan)
九寨沟	Jiuzhai Valley (Sichuan)
九寨沟国家公园	Jiuzhaigou Valley National Park (Sichuan)
九族文化村	Formosa Aboriginal Culture Village (Taiwan)
酒池肉林	〈成〉extravagant orgy; steeped in wine and surrounded by women; unbridled debauchery and licentiousness
酒德	good drinking-manners (a person should have when drinking)
酒店冶铁遗址	Jiudian Iron Smelting Site (He'nan)
酒基	→基酒[酒基]
酒禁	alcohol prohibition; (of feudal China) prohibition of liquor production
酒礼	manners of drinking; proprieties of drinking
酒令	〈民俗〉drinking game; drinkers' wager game
酒篓	liquor container made of bamboo; basket work for reserve distillate
酒满茶半	〈礼〉full cup of spirit and half cup of tea
酒旗	〈民俗〉signs hung high near the entrance of an inn; tavern sign in the form of a streamer; wine flag
酒器	drinking vessel
酒泉卫星发射中心	Jiuquan Satellite Launch Centre; JSLC (Gansu) →东风航天城
酒泉夜光杯	Jiuquan luminous wine glass
酒税	taxes on wine; wine duty
旧北区理民府	Old District Office North (Hong Kong)
旧石器	paleolith; old stone
旧石器时代	Paleolithic/Palaeolithic Age; Paleolithic/Palaeolithic Period; Old Stone Age
旧湾仔邮政局	Old Wan Chai Post Office (declared monument of Hong Kong)
救人一命胜造七级浮屠	〈佛〉saving a life better than building a seven-storey pagoda; there is greater merit in saving one life than in building a seven-tier pagoda

救生泉	Lifesaving Spring (Shandong)
鹫峰山	Jiufeng Mountain (Hebei)
居丧	〈旧〉jusang (to stay in mourning after the death of one's elder relatives); to be in mourning for one's dead parent
居石侯公祠	Hau Ku Shek Ancestral Hall (Hong Kong)
居延文化遗址	Juyan Culture Site; Juyan Visiting Ancient Culture Tour (Gansu, Inner Mongolia)
居庸关	Juyong Guan; Juyong Pass (of Great Wall) (Beijing)
居庸关云台	Cloud Terrace in JuyongPass (Beijing)
局址岛景区	Juzhi Island Tourism Spot (Jilin)
菊花岛	Chrysanthemum Island (Liaoning)
菊花节	chrysanthemum festival
菊圃	chrysanthemum garden
橘子洲	Juzi Island; Orange Island (Hu'nan)
沮河湿地公园	Juhe River Wetland Park (Hubei)
莒光楼	Chukuang Tower; Juguang Tower (Fujian)
巨灵神	(of legend) Mighty Miracle God (a role in Journey to the West)
巨蟒出山	Python out of the Mountain (Jiangxi)
巨树岛	Giant Tree Island (Heilongjiang)
巨型睡佛	Colossal Lying Buddha (Sichuan)
拒马河	Juma River (Hebei)
具服台	(of Temple of Heaven) Robing Platform; Dressing Platform (where the emperor changed sacrificial clothes when he went to the Hall of Prayer for Good Harvest)
聚鹤峰	(of Three Gorges) Juhe (Crane Gathering) Peak
聚仙谷	Juxian (Immortal Gathering) Valley (Hebei)
聚星楼	Tsui Sing Lau Pagoda (Hong Kong)
卷棚式庑廊	Veranda of Round Ridge Roof (Heilongjiang)
倦勤斋	(of Imperial Palace) Studio of Retirement from Diligent Service

觉山寺	Mount Jueshan Temple (Shanxi)
觉生寺	Juesheng Temple (Beijing)
绝壁栈道	cliffside plank path; plank road built along a cliff
厥子腿	Horse kick
蹶鼠	〈动〉*Sicista*
军礼	〈古〉military rites; etiquettes of military activities (one of Five Etiquettes of Western Zhou Dynasty)
军坡节	〈黎族〉Junpo Festival
君为臣纲	〈古〉ruler as the guide of subject (one of the three cardinal guides) →三纲五常
君子九容	〈古〉nine manners of gentleman
钧瓷	〈古〉Jun-Ware; Jun Porcelain (one of the five famous chinawares in ancient China)
钧台钧窑遗址	Juntai Jun Kiln Site (He'nan)
钧窑	〈古〉Jun Kiln (one of the five famous kilns in ancient China)

K

喀尔喀语	Khalkha dialect
喀拉汗王朝王庭遗址	Royal Court Site of Qara-Khanid Khanate; Ruins of Karakhan Dynasty (Xinjiang)
喀拉峻国家公园	Kalajun National Park (Xinjiang)
喀拉喀什河	Karakash River; Qaraqash River (Qinghai)
喀拉库勒湖	Karakul (Black) Lake (Xinjiang)
喀喇昆仑公路	Karakorum/Karakoram Highway; KKH
喀喇昆仑沙漠	Karakoram Desert (Xinjiang)
喀喇昆仑山	Karakorum/Karakoram Mountain (Xinjiang)
喀喇昆仑山脉	Karakoram Mountains/Range; Har Goolun Range
喀喇沁亲王府	Prince Kharqin's Mansion (Inner Mongolia)
喀纳斯河	Kanas River (Xinjiang)
喀纳斯湖	Kanas Lake (Xinjiang)
喀纳斯湖怪	Kanas Lake monster
喀什大巴扎	Kashgar Bazaar (Xinjiang)
喀什大集市	Kashgar Grand Bazaar (Xinjiang)
喀什噶尔河	Kashgar River (Xinjiang)
喀什民俗园	Kashgar Folk Custom Garden (Xinjiang)
喀斯特地貌	karst landform
喀斯特地质博物馆	Karst Geological Museum (Yunnan)
卡若拉冰川	Karuola Glacier; Khari La Glacier (Tibet)
卡若文化遗址	Karuo Cultural Site (Tibet)
卡瓦格博峰	(of Taizi Snow Mountain) Kawakarpo (Peak)
卡瓦格博雪山	Kawagebo Snow Mountain (Yunnan)

开吊	〈丧〉(of a funeral) kaidiao (friends and relatives come to offer their condolences); to hold a memorial service or funeral rites
开都河	Kaidu River; Karaxahar River (Xinjiang)
开封汴绣	Bian Embroidery of Kaifeng
开合手	(of Tai Chi) Open-close hands
开垦祭	〈高山族〉Reclamation Sacrifice (during the 10th lunar month)
开路神	〈丧〉a divinity that leads the way (picture carried at the head of a funeral procession) path-breaker for the deceased
开滦矿务局大楼	Kailuan Mining Bureau Building (Tianjin)
开门[出夏]节	Gate Opening Festival; Open-Door Day (a traditional festival of the Dai, Bulang, De'ang and Wa ethnic groups on the 15th day of the 12th month according to Dai calendar)
开面	〈婚〉kaimian (wash the bride's face and make her up before the wedding)
开平碉楼	Kaiping Diaolou (Watchtower) (Guangdong)
开善寺	Kaishan Temple (Hebei)
开业酒	business opening banquet
开渔节	fishing festival; fishery-day opening festival
开元寺	kaiyuan temple
开元寺东西二塔	East and West Pagodas of Kaiyuan Temple; Twin Pagodas of Kaiyuan Temple
开元寺天王殿	Hall of the Heavenly King of the Kaiyuan Temple
开元寺钟楼	Bell Tower of Kaiyuan Temple (Hebei)
开源森林公园	Kaiyuan Forest Park (He'nan)
开斋节	〈维吾尔族〉Lesser Bairam; Festival of Fast-Breaking
凯达格兰大道	Ketagalan Boulevard (Taiwan)
坎布拉森林公园	Kanbula Forest Park (Qinghai)
坎儿井	Karez Wells (underground network of irrigation) (Xinjiang)
坎离宫	Kanli Palace (Jilin)

砍火星节	〈苗族〉Spark-Hacking Day (from the 8th lunar month to the 9th one)
看经寺	(of Longmen Grottoes) Sutra Reading Temple
看山楼	(of Surging Waves Pavilion) Mountain-Watching Tower
看松读画轩	(of Master-of-Nets Garden) Studio of Pine-Watching and Painting-Appreciation
阚家塘古村	Kanjiatang Ancient Village (Hubei)
瞰胜楼	Kan Sheng Pavilion; Scenic Beauty Pavilion (Chongqing)
康巴地区	Khampa area (Tibet) →康区
康巴喇嘛	〈佛〉Khamba Lama
康巴人	Khamba (a Tibetan or Sichuan people from Kham)
康定情歌景区	Kangding Love Song Scenic Area (Sichuan)
康公庙	Kanggong Temple (Macao)
康区	Kham-Tibetan area (Tibet) →康巴地区
康西草原	Kangxi Prairie; Kangxi Grassland (Beijing)
康熙皇帝	Emperor Kangxi (1654–1722, reigning from 1661 to 1722 in the Qing Dynasty)
康熙御碑亭	(of Surging Waves Pavilion) Pavilion of Kangxi Imperial Stele
康县隆肛蛙	〈动〉*Feirana kangxianesis*; Kangxian paa frog
抗战胜利纪功碑	Monument to the Victory of Anti-Japanese War (Chongqing) →人民解放纪念碑
抗战受降纪念坊	Memorial Archway of Anti-Japanese War Victory and Surrender Acceptance; Memorial Archway for the Victory of Anti-Japanese War and Acceptance of Japanese Surrender (Hu'nan)
抗震纪念碑	Earthquake Monument (Hebei, Tianjin)
烤包子	samsa; gox garda; baked bun (a special snack in Xinjiang)
烤全羊	(of Xinjiang food) roast whole lamb; baked whole sheep

柯尔克孜族	Kirgiz ethnic group; Kirgiz
科尔沁草原	Horqin Grassland (Inner Mongolia)
科尔沁沙地	Horqin Sandy Land (Inner Mongolia)
蚵仔煎	oyster omelette (a special snack in Fujian, Chaozhou and Taiwan)
磕寿头	〈民俗〉to kowtow to the old on their birthdays
磕头	〈礼〉kowtow
可可沙炼铁遗址	Remains of Kekesha Iron Smelting Workshop; Kekesha Iron Smelting Site (Xinjiang)
可可托海	Koktokay River Bend (Xinjiang)
可可托海景区	Koktokay Valley Scenic Area (Xinjiang)
可可西里冰川	Hoh Xil Glacier
可可西里自然保护区	Hoh Xil Nature Reserve (Qinghai)
克拉玛依戈壁	Karamay Gobi (Desert) (Xinjiang)
克里雅河	Keriya River (Xinjiang)
克鲁伦河	Kherlen River (Heilongjiang)
克什克腾旗	Hexigten Banner
克什克腾世界地质公园	Hexigten Global Geopark (Inner Mongolia)
克孜尔尕哈烽燧	Kizilgaha Beacon Tower (Xinjiang)
克孜尔千佛洞[石窟]	Kizil/Kezil Thousand-Buddha Caves/Grottoes (Xinjiang)
克孜勒苏河	Kirzlesu River (Xinjiang)
克孜利亚大峡谷	Kiziliya Grand Canyon (Xinjiang)
克孜利亚炼铜遗址	Remains Of The Kiziliya Copper Smeltery; Kiziliya Copper Smelting Site (Xinjiang)
客家	Hakka
客家话	Hakka dialect; Hakkanese
客家人	Hakkanese; Hakkas
客堂	visitor's hall (management center of a temple; a reception room for guests)
肯氏小树蛙	〈动〉*Philautus kempii*; Kemp's small tree frog
垦丁国家公园	Kenting National Park (Taiwan)
空腹不送丧	〈丧〉don't take part in a funeral procession with an empty stomach

空首	〈古〉kongshou (one of the nine ways of kowtows)
空心潭	(of Zhangjiajie) Hollow Pond
空中飞人	flying trapeze (artist)
空中走廊	(of Zhangjiajie) Corridor in Air
崆峒山	Kongtong Mountain (Gansu)
崆峒水库	Kongdong Reservoir (Gansu)
崆岭[空冷]峡	Kongling Gorge (Hubei)
崆山白云洞	White Cloud Cave of Kongshan Mountain (Hebei)
孔唇兰	〈植〉*Porolabium biporosum*
孔府	Confucian Mansion; Kong Family Mansion (Shandong)
孔府花园	Confucius Mansion Garden (Shandong)
孔伋墓	Tomb of Kong Ji (Shandong)
孔鲤墓	Tomb of Kong Li (Shandong)
孔林	Cemetery of Confucius (and his descendants); Confucian Graveyard (Shandong)
孔(子)庙	Confucius temple; temple of Confucius
孔明	Kong Ming (Zhuge Liang, the representative of loyal officials and wisdom in traditional Chinese culture)
孔明灯	kongming lantern (a weather-roof portable lantern for making a wish) →天灯
孔雀河	Konque River; Peacock River (Xinjiang)
孔雀河道	(of Jiuzhai Valley) Peacock River Course
孔雀山	Peacock Mountain (Guangxi)
孔雀园	Peacock Garden (Zhejiang)
孔望山摩崖造像	Sculptures on the Cliff of Kongwangshan; Kongwangshan Cliffside Images (Jiangsu)
孔子故里[乡]	Hometown/Birthplace of Confucius (Shandong) →曲阜市
孔子墓	Tomb of Confucius (Shandong)
恐龙博物馆	dinosaur museum
恐龙蛋化石	Dinosaur egg fossil

恐龙山镇	Dinosaur Town (Yunnan)
口嚼酒	〈高山族〉chewed grain wine
口容止	〈古〉immobility of mouth (the mouth should be immobile when one is not speaking or eating)(a saying from The Book of Rites) →君子九容
叩头［首］	〈礼〉kowtow (worship on bended knees)
叩指礼	etiquette of kowtow with fingers (to tap your fingers on the table to show your gratitude when the host serves you wine or tea)
扣腿平衡	〈武术〉balance with legs buckling
枯井园	Dry Well Garden (Anhui)
哭(出)嫁	〈婚〉crying marriage; bride crying (the crying and singing ceremony performed when the bride gets married)
苦酒节	〈侗族〉Bitter Alcohol Festival (September)
库布齐沙漠	Kubuqi Desert (Inner Mongolia)
库车大峡谷	Kuqa Grand Canyon (Xinjiang)
库车河	Kuqa River (Xinjiang)
库鲁克塔格沙漠	Kuruktag Desert (Xinjiang)
库伦旗	Kulun Banner (Inner Mongolia)
库姆塔格沙漠	Kumtage Desert (Xinjiang)
库姆［吾］孜	〈乐〉Kumzi; Kumuz (a string and pipe music instrument of Kirgiz ethnic group)
库姆孜弹唱	Kumzi/Kumuz performance
库木库里盆地	Kumkor Basin; Kumkor Depression (Xinjiang)
库木吐拉［喇］千佛洞	Kumutula Thousand-Buddha Caves (Xinjiang)
库扎节	〈拉祜族〉Kuzha Festival (in the 3rd month or the early 4th month according to Dai calendar)
跨火	〈民俗〉to cross fire (a folk custom that crossing the fire can get rid of filth and will have good fortune)
跨火盆	〈礼〉to cross fire plate; to stride the fire pan (for seeking good fortune and avoiding disaster

跨马鞍	〈婚〉(of a bride in the wedding) to step on the saddle
会稽山	Kuaiji Mountain (Zhejiang)
快板	kuaiban; clapper talk →数来宝
快活谷马场	→跑马地［快活谷］马场
筷子文化	chopsticks culture
宽脊疣螈	〈动〉*Tylototriton broadoridgus*
宽阔水拟小鲵	〈动〉*Pseudohynobius kuankuoshuiensis*; Kuankuoshui salamander
宽阔水自然保护区	Kuankuoshui Nature Reserve (Guizhou)
狂欢嘉年华游乐区	Carnival Recreation Area (Zhejiang)
魁星塔	Kuixing Tower (Hai'nan)
夔门	Kuimen Gate (Chongqing)
坤宁宫	(of Imperial Palace) Palace of Earthly Tranquility
坤宁门	(of Imperial Palace) Gate of Earthly Tranquility
昆承湖景区	Kuncheng Lake Scenic Area (Jiangsu)
昆剧票友	Kunqu Opera fan/amateur; amateur performer of Kunqu Opera
昆仑河	Kunlun River
昆仑决	〈武术〉Kunlun Fight
昆仑拳	〈武术〉Kunlun Boxing
昆仑山(脉)	Kunlun Mountains; Kunlun Range (Xinjiang, Qinghai and Tibet)
昆仑山口	Kunlun Mountain Pass (Qinghai)
昆仑(山)神话	Mythology of Kunlun Mountains
昆仑武术	Kunlun Martial Arts
昆仑药用植物观光园	Kunlun Medicinal Plant Sightseeing Park (Taiwan)
昆明湖	(of Summer Palace) Kunming Lake
昆明湖景区	Kunming Lake Area (Beijing)
昆明金殿	Kunming Golden Palace; Kunming Golden Temple (Yunnan)
昆曲［剧］	Kunqu Opera
昆曲表演	Kunqu Opera performance

昆曲剧团	Kunqu Opera troupe
昆曲艺术	Kunqu Opera art
阔时节	〈傈僳族〉Kuoshi Festival (from the 5th day of the 12th lunar month to the 10th day of the 1st lunar month next year)
阔褶水蛙	〈动〉*Hylarana latouchii*; broad-folded frog
廓如亭	(of Summer Palace) Pavilion of Broad View

L

拉卜楞寺	Labrang Monastery; Labuleng Temple (Gansu)
拉法山森林公园	Lafa Mountain Forest Park (Jilin)
拉歌节	〈傈僳族〉Chorus Competition Day (on the 5th or 6th day of the 1st lunar month)
拉轨冈日山脉	Laguigangri Mountains (Tibet)
拉祜族	Lahu ethnic group; Lahu
拉祜族米酒	Lahu rice liquor
拉鲁岛	Lalu Island (Taiwan)
拉木鼓节	〈佤族〉Wooden Drum Festival (in December)
拉萨布达拉宫历史建筑群	Historic Ensemble of the Potala Palace in Lhasa (Tibet)
拉萨河	Lhasa River (Tibet)
拉萨河谷	Lhasa River Valley (Tibet)
拉市海湿地	Lashi Lake Wetland (Yunnan)
喇嘛教	〈佛〉Lamaism (a form of Buddhism practiced in Tibet and Mongolia) →藏传佛教
喇嘛庙[寺]	lamasery; lama temple
腊八(节)	Laba Rice Porridge Festival (on the 8th day of the 12th lunar month)
蜡梅	〈植〉*Chimonanthus praecox*; winter sweet
蜡染	Batik; Wax Printing (a traditional handicraft)
蜡染布	batik fabric; wax dye cloth
蜡像馆	wax figure gallery; wax (work) museum
辣白酒	〈彝族〉spicy liquor; light liquor
来凤轩[阁]	Laifeng Pavilion (Sichuan)
莱州湾	Laizhou Bay (Shandong)

兰桂坊	Lan Kwai Fong (Hong Kong)
兰亭八柱亭	(of Zhongshan Park) Lanting Octa-pillar Pavilion
兰亭碑	Orchid Pavilion Stele (Beijing)
兰亭书法博物馆	Orchid Pavilion Calligraphy Museum (Zhejiang)
兰亭书法节	Orchid Pavilion Calligraphy Festival (on the 3rd day of the 3rd lunar month)
兰屿岛	Lanyu Island (Taiwan)
兰州水车园	Lanzhou Waterwheel Garden (Gansu)
兰渚山	Lanzhu Mountain (Zhejiang)
拦路酒	〈苗族〉lanlu wine (a welcoming etiquette to block the guests' way unless they drink the served wine)
蓝宝石婚	sapphire wedding (the 45th anniversary of marriage)
蓝采和	〈神话〉Lan Caihe (one of the Eight Immortals)
蓝马鸡	〈动〉*Crossoptilon auritum*; blue eared pheasant
蓝田汤峪(温泉)	Lantian Tangyu Spa (Shaanxi)
蓝田猿人遗址	Ruins of Lantian Man; Lantian Apeman Site (Shaanxi)
蓝尾蝾螈	〈动〉*Cynops cyanurus*; blue-tail cynops
蓝屋	Blue House (the first-class historical building of Hong Kong)
蓝鹇	〈动〉*Lophura swinhoii*; Taiwan blue pheasant; Swinhoe's pheasant
澜沧江	Lancang River
澜沧江高峡百里长湖景区	Baili (100 li) Lake Scenic Area in the Narrow Gorges of Lancang River (Yunnan)
澜沧江流域	Lancang River basin
澜沧江–湄公河	Langcang-Mekong River
揽胜阁	(of Garden of Quiet Meditation) Landscape-Viewing Pavilion
揽月亭	(of Beishan Park) Lanyue Pavilion
郎木寺	Langmu Temple (Gansu)
郎扎热甲节	〈藏族〉Langzharejia Fair (on the 4th day of the 5th lunar month)

狼山景区	Langshan Mountain Scenic Area (Jiangsu)
琅琊古道	Langya Ancient Avenue (Anhui)
琅琊山	Langya Mountain (Anhui)
琅琊寺	Langya Temple (Anhui)
榔梅祠	(of Mount Wudang) Langmei Shrine
榔[小叶]榆	〈植〉*Ulmus parvifolia*; Chinese elm
崀山	Langshan Mountain; Mount Lang (Hu'nan)
劳动公园观景台	Observation Platform of Labor Park; Sightseeing Stand of Labor Park (Liaoning)
劳动节	Labor Day; International Worker's Day (on May 1st)
劳动人民文化宫	Working People's Cultural Palace (Beijing)
崂山	Laoshan Mountain (Shandong)
崂山道士	(of an old story) Laoshan Taoist; Taoist priest in Laoshan Mountain
老城厢	Old City Area; Historical City Core Building (Shanghai)
老旦	〈戏〉Laodan (an old female character type in Beijing Opera)
老道拜月	Old Taoist Praying to the Moon (Jiangxi)
老观湖湿地公园	Laoguan Lake Wetland Park (Hubei)
老官台文化	Laoguantai culture (5000-6000 B.C., early Neolithic culture in the Middle Reaches of the Yellow River)
老哈河流域	Laoha River basin
老虎石海上公园	Tiger Stone/Rock Marine Park (Hebei)
老虎滩海洋公园	Laohutan Ocean Park (Liaoning)
老君阁	(of Mount Qingcheng) Laojun Pavilion
老君犁沟	(of Mount Huashan) Laojun Ploughed-Furrow (one of the Three Major Risks Mount Huashan)
老君山	Laojun Mountain (He'nan)
老君堂	(of Mount Wudang) Hall of Supreme Patriarch; Palace of Lord Lao Zi
老君岩造像	〈道〉Rock Image of Lao Jun (Fujian)

老龙池	Laolong Pool; Old Dragon Pool (Shaanxi)
老龙潭	Old Dragon Pond (Ningxia)
老龙头	Old Dragon's Head (Hebei)
老妈[天后]宫	Palace-Temple of Old Mother; Mazu Palace (Guangdong)
老人节	Seniors' Day (on the 9th day of the 9th lunar month) →重阳节
老舍茶馆	Laoshe Teahouse (Beijing)
老舍纪念馆[故居]	Laoshe Memorial Hall; Memorial Museum of Laoshe (Beijing)
老生	〈戏〉Laosheng (an old male character with a black or white beard of Beijing Opera)
老司城	Laosi Town (Hu'nan)
老孙家	Lao Sun Family (one of the best-known restaurants in Xi'an that serve Pita Bread Soaked in Lamb Soup)
老铁山灯塔	Lighthouse at Laotie Mountain (Liaoning)
老围	Lo Wai (declared monument of Hong Kong)
老鹰嘴	(of Zhangjiajie) Eagle's Beak
老子	〈道〉Laozi; Lao-Tzu (an ancient Chinese thinker, philosopher, litterateur and historian)
老子雕像	〈道〉Laozi statue
老子像碑	〈道〉Statue Tablet of Laozi (Jiangsu)
老字号	long-established store or brand; time-honored shop or brand
乐亭海滨旅游区	Laoting Coastal Tourist Area (Hebei)
乐成阁	(of Chengde Mountain Resort) Pavilion of Peace and Harvest Enjoyment
乐东蟾蜍	〈动〉*Bufo ledongensis*; Ledong toad
乐东拟单性木兰	〈植〉*Parakmeria lotungensis*; Ledong lotus tree
乐山大佛	Leshan Giant Buddha (Sichuan)
乐寿堂	(of Imperial Palace) Hall of Joyful Longevity; Hall of Happiness and Longevity
乐贤堂	Lexian Hall (Anhui)

乐业天坑	Leye Tiankeng; Leye Cenote/Doline (Guangxi)
勒巴沟岩画	Lebagou Cliff/Rock Painting (Qinghai)
鳓鱼	〈动〉*Ilisha elongata*; Chinese herring; long-finned herring
雷洞坪	(of Mount Emei) Thunder Caves Terrace
雷峯夕照	→雷峰夕照
雷峰塔	Leifeng Pagoda (Zhejiang)
雷峰夕照	(of West Lake) Sunset Glow at Leifeng Pagoda; Leifeng Pagoda in the Sunset; Leifeng Pagoda in Evening Glow
雷公	〈神话〉Thunder God
雷公祠	Leigong (Thunder God) Temple (Liaoning)
雷公山	Leigong (Thunder God) Mountain (Guizhou)
雷公峡	Leigou (Thunder God) Gorge (Guangdong)
雷龙胜境	Leilong Wonderland (Guangxi)
雷劈山	Leipi (thunder-struck) Mountain (Jilin)
雷山髭蟾	〈动〉*Vibrissaphora leishanense*; Leishan spiny/moustache toad toad
雷神	〈神话〉Thunder God
雷神洞	(of Mount Wudang) Cave of Thunder God
雷台汉墓	Leitai Han Tombs (Gansu)
雷台景区	Leitai Scenic Area (Gansu)
《雷塘祷雨文》	*Pray for Rain in Thunder Pool* (Liu Zongyuan, 815)
雷音寺	(of Mount Emei) Leiyin Temple
擂茶	lei cha; ground tea (including mashed tea leaves, rice, peanut, sesame, mung bean, salt, litsea cubeba and ginger, etc.)
擂鼓墩古墓群	Leigudun Ancient Tombs (Hubei)
罍	〈古〉lei (a traditional large wine-drinking and sacrificial vessel)
冷泉亭	(of Master-of-Nets Garden) Lengquan Pavilion; Cold Spring Pavilion
冷水河	Lengshui River; Cold Water River

冷水瀑布	Lengshui Waterfall; Cold Water Waterfall (Guangxi)
冷香亭	(of Chengde Mountain Resort) Pavilion of Cool Fragrance
《离骚》	*Li Sao*; *Encountering Sorrow* (a Chuci-style poetry, by Quyuan in the late Warring States Period)
骊靬遗址	Liqian Ruins (Gansu)
骊山	Lishan Mountain; Mount Li (Shaanxi)
梨花伴月	(of Chengde Mountain Resort) Pear Blossoms under Moonlight
梨花湖	Lihua Lake; Pear Blossom Lake (Hubei)
梨花会	〈白族〉Pear Blossom Festival (March)
梨园	〈旧〉Liyuan (old nickname of opera troupe) →戏班子
梨园戏	〈戏〉Liyuan Opera
犁头[铧]节	〈塔塔尔族〉Plowshare Festival →撒班节
漓江	Lijiang River (Guangxi)
漓山	〈旧〉→象鼻山
黎族	Li ethnic group; Li
礼	li (ceremonial observances in general); courtesy; etiquette
《礼记》	*Classic of Rites* (a Confucian scripture, by Dai Sheng in the Western Han Dynasty)
礼书	〈婚〉gift letter →三书
李冰圆雕石像	Stone Statue of Li Bing (Sichuan)
李纯祠堂	Li Chun's Ancestral Temple (Tianjin)
李大钊故居	Former Residence of Li Dazhao (Beijing)
李家峡水电站	Lijiaxia Hydropower Station (Qinghai)
李坑古村	Li Keng Ancient Village (dominated by the residents surnamed Li) (Jiangxi)
李满柱	Li Manzhu (the third king of Jurchen, established the Manchu kingdom in 1424)
李叔同书法碑林	Li Shutong's Calligraphic Forest of Steles (Tianjin)
李子节	plum festival

李自成墓	Tomb of Li Zicheng (Hubei)
李自成行宫	Li Zicheng Imperial Palace (Shaanxi)
里合腿	〈武术〉inside kick
里合腿接弓步	〈武术〉inside kick into bow stance
里玛主节	〈哈尼族〉Limazhu Festival (in the 3rd month of lunar year)
里耶古城遗址	Ancient Town of Liye (Hu'nan)
理县湍蛙	〈动〉*Amolops lifanensis*; Lifan torrent/sucker frog
鲤鱼	〈动〉*Cyprinus carpio*; common carp; carp
鲤鱼打挺	〈武术〉carp skip-up; carp flip
鲤鱼门公园及度假村	Lei Yue Mun Park and Holiday Village (Hong Kong)
鲤跃龙门	〈成〉a carp leaping over the dragon gate (a metaphor for success or promotion)
历代帝王庙	Temple of Ancient Monarchs; Imperial Temple of Emperors of Successive Dynasties (Beijing)
历代艺术馆	(of Imperial Palace) Museum of Art History
立春	〈节气〉Beginning of Spring; Spring Begins (1st solar term)
立冬	〈节气〉Beginning of Winter; Winter Begins (19th solar term)
立秋	〈节气〉Beginning of Autumn; Autumn Begins (13rd solar term)
立容德	〈古〉Lirongde (to maintain neutrality and show impartial and moral demeanour) (a saying from The Book of Rites) →君子九容
立夏	〈节气〉Beginning of Summer; Summer Begins (7th solar term)
立夏节	Beginning of Summer Festival
立雪堂	(of Lion Forest Garden) Hall of Standing in Snow
立鱼峰景区	Liyu Peak Scenic Area (Guangxi)
丽豆	〈植〉*Calophaca sinica*
丽港公园	Laguna Park (Hong Kong)
丽江古城	Lijiang Ancient/Old Town (Yunnan)

丽江玉泉公园	Lijiang Yuquan Park; Lijiang Jade Spring Park (in Black Dragon Pond) (Yunnan)
丽江云杉	〈植〉*Picea likiangensis*; Lijiang spruce
丽景轩	(of Imperial Palace) Bower of Enchanting Scenery
丽水异角蟾	〈动〉*Xenophrys lishuiensis*; Lishui horned toad
丽正门	(of Chengde Mountain Resort) Gate of Beauty and Righteousness
利川齿蟾	〈动〉*Oreolalax lichuanensis*; Lichuan toothed toad
利川铃蟾	〈动〉*Bombina lichuanensis*; Lichuan bell toad
利华大楼	Leopold Building (cultural relics protection unit of Tianjin)
利是	laisee (distributing laisee is a New Year custom in Guangdong) →红封包
利是钱	lucky money
荔波异角蟾	〈动〉*Xenophrys liboensis*; Libo horned toad
荔枝	〈植〉*Litchi chinensis*; lychee
荔枝节	litchi festival
栗齿鼩鼱	〈动〉*Sorex daphaenodon*; Siberian large-toothed shrew
栗子坪自然保护区	Liziping Nature Reserve (Sichuan)
笠亭	(of Humble Administrator's Garden) Bamboo Hat Pavilion
傈僳族	Lisu ethnic group; Lisu
傈僳族同心酒	〈傈僳族〉Lisu tongxin wine (two persons hold the same drinking vessel, and drink at the same time with their mouths getting closely together)
莲池[花]潭	Lotus Pond (Taiwan)
莲峰庙[寺]	Lin Fong Temple (Macao)
莲湖公园	Lianhu (Lotus Lake) Park (Guangdong)
莲花倒挂	Inverse Lotus Peak (Zhejiang)
莲花洞	(of Longmen Grottoes) Lotus Flower Cave
莲花峰	(of Mount Huangshan) Lotus Peak (one of three main peaks)

莲花峰景区	Lotus Peak Scenic Area (Guangdong)
莲花湖湿地公园	Lotus Lake Wetland Park (Hubei)
莲花山	Lotus Mountain (Guangdong)
莲花山滑雪场	Lianhua Mountain Skiing Spot in Changchun (Jilin)
莲花山自然保护区	Lianhuashan Nature Reserve (Gansu)
莲花塔	Lotus Tower (Guangdong) →省会华表
莲花潭	→莲池[花]潭
莲花岩	Lotus Rock (Guangxi)
莲沱九四暴动革命烈士纪念碑	Revolutionary Martyrs Monument of 1994 Liantuo Uprising (Hubei)
莲溪庙	Lin Kai Temple (Macao)
莲子	〈中药〉Lotus Seed
莲宗寺	Lianzong Temple (Tianjin)
联峰山景区	Lianfeng Mountain Scenic Area (Hebei)
鲢鱼	〈动〉*Hypophthalmichthys molitrix*; chub
脸谱	〈戏〉Lianpu (face painting of Peking Opera)
练功台	exercise platform; training platform
炼丹峰	(of Mount Huangshan) Alchemy Peak
恋爱巷	Love Lane; Travessa da Paixão (Macao)
楝树	〈植〉*Melia azedarach*; Chinaberry; China tree
良辰吉日	auspicious occasion
良口景区	Liangkou Scenic Area (Guangxi)
良渚(古城)遗址	Liangzhu Site; Liangzhu Archaeological Ruins (Zhejiang)
凉北齿蟾	〈动〉*Oreolalax liangbeiensis*; Liangbei toothed toad
凉山湍蛙	〈动〉*Amolops liangshanensis*; Liangshan torrent/sucker frog
凉州风情园	Liangzhou Amorous Feelings Garden (Gansu)
梁朝	Liang Dynasty (502-557)
梁莫峡谷	Liangdian Gorge (Ningxia)
梁王山	Liangwang Mountain (Yunnan)
梁祝化蝶	(of a love story) Butterfly Lovers

粮蔗之乡	Land of Grain and Sugarcane (referring to Yingjiang County in Yunnan)
两广总督	〈古〉Viceroy of Guangdong and Guangxi Provinces (in the Qing Dynasty)
两江四湖景区	Scenic Area of Two Rivers and Four Lakes (Guangxi)
两蒋文化园区	Two Chiangs' (Chiang Kai-shek and Chiang Chingkuo) Cultural Park (Taiwan)
亮掌	〈武术〉Palm turning
晾桥节	〈苗族〉Liangqiao Festival (on the 2nd day of the 2nd lunar month)
辽代壁画墓群	Mural Tombs of Liao Dynasty (Hebei)
辽代仿瓷	imitated porcelain of Liao Dynasty
辽东湾	Liaodong Bay (Bohai Sea)
辽河流域	Liaohe River basin
辽陵及奉陵邑	Mausoleums of the Liao Dynasty and their Memorial Cities (Inner Mongolia)
辽宁爪鲵	〈动〉*Onychodactylus zhaoermii*; Liaoning clawed salamander
辽上京遗址	Upper Capital Site of the Liao Dynasty; Site of Liao Dynasty's Upper Capital (Inner Mongolia)
辽砚	Liao ink-stone
辽阳白塔	Liaoyang White Pagoda (Liaoning)
辽阳(汉魏)壁画墓群	Liaoyang Mural Tombs; Liaoyang Murals in Han and Wei Dynasties' Tombs (Liaoning)
辽源魁星楼	Kuixing Building in Liaoyuan (Jilin)
辽中京遗址	Middle Capital Site of the Liao Dynasty; Site of Liao Dynasty's Middle Capital (Inner Mongolia)
撩拳	〈武术〉Uppercut palm
廖万石堂	Liu Man Shek Tong (Ancestral Hall) (Hong Kong)
烈士公园	martyr memorial park; martyr's park
烈士陵园	martyrs cemetery
烈士墓及昭忠祠	Martyr's Tomb and Zhaozhong Temple (Fujian)

猎日节	〈蒙古族〉Hunting Day (on the 5th day of the 5th lunar month)
林村天后庙	Lam Tsuen Tin Hau Temple (Hong Kong)
林村许愿树	Lam Tsuen Wishing Trees (Hong Kong)
林琴蛙	〈动〉*Nidirana lini*; Jiangcheng music frog
林泉耆硕之馆	(of Lingering Garden) Old Hermit Scholars' House
林麝	〈动〉*Moschus berezovskii*; dwarf musk deer; Chinese forest musk deer
林氏角蟾	〈动〉*Megophrys lini*; Lin's horned toad
林蛙	〈动〉*Rana amurensis*; wood frog
林王节	〈侗族〉Forest King's Day
林猬	〈动〉*Mesechinus sylvaticus*; Hugh's hedgehog
林则徐销烟池与虎门炮台旧址	Site of Lin Zexu's Opium Destroying Pool and the Humen Batteries (Guangdong)
林芝湍蛙	〈动〉*Amolops nyingchiensis*
临沧茶文化风情园	Lincang Tea Culture and Custom Garden (Yunnan)
临芳墅	(of Chengde Mountain Resort) Villa Surrounded with Fragrant Flowers and Plants
临汾尧庙	Linfen Yao Temple (Shanxi)
临汉门	Linhan Ancient City Gate (Hubei)
临墙为好	〈礼〉the seat against the wall is the seat of honour
临时大总统办公室	Office of the Provisional President (Jiangsu)
临台为上	〈礼〉the seat near the platform is the seat of honour
临溪亭	(of Imperial Palace) Over-Pool Pavilion
临淄齐国故城	Linzi Unearthed City of Qi State; Linzi Site of Qi State (Shandong)
鳞皮小蟾	〈动〉*Parapelophryne scalpta*; Hai'nan flathead toad
蔺相如回车巷	Lin Xiangru's Huiche Alley/Lane (Hebei)
灵宝塔	Lingbao Pagoda (Sichuan)

灵渡寺	〈佛〉Lingdu Temple (Hong Kong)
灵峰	(of Mount Yandang) Lingfeng Peak; Spiritual Peak
灵峰寺	Lingfeng Temple (Zhejiang)
灵谷(禅)寺	〈佛〉Linggu Temple (Jiangsu)
灵光塔	Lingguang Pagoda (Jilin)
灵柩	(of funeral) a coffin containing a corpse; bier
灵鹫山	Lingjiu Mountain (Sichuan)
灵前忌猫	〈丧〉no cats in the mourning hall
灵丘桃花山	Lingqiu Peach Mountain (Shanxi)
灵泉(禅)寺	〈佛〉Lingquan Temple (Taiwan)
灵泉寺石窟	Grottoes of Lingquan Temple (He'nan)
灵山	Lingshan Mountain; Soul Mountain (Jiangxi)
灵山大佛	Lingshan Grand Buddha (Jiangsu)
灵山大照壁	Great Screen Wall at Lingshan (Jiangsu)
灵山胜境	Lingshan Buddhist Scenic Spot (Jiangsu)
灵山寺	Lingshan Temple (He'nan)
灵山自然景区	Lingshan Mountain Natural Scenic Area (Beijing)
灵塔殿	Stupa Hall (Tibet)
灵堂	〈丧〉mourning hall
灵秀苑	Lingxiu Amusement Park (Sichuan)
灵虚岩	(of Mount Wudang) Lingxu Rock (Cave); Overhang Rock
灵岩	Linyan Rock; Spiritual Rock (Zhejiang)
灵岩山	Lingyan Mountain; Divine Cliff Hill (Jiangsu)
灵岩寺	(of Mount Taishan) Lingyan Temple; Divine Rock Temple
灵岩寺旅游区	Lingyan Temple Tourist Area; Divine Rock Temple Tour Zone (Shandong)
灵隐禅踪	(of West Lake) Buddhism in Lingyin Monastery; Zen Aroma of Lingyin Temple
灵隐佛国	Lingyin Buddhist Kingdom (Zhejiang)
灵隐山	〈佛〉Lingyin Mountain (Zhejiang)

灵隐寺	Lingyin Temple; Temple of Soul's Retreat (Hangzhou)
灵应岩	(of Mount Wudang) Lingying Rock; Efficacious Rock
灵芝草	〈中药〉*Ganoderma lucidum*; glossy ganoderma; felicitous plant (dark-brown fungus credited with miraculous powers)
灵芝岩	ganoderma rock
玲珑馆	(of Humble Administrator's Garden) Exquisite Hall
凌冰岩	Cryolite-like Rock (Sichuan)
凌太虚	(of Chengde Mountain Resort) Pavilion Soaring to the Skies
凌霄阁	Peak Tower (Hong Kong)
凌霄花	〈植〉*Campsis grandiflora*; Chinese trumpet creeper
凌霄塔	Lingxiao Pagoda; Stratosphere Tower (Hebei, Shaanxi)
凌云白塔	Lingyun White Pagoda (Sichuan)
凌云禅院	Lingyun Temple (Sichuan)
凌云山	Lingyun Mountain (Sichuan)
凌云山景区	Lingyun Mountain Scenic Area (Sichuan)
凌云栈道	Lingyun Plank Road (Sichuan)
陵山	Lingshan Mountain (Hebei)
陵水椰子岛	Lingshui Coconut Island (Hai'nan)
菱角	〈植〉*Trapa bispinosa*; water caltrop
菱角湖湿地公园	Lingjiao Lake Wetland Park (Hubei)
棂星门	lingxing gate
羚牛	〈动〉*Budorcas taxicolor*; takin
裬恩殿	→隆[裬]恩殿
裬恩门	→隆[裬]恩门
领羊	〈民俗〉(of superstitious customs in Gansu) a goat for sacrifice (it is believed that the goat body would be possessed by the deceased's spirit)
刘公岛	Liugong Island (Shandong)

刘公岛甲午战争纪念地	Liugongdao Memorial Places of the Jiawu War; Commemorative Site of Sino-Japanese War in Liugong Island (Shandong)
刘家湾赶海园	Liujiawan Beachcombing Park (Shandong)
刘家峡大坝	Liujiaxia Dam; Liujia Gorge Dam (Gansu)
刘家峡水电站	Liujiaxia Hydropower Station (Gansu)
刘少奇故居	Former Residence of Liu Shaoqi (Hu'nan)
刘氏泰诺蛙	〈动〉*Limnonectes liui*; menglun eastern frog
刘氏掌突蟾	〈动〉*Leptobrachella laui*; lau's leaf litter toad
浏阳河	Liuyang River (Hu'nan)
浏阳疣螈	〈动〉*Tylototriton liuyangensis*; Liuyang knobby newt
留拉酒节	〈瑶族〉Liula Wine Festival (on the 14th day of the 7th lunar month)
留听阁	(of Humble Administrator's Garden) Stay and Listening Pavilion
流动性大沙漠	shifting sand dunes
流浮山	Lau Fau Shan (Hong Kong)
流红	floating red; floating flower
流徽榭	Liuhui Waterside Pavilion (Jiangsu)
流沙河	Liusha (Flowing Sand) River (in Journey to the West)
流觞曲水	〈古〉floating cup on a winding brook (a game of men of letters in which a cup is flowing on a winding canal, and whoever has to drink when the cup stops before him)
流霞	〈易〉Liu Xia (a symbol of physical injury)
琉璃厂文化街	Liulichang Culture Street (Beijing)
琉璃塔	glazed stupa
琉璃影壁	glazed screen wall
柳侯祠	Liuhou Memorial Temple (a memorial temple to Liu Zongyuan) (Guangxi)
柳侯公园	Liuhou Park (Guangxi)
柳浪闻莺	(of West Lake) Orioles Singing in the Willows; Listening to Orioles Singings in the Willows

柳青庄园	Liuqing Manor (Tianjin)
柳阴路曲	(of Humble Administrator's Garden) Zigzag Pathway with Willow Shade
柳子庙	Temple of Master Liu (a memorial temple to Liu Zongyuan) (Hu'nan)
六顶山古墓群	〈佛〉Ancient Tombs at Liudingshan (Jilin)
六峰山	Liufeng (six-peak) Mountain (Guangxi)
六峰山景区	Liufeng Mountain Scenic Area (Guangxi)
六福村主题乐园	Leofoo Village Theme Park (Taiwan)
六合拳	〈武术〉Liuhe Quan; Six Combination Boxing
六合夜市	Liuhe Night Market (Taiwan)
六和塔	〈佛〉Liuhe (Six Harmonies) Pagoda; Pagoda of Six Harmonies (Zhejiang)
六和听涛	(of West Lake) Hearing the Roaring of Qiantang River at Liuhe Pagoda
六虎山茶园	Liuhushan Tea Garden (Hubei)
六角亭	Hexangular Pavilion (Hubei)
六礼	〈婚〉Six Etiquettes; Six Rituals (matchmaker's proposal, birthday matching, exchange of birthdays and family tree, betrothal gifts presentation, agreement upon the wedding date, personal escort to the bride) →纳采, 问名, 纳吉, 纳征, 请期, 亲迎
六里坪森林公园	Liuliping Forest Park (Hebei)
六龙山	Liulong (six-dragon) Mountain (Guizhou)
六盘齿突蟾	〈动〉*Scutiger liupanensis*; Liupan alpine toad
六盘山	Liupan Mountain (Gansu, Ningxia)
六盘山森林公园	Liupan Mountain Forest Park (Ningxia)
六奇阁	(of Zhangjiajie) Six Wonders Pavilion
六曲	〈中药〉*Massa Medicata Fermentata*; medicated leaven
六榕寺	Liurong Temple; Six Banyan Temple (Guangdong)
六世祖祠	Sixth Ancestor Hall (Guangdong)

六一纪念亭	6·1 Memorial Pavilion (Hubei)
六月会	June Festival (a large-scale sacrificial performance activity prevailing among Tibetan and Tu ethnic groups from the 17th day to 25th day of the 6th lunar month)
六月节	〈壮族〉Liuyue Festival (on the 1st day of the 6th lunar month)
六月六	〈汉族、布依族〉Double Sixth Festival
龙	loong; Chinese dragon
龙鼻洞	Dragon Nose Cave (Zhejiang)
龙布寺	→绒[龙]布寺
龙昌峡	(of Shenlong River) Longchang Gorge
龙池森林公园	Longchi Forest Park (Sichuan)
龙川大峡谷	(of Mount Wuyi) Longchuan Grand Canyon
龙川胡氏宗祠	Longchuan Ancestral Temple of Hu Family (Anhui)
龙船节	〈苗族〉Chinese Dragon Boat Festival (from the 24th day to the 27th day of the 5th lunar month)
龙达温泉生态城	Longda Hot Spring Eco-City (Tianjin)
龙的传人	descendants of Loong (Chinese dragon, referring to the Chinese nation)
龙的故乡	Loong's home; hometown of Chinese dragon
龙灯舞	〈舞〉Dragon Lantern Dance
龙滴水	(of Huanglong Valley) Dragon Trickles
龙洞山溪鲵	〈动〉*Batrachuperus londongensis*; Longdong stream salamander
龙凤谷温泉	Longfeng Valley Hot Spring (Sichuan)
龙凤门	Dragon and Phoenix Gate (Beijing)
龙凤石	Marble of Dragon and Phoenix (Beijing)
龙凤水法	(of Yuanming Garden) Dragon-Phoenix Fountain
龙宫	Loong Palace; Chinese Dragon Palace
龙宫玉珠	(of Xingtai Canyon group) Dragon Palace and Jade Pearls
龙骨	dragon bone; keel

龙骨坡遗址	Longgupo Site (Chongqing)
龙骨山	Dragon Bone Hill (Beijing)
龙鼓滩	Lung Kwu Tan (Hong Kong)
龙洪自然景区	Longhong Natural Scenic Area (Guangxi)
龙湖公园	Longhu Lake Park; Dragon Lake Park (Anhui)
龙湖[泉]山	Longhu Mountain (Fujian)
龙虎殿	(of Mount Wudang) Hall of Green-Blue Dragon and White Tiger
龙虎山	〈道〉Mount Longhu; Dragon and Tiger Mountain (Jiangxi)
龙虎山郊野公园	Lung Fu Shan Country Park (Hong Kong)
龙虎塔	Dragon and Tiger Pagodas (Shandong, Taiwan)
龙华革命烈士纪念地	Longhua Memorial Place of Revolutionary Martyrs (Shanghai)
龙华寺	Longhua Temple (Shanghai)
龙华塔	Longhua Pagoda (Shanghai)
龙剑峰	(of Tiantang Zhai) Dragon Sword Peak
龙进溪	Longjin Brook (Hubei)
龙井(茶)	Longjing; Loong Well tea; Dragon Well tea
龙井茶园	Longjing Tea Plantation (Zhejiang)
龙井问茶	(of West Lake) Enjoying Tea at Dragon Well; Inquiring about Tea at Dragon Well
龙井峡[河]	Longjing Gorge/River (Anhui)
龙口南山景区	Longkou Nanshan Scenic Spot (Shandong)
龙里瘰螈	〈动〉*Paramesotriton longliensis*; Chinese warty newt
龙銮潭	Longluan Beach Wetland (Taiwan)
龙脉	〈易〉Loong Vein; Chinese Dragon Vein
龙门	longmen; dragon gate (gateway to success)
龙门古镇	Longmen Ancient Town (Zhejiang)
龙门激浪	Longmen Surf (Hai'nan)
龙门瀑布	longmen waterfall; dragon gate waterfall
龙门石窟	Longmen Grottoes (He'nan)
龙门天关	Longmen Natural Pass (Hebei)

龙门峡	(of Lesser Three Gorges) Longmen Gorge
龙门峡谷	Longmen Canyon; Dragon Gate Canyon (Zhejiang)
龙门峡景区	(of Guanmen Mountain) Longmen Valley Scenic Area
龙眠山	Longmian Mountain (Anhui)
龙年	Year of the Dragon (one of the 12 Chinese Zodiac)
龙栖湿地生态园	Longqi Wetland Ecopark (Anhui)
龙泉观	〈道〉Longquan Temple; Dragon Spring Taoist Temple (Yunnan)
龙泉湖	longquan lake; dragon spring lake
龙泉山	→龙湖[泉]山
龙泉神女宫	Longquan Goddess Palace (Sichuan)
龙泉寺	〈佛〉Longquan Temple; Longquan Monastery; Dragon Spring Temple (Beijing)
龙泉探幽	(of Swallow Cave) Dragon Spring Exploration
龙泉岩	Longquan Rock; Dragon Spring Rock (Guangdong)
龙山	Longshan Mountain; Dragon Mountain (Shandong)
龙山湖景区	Longshan Lake Scenic Area (Jilin)
龙山湖湿地公园	Longshan Lake Wetland Park (He'nan)
龙山寺	longshan temple
龙山文化	Longshan Culture (3000-2000 B.C.) (successor to Yangshao Culture)
龙身凤尾虾	〈烹饪〉Prawn with Dragon's Body and Phoenix's Tail
龙神祠	Dragon God Temple (Yunnan)
龙首崖	(of Mount Lushan) Dragon Head Cliff
龙抬头	Loong Taitou Festival; Dragon Head-Raising Day; Double-Second Festival (on the 2nd day of the 2nd lunar month) →春耕节, 春龙节
龙潭	dragon pond
龙潭大峡谷	Longtan Grand Canyon; Dragon Pond Grand Canyon (He'nan)

龙潭洞	Longtan Cave; Dragon Pond Cave (Anhui)
龙潭山鹿场	Longtan Mountain Deer Farm (Jilin)
龙潭水库	(of Mount Taishan) Dragon Pond Reservoir
龙亭大殿	Longting Hall; Dragon Pavilion Hall (He'nan)
龙亭公园	Longting Park; Dragon Pavilion Park (He'nan)
龙头峰	(of Zhangjiajie) Dragon Head Peak
龙头山	Longtou Mountain; Dragon Head Mountain (Chongqing)
龙头山古墓群	Ancient Tombs at Longtou Mountain (Jilin)
龙湾火山湖	Longwan Crater Lake; Longwan Volcanic Lake (Jilin)
龙湾群森林公园	Longwanqun Forest Park (Jilin)
龙王	〈神话〉Dragon King; God of Rain
龙王殿	longwang palace; dragon king palace
龙王(庙)会	〈纳西族〉Dragon King Temple Fair (on the 15th day of the 3rd lunar month)
龙王庙	longwang temple; dragon king temple
龙王峡	Longwang Gorge; Dragon King Gorge (Hubei)
龙溪黄土高原	Longxi Loess Plateau (Gansu)
龙虾花	〈植〉*Impatiens spp*; lobster flower
龙虾湾石刻	Lobster Bay Stone Carving (Hong Kong)
龙兴寺	longxing temple
龙形神道	Divine Path of Dragon Scale (Hubei)
《龙须沟》	〈戏〉*Longxu Ditch; Dragon Beard Ditch* (Lao She, 1950)
龙须山	Longxu Mountain (Anhui)
龙眼	〈植〉*Dimocarpus longan*
龙羊峡大坝	Longyang Gorge Dam (Qinghai)
龙羊峡水电站	Longyang Gorge Hydropower Station (Qinghai)
龙璋山	Longzhang Mountain (Hu'nan)
龙舟	Chinese dragon boat
龙舟队	Chinese dragon boat team
龙舟节	Chinese Dragon Boat Festival (on the 5th day of the 5th lunar month) →端午节

龙舟赛	〈民俗〉Chinese dragon boat race; Chinese dragon boat competition
龙子湖	Longzi Lake; Dragon Son Lake (Anhui)
龙子湖景区	Longzi Lake Scenic Area (Anhui)
隆德节	〈珞巴族〉Longde Festival (on the 4th or 5th month according to Tibetan calendar)
隆[祾]恩殿	Hall of Eminent Favor (Hebei)
隆[祾]恩门	Gate of Eminent Favor (Hebei)
隆肛蛙	〈动〉*Feirana quadranus*; Kwang-yang Asian frog; swelled vent frog
隆务寺	Longwu Temple (Qinghai)
隆兴寺	Longxing Temple (Hebei)
隆枕蟾蜍	〈动〉*Bufo cyphosus*; occipital bulged toad
《隆中对》	Longzhong Plan; Longzhong Strategy (strategies and plans offered to Liu Bei by Zhuge Liang in Longzhou) (Chen Shou, 207-208)
隆中山	Longzhong Mountain (where Zhouge Liang lived on farming) (Hubei)
隆中植物园	Longzhong Botanical Garden (Hubei)
隆宗门	(of Imperial Palace) Gate of the Thriving Imperial Clan; Gate of Imperial Prosperity
陇川大头蛙	〈动〉*Limnonectes longchuanensis*; Longchuan big-headed frog
陇端节	〈壮族〉Longduan Festival (on the 25th day to 28th day of the 3rd lunar month)
陇海铁路	Longhai Railway; Lanzhou-Lianyungang Railway
陇戛石林	Longjia Stone Forest (Guizhou)
楼兰古国	Loulan Ancient City (Xinjiang)
楼兰故城遗址	Site of Ancient Loulan City (Xinjiang)
楼梯街	Ladder Street (Hong Kong)
搂膝拗步	(of Tai Chi) Brushing keen and twisting step
卢[芦]沟桥	Lugou Bridge; Marco Polo Bridge (Beijing)
卢家大屋	Casa de Lou Kau; Lou Kau Mansion (Macao)
卢浦大桥	Lupu Bridge (Shanghai)

卢崖瀑布	(of Shaolin Temple) Luya Cliff Waterfall
卢崖瀑布景区	Luya Waterfall Scenic Area (He'nan)
卢(廉若公)园	Jardim Lou Lim; Lou Lim Lok Garden (Macao)
芦笛岩	Reed Flute Cave (Guangxi)
芦柑	(of a fruit) Chinese honey
芦花荡公园	Luhuadang Park (Zhejiang)
芦花鸡	〈动〉*Gallus domestiaus*; plymouth rock (domestic fowl)
芦林湖	(of Mount Lushan) Lulin Lake
芦笙	〈乐〉Lusheng pipe (a reed-pipe wind instrument)
芦笙节	Lusheng (reed-pipe wind instrument) Festival (a traditional festival of the Miao and Dong ethnic groups from the early 1st lunar month to the late 2nd one)
芦苇海	(of Jiuzhai Valley) Reed Lake
庐山	Mount Lushan; Lushan Mountain (Jiangxi)
庐山博物馆	Lushan Museum (Jiangxi)
庐山国家公园	Lushan National Park (Jiangxi)
庐山会议	Lushan Conference; Lushan Plenum (1959)
庐山会议旧址	Former Site of Lushan Conference (Jiangxi)
《庐山恋》	*Love/Romance on Lushan Mountain* (Shanghai Film Studio, 1980)
庐山瀑布	Waterfall on Lushan Mountain (Jiangxi)
庐山西海	Lushan West Sea (Jiangxi)
庐山植物园	Lushan Botanical Gardens (Jiangxi)
泸定[大渡]桥	Luding Bridge; Luding Chain Bridge (Sichuan)
泸沽湖	Lugu Lake (Yunnan)
泸沽三岛	Three Islands of Lugu Lake (Yunnan)
泸江	Lujiang River
泸溪河	Luxi River (Jiangxi)
泸州大曲老窖池	Old Pit of Luzhou Daqu Liquor (Sichuan)
鸬鹚潭	Cormorant Pond (Zhejiang)
鲈鱼	〈动〉*Lateolabrax japonicus*; common sea perch; weever; bass

鲁	Lu (abbreviation for Shandong Province)
鲁班节	〈蒙古族〉Luban Festival (on the 2nd day of the 4th lunar month, for the worship of the master of Chinese carpenter, Luban)
鲁班(先师)庙	Lo Pan Temple (Hong Kong)
鲁布革三峡	Lubuge Three Gorges (Yunnan)
鲁国	State of Lu (1043 -249 B.C.)
鲁土司衙门旧址	Site of Chieftain Lu's Office (Gansu)
鲁王城遗址	Site of Luwang City (Inner Mongolia)
鲁迅公园	Lu Xun Park (Shanghai, Shandong)
鲁迅故居	Former Residence of Lu Xun (Shanghai, Beijing)
鲁迅纪念馆	Lu Xun Memorial Hall; Lu Xun Museum (Shanghai)
鲁迅墓	Tomb of Lu Xun (Shanghai)
陆和村茶艺博物馆	Tea Art Museum in Luhe Village (Anhui)
陆家嘴	Lujiazui (national financial center of the Yangtze River economic belt of China) (Shanghai)
陆良彩色沙林	Luliang Colorful Sand Forest (Yunnan)
陆水水库	Lushui Reservoir (Hubei)
陆游泉	Lu You Spring (Hubei)
鹿峰山	Lufeng Mountain (Guangxi)
鹿回头山顶公园	Luhuitou Mountain Park (Hai'nan)
鹿颈	Luk Keng (an ecotourism area of Hong Kong)
鹿门寺国家森林公园	Lumen Temple National Forest Park
鹿蹄草	〈植〉*Pyrola calliantha*; wintergreen
鹿院坪峡谷	Luyuanping Valley (Hubei)
禄丰恐龙化石	dinosaur fossils of Lufeng
路环村[市区]	Vila de Coloane; Coloane Village (Macao)
路环岛	Coloane Island (Macao)
路环圣方济各圣堂	Coloane St. Francis of Assisi Church; Chapel of St. Francis Xavier (Macao)
路祭	〈表〉to offer sacrifices on the route of a funeral procession
路神生日	birthday of road god (a wealth god) (the 5th day of the 1st lunar month)

潞王陵	Mausoleum of King Lu (He'nan)
鹭鸶草	〈植〉*Diuranthera major*; egret grass
麓山寺	Lushan Temple (Hu'nan)
吕洞宾	LüDongbin (one of the Eight Immortals)
吕梁山	Lüliang Mountain (Shanxi)
捋挤式	(of Tai Chi) Deflecting pushing and squeezing
旅顺监狱旧址	Site of Lüshun Prison (Liaoning)
旅行社	tourist agency; travel agency/service
旅游局	tourism administration
绿宝石公园	Emerald Park (Tianjin)
绿宝石婚	emerald wedding (the 55th anniversary of marriage)
绿茶	green tea
绿春溪蟾	〈动〉*Torrentophryne luchunnica*
绿岛	Green Island (Taiwan)
绿岛公园	Green Island Park (Zhejiang)
绿点湍蛙	〈动〉*Amolops viridimaculatus*; green-spotted torrent frog; Dahaoping sucker frog
绿色爆竹	green firecracker
绿色旅游	green tourism
绿色世界生态园	Green World Ecopark (Tianjin)
绿色仙境	green fairyland
绿松石雕	turquoise carving
绿尾虹雉	〈动〉*Lophophorus lhuysii*; Chinese monal
绿荫	(of Lingering Garden) Green Shade Pavilion
葎叶蛇葡萄	〈植〉*Ampelopsis humulifolia*
栾树	〈植〉*Koelreuteria paniculata*; golden rain tree
滦河	Luanhe River (Hebei)
抡臂砸拳	〈武术〉Circle arms into smash punch
罗布泊	Lop Nor/Nur; Lopnor Lake (Xinjiang)
罗布林卡	〈佛〉Norbulingka Summer Palace (summer residence of Dalai Lamas in Lhasa) (Tibet)
罗布林卡寺	Norbu Lingka (Tibet)
罗布人	Lop Nur villagers (Xinjiang)

罗池八景	Eight Views of Luochi Pool (Guangxi)
罗池庙	Luochi Temple (Zhejiang)
罗东舒祠	Luo Dongshu Ancestral Temple (Anhui)
罗汉峰	(of Mount Huangshan) Luohan Peak; Arhat Peak
罗汉山	Arhat Mountain (Hebei)
罗汉唐卡	〈佛〉Luohan Tangka (a religious scroll painting)
罗汉堂	〈佛〉Luohan Hall; Arhat Hall
罗汉崖	(of Mount Taishan) Arhat Cliff
罗汉迎宾	(of Zhangjiajie) Guest Welcoming Arhat
罗汉竹	→佛肚竹
罗睺罗	〈佛〉Rahula (the only son and one of the ten disciples of the Buddha, best-known for his esoteric practices)
罗默刘树蛙	〈动〉*Liuixalus romeri*; Romer's tree frog
罗平螺丝田	Screw-Shaped Field (Yunnan)
罗平油菜花旅游节	Luoping Rapeseed Flower Tourism Festival (from February 3rd to April 10th)
罗让扎花节	〈藏族〉Keba Memorial Day (on the 25th day of the 10th lunar month according to Tibetan calendar)
罗斯坦棘蛙	〈动〉*Paa rostandi*; Dubois' paa frog; Rostand's paa frog
罗霄山	Luoxiao Mountain (Hu'nan, Jiangxi)
罗阳瀑布	Luoyang Waterfall (Zhejiang)
锣	〈乐〉Chinese gong
骡马会	→七月[骡马]会
螺髻亭	(of Garden of Harmony) Pavilion of Snail-Shaped Bun
螺丝山[马交石]公园	Garden of Montanha Russa (Macao)
螺旋掌	Spiraling palm; Revolving palm
裸婚	naked marriage; bare marriage (a simple way of getting married without purchasing a house and car)
裸芸香	〈植〉*Psilopeganum sinense*
洛川会议纪念馆	Memorial Hall of Luochuan Meeting (Shaanxi)

洛带古镇	Luodai Ancient Town (Sichuan)
洛南文庙	Luonan Confucius Temple (Shaanxi)
洛阳白园	Luoyang Baiyuan Garden; Cemetery of Bai Juyi in Luoyang (built in memory of Bai Juyi, a great poet of Tang Dynasty) (He'nan)
洛阳牡丹节	Luoyang Peony Festival (April, May)
洛阳桥	Luoyang Bridge (He'nan, Fujian)
洛阳青要山景区	Qingyao Mountain Scenic Area in Luoyang (He'nan)
骆驼城遗址	Camel City Site (Gansu)
骆驼峰	(of Zhangjiajie) Camel Peaks
珞巴族	Lhoba ethnic group; Lhoba
落红	fallen red (fallen flower)
落蟒布依寨	Luomang Village of Buyi Ethnic Group (Guizhou)
落雁岛	Luoyan Island; Landing Wild Goose Island (Hubei)
落雁峰	(of Mount Huashan) Landing Wild Goose Peak
落叶兰	〈植〉*Cymbidium defoliatum*

M

妈阁庙	Ma Kok Miu; A-Ma Temple (Macao)
妈祖	Mazu (the Goddess of Sea)
妈祖庙	Mazu Temple (a temple for offering sacrifice to Mazu) (Fujian)
妈祖文化村	Mazu Culture Village (Macao)
麻城浮桥河水利景区	Fuqiao River Water Conservancy Scenic Area in Macheng (Hubei)
麻城孔庙	Macheng Confucius Temple (Hubei)
麻城狮子峰	Macheng Lion Peak (Hubei)
麻浩岩墓	Mahao Cliff Tombs; Cave Tombs on the Mahao River (Sichuan)
麻将	mahjong
麻皮河	Mapi River (Qinghai)
马鞍岭火山口	Ma'anling Crater (Hai'nan)
马鞍山海滨长廊	Ma On Shan Waterfront Promenade (Hong Kong)
马鞍山郊野公园	Ma On Shan Country Park (Hong Kong)
马堡店生态旅游区	Mabudian Eco-tourism Resort (Inner Mongolia)
马布	〈乐〉Mabu (a single-reed musical instrument of Yi ethnic group)
马步	〈武术〉Horse stance; Horse-riding stance
马步冲拳	〈武术〉Thrust punch in horse stance
马步靠	〈武术〉(of Tai Chi) Horse riding step pushing forearm
马厂塬遗址	Machangyuan Site (Qinghai)
马齿毛兰	〈植〉*Eria szetschuanica*

马骨胡	〈乐〉Maguhu (a two-stringed musical instrument made of horse bone and used in Zhuang ethnic group)
马国师陵园	Mausoleum of Ma Guoshi (Hai'nan)
马家窑文化	Majiayao Culture (3300 –2050 B.C., a local type of Yangshao Culture in the Western China) (Gansu)
马家窑遗址	Majiayao Site (Gansu)
马江海战炮台	Majiang Naval Battle Fort (Fujian)
马交石公园	→螺丝山[马交石]公园
马口陶瓷	Makou Pottery
马兰峪清孝陵	Malanyuan Xiaoling Mausoleum of the Qing Dynasty (Hebei)
马礼逊教堂	Protestant Chapel; Morrison Chapel (Macao) → 圣公会马礼逊堂
马莲河	Malian River (Gansu)
马岭河峡谷	Maling River Canyon (Guizhou)
马岭山	Maling Mountain (Hai'nan)
马马岩壁画	Mamayan Rock Painting; Mamayan Horse Murals (Guizhou)
马马岩瀑布	Mamayan Waterfall (Guizhou)
马门溪龙	〈动〉*Mamenchisaurus (a kind of dinosaurs)*
马面石	horse-faced rock (Gansu)
马奶节	〈蒙古族〉Mare's Milk Festival (within the last ten-day period of the 8th lunar month)
马奶酒	〈蒙古族〉kumis
马胖鼓楼	Mapang Drum Tower (Guangxi)
马桥手狮舞	〈舞〉Maqiao Hand Lion Dance
马仁奇峰	Maren Striking Peak (Anhui)
马上拔河	〈哈萨克族〉(of sports activity) tug-of-war on horseback
马蹄芹	〈植〉*Dickinsia hydrocotyloides*
马蹄寺石窟群	〈佛〉Mati Temple Grottoes (Gansu)
马蹄香	〈植〉*Saruma henryi*; upright wild ginger
马蹄峪	(of Mount Taishan) Horse Hoof Ravine
马田鼓楼	Matian Drum Tower (Hu'nan)

马头琴	〈乐〉Matouqin (a four-stringed musical instrument with carved horsehead)
马头岩	(of Mount Wuyi) Horse Head Rock
马湾公园	Ma Wan Park (Hong Kong)
马王堆 T 型非衣帛画	Mawangdui T-Shaped Non-cloth Painting on Silk (Hu'nan)
马王堆汉墓	Mawangdui Tombs of Han Dynasty (Hu'nan)
马王节	〈满族〉Horse King Festival (on the 23rd day of the 6th lunar month)
马尾松	〈植〉*Pinus massoniana*; masson pine; Chinese red pine
马戏游乐园	(of Wuqiao Acrobatics World) Circus amusement park
马祖列岛	Matsu Islands (Fujian)
玛纳斯河	Manas River (Xinjiang)
玛尼石堆	Mani Stone Pile (Tibet)
玛旁雍措（湖）	Lake Manasarovar (known as the clearest freshwater lake in China) (Tibet)
玛卿岗日峰	Machen Kangri Peak (Qinghai)
玛雅水公园	maya water park
蚂蚱腿子	〈植〉*Myripnois dioica*; Myripnois bunge
买年货	〈民俗〉special purchases for the Spring Festival; to do Spring Festival shopping
麦吊云杉	〈植〉*Picea brachytyla*; sargent spruce
麦盖提刀郎人	Makit Uyghur Dolans
麦积山	Maiji Mountain; Mount Maiji (Gansu)
麦积山石窟	Maiji Mountain Grottoes (Gansu)
麦秀山	Maixiu Mountain (Qinghai)
麦秀原始森林	Maixiu Virgin Forest (Qinghai)
满城汉墓	Mancheng Han Tombs (Hebei)
满江红	〈植〉*Azolla imbricata*; floating fern
满陇桂雨	(of West Lake) Rains of Sweet-Scented Osmanthus Over Hills; Sweet Osmanthus rain at Manjuelong Village

满堂客家大围	Mantang Hakka Manor House (Guangdong)
满月酒	〈民俗〉one-month banquet; full moon feast; red egg and ginger party (for celebrating the first month of a newborn baby)
满月宴	〈民俗〉full moon banquet →满月酒
满洲人	Manchu
满洲语	Manchu language
满族	Manchu ethnic group; Manchu
满族风情园	Manchu Folk-Custom Garden (Heilongjiang)
满族人	Manchurian; Manchus
满族文化	Manchu Culture
曼德拉山岩画	Mandela Mountain Rock Murals/Paintings (Inner Mongolia)
曼飞龙塔	Manfeilong Pagoda (Yunnan)
曼陀大佛	Mantuo Great Buddha (Inner Mongolia)
曼陀山庄	Mantuo Mountain Villa (Inner Mongolia)
幔亭峰	(of Mount Wuyi) Curtain Booth Peak
芒苞草	〈植〉*Acanthochlamys bracteata*
芒种	〈节气〉Grain in Ear (9th solar term)
莽山角蟾	〈动〉*Megophrys mangshanensis*; Mangshan horned toad
莽山烙铁头	〈动〉*Protobothrops mangshanensis*; Mangshan pit-viper
莽山疣螈	〈动〉*Tylototriton lizhengchangi*; Mangshan crocodile newt
猫鼻头公园	Maobitou (Cat Nose) Park (Taiwan)
猫儿蹲	Cat Squatting (Sichuan)
猫儿山小鲵	〈动〉*Hynobius maoershanensis*; Xingan salamander
猫儿山掌突蟾	〈动〉*Paramegophrys maoershanensis*
毛白杨	〈植〉*Populus tomentosa*; Chinese white poplar
毛笔圣地	Holy Land of Writing Brush (referring to Hengshui, Hebei)
毛梗红毛五加	〈植〉*Acanthopanax giraldii*

毛冠鹿	〈动〉*Elaphodus cephalophus*; tufted deer
毛南族	Maonan ethnic group; Maonan
毛女洞	(of Mount Huashan) Maonü Fairy Cave
毛衫树歌节	〈布依族〉Maoshan Shu Song Festival (on the 3rd day of the 3rd lunar month)
毛乌素沙漠	Mu Us Desert (Shaanxi)
毛樱桃	〈植〉*Cerasus tomentosa*; nanking cherry
毛泽东纪念馆	Mao Zedong Memorial Museum (Hu'nan)
毛泽东主席故居	Former Residence of Chairman Mao Zedong (Hu'nan)
毛竹	〈植〉*Phyllostachys edulis*; moso bamboo
毛主席纪念堂	Chairman Mao Memorial Hall (Beijing)
茅盾故居	Former Residence of Mao Dun (Beijing, Zhejiang)
茅湖山观测台	Maohu Mountain Observatory (Hong Kong)
茅兰沟自然景区	Maolan Valley Scenic Area (Heilongjiang)
茅坪	Maoping (an important part of Jinggang Mountain Revolutionary Base and one of the main birthplaces of Jinggang Mountain Spirit)
茅台	Maotai; Moutai (traditional Chinese liquor)
茅岩河	Maoyan River (Hu'nan)
茅岩河风光	scenery of Maoyan River
牦牛	〈动〉*Bos mutus*; wild yak
卯节	〈水族〉Mao Festival (on the 9th or 10th month according to the calendar of Shui ethnic group)
茂兰瘰螈	〈动〉*Paramesotriton maolanensis*; Maolan warty newt
冒都点地梅	〈植〉*Androsace bisulca*
帽儿胡同	Maoer Hutong (Beijing)
帽儿山墓地	Maoer Mountain Cemetery (Jilin)
帽儿山森林公园	Maoer Mountain Forest Park (Jilin)
帽盒峰	→松峦峰
帽天山	Maotian Mountain (Yunnan)
玫瑰堂圣物宝库	Treasure of Sacred Art Museum (Macao)

眉柳	〈植〉*Salix wangiana*; brow willow
梅川水库水利景区	Meichuan Reservoir Water Conservancy Scenic Area (Hubei)
梅江公园	Meijiang Park (Tianjin)
梅兰芳纪念馆	Mei Lanfang Memorial Museum (Beijing)
梅里雪山	Meili Snow Mountain (Xizang, Yunnan)
梅岭	Meiling Hill (Jiangxi)
梅瓶	prunus vase; plum bottle (a vase with blue and white prunus blossom design)
梅山铁线蕨	〈植〉*Adiantum meishanianum*
梅树坑公园	Mui Shue Hang Park (Hong Kong)
梅树坑游乐场	Mui Shue Hang Playground (Hong Kong)
梅窝	Mui Wo (a seaside view of Hong Kong)
梅坞春早	(of West Lake) Meijia Cove in Early Spring
梅溪(石)牌坊	Meixi Royal Stone Archway (Guangdong)
梅雨	plum rain (long-lasting cloudy and rainy weather)
梅雨季节	plum rain season
梅园	Plum Garden (Jiangsu)
梅园新村纪念馆	Meiyuan Xincun Memorial Hall (Jiangsu)
梅竹山庄	Plum and Bamboo Villa (Zhejiang)
湄沱湖	Meituo Lake (Heilongjiang)
湄州湾	Meizhou Bay (Fujian)
湄洲妈祖庙	Meizhou Mazu Temple (Fujian)
媒婆	〈旧〉woman matchmaker
美岱召藏传佛教寺院	Meidaizhao Lamasery (Inner Mongolia)
美岱召庙会	Meidaizhao Temple Fair
美利楼	Murray House (Hong Kong)
美龄宫	〈旧〉Meiling Palace (Jiangsu)
美庐	Meilu Villas; Beauty Houses (Jiangxi)
美庐别墅	(of Mount Lushan) Meilu Villa
美女峰	Beauty Peak (Guizhou)
美人松苑	Changpai Scotch Pine Garden (Jilin)
美容茶	cosmetic tea; beauty tea
美食节	gourmet festival

门巴族	Menba ethnic group; Menba
焖锅酒	〈哈尼族〉menguo (stew pot) wine
勐仑热带植物园	Menglun Tropical Botanical Garden (Yunnan)
勐养湍蛙	〈动〉*Amolops mengyangensis*
猛洞河	Mengdong River (Hu'nan)
猛洞河景区	Mengdong River Scenic Area (Hu'nan)
猛虎啸天	(of Zhangjiajie) Tiger Roaring at the Sky
蒙古包	Mongolian yurts
蒙古刺绣	Mongolian embroidery
蒙古刀	Inner Mongolian knife
蒙古利亚人种	Mongoloid race
蒙古皮画	Inner Mongolian leather painting
蒙古人	Mongols
蒙古银器	Inner Mongolian silverware
蒙古语	Mongolian
蒙古族	Mongolian/Mongol ethnic group; Mongolians/Mongols
蒙山	Mengshan Mountain (Shandong)
孟达天池	Mengda Tianchi; Mengda Heavenly Lake (Qinghai)
孟达天池自然保护区	Mengda Tianchi Nature Reserve (Qinghai)
孟店民宅	Mengdian traditional dwelling houses (Shaanxi)
孟姜女庙	Meng Jiangnü Temple; Temple of Lady Meng Jiang (Hebei)
孟连溪蟾	〈动〉*Torrentophryne mengliana*; long-snout torrent frog
孟连细狭口蛙	〈动〉*Kalophrynus menglienicus*; Menglian narrow-mouthed frog
孟良梯	Meng Liang Ladder; Meng Liang Staircase (on the cliff of Qutang Gorges) (Hubei)
孟门山	Mengmen Mountain (Shaanxi)
孟门夜月	Mengmen Night Moon (Shanxi)
孟婆桥	→奈何[孟婆]桥
《孟子》	Mencius (a Confucian classic, by Mencius and his students in the mid-period of Warring States)

孟子	Mencius (372 -289 B.C., a Confucian representative in the Warring States Period)
梦笔生花	(of Mount Huangshan) Writing Brush as Dreamy Flower; Dreamy Flowery Writing Brush (a scenic spot)
梦幻世界	(of Swallow Cave) Fantasy Land
梦幻西游	(of an online game) Fantasy Westward Journey (Net Ease, 2001)
弥勒(佛)殿	Maitreya Hall (Inner Mongolia)
弥勒佛像	Maitreya Buddha
弥勒石像	Maitreya stone statue
弥里塘草场	Militang Pasture (Yunnan)
弥陀殿	Pavilion of Great Benevolence; Hall of Amitabha (Shanxi)
迷魂台	(of Zhangjiajie) Enchanting Stand
迷踪拳	Mizong Quan; Mizong Boxing
猕猴谷	Macaque Valley (He'nan)
猕猴桃	〈植〉*Actinidia chinensis*; Chinese gooseberry; kiwi fruit
糜子酒	〈满族〉millet wine
麋鹿	〈动〉*Elaphurus davidianus*; Père David's deer; elk
米阔鲁节	〈鄂温克族〉Mikuolu Festival (on the 22nd day of the 5th lunar month)
米拉日巴	Milareba (the most famous Buddhist practitioner in Tibet and the protagonist of many Tibetan folklores)
米埔湿地	Mai Po Wetland (Hong Kong)
米埔自然保护区	Mai Po Nature Reserve (Hong Kong)
汨罗江	Miluo River (Hu'nan)
汨罗山古墓群	Tombs (of Qu Yuan) in Miluo Mountain →屈原墓群
密云水库	Miyun Reservoir (Beijing)
密枝节	〈彝族〉Mizhi Festival
密祉花灯元宵灯会	Mizhi Lantern Festival (on the 15th day of the 1st lunar month)

密宗	〈佛〉Mi Zong (one of the sect of Buddhism)
蜜月	honeymoon (the sweet life of newlyweds)
眠云亭	(of Garden of Quiet Meditation) Pavilion with Towering Trees in Cloud
绵竹峡	Mianzhu Gorge (Hubei)
棉布婚	calico wedding (the 2nd anniversary of marriage)
免治肉	Mince (a traditional dish from Macao)
勉	Mien (self appellation of Yao ethnic group)
面壁亭	(of Garden of Harmony) Cliff-Facing Pavilion
面门为上	〈礼〉the seat facing the front door is the seat of honor
面人儿	dough figurine
苗岭	Miaoling Mountain (Guizhou)
苗年	〈苗族〉Miao's New Year
苗族	Miao ethnic group; Miao
苗族古村落	ancient villages of Miao ethnic group
苗族人	Miao; Miao people
苗族语	Miao language
妙道山	Miaodao Mountain (Anhui)
妙道山森林公园	Miaodao Mountain Forest Park (Anhui)
妙峰山景区	Miaofeng Mountain Scenic Area (Beijing)
妙利普明塔院	〈佛〉Miaoli Puming Temple (Jiangsu)
妙应寺	Miaoying Temple (Beijing) →白塔寺
妙应寺白塔	White Pagoda of Miaoying Temple (Beijing)
庙后山	Miaohou Mountain (Liaoning)
庙后山遗址	Miaohou Mountain Relics (Liaoning)
庙会	temple fair
庙街	Temple Street (Hong Kong)
庙南宽谷	Miaonan Wide Valley (Hubei)
民间传说	folk legend; folklore
民间习俗	folk custom; folkways
民俗	→民间习俗
民俗馆	Folk Custom Hall (Zhejiang)
民俗文化节	folk culture festival
民谣	〈乐〉folk rhyme/song; ballad

民族工业园	national industrial park
民族工艺品	national craft
民族文化宫	Cultural Palace of Nationalities (Beijing)
岷江	Minjiang River
岷江柏木	〈植〉*Cupressus chengiana*
岷山	Minshan Mountain (Gansu, Sichuan)
闵行体育公园	Minhang Sports Park (Shanghai)
闽方言	Min dialect; Fujian dialect
闽江三角洲	Minjiang River Delta
闽南	southern Fujian
闽南小九寨	Small Jiuzhai (Valley) in southern Fujian (Fujian)
闽南语	Hokkien; southern Fujian dialect
闽浙赣省委机关旧址	Former Site of the Fujian-Zhejiang-Jiangxi Provincial Party Committee (Jiangxi)
敏珠(竹)林寺	〈佛〉Mindroling Monastery (Tibet)
名洋湖生态庄园	Mingyang Lake Eco-Manor (Tianjin)
明长城	Ming Great Wall; Great Wall of the Ming Dynasty
明朝	Ming Dynasty (1368-1644)
明城墙遗址公园	Ming City Wall Ruins Park; City Wall Relics Park of Ming Dynasty (Beijing)
明道堂	(of Surging Waves Pavilion) Scholar Lecture Hall
明定陵	Dingling Mausoleum/Tombs of the Ming Dynasty (Beijing)
明鼓清碑	Drum of Ming Dynasty and Stele of Qing Dynasty (Jiangsu)
明故宫	Ming Palace; Ming Palace Museum (Jiangsu) → 南京故宫
明故宫遗址	Ming Palace Ruins; Ming Palace Museum (Jiangsu)
明故宫遗址公园	Ruins of the Ming Palace (Jiangsu)
明皇陵	Ming Tombs of Imperial Family (Anhui)
明镜湖	Mirror Lake (Jiangsu)
明末清初时期	late Ming and early Qing Dynasties (1600-1700)
明前龙井	〈茶〉pre-Qingming Longjing
明清城墙	City Walls of the Ming and Qing Dynasties

明清工艺美术馆	(of Imperial Palace) Art and Craft Exhibition Hall of Ming and Qing Dynasties
明清古街	Ancient Street of the Ming and Qing Dynasties
明清皇宫	Imperial Palace of the Ming and Qing Dynasties (Beijing)
明清皇家陵寝	Imperial Tombs of the Ming and Qing Dynasties
明清建筑	architecture of Ming and Qing Dynasties
明清商业街	Commercial Street of the Ming and Qing Dynasties (Jiangxi)
明清时期	Ming and Qing Dynasties (1368-1912)
明瑟搂	(of Lingering Garden) Pellucid Tower
明山水利景区	Mingshan Water Conservancy Scenic Area (Hubei)
明十三陵	Ming Tombs; Imperial Tombs of the Ming Dynasties (Beijing)
明仕河	Mingshi River (Guangxi)
明仕景区	Mingshi Scenic Area (Guangxi)
明誓血酒	〈古〉drinking blood wine to swear an oath (a traditional custom that people usually drink a bowl of liquor mixed with chicken blood after taking an oath when they want to make sworn brothers with each other)
明蜀王陵	Mausoleum of King Shu of the Ming Dynasty (Sichuan)
明显陵	Xianling Mausoleum of the Ming Dynasty (Hubei)
明孝陵	Ming Xiaoling Mausoleum; Xiaoling Tomb of Ming Dynasty (Jiangsu)
明永冰川	Mingyong Glacier (Yunnan)
明月岛	Mingyue Island; Bright Moon Island (Heilongjiang)
明月湖	mingyue lake; clear moon lake
明中都皇故城及皇陵石刻	Site of the Imperial City and Stone Sculptures at the Royal Tombs in the Middle Capital of the Ming Dynasty (Anhui)

明祖陵	Ming Ancestors Mausoleum; Ancestors' Mausoleum of the Ming Dynasty (Jiangsu)
鸣凤山	Mingfeng Mountain (Hubei)
冥婚	〈民俗〉(of a superstitious practice) ghost marriage; posthumous marriage (finding a spouse for the dead and holding a wedding ceremony)
冥钱	〈民俗〉hell money; paper money in the netherworld; joss paper
命子花	→膀胱豆
摸橘	〈婚〉(of the bride in the wedding) moju; to touch the orange in a child's hand (meaning the new couple will have many children and grandchildren, as there are so many seeds (籽、子) in the orange)
摹拓品	rubbing
模印砖画	moulded relief brick sculpture
膜拜	〈礼〉to prostrate oneself in worship; to pay homage to
摩诃迦叶	〈佛〉Mahakasyapa (one of the ten disciples of the Buddha, best-known for his buddhist recluse/ ascetism)
摩罗街	Lascar Row (an antiques street in Hong Kong)
摩尼殿	Hall of Manichaean (Hebei)
摩尼石刻	Mani Stone Inscription (Qinghai)
摩士公园	Morse Park (Hong Kong)
摩梭人	Mosuo People; Mosuo
摩天峰	(of Zhangjiajie) Skyscraping Peak
摩天岭	motian (skyscraping) ridge
摩西会堂	Ohel Moshe Synagogue (Shanghai)
摩崖石刻	inscriptions on cliffs
磨针井	(of Mount Wudang) Needle Grinding Well
魔术迷幻宫	(of Wuqiao Acrobatics World) Palace of Fascinated Magic
魔芋豆腐	konjac tofu

抹黑节	〈锡伯族〉Smearing Black Festival (on the 16th day of the 1st lunar month)
末角	〈戏〉(of Beijing Opera role) role of Mo (middle-aged male character)
莫愁湖	Mochou Lake (Jiangsu)
莫尔寺遗址	〈佛〉Mor Temple Site/Vestige (Xinjiang)
莫干山	Mogan Mountain (Zhejiang)
莫高窟	Mogao Caves; Mogao Grottoes (Gansu)
莫拉布山	Molabu Mountain (Heilongjiang)
莫力庙水库	Molimiao Reservoir (Inner Mongolia)
莫氏肥螈	〈动〉*Pachytriton moi*; Mo's stout newt
墨兰	〈植〉*Cymbidium sinense*; Chinese cymbidium
墨脱棘蛙	〈动〉*Nanorana medogensis*; Medog spiny frog
墨脱舌突蛙	〈动〉*Liurana medogensis*; Medog tongue frog
墨脱湍蛙	〈动〉*Amolops medogensis*
墨脱异角蟾	〈动〉*Xenophrys medogenis*; Medog horned toad
墨鱼	→乌贼
磨盘峰	(of Mount Huangshan) Mopan Peak
磨盘山森林公园	Mopan Mountain Forest Park (Yunnan)
磨秋节	〈哈尼族〉Moqiu Festival; Mill-Swing Festival (in Mid-May) →五月年
磨子沟景区	Mozi (millstone) Ditch Scenic Area (Hubei)
牟尼沟景区	Mouni Valley Scenic Area (Sichuan)
牟氏庄园	Manor of Mou Family (Shandong)
母恩池	Muen Pool; Mother's Kindness Pool (Liaoning)
母子峰	(of Zhangjiajie) Peaks of Mother and Child
牡丹	〈植〉*Paeonia suffruticosa*; mudan
牡丹峰自然保护区	Mudanfeng Natural Reserve (Heilongjiang)
牡丹江	Mudan River (Heilongjiang)
《牡丹亭》	*Peony Pavilion*; *Mudan Pavilion* (a legend kunqu opera, by Tang Xianzu in the Ming Dynasty)
牡丹文化节	peony cultural festival
牡蛎滩	Oyster Bank; Oyster Beach (ancient coastal relics) (Tianjin)

亩	mu (a unit of area for about 0.165 acres)
木雕	Wooden Carving
木渎古镇	Mudu Ancient Town (Jiangsu)
木府	Mufu Mansion; Chieftain Mu's Mansion (Yunnan)
木格措	Mugecuo Lake (Sichuan) →野人海
木婚	wood wedding (the 5th anniversary of marriage)
木兰	〈植〉*Magnolia liliflora*; magnolia
木兰祠[庙]	Temple of Hua Mulan (He'nan)
木兰玫瑰园	Mulan Rose Garden (Hubei)
木兰天池	Mulan Heaven Pool (Hubei)
木兰天池景区	Mulan Heaven Pool Scenic Area (Hubei)
木兰湾	Mulan Bay (Hai'nan)
木兰围场	Mulan Hunting Ground (Hebei)
木里齿突蟾	〈动〉*Scutiger muliensis*
木林子自然保护区	Mulinzi Nature Reserve (Hubei)
木龙湖	Mulong Lake; Wooden Dragon Lake (Guangxi)
木牛流马	wooden ox and gliding horse (a vehicle invented by Zhuge Liang, used to transport material and food for his troop)
木牌坊	Wooden Memorial Archway (Zhejiang)
木琴	〈乐〉xylophone
木它梅玛山	Mutameima Mountain (Qinghai)
木塔寺	Wooden Pagoda Temple (Shaanxi, Gansu)
木鱼	〈乐〉wooden fish; wooden knocker (a percussion instrument made of a hollow wooden block, originally used by Buddhist priests to beat rhythm when chanting scriptures)
木鱼石	muyu rock (a precious hollow ore containing microelements, used to make tea sets, drinking utensils and so on)
木扎尔特冰川	Muzart Glacier (Xinjiang)
木扎尔特河谷	Muzart River Valley (Xinjiang)
木扎提河	Muzati River (Xinjiang)

目犍连	〈佛〉Maudgalyayana (one of the ten disciples of the Buddha, best-known for his super power)
目瑙[脑]纵歌(节)	〈景颇族〉Munao Dance and Song Festival (on the 15th day of the 1st lunar month)
目容端	〈古〉Murongduan (to look steadily forward with concentration when observing things) (a saying from Book of Rites) →君子九容
仫佬族	Mulao ethnic group; Mulao
沐浴节	〈藏族〉Bathing Festival; Showering Festival (within the first ten-day period of the 7th month according to Tibetan calendar)
牧马滩	Herd Horse Grassland (Gansu)
牧童节	〈布依族〉Shepherd Boy Festival (on the 8th day of the 4th lunar month)
墓穴安放法	〈丧〉to put the deceased in an appropriate place
墓葬	〈丧〉tomb burial
睦南道	Munan Road (Tianjin)
慕士塔格峰	Muztagh Ata; Muztag Peak (Xinjiang)
慕田峪	Mutianyu Section (Beijing)
慕田峪长城	Mutianyu Great Wall (Beijing)
穆陵关	(of the Great Wall of Qi) Muling Guan; Muling Pass (Shandong)
穆斯林广场	〈回族〉Muslim Square (Hai'nan)

N

那达慕大会	〈蒙古族〉Nadam Fair; Naadam (on the 4th day of the 6th lunar month) →那达慕节
那达慕节	〈蒙古族〉Nadam Festival (a traditional entertainment festival) →那达慕大会
那拉提草原	Nalati/Narati Grassland (Xinjiang)
那拉提山	Nalati/Narati Mountain (Xinjiang)
纳采	〈婚〉matchmaker's proposal; to propose a marriage (with a gift given to the girl's family at time of betrothal) →六礼
纳顿节	〈土族〉Nadun Festival (from the 12th day of the 7th lunar month to the 15th day of the 9th lunar month)
纳吉	〈婚〉exchange of birthdays and family tree; to propose an engagement upon an appropriateness and luck divination (according to the birthdays of the two persons involved) →六礼
纳楼长官司署	〈古〉Nalou Justice Department of Senior Officer (Yunnan)
纳木错	Namtso Lake (the third largest salt water lake in China) (Tibet)
纳吾肉孜节	→诺鲁孜节
纳西古乐	Naxi ancient music
纳西文化	Naxi culture
纳西族	Naxi ethnic group; Naxi

纳征	〈婚〉betrothal gifts presentation; to present betrothal gifts to the bride's family →六礼
娜允古城	Nayun Ancient Town (Yunnan)
乃琼寺	Nechung Monastery (Tibet)
奶酒	milk wine
奶诺戈汝冰川	→明永冰川
奈何[孟婆]桥	(of Taoism and folk legend) Naihe Bridge (the bridge to Hell); Abyss Bridge; Bridge of Helplessness
南安寺塔	Nanan Temple Pagoda (Hebei)
南岸嘴	South Bank Peninsula (Hubei)
南澳岛	Nan'ao Island (South China Sea)
南北朝	Southern and Northern Dynasties (420-589)
南北格拉球山	southern and northern Gelaqiu Mountain (Heilongjiang)
南北吉祥寺	North and South Jixiang (auspicious) Temple (Shanxi)
南北孔氏家庙	Ancestral Temples for the Confucius Family
南禅寺大殿	Main Hall of Nanchan Temple (Shanxi)
南昌八一起义纪念馆	Nanchang August 1st Memorial Hall (Jiangxi)
南长城	South-Great Wall (Miao frontier wall) (Hu'nan)
南朝石刻	stone carving/sculpture of the Southern Dynasties
南川木菠萝	〈植〉*Artocarpus nanchuanensis*; Nanchuan jackfruit
南大港湿地	Nandagang Wetland (Hebei)
南大屿郊野公园	Lantau South Country Park (Hong Kong)
南戴河旅游度假区	Nandai River Tourism Resort (Hebei)
南方澳渔港	Nanfang'ao Fishing Port (Taiwan)
南方丝绸之路	Southern Silk Road; The Silk Road in the Southeast China
南风	(of mahjong) South Wind
南宫寺	Nangong Temple (Zhejiang)

南瓜节	〈毛南族〉Pumpkin Festival (on the 9th day of the 9th lunar month)
南关清真寺	〈伊斯兰〉Nanguan Mosque
南蛤蟆塘旅游景区	Nanhamotang Scenic Area (Heilongjiang)
南海	South China Sea
南海禅寺	Nanhai-Buddhist Temple (the largest Buddhist temple in China) (He'nan)
南海公园	Nanhai Park (Inner Mongolia)
南海观音	〈佛〉South China Sea Guanyin (Avalokitesvara Bodhisattva) (Zhejiang, Guangdong)
南海观音文化苑	Nanhai Guanyin Culture Garden (Guangdong)
南海海域	South China Sea area
南海环礁	South China Sea atoll
南海龙王	〈神话〉Dragon King of South China Sea
南海圣境	South China Sea Holyland (Putuo Mountain)
南湖公园	south lake park
南湖柳叶菜	〈植〉*Epilobium nankotaizanense*
南湖山椒鱼	〈动〉*Hynobius glacialis*
南湖书院	〈古〉Nanhu (South Lake) Academy (Anhui)
南湖小鲵	〈动〉*Hynobius glacialis*; Nanhu salamander
南汇嘴观海公园	Nanhuizui (Beach) Park (Shanghai)
南迦巴瓦峰	Namcha Barwa Peak (Tibet)
南江齿蟾	〈动〉*Oreolalax nanjianggensis*
南江无耳蟾	〈动〉*Atympanophrys nankiangensis*
南江峡谷	Nanjiang Canyon (Guizhou)
南街村文化园	Nanjie Village Cultural Park (He'nan)
南津关大峡谷景区	Nanjinguan Grand Valley Scenic Resort (Hubei)
南京大屠杀死难者国家公祭日	National Memorial Day for Nanjing Massacre Victims (the 13th December)
南京都市圈	Nanjing Metropolitan Coordinating Region
南京夫子庙	Nanjing Confucius Temple (Jiangsu)
南京故宫	Forbidden City of Nanjing; Nanjing Palace Museum (Jiangsu) →明故宫
南京江东门纪念馆	→侵华日军南京大屠杀遇难同胞纪念馆

南京路步行街	Nanjing Road Walkway; Nanjing Road Pedestrian Street (Shanghai)
南京明城墙	Nanjing City Wall (Jiangsu)
南京南朝陵墓石刻	Stone Carvings/Sculptures at Mausoleums of the Southern Dynasties in Nanjing (Jiangsu)
南京市博物馆	Nanjing Municipal Museum (Jiangsu)
南京西路	West Nanjing Road (Shanghai)
南京中华门	Nanjing Zhonghua Gate; China Gate of Nanjing
南京总统府	Nanjing Presidential Palace (Jiangsu)
南开区烈士陵园	Martyrs Cemetery in Nankai District (Tianjin)
南开学校旧址	Site of Nankai School (Tianjin)
南龛摩崖造像	〈佛〉Southern Niche Cliffside Images (Sichuan)
南丽湖	Nanli Lake (Hai'nan)
南丽湖旅游区	Nanli Lake tourism area (Hai'nan)
南莲园池	Nan Lian Garden (Hong Kong)
南锣鼓巷	South Luogu Lane (Beijing snack pedestrian street) (Beijing)
南锣鼓巷戏剧节	Nanluoguxiang Performance Arts Festival
南明山	Nanming Mountain (Zhejiang)
南宁孔庙	Nanning Confucian Temple (Guangxi)
南宁南湖公园	Nanning Nanhu Park; Nanning South Lake Park (Guangxi)
南盘江	Nanpan River
南屏村	Nanping Village (Anhui)
南屏山	Nanping Mountain (Zhejiang)
南屏晚钟	(of West Lake) Evening Bell at Nanping Hill
南浦大桥	Nanpu Bridge (Shanghai)
南普陀寺	Nanputuo Temple; South Putuo Temple (Fujian)
南(方)拳	〈武术〉Nan Quan; Southern Style Boxing
南沙群岛	(of South China Sea) Nansha Islands
南沙群岛岛链	Nansha Island chain
南山积雪	(of Chengde Mountain Resort) Snow-Capped South Hills
南山路艺术休闲特色街	Nanshan Road Arts and Leisure Street (Zhejiang)

南山摩崖造像	Nanshan Cliffside Statue (Zhejiang)
南山寿翁	God of Longevity on South Mountain (Jiangsu)
南山文化旅游区	Nanshan Culture Tourism Zone (Hai'nan)
南山竹海	South Mountain Bamboo Ocean (Jiangsu)
南生围	Nam Sang Wai (Hong Kong)
南石窟寺	Southern Grottoes Temple (Gansu)
南市食品街和旅馆街	Nanshi Food Street and Hotel Street (Tianjin)
南寺唐塔	South Temple Pagoda of the Tang Dynasty (Shaanxi)
南宋	Southern Song Dynasty (1127–1279)
南宋皇城遗址	Site of the Imperial City of Southern Song Dynasty (Zhejiang)
南唐	Southern Tang Dynasty (A.D. 937–975)
南唐二陵	Two Mausoleums of the Southern Tang Dynasty; Two Tombs of Southern Tang (Li Bian's Qinling Mausoleum and Li Jing's Shunling Mausoleum) (Jiangsu)
南堂岛	Tung Lung Island (Hong Kong) →东龙洲
南天门	1〈神话〉South-Sky Gate; South Gate of Heaven 2(of Mount Taishan and Wudang) Heavenly Southern Gate
南天一柱	(of Zhangjiajie) South Heaven Pillar; Column of Southern Sky
南天竺寺	Nam Tin Chuk Temple (Hong Kong)
南坨	→驼梁
南湾猴岛	Nanwan Monkey Island; Monkey Island (the only nature reserve for macaque monkeys in the world) (Hai'nan)
南湾森林公园	Nanwan Forest Park (He'nan)
南无阿弥陀佛	Namo Amituofo; Namo Amita Buddha
南浔史馆	Nanxun Museum (Zhejiang)
南浔丝业会馆	Nanxun Silk Assembly Hall (Zhejiang)
南丫岛	Lamma Island (Hong Kong)
南岩宫	(of Mount Wudang) South Cliff Palace (Wudang Sect temple of the Chinese taoist)

南岩景区	(of Mount Wudang) South Cliff Scenic Area
南岩寺景区	Nanyan Temple Scenic Area (Jiangxi)
南燕湾	Nanyan Bay (Hai'nan)
南阳公主祠	(of Fuqing Temple) Nanyang Princess Memorial Hall; Memorial Hall of Princess Nanyang
南阳角梳	Nanyang horn comb
南伊诺勒切克冰川	South Inilchek Glacier (Xinjiang)
南岳大庙	Grand Temple of South Hengshan (Hu'nan)
南岳衡山	Southern Mount Hengshan; Southern Hengshan Mountain (as the South One of the Five Sacred Mountains in China) (Hu'nan)
南越[粤]国	Nanyue Kingdom (204 -111 B.C.)
南越国宫署遗址	Site of Nanyue Kingdom Palace (Guangdong)
南越国遗址	Site of Nanyue Kingdom (Guangdong)
南越文化	Nanyue culture
南越文王墓	Tomb of King Wen of the Nanyue Kingdom (Guangdong)
南诏(国)	Nanzhao Kingdom (738- 937) (Yunnan)
南宗尼姑寺	Nanzong (Buddhist) Nunnery (Qinghai)
南宗扎寺	Nanzongzha Temple (Qinghai)
南佐遗址	Nanzuo Ruins (of large buildings in the Neolithic Age) (Gansu)
难老泉亭	Longevity Spring Pavilion (Shanxi)
楠木	〈植〉*Phoebe zhennan*; nanmu
楠溪江景区	Nanxi River Scenic Area (Zhejiang)
囊花马兜铃	〈植〉*Aristolochia utriformis*
闹洞房	〈婚〉rough horseplay at weddings; to tease the bride on a wedding night
闹红一舸	(of Garden of Quiet Meditation) Boat-shaped Pavilion in Blooming Lotuses
闹羊花	〈中药〉*Flos Rhododendri Mollis*; Chinese azalea
哪吒洞	Nezha Cave (Sichuan)
哪吒庙	Na Tcha Temple (Macao)
哪吒行宫	Nezha Palace (Sichuan)

内画鼻烟壶	inside-painted snuff bottle
内家拳	〈武术〉Internal Style Boxing
内金水桥	(of Imperial Palace) Inner Golden Water Bridge
内蒙古地毯	Inner Mongolian carpet
内蒙古高原	Inner Mongolian Plateau
内蒙亚菊	〈植〉*Ajania alabasica*; Inner Mongolia chrysanthemum
内明堂	〈风水〉inside-door space
内三关	Three Passes of the Inner Great Wall (Juyong Pass, Zijing Pass and Daoma Pass in Hebei)
内五龙桥	(of Nanjing Ming Palace) Inner Five-Dragon Bridge
嫩江	Nenjiang River (Heilongjiang)
嫩江旅游度假村	Nengjiang River Tourism Resort (Jilin)
能源植物园	Energy Plant Garden (Yunnan)
尼勒克喇嘛庙[寺]	Nileke Lamasery (Xinjiang)
尼山古代建筑群	Nishan Ancient Constructions (Shandong)
尼乌节	〈珞巴族〉Niwu Festival (ceremony for starting sowing)
尼雅河	Niya River (Xinjiang)
尼雅遗址	Niya Ruins (Jingjue Kingdom in the Han and Jin Dynasties) (Xinjiang)
泥凼石林	Nidang Stone Forest (Guizhou)
泥凼石林景区	Nidang Stone Forest Scenic Attraction (Guizhou)
泥河湾遗址	Nihewan Site (of early human fossils) (Hebei)
泥鳅	〈动〉*Misgurnus anguillicaudatus*; loach
泥人	clay figurine; clay figure
泥人王村	Niren (clayfigurine) Wang Village (Hubei)
泥人张	Niren (clay figurine) Zhang
泥人制作	clay figurine making
年(夜)饭	〈民俗〉New Year's Eve dinner →团圆饭
年画	New Year painting/picture
年兽	〈神话〉monster Nian; Nian (the evil beast in ancient Han myths and legends)

年终大扫除	year-end (household) cleaning
念八峡	Nianba Gorge (Guangxi)
念青唐古拉山(脉)	Mount Nyainqen Tanglha; Nyenchen Tanglha Mountains/Range (Tibet)
娘子洞景区	Niangzi Cave Scenic Area (Hubei)
娘子关	Niangziguan Pass (Shanxi)
鸟巢	Bird's Nest (the main stadium for the 2008 Olympic Games) (Beijing) →国家体育场
鸟岛	Bird Island (Qinghai)
鸟鸣林	bird-singing forest
聂耳墓	Tomb of Nie Er (Yunnan)
宁都起义指挥部旧址	Site of the Ningdu Uprising Headquarters (Jiangxi)
宁金抗沙峰	Ningjin Kangsha Peak (Tibet)
宁静斋	(of Chengde Mountain Resort) House of Serenity Tranquility
宁陕齿突蟾	〈动〉*Scutiger ningshanensis*; Ningshan alpine toad
宁寿宫	(of Imperial Palace) Palace of Tranquility and Longevity
宁寿宫花园	(of Imperial Palace) Garden of the Palace of Tranquility and Longevity
宁寿门	(of Imperial Palace) Gate of Tranquility and Longevity
宁远文庙	Ningyuan Confucius Temple (Hu'nan)
凝香亭	(of Imperial Palace) Pavilion of Concentrated Fragrance
拧酒令儿	〈古〉to play a drinker's wager game
牛池湾公园	Ngau Chi Wan Park (Hong Kong)
牛房仓库	Ox Warehouse (art exhibition) (Macao)
牛肝马肺峡	Niugan Mafei Gorge; Ox Liver and Horse Lung Gorge (Hubei)
牛河梁文化遗址	Niuheliang Cultural Site; Niuheliang Archaeological Site (Liaoning)

牛魂[王]节	Ox Soul Festival (a traditional festival of the Zhuang, Dong, Mulao and Gelao ethnic groups mainly on the 8th day of the 4th lunar month)
牛角酒	〈苗族〉ox horn wine
牛角兰	〈植〉*Ceratostylis Hainanensis*; Hai'nan ceratostylis
牛街礼拜[清真]寺	Niujie Mosque (Beijing)
牛(王)节	〈仡佬族〉Ox Festival (on the 1st day of the 10th lunar month)
牛郎	〈神话〉(of a love legend) Niulang; Cowboy; Cowherd
牛魔王	〈神话〉Bull Demon King (a character in Journey to the West)
牛年	Year of the Ox (one of the 12 Zodiac Years)
牛棚艺术村	Cattle Depot Artist Village (Hong Kong)
牛首山	Niushou (Ox Head) Mountain (Jiangsu)
牛头碑	Cow Head Stele (source of Yellow River) (Qinghai)
牛膝草	〈植〉*Hyssopus officinalis*; cowslip
牛心寺	Niuxin (Bull Heart) Temple (Sichuan)
扭秧歌	〈舞〉to do the Yangko Dance
农具会	〈纳西族〉Farm Tool Fair (on the 20th day of the 1st lunar month)
农历	traditional Chinese calendar; lunar calendar; Chinese calendar
农历年	lunar (calendar) year
农历新年	Chinese new year; Chinese lunar new year; lunar new year
农历月(份)	lunar month
农民艺术画画廊	farmer painting gallery
农特产	agricultural speciality
农田景观旅游	agricultural landscape tourism
弄岗狭口蛙	〈动〉*Kaloula nonggangensis*; Nonggang narrow-mouthed frog
弄岗自然保护区	Nonggang Nature Reserve (Guangxi)
怒江大峡谷	Nujiang Grand Canyon; Grand Canyon of Nujiang River (Yunnan)

怒族	Nu ethnic group; Nu
怒族鲜花节	Nu Flower Festival (on the 15th day of the 3rd lunar month)
女儿会	〈土家族〉Lady Party; Girls' Fair (on the 12th day of the 7th lunar month)
女儿节	Daughter' Festival (on the 3rd day of the 3rd lunar month, and on the 7th day of the 7th lunar month, etc.)
女人岛	Island of Women (Fujian) →大嶝岛
女人街	women's street; lady street
女娲	〈神话〉Nüwa (the Goddess of Creation in ancient Chinese mythology); Goddess of Sky-Patching
女娲补天	〈神话〉Goddess Nüwa mending/patching the sky
女娲庙	Nüwa temple
女娲山景区	Nüwa Mountain Scenic Spot (Hubei, Shaanxi)
女真族酒宴	Jurchen banquet
暖溜暄波	(of Chengde Mountain Resort) Hot Spring with Ripples and Mist Spray
傩舞	〈舞〉Nuo Dance (for worshiping gods, driving away pestilences and epidemics, and praying for peace)
傩[鬼]戏	〈戏〉Nuo Opera
傩戏面具	Nuo Opera mask
诺劳孜节	〈柯尔克孜族〉Nuolaozi Festival (traditional festivities like those in the Spring Festival for Han Nationality) (in March)
诺鲁孜节	Day of Nowruz (a traditional festival of the Uygur, Kazak, Uzbek and Taijik ethnic groups)
诺敏风城	Nuomin Wind City (Xinjiang) →诺敏魔鬼城
诺敏魔鬼城	Nuomin Ghost City (Xinjiang) →诺敏风城
诺日朗瀑布	(of Jiuzhai Valley) Nuorilang Waterfall
诺日朗群海	(of Jiuzhai Valley) Nuorilang Group Lakes

O

欧罗巴世界乐园　　Europa World Amusement Park (Shanghai)
耦[涉]园　　　　　Ouyuan Garden; Garden of Couple's Retreat (Jiangsu)

P

啪嘎节	〈瑶族〉Paga Festival (on the 2nd day of the 10th lunar month)
爬坡节	〈苗族〉Papo Festival; Climbing Day (on the 19th day of the 6th lunar month)
爬山节	〈苗族〉Mountain-Climbing Festival
帕拉鲁布	Palalumpuk (Tibet)
帕米尔高原	Pamir Plateau; Pamirs of China (Xinjiang)
排云殿	(of Summer Palace) Hall of Dispelling Clouds
排云亭	(of Mount Huangshan) Cloud Dispelling Pavilion
牌匾	plaque; horizontal inscribed board
牌坊	memorial archway
牌九	(of a folk game) pai gow; Chinese domino
牌楼门	pailou gate; decorated archway
牌位	memorial tablets
潘集湖湿地公园	Panji Lake Wetland Park (Hubei)
潘家口水库	Panjiakou Reservoir (Hebei)
潘家园旧货市场	Panjiayuan Antique Market (Beijing)
潘家园收藏市场	Panjiayuan Collection Market (Beijing)
攀龙书院	〈古〉Panlong Academy (Jiangxi)
盘古村自然公园	Pangu Village Nature Park (Hebei)
盘谷蟾蜍	〈动〉*Bufo bankorensis*; bankor toad
盘锦红海滩	Panjin Red Beach (Liaoning)
盘龙城遗址	Site of Panlong City (Hubei)
盘[蟠]门	Panmen Gate (Jiangsu)
盘山景区	Panshan Mountain Scenic Area (Tianjin)
盘腿跌	〈武术〉Inside crescent falling kick

蟠门	→盘[蟠]门
膀胱豆	〈植〉*Coluteadelavayi*; dalavay bladdersenna
抛绣球	〈婚〉to throw an embroidered ball (for choosing a husband)
跑马地[快活谷]马场	Happy Valley Racecourse (Hong Kong)
醅酒	〈普米族〉peijiu (unfiltered liquor)
沛县汉城[宫]	Han City in Peixian County; Han Palace in Peixian County (Jiangsu)
盆景	potted landscape; bonsai; miniature trees and rockery
盆景池	(of Huanglong Scenic Area) Bonsai Pond; Bonsai Pool
盆景滩[海]	(of Jiuzhai Valley) Bonsai Shoal; Bonsai beach
盆景园	penjing garden; bonsai garden
彭福公园	Penfold Park (Hong Kong)
彭家垴革命烈士纪念园	Pengjianao Revolutionary Martyrs Memorial Cemetery (Hubei)
彭刘杨三烈士亭	Peng Liu Yang Three Martyrs Pavilion (Hubei)
蓬岛瑶台	(of Yuanming Garden) Immortal Abode on Penglai Island
蓬莱岛	1(of a legend) Penglai Island 2(of Summer Palace) Penglai Isle
蓬莱阁	Penglai Pavilion (Shandong)
蓬莱山	(of Chinese legend) Penglai Mountain (referring to fairyland where the immortals live)
蓬莱水城	Penglai Water City (Shandong)
澎湖国家景区	Penghu Lake National Scenic Area
澎湖列[群]岛	Penghu Islands; Penghu Archipelago
澎湖天后宫	Penghu Thean Hou Temple
披麻戴孝	〈丧〉to wear mourning clothes; to be dressed in the coarse hempen cloth of mourning; to put on mourning apparel
披针耳蕨	〈植〉*Polystichum deltodon*
劈挂拳	〈武术〉Pigua Boxing

劈拳	〈武术〉Hammer fist; Chopping fist
劈山救母	1(of a legend)Hewing the Mountain to Rescue Mother →宝莲灯 2 (of Zhangjiajie) Cleaving the Mountain to Save the Holy Mother
劈掌	Chopping palm
皮革婚	leather wedding (the 3rd anniversary of marriage)
皮影(戏)	〈戏〉Shadow Play (leather-silhouette show)
枇杷	〈植〉*Eriobotrya japonica*; loquat
枇杷园	(of Humble Administrator's Garden) Loquat Garden
毗卢寺	〈佛〉Pilu Temple (Jiangsu)
啤酒泉	beer fountain
琵琶	〈乐〉pipa (a four-stringed plucked string instrument with a fretted fingerboard); Chinese lute/banjo
《琵琶记》	*Story of Pipa* (by Gaoming in Yuan Dynasty)
貔貅	Pixiu (a fierce beast); brave troop (used for exorcising evil spirits)
偏观寺山	Pianguan Temple Mountain (Hubei)
偏岩古镇	Pianyan Ancient Town (Chongqing)
片马湍蛙	〈动〉*Amolops bellulus*; Pianma torrent frog
撇身捶	〈武术〉(of Tai Chi) Flank attack
聘礼	〈婚〉betrothal present; betrothal gift; bride price
聘书	〈婚〉betrothal letter; engagement letter →三书
平安古堡	→安平[平安]古堡
平城遗址	Site of Pingcheng City (Shanxi)
平顶山惨案遗址	Site of Pingdingshan Massacre (Liaoning)
平顶山景区	Pingdingshan Scenic Area (He'nan)
平湖秋月	(of West Lake) Autumn Moon on/over Calm Lake; Moon over the Peaceful Lake in Autumn
平江起义旧址	Site of Pingjiang Uprising (Hu'nan)
平粮台古城遗址	Ancient City Site at Pingliangtai (He'nan)
平罗峡	Pingluo Gorge (Hubei)

平山温泉	Pingshan Hot Spring (Hebei)
平武齿突蟾	〈动〉*Scutiger pingwuensis*; Pingwu alpine toad
平型关	(of inner Great Wall) Pingxingguan Pass (Shanxi)
平遥城墙	Pingyao City Wall (Shanxi)
平遥古城	Pingyao Ancient City (Shanxi)
平遥碗团[托]	Pingyao Wantuan (a traditional pasta snack on special plate)
评话	〈戏〉pinghua (storytelling in a local dialect)
评剧	〈戏〉Pingju Opera; Pingju (a local opera of north and northeast China)
评[说]书	pingshu (story-telling)
坪輋天后古庙	Tin Hau Ancient Temple in Pingshe (Hong Kong)
坪洲岛	Peng Chau Island (Hong Kong)
屏山文物径	Ping Shan Heritage Trail (Hong Kong)
屏山杨侯古庙	Pingshan Yeung Hau Temple; Pingshan Duke Yang Ancient Temple (Hong Kong)
萍香泭	(of Chengde Mountain Resort) Bank of Duckweed Fragrance
坡鹿	〈动〉*Rucervus eldii*; Eld's deer
泼水节	Water-Splashing Festival; Water-Sprinkling Festival (from the 13th to 15th day of April, typically celebrated by Dai people and other ethnic groups)
婆罗科努山	Borohoro Mountain (Xinjiang)
鄱阳湖	Poyang Lake (the largest fresh lake in China) (Jiangxi)
珀普短腿蟾	〈动〉*Brachytasophrys popei*; bopu short-leg toad
仆步	〈武术〉Crouch stance; Crouch step; Half-squat stance
仆步穿掌	〈武术〉Threading palm in crouch stance/step
仆步抡拍	〈武术〉Circle arms and slap floor in crouch stance/step
菩提禅院	Pou Tai Temple (Macao)

菩提大佛	Bodhi Buddha
菩提岛	Bodhi Islet (Hebei) →石臼[十九]坨
菩提寺	〈佛〉Bodhi Monastery (He'nan)
葡萄沟	Grape Valley (Xinjiang)
蒲剧	〈戏〉Puju Opera
蒲类海	〈古〉Pulei Sea (Xinjiang) →巴里坤湖
蒲台岛	Po Toi Island (Hong Kong)
蒲峪路故城遗址	Old City Site on Puyu Road (Heilongjiang)
蒲州古城	Puzhou Ancient Town (Shanxi)
普达措国家公园	Potatso National Park (Yunnan)
普达措森林公园	Potatso Forest Park (Yunnan)
普洱景迈山古茶园	Ancient Tea Garden on Jingmai Mountain in Pu'er (Yunnan)
普光明寺	Puguangming Temple (Hong Kong)
普哈丁墓	Tomb of Puhaddin (Jiangsu)
普济寺	(of Mount Putuo) Puji Temple
普米族	Pumi ethnic group; Pumi
普氏原羚	〈动〉*Procapra przewalskii*; Przewalski's gazelle
普通朱雀	〈动〉*Carpodacus erythrinus*; rosefinch
普陀鹅耳枥	〈植〉*Carpinus putoensis*; Putuo hornbeam
普陀山	〈佛〉Putuo Mountain (Zhejiang)
普陀山景区	Putuo Mountain Scenic Area (Zhejiang)
普陀石林	Putuo Stone Forest (Guangxi)
普陀宗乘之庙	Putuo Zongcheng Temple; Temple of Potaraka Doctrine (Hebei) →小布达拉宫
普贤菩萨	〈佛〉Samantabhadra
普雄齿蟾	〈动〉*Oreolalax puxiongensis*; Puxiong toothed toad
普雄原鲵	〈动〉*Protohynobius puxiongensis*; Puxiong salamander
普照寺	(of Mount Taishan) Puzhao Temple; Universal Light Temple
普者黑湖	Puzhehei Lake (Yunnan)
普者黑民族旅游景区	Puzhehei Ethnic Tourism Resort (Yunnan)

溥仪	Puyi (1906-1967, the last emperor in the Qing Dynasty)
瀑布寺	waterfall temple
瀑布钟	Waterfall Clock (Shanghai)

Q

七宝古镇	Qibao Ancient Town (Shanghai)
七宝老街	Shippo Ancient Street (Shanghai)
七宝皮影戏	Qibao Shadow Play
七佛潭	Seven-Buddha Pool (Zhejiang)
七孔桥	Seven-Arch Bridge (Beijing)
七巧板	tangram (a Chinese puzzle consisting of a square divided into seven pieces that must be arranged to match particular designs)
七[乞]巧节	Qiqiao Festival; Begging-for-Dexterity Festival (on the 7th day of the 7th lunar month) →七夕(节)
七曲山	Mount Qiqu; Qiqu Mountain (Sichuan)
七色海	Seven-Color Sea (Sichuan)
七省通衢	thoroughfare of seven provinces; major juncture of seven provinces (especially referring to Lanxi of Zhejiang Province)
七圣宫古庙	Seven Sage Palace Ancient Temple (Hong Kong)
七夕(节)	Qixi Festival; Double Seventh Festival; Chinese Valentine's Day (on the 7th day of the 7th lunar month) →七[乞]巧节
七夕桥	(of legend) Qixi Bridge (across the Milky Way where the Cowherd and Weaver met on the 7th evening of the 7th lunar month)
七夕情人节	Chinese Valentine's Day →七夕(节)
七仙[指]岭	Qixian Ridge (Hai'nan)
七仙女	(of legend) Seven Fairies
七星古墓群	Seven-Star Ancient Tomb Group (Guangxi)

七星湖沙漠生态区	Seven-Star Lake Eco-Zone (Inner Mongolia)
七星石	(of Temple of Heaven) Seven-Star Stones
七星潭	Chisingtan; Seven-Star Pond (Taiwan)
七星岩	Seven-Star Crags; Seven-Star Hill (Guangdong)
七星燕窝岭	Seven-Star Bird's Nest Ridge (Hai'nan)
七星寨景区	Qixingzhai Scenic Area (Hubei)
七雄混战	〈古〉(of Warring States) Rebellion of the Seven Princes
七一冰川	Qiyi Glacier; July 1st Glacier (Gansu)
七月半	Festival in July and A Half →鬼节，中元节
七月[骡马]会	〈纳西族〉Mule and Horse Fair in July; July Fair
七指岭	→七仙[指]岭
七子花	〈植〉*Heptacodium miconioides*; seven-son flower
栖兰森林游乐区	Qilan Forest Recreation Area (Taiwan)
栖霞山	Qixia Mountain (Jiangsu)
栖真寺	Qizhen Temple (Zhejiang)
戚城文化遗传公园	Qicheng Cultural Relics Park (He'nan)
戚城遗址	Site of Qicheng City (He'nan)
戚继光石雕	Qi Jiguang stone statue
漆器艺术馆	Museum of Lacquer Art (Shanxi)
齐长城遗址	Remains Great Wall of Qi State (Shandong)
齐国	Qi State (1044 –221 B.C.)
齐家坪遗址	Qijiaping Culture Site (of the Late Neolithic Age) (Gansu)
齐家文化	Qijia culture (2000 –1900 B.C., the Late Neolithic Culture centered on Gansu Province)
齐鲁文化	Qilu culture; culture of Qi and Lu (States)
齐云山	Qiyun Mountain (Anhui)
祁连山	Qilian Mountains; Qilian Range (Qinghai, Gansu)
祈谷坛	(of Temple of Heaven) Altar of Praying for Grain
祈年殿	(of Temple of Heaven) Hall of Prayer for Good Harvest
淇澳岛	Qi'ao Island (Guangdong)
棋类	board games

棋盘	chessboard; chequerboard; draughtboard
棋盘洞	chessboard cave
棋盘山	Qipan Mountain; Chessboard Mountain (Liaoning)
棋盘石窟	〈佛〉Qipan Grottoes (Xinjiang)
棋子湾	Qizi Bay (Hai'nan)
旗后要塞和灯塔	Qihou Fortress and Lighthouse (Taiwan)
旗人	〈满族〉banner man (a member of any one of the "Eight Banners" during the Qing Dynasty)
麒麟	(of legend) kylin; kirin; Chinese unicorn (a traditional auspicious animal)
麒麟山	Kirin Mountain (Heilongjiang)
乞巧节	→七[乞]巧节
杞麓湖	Qilu Lake (Yunnan)
启祥门	(of Imperial Palace) Gate of Lucky Auspice
起跑线	starting line for a race (usually used for young child's education)
起势	〈武术〉(of Tai Chi) Starting posture; Preparation
起云峰	(of Three Gorges) Qiyun Peak
绮春园宫门	(of Yuanming Garden) Palace Gates of Qichun Garden
绮春园石残桥	(of Yuanming Garden) Remnants of a Stone Bridge
绮望楼	(of Chengde Mountain Resort) Tower of Enchanting View
气功	qigong (a centuries-old system of coordinated body-posture and movement, breathing, and meditation used for the purposes of health, spirituality, and martial-arts training)
气功大师	qigong master
气容肃	〈礼〉Qirongsu (to breathe calmly and smoothly and do not pant or gasp) (a saying from Book of Rites) →君子九容
迄脱乞迪尔节	〈塔吉克族〉Festival of Cleaning up Smoke and Dust (March)

契丹帝国	Khitan Empire (1124–1211, a minority's regime in northern China during the Five Dynasties)
器械对练	Armed combat
洽川景区	Qiachuan Scenic Area (Shaanxi)
恰克玛克河	Qiakmakh/Qiakemake River (Xinjiang)
千尺雪	(of Chengde Mountain Resort) Thousand-Feet Snow; Thousand-Feet of Waterfall
千尺幢	(of Mount Huashan) Qianchi Precipice; Thousand-foot Precipice (one of the Three Major Risks Mount Huashan)
千岛湖	Qiandao Lake; Thousand-Island Lake (Zhejiang)
千岛湖区	Thousand-Island Lake area/region (Zhejiang)
千灯节	Thousand Lanterns Festival (a traditional festival of the Mongol and Daur ethnic groups on the 25th day of the 10th lunar month)
千佛殿	Thousand-Buddha Hall (Sichuan, Shandong)
千佛顶	(of Mount Emei) Thousand Buddha Peak
千佛洞	thousand-Buddha grottoes
千佛山	Qianfo Mountain; Thousand-Buddha Mountain (Shandong)
千佛崖	Thousand-Buddha Cliff (Sichuan)
千佛崖造像	Thousand-Buddha Cliffside Statues (Shandong)
千佛岩	Thousand-Buddha Rock; Cliff of Thousand Buddhas (Jiangsu, Sichuan)
千佛院	thousand-buddha temple
千家洞自然保护区	Qianjiadong Nature Reserve (Guangxi)
千家寨景区	Qianjiazhai Scenic Area (Yunnan)
千灵山	Qianling Mountain (Beijing)
千龙洞	Qianlong Karst Cave (Hai'nan)
千米枯木长堤	Thousand-Meter Long Bank with Withered Trees (Xinjiang)
千鸟园	Thousand-Bird Garden (Jiangsu)
千秋墓	Qianqiu Mausoleum; Thousand-Year Mausoleum (Jilin)

千秋亭	(of Imperial Palace) Pavilion of Thousand Autumns
千人石	Thousand-Men Stone (Jiangsu)
千沙	Thousand-Step Sand Beach (Zhejiang)
千山	Qianshan Mountain (Liaoning)
千山景区	Qianshan Mountain Scenic Area (Liaoning)
千手观音	〈佛〉Thousand-Hand Goddess of Mercy; Thousand-Hand Bodhisattva
千手观音殿	(of Hongluo Temple) Hall of Thousand-Hand Guanyin
千唐志斋博物馆	Qiantang Zhizhai Museum; Qiantang Epigraph Museum (He'nan)
千唐志斋石刻	Qiantang Zhizhai Stone Inscription; Qiantang Epigraph Inscription on Stone (He'nan)
千童祠	Qiantong Ancestral Temple (Hebei)
千丈岩瀑布	Qianzhang Cliff Waterfall (Zhejiang)
牵新	〈婚〉qianxin; to lead the bride (a blessed elder on the bridegroom's side supports with hands the bride entering the hall)
前鼓楼苑胡同	Qiangulouyuan Hutong; Front Hutong of Drum Tower (Beijing)
前滚翻	〈武术〉Forward roll
前九广铁路钟楼	Former Kowloon-Canton Railway Clock Tower (Hong Kong)
前空翻	〈武术〉Front somersault; Front flip
前扫堂腿	〈武术〉Forward floor sweep kick
前扫腿	〈武术〉Front sweep
前手抄拳	〈武术〉Front fist upper cut
前手冲拳	〈武术〉Front fist jab
前手贯拳	〈武术〉Front fist side hook
前压腿	〈武术〉Front stretching of the leg
钱祠表忠	(of West lake) Honoring Devotion Stele of King Qian's Temple
钱塘[江]潮	Qiantang River Tide

钱塘江	Qiantang River (Zhejiang)
钱塘江(大)桥	Qiantang River Bridge (Zhejiang)
乾隆大钟	Big Bell of Emperor Qianlong (Beijing)
乾清宫	(of Imperial Palace) Palace of Heavenly Purity (Beijing)
乾清门	(of Imperial Palace) Gate of Heavenly Purity
潜溪寺	(of Longmen Grottoes) Qianxi Temple
黔金丝猴	〈动〉*Rhinopithecus brelichi*; Guizhou golden monkey; gray snub-nosed monkey
黔灵山	Qianling Mountain (Guizhou)
黔西南	southwestern Guizhou
浅浮雕	shallow-relief carving
浅水湾	Repulse Bay (Hong Kong)
羌塘草原	Changtang Grassland; Qiangtang Grassland (Tibet)
羌族	Qiang ethnic group; Qiang
羌族部落	Qiang tribe
羌族服饰	Qiang costume
枪术	〈武术〉spear-playing art; spear form
强巴格桑	Qiangba Gesang (1930–1995, a master of arts and crafts in Tibet)
强巴林寺	〈佛〉Qiangbalin Monastery; Galden Jampaling Monastery (Tibet)
强婚刺铃蟾	〈动〉*Bombina fortinuptialis*
抢春水	〈仡佬族〉Spring Water Scrambling Festival (Beginning of Spring)
乔戈里峰	(of Kunlun Mountains) Chogori Peak
乔家大院	Qiao's Grand Courtyard; Qiao Family Courtyard (Shanxi)
乔迁酒	〈民俗〉house-warming party; relocation banquet
乔铁汉故居	Former Residence of Qiao Tiehan (Tianjin)
巧克力开心乐园	Chocolate Happy Land (Shanghai)
钦安殿	(of Imperial Palace) Hall of Imperial Peace
钦江	Qinjiang River (Guangxi)

钦州坭兴陶	Qinzhou nixing pottery
侵华日军东北要塞	military fortress built by Japanese invader in Northeast (which is called the Oriental Maginot Line by Japanese invaders) (Heilongjiang)
侵华日军南京大屠杀遇难同胞纪念馆	Memorial Hall of the Victims in Nanjing Massacre by Japanese Invaders (Jiangsu)
亲迎	〈婚〉(of the bridegroom) personal escort to the bride; to welcome the bride personally (to meet the bride at her home and escort her back for the wedding) →六礼
秦巴巴鲵	〈动〉*Liua tsinpaensis*; Sichuan salamander
秦巴山区	Qinba Mountain area (Gansu)
秦长城	Qin Great Wall; Great Wall of the Qin Dynasty
秦长城遗址［迹］	Remains of Qin Great Wall (Gansu)
秦朝	Qin Dynasty (221-207 B.C.)
秦公一号大墓	Tomb No.1 of Dukes of Qin (Shaanxi) →秦景公之墓
秦汉风格建筑	architecture of Qin and Han dynasties
秦淮河	Qinhuai River (Jiangsu)
秦皇岛桃林口景区	Taolinkou Water Conservancy Scenic Zone in Qinhuangdao (Hebei)
秦皇岛野生动物园	Qinhuangdao Wildlife Zoo (Hebei)
秦皇古驿道	Qinhuang Ancient Road; Ancient Road of the Qin Dynasty (Hebei)
秦景公之墓	Tomb of Duke Jing of Qin (Shaanxi) →秦公一号大墓
秦岭（山脉）	Qinling/Tisnling; Qinling Mountains (boundary of northern China and southern one)
秦岭党参	〈植〉*Codonopsis tsinglingensis*; Qinling/Tsinling root of hairy asiabell
秦岭火绒草	〈植〉*Leontopodium giraldii*; Qinling/Tsinling edelweiss
秦岭冷杉	〈植〉*Abies chensiensis*; Qinling/Tsinling fir
秦岭羚牛	〈动〉*Budorcas bedfordi*; Qinling/Tsinling takin

秦岭木姜子	〈植〉*Litsea tsinlingensis*; Qinling/Tsinling pungent litse fruit
秦岭藤	〈植〉*Biondia chinensis*; Qinling/Tsinling vine
秦岭无心菜	〈植〉*Arenaria giraldii*
秦岭雨蛙	〈动〉*Hyla tsinlingensis*; Qinling/Tsinling tree toad
秦腔	〈戏〉Qin Opera; Shaanxi Opera
秦人古洞	Ancient Cave of Qin People (Hu'nan)
秦始皇	Qin Shi Huang; First Emperor of Qin; Emperor Qin Shihuang (259-210 B.C., the first to unify the six nations of China
秦始皇兵马俑	Qin terracotta warriors and horses; Qin terracotta army (Shaanxi)
秦始皇帝陵博物院	Emperor Qinshihuang's Mausoleum Site Museum (Shaanxi)
秦始皇陵	Mausoleum of First Emperor of Qin; Mausoleum of Emperor Qin Shihuang (Shaanxi)
秦王宫	Emperor Qin's Palace; Qin Palace (Zhejiang)
秦王湖	Qinwang Lake (Hebei)
琴丝竹	〈植〉*Bambusa multiplex*; qinsi Bamboo
琴台大剧院	Qintai Grand Theatre (Hubei)
琴台公园	Qintai Park (Hubei)
勤政殿	(of Chengde Mountain Resort) Hall of Industrious Administration
青城山	Mount Qingcheng; Qingcheng Mountain (one of the birthplaces of Taoism) (Sichuan)
青瓷	celadon porcelain
青岛东部旅游区	Qingdao eastern tourist area
青岛国际啤酒节	Qingdao International Beer Festival (the second week of August)
青岛海军博物馆	Qingdao Naval Museum (Shandong)
青岛崂山	Qingdao Laoshan Mountain (Shandong)
青岛啤酒博物馆	Qingdao Beer Museum (Shandong)
青枫绿屿	(of Chengde Mountain Resort) Lush Maple on Green Islet

青姑娘节	〈白族〉Green Girl Festival (on the 15th day of the 1st lunar month)
青果	〈植〉*Fructus canarii*; Chinese olive
青海湖	Qinghai Lake (Qinghai)
青海田鼠	〈动〉*Microtus fuscus*; plateau vole
青花瓷	blue and white porcelain
青礁慈济宫	Qingjiao Ciji Palace (Fujian)
青稞酒	(of Tibetan) highland barley wine
青龙大瀑布	(of Mount Wuyi) Qinglong Waterfall
青龙湖湿地公园	Qinglong Lake Wetland Park (Hebei)
青龙山森林公园	Qinglong Mountain Forest Park (Hubei)
青龙寺	qinglong temple
青龙潭旅游景区	Qinglong Pond Tourism Scenic Area (Hebei)
青龙峡	Qinglong Gorge (Beijing)
青龙峡旅游度假村	Qinglong Gorge Tourist and Holiday Village (Beijing)
青苗会	Young Crops Association (traditional festival of Tu and Tibetan ethnic groups)
青南牧区	Qingnan Pasture; Southern Pasture of Qinghai
青年节	Youth Day (on the May 4th)
青年路北湖公园	North Lake Park on Youth Road (Hubei)
青年志愿者服务日	Youth Volunteer Service Day (March 5th) → 学（习）雷锋日
青钱柳	〈植〉*Cyclocarya paliurus*; wheel wingnut
青雀舫	(of Chengde Mountain Resort) Decorated Boat with Aquatic Bird Qingque
青山	Castle Peak (Hong Kong)
青山禅院	Tsing Shan Monastery; Castle Peak Monastery (Hong Kong)
青山飞瀑	Qingshan Waterfall (Liaoning)
青山沟	Qingshan Valley (Liaoning)
青山关景区	Qingshan Pass Scenic Area (Hebei)
青山湖景区	Qingshan Lake Scenic Area (Jiangxi)
青山湿地公园	Qingshan Wetland Park (Hubei)

青狮岩	Green Lion Rock (Fujian)
青石林	Green Stone Forest (Chongqing)
青松岭旅游区	Qingsongling Tourim Area (Hebei)
青[新]滩	(of Three Gorges) Qing Shoal
青檀	〈植〉*Pteroceltis tatarinowii*; wingceltis
青铜工艺品	bronze handicraft
青铜馆	Bronze Ware Hall; Bronze Vessel Gallery (Beijing)
青铜器	bronze ware; bronze vessel
青铜时代	Bronze Age
青铜峡 108 塔	Qingtongxia 108 Tower (Ningxia)
青岩古镇	Qingyan Ancient Town (Guizhou)
青阳巷 18 号革命旧址	Revolutionary Site of No. 18 Qingyang Lane (Hubei)
青衣	〈戏〉(of a Beijing Opera) Tsing Yi (a faithful wife character, lover or maiden in distress)
青衣东北公园	Tsing Yi Northeast Park (Hong Kong)
青衣公园	Tsing Yi Park (Hong Kong)
青衣海滨公园	Tsing Yi Promenade (Hong Kong)
青衣山	Tsing Yi Peak (Hong Kong) →三支香
青衣运动场	Tsing Yi Sports Ground (Hong Kong)
青云山	Qingyun Mountain (Shandong)
青藏高原	Qingzang Plateau; Qinghai-Tibet Plateau; Tibet Plateau (located in southeast China)
青藏铁路	Qingzang Railway; Qinghai-Tibet Railway
清朝	Qing Dynasty (1636-1912)
清朝中期	Middle Qing Dynasty
清代皇陵	Imperial Mausoleum of the Qing Dynasty (Hebei)
清东陵	Eastern Qing Mausoleum; Eastern Royal Tombs of the Qing Dynasty (Hebei)
清风池馆	(of Lingering Garden) Refreshing Breeze Pavilion by the Lake
清风楼	Cool Breeze Tower (Hebei)
清风亭	(of Zhangjiajie) Fresh Breeze Pavilion

清河坊古街	Qinghefang Ancient Street (Zhejiang)
清晖亭	(of Chengde Mountain Resort) Pavilion of Lucid Light
清江	Qingjiang River (Hubei)
清江古城	Qingjiang Ancient City (Hubei)
清江古河床	Qingjiang Ancient River Bed (Hubei)
清江景区	Qingjiang River Scenic Area (Hubei)
清净［圣友］寺	〈伊斯兰〉Qingjing Mosque (Fujian)
清澜港	Qinglan Harbor (Hai'nan)
清凉山	Bracing Mountain (Shanxi) →五台山
清凉山新闻出版革命纪念馆	Revolutionary Memorial Hall for Journalism and Publication at Qingliang Hill (Shaanxi)
清烈公祠	Qingliegong Ancestral Hall (Hubei) →屈原祠
清明	〈节气〉Qingming; Clear and Bright (5th solar term)
清明节	Qingming Festival; Ching Ming Festival; Tomb Sweeping Day (around April 5th）
清明上河街	Qingming Riverside Landscape Street (Jiangsu)
清明上河图	(of a painting) Riverside Scene at Qingming Festival; Qingming Festival by the Riverside (Zhang Zeduan, 1104)
清明上河图再现区	Reappearance Area of "Riverside Scene at Qingming Festival" (Zhejiang)
清明上河园	Qingming Riverside Landscape Garden; Millennium City Park (He'nan)
清泉飞瀑	Clear Spring and Flying Waterfall (Hebei)
清舒山馆	Pure Comfort Hill Villa (Hebei)
清暑轩	Ching Shu Hin (Hong Kong)
清水断崖	Chingshui Cliff (clear water and steep cliff) (Taiwan)
清水河峡谷	Qingshui River Ravine (Guizhou)
清水湾郊野公园	Clear Water Bay Country Park (Hong Kong)
清泰陵	Tailing Mausoleum of Qing Emperor Yongzheng (Hebei)
清潭峰	(of Mount Huangshan) Clear Pond Peak

清汤鹿尾	〈烹饪〉Deer's Tail of Clear Soup
清西陵	Western Qing Mausoleum; Western Royal Tombs of the Qing Dynasty (Hebei)
清香馆	(of Surging Waves Pavilion) Pure Fragrance Hall
清孝陵	Xiaoling Mausoleum of the Qing Dynasty (Hebei)
清虚阁	Qingxu Pavilion (Shanxi)
清晏舫	(of Summer Palace) Clear and Calm Boat, Qingyan Stone Boat (Beijing)
清音阁	(of Mount Emei) Qingyin Pavilion; Clear Sound Pavilion
清音阁景区	(of Mount Emei) Clear Sound Pavilion area
清源山	Qingyuan Mountain; Mount Qingyuan (Fujian)
清远楼	Qingyuan Pavilion (Hebei) →钟楼
清真大寺	Great Mosque of Hohhot (Inner Mongolia)
清真寺	mosque
清政府	Qing government
情侣峰	Lovers' Peak (Anhui)
情侣路	Lover Road (Guangdong)
情人谷	lover's valley; valentine valley
晴川阁	Qingchuan Pavilion (Hubei)
晴川桥	Qingchuan Bridge (Hubei)
晴川书院遗址	〈古〉Qingchuan Academy Site (Hubei)
擎天柱	Qingtian Pillar; Optimus Prime (Guizhou)
请佛	to worship in the temple
请柬	invitation card
请期	〈婚〉agreement upon the wedding date; to reach an agreement between the bride's and groom's families on the date of the wedding →六礼
请山神	〈民俗〉to invite the god of mountains
请帖	invitation card
庆林寺塔	Qinglin Temple Pagoda (Hebei)
庆王府	Qingwang Mansion Holiday Resort (Tianjin)
庆云寺	Qingyun Temple (Guangdong)

筇竹	〈植〉*Qiongzhuea tumidinoda*; walking stick bamboo
琼海(市)	Qionghai (Hai'nan)
琼海卷柏	〈植〉*Selaginella Hai'nanensis*; Qionghai spikemoss
琼浆	Qiongjiang; nectar; jadelike wine (good wine)
琼台观	(of Mount Wudang) Qiongtai Temple
琼台景区	Qiongtai Scenic Area (Zhejiang)
琼台书院	〈古〉Qiongtai Academy (Hai'nan)
琼州海峡	Qiongzhou Strait (Hai'nan)
琼[陈]棕	〈植〉*Chuniophoenix Hainanensis*
龟兹壁画	Qiuci Frescoes (Xinjiang)
龟兹都城遗址	Ruins/Site of the Capital City of Ancient Qiuci State (Xinjiang)
秋分	〈节气〉Autumn Equinox (16th solar term)
秋霞圃	Qiuxia Garden (Shanghai)
求签	〈佛〉to draw lots before idols (for good fortune); to pray and draw divination sticks at a temple
球形乌龙	〈茶〉pelleted Oolong
驱厄运	to sweep away ill fortune; to get rid of bad luck
驱鬼节	〈藏族〉Lemuralia; Silvester-Klause Festival (on the 29th day of the 12th month in Tibetan calender)
屈原祠	Qu Yuan Ancestral Hall (Hubei) →清烈公祠
屈原纪念馆	Qu Yuan Memorial Hall (Hubei)
屈原庙	Qu Yuan Temple (Hu'nan) →屈子祠
屈原墓群	Qu Yuan Tombs (Hu'nan) →汨罗山古墓群
屈原问天	(of Tiantang Zhai) Qu Yuan Questioning Heaven
屈子祠	Memorial Temple of Master Qu (Hu'nan) →屈原庙
屈子行吟	(of Zhangjiajie) Master in Poem Composing
渠家大院	Qu Family Courtyard (Shanxi)
瞿塘峡	Qutang Gorge (Hubei)
鼩猬	〈动〉*Neotetracus*; shrew-hedgehog
鼩鼱	〈动〉*Uropsilus soricipes*; Chinese shrew mole
衢州南宗孔庙	Confucius Temple of South Sect; Confucius Temple at Quzhou (Zhejiang)

曲阜孔府	Kong Family Mansion in Qufu; Qufu Confucius Temple (Shandong)
曲阜市	Qufu City (Shandong) →孔子故里［乡］
曲江公园	Qujiang Park (Jiangsu)
曲江海洋世界	Qujiang Ocean World (Shaanxi)
曲江寒窑遗址公园	Qujiang Cool Cave Heritage Park (Shaanxi)
曲茎石斛	〈植〉*Dendrobium flexicaule*
曲科节	〈门巴族〉Quke Festival (June)
曲廊	(of Lingering Garden) Zigzag Walkway
曲水荷香	(of Chengde Mountain Resort) Lotus Fragrance over Winding Water
曲溪楼	(of Lingering Garden) Zigzag Stream Tower
曲艺	〈戏〉quyi (Chinese folk performing art, including ballad singing, storytelling, comic dialogues, clapper talks, cross talks, etc.)
曲苑风荷	(of West Lake) Lotus in the Breeze at Crooked Courtyard; Lotus Flowers in the Breezing Winding Courtyard
取新火节	〈佤族〉New Fire Festival
趣联	humorous couplet
圈养大熊猫	captive giant panda; giant panda in captivity
圈椅淌湿地公园	Quanyitang Wetland Park (Hubei)
权星门	quanxing gate
全福庙会	Quanfu Temple Fair (the last ten-day period of April)
全国爱耳日	National Ear Care Day (March 3rd)
全国爱牙日	Chinese Teeth Care Day (September 20th)
全国爱眼日	National Eye Care Day; National Sight Day (June 6th)
全国法制宣传日	National Legal Publicity Day (December 4th)
全国高血压日	National Hypertension Day (October 8th)
全国双拥模范城市	national double support model city
全国糖酒（商品交易）会	China Food & Drinks Fair; CFDF
全国土地日	National Land Day (June 25th)
全国学生营养日	National Students Nutrition Day (May 20th)

全国重点文物保护单位	key monuments under national protection; major historical and cultural sites protected at the national level
全国助残日	National Disabled Day; National Day of Disabled people (the 3rd Sunday in May)
全民国防教育日	Nationwide National Defense Education Day (the 3rd Saturday in September)
全芽心	〈茶〉all-bud
全真道观	(of Mount Qingcheng) Quanzhen Taoist Temple
全真教	〈道〉Quanzhen Taoism
全真岩	(of Mount Huashan) Quanzhen Block Rock
荃湾广场	Tsuen Wan Plaza (Hong Kong)
荃湾赛马会德华公园	Tsuen Wan Jockey Club Tak Wah Park (Hong Kong)
泉城	City of Springs (referring to Jinan, Shandong)
泉山森林公园	Quanshan (Mountain) Forest Park (Jiangsu)
泉源石壁	(of Chengde Mountain Resort) Springs Dripping from Stone Cracks
泉州海外交通史博物馆	Quanzhou Maritime Museum (Fujian)
拳法	〈武术〉fist position; boxing art
拳术	〈武术〉Chinese boxing
犬王节	〈瑶族〉God-of-Dog Festival (on the 29th day of the 10th lunar month)
劝酒	〈民俗〉to urge sb to drink
却依拉殿	〈佛〉(of Wudangzhao Monastery) Queyila Hall
雀可节	〈门巴族〉Queke Festival (for preventing natural disasters and welcoming a bumper harvest) (in the 7th or 8th month of Tibetan calender)

R

然乌湖景区	Ranwu Lake Scenic Area (Tibet)
燃灯节	〈藏族〉Butter Lamp Festival (on the 25th day of the 10th month in Tibetan calender)
燃放鞭炮	〈民俗〉to set off firecrackers; to ignite firecrackers
冉庄地道战纪念馆	Museum of the Tunnel Warfare at Ranzhuang (Hebei)
绕三灵	〈白族〉Raosanling Ceremony (worship of three divinities) (from the 23th day to the 25th day of the 4th lunar month)
热带雨林馆	Tropical Rain Forest Hall (Liaoning)
热带植物观光园	Tropical Plants Sightseeing Garden (Tianjin)
热带植物区	tropical plants area
热贡六月会	June Festival of Regong (traditional festival of Tibetan and Tu ethnic groups from the 17th day to the 25th one of the 6th lunar month)
热河泉	(of Chengde Summer Resort) Rehe Hot Spring; Hot Spring Villa
热河行宫	Rehe Palace (Hebei) →承德避暑山庄
热瓦克佛寺遗址	Rewak Vestige of Buddhist Temple (Xinjiang)
人民大会堂	Great Hall of the People (Beijing)
人民大礼堂	People's Auditorium (Chongqing)
人民广场	People's Square (Shanghai)
人民解放纪念碑	Monument to the People's Liberation (Chongqing) →抗战胜利纪功碑
人民英雄纪念碑	Monument to the People's Heroes (Beijing)

人日[胜]节	Renri Festival; Human Day (birthday of humankind) (on the 7th day of the 1st lunar month)
人字瀑	(of Mount Huangshan) Herringbone Waterfall
仁寿殿	(of Summer Palace) Hall of Benevolence and Longevity
仁宗皇帝	Emperor Renzong (1010-1063, reigning from 1022 to 1063 in the Song Dynasty)
日光菩萨	Sunlight Bodhisattva
日光岩	Sunlight Rock (Fujian)
日喀则新年	→西藏农耕新年
日喀则展佛节	〈藏族〉Thangka Festival in Shigatse (from the 14th day to the 16th day of the 5th month in Tibetan calender)
日月谷温泉	Riyuegu Hot Spring (Fujian)
日月山	Riyue Mountain; Sun Moon Mountain (Qinghai)
日月潭	Riyue Pond; Sun Moon Lake (Taiwan)
日月潭邵族	Thao People of Sun Moon Lake
日月湾	Riyue Bay; Sun-Moon Bay (Hai'nan)
日则沟风景线	(of Jiuzhai Valley) Rize Gully tourist route
日知会旧址	Site of Rizhihui (a revolutionary association in the Late Qing Dynasty) (Hubei)
荣宝斋	Rongbaozhai Art Gallery; Studio of Glorious Treasures (most famous shop in the Liulichang Street of Chinese Culture since 1672) (Beijing)
荣成天鹅湖	Rongcheng Swan Lake (Shandong)
绒布冰川区	Rongbuk Glacier Zone (Tibet)
绒布河	Rongbuk River (Tibet)
绒[龙]布寺	Rongbuk Monastery (Tibet)
绒毛皂荚	〈植〉*Gleditsia japonica*; Gleditsia vestita
榕[鉴]湖	Ronghu Lake (Guangxi)
榕树湾	Yung Shue Wan (Hong Kong)
融和门	Ronghe Gate; Gate of Understanding (Macao)
肉桂	〈中药〉*Cinnamomum Cassia Presl*; cinnamon; cassia bark

肉桂树	〈植〉*Cinnamomum cassia*; cinnamon tree
肉叶猕猴桃	〈植〉*Actinidia carnosifolia*
肉孜节	→开斋节
如风似闭	(of Tai Chi) Pushing one's hands forward in defense
如意湖	(of Chengde Mountain Resort) Lake of Happiness
如意湖亭	(of Chengde Mountain Resort) Pavilion of Happiness Lake
如意金箍棒	Monkey King Bar; MKB (a weaponry with tremendously supernatural power used by Sun Wukong in Journey to the West) →定海神针
儒家[教]	Confucianism; Confucian School
汝南麦草画	Runan wheatgrass painting
汝窑	〈古〉Ru Kiln (one of the five famous kilns in ancient China)
汝窑瓷器	〈古〉Ru-Ware; Ru Porcelain (one of the five famous chinawares in ancient China)
乳[小]名	infant name; milk name (used for children in their childhood)
乳山银滩	Rushan Silver Beach (Shandong)
入土为安	〈丧〉burial/prayer brings peace to the deceased
入座之礼	seating etiquette
阮墩环碧	(of West Lake) Ruan Mound in Green; Ruangong Islet Submerged in Greenery
瑞蚨祥	Refosian; Ruifuxiang Silk (Beijing's best cheongsam tailor and the most famous silk store since 1862)
瑞丽江	Ruili River (Yunnan)
瑞雪兆丰年	a timely snow promises a good harvest; a fall of seasonable snow gives promise of a fruitful year; winter snow signifies a year of good crops
闰年	leap year; intercalary year; bissextile year
闰日	leap day; intercalary day (February 29th in a leap year)
闰月	leap month; intercalary month (in the lunar calendar)

S

撒拉族	Salar ethnic group; Salar
撒尼人	Sani People; Sani
撒班节	〈塔塔尔族〉Saban Festival (in memory of the inventor of the new plow–Saban) →犁头［铧］节
撒买路钱	〈丧〉to scatter paper money as the funeral procession passes by
撒种节	〈阿昌族〉Sowing Day (on the 10th day of the 3rd lunar month)
萨嘎达瓦节	〈藏族〉Saga Dawa Festival (a traditional festival of Tibetan Buddhism, on the 15th day of the 4th month in Tibetan calendar) →佛吉祥日
萨迦寺	Sakya Kloster; Sakya Monastery (Tibet)
萨满仪式	shamanic ceremony
塞北第一庄	The First Villa of Saibei (Inner Mongolia)
塞外蟠龙湖	Panlong Lake outside the Great Wall (Hebei)
赛里木湖	Sayram Lake (Xinjiang)
赛龙舟	〈民俗〉to hold Chinese dragon boat races; Chinese dragon boat race
赛马会创意艺术中心	Jockey Club Creative Arts Centre; JCCAC (Hong Kong)
赛马节	Horse Racing Festival (a traditional festival of Tibetan and Mongolian ethnic groups)
赛西湖公园	Choi Sai Woo Park (Hong Kong)
赛衣［服装］节	〈彝族〉Saiyi Festival; Garment Festival (on the 28th day of the 3rd lunar month)

赛装节	〈彝族〉Saizhuang Festival; Costume Competition Festival (on the 15th day of the 1st lunar month)
三把刀景区	Three-Knife Scenic Area (Hubei)
三宝侗寨	Sanbao Dong Village (Guizhou)
三步桥	Three-Step Bridge (Jiangsu) →引静桥
三岔旅游村	Sancha Tourist Village (Gansu)
三刺草	〈植〉*Aristida triseta*
三大石窟	Three Famous Buddhist Grottoes (Mogao Grottoes, Longmen Grottoes and Yungang Grottoes)
三道茶	〈白族〉Three-Course Tea
三道关森林公园	Sandao Guan Forest Park (Heilongjiang)
三叠峰	(of Mount Wuyi) Three Tiers Peak
三叠泉	(of Mount Lushan) Three-Stepped Fall
三朵[多]节	〈纳西族〉Sanduo Festival (for sacrifice to the God Sanduo) (on the 8th day of the 2nd lunar month)
三港雨蛙	〈动〉*Hyla sanchiangensis*; San Chiang tree frog
三顾茅[草]庐	Three Humble Visits to the Thatched Cottage (in Records of the Three Kingdoms)
三顾堂	(of Longzhong) Sangu Hall; Hall of Three Calls (Hubei)
三国	〈古〉Three Kingdoms
三国城	Three Kingdoms Town/City (Jiangsu)
三国圣地	Shrine of the Three Kingdoms period (Sichuan) →武侯祠
三国时期	Three Kingdoms period (220-280)
《三国演义》	*Romance of the Three Kingdoms* (a historical romance novel, by Luo Guanzhong in the Later Yuan and the Early Ming Dynasty)
《三国志》	*Records of Three Kingdoms* (Chen Shou, A.D. 280-290)
三河口水利景区	Sanhekou Water Conservancy Scenic Area (Hubei, Shaanxi)
三湖书院	Three Lakes Academy (Guangdong)

三花五罗	〈动〉Fishes of Three "Hua" and Five "Luo" (eight types of fishes)
三花紫菊	〈植〉*Notoseris triflora*; three flower kalimeris herb
三皇五帝	〈神话〉Three Sovereigns and Five Emperors
三甲港海滨乐园	Sanjiagang Waterfront Park (Shanghai)
三剑峰	Sanjian Peak; Three Swords Peak (Fujian)
三江并流景观	Three Parallel Rivers landscape (Jinsha River, Lancang River and Nujiang River) (Yunnan)
三江口	sanjiangkou; three rivers estuary
三江口景区	Sanjiangkou Scenic Area; Three-River-Estuary Resort/Area
三江平原湿地	Sanjiang Plains Wetland (Heilongjiang)
三江源	Sanjiangyuan; Three-River-Source (source of Yangtze, Yellow and Lancang Rivers) (Qinghai)
三江源地区	Sanjiangyuan area; source region of the Three Rivers (Qinghai)
三江源国家公园	Sanjiangyuan National Park; Three-River-Source National Park (Qinghai)
三江源自然保护区	Sanjiangyuan Nature Reserve; Three-River-Source Nature Reserve (Qinghai)
三角龙湾景区	Sanjiao Longwan (Bay) Scenic Area (Jilin)
三节棍	〈武术〉three-section cudgel/staff
三姐妹峰	(of Zhangjiajie) Three Sisters Peak
三句半	(of Chinese folk art form) san juban; three-and-a-half-line ballad
三里屯	Sanlitun (bar street) (Beijing)
三菱湖湿地公园	Sanlinhu Lake Wetland Park (Hubei)
三龙出海	Three Dragons Rising from the Sea (Jiangxi)
三门峡中日友好苑	Sino-Japanese Friendship Garden in Sanmen Xia (He'nan)
三七之乡	Hometown of Panax Notoginseng (Yunnan)
三清阁	〈道〉Three-purity Pavilion (Yunnan)
三清[少华]山	〈道〉Sanqing Mountain; Mount Sanqing (Jiangxi)

三清山国家公园	Mount Sanqing National Park (Jiangxi)
三曲	〈古〉sanqu (three transitions in rhythm or melody)
三生汤	→擂茶
三圣堂	three-saint hall
三盛公黄河水利枢纽	Sanshenggong Water Conservancy Project on Yellow River (Inner Mongolia)
三十六鸳鸯馆	(of Humble Administrator's Garden) Hall of 36 Pairs of Mandarin Ducks
三十七部会盟碑	Alliance Stele of the 37 Tribes (Yunnan)
三世佛	Trikalea Buddhas (Buddhas of the Past, Present and Future); Buddhas of Three Periods
三书	〈婚〉Three Letters (betrothal letter, gift letter and wedding letter)
三书六礼	〈婚〉Three Letters and Six Etiquettes
三梳子孙满堂	(of wedding) the third combing, blessed with lots of offspring
三苏祠	Three Sus' Memorial Temple (former residence of three famous writers as Su Xun, Su Shi and Su Zhe in the Northern Song Dynasty) (Sichuan)
三苏坟	Tombs of Three Sus (three famous writers as Su Xun, Su Shi and Su Zhe in the Northern Song Dynasty) (He'nan)
三台云水	(of West Lake) Suffusing Clouds and Gurgling Waters of Santai Mountain
三潭印月	(of West Lake and Yuanming Garden) Three Pools Mirroring the Moon
三王	〈古〉Three Kings (kings of the Xia, Shang and Zhou Dynasties)
三味书屋	Sanwei Study; Shamisen Bookstore (Zhejiang)
三五九旅屯垦纪念馆	Memorial Hall of 359th Brigade Reclamation (Xinjiang)
三五九旅文化旅游区	Cultural Tourism Area of 359th Brigade (Xinjiang)
三希堂	(of Imperial Palace) Room of Three Rare Treasures (Beijing)

三峡	(of Yangtze River) Three Gorges
三峡大坝	Three Gorges Dam (Hubei)
三峡大老岭	Dalaoling in the Three Gorges (Hubei)
三峡工程	Three Gorges Project (Hubei) →长江三峡水利枢纽工程
三峡猴溪	Three Gorges Monkey Creek (Hubei)
三峡水乡水利景区	Three Gorges Water Town Water Conservancy Scenic Area (Hubei)
三仙洞	Cave of Three Immortals; Three-Immortal Caves (Buddhist caves of the Han Dynasty) (Xinjiang)
三仙台	Sanhsientai (Taiwan)
三弦	〈乐〉sanxian (a three-stringed plucked instrument)
三亚湾	Sanya Bay (Hai'nan)
三仰峰	(of Mount Wuyi) Sanyang Peak; Three Rises Peak
三叶崖爬藤	〈中药〉*Tetrastigma hemsleyanum*
三音石	(of Temple of Heaven) Triple Sound Stone; Three Echo Stone
三游洞	Sanyou Cave; Three Travelers' Cave (Hubei)
三月会	〈纳西族〉March Festival (in the 3rd lunar month)
三月街	〈白族〉The Third Month Fair (within the 15th-21st day of the 3rd lunar month) →观音市[街]
三月三	March Third Festival (worship of ancestors)
三月桃花会	peach blossom festival in March
三朝	1〈婚〉the third day after marriage (the day when the bride returns to her mother's home) 2〈民俗〉the third day after one's birth
三朝回门	〈婚〉return of a bride to her mother's home on the third day after the wedding
三朝礼	〈婚〉gift of the third day (after one's birth or marriage)
三折瀑	(of Mount Yandang) Sanzhe Waterfall; Three-Step/Fold Waterfall (Zhejiang)

三支香	Sam Chi Heung (Hong Kong) →青衣山
三姊妹峰	(of Zhangjiajie) Three Sister Peaks
伞花木	〈植〉*Eurycorymbus cavaleriei*
散打	free combat
散曲	〈古〉sanqu; non-dramatic song (a type of verse with tonal patterns modelled on tunes drawn from folk music)
散手道长拳	Sanshou Dao Long Fist
散花坞	(of Mount Huangshan) Flower Scattering Basin
丧服	〈丧〉mourning apparel
丧葬酒	〈丧〉mourning wine
丧葬习俗	funeral practice; funeral custom; burial custom
桑丁寺	Samding Kloster; Sandin/Sangding Temple (Tibet)
桑干河	Sanggan River (Hebei)
桑耶寺	Samye Monastery; Samye Kloster (Tibet)
桑植角蟾	〈动〉*Megophrys sangzhiensis*; Sangzhi horned toad
扫尘日	〈民俗〉Cleaning Day (year-end cleaning on the 24th day of the 12th lunar month) →大扫除
扫墓	〈民俗〉to pay respect to a dead at his/her tomb; to sweep a tomb
色拉崩钦节	Sera Bengqin Festival (a religious festival unique to Sera Monastery, on December 27th in Tibetan calendar)
色拉寺	Sera Monastery (Tibet)
色拉寺金刚橛节	〈藏族〉Vajrakila Worship Festival of Sera Monastery (on December 27th in Tibetan calendar)
色木槭	〈植〉*Acer mono*; painted maple
色扎寺	→南宗扎寺
瑟宾节	〈鄂温克族〉Sebin Festival (in the mid-to-late of the 5th lunar month)
僧侣生活	monasticism
僧王府	Prince Seng Mansion (Beijing)

沙冬青	〈植〉*Ammopiptanthus mongolicus*; Mongolian Ammopiptanthus Leaf
沙湖景区	Sand Lake Scenic Resort (Ningxia)
沙湖湿地公园	Shahu Wetland Park (Hubei)
沙画	sand painting; sand draw
沙棘	〈中药〉*Hippophae rhamnoides*; sea buckthorn
沙家浜阿庆嫂民俗风情旅游节	Folk Tourism Festival of Aunt A-Qing in Shajiabang
沙家浜阳澄湖大闸蟹美食节	Gourmet Festival of Yangcheng Lake Hairy Crabs in Shajiabang
沙咀道游乐场	Sha Tsui Road Playground (Hong Kong)
沙梨	〈植〉*Pyrus pyrifolia*; sand pear; Chinese pear
沙鲁寺	Shalu Monastery; Schalu Kloster (Tibet)
沙面岛	Shamian Island (Guangdong)
沙漠之谜	〈古〉Mystery of Desert (in the Xia Dynasty)
沙皮狗	〈动〉*Canis lupus familiaris*; Chinese shar-pei; shar pei
沙坪无耳蟾	〈动〉*Atympanophrys shapingensis*
沙坡头风景[旅游]区	Shapotou Scenic Spot; Shapotou Tourist Area (Ningxia)
沙坡头自然保护区	Shapotou Nature Reserve (Ningxia)
沙生柽柳	〈植〉*Tamarix taklamakanensis*
沙滩浴场	sand beach bathing place
沙田车公庙	Che Kung Temple in Sha Tin (Hong Kong)
沙田大会堂	Sha Tin Town Hall (Hong Kong)
沙田大围侯王宫	Tai Wai Marquis Palace at Sha Tin (Hong Kong)
沙田公园	Sha Tin Park (Hong Kong)
沙田马场	Sha Tin Racecourse (Hong Kong)
沙头角	Shatoujiao; Sha Tau Kok (Guangdong)
沙溪湖	Sand Creek Lake (Chongqing)
砂刀沟风景线	(of Zhangjiajie) Shadao Valley scenic route
鲨鱼馆	shark aquarium
晒布岩	(of Wuyi Mountain) Cloth Drying Rock
晒草湾游乐场	Sai Tso Wan Recreation Ground (Hong Kong)

晒佛节	〈藏族〉Thangka Festival (from the 29th June to the 1st July of the Tibetan calendar)
晒经石	Rock of Sutra Drying; Sutra Drying Rock (Sichuan)
晒龙袍	→天贶节
晒衣节	〈民俗〉Clothes Drying Day (on the 6th day of the 6th lunar month)
山白树	〈植〉*Sinowilsonia henryi*
山城夜景	night views of the hilly city
山顶公园	Victoria Peak Garden (Hong Kong)
山顶缆车	Peak Tram (Hong Kong)
山东地下大峡谷	Shandong Underground Grand Canyon
山东[竹板]快书	〈曲艺〉Shandong Clapper Ballad
山拐枣	〈植〉*Poliothyrsis sinensis*; Chinese pearl bloom tree
山海关	Shanhaiguan; Shanhai Pass (Hebei) →天下第一关
山海天旅游度假区	Shanhai Tian Tourism Resort (Shandong)
山茴香	〈植〉*Carlesia sinensis*; dentate wampee leaf/root
山橘	〈植〉*Fortunella hindsii*; hybrid oval kumquat
山抗节	〈布朗族〉Shankang Festival (on April 15th)
山蜡树	Chinese privet
山林节	〈怒族〉Mountain Forest Worship (on the 4th or 5th day of the 1st lunar month)
山林景观	mountain forest landscape
山门	mountain gate; gate to a monastery (an ornamental archway usually decorated with stone dragons)
山门景区	Shanmen Scenic Area; Mountain Gate Tourist Resort (Jilin)
山门水库	Mountain Gate Reservoir (Jilin)
山珊瑚	〈植〉*Galeola faberi*
山神庙	Shanshen Temple; Mountain Deity Temple (Shandong)
山桃	Chinese wild peach
山铜材	〈植〉*Chunia bucklandioides*; mountain copper

山西高原	Shanxi Plateau
山溪鲵	〈动〉*Batrachuperus pinchonii*; stream salamander
山楂	〈植〉*Crataegus pinnatifida*; haw
山茱萸	〈植〉*Cornus officinalis*
杉湖	Shanhu (Fir) Lake (Guangxi)
杉林幽径	(of Zhangjiajie) Fir Forest Path
杉木	〈植〉*Cunninghamia lanceolate*; Chinese fir
珊瑚婚	coral wedding (the 35th anniversary of marriage)
舢板	sampan (a kind of boat)
陕北黄土高原	Northern Shaanxi Loess Plateau
陕北剪纸	Northern Shaanxi Paper-Cut
陕北民歌	Northern Shaanxi Folk Song
陕北说书	Northern Shaanxi Storytelling
陕北窑洞	Northern Shaanxi cave dwelling
陕西杜鹃	→太白山[陕西]杜鹃
陕西歌舞大剧院	Shaanxi Grand Opera House
陕西槭	〈植〉*Acer shensiense*; Shaanxi maple
陕西小檗	〈植〉*Berberis shensiana*; Shaanxi berberis
陕州地坑院景区	Shanzhou Silo-Cave Scenic Area (He'nan)
扇蕨	〈植〉*Neocheiropteris palmatopedata*
扇面亭	(of Lion Forest Garden) Fan-Shaped Pavilion
扇子崖景区	(of Mount Taishan) Fan Cliff tour zone
善化寺	Shanhua Temple (Shanxi)
商城肥鲵	〈动〉*Pachyhynobius shangchengensis*; Shangcheng stout salamander
商丘古城	Shangqiu Ancient Town (He'nan)
商丘日月湖景区	Sun Moon Lake Scenic Area in Shangqiu (He'nan)
赏花节	〈藏族〉Flower-Admiring Day
赏菊	〈民俗〉to enjoy chrysanthemum; to admire the beauty of chrysanthemum
赏月	〈民俗〉to enjoy the glorious full moon; to appreciate the glorious full moon
上步盖掌	Backhand stroke in bow step
上步七星	(of Tai Chi) Stepping forward with seven stars

上方山森林公园	Shangfang Mountain Forest Park (Jiangsu, Beijing)
上丰花果山	Mountain of Flowers and Fruits at Shangfeng (Anhui)
上瓜景区	Shanggua Scenic Area (Guizhou)
上海 1930 风情街	Shanghai 1930 Fengqing Street; Shanghai 1930 Leisure Street
上海滨江森林公园	Shanghai Riverside Forest Park
上海博物馆	Shanghai Museum
上海菜	〈烹饪〉Shanghai cuisine
上海长江隧桥	Yangtze River Tunnel and Bridge of Shanghai
上海辰山植物园	Shanghai Chenshan Botanical Garden
上海迪士尼度假区	Shanghai Disney Resort
上海迪士尼乐园	Shanghai Disneyland Park
上海儿童博物馆	Shanghai Children's Museum
上海法租界	French Concession in Shanghai
上海方言	Shanghai dialect →上海话
上海歌剧院	Shanghai Opera House
上海国际电影节	Shanghai International Film Festival
上海国际赛车场	Shanghai International Circuit
上海国际艺术节	Shanghai International Arts Festival
上海国际音乐烟花节	Shanghai International Music Fireworks Festival
上海海湾森林公园	Shanghai Bay Forest Park
上海海洋水族馆	Shanghai Ocean Aquarium
上海和平公园	Shanghai Peace Park
上海沪剧院	Shanghai Huju Opera Theatre
上海滑稽剧团	Shanghai Farce Troupe
上海话	Shanghainese →上海方言
上海话剧艺术中心	Shanghai Dramatic Arts Centre
上海欢乐谷	Shanghai Happy Valley
上海环球金融中心	Shanghai World Financial Centre
上海基督教诸圣堂	All Saint Church
上海金茂大厦	Shanghai Jinmao Tower
上海科技馆	Shanghai Science and Technology Museum

上海老街	Shanghai Old Street
上海历史博物馆	Shanghai History Museum
上海旅游节	Shanghai Tourism Festival
上海马戏城	Shanghai Circus World
上海玛雅海滩水公园	Playa Maya Water Park at Shanghai; Shanghai Maya Beach Water Park
上海美术馆	Shanghai Art Museum
上海浦东国际机场	Shanghai Pudong International Airport
上海人民广场	People's Square of Shanghai
上海石库门	Shanghai Shikumen
上海世博会	2010 Shanghai World Expo; Shanghai World Expo 2010
上海世博展览馆	Shanghai World Expo Exhibition & Convention Centre
上海世纪公园	Shanghai Century Park
上海唐墓桥露德圣母堂	Shanghai Lude Chapel of Our Lady; Shanghai Church of Our Lady of Lourdes
上海体育馆	Shanghai Stadium
上海外滩	Waitan; Shanghai Bund (Shanghai)
上海文化广场	Shanghai Culture Square
上海文庙	Shanghai Confucian Temple
上海鲜花港	Shanghai Flower Port
上海新国际博览中心	Shanghai New International Expo Centre
上海新天地	Shanghai Xintiandi; New World of Shanghai
上海寻梦园香草农场景区	Scenic Area of Dream Garden Vanilla Farm in Shanghai
上海野生动物园	Shanghai Wild Animal Park
上海音乐厅	Shanghai Concert Hall
上海越剧院	Shanghai Yueju Opera House
上海展览中心	Shanghai Exhibition Centre
上海植物园	Shanghai Botanical Garden
上海朱家角古镇	Shanghai Zhujiajiao Ancient Town
上海自然博物馆	Shanghai Natural History Museum
上虎跳峡	Upper Tiger Leaping Gorge (Yunnan)

上季节海	(of Jiuzhai Valley) Upper Seasonal Lake
上九节	〈藏族〉Shangjiu Festival (on the 9th day of the 1st lunar month)
上联	(of a couplet) left roll
上梁酒	〈习俗〉shangliang banquet; beam-framing wine
上马酒	〈蒙古族〉up-horse wine; stirrup-cup
上马石	horse-mounting stone
上清宫	Shangqing Palace; Lofty Purity Palace (He'nan, Sichuan)
上清古镇	Shangqing Ancient Town (Jiangxi)
上泉寺	Shangquan Temple (Sichuan; Hubei)
上涉湖湿地国家自然保护区	Shangshe Lake Wetland Nature Reserve (Hubei)
上巳节	Shangsi Festival →三月三
上碗窑樊仙宫	Fan Sin Temple of Sheung Wun Yiu (Hong Kong)
上香	to burn joss sticks (before an idol or a spirit tablet); to burn incense (for praying)
上窑森林公园	Shangyao Forest Park (Anhui)
上元节	Lantern Festival (on the 15th day of the 1st lunar month) →元宵节
尚湖太公美食节	Taigong Food Festival of Shanghu Lake
烧百期	〈丧〉to hold a memorial ceremony on the hundredth day of a deceased
烧三年纸	〈丧〉to hold a memorial ceremony on the third anniversary of a deceased
烧头年纸	〈丧〉to hold a memorial ceremony on the first anniversary of a deceased
烧香	to burn joss sticks (before an idol)
烧香港	Shaoxiang Harbour; Incense Burning Harbour (Zhejiang)
烧纸(钱)	〈丧〉to burn joss paper (a mourning for the deceased)
筲箕湾谭公庙	Tam Kung Temple of Shau Kei Wan (Hong Kong)
筲箕湾天后庙	Tin Hau Temple of Shau Kei Wan (Hong Kong)

勺鸡	〈动〉*Pucrasia macrolopha*; koklass pheasant
芍药	〈植〉*Paeonia lactiflora*; peony
韶峰耸翠	Green Pines on the Apex (one of the Eight Scenes on Shaoshan, Hu'nan)
韶山	Shaoshan; Shaoshan Mountain (hometown of Mao Zedong) (Hu'nan)
韶山八景	Eight Scenes on Shaoshan (Hu'nan)
少数民族文化	minority culture
少昊陵	Shaohao Tomb (Shandong)
少华山	1 Shaohua Mountain (Shaanxi) 2 →三清[少华]山
少华山森林公园	Shaohua Mountain Forest Park (Shaanxi)
少林功夫	〈武术〉Shaolin kung-fu
少林寺	Shaolin Temple; Shaolin Monastery (He'nan)
少林(寺)塔林	Pagoda Forest at Shaolin Temple (He'nan)
少年节	〈高山族〉Juvenile Festival (within the 3rd lunar month)
少室山景区	(of Shaolin Temple) Shaoshi Mountain Scenic Area
邵族部落	Thao ethnic tribe
邵族祭典	Thao religious ceremonies
绍兴花雕酒	Shaoxing Huadiao Medium Sweet Wine
绍兴黄酒	Shaoxing rice wine
绍兴兰亭	Shaoxing Orchid Pavilion (the garden residence of Wang Xizhi, a famous calligrapher in the Eastern Jin Dynasty) (Zhejiang)
绍兴戏	Shaoxing Opera →越剧
猞猁	〈动〉*Lynx lynx*; lynx
畲族	She ethnic group; She
舌喙兰	〈植〉*Hemipilia cruclata*
舌柱麻	〈植〉*Archiboehmeria atrata*
舌子岩	(of Zhangjiajie) Tongue Rock
佘山国家旅游度假区	Sheshan Mountain National Tourist Resort (Shanghai)
佘太君庙	She Taijun Temple (Beijing)

蛇年	Year of the Snake (one of 12 zodiac signs)
蛇山	Snake Hill (Hubei)
蛇山炮台	Snake Hill Fort (Hubei)
舍利殿[堂]	Buddha's relics hall
舍利弗	〈佛〉Sariputra (one of the ten disciples of the Buddha, best-known for his wisdom)
舍利塔	Buddha's relics tower
设灵	〈丧〉to set up a mourning hall
社稷坛	(of Zhongshan Park) Imperial Divine Temple; Altar of the Land and Grain
射雕影视城	Shediao Film and TV City; Film and TV City for the Legend of Condor Hero (Zhejiang)
射干	〈植〉*Belamcanda chinensis*; blackberry lily; leopard flower
射轿帘	〈婚〉(of wedding) empty arrow-shootings at the air, ground and the bride (symbolizing good luck and getting rid of evil)
射弩会	〈傈僳族〉Crossbow-Shooting Day
射鸭廊	(of Master-of-Nets Garden) Duck Shooting Corridor
涉园	〈旧〉Sheyuan Garden (Jiangsu) →耦[涉]园
摄山	〈旧〉Sheshan Mountain (Jiangsu) →栖霞山
歙砚	Shezhou ink-stone; She ink-stone (one of the four famous ink-stones in China, which is produced in Shezhou, Anhui)
麝	〈动〉*Noschus noschiferus*; musk deer
麝香猫	〈动〉*Viverra zibetha*; civet cat
麝鼹	〈动〉*Scaptochirus moschatus*; desman
深水湾	Deep Water Bay (Hong Kong)
深潭凝碧三角岩	(of Nanxi River Scenic Area) Triangle Rock of Deep Pool
深圳碧梧栖景区	Scenic Area of Parasol Tree and Phoenix Perching in Shenzhen (Guangdong)

深圳东部华侨城	Overseas Chinese Town in Eastern Shenzhen (Guangdong)
深圳东湖公园景区	East Lake Park Scenic Area in Shenzhen (Guangdong)
深圳凤谷鸣琴景区	Fenggu Mingqin Scenic Area in Shenzhen (Guangdong)
深圳河	Shenzhen River (Guangdong)
深圳明思克航母世界	Shenzhen Minsk World (Guangdong)
深圳生态保护区	Eco-Protection Zone in Shenzhen (Guangdong)
深圳梧桐烟云景区	Clouds Scenic Area on Top of Wutong Mountain in Shenzhen (Guangdong)
深圳仙湖植物园	Fairy Lake Botanical Garden in Shenzhen (Guangdong)
神厨	(of Temple of Heaven and Zhongshan Park) Divine Kitchen
神墩岗古文化遗址	Shendun Gang Ancient Culture Site (Hubei)
神功圣德碑亭	Stele Pavilion of Divine Merits (Jiangsu)
神库	(of Zhongshan Park) Divine Storehouse
神龙戏松	(of Mount Sanqing) Holy Dragon Playing with the Pine
神龙峡景区	Dragon Gorge Scenic Area (Chongqing)
神路十二生肖	(of Wanfo Garden) Sacred Twelve Chinese Zodiac Signs
神牛泉	Immortal Ox Spring (Hubei)
神农祠	Shennong (Emperor Yan) Temple (Shaanxi)
神农顶	Shennong Peak (Hubei)
神农顶神秀台	(of Shennongjia) Shenxiu Platform of Shennong Peak
神农祭坛	(of Shennongjia) Shennong Altar
神农架	Shennongjia (Hubei)
神农架山	Shennongjia Mountain (Hubei)
神农架自然保护区	Shennongjia Nature Reserve (Hubei)
神农溪	Shennong Stream; Shennong River (Hubei)
神农溪纤夫文化	Tracker Cultural of Shennong River (Hubei)

神女峰	(of Three Gorges) Goddess Peak; Peak of Goddess →望霞峰
神拳门	Shenquan Sect; Divine Boxing Sect (from The Heaven Sword and Dragon Saber written by Jin Yong)
神树	trees of miracle
神堂湾	(of Zhangjiajie) Shentang Bay
神荼	〈道〉Shen Tu (an ancient immortal)
神武门	(of Imperial Palace) Gate of Divine Prowess
神仙池景区	(of Jiuzhai Valley) Shenxianchi Scenic Area; Fairy Pool Scenic Area (Sichuan)
神仙洞	Immortals Cave
神仙谷	(of Tiantang Zhai) Immortal Valley
神香草	→牛膝草
神鹰护鞭	(of Zhangjiajie) Hawk Guarding the Golden Whip
神鹰峡	Shenying Gorge (Chongqing)
神乐署	(of Temple of Heaven) Divine Music Administration
神州荒漠野生动物园	Shenzhou Desert Wildlife Park (Gansu)
沈丛文故居	Former Residence of Shen Congwen (Hu'nan)
沈阳道古玩市场	Shenyang Dao (Road) Antique Market (Tianjin)
沈阳故宫	Shenyang Imperial Palace (Liaoning) →后金故宫
沈阳故宫博物院	Imperial Palace Museum of Shenyang (Liaoning)
沈阳怪坡	Shenyang Magic Slope (Liaoning)
沈阳森林公园	Shenyang Forest Park (Liaoning)
肾盖铁线蕨	〈植〉*Adiantum erythrochlamys*
升庵桂湖	Sheng'an Guihu Lake; Sheng'an Laurel Lake (Sichuan)
升仙坊	(of Mount Taishan) Shengxian Bridge; Arch of Ascending Immortals
生旦净末丑	〈戏〉(of Beijing Opera) Sheng, Dan, Jing, Mo, Chou
生态猴区	(of Mount Emei) Eco-Zone of monkeys
生态缓冲区	ecological buffer area; zoological buffer area

生肖	Chinese zodiac; Chinese zodiac sign (representing any of the twelve Earthly Branches to symbolize the year in which a person is born)
生肖动物	zodiac animal
声容静	〈古〉Moderateness of Voice (to speak and behave quietly) (a saying from Book of Rites)
省博物馆	provincial museum
省会华表	Ornamental Pillar of The Provincial Capital (Guangdong) →莲花塔
圣公会马礼逊堂	Macau Protestant Chapel (a house of prayer for all nations) →马礼逊教堂
圣湖	Holy Lakes (Tibet)
圣火广场	Plaza of Holy Fire (Beijing)
圣纪[忌]节	〈伊斯兰〉Mauludin Nabi; Mawlid (one of the three major Islamic festivals, on March 12th in the Islamic calendar)
圣经山	Holy Classics Mountain (Shandong)
圣境山	Shengjing Mountain; Sacred Landscape Mountain (Hubei)
圣母殿	(of Jinci Temple) Hall of Saintly Mother
圣泉峰	Shengquan Peak (Chongqing; Anhui)
圣时门	Gate of Sage Time (Shandong)
圣水阁	(of Mount Emei) Holy Water Pavilion
圣岩寺	Shengyan Temple (Zhejiang)
圣友寺	→清净[圣友]寺
圣佑庙	Shengyou Lamasery (Xinjiang)
圣源寺	Shengyuan Temple (Yunnan)
圣约翰大教堂	St. John's Cathedral (Hong Kong)
胜天生态农庄	Shengtian Ecological Farm (Hubei)
盛京故宫	Shengjing Imperial Palace (Liaoning) →沈阳故宫
盛宴美食街	Food Feast Street; Street-Food Delicacies (Chongqing)
嵊山岛	Shengshan Island (Zhejiang)
嵊泗列岛	Shengsi Islands (Zhejiang)
诗碑亭	shibei pavilion; poem stele pavilion

狮头峡	Shitou Gorge; Lion Head Gorge (Chongqing)
狮(子)舞	〈舞〉Lion Dance
狮子峰	(of Mount Huangshan) Lion Peak
狮子狗	Pekingese; peke; lion dog
狮子吼	〈武术〉Lion howling (one of Shaolin's 72 Stunts)
狮子林	Lion Forest Garden; Lion Grove Garden (Jiangsu)
狮子山	Shizi Mountain; Lion Mountain (Hong Kong)
狮子山郊野公园	Lion Rock Country Park (Hong Kong)
狮子亭	Lion Pavilion (Hong Kong)
狮子岩	(of Nanxi River Scenic Area) Lion Rock
十八重溪石林	Eighteen Streams and Stone Forest (Fujian)
十八乱冢	Eighteen Disorderly Tombs (Hebei)
十八罗汉	〈佛〉Eighteen Arhats
十八曼陀罗花馆	(of Humble Administrator's Garden) Hall of 18 Thorn-Apples
十八盘	(of Mount Taishan) Eighteen Bends
十渡景区	Shidu Scenic Area (Beijing)
十二生肖公园	Chinese Zodiac Garden (Beijing)
十二生肖兽首	heads of twelve zodiac animal
十二属相	twelve symbolic animals; twelve zodiac signs
十方禅院	Shifang Buddhist Temple (Jiangsu)
十九坨	→石臼[十九]坨
十里画廊	(of Zhangjiajie) Art Gallery of Ten Miles; Miles Long Gallery
十里潜溪景区	Shi Li Qian Xi Scenic Area (Zhejiang)
十六浦主题公园	Ponte 16 Theme Park (Macao)
十七孔桥	(of Summer Palace) Seventeen-Arch Bridge
十全街	Shiquan Street (Jiangsu) →十泉街
十泉街	〈旧〉Ten Spring Well Street (Jiangsu) →十全街
十三陵	Ming Tombs (tombs of 13 Ming emperors built outside Beijing during 15-17th centuries) (Beijing)
十三陵水库	Ming Tombs' Reservoir (Beijing)

十万大山	Shiwan Dashan Mountain; Shiwan Grand Mountain (Guangxi)
十万大山刘树蛙	〈动〉*Liuixalus shiwandashan*
十万大山森林公园	Shiwan Grand Mountain Forest Park (Guangxi)
十王亭	Shiwang Pavilion; Pavilions of Ten Kings (Liaoning)
十堰四方山植物园	Shiyan Sifang Mountain Botanical Garden (Hubei)
十月年	〈哈尼族〉Hani Yearly Festival (in the 10th lunar month)
十字手	(of Tai Chi) Cross hands
什锦丁香	〈植〉*Syringa chinensis*; Chinese lilac
石澳泳滩	Shek O Beach (Hong Kong)
石板房	flagstone house
石宝山	Shibao Mountain (Yunnan)
石宝山歌会	Song Meeting in Shibao Mountain
石壁流泉	Stream of Spring Water from Rock Cracks (one of the Eight Scenes on Shaoshan, Hu'nan)
石壁泻珠	Water Dropping Cliff (Tulugou, Gansu)
石城古刹	Shicheng Ancient Buddhist Temple (Zhejiang) →新昌大佛寺
石城门	Stone Gate (one of the thirteen inner city gates of the Ming Dynasty in Nanjing) (Jiangsu)
石城山	Shicheng Mountain (Zhejiang)
石岛	Rocky Island (Hai'nan)
石雕	stone sculptures
石洞古庙	Ancient Stone Cave Temple (Guangdong)
石舫	1 (of Lion Forest Garden) Stone-Boat-Shaped Pavilion 2 →清晏舫
石佛寺	shifo temple; stone buddha temple
石鼓瀑	Shigu Waterfall; Stone Drum Waterfall (Sichuan)
石花菜	〈植〉*Gelidium amansii*; Chinese Gelatin
石花洞景区	Shihua Cave Scenic Area (Beijing)
石花瓶	carved stone flower vase

石矶观鱼	(of Chengde Mountain Resort) Watching Fish on Rocky Ledge
石鸡	〈动〉*Alectoris chukar*; partridge
石家大院	Shi Family Courtyard (Tianjin)
石经墙	stone scripture wall
石经寺	Shijing Temple; Stone Scripture Temple (Sichuan)
石景山游乐园	Shijingshan Amusement Park (Beijing)
石臼[十九]坨	Shijiutuo Islet (Hebei) →菩提岛
石臼坨岛	Shijiu Tuo Island (Hebei)
石窟建筑	Sacred Grottoes (Xinjiang)
石窟寺	Grotto Temples (Gansu)
石库门博物馆	Shikumen House Museum (Shanghai)
石廊	stone gallery
石廊峡谷景区	Stone Corridor Canyon Scenic Area (Fujian)
石梁瀑布	Shiliang Waterfall (Zhejiang)
石林	Stone Forest (Yunnan)
石林峡	Stone Forest Gorge (Beijing)
石林峡景区	Shilin Gorge Scenic Area; Scenic Area of Stone Forest Gorge (Beijing)
石榴	〈植〉*Punica granatum*; pomegranate
石龙沟景区	Shilong Gully Scenic Area; Stone Dragon Valley Scenic Area (He'nan)
石路步行街	Shilu Walking Street; Stone-Paved Walking Street (Jiangsu)
石马关	(of Huanglong Valley) Stone Horse Pass
石漫滩公园	Shiman Beach Park (He'nan)
石漫滩水库景区	Shimantan Reservoir Scenic Area (Henan)
石门涧	(of Mount Lushan) Rock Gate Gully
石门山	Shimen Mountain (Gansu)
石门水库	Shimen Reservoir (Shaanxi)
石排湾郊野公园	Shek Pai Wan Country Park (Macao)
石牌坊	stone memorial arch
石盘水库	Shipan Reservoir (Fujian)

石棚山	Shipeng Mountain (Jiangsu)
石棋盘	stone chessboard
石阡万寿宫	Shiqian Wanshou Palace; Shiqian Longevity Palace (Guizhou) →豫章合省会馆
石人山	Shiren Mountain; Human-Shaped Stone Mountain (He'nan) →尧山景区
石人山景区	(of Shaolin Temple) Shiren (Stone Man) Mountain Scenic Area
石山木莲	〈植〉*Manglietia calcarea*
石塔斜影	Pond Reflection of Leaning Pagoda (Zhangjiajie, Hu'nan)
石塔镇海	(of Huanglong Valley) Stone Pagoda Guarding Lake
石听琴室	(of Garden of Harmony) Studio of Slumped Man Listening to Streaming Sound
石头城	Stone Castle (ancient Pantuo State) (Xinjiang)
石屋清风	Stone House (one of the Eight Scenes on Shaoshan, Hu'nan)
石像生	stone animal; stone (human) statue (installed in front of imperial mausoleums) →翁仲
石燕岩	(of Tiantang Zhai) Swallow-Like Rock
石羊河流域	Shiyang River Basin
石雨伞	Stone Umbrella (Taiwan)
石钟寺	Shizhong Temple (Yunnan)
石竹山	Shizhu Mountain (Fujian)
食草动物区	herbivore zone
史氏小姬蛙	〈动〉*Micryletta steinegeri*; stejneger's paddy frog; stejneger's narrow-mouthed toad
始信峰	(of Mount Huangshan) Convincing Peak
士林官邸	Shilin Official Residence; Chiang Kai-shek Shilin Residence (Taiwan)
士林夜市	Shilin Night Market (Taiwan)
世博轴	Expo Axis (Shanghai)
世纪公园	Century Park (Shanghai)

世纪广场	Century Square (Shanghai)
世纪花钟	Flower Clock of the Century (Shanghai)
世界魔鬼城	World Ghost Town (Xinjiang)
世界烧香节	〈藏族〉World Incense Festival
世界屋脊	Rooftop of the World →青藏高原
世界休博园	World Leisure Expo Garden (Zhejiang)
世界艺术馆	World Art Museum (Beijing)
世界园艺博览园	World Horti-Expo Garden (Yunnan)
世界之窗	Window of the World (Guangdong; Hu'nan)
世贸中心	World Trade Centre (Zhejiang)
世系宗祠	ancestral lineage hall
世运公园	Olympic Garden (Hong Kong)
市政局百周年纪念花园	Urban Council Centenary Garden (Hong Kong)
试马埭	(of Chengde Mountain Resort) Racecourse for Horse Testing
柿子	〈植〉*Diospyros kaki*; persimmon
释迦牟尼	〈佛〉Sakyamuni
释迦牟尼殿	〈佛〉Sakyamuni Buddha Hall
释迦牟尼佛像	〈佛〉Buddha statue of Sakyamuni
释迦文舍利宝塔	〈佛〉Shijiawen Pagoda
收获[丰收]祭	〈高山族〉Harvest Festival
收获节	〈傈僳族〉Harvest Day
收势	(of Tai Chi) Closing form
手工织锦	handmade tapestry
手挥琵琶	(of Tai Chi) Hand strumming the lute
手婚	hand wedding (the 7th anniversary of marriage) →铜婚
手容恭	〈古〉politeness of hand manner (the fingers should not act randomly in etiquette activities) (a saying from The Book of Rites) →君子九容
守灵[铺]	〈丧〉to stand as guards at the bier; to keep vigil beside the coffin
守岁	〈民俗〉to stay up late or all night on New Year's Eve

守制	〈旧〉to go into mourning for one's parents →丁忧守制
首阳山景区	Shouyang Mountain Scenic Area (Gansu)
寿安宫	(of Imperial Palace) Palace of Peace and Longevity
寿安寺	Shou'an Temple (Shanghai)
寿诞礼	birthday ceremony
寿康宫	(of Imperial Palace) Palace of Longevity and Health
寿联	birthday couplests; longevity couplets
寿鹿山国家森林公园	Shoulu Mountain National Forest Park (Gansu)
寿丘黄帝诞生地	Birth Place of Emperor Huangdi in Shouqiu (Shandong)
寿终正寝	to die a natural death; to die peacefully in bed
寿州窑遗址	Shouzhou Kiln Relics
瘦房兰	〈植〉*Ischnogyne mandarinorum*; mandarin ischnogyne
瘦西湖	Slender West Lake (Jiangsu)
书法博物馆	calligraphy museum
书院门文化街	Shuyuan Men (Gate) Culture Street (Shaanxi)
梳妆楼	Shuzhuang Hall (Shanxi) →水母楼
舒啸亭	(of Lingering Garden) Shuxiao Pavilion
疏花水柏枝	〈植〉*Myricaria laxiflora*
蜀汉	Shu Han Kingdom (221-263, a regime in the Three Kingdoms period)
蜀山森林公园	Shushan Forest Park (Anhui)
蜀藏兜蕊兰	〈植〉*Androcorys spiralis*
鼠年	Year of the Rat; Year of the Mouse (one of 12 zodiac signs)
数来宝	rhythmic storytelling to clapper accompaniment →快板
树正沟风景线	(of Jiuzhai Valley) Shuzheng Gully tour route
树正瀑布	(of Jiuzhai Valley) Shuzheng Waterfall
树正群海	(of Jiuzhai Valley) Shuzheng Lakes
树正寨	(of Jiuzhai Valley) Shuzheng Village

竖掌	〈武术〉Upright palm
庶族	common people; a family of commoners
漱芳斋	(of Imperial Palace) Hall of Imperial Entertainment
漱芳斋戏台	(of Imperial Palace) Stage of the Hall of Imperial Entertainment
耍海会	〈白族〉Lake-Playing Meetings (starting on the 24th and 6th lunar month)
摔跤节	〈侗族〉Wresting Day (on the 15th day of the 2nd lunar month)
涮羊肉	instant-boiled mutton →羊肉火锅
双墩文化	Shuangdun Culture (about 7000 B.C., one of the important sources of the origin of Chinese characters)
双盾木	〈植〉*Dipelta floribunda*; rosy dipelta
双峰插云	(of West Lake)Twin Peaks Soaring through the Clouds; Twin Peaks Piercing the Clouds
双峰贯耳	(of Tai Chi) Striking opponent's ears with both fists
双峰林场	Shuangfeng Forestry Centre (Heilongjiang)
双合洞	(of Zhangjiajie) Shuanghe Karst Cave; Joined Couple Cave
双湖夹镜	(of Chengde Mountain Resort) Twin Lakes with a Dike-Bridge in Between
双环万寿亭	Double-Circle Longevity Pavilion (Beijing)
双节棍	〈武术〉nunchakus; nunchucks
双林寺	Shuanglin Temple (Shanxi)
双龙大桥	shuanglong bridge; twin dragon bridge
双龙洞	Shuanglong Cave; Twin Dragon Cave (Zhejiang)
双龙海	(of Jiuzhai Valley) Twin Dragons Lake
双龙湖	Shuanglong Lake; Twin Dragon Lake (Chongqing)
双龙湖景区	Shuanglong Lake Scenic Area (Hubei)
双龙溶洞	Shuanglong Karst Cave (Shaanxi)

双龙潭	(of Mount Lushan) Twin Dragon Ponds
双拍脚	Double slap kick
双乳峰	(of Mount Wuyi) Peak of Two Breasts
双塔山	Shuangta Mountain; Twin Peak (Hebei)
双塔寺	Twin Pagoda Temple
双团棘胸蛙	〈动〉*Paa yunnanensis*; bi-lump spined-breasted frog
双尾褐凤蝶	〈动〉*Bhutanitis mansfieldi*; mansfield's three-tailed swallowtail
双喜	double happiness; double strokes of luck
霜降	〈节气〉Frost's Descent; Hoar-Frost Falls (the 18th solar term)
水车博览园	Waterwheel Exhibition Garden (Gansu)
水城拟小鲵	〈动〉*Pseudohynobius shuichengensis*; Shuicheng salamander
水城异角蟾	〈动〉*Xenophrys shuichengensis*; Shuicheng horned toad
水芳岩秀	(of Chengde Mountain Resort) Limpid Water and Charming Rockery
水丰景区	Shuifeng Scenic Area (Liaoning)
水府庙	Shuifu Temple; Waterland Temple (Hu'nan)
水光石	Iron Slab Peak (Fujian)
水龟石	Turtle Rocks (Fujian)
水浒城	Water Margin Town (Jiangsu)
水晶宫	Crystal Palace (Jiangxi)
水晶婚	crystal wedding (the 15th anniversary of marriage)
水镜台	Water Mirror Stage (Shanxi)
水口瀑布	Shuikou Waterfall (Jiangxi) →彩虹瀑
水口寺瀑布	Waterfall of the Shuikou Temple (Chongqing)
水立方	Water Cube (Beijing) →国家游泳中心
水帘长廊	Water Shade Long Corridor (Beijing)
水帘洞	Shuilian Cave; Water Curtain Cave (Gansu)

水流云在	(of Chengde Mountain Resort) Floating Clouds over Running Stream
水陆庵	Shuilu Nunnery (Shaanxi)
水磨沟	Watermill Valley (Xinjiang)
水母宫	Palace of Water Goddess (Hebei)
水母楼	River Goddess Building (Shanxi) →梳妆楼
水泡甜酒	〈纳西族〉Naxi bubble liqueur
水泊梁山	Marshes of Mount Liang; Marshes of Liangshan Mountain (cradle of Water Margin) (Shandong)
水绕四门	(of Zhanjiajie) Waters around Four Gates
水杉	〈植〉*Metasequoia glyptostroboides*; dawned redwood
水上乐园	water paradise
水生植物园	aquatic plant collection/garden
水松	〈植〉*Glyptostrobus pensilis*; water pine
水下长城	Submerged Section of the Great Wall (Hebei)
水香榭	(of Garden of Quiet Meditation) Water Fragrance Pavilion
水心榭	(of Chengde Mountain Resort) Pavilions at the Center of Lake
水岩	water rock (one of the famous pits of Duanyan)
水源洞	Shuiyuan Cave (Guangxi)
水源亭	Shuiyuan Pavilion; Riverhead Pavilion (Hu'nan)
水月洞	Shuiyue Cave; Water-Moon Cave (Guangxi)
水月宫	Shuiyue Palace (Guangdong)
水葬	〈丧〉water burial
水族	Shui ethnic group; Shui
睡莲	〈植〉*Nymphaea tetragona*; water lily
舜耕山	Mount Shungeng (Anhui)
说法堂	sermon hall
说媒	〈婚〉(of a marriage) match-making
说书	→评[说]书
司东康宫	Shidoukhan Palace (Tibet)
司马库斯部落	Smangus tribe

司马迁祠	Ancestral Temple of Sima Qian; Sima Qian Ancestral Temple (Shaanxi)
司马台长城	Simatai Great Wall (Beijing)
丝绸之府	home of the silk
丝绸之路	Silk Road (ancient trade route between China and the West)
丝绸之路博览会	Silk Road Expo
丝绸之路艺术节	Silk Road Art Festival
丝婚	silk wedding (the 4th anniversary of marriage) →象牙婚
思南公馆	Sinan Mansion (Shanghai)
缌麻	〈表〉gown of fine linen (one of five funeral garments) →五服
"四·八"烈士陵园	"April 8th" Revolutionary Martyrs' Mausoleum (Shaanxi)
四川侧柏	〈植〉*Thuja sutchuenensis*; Sichuan thuja →崖柏
四川独蒜兰	〈植〉*Pleione limprichtii*; hardy Chinese orchid
四川短尾鼩	〈动〉*Anourosorex squamipes*; Sichuan short-tailed shrew
四川棘蛙	〈动〉*Nanorana sichuanensis*; Szechuan paa liebigii
四川林跳鼠	〈动〉*Eozapus setchuanus*; Sichuan jumping mouse
四川毛尾睡鼠	〈动〉*Chaetocauda sichuanensis*; Sichuan dormouse
四川山鹧鸪	〈动〉*Arborophila rufipectus*; Sichuan partridge
四川湍蛙	〈动〉*Amolops mantzorum*; Sichuan torrent frog
四川狭口蛙	〈动〉*Kaloula rugifera*; Sichuan digging frog; Szechwan narrowmouth toad
四川雉鹑	〈动〉*Tetraophasis szechenyii*; verreaux's monal partridge
四大部洲	1〈佛〉Four Great Continents 2 (of Summer Palace) Four Continents (Han-Tibetan building complex)

四大道教圣地	four Taoist holy places (referring to Wudang Mountain, Longhu Mountain, Qincheng Mountain and Qiyun Mountain)
四大金刚	〈佛〉Four Heavenly Guardians
四大名山	〈佛〉Four Holy Mountains (Mount Wutai in Shanxi, Mount Putuo in Zhejiang, Mount Emei in Sichuan and Jiuhua Mountain in Anhui)
四洞峡	Sidong Valley; Four Cave Valley (Hubei)
四方顶子山	Square-Top Mountain (Jilin)
四福花	〈植〉*Tetradoxa omeiensis*
四合木	〈植〉*Tetraena mongolica*; oil firewood
四合院	siheyuan; courtyard dwellings; quadrangle dwellings (a courtyard with houses on all sides)
四季豆	〈植〉*Phaseolus vulgaris*; green beans
四季青	〈植〉*Ilex chinensis*; Chinese holly
四烈士纪念碑	Monument of Four Martyrs (Tianjin)
四裂无柱兰	〈植〉*Amitostigma basifoliatum*; basal leaved amitostigma
四面山	Simian Mountain (Chongqing)
四面云山	(of Chengde Mountain Resort) Pavilion among Clouds and Mountains
四神墓群	Sishen Tomb Group; Four Gods Tombs (Jilin)
四时潇洒亭	(of Garden of Harmony) Pavilion with Fine Bamboo in all Seasons
四世同堂	sishi tongtang; four generations under one roof
四梳白发齐眉	(of wedding) the fourth combing, blessed with longevity
四帅殿	Four Generals Hall (Hebei)
四天下	〈佛〉→四大部洲
四维影院	four-dimension cinema
四弦琴	〈乐〉four-stringed lute
四月八(节)	〈苗族〉Siyueba Festival; Eighth of the Fourth Month Festival; "Fourth Month 8" Festival

寺洼文化	Siwa Culture (1400–1100 B.C., the Bronze Age culture in Northwest China)
泗河湿地公园	Sihe River Wetland Park (Hubei)
松谷庵	(of Mount Huangshan) Pine Valley Nunnery
松谷景区	Pine Valley Scenic Area (Anhui)
松鹤清樾	(of Chengde Mountain Resort) Hall of Melodious Resonance of Pines and Cranes
松鹤斋	(of Chengde Mountain Resort) Hall of Pines and Cranes
松花湖	Songhua Lake (Jilin)
松花江	Songhua River (Heilongjiang)
松花江流域	Songhua River basin/valley
松卷绿茶	curled green tea
松辽平原	Songliao Plains
松林山	Songlin Mountain; Pinery Mountain (Hubei)
松岭邓公祠	Tang Chung Ling Ancestral Hall (Hong Kong)
松峦峰	Songluan Peak (Chongqing)
松鸣岩森林公园	Songming Rock Forest Park (Gansu)
松嫩平原	Songnen Plains
松浦大桥	Songpu Bridge (Shanghai)
松山缆车	Guia Cable Car (Macao)
松山战役	Songshan Mountain Campaign (1944)
松山自然保护区	Songshan Nature Reserve (Beijing)
松狮犬	chow chow
松鼠跳天都	(of Mount Huangshan) Squirrel Skipping to Celestial Capital
松涛水库	Songtao Reservoir (Hai'nan)
松州城遗址	Remains of the Songzhou Ancient Town (Sichuan)
嵩山	Mount Songshan; Songshan Mountain (He'nan)
嵩阳书院	(of Shaolin Temple) Songyang Academy
宋璟碑	Songjing Monument (Hebei)
宋庆龄故居	Former Residence of Soong Ching-ling (Beijing)
宋庆龄陵园	Soong Ching-ling Mausoleum Park (Shanghai)

宋庆龄上海故居	Soong Ching-ling Memorial Residence in Shanghai
宋王台	Sung Wong Toi (Hong Kong)
宋绣	Song Embroidery (traditional fine arts in Kaifeng, He'nan)
宋玉生公园	Dr. Carlos d'Assumpcao Park (Macao)
送灵	〈丧〉to offer one's condolences to a deceased by joining the funeral procession
送龙节	〈傣族〉Sacrifice to Dragon Festival
送亲	〈婚〉to accompany the bride to the bridegroom's family on wedding day
送入洞房	〈婚〉(of wedding) to be sent to the bridal chamber
送丧饭	food for funeral procession
送丧酒	〈彝族〉mourning wine; banquet for funeral ceremony
送行酒	farewell banquet
送妆	〈婚〉songzhuang; dowry offering (the bride's family sends the dowry to the bridegroom's home)
诵经	〈佛〉chanting
苏巴什佛寺遗址	Subash Buddhist Temple Ruins (Xinjiang)
苏堤	(of West Lake) Su Causeway
苏堤春晓	(of West Lake) Spring Dawn at Sudi Causeway
苏公祠	Sugong Memorial Temple (Hai'nan)
苏公塔	Sugong Pagoda (Xinjiang) →额敏塔
苏理玛酒	〈普米族、摩梭人〉Sulima wine
苏宁喜节	〈水族〉Mother Worship Festival (on Chou day of the 12th lunar month)
苏颂故居	Former Residence of Su Song (Fujian)
苏仙岭	Suxian Immortal Ridge (Hu'nan)
苏州河	Suzhou Creek; Suzhou River (Shanghai)
苏州街	(of Summer Palace) Suzhou Street

苏州留园	Suzhou Liuyuan Garden; Suzhou Lingering Garden (Jiangsu) →寒碧山庄
苏州市金鸡湖	Suzhou Jinji Lake (Jiangsu)
苏州太湖国家旅游度假区	Taihu Lake National Tourism Resort in Suzhou (Jiangsu)
苏州旺山九龙潭景区	Wangshan and Jiulong Pond Scenic Area in Suzhou (Jiangsu)
苏州园林	Classical Gardens of Suzhou (Jiangsu)
苏州拙政园	Zhuozheng Garden of Suzhou; Humble Administrator's Garden of Suzhou (Jiangsu)
酥油茶	butter tea; yak butter tea
酥油花	〈藏族〉butter sculpture
酥油花灯节	〈藏族〉Butter Lamp Festival
酥油花堂	〈藏族〉Hall of Butter Sculptures
素尚斋	(of Chengde Mountain Resort) House of Advocation for Simplicity
宿根花卉园	Perennial Flowers Park (Beijing)
宿云檐	(of Chengde Mountain Resort) Eaves with Clouds Lodged on
粟米草	〈植〉*Mollugo stricta*; carpet weed
酸辣汤	〈烹饪〉Hot and Sour Soup
酸竹	〈植〉*Acidosasa chinensis*; acid bamboo
蒜头果	〈植〉*Malania oleifera*; garlic fruit
算盘	abacus; counting frame
绥江金沙水上乐园	Suijiang Golden Sand Water Park
隋仁寿宫	Ruins of Renshou Palace of the Sui Dynasty (Shaanxi)
随礼[份子]	〈民俗〉to give money/cash as a wedding gift; to give presents in return
随州市新四军第五师尹家湾革命旧址群	Yinjiawan Revolutionary Sites of, the Fifth Division of the New Fourth Army in Suizhou (Hubei)

岁币	〈古〉suibi; annual tribute (the money and goods that the imperial court presents to foreign nations, or that the local government to the central authority each year)
岁寒草庐	(of Garden of Harmony) Thatched Cottage with Luxuriant Plants in Winter
岁酒	〈朝鲜族〉New Year Wine (prepared for New Year's Day)
岁首节	〈朝鲜族〉New Year's Day
岁岁平安	(of idiom) peace all year round; everlasting peace year after year
穗花杉	〈植〉*Amentotaxus argotaenia*; Chinese flowering yew
孙传芳故居	Former Residence of Sun Chuanfang (Tianjin)
孙中山故居	Former Residence of Sun Yat-sen (Guangdong)
孙中山故居纪念馆	Museum of Dr. Sun Yat-sen (Guangdong)
孙中山纪念馆	→国父[孙中山]纪念馆
孙中山市政纪念公园	Sun Yat-sen Municipal Memorial Park (Macao)
索罟湾	Sok Kwu Wan (Hong Kong)
索溪峪景区	(of Zhangjiajie) Suoxi Valley Scenic Area
索溪峪自然保护区	Suoxi (Stream) Valley Nature Reserve (Hu'nan)
唢呐	〈乐〉suona horn; Chinese horn (two-reed woodwind instrument)
唢呐瀑布	suona-sound waterfall
锁龙瀑	Dragon-Locking-Waterfall (Shaanxi)
锁绿轩	(of Garden of Harmony) Green-Locking Pavilion

T

塔川村	Tachuan Village (Anhui)
塔尔寺	Ta'er Monastery; Kumbum Monastery (Qinghai)
塔虎城遗址	Tahu Town Relics (Jilin)
塔虎古城	Tahu Ancient Town (Jilin)
塔吉克语	Tajik language
塔吉克族	Tajik ethnic group; Tajik
塔克拉玛干沙漠	Taklimakan/Taklamakan Desert (Xinjiang)
塔里木河	Tarim River (Xinjiang)
塔里木盆地	Tarim Basin; Tarim Depression (Xinjiang)
塔里木沙拐枣	〈植〉*Calligonum roborovskii*
塔林	(of Shaolin Temple) Pagoda Forest
塔岭晴霞	(of Shaoshan) Clear Sunglow over Tower Mountain
塔坪寺	Taping Temple (Chongqing)
塔石广场	Tashi Square (Macao)
塔塔尔族	Tartar ethnic group; Tartar
塔湾金沙	Tawan Golden Sand Beach (Zhejiang)
塔影亭	(of Humble Administrator's Garden) Tower Shadow Pavilion
踏青	〈民俗〉to go for outings; to have an outing in spring; to go for a countryside walk in spring
台北都会区	Taipei metropolis; Taipei metropolitan area →大台北地区
台北故宫	Taipei Palace Museum (Taiwan)
台北国际金融大楼	Taipei International Financial Centre (Taiwan)
台海	→台湾海峡
台南孔庙	Tainan Confucius Temple (Taiwan)

台湾堆	→吉贝屿
台湾海峡	Taiwan Strait
台湾黑熊	〈动〉*Ursus thibetanus formosanus*; formosan black bear
台湾猴	〈动〉*Macaca cyclopis*; Taiwanese macaque; formosan rock macaque
台湾厚唇兰	〈植〉*Epigeneium nakaharaei*; waxen flower epigeneium
台湾家酿果酒	Taiwan home-brewed fruit wine
台湾金狗毛蕨	〈植〉*Cibotium taiwanianum*; Taiwanense cibotium
台湾鬣羚	〈动〉*Capricornis swinhoei*; Taiwan serow
台湾牛齿兰	〈植〉*Appendicula formosana*; Taiwan stream orchids
台湾枪乌贼	〈动〉*Loligo formosana*; Taiwan calamari
台湾[长叶]蜻蜓兰	〈植〉*Tulotis devolii*
台湾曲轴蕨	〈植〉*Paesia taiwanensis*
台湾人	Taiwanese; Taiwan people
台湾山椒鱼	〈动〉*Hynobius formosanus*; Taiwan salamander
台湾石豆兰	〈植〉*Bulbophyllum aureolabellum*; tongued bulbophyllum
台湾鼠耳蝠	〈动〉*Myotis taiwanensis*
台湾水韭	〈植〉*Isoetes taiwanensis*
台湾水青冈	〈植〉*Fagus hayatae*; Taiwan beech
台湾穗花杉	〈植〉*Amentotaxus formosana*; Taiwan catkin yew
台湾田鼠	〈动〉*Microtus kikuchii*; Taiwan vole
台湾头蕊兰	〈植〉*Cephalanthera taiwaniana*
台湾无尾叶鼻蝠	〈动〉*Coelops frithi formosanus*; Chinese tailless leaf-nosed bat
台湾无柱兰	〈植〉*Amitostigma alpestre*
台湾虾脊兰	〈植〉*Calanthe arisanensis*; Mount A-Li calanthe
台湾小黄鼠狼	〈动〉*Mustela nivalis formosana*; Taiwan least weasel
台湾小鲵	→台湾山椒鱼
台湾云豹	〈动〉*Neofelis nebulosa brachyurus*; formosan clouded leopard

抬官节	〈侗族〉Official-Parade Day (to carry the official in an armchair for a parade) (on the 7th day of the 1st lunar month)
太白柴胡	〈植〉*Bupleurum dielsianum*; Taibai sickle-leaved hare's-ear
太白飞蓬	〈植〉*Erigeron taipeiensis*; Taibai fleabane
太白风毛菊	〈植〉*Saussurea taipaiensis*
太白红杉	〈植〉*Larix chinensis*
太白虎耳草	〈植〉*Saxifraga josephii*; Taibai rockfoil
太白龙胆	〈植〉*Gentiana apiata*; Taibai rough gentian
太白忍冬	〈植〉*Lonicera taipeiensis*; Taibai honeysuckle
太白山	Taibai Mountain (Shaanxi)
太白山[陕西]杜鹃	〈植〉*Rhododendron taibaiense*
太白山汤浴温泉	Tangyu Hot Spring in Taibai Mountain (Shaanxi)
太白山五加	〈植〉*Acanthopanax stenophyllus*
太白山溪鲵	〈动〉*Batrachuperus taibaiensis*; Taibai stream salamander
太白书屋	Taibai Book Hall (Sichuan)
太白野豌豆	〈植〉*Vicia taipaica*; Taibai vetch
太常观	(of Mount Wudang) Taichang Taoist Temple
太行大峡谷	Taihang Grand Canyon
太行花	〈植〉*Taihangia rupestris*
太行菊	〈植〉*Opisthopappus taihangensis*; Taihang Chrysanthemum
太行隆肛蛙	〈动〉*Feirana taihangnica*; Taihangshan swelled-vented frog
太行平湖	(of Taihang Grand Canyon) Taihang Pinghu Lake
太行山	Taihang Mountain
太行山大峡谷	Taihang Grand Canyon (Shanxi)
太行天路	Taihang Celestial Road
太昊陵	Taihao Mausoleum (He'nan)
太和茶楼	taihe teahouse
太和殿	(of Imperial Palace) Taihe Palace; Hall of Supreme Harmony →金銮殿

太和殿广场	(of Imperial Palace) Square of Hall of Supreme Harmony
太和宫	(of Mount Wudang) Taihe Palace
太和门	(of Imperial Palace) Gate of Supreme Harmony
太湖	Taihu Lake (the third largest fresh lake in China) (Jiangsu)
太湖景区	Taihu Lake Scenic Resort (Jiangsu)
太湖新银鱼	〈动〉neosalanx taihuensis; Taihu Lake silver fish
太极殿	(of Imperial Palace) Hall of Supreme Authority
太极剑	〈武术〉Tai Chi straight sword form
太极剧场	Tai Chi Theatre (Hubei)
太极拳	〈武术〉Tai Chi Chuan/Quan; Hexagram Boxing; Chinese Shadow Boxing
太极之乡	Cradle of Tai Chi (referring to Yongnian District of Handan, Hebei)
太姥山	Taimu Mountain (Fujian)
太鲁阁公园	Taroko National Park (Taiwan)
太庙	Taimiao Temple; Imperial Ancestral Temple (Beijing)
太平山顶	Victoria Peak (Hong Kong)
太平山国家森林游乐区	Taipingshan National Forest Recreation Area (Taiwan)
太平寺塔	Taiping Temple Pagoda (Shaanxi)
太平天国历史博物馆	Historical Museum of Taiping Heavenly Kingdom (Jiangsu)
太平湾景区	Taiping Wan Scenic Area (Liaoning)
太平湾水电站	Taipingwan Power Station (Liaoning)
太平兴国禅寺	Taiping Xingguo Temple; National Rejuvenation Temple (Jiangsu)
太平岩	(of Nanxi River Scenic Area) Taiping Rock
太平洋水下世界博览会	Pacific Underwater World Expo (Beijing)
太平寨	Taiping Mountain Stronghold (Tianjin)
太平钟楼	Taiping Bell Tower (Jilin)
太上老君	Taishang Laojun; Moral Lord (Ancestor of Taoism)

太室山景区	(of Shaolin Temple) Taishi Mountain Scenic Area
太王陵	Taiwang Mausoleum; Tomb of King Haotai (of Goguryeo) (Jilin)
太武山景区	Taiwu Mountain Scenic Area (Taiwan)
太阳岛公园	Sun Island Park (Heilongjiang)
太阳岛景区	Sun Island Scenic Area (Heilongjiang)
太阳日	〈满族〉Sun's Day (the 1st day of the 2nd lunar month)
太乙山	Taiyi Mountain (Shaanxi) →终南山
太原晋祠	Taiyuan Jinci Temple (Shanxi)
太子殿	Prince Hall (Shanxi)
太子坪	(of Mount Emei) Prince Terrace
太子坡	(of Mount Wudang) Prince Hillside →复真观
太子坡景区	(of Mount Wudang) Prince Hillside scenic area →复真观
太子雪山	Prince Snow Mountain (Yunnan)
泰丰公园	Taifeng Park (Tianjin)
泰陵	Tailing Mausoleum (Hebei)
泰山	Mount Taishan; Taishan Mountain (Shandong)
泰山神启跸回銮图	(of Mount Taishan) Mural of Taishan's God Returning to the Palace after an Inspection Tour
泰雅人	(of indigenous Taiwanese) Atayal; Tayal (belonging to the Gaoshan ethnic group)
滩口牌坊	Tankou Memorial Arch (Chongqing) →川东第一牌坊
弹琴蛙	〈动〉*Hylarana adenopleura*
弹拳	〈武术〉Spring horizontal back fist/boxing
弹跳力	〈武术〉jumping ability; spring ability
弹腿	〈武术〉Spring kick; Snap kick
弹腿冲拳	〈武术〉Snap kick with thrust punching/boxing
汤瓶(壶)	〈回族〉hot water pitcher
汤泉池景区	Tangquan Pond Scenic Spot; Hotspring Pond Scenic Area (He'nan)
汤泉行宫	Tangquan Palace; Hotspring Palace (Hebei)

汤山温泉	Tangshan Hot Spring (Jiangsu)
汤旺河国家公园	Tangwang River National Park (China's First National Park) (Heilongjiang)
汤玉麟故居	Former residence of Tang Yulin (Tianjin)
唐布拉草原	Tangbula Grassland (Xinjiang)
唐长安城	Tang Chang'an City (Shaanxi)
唐城	Tangcheng City (Jiangsu, Hubei)
唐城墙遗址公园	City Wall Heritage Park of Tang Dynasty (Shaanxi)
唐古拉山	Tanggula Mountains (Tibet, Qinghai)
唐古拉山口	Tanggula Mountain Pass (Tibet, Qinghai)
唐古拉山镇	Tanggula Town (Qinghai)
唐古特白刺	〈植〉*Nitraria tangutorum*
唐井遗址	Tangjing Site; Tang Well Site (Shaanxi)
唐九成宫遗址	Ruins of Jiucheng Palace of the Tang Dynasty (Shaanxi)
唐卡画	Thangka (a religious scroll painting decorated with colorful satin and hung for worship, and regarded as a masterpiece of Tibetan culture)
唐口公园	Tangkou Park (Tianjin)
唐睿宗桥陵	Qiaoling Tomb of Emperor Tang Ruizong (Shaanxi)
唐三彩	Tang San Cai; Tri-color Glazed Porcelain of the Tang Dynasty
唐山地震遗址纪念公园	Tangshan Earthquake Memorial Park (Hebei)
唐山抗震纪念馆	Tangshan Earthquake Memorial Hall (Hebei)
唐泰陵	Tailing Mausoleum of Emperor Tang Xuanzong (Shaanxi)
唐玄奘纪念堂	Memorial Hall of Xuanzang (Jiangsu)
唐崖寺村	Tangya Temple Village (Hubei)
塘沽堂	Tanggu Christian Church (Tianjin)
糖婚	candy wedding (the 6th anniversary of marriage) →铁婚
螳螂拳	Mantis Boxing; Mantis Style Boxing
趟拢门	push-pull bar door

洮砚	Tao ink-stone (one of the four famous ink-stones in China, which is produced in Gannan Tibetan Autonomous Prefecture, Gansu)
桃花岛	Taohua Island; Peach Blossom Island (Zhejiang)
桃花堤	Taohua Dyke; Peach Blossom Garden (Tianjin)
桃花洞	Taohua Cave; Peach Blossom Cave (Shanxi)
桃花谷	(of Taihang Grand Canyon) Peach Blossom Valley
桃花山	peach hill; peach blossom mountain
桃花溪	Taohua Stream; Peach Blossom Stream (Hu'nan)
桃花峪	Taohua Valley; Peach Blossom Ravine (Shandong)
桃花峪景区	(of Mount Taishan) Peach Blossom Ravine scenic area
桃花源	Peach Blossom Valley; Land of Peach Blossom (Hu'nan)
桃李园	garden of peach and plum
桃坪羌寨	Taoping Qiang Village (Sichuan)
桃叶渡	Taoye Ferry; Peach Leaves Ferry (Jiangsu)
桃园蝙蝠洞	Taoyuan Bat Cave (Taiwan)
桃园洞	(of Mount Wuyi) Peach Blossom Cave
桃源洞	taoyuan cave; peach land cave
桃源洞景区	Taoyuan Cave Scenic Area (Fujian)
陶瓷塔	pottery pagoda
陶婚	pottery wedding (the 9th anniversary of marriage)
陶然亭	Joyous Pavilion (Beijing)
讨喜	〈婚〉taoxi (friends of the bride ask money from the bridegroom before allowing him to see the bride); to ask for lucky money
腾冲饵块	Tengchong Erkuai (one of the most famous local snacks, its process is to wash, soak, steam, pound the rice, and knead it into various shapes)
腾冲火山	Tengchong Volcano (Yunnan)
腾冲火山地质公园	Tengchong Volcano Geological Park (Yunnan)

腾冲拟髭蟾	〈动〉*Leptobrachium tengchongense*
腾冲热海	Tengchong Thermal Lake (Yunnan)
腾冲掌突蟾	〈动〉*Paramegophrys tengchongensis*; Tengchong leaf litter toad
腾格里沙漠	Tengger Desert (Inner Mongolia)
腾格里沙漠通湖草原	Tonghu Grassland in Tengger Desert (Inner Mongolia)
腾格里月亮湖沙漠生态旅游区	Moon Lake Ecotourism Area in Tengger Desert (Inner Mongolia)
腾空摆莲	〈武术〉Jumping lotus kick; Outward leg swing in flight
腾空侧踹	〈武术〉Jumping with side kick
腾空蹬腿	〈武术〉Jumping with heel kick
腾空飞脚	〈武术〉Jumping/Flying front kick
腾空箭弹	〈武术〉Jumping with spring kick
腾空双侧踹脚	〈武术〉Jumping with both legs side kick
腾空旋风脚	〈武术〉Jumping with whirlwind kick
腾空正踢腿	〈武术〉Jumping/Flying front raise kick
滕王阁	Tengwang Pavilion; Pavilion of Prince Teng (Jiangxi)
藤山草场	Cane Hill Grassland (Fujian)
藤山柳	〈植〉*Clematoclethra lasioclada*; Tengshan willow
藤王	(of Zhangjiajie) King Vine
藤溪潭瀑	Waterfalls of Tengxi Pond (Zhejiang)
踢轿门	〈婚〉(of wedding) to kick the curtain of the sedan chair
提手	〈武术〉(of Tai Chi) Hand lifting
提膝平衡	〈武术〉Balance with one knee raised
体和殿	(of Imperial Palace) Hall of Manifest Harmony
体仁殿	(of Imperial Palace) Hall of Benevolence Embodiment
体仁阁	(of Imperial Palace) Belvedere of Benevolence Embodiment
体育运动委员会	physical culture and sports commission

天安门	Tian'anmen; Gate of Heavenly Peace (Beijing)
天安门城楼	Tian'anmen Rostrum (Beijing)
天安门广场	Tian'anmen Square (Beijing)
天波府	Tian Bo Mansion (He'nan)
天池	(of Zhangjiajie) Heaven Pond
天池山	Tianchi Mountain (Jiangsu, He'nan)
天赐湖	Tianci Lake (Heilongjiang)
天灯	sky lantern →孔明灯
天地广场	(of Mount Taishan) Heaven and Earth Square
天都峰	(of Mount Huangshan) Celestial Capital peak (one of three main peaks)
天鹅海	(of Jiuzhai Valley) Swan Lake
天府之国	Land of Abundance (reffering to Chengdu Plains)
天干地支	Heavenly Stems and Earthly Branches; Chinese Era
天罡拳	〈武术〉Tiangang Quan; Tiangang Boxing
天国	〈道〉Heavenly Kingdom
天海	(of Mount Huangshan) Heaven Sea
天河潭	Tianhe Pond (Guizhou)
天后宫	1 Tianhou Palace; Heavenly Empress Palace 2 → 老妈[天后]宫
天后庙	Tin Hau Temple (Hong Kong)
天湖湿地公园	Tianhu Lake Wetland Park (Hu'nan)
天际100香港观景台	Sky 100 Hong Kong Observation Deck (Hong Kong)
天街撷美	(of Swallow Cave) Enjoying Beauty in Heavenly Streets
天津北少林寺	Tianjin North Shaolin Temple
天津古文化街	Tianjin Ancient Culture Street
天津广播电视塔	Tianjin Radio and Television Tower
天津欢乐谷	Tianjin Happy Valley
天津欢乐水魔方	Tianjin Aquamagic
天津欢乐水世界	Tianjin Happy Water World

天津抗震纪念碑	Tianjin Earthquake Monument
天津泥人	Tianjin clay figurine
天津首届精武冰雪文化嘉年华	First Carnival of Jingwu Ice and Snow Culture in Tianjin
天津戏剧博物馆	Tianjin Opera Museum
天津盐业银行旧址	Former Site of Tianjin Salt Bank
天津意库创意产业园	Tianjin Yicoo Creative Park
天井峡景区	Tianjing Valley Scenic Spot (Gansu)
天贶殿	Palace of Heavenly Blessings (Shandong)
天贶节	Tiankuang Festival (on the 6th day of the 6th lunar month) →晒衣节
天龙山石窟	Tianlong Mountain Grottoes (Shanxi)
天龙湾湿地公园	Tianlong Wan (Bend) Wetland Park (Hubei)
天麻糯米酒	rhizoma gastrodiae glutinous rice wine
天门山森林公园	Tianmen Mountain Forest Park (Hu'nan)
天门山峡谷生态旅游景区	Eco-tourist Attraction of Tianmen Mountain Canyon (Fujian)
天目湖	Tianmu Lake (Jiangsu)
天目湖山水园景区	Tianmu Lake Natural Scenery Park (Jiangsu)
天目木姜子	〈植〉*Litsea auriculata*; fruit of Tianmu Mountain litse; Tianmushan litse
天目山	Taimu Mountain (Zhejiang)
天目铁木	〈植〉*Ostrya rehderiana*
天宁阁	tianning pavilion
天桥	(of Zhangjiajie) Natural Bridge
天桥遗墩	(of Zhangjiajie) Deserted Piers of Heaven Bridge
天然壁画	(of Zhangjiajie) Natural Murals
天然图画	(of Mount Qingcheng) Natural Pictures
天然氧吧	natural oxygen bar
天山	Tianshan Mountain
天山大峡谷	Tianshan Grand Canyon (Xinjiang)
天山景区	Tianshan Mountain Scenic Area (Xinjiang)
天山天池传说	Legend of Tianchi Lake in Celestial Mountain; Legend of Tianshan Heavenly Lake (Xinjiang)

天山云杉	〈植〉*Picea schrenkiana*; Tianshan Mountain spruce
天师洞	Heavenly Master Cave (Sichuan)
天师府	Heavenly Master's Residence (Jiangxi)
天书宝匣	(of Zhangjiajie) Treasure Box of Celestial Books
天水伏羲文化旅游节	Tianshui Fuxi Culture and Tourism Festival (Gansu)
天水围公园	Tin Shui Wai Park (Hong Kong)
天台粗皮蛙	〈动〉*Rugosa tientaiensis*
天台山	Tiantai Mountain (Zhejiang)
天台山景区	Tiantai Mountain Scenic Area (Zhejiang)
天台蛙	〈动〉*Rana tientaiensis*
天坛(公园)	Tiantan Park; Temple of Heaven (Park) (Beijing)
天坛大佛	Tian Tan (Big) Buddha (Hong Kong)
天堂寨	Tiantang Zhai; Tiantang Stronghold (Anhui)
天梯山石窟	Tianti Mountain Grottoes (Gansu)
天庭[廷]	〈神话〉Celestial Kingdom
天童寺	Tiantong Temple (Zhejiang)
天外村	Tianwai Village; Sky Village (Shandong)
天王殿	(of Shaolin Temple) Heavenly King's Hall; Hall of Heavenly King
天王府	Palace of the Heavenly King (Jiangsu)
天下第一城	Grand Epoch City (Hebei)
天下第一洞房	(of Mount Huashan) the Best Bridal Chamber in the World
天下第一墩	First Fire Pier of the Great Wall (Gansu)
天下第一关	First Pass under Heaven (in the world) (Hebei) →山海关
天下第一桥	(of Zhangjiajie) the First Bridge of the World
"天下名山"牌坊	(of Mount Emei) Archway of "Famous Mountain under Heaven"
天仙圣母	(of Mount Taishan) Heavenly Immortal Goddess
天仙玉女	〈道〉(of Mount Taishan) Heavenly Immortal Jade Maiden →碧霞元君
天险河漂流	Tianxian River Drifting (Anhui)

天心石	(of Temple of Heaven) Heart of Heavenly Stone; Heavenly Heart Stone
天心岩景区	Heaven Heart Rock Scenic Area (Fujian)
天兴洲	Tianxing Sandbar (Hubei)
天悬白练	(of Zhangjiajie) Silver Ribbon Pendent from Heaven
天涯海角	Tianya Haijiao; Ends of the Earth (Hai'nan)
天演广场	Tian Yan Square (Tianjin)
天游峰	(of Mount Wuyi) Henvenly Tour Peak
天游峰景区	(of Mount Wuyi) Heavenly-Tour Peak Scenic Area
天宇咸畅	(of Chengde Mountain Resort) Towering Pavilion and Vast Sky View
天葬	〈藏族、蒙古族〉tianzang; sky burial; celestial burial (intentionally exposing the bodies to birds of prey or beasts)
天竺山	Mount Tianzhou; Tianzhu Mountain (Fujian)
天竺山森林公园	Tianzhu Mountain Forest Park (Fujian)
天烛峰	(of Mount Taishan) Heaven Candle Peak
天柱峰	heavenly pillar peak
天柱山景区	Tianzhu Mountain Scenic Spot (Anhui)
天子井	(of Zhangjiajie) Emperor's Well
天子山自然保护区	(of Zhangjiajie) Emperor Mountain Natural Reserve
天子山自然景区	(of Zhangjiajie) Tianzi Mountain Nature Reserve; Emperor Mountain Nature Reserve
添仓节	〈满族〉Tiancang Festival; Fillpositions Insection (on the 25th day of the 1st lunar month)
田螺坑村	Tianluokeng Village (Fujian)
田螺坑土楼群	Tianluokeng earth building cluster (Fujian)
田中玉故居	Former Residence of Tian Zhongyu (Tianjin)
甜水沟遗址	Tianshuigou Paleolithic Ruins (Shaanxi)
甜藤粑节	〈侗族〉Sweet Tengba Festival (on the 3rd day of the 3rd lunar month)

挑盖头	〈婚〉(of wedding) to uncover the red veil
调景岭	Tiu Keng Leng (Hong Kong)
跳墩河湿地	Tiaodun River Wetland (Yunnan)
跳棋	Chinese chequers; Chinese draughts
跳月节	〈苗族、彝族〉Moon-Dance Festival
贴春联	〈民俗〉to paste Spring Festival couplets; to put up antithetical couplets
铁鞭古祠	Iron Whip Ancient Temple (Hubei)
铁佛寺	Iron Buddha Statue Temple
铁拐李	〈道〉Iron-Crutch Li (one of the Eight Immortals)
铁棺峡	Hanging Coffin Gorge (Chongqing)
铁婚	iron wedding (the 6th anniversary of marriage) →糖婚
铁人王进喜纪念馆	Memorial Hall of Iron-Man Wang Jinxi (Heilongjiang)
铁扇关	(of Huanglong Valley) Iron Fan Pass
汀九桥	Ting Kau Bridge (Hong Kong)
听鹂馆	(of Summer Palace) Hall of Oriole Singing
听橹楼	(of Couple's Retreat Garden) Tower of Scull-Sounding
听松风处	(of Humble Administrator's Garden) Place for Listening to Pine-Waves
听雨轩	(of Humble Administrator's Garden) Pavilion of Rain Listening
停棺	〈丧〉(of funeral) to keep the coffin in the house (in order to pick an auspicious day to bury the deceased)
停丧待葬	〈丧〉to lay down a coffin waiting for a due burial time
通海秀山	Tonghai Xiushan Mountain (Yunnan)
通灵大瀑布	Tongling Grand Waterfall (Guangxi)
通灵大峡谷	Tongling Grand Canyon (Guangxi)
通灵峡	Tongling Gorge (Guangxi)
通山石龙峡	Tongshan Shilong Valley (Hubei)

通山无量寿禅寺	Wuliangshou Buddhist Temple of Tongshan (Hubei)
通天洞	Tongtian Cave (Guangxi)
通天河	Tongtian River (Qinghai)
通天河大桥	Tongtian River Bridge (Qinghai)
通天河森林公园	Tongtian River Forest Park (Shaanxi)
通天桥	(of Mount Taishan) Heavenward Bridge
通脱木	〈植〉*Tetrapanax papyrifer*; rice-paper plant
通玄寺	Tongxuan Temple (Jiangsu)
同安野山谷热带雨林	Wild Valley Tropical Rainforest of Tong'an (Fujian)
同道堂	(of Imperial Palace) Hall of Like-Minded People
同里古镇	Tongli Ancient Town (Jiangsu)
铜锤	〈戏〉(of Beijing Opera) Tongchui (a painted face) →正净
铜鼎	bronze ding-tripod; bronze tripot
铜鼓节	〈壮族〉Bronze Drum Festival (on the 1st, 15th and 30th day of the 1st lunar month)
铜鼓岭景区	Tonggu Mountain Scenic Area (Hai'nan)
铜鼓山歌艺术节	〈壮族〉Tonggu Folk Song Art Festival (from the 3th to 5th December)
铜婚	copper wedding (the 7th anniversary of marriage)
铜锣坝森林公园	Tongluoba Forest Park (Yunnan)
铜锣湾	Tung Lo Wan; Causeway Bay (Hong Kong)
铜锣湾避风塘	Causeway Bay Typhoon Shelter (Hong Kong)
统万城遗址	Tongwan City Site (the ruins of the capital of Huns) (Shaanxi)
筒距兰	〈植〉*Tipularia szechuanica*
头七	〈丧〉the seventh day after a person's death (it is believed that the souls of the deceased will return home on that day)
投壶	〈古〉touhu (a Chinese game in which people who throw more arrows into the pot are winners)

突厥石人	〈古〉Turkic stone figurines (sacrificial objects in front of a tomb)
图们江	Tumen River
图们口岸	Tumen Port (Jilin)
图瓦人	Tuwa People; Tuwa
土登嘉措	Thubten Gyatso (1876–1933, the 13th Dalai Lama)
土地公	God of Earth →福德正神
土皇节	〈侗族〉Soil Emperor Festival (two or three days before Grain Rain) →土王节
土家农事酒	〈土家族〉Tujia farming wine
土家甜酒	〈土家族〉Tujia sweet wine
土家族	Tujia ethnic group; Tujia
土楼	(of Hakkas) earth building
土王节	〈侗族〉Tu Wang Festival (two or three days before Grain Rain) →土皇节
土窑洞	loess cave dwelling
土葬	〈丧〉burial in the ground; inhumation
土族	Tu ethnic group; Tu
土族民俗文化村	folk culture village of Tu ethnic group (Qinghai)
吐鲁番盆地	Turpan Basin; Turfan/Turpan Depression (Xinjiang)
吐鲁番葡萄沟	Grape Valley in Turpan (Xinjiang)
吐鲁番葡萄节	Turpan Grape Festival (on the 20th August)
吐鲁沟森林公园	Tulug Valley Forest Park (Gansu)
吐鲁沟掌草原游乐区	Tulu Valley Pasture Pleasure Place (Gansu)
吐露港	Tolo Harbour (Hong Kong)
吐曼河	Tuman River
吐峪沟	Tuyu Valley (Xinjiang)
吐峪沟石窟	Tuyu Valley Grotto (Xinjiang)
兔儿望月	(of Zhangjiajie) Rabbit Watching the Moon
兔年	Year of the Rabbit (one of 12 zodiac signs)
兔子灯	rabbit-shaped lantern
团泊湖温泉	Tuanbo Lake Hot Spring (Tianjin)
团城山公园	Tuancheng Mountain Park (Hubei)

团湖	Tuanhu Lake (Hu'nan)
团圆	〈习俗〉family reunion; reunion
团圆饭	〈习俗〉family reunion dinner (on Lunar New Year's Eve)
推掌	〈武术〉Pushing palm
腿部爆发力	〈武术〉explosive leg strength
退步穿掌	〈武术〉(of Tai Chi) Stepping backward and penetrating palm
退步跨虎	〈武术〉(of Tai Chi) Stepping backward and straddling on tiger
退思草堂	(of Garden of Quiet Meditation) Thatched Cottage of Quiet Meditation
退思园	Tuisi Garden; Garden of Quiet Meditation (Jiangsu)
屯门公园	Tuen Mun Park (Hong Kong)
屯门善庆洞	Tuen Mun Sin Hing Tung; Sin Hing Taoist Temple (Hong Kong)
屯溪老街	Tunxi Antique Street (Anhui)
托林寺	〈佛〉Tuolin Monastery (Tibet)
托木尔峰	Mount Tomur; Tomur Mountain (Xinjiang)
陀螺	spinning top; whipping top
陀螺节	〈壮族〉Gyro Festival; Gyroscopic Festival (from two or three days before Spring Festival Eve to the 16th day of the 1st lunar month)
沱沱河	Tuotuo River (Qinghai)
驼梁	Tuoliang; Hump Mountain (Hebei, Shanxi)
鼍	〈动〉*Alligator sinensis*

W

娃娃生	〈戏〉(of Beijing Opera) Wawasheng (a child character)
娃娃鱼	〈动〉*Andrias davidianus*; giant salamanders → 大鲵
瓦仓起义革命烈士陵园	Wacang Uprising Revolutionary Martyrs Cemetery (Hubei)
瓦屋无耳蟾	〈动〉*Atympanophrys wawuensis*
瓦窑堡革命旧址	Revolutionary Site at Wayaobao (Shaanxi)
瓦窑堡会议旧址	Site of Wayaobao Meeting (Shaanxi)
佤族	Wa ethnic group; Wa
外白渡桥	Waibaidu Bridge; Garden Bridge (Shanghai)
外摆腿	〈武术〉Outside circle kick
外港新填海区	New Reclamation Area in Outer Harbour (Macao)
外家拳	〈武术〉External Style Boxing
外木山滨海步道	Waimu Mountain Coastal Trail (Taiwan)
外滩观光隧道	Bund Sightseeing Tunnel (Shanghai)
外滩情人墙	Bund Valentine's Wall (Shanghai)
外滩万国建筑博览群	exotic building clusters in the Bund of Shanghai
外五龙桥	(of Nanjing Ming Palace) Outer Five-Dragon Bridge
弯齿盾果草	〈植〉*Thyrocarpus glochidiatus*
弯弓射虎	(of Tai Chi) Tiger shooting bow
湾仔北帝庙	Wan Chai Pak Tai Temple (Hong Kong)
湾仔洪圣古庙	Wan Chai Hung Shing Temple (Hong Kong)
湾仔锡克教庙	Sikh Temple in Wan Chai (Hong Kong)

挽联	elegiac couplets
晚对峰	(of Mount Wuyi) Wandui Peak; Evening View Peak
皖南古村落	Ancient Villages in Southern Anhui (referring to Xidi and Hongcun Villages)
畹香楼	(of Garden of Quiet Meditation) Wan Xiang Tower
万部华严经塔	Pagoda of Ten Thousand Huayan Buddhist Scriptures; Pagoda of Ten Thousand Avatamsaka Sutras (Inner Mongolia)
万朝山自然保护区	Wanchao Mountain Nature Reserve (Hubei)
万春亭	(of Imperial Palace) Pavilion of Myriad Springs
万春园	(of Mount Wuyi) All Spring Garden
万佛顶	(of Mount Emei) Wanfo Peak; Ten Thousand Buddha Peak
万佛洞	(of Longmen Grottoes) wanfo caves; Cave of Ten Thousand Buddhas
万佛寺	wanfo temple; ten thousand buddhas monastery
万佛园	Wanfo Garden; Ten-Thousand Buddha Park (Hebei) →燕山塔陵
万壑松风	(of Chengde Mountain Resort) Pine-Soughing from Ten-Thousand Ravines
万华岩	All-Splendor Rock (Hu'nan)
万卷堂	(of Master-of-Nets Garden) Hall of Scrolls
万里长城	the Great Wall
万里长城第一墩	the First Frustum of the Great Wall
万绿园	Wanlu Park; Evergreen Park (Hai'nan)
万年寺	(of Mount Emei) Myriad Years Temple
万年寺景区	Myriad Years Temple Scenic Area (Sichuan)
万平口景区	Wanpingkou Scenic Area (Shandong)
万泉河	Wanquan River (Hai'nan)
万乳崖	Wanru Cliff (Guangxi)
万盛石林	Wansheng Stone Forest (Chongqing)
万石山	Wan Shi (Ten Thousand Rocks) Mountain (Fujian)
万寿八仙宫	〈道〉Wanshou Eight Immortals Palace (Shaanxi) →八仙庵

万寿宫	Wanshou Palace; Palace of Longevity; Longevity Palace (Jiangxi)
万寿山	(of Summer Palace) Longevity Hill
万寿寺	Wanshou Temple; Temple of Longevity; Longevity Temple (Beijing)
万寿园	Wanshou Garden; Longevity Garden (Jiangxi)
万树园	(of Chengde Mountain Resort) Ten-Thousand-Tree Garden
万松书缘	(of West Lake) Conjugal Felicity at Wansong Academy
万岁寺	Longevity Temple (Fujian, Shanxi)
万仙楼	(of Mount Taishan) All Immortals Gathering Tower; Ten Thousand Immortals Tower
万仙山	Wanxian Mountain (He'nan)
万洋洲湿地公园	Wanyang Zhou Wetland Parkg (Hubei)
万宜水库	High Island Reservoir (Hong Kong)
万源龙顺度假庄园	Wanyuan Longshun Holiday Resort (Tianjin)
万丈盐桥	Wanzhang Salt Bridge (Qinghai)
万州大瀑布	(of Mount Wuyi) Wanzhou Waterfall
万子鞭	〈古〉wanzi fireworks (to set off fireworks, announcing to parents-in-law about the new birth)
亡灵	〈丧〉departed soul
亡灵祭酒	〈丧〉sacrifice wine to the dead
王府井大街	Wangfujing Street (Beijing)
王家大院	Courtyard of the Wang Family (Shanxi)
王家坪革命旧址	Wangjiaping Revolutionary Site (Shaanxi)
王家坪旧址	Former Revolutionary Headquarter of Wangjiaping (Shaanxi)
王朗齿突蟾	〈动〉*Scutiger wanglangensis*
王母池	Wangmu Pool; Pool of Heavenly Queen Mother (Shandong)
王母宫山	Wangmu Palace Mountain; Queen Mother Palace Mountain (Gansu)

王母宫石窟	Wangmu Palace Grottoes; Queen Mother Palace Grottoes (Gansu)
王屋村民宅	Wangwu Village-Dwelling (Hong Kong)
王羲之故居	Former Residence of Wang Xizhi (Shandong)
王羲之纪念馆	Wang Xizhi Memorial Hall (Zhejiang)
王相岩	(of Taihang Grand Canyon) Wang-Xiang Rock; (of Taihang Grand Canyon) Rock of Kings and Prime Ministers
王祥求鲤	(of Chinese fortune sticks) Wang Xiang Praying for a Carp
王星记扇庄	Wangxingji Fan Store (Zhejiang)
王星记扇子	Wangxingji fan
王益孙旧居	Former Residence of Wang Yisun (Tianjin)
王占元故居	Former Residence of Wang Zhanyuan (Tianjin)
王仲山旧宅	Former Residence of Wang Zhongshan (Tianjin)
网师园	Master-of-Nets Garden (Jiangsu)
网藤蕨	〈植〉*Lomagramma matthewii*
网纹舌突蛙	〈动〉*Liurana reticulata*
旺波日山	Wangpori Mountain (Tibet)
旺角花墟	Mong Kok Flower Market (Hong Kong)
旺角女人街	Mong Kok Lady's Street (Hong Kong)
望德圣母堂	St. Lazarus Church (Macao)
望德圣母湾湿地生态观赏区	Eco-Scenic Area of Virgin Mary Wetland (Macao)
望德圣母湾湿地生态区	Virgin Mary Wetland Eco-Zone (Macao)
望德堂区	St. Lazarus Parish (Macao)
望灯杆	〈古〉Lamp Post (a name of sacrificial device) (Beijing)
望夫石	Amah Rock (Hong Kong)
望夫崖	Wangfu Cliff (longing for husband to return)
望果节	〈藏族〉Ongkor (Bumper Harvest) Festival; Wangguo Festival
望海峰	Peak Overlooking the Sea (Shanxi)
望海观音	Guanyin Overlooking the Sea (Guangzhou)
望海楼	sea-facing building

望海楼教堂	Wanghailou Church (Tianjin)
望海山临潮湖公园	Wanghai Hill and Linchao Lake Park
望海亭	Wanghai Pavilion; Seaside Pavilion
望郎峰	(of Zhangjiajie) Beloved Watching Peak
望女成凤	to hope one's daughter to grow up into a phoenix (a person of unsurpassed excellence)
望天鹅景区	Wang Tian'e Scenic Area (Jilin)
望霞峰	→神女峰
望厦炮台	Mong-Há Fort (Macao)
望厦山（市政）公园	Mong Há Hill Municipal Park; (of Portuguese) Parque Municipal da Colina de Mong Há (Macao)
望仙台石窟	Wangxiantai Grottoes (Guizhou)
望乡台瀑布	Wangxiangtai Waterfall (Chongqing)
望月平衡	〈武术〉Balance with the back leg hooked up
微蹼铃蟾	〈动〉*Bombina microdeladigitora*; Hubei firebelly toad
微小耳蕨	〈植〉*Polystichum minutissimum*
巍宝山	Weibao Mountain (one of the birthplaces of the ancient Nanzhao State) (Yunnan)
巍宝山朝山节	〈纳西族〉Pilgrimage Festival at Weibao Mountain (from the 1st day to the 15th day of the 2nd lunar month)
巍山古城	Ancient City of Weishan (Yunnan)
韦驮雕像	Statue of Skanda (Shanxi)
围棋	Weiqi (a game played with black and white pieces on a board of 361 crosses); a go chess game
维多利亚港	Port Victoria; Victoria Harbour (Hong Kong)
维多利亚公园	Victoria Park (Hong Kong)
维吾尔族	Uyghur/Uighur ethnic group; Uyghur/Uighur
维吾尔族穆斯林	Uyghur/Uighur Muslim
潍坊风筝节	Weifang Kite Festival (on the 3rd Saturday of April)
伪满皇宫	Puppet Emperor's Imperial Palace; Imperial Palace of Manchu State (Jilin)

伪满皇宫博物院	Museum of Imperial Palace of Manchu State (Jilin)
伪满洲国	The puppet state of Manchukuo; Manchu Kingdom (the puppet regime supported by Japanese imperialism during World War II) (1932-1945)
伪满洲国国务院旧址	Former Site of the State Council of the Puppet Manchukuo (Jilin)
尾斑瘰螈	〈动〉*Paramesotriton caudopunctatus*; spot-tailed warty newt
尾囊草	〈植〉*Urophysa henryi*
尾突角蟾	〈动〉*Megophrys caudoprocta*; convex-tailed horned toad
尾牙宴	〈习俗〉year-end party (on the 16th day of the 12th lunar month)
卫奕信径	Wilson Trail (Hong Kong)
未央湖游乐园	Weiyang Lake Amusement Park (Shaanxi)
位育斋	(of Imperial Palace) Studio of Situational Adaptation
渭河	Weihe River
渭河公园	Weihe River Park (Shaanxi)
渭河谷地	Weihe River Valley
渭河平原	Weihe River Plain (the fourth largest plain in China, Shaanxi) →关中平原
蝟实	〈植〉*Kolkwitzia amabilis*; beauty bush
魏国	Kingdom of Wei (403-225 B.C.)
魏晋壁画墓	Wei-Jin Tomb Murals; Mural Painting Tombs of the Wei and Jin Dynasties (Gansu)
魏氏齿蟾	〈动〉*Oreolalax weigoldi*; Weigold's toothed toad
魏源故居	Former Residence of Wei Yuan (Hu'nan)
温泉寺	wenquan temple
文昌阁	(of Summer Palace) wenchang pavilion; Pavilion of Flourishing Culture
文昌宫	wenchang palace
文昌孔庙	Wenchang Confucius Temple (Hai'nan)

文成公主庙	Temple of Princess Wencheng (Qinghai)
文旦柚	Wendan pomelo; citrus grandis
文房四宝馆	museum of Chinese stationery
文峰塔	Wenfeng Tower (Hu'nan)
文华殿	(of Imperial Palace) Hall of Literary Glory/Brilliance
文华书院	〈古〉Boone Memorial School (founded on October 20, 1871) (Hubei)
文化广场	culture square
文敬	〈礼〉Wen Jing (a manifestation of traditional alcoholic morality, i.e. to advise courteously guests to drink)
文庙	→孔(子)庙
文殊寺	Manjusri Temple (Gansu)
文塔	→聚星楼
文天祥碑亭	(of Lion Forest Garden) Pavilion of Wen Tianxiang Stele
文武殿	(of Mount Qingcheng) Wenwu Hall
文武庙	Man Mo Temple (Hong Kong)
文咸街	Bonham Strand (Hong Kong)
文县疣螈	〈动〉*Tylototriton wenxianensis*; Wenxian crocodile newt
文学社旧址	Former Site of Literacy Association (Hubei)
文渊阁	(of Imperial Palace) Belvedere of Literary Profundity
文园狮子林	Lion Forest of Literary Garden (Hebei)
闻木樨香轩	(of Lingering Garden) Osmanthus Fragrance Pavilion
问梅阁	(of Lion Grove Garden) Pavilion of Plum Blossom
问名	〈婚〉birthday matching; to ask for the name and horoscope of a prospective bride →六礼
问泉亭	(of Mountain Villa with Embracing Beauty) Spring-Questioning Pavilion

翁仲	bronze or stone man in front of a mausoleum → 石像生
瓮棺葬	urn-burial; hydriotaphia
窝罗节	〈阿昌族〉Woluo Festival (on the 4th day of the 2nd lunar month)
沃沱罗	〈苗族〉Wotuoluo (a ceremonial wine)
卧佛寺	Lying Buddha Temple (Beijing)
卧虎山	Wohu Mountain; Crouching Tiger Mountain (Guangxi)
卧龙大熊猫博物馆	Wolong Panda Museum (Sichuan)
卧龙谷	Crouching Dragon Valley (Jiangxi)
卧龙海	(of Jiuzhai Valley) Lying Dragon Lake
卧龙桥	Crouching Dragon Bridge (Zhejiang)
卧龙山	Wolong Mountain; Lying Dragon Mountain
卧龙自然保护区	Wolong Nature Reserve (Sichuan)
卧峡晴虹	(Xingtai Canyon group) Woxia Gorge Clear Bow
乌饭节	Black Rice Day; Black Rice Festival (on the 8th day of the 4th lunar month by the Miao, Yao and Dong ethnic groups)
乌龟山遗址	Turtle Mountain Ruins (cultural remains of the Shang and Zhou dynasties) (Zhejiang)
乌江	Wujiang River (Guizhou, Chongqing)
乌拉泊水上公园	Urabo Water Park (Xinjiang)
乌拉山	Ula/Wula Mountain (Inner Mongolia)
乌兰布和沙漠	Ulan Buh Desert; Wulanbuhe Desert (Inner Mongolia)
乌兰布统草原	Wulanbutong Grassland (Inner Mongolia)
乌鲁木齐河	Urumqi River (Xinjiang)
乌鲁木齐烈士陵园	Urumqi Cemetery of Revolutionary Martyrs (Xinjiang)
乌伦古河	Ulungur River (Xinjiang)
乌伦古湖	Ulungur Lake (Xinjiang) →布伦托海
乌蒙山	Wumeng Mountain (Yunnan, Guizhou)
乌苏里江	Ussuri River (Heilongjiang)

乌孙古墓	Usun Ancient Tomb (Xinjiang)
乌贼	〈动〉*Sepia officinalis*; cuttle fish
乌镇古镇	Ancient Town of Wuzhen (Zhejiang)
乌孜别克族	Ozbek ethnic group; Ozbek
巫山	Mount Wushan; Wushan Mountain (Chongqing)
巫山巴鲵	〈动〉*Liua shihi*; Wushan salamander
巫山北鲵	〈动〉*Ranodon shihi*; Wushan north salamander
巫山角蟾	〈动〉*Megophrys wushanensis*; Wushan horned toad
巫山十二峰	twelve peaks of the Wushan Mountain (Hubei; Chongqing)
巫山猿人遗址	Wushan Ape-Man Site (Chongqing) →龙骨坡遗址
巫师城堡	Wizard Castle (Zhejiang)
巫溪叶底珠	〈植〉*Securinega wuxiensis*
巫峡	(of Three Gorges) Wuxia Gorge
无斑肥螈	〈动〉*Pachytriton labiatus*
无斑瘰螈	〈动〉*Paramesotriton labiatus*; spotless stout newt
无斑山溪鲵	〈动〉*Batrachuperus karlschmidti*; spotless mountain salamander
无斑雨蛙	〈动〉*Hyla immaculata*; spotless tree toad
无车日	No Car Day; Car Free Day (the 22nd September)
无棘溪蟾	〈动〉*Torrentophryne aspinia*
无距虾脊兰	〈植〉*Calanthe tsoongiana*
无梁(大)殿	Beamless Hall; Hall without Beams (Beijing)
无蹼齿蟾	〈动〉*Oreolalax schmidti*
无暑清凉	(of Chengde Mountain Resort) Hall of Coolness and tranquility
无为寺	Inaction Temple (Yunnan)
无锡蠡园	Zhiyuan Garden in Wuxi (Jiangsu)
无锡影视基地	Wuxi Movie & TV Base (Jiangsu)
无字碑	Wordless Tablet; Tablet without Inscription (Wu Zetian's monument)
毋歠醢	〈礼〉don't drink seasoning sauce
毋刺齿	〈礼〉don't pick teeth while eating

毋反鱼肉	〈礼〉don't put the meat or fish you set your mouth on back to the bowl
毋放饭	〈礼〉don't put the food that you set your mouth on back to the bowl
毋固获	〈礼〉don't keep eating exclusively one dish
毋口它食	〈礼〉don't make noises when chewing
毋流歠	〈礼〉don't eat eagerly with a great speed
毋啮骨	〈礼〉don't chew on bone
毋嚃羹	〈礼〉don't gobble up thick soup or make a loud noise
毋投与狗骨	〈礼〉don't throw a bone to a dog
毋抟饭	〈礼〉don't gobble food
毋絮羹	〈礼〉don't season your own soup
毋扬饭	〈礼〉don't stir up the rice in your bowl to cool it
毋嘬炙	〈礼〉don't devour a piece of roast meat at a time
芜湖方特欢乐世界	Wuhu Fantawild Adventure Theme Park (Anhui)
吾爱亭	(of Couple's Retreat Garden) Self-love Pavilion
吴桥杂技大世界	Wuqiao Acrobatic Grand World (Hebei)
吴山森林公园	Wushan Mountain Forest Park (Shaanxi)
吴山天风	(of West Lake) Heavenly Wind over Wushan Mountain
吴氏齿突蟾	〈动〉*Scutiger wuguanfui*
吴氏肥螈	〈动〉*Pachytriton wuguanfui*; Wu's paddle-tail newts
吴王宫	King Wu's Palace; Palace of King Wu (Anhui)
吴文化公园	Wu Culture Garden (Jiangsu)
浯溪石刻	Rock Carvings along the Wu Stream (Hu'nan)
梧桐	〈植〉*Firmiana simplex*; Chinese parasol tree
梧桐山	Wutong Mountain (Guangdong)
梧桐寨瀑布	Ng Tung Chai Waterfall (Hong Kong)
蜈支洲岛	Wuzhizhou Island (Hai'nan)
五百罗汉堂	Five-Hundred-Arhat Hall (Anhui)
五百罗汉园	(of Hongluo Temple) Five Hundred Luohans Garden

五彩池	(of Jiuzhai Valley) Five-Color Pond; Colorful Pond
五彩湖	(of Guanmen Mountain) Five-Colored Lake
五常龙舟胜会	Exhibition of Wuchang Dragon Boat Culture (on the 5th day of the 5th lunar month)
五唇兰	〈植〉*Doritis pulcherrima*
五大连池景区	Wudalianchi Scenic Area (Heilongjiang)
五当召	Wudang Lamasery (a sacred place of Tibetan Buddhism in Inner Mongolia)
五毒衣[裤]	〈民俗〉(of Dragon Boat Festival) coats/trousers with the patterns of the five poisons (for exorcising poisonous substances)
五朵峰自然保护区	Wuduofeng Nature Reserve (Hubei)
五朵山景区	Wuduo Mountain Scenic Attraction (He'nan)
五方[智]佛	Five Directions Buddhas; Five Dhyani Buddhas
五峰兰科植物保护区	Orchid Plant Reserve in Wufeng (Hubei)
五峰山原始森林公园	Wufeng Mountain Virgin Forest Park (Yunnan)
五峰书屋	(of Master-of-Nets Garden) Wufeng Study Room; Five Peaks Library
五峰仙馆	(of Lingering Garden) Celestial Hall of Five Peaks
五凤楼	Five-Phoenix Pavilion (Yunnan) →法云阁
五佛顶景区	Five-Buddha Summit Scenic Area (Liaoning)
五服	1 〈丧〉wufu; five funeral garments (differed according to the social distance to the deceased person) 2 wufu; five kinds of kinship (referring to the five generations of great-great-grandfather, great grandfather, grandfather, father and oneself)
五福花	〈植〉*Adoxa moschatellina*; flower of five happiness
五盖山	Wugai Mountain; Five Canopies Mountain (the summit is always covered with frost, snow, clouds, fog, and dew) (Hu'nan)

五公祠	Wugong Temple; Temple of Five Lords (Hai'nan)
五虎岛旅游景区	Wuhu Island Tourist Attraction; Tourist Attraction of Five Tigers' Island (Jilin)
五花海	(of Jiuzhai Valley) Five-colored Lake
五华洞	Wuhua Caves; Five Magnificent Caves (Shanxi)
五华山	Wuhua Mountain (Yunnan)
五尖槭	〈植〉*Acer maximowiczii*
五间房水岛乐园	Wujianfang Water Island Paradise (Jilin)
五盔墓群	Wukui Tomb Group (Jilin)
五老峰	(of Mount Lushan) Wulao Peaks; Five Seniors Peak
五老山森林公园	Wulao Mountain Forest Park (Yunnan)
五龙洞森林公园	Wulongdong Forest Park (He'nan)
五龙宫	Wulong Palace; Five Dragons Palace (Hubei)
五龙景区	(of Mount Wudang) Five-Dragon Palace Area
五龙山	Wulong Mountain; Five Dragons Mountain (Liaoning)
五龙山森林公园	Wulong (Five Dragons) Mountain Forest Park (Liaoning)
五龙潭	(of Mount Huangshan) Five Dragons Pond
五龙潭公园	Five Dragon Pool Park (Shandong)
五龙潭瀑布	Waterfalls in the Five Dragon Pond (Jiangxi)
五龙亭	Five Dragon Pavilion (Guangxi)
五年祭	〈高山族〉Five-Year Sacrifice (in the 9th lunar month every five years)
五女拜寿	(of Zhangjiajie) Birthday Courtesy of Five Daughters
五女峰森林公园	Wunüfeng (Peak) Forest Park (Jilin)
五曲更衣台	(of Wuyi Mountain)Scenery of Dressing Terrace at Bend Five
五泉公园	Five Springs Park (Gansu)
五泉山	Five Springs Mountain (Gansu)
五色花	(of Zhangjiajie) Five Colored Flowers
五色梅	〈植〉*Lantana camara*; five-color flower

五色丝线	five-color silk thread (wore in Dragon Boat Festival for exorcising evil spirits)
五四广场	May Fourth Square (Shandong)
五四青年节	Youth Day (on the 4th May) →中国青年节
五松园	Five Pines Garden (Gansu)
五塔寺	Five-Pagoda Temple (Inner Mongolia)
五台山	Mount Wutai; Wutai Mountain (Shanxi) →清凉山
五羊石像	Stone Statue of the Five Rams (Guangdong)
五一广场	wuyi square
五音桥	Five-Tone Bridge (Hebei)
五营森林公园	Wuying Forest Park (Heilongjiang)
五月庙节	〈毛南族〉Temple Festival in May
五月年	〈哈尼族〉May Festival
五云山	Wuyun Mountain (Zhejiang)
五丈原诸葛亮庙	Zhuge Liang Ancestral Temple on Wuzhang Plains (Shaanxi)
五指峰	Five-Finger Peaks (Jiangxi)
五指山景区	Wuzhi Mountain Scenic Area; Five-Finger Mountain Scenic Area (Hai'nan)
五指石景区	Wuzhishi Scenic Area; Five-Finger Rock Cliff Scenic Area (Guangdong)
五智佛	→五方[智]佛
五竹亭	(of Yuanming Garden) Five Bamboo Pavilions
五柱红砂	〈植〉*Reaumuria kaschgarica*
午门	(of Imperial Palace) Meridian Gate
伍龙寺	Wulong Temple (Guizhou)
武昌江滩	Wuchang river beach (Hubei)
武昌廉政文化公园	Wuchang Anti-Corruption Culture Park (Hubei)
武大樱花	cherry blossom in Wuhan University (Hubei)
武当拳	〈武术〉Wudang Quan; Wudang Boxing
武当山	Mount Wudang; Wudang Mountain (Hubei)
武当山景区	Wudang Mountain Scenic Area (Hubei)
武德	〈武术〉wushu morality; martial arts morality/virtue
武帝阁	Wudi Pavilion (Guangxi)

武关	Wuguan Pass (Shaanxi)
武汉白云阁	Wuhan White Cloud Tower (Hubei)
武汉长江大桥	Wuhan Yangtze River Bridge (Hubei)
武汉长江大桥建成纪念碑	Monument of Wuhan Yangtze River Bridge (Hubei)
武汉长江二桥	The Second Wuhan Yangtze River Bridge (Hubei)
武汉崇真堂	Chongzhen Church in Wuhan (Hubei)
武汉东湖牡丹园	Donghu Peony Garden in Wuhan; Peony Garden at East Lake in Wuhan (Hubei)
武汉桂园	Guiyuan Garden in Wuhan (Hubei)
武汉国际博览中心	Wuhan International Expo Centre (Hubei)
武汉江滩	Wuhan River Beach (Hubei)
武汉九峰森林动物园	Jiufeng Forest Zoo in Wuhan (Hubei)
武汉抗战纪念园	Anti Japanese War Memorial Park in Wuhan; Wuhan Memorial Park of Anti-Japanese War (Hubei)
武汉莲花湖公园	Lotus Lake Park in Wuhan (Hubei)
武汉体育中心	Wuhan Sports Centre (Hubei)
武汉铁门关	Tiemen Pass in Wuhan (Hubei)
武汉铜锣	〈乐〉Wuhan Gong
武汉西大街	Wuhan West Street (Hubei)
武汉意大利风情街	Wuhan Italian Style Street (Hubei)
武汉园博园	Wuhan Garden Expo Park (Hubei)
武侯祠	Temple of Marquis Wu; Memorial Temple of Zhuge Liang (Sichuan) →三国圣地
武华山	Wuhua Mountain (Hebei)
武陵瘰螈	〈动〉*Paramesotriton wulingensis*; Wuling warty newt
武陵山	Wuling Mountain (Hu'nan)
武陵源景区	Wulingyuan Scenic Area (Hu'nan)
武强年画	Wuqiang New Year Painting
武山	Wushan Mountain (Zhejiang)
武山湖	Wushan Lake (Hubei)

武术	wushu; martial arts
武术传统套路	wushu traditional routines; traditional routines of martial arts
武术动作	wushu movements; wushu actions; actions of martial arts
武术基本功	wushu basic techniques; basic skills of martial arts
武术节	wushu festival; martial arts festival
武术竞赛套路	wushu competition routines; competition routines of martial arts
武术之乡	country of martial arts
武夷宫	(of Mount Wuyi) Wuyi Palace
武夷宫景区	(of Mount Wuyi) Wuyi Palace Scenic Area
武夷精舍	(of Mount Wuyi) Wuyi Elite House
武夷山历史文物陈列馆	Exhibition of Historic Relics in Mount Wuyi (Fujian) →武夷精舍
武夷山自然保护区	Wuyi Mountain Nature Reserve (Fujian)
武夷书院	(of Mount Wuyi) Wuyi Academy
武夷湍蛙	〈动〉*Amolops wuyiensis*; Wuyi torrent frog
武英殿	(of Imperial Palace) Hall of Martial Valor
武英门	(of Imperial Palace) Gate of Martial Valor
舞春牛	〈壮族〉Spring Cattle Dance
舞火狗节	〈瑶族〉Festival of Huogou Dance; Festival of Dance for Worshipping the Fire God and Dog (on the 15th day of the 8th lunar month)
舞龙	dragon dance
舞龙灯	dragon lantern dance
舞狮	lion dance
舞狮团	lion dance troupe
舞阳河景区	Wuyang River Scenic Area (Guizhou)
舞阳三峡	Wuyang Three Gorges (Guizhou)
婺源金山生态茶业观光园	Jingshan Eco-Tea Tourist Park of Wuyuan (Jiangxi)

雾灵山玉皇顶	Green Pearl East of Beijing (the first peak among the east of Beijing)
雾灵山自然保护区	Wuling Mountain Nature Reserve (Hebei)
雾凇岛	Wusong Island; Rime Island (Jilin)

X

夕九节	〈瑶族〉Xijiu Festival (New Year's Eve of the Yao ethnic group on the 29th day of the 5th lunar month)
夕照山	(of West Lake) Sunset Hill
西安碑林博物馆	Xi'an Beilin Museum; Xi'an Forest of Stone Steles Museum (Shaanxi)
西安(古)城墙	Xi'an (Ancient) Circumvallation; Xi'an (Ancient) City Wall (Shaanxi)
西安大清真寺	Great Mosque of Xi'an (Shaanxi)
西安古玩市场	Xi'an Antique Market (Shaanxi)
西安鼓楼	Xi'an Drum Tower (Shaanxi)
西安门	Xi An Gate (the West Gate of the Imperial City during the Ming and Qing dynasties) (Beijing)
西柏坡景区	Xibaipo Scenic Area (a sacred place of revolution, Hebei)
西北湖绿化广场	Northwest Lake Green Square (Hubei)
西伯利亚虎	→东北[西伯利亚]虎
西禅寺	Xichan Temple (Sichuan)
西大殿	(of Potala Palace) Great West Hall
西堤六桥	(of Summer Palace) Six Bridges of West Dyke
西方三圣殿	Western Trinity; Three Saints Hall of the West
西方寺	Western Monastery (Hong Kong)
西风	(of mahjong) West Wind
西贡海滨公园	Sai Kung Waterfront Park (Hong Kong)
西瓜节	Watermelon Festival (on the 28th May)
西关大屋	Sai Kwan Mansion; Xiguan Mansion (Guangdong)

西海	→青海湖
西汉帝陵	Imperial Mausoleum of the Western Han Dynasty (Shaanxi)
西汉酒泉胜迹	Jiuquan Scenic Spot of the Western Han Dynasty (Gansu)
西汉南越王博物馆	Museum of the Nanyue King Mausoleum of the Western Han Dynasty (Guangdong)
西汉南越王墓	Tomb of Nanyue King of the Western Han Dynasty (Guangdong)
西湖	West Lake (Zhejiang)
西湖景区	West Lake Scenic Area (Zhejiang)
西湖十景	Ten Views of the West Lake; Ten Top Scenic Spots of the West Lake (Zhejiang)
西华门	(of Imperial Palace) West Prosperity Gate
西江	Xijiang River; West River
西江千户苗寨	Xijiang Miao Village with Thousand Households; One-Thousand-Household Miao Village of Xijiang (Guizhou)
西津渡	Xijin Ferry (Jiangsu)
西开教堂	St. Joseph's Cathedral Church (Tianjin)
西泠印社	Xiling Seal Art Society (Zhejiang)
西陵长江大桥	Xiling Yangtze River Bridge; Xiling Changjiang Bridge (Hubei)
西陵峡	(of Three Gorges) Xiling Gorge
西岭晨霞	(of Chengde Mountain Resort) Morning Sunglow over West Mountains
西六宫	(of Imperial Palace) West Six Halls
西南边陲大观园	Grand View Garden at Southwest Border (Yunnan)
西南大都会	southwest metropolis; metropolis of the southwest
西南绒鼠	〈动〉*Eothenomys custos*
西南丝路	Southwest Silk Road
西南无心菜	〈植〉*Arenaria forrestii*

西排子湖湿地公园	Xipaizi Lake Wetland Park (Hubei)
西樵山白云洞景区	White Cloud Cave Scenic Spot at Xiqiao Mountain (Guangdong)
西樵山碧玉洞景区	Jasper Cave Scenic Spot at Xiqiao Mountain (Guangdong)
西樵山翠岩景区	Green Rock Scenic Spot at Xiqiao Mountain (Guangdong)
西樵山景区	Xiqiao Mountain Scenic Area (Guangdong)
西沙群岛	(of South China Sea) Xisha Islands
西山景区	Xishan Mountain Scenic Area (Guangxi, Hubei)
西双版纳堆花酒	Xishuangbanna hops-piled wine
西双版纳热带植物园	Xishuangbanna Tropical Botanical Graden (Yunnan) →勐仑热带植物园
西塘古镇	Xitang Ancient Town (Zhejiang)
西天门	(of Zhangjiajie) West Heaven Gate
西天取经	(of Zhangjiajie) Pilgrims to the West
西湾河海滨公园	Waterfront Park of Sai Wan Ho (Hong Kong)
西湾湖广场	West Bay Plaza (Macao)
西王母	〈道〉Queen Mother of the West
西溪湿地公园	Xixi Wetland Park (Zhejiang)
西狭颂	Xixia Song (Cliff Carvings); Ode to Western Valley (by Qiu Jing in the Eastern Han Dynasty)
西夏王陵	Western Xia Imperial Tombs; Royal Mausoleum of the Western Xia Kingdom (Ningxia)
西秀海滩公园	Xixiu Seaside Park (Hai'nan)
西洋楼景区	(of Yuanming Garden) European Palaces
西屿古堡	Xiyu Ancient Castle (Taiwan)
西域湍蛙	〈动〉*Amolops afghanus*
西岳华山	Mount Huahan; Huahan Mountain (as the Western One of the Five Sacred Mountains in China) (Shaanxi)
西岳庙	(of Mount Huashan) Xiyue Temple
西藏朝山节	Tibetan Mountain Worship Festival (on the 4th June in Tibetan calendar)

西藏齿突蟾	〈动〉*Scutiger boulengeri*; Tibetan toothlet toad
西藏地毯	Tibetan carpet (traditionally made from Tibetan highland sheep's wool)
西藏高原	Tibetan Plateau; Tibet Plateau
西藏农耕新年	Tibetan New Year in Shigatse Area
西藏庞贝古城	Ancient City of Pompeii in Tibet
西藏山溪鲵	〈动〉*Batrachuperus tibetanus*; alpine stream salamander
西藏杓兰	〈植〉*Cypripedium tibeticum*
西藏舌突蛙	〈动〉*Liurana xizangensis*
西藏无柱兰	〈植〉*Amitostigma tibeticum*; Tibetan amitostigma
西藏野驴	〈动〉*Equus kiang*; Tibetan wild ass
西藏自治区	Tibet Autonomous Region
西周五礼	〈古〉Five Etiquettes of Western Zhou Dynasty
西周燕都遗址博物馆	Yan Capital Site Museum of Western Zhou Dynasty; Museum of Yan Capital Remains of the Western Zhou Dynasty (Beijing)
希拉穆仁草原	Xilamuren Grassland (Inner Mongolia)
希日塔拉草原度假区	Xiri Tala Grassland Holiday Resort (Inner Mongolia)
牺牲所	1 〈旧〉House of Sacrifice (an office of the Imperial Household Department in the Qing Dynasty) 2 (of Temple of Heaven) House for Raising Sacrificed Animals
息心所	(of Mount Emei) Mind Becalming Place
犀牛海	(of Jiuzhai Valley) Rhinoceros Lake
犀牛山	Xiniu Mountain (Sichuan)
锡伯族	Xibe/Sibe ethnic group; Xibe/Sibe
锡达布逊盐湖	Xidabuxun Salt Lake (Qinghai)
锡惠公园	Xihui Park (Jiangsu)
锡婚	tin wedding (the 10th anniversary of marriage)
锡林郭勒大草原	Xilin Gol Grassland (Inner Mongolia)
锡林郭勒赛马场	Xilin Gol Racecourse (Inner Mongolia)

溪水森林公园	Xishui Forest Park (Heilongjiang)
溪头景区	Xitou Scenic Area (Taiwan)
溪头石豆兰	〈植〉*Bulbophyllum chitouense*
膝柄木	〈植〉*Bhesa robusta*
习礼亭	(of Zhongshan Park) Pavilion of Imperial (of Zhongshan Park) Etiquette Exercises
洗牛节	〈侗族〉Cattle-Washing Festival (on the 6th day of the 6th lunar month)
洗三	〈习俗〉Xisan (to bath infants on the 3rd day of their birth)
洗身洞	(of Huanglong Valley) Body Washing Grotto
洗象池	(of Mount Emei) Elephant Bathing Pond
洗澡节	〈藏族〉Bathing Festival (in early July of Tibetan calendar)
玺	〈古〉ruler's seal
喜得贵子	used to to bless a baby's birth; to congratulate sb. on the birth of a baby
喜峰口旅游度假区	Xifengkou Tourist Resort (Hebei)
喜酒	wedding wine; wedding banquet
喜联	wedding couplets
喜马拉雅旱獭	〈动〉*Marmota himalayana*; Himalayan marmot
喜马拉雅沙参	〈植〉*Adenophora himalayana*
喜马拉雅鼠兔	〈动〉*Ochotona himalayana*; Himalayan pika
喜树	〈植〉*Camptotheca acuminata*
喜帖	wedding invitation
喜雨草	〈植〉*Ombrocharis dulcis*
禧庐	→景贤里
戏班子	〈旧〉theatrical troupe →梨园
戏楼	opera tower (stage in an ancestral hall or temple for performances)
戏曲联欢晚会	opera gala
戏台	→戏楼
细刺水蛙	〈动〉*Hylarana spinulosa*

细刺蛙	〈动〉*Rana spinulosa*; fine-spined frog
细梗紫菊	〈植〉*Notoseris gracilipes*
细叶凤尾蕨	〈植〉*Pteris angustipinna*
细痣疣螈	〈动〉*Tylototriton asperrimus*; black knobby newt
峡谷大观园	valley showplace; grand canyon showplace
峡谷浮石林	Canyon Pumice Forest (Jilin)
狭叶含笑	〈植〉*Michelia angustioblonga*
狭叶金粟兰	〈植〉*Chloranthus angustifolius*
下白泥碉堡	Xia Baini Blockhouse (Hong Kong)
下季节海	(of Jiuzhai Valley) Lower Seasonal Lake
下联	(of a couplet) right roll
下马碑	horse-dismounting stele
下马酒	〈蒙古族〉down horse wine
下梅古民居	(of Mount Wuyi) ancient dwellings of Xiamei Village
夏蜡梅	〈植〉*Calycanthus chinensis*; Chinese sweetshrub
夏鲁寺	Schalu Kloster; Shalu Monastery (Tibet)
夏至	〈节气〉Summer Solstice (the 10th solar term)
厦门大桥	Xiamen Bridge (Fujian)
厦门古避暑洞	Ancient Cave of Summer Resort in Xiamen (Fujian)
厦门观海园	Xiamen Sea-Watching Garden (Fujian)
厦门皓月园	Xiamen Bright Moon Garden (Fujian)
厦门胡里山炮台	Xiamen Hulishan Fortress; Huli Mountain Canon Platform in Xiamen (Fujian)
厦门华侨博物院	Xiamen Overseas Chinese Museum (Fujian)
厦门莲花森林公园	Xiamen Lotus Forest Park (Fujian)
厦门南普陀寺	Xiamen Nanputuo Temple (Fujian)
厦门日光岩	Xiamen Sunlight Rock (Fujian)
厦门万石植物园	Wanshi Botanical Garden of Xiamen (Fujian) → 厦门园林植物园
厦门英雄三岛	Xiamen Three Heroic Islets (Fujian)
厦门园林植物园	Xiamen Botanical Garden (Fujian) →厦门万石植物园

厦门战地观光园	Xiamen Battleground Sightseeing Garden (Fujian)
仙安石林	Xian'an Stone Forest (Hai'nan)
仙岛湖观音洞	Guanyin Cave at Xiandao Lake (Hubei)
仙岛湖野人岛	Savage Island in Xiandao Lake (Hubei)
仙都山	Xiandu Mountain (Zhejiang)
仙峰寺	(of Mount Emei) Xianfeng Temple; Immortal Peak Temple
仙景台景区	Xianjingtai Scenic Area (Jilin)
仙居河湿地公园	Wetland Park at Xianju River (Hubei)
仙龙岛	Xianlong Island (Beijing)
仙米森林公园	Xianmi Forest Park (Qinghai)
仙女茅庵	Fairy Thatch Hut (Hu'nan)
仙女山	Fairy Maiden Mountain (Chongqing)
仙女岩	Fairy Maiden Rock (Guangxi)
仙瀑洞	Fairy Waterfall Cave (Zhejiang)
仙琴蛙	〈动〉*Hylarana daunchina*; *Nidirana daunchina*; Emei music frog
仙人承露台	(of Yuanming Garden) Platform of Immortal Collecting Heavenly Dew
仙人洞	fairy cave; immortal cavern
仙人桥	(of Zhangjiajie) Fairy Bridge; Immortals Bridge
仙人台景区	Xianren Tai Scenic Spot; Immortal Summit Scenic Spot (Liaoning, Hubei)
仙人台森林公园	Xianrentai Forest Park (Liaoning)
仙台山	Xiantai Mountain (Hebei, He'nan)
仙霞铁线蕨	〈植〉*Adiantum juxtapositum*; Chinese maidenhair
先干为敬	〈礼〉to drink first to show one's respect
先秦官学祭祀	Memorial Ceremony of Official Schools in Pre-Qin
祅[玄]神楼	Xianshen Tower (Shanxi)
咸福宫	(of Imperial Palace) Palace of Universal Happiness
咸宁金桂湖	Jingui Lake in Xianning (Hubei)
咸宁太乙观	Taiyi Taoist Temple in Xianning (Hubei)

咸宁向阳湖国家湿地公园	Xiangyang Lake National Wetland Park in Xianning (Hubei)
线法画	(of Yuanming Garden) Perspective Landscapes
线法山	(of Yuanming Garden) Hill of Perspective
献县单桥石桥	Danqiao Stone Bridge of Xian County (Hebei)
乡城齿蟾	〈动〉*Oreolalax xiangchengensis*; Xiangcheng lazy/toothed toad
相国寺	Xiangguo Temple (He'nan)
香菜	〈植〉*Coriandrum sativum*; Chinese parsley; coriander
香雕绍兴酒	Xiangdiao Shaoxing Medium Sweet Wine
香妃墓	Tomb of Xiangfei; Fragrant Imperial Concubine Tomb (Xinjiang) →阿帕克霍加墓
香港长山古寺	Hong Kong Changshan Ancient Temple
香港大会堂	Hong Kong City Hall
香港大球场	Hong Kong Stadium
香港迪士尼乐园	Hong Kong Disneyland
香港电影资料馆	Hong Kong Film Archive
香港东林念佛堂	Donglin Buddhist Hall of Hong Kong
香港东涌罗汉寺	Tung Chung Lohan Temple of Hong Kong
香港动植物公园	Hong Kong Zoological and Botanical Garden
香港杜莎夫人蜡像馆	Madame Tussauds in Hong Kong
香港芙蓉山烈女宫	Hong Kong Women's Palace at Furong Mountain
香港港	Hong Kong Port
香港公园	Hong Kong Park
香港观宗寺	Hong Kong Guanzong Temple
香港国际机场	Hong Kong International Airport
香港国际七人榄球赛	Hong Kong Rugby Sevens
香港海洋公园	Hong Kong Ocean Park
香港环球贸易广场	Hong Kong International Commercial Centre
香港黄金海岸	Hong Kong Gold Coast
香港回归祖国纪念碑	Monument of Hong Kong's Return to the Motherland
香港会议展览中心	Hong Kong Convention and Exhibition Centre

香港机场核心计划展览中心	Airport Core Programme Exhibition Centre of Hong Kong
香港锦田树屋	Kam Tin Tree House in Hong Kong
香港科学园	Hong Kong Science Park; HKSP
香港礼宾府	Hong Kong Government House
香港瘰螈	〈动〉*Paramesotriton hongkongensis*; Hong Kong newt
香港妙法寺	Hong Kong Miao Fa Temple
香港赛马会大熊猫园	Giant Panda Habitat of Hong Kong Jockey Club
香港沙田彭福公园	Sha Tin Penfold Park in Hong Kong
香港湿地公园	Hong Kong Wetland Park
香港石板街	Hong Kong Slate Street
香港世界地质公园	Hong Kong Global Geopark
香港视觉艺术中心	Hong Kong Visual Arts Centre
香港太空馆天文公园	Hong Kong Space Museum Astropark
香港湍蛙	〈动〉*Amolops hongkongensis*; Hong Kong cascade-frog
香港文化中心	Hong Kong Cultural Centre
香港西林寺	Hong Kong Xilin Temple
香港延庆寺	Hong Kong Yanqing Temple
香港艺术节	Hong Kong Arts Festival
香港圆玄学院	Hong Kong Yuen Yuen Institute
香港仔海滨公园	Hong Kong Aberdeen Seaside Park
香港仔郊野公园	Hong Kong Aberdeen Country Park
香港中央图书馆	Hong Kong Central Library
香格里拉大峡谷	Shangri-la Grand Canyon (Yunnan)
香格里拉葛丹·松赞林寺	Gedan-Songzanlin Monastery in Shangri-la (Yunnan)
香果树	〈植〉*Emmenopterys henryi*; Chinese emmenopterys
香积寺	Xiangji Temple (Shaanxi)
香兰	〈植〉*Haraella retrocalla*; Chinese cymbidium
香龙洞景区	Xianglong Cave Scenic Area (Hubei)
香炉峰	Incense Burner Peak (Zhejiang)
香炉寺	Xianglu Peak; Incense Burner Temple (Shaanxi)
香山	Xiangshan Mountain; Fragrance Mountain (Beijing)

香山公园	Xiangshan Mountain Park; Fragrance Mountain Park (Beijing)
香山湖水利生态旅游区	Water Conservancy Ecotourism Area of Xiangshan Lake (He'nan)
香溪洞	Xiangxi Cave (Shaanxi)
香油湾	(of Mount Taishan) Sesame Oil Valley
香橼	〈植〉*Citrus medica*
香远益清	(of Chengde Mountain Resort) Widely Spreading and Refreshing Fragrance
湘菜	Xiang cuisine →湖南菜
湘楚文化	Xiangchu culture; Hu'nan culture
湘江	Xiangjiang River (Hu'nan)
湘江流域	Xiangjiang River basin; Xiangjiang River valley
湘西明珠	Pearl of West Hu'nan (referring to Ancient Town of Fenghuang) →凤凰古城
襄阳唐城	City of Tang Dynasty in Xiangyang
襄阳唐城影视基地	Tangcheng Film and Television Base in Xiangyang (Hubei)
襄阳引丹水利景区	Danjiang to Xiangyang Water Conservancy Scenic Area (Hubei)
襄阳钟鼓楼	Xiangyang Bell and Drum Tower (Hubei)
翔安旅游区	Xiang'an Tourist Area (Fujian)
翔龙湖	Xianglong Lake (Guangdong)
响浪节	〈藏族〉Firewood-Collection Day (from the 4th day to the 17th day of the 6th lunar month)
响沙湾	Resonant Sand Bay (Inner Mongolia)
响堂山景区	Xiangtang Hill Scenic Area (Hebei)
响堂山[寺]石窟	Xiangtang Hill Grottoes; Xiangtang Temple Grottoes (Hebei)
向海自然保护区	Xianghai Nature Reserve (Jilin)
象鼻山	Elephant Trunk Hill (Guangxi) →漓山
象河景区	Xianghe River Scenic Area (Hubei)
象棋	Chinese chess
象山	Xiangshan Mountain (Jiangsu)

象牙婚	ivory wedding (the 14th anniversary of marriage) →丝婚
象眼岩	Elephant's Eye Rock (Elephant Trunk Hill, Guangxi)
消防宣传日	Fire Publicity Day (November 9th)
消灾祈福	to avert calamities and pray for blessings
宵夜	→夜宵
萧太后梳妆楼	Dressing House of Empress Dowager Xiao (Hebei)
潇湘八景	Eight Views of Hsiao and Hsiang; Eight Grand Sights of Xiaoxiang (Hu'nan)
小布达拉宫	Small Potala Palace (Hebei) →普陀宗乘之庙
小沧浪	(of Humble Administrator's Garden) Small Pavilion of Quiet Meditation
小沧浪亭	(of Garden of Harmony) Small Pavilion of Surging Waves
小藏峰	(of Mount Wuyi) Small Hiding Peak
小大昭寺	Small Jokhang Temple (Sichuan)
小叮当科学游乐区	Little Ding-Dong Science Park; Xiao Dingdang Science Recreation Area (Taiwan)
小飞虹	(of Humble Administrator's Garden) Small Flying Rainbow
小功	〈丧〉gown of thin flax; mourning apparel (of the 4th class of wufu in ancient China); minor merit →五服
小勾儿茶	〈植〉*Berchemiella wilsonii*; little supplejack
小鼓	〈乐〉small drum
小锅酒	〈彝族〉small pot shochu
小寒	〈节气〉Slight Cold; Lesser Cold; Minor Cold (the 23rd solar term)
小河沿文化	〈古〉Xiaoheyan Culture (3000–2500 B.C., late Neolithic Culture)
小华山	(of Tiantang Zhai) Lesser Mount Huashan

小黄山景区	(of Guanmen Mountain) Lesser Mount Huangshan Scenic Area
小棘蛙	〈动〉*Quasipaa exilispinosa*; common/lesser spiny frog
小麂	〈动〉*Muntiacus reevesi*; Chinese muntjac
小蓟	〈中药〉*Cirsium Setosum*; Herba Cirsii; Field Thistle
小角蟾	〈动〉*Megophrys minor*
小金瓦寺	(of Ta'er Monastery) Xiaojinwa Temple; Lesser Hall of the Golden Roof →护法神殿
小兰亭	Small Orchid Pavilion (Zhejiang)
小浪底黄河水利枢纽	Xiao Langdi Water Conservancy Project on Yellow River (He'nan)
小莲庄	Lesser Lotus Villa (national key cultural relics protection unit) (Zhejiang)
小殓	〈丧〉xiaolian (the funeral process of purifying and dressing the deceased)
小龙湫	Small Dragon Waterfall (Zhejiang)
小龙潭	Small Dragon Pond (Hubei)
小满	〈节气〉Grain Full; Lesser Fullness (the 8th solar term)
小梅沙海滨旅游景区	Xiaomeisha Coastal Tourist Area (Guangdong)
小米蕉	→粉蕉
小名	→乳[小]名
小南海古地震遗址	Site of Xiaonanhai Earthquake Heritage (Chongqing)
小年	Kitchen God's Day; Festival of the Kitchen God; Little/Minor New Year (on the 23rd or 24th day of the 12th lunar month)
小蓬莱	(of Lingering Garden) Small Fairy Isle
小三峡	Lesser Three Gorges (Hubei)
小山丛桂轩	(of Master-of-Nets Garden) Small Hill and Osmanthus Fragrance Pavilion; Small Hill and Fragrans Pavilion

小暑	〈节气〉Slight Heat; Lesser Heat (the 11th solar term)
小天池	(of Mount Lushan) Lesser Heaven Pond
小天门	(of Zhangjiajie) Minor Heaven Gate
小湍蛙	〈动〉*Amolops torrentis*; little torrent frog; small cascade-frog
小兴安岭	Lesser Khingan Mountains; Lesser Xing'an Mountains (Heilongjiang)
小兴安岭驯鹿	Lesser Khingan reindeer
小雪	〈节气〉Slight Snow; Minor Snow (the 20th solar term)
小雁塔	Small Wild Goose Pagoda (Shaanxi)
小野柳地形景观区	Xiaoye Liu Topographic Landscape Area (Taiwan)
小叶钩毛蕨	〈植〉*Cyclogramma flexilis*
小叶锦鸡儿	〈中药〉*Caragana Microphylla*
小叶榆	→榔[小叶]榆
小叶中国蕨	〈植〉*Sinopteris albofusca*
小昭寺	Ramoche Temple; Ramoche Monastery (Tibet)
孝灯	〈丧〉filial piety lamp; funeral lamp
孝登寺	Shaten Monastery; Xiaodeng Monastery (Tibet)
孝联	filial piety couplets
孝顺竹	〈植〉*Bambusa multiplex*
歇步	〈武术〉resting stance
歇步勾手亮掌	〈武术〉Hook hand and flash palm in resting stance
歇步擒打	〈武术〉(of Tai Chi) Catching and hitting in cross-legged crouching stance
斜萼草	〈植〉*Loxocalyx urticifolius*
斜飞势	〈武术〉(of Tai Chi) Oblique flying gesture
谐联	facetious couplet
谐奇趣	(of Yuanming Garden) Harmonious Wonder
谐趣园	(of Summer Palace) Garden of Harmonious Interests
撷绣楼	(of Master-of-Nets Garden) Beauty-View Tower

谢师酒［宴］	teacher appreciation banquet; to propose a toast to teachers for gratitude
心形潭	Heart-Shaped Pond (Chongqing)
心意六合拳	〈武术〉Heart-and-will Six Harmony Boxing
心意拳	〈武术〉Xinyi Quan; Mind Boxing
辛亥首义人物群雕像	Statues of the First Xinhai Uprising Figures (Hubei)
新澳凼大桥	Friendship Bridge; Amizade Bridge (of Portuguese) Ponte de Amizade (Macao)
新昌大佛寺	Xinchang Grand Buddha Temple (Zhejiang) →石城古刹
新场古镇	Xinchang Ancient Town (Shanghai)
新谷节	〈壮族〉Newly-Harvested Millet Day (on the 1st day after harvest in the 10th lunar month)
新谷酒	〈哈尼族〉Xin'gu wine; new grain wine
新禾节	〈苗族〉Rice Harvest Festival
新华丝绸市场	Xinhua Road Silk Market (Zhejiang)
新华土林	Xinhua Soil Forest (Yunnan)
新婚节	〈侗族〉New Wedding Day (in the 10th lunar month)
新疆国际大巴扎	Xinjiang International Grand Bazaar
新疆国际舞蹈节	Xinjiang International Dance Festival
新疆丝绸之路博物馆	Xinjiang Silk Road Museum
新疆天山自然遗产地	Xinjiang Tianshan Mountain Natural Heritage
新疆维吾尔自治区	Xinjiang Uygur/Uyghur Autonomous Region
新疆西域民俗风情园	Xinjiang Western Region Folk Custom Garden
新界	New Territories (Hong Kong)
新灵峡	Xinling Valley (Guangxi)
新米节	Newly-Harvested Rice Festival; New Rice Festival (in the 9th lunar month for the Miao and Jinuo ethnic group, and on the 14th day of the 8th lunar month for the Wa ethnic group)
新民园广场	New Minyuan Square (Tianjin)
新年倒数仪式	New Year countdown ceremony
新年祭	〈高山族〉New Year's Day Ceremony

新葡京酒店	Grand Lisboa Hotel (engaged in the gambling industry) (Macao)
新世纪广场	New Century Plaza (Hong Kong)
新四军第五师纪念馆	Memorial Hall of the New Fifth Division of of the New Fourth Army (Hubei)
新滩	→青[新]滩
新唐风	New Tang Style (a new Chinese architectural form)
新田遗址	Xintian Site (Shanxi) →侯马晋国遗址
新五师旧址	Site of the Fifth-Division of the New Fourth Army (Hubei)
新西湖十景	New Ten Views of West Lake (Zhejiang)
新乡八里沟	Xinxiang Bali Valley (He'nan)
信义宗神学院	Lutheran Theological Seminary (Hong Kong)
兴安杜鹃花	〈植〉*Rhododendron dauricum*; Xing'an azalea
兴安落叶松	〈植〉*Larix gmelinii*; Xing'an larch
兴畜节	〈蒙古族〉Livestock Festival (on the 16th day of the 1st lunar month)
兴海湖鸟类保护区	Xinghai Lake Bird Sanctuary (Tianjin)
兴凯湖	Xingkai Lake; Khanka Lake (Heilongjiang)
兴隆观测站	Xinglong Observation Station (Hebei)
兴隆热带植物园	Xinglong Tropical Botanical Garden (Hai'nan)
兴隆山黄榆景区	Xinglongshan Yellow Elm Scenic Spot (Jilin)
兴坪古街	Xingping Ancient Street (Guangxi)
兴坪古镇	Xingping Ancient Town (Guangxi)
兴庆宫公园	Xingqing Palace Park; Park of Xingqing Palace (Shaanxi)
星光大道	Avenue of Stars (Hong Kong)
星海公园	Xinghai Park (Liaoning)
星海广场	Xinghai Square (Liaoning)
星毛短舌菊	〈植〉*Brachanthemum pulvinatum*
星云湖	Xingyun Lake (Yunnan)
邢台大峡谷	Xingtai Grand Canyon (Hebei)

行宫	〈古〉imperial palace for short stays (away from the capital); temporary dwelling palace of an emperor used for his tours
行酒令	to play drinking games
行三跪九叩之礼	〈古〉to perform three kneels and nine kowtows; to perform the most respectful courtesy/etiquette
行中书省	〈古〉executive secretariat (a central government department in the Yuan Dynasty)
行走之礼	walking etiquette
形意拳	〈武术〉Xingyi Quan; Xingyi Boxing; Form-and-Will Boxing
省善真堂	Shang Sin Chun Tong (Hong Kong)
兴福寺新年听钟声活动	to wait for New Year Bell at Xingfu Temple
凶拜	〈丧〉Xiongbai (one of the nine ways of kowtows)
凶礼	〈古〉etiquette for mourning and disasters (one of Five Etiquettes of Western Zhou Dynasty)
胸佩白花	〈丧〉to wear white flowers
胸腺齿突蟾	〈动〉*Scutiger glandulatus*; chest gland cat-eyed toad
熊猫	〈动〉*Ailuropoda melanoleuca*; panda
熊猫海	(of Jiuzhai Valley) Panda Lake
熊猫海瀑布	(of Jiuzhai Valley) Panda Lake Waterfall
修顿球场	Southorn Playground; Southorn Stadium (Hong Kong)
修竹阁	(of Lion Forest Garden) High Pavilion with Flowing Water
秀峰	(of Mount Lushan) Grace Peak
秀水街	Xiushui Street; Silk Street (international tourism shopping market) (Beijing)
绣林山	Xiulin Mountain; Mountain of Oriflamme Forest (Hubei)
绣楼	〈古〉embroidery tower; embroidery building
绣绮亭	(of Humble Administrator's Garden) Peony Pavilion; Pavilion of Splendid Landscape

须弥福寿之庙	Temple of Sumeru Happiness and Longevity (Hebei)
须弥山石窟	Sumeru Mountain Grottoes (Ningxia)
须菩提	〈佛〉Subhuti (one of the ten disciples of the Buddha, best-known for his understanding of kong [emptiness])
虚步	〈武术〉Empty stance; Empty step
虚步压掌	(of Tai Chi) Empty step downward palm; Downward palm in empty step/stance
徐悲鸿博物馆	Xu Beihong Museum (Beijing)
徐悲鸿故居	Former Residence of Xu Beihong (Guangxi)
徐悲鸿纪念馆	Xu Beihong Memorial Hall (Beijing)
徐东商业街	Xudong Commercial Street (Hubei)
徐家汇藏书楼	Xujiahui Treasure Book Tower (Shanghai)
徐州汉城	Xuzhou Han City (Jiangsu)
许国石坊	Xu Guo Stone Archway (Anhui)
许氏旧居	Former Residence of the Xu Family (Tianjin)
旭独龙节	〈珞巴族〉Xudulong Festival (in February of Luoba calendar, for celebrating a peaceful year and good harvest)
蓄水节	〈壮族〉Water Storage Day (on the 7th day of the 7th lunar month)
轩辕黄帝	Emperor Xuanyuan; Yellow Emperor (the leader of the ancient Chinese tribal alliance, honored as the primitive ancestor of Chinese nation)
轩辕庙	Xuanyuan Temple (Shaanxi) →黄帝庙
宣城新四军军部旧址纪念馆	Memorial Hall of the Former Military Headquarter of New Fourth Army in Xuancheng (Anhui)
宣化店谈判旧址	Xuanhuadian Negotiation Site (Hubei)
玄帝殿	(of Mount Wudang) Emperor Xuan's Temple
玄妙观	〈道〉Xuanmiao (Taoist) Temple (Jiangsu)
玄神楼	→袄[玄]神楼
玄武湖	Xuanwu Lake (Jiangsu)
玄武门	Xuanwu Gate (Shaanxi, Jiangsu)

玄岳门	(of Mount Wudang) Xuanyue Archway; Portal of Entry
悬臂长城	Xuanbi Great Wall; Overhanging Great Wall (Gansu)
悬棺	xuanguan; hanging coffin; coffin on cliff
悬棺葬	precipice coffin burying
悬空寺	Suspended Temple (Shanxi)
旋风脚	〈武术〉Whirlwind kick; Tornado kick
旋子脚	〈武术〉Butterfly kick
旋子转体	〈武术〉Butterfly twist
选茔	〈丧〉to choose a graveyard
学步桥	Xuebu Bridge; Walk-Learning Bridge (Hebei)
学宫	〈古〉xue gong; palace of learning; Confucian academy (schools set up by local governments in ancient times)
学(习)雷锋日	Learning from Lei Feng Day (March 5th) →青年志愿者服务日
学堂洞	School Cave (Hubei)
雪窦瀑布	Xuedou Waterfall (Zhejiang)
雪顿节	〈藏族〉Sho Ton Festival (from 29th June to 1st July of the Tibetan calendar)
雪峰山	Xuefeng Mountain (Hu'nan)
雪山飞瀑	Xueshan Mountain Waterfall; Snow Mountain Waterfall (Guangxi)
雪香云蔚亭	(of Humble Administrator's Garden) Prunus Mume Pavilion; Pavilion of White Plum Blossoms
血水草	〈植〉*Eomecon chionantha*; snow poppy
血雉	〈动〉*Ithaginis cruentus*; blood pheasant
薰衣草风情园	Lavender Flavour Park; Lavender-Featured Botanical Garden (Hubei)
浔江	Xunjiang River (Guangxi)
鲟鱼	〈动〉*Acipenser sinensis*; sturgeon
讯号山	Signal Hill (Hong Kong) →黑头角
驯鹿坡	(of Chengde Mountain Resort) Hillside of Domesticated Deer

Y

丫山花海石林	Flower Ocean and Stone Forest on Yashan Mountain (Anhui)
压岁钱	New Year lucky money (given to children as a Lunar New Year gift)
鸭淀水库	Yadian Reservoir (Tianjin)
鸭绿江	Yalu River (Liaoning)
鸭绿江大桥	Yalu River Bridge (Liaoning)
鸭绿江大峡谷	Yalu River Grand Canyon (Jilin)
崖柏	〈植〉*Thuja sutchuenensis* →四川侧柏
崖下库含羞瀑	(of Yaxiaku) Bashful Waterfall from Cliff (Zhejiang)
崖下库景区	Yaxiaku Scenic Spot (Zhejiang)
崖葬	〈丧〉cliff burial
雅丹地貌	yadan/yardang landform
雅丹奇观	yadan/yardang spectacle
雅鲁藏布大峡谷	Yarlung Zangbo Grand Canyon (the deepest canyon in the world) (Tibet)
雅鲁藏布大峡谷国家公园	National Park of Yarlung Zangbo Grand Canyon (Tibet)
雅鲁藏布江	Yalu Zangbo River (the largest plateau river in China) (Tibet)
雅玛里克山	Yamalike Mountain (Xinjiang)
亚布力国际滑雪旅游度假区	Yabuli International Ski Resort (Heilongjiang)
亚龙湾国家旅游度假区	Yalong Bay National Tourist Resort (Hai'nan)
亚龙湾中心广场	Yalong Bay Central Square (Hai'nan)

亚欧大陆	Euro-Asia Continent; Eurasian Continent
亚婆井前地	Yapo Well Front Ground; (of Portuguese) Largo do Lilau (Macao)
娅拜节	〈壮族〉Ya Bai Festival (on the 4th day of the 4th lunar month, for the worship of a heroine named Yabai)
胭脂古井	Ancient Kermes Well (Hu'nan)
烟波致爽	(of Chengde Mountain Resort) Hall of Refreshing Mist and Ripples
烟花爆竹	firework and firecracker
烟雨楼	Tower/Pavilion of Mist and Rain (Zhejiang)
焉支山森林公园	Yanzhi Mountain Forest Park (Gansu)
延安宝塔山	Yan'an Pagoda Hill (Shaanxi)
延安凤凰山革命旧址	Revolution Site of Fenghuang Mountain in Yan'an (Shaanxi)
延安革命纪念馆	Memorial Hall of Revolutionary Activities in Yan'an (Shaanxi)
延安古城墙遗址	Ruins of the Ancient City Wall of Yan'an (Shaanxi)
延晖阁	(of Imperial Palace) Belvedere of Prolonging Splendor
延平故垒	Yanping Old Fort (Fujian)
延平郡王祠	Temple of Yanping King; Koxinga Shrine (Taiwan)
延禧宫	(of Imperial Palace) Palace of Prolonging Happiness
延薰山馆	(of Chengde Mountain Resort) Hall of Tree-Shade and Breeze Coolness
岩洞葬	〈丧〉grotto burial
岩画	rock painting; cliff painting; petrogram
岩画长廊	Long Gallery of Rock Paintings/Petroglyphs (Xinjiang)
岩生耳蕨	〈植〉*Polystichum rupicola*
岩松鼠	〈动〉*Sciurotamias davidianus*; David's rock squirrel

岩羊	〈动〉Peseudois nayaur; bharal
炎帝陵	Emperor Yandi Mausoleum (Shaanxi, Hu'nan)
盐锅峡水电站	Yanguoxia Hydropower Station (Gansu)
盐湖博物馆	Salt Lake Museum (Qinghai)
盐业风情游览区	Salt Industry Tour Area (Tianjin)
盐源山溪鲵	〈动〉Batrachuperus yenyuanensis; yenyuan stream salamander
颜惠庆故居	Former Residence of Yan Huiqing (Tianjin)
衍圣公府	→孔府
掩手肱捶	〈武术〉(of Tai Chi) Covering hands and striking with arms
眼斑刘树蛙	〈动〉Liuixalus ocellatus
罨画窗	(of Chengde Mountain Resort) Window of Colorful Natural Pictures
演武厅	wushu-practicing hall
艳湖公园	Yanhu Park (Hubei)
堰工石像	Stone Statue of Weir Labourer (Sichuan)
堰塞湖	barrier lake; dammed lake; quake lake
雁荡山	Mount Yandang; Yandang Mountain (Zhejiang)
雁荡山畲族民俗风情园	Folk-Custom Garden of She ethnic group in Yandang Mountain (Zhejiang)
雁湖	Wild Goose Lake (Zhejiang)
雁门关	Yanmen Pass (Shanxi)
燕伋望鲁台	Yanji Wanglu Fort (Shaanxi)
燕皮	〈烹饪〉Yanpi (a special traditional snack in Fuzhou, Fujian)
燕青拳	Yanqing Quan; Yanqing Boxing
燕塞湖景区	Yansai Lake Scenic Area (Hebei)
燕山	Mount Yanshan; Yanshan Mountain (Beijing)
燕山塔陵	Tower-Shaped Mausoleum at Yanshan Mountain (Hebei) →万佛园
燕射	〈礼〉shooting at banquet (gratitude for guests in the banquet)
燕式平衡	〈武术〉Swallow-style balance while leaning forward and extending one leg

燕王湖湿地生态园	Yanwang Lake Wetland Ecopark (Tianjin)
燕窝节	Bird's Nest Festival (on the 8th August in Yunnan)
燕下都古城	Ancient City of Yanxia Capital (Hebei)
燕下都遗址	Site of the Yanxia Capital (Hebei)
燕誉堂	(of Lion Forest Garden) Hall of Pleasant Entertainment
燕子洞	Swallow Cave (Yunnan)
央视春节联欢晚会	CCTV Spring Festival Gala
秧歌	〈舞〉Yangko; Yangko dance (in Northern China)
扬州八怪	〈古〉Yangzhou Eight Eccentric Painters (in the Qing Dynasty)
扬州古城	Yangzhou Ancient City (Jiangsu)
扬子鳄	〈动〉*Alligator sinensis*; Chinese alligator; Yangtze alligator
扬子江	Yangtze River
羊年	Year of the Goat/Ram; Year of the Sheep (one of 12 zodiac signs)
羊肉火锅	Mutton Slices in a Hot Pot; Thin Slices of Mutton Boiling in a Hot Pot →涮羊肉
羊踯躅	〈植〉*Rhododendron molle*; Chinese azalea →黄杜鹃
羊卓雍措	Yamdrok Yumtso Lake (Tibet)
阳春古戏台	Yanchun Ancient Stage (Jiangxi)
阳历	solar calendar; Gregorian calendar
阳明山国家公园	Yangmingshan National Park (Taiwan)
阳元山	Yangyuan Mountain (Guangdong)
阳元石	(of Mount Danxia) Yangyuan Stone; Yangyuan Column; Masculine Stone
阳宗海	Yangzong Lake (Yunnan)
杨村小世界	Small World Entertaining Park of Yangcun (Tianjin)
杨堤景行	(of West Lake) Strolling along Scenic Yanggong Causeway
杨贵妃墓	Tomb of Yang Guifei; Tomb of Imperial Concubine Yang (Shaanxi)

杨家界景区	(of Zhangjiajie) Yangjiajie scenic area
杨家岭革命旧址	Yangjialing Revolutionary Site (Shaanxi)
杨靖宇烈士陵园	Yang Jingyu Cemetery; Cemetery Revolutionary Martyrs of Yang Jingyu (Jilin)
杨靖宇殉国地	Yang Jingyu's Martyrdom Site (Jilin)
杨连弟公园	Yang Liandi Park (Tianjin)
杨柳青古镇	Yang Liuqing Ancient Town (Tianjin)
杨柳青画社	Yang Liuqing Painting Workshop (Tianjin)
杨柳青庄园	Yang Liuqing Manor (Tianjin)
杨浦大桥	Yangpu Bridge (Shanghai)
杨式太极	〈武术〉Yang-Style Tai Chi
洋货市场	Exotic Cargo Market (Tianjin)
仰韶村文化遗址	Site of Yangshao Culture (He'nan) →仰韶文化
仰韶文化	〈古〉Yangshao Culture (5000-3000 B.C., an important Neolithic Pottery Culture in the middle reaches of the Yellow River)
仰掌	Upward palm
养雀笼	(of Yuanming Garden) Western Gate with Aviary
养生	health cultivation
养心殿	(of Imperial Palace) Hall of Mental Cultivation
养性斋	(of Imperial Palace) Studio of Spiritual Cultivation
腰鼓	〈乐〉waist drum
腰鼓舞	〈舞〉waist drum dance
腰子寨风景线	(of Zhangjiajie) Yaozi Zhai Scenic line
尧山景区	Yaoshan Mountain Scenic Spot (He'nan) →石人山景区
瑶池妆台	(of Xingtai Canyon group) Yaochi Dressing Table
瑶山肥螈	〈动〉*Pachytriton inexpectatus*; Yaoshan stout newt
瑶山苣苔	〈植〉*Dayaoshania cotinifolia*
瑶寨	Yao village; village of the Yao ethnic group (Guangdong)
瑶族	Yao ethnic group; Yao

咬春	〈习俗〉bite-the-spring (a custom of eating spring pancake, and raw radishes on Beginning of Spring in ancient Beijing and Tianjin)
咬秋	〈习俗〉bite-the-autumn (a custom of eating melons on Beginning of Autumn in ancient Beijing and Tianjin)
药池沸泉	(of Mugecuo Scenic Area) Medicine Pool with Boiling Spring; Medicine Pool with Curative Effect
药方洞	(of Longmen Grottoes) Medical Formulas Cave; Medical Prescription Cave
药师殿	〈佛〉Pharmaceutical Master Hall (dedicated to the Pharmacist Buddha of Oriental pure glazed world)
药师佛	Pharmacist Buddha
药师佛塔	Pharmacist Buddhist Tower (Jiangsu)
药师节	〈壮族〉Medicine Master Festival (on the 5th day of the 5th lunar month) →药王节
药师如来圣诞法会	〈佛〉Medicine Buddha Dharma Assembly
药王故里	Yaowang's Hometown; Hometown of King Medicine (Shaanxi)
药王节	〈壮族〉Medicine King Festival (on the 5th day of the 5th lunar month) →药师节
药王庙	King Medicine temple
药王山	King Medicine mountain
药香节	〈满族〉Medicine Fragrance Day (on the 5th day of the 5th lunar month)
药用植物	medicinal plant
药用植物园	medicinal plant garden
鹞子翻身	〈武术〉(of Mount Huashan) Pigeon's Over-Turn (a narrow place where you should turn your body left and right to pass)
椰胡	〈乐〉yehu (two-stringed Chinese violin)
椰子王国	Kingdom of Coconuts (Hai'nan)

野慈姑	〈植〉*Sagittaria trifolia*; threeleaf arrowhead
野芳园	Wild Fragrance Park (Anhui)
野浪谷景区	Yelang Valley Scenic Area (Hubei)
野马分鬃	〈武术〉(of Tai Chi) Parting the wild horse's mane
野猫水村	Yemao/Wild Cat Water Village (with Chinese ethnic minority characteristics) (Hubei)
野牦牛	〈动〉*Bos mutus*; wild yak
野牛沟	Wild Yak Valley (Sichuan)
野人海	Wild Man Lake (Sichuan) →木格措
野三坡景区	Ye San Po (Wild Three Hillsides) Nature Scenic Area (Hebei)
野三坡森林公园	Yespo Forest Park (Hebei)
野生大熊猫	wild giant panda
野生东北虎	wild Siberian tiger; wild Amur tiger
野生荷花世界旅游区	Wild Lotus World Tourist Area (Hu'nan)
野生金丝猴	wild golden monkey
野象谷	Wild Elephant Valley (Yunnan)
叶定仕故居	Former Residence of Ye Dingshi (Tianjin)
叶尔羌河	Yarkent/Yarkand River (Xinjiang)
叶赫那拉古城	Yehenala Ancient City (Jilin)
叶氏隆肛蛙	〈动〉*Paa feirana yei*; Ye's spiny-vented frog
邺城	Yecheng City (one of the five great capitals in ancient times)
夜宵	late night snack; midnight snack; bedtime snack
夜莺	〈动〉*Luscinia megarhynchos*; nightingale
腋序苎麻	〈植〉*Boehmeria glomerulifera*
一拜天地,二拜高堂	〈婚〉(of wedding) the first bow to the heaven and the earth, the second bow to mutual parents
一步难行	(of Zhangjiajie) One Dangerous Step
一方有难八方支援	〈成〉when one place is in difficulty, help comes from all sides
一片云	(of Chengde Mountain Resort) Tower of a Patch of Cloud
一梳梳到尾	(of wedding) the first combing, together for all your lives

一天门	(of Mount Wudang) The First Gate of Heavenly Palace
一线天	(of Mount Wuyi) Yixian Tian; Narrow Path between Rocks; a Tread of Heavenly Light
一线天栈道	(of Mount Emei) Walkway of One Thread of Sky
伊春水上公园	Yichun Water Park (Heilongjiang)
伊河	Yihe River
伊勒呼里山	Yilehuli Mountain (Heilongjiang)
伊犁草原	Ili Grassland (Xinjiang)
伊犁河	Ili River (Xinjiang)
伊犁河谷	Ili Valley (Xinjiang)
伊犁鼠兔	〈动〉*Ochotona iliensis*; Ili pika
伊岭岩景区	Yilingyan Scenic Area (Guangxi)
伊通火山群	Yitong Volcano Group (Jilin)
伊通满族民俗博物馆	Manchu Folk Custom Museum of Yitong (Jilin)
衣冠葬	to bury only the dead's hats and clothes
医圣祠	Temple of Medical Sage (He'nan)
医学史博物馆	Museum of Medical History (Shanghai)
依饭节	〈仫佬族〉Yifan Festival (after Beginning of Winter every three to five years)
依连哈比尔尕山	Eren Habirga Mountains (Xinjiang)
揖峰轩	(of Lingering Garden) Pavilion Facing Unique Mountain Peak
揖让	→作揖礼
沂蒙山区	Yimeng Mountain Area (Shandong)
怡和午炮	Jardine Noonday Gun (Hong Kong)
怡湖山庄	Yihu Mountain Resort (Hubei)
怡园	Yiyuan Garden; Garden of Harmony (Jiangsu)
宜昌橙	〈植〉*Citrus ichangensis*; Ichang papeda
宜昌大撤退纪念园	Yichang Great Retreat Memorial Park (Hubei)
宜昌清江画廊	Qingjiang River Gallery at Yichang (Hubei)
宜两亭	(of Humble Administrator's Garden) Pavilion for Two-Family Setting
贻贝	〈动〉*Mytilus edulis*; mussel

遗鸥自然保护区	Relict Gull Nature Reserve (Inner Mongolia)
颐和轩	(of Imperial Palace) Bower of Rejuvenative Harmony
颐和园	Summer Palace (Beijing)
颐志堂	(of Chengde Mountain Resort) Hall of Self-Cultivation
彝族	Yi ethnic group; Yi
以茶代酒	(of table etiquette) substitution of tea for wine; to drink tea instead of wine (for those who gets drunk easily)
以茶代礼	〈习俗〉to give sb. tea as gifts
以右为尊	(of table etiquette) to take the right side as superiority
以远为上	〈礼〉(of table etiquette) the farther, the more honored; to take the farthest comer/guest as superiority
倚玉轩	(of Humble Administrator's Garden) Pavilion Leaning on Beautiful Bamboo and Stone
亿载金城	Eternal Golden Castle (Taiwan)
义气	code of the brotherhood; personal loyalty
义乌小鲵	〈动〉*Hynobius yiwuensis*; Yiwu salamander
艺圃	Garden of Cultivation (Jiangsu)
艺园	Garden of the Arts (Taiwan)
议事亭前地	Senado Square; (of Portuguese) Largo do Senado (Macao)
异龙湖	Yilong Lake (Yunnan)
异野芝麻	〈中药〉*Heterolamium Debile*
翊坤宫	(of Imperial Palace) Palace of Earthly Honor
翼蓼	〈植〉*Pteroxygonum giraldii*
因缘故事	〈佛〉nidana stories
阴曹地府	〈道〉palace of hell; land of darkness
阴历	Chinese calendar; lunar calendar
阴山荠	〈植〉*Yinshania albiflora*
阴山山脉	Yinshan Mountains (Inner Mongolia)

阴元石	(of Mount Danxia) Yinyuan Stone; Feminine Stone
荫翠峡	Green Shady Valley (Yunnan) →情人谷
音乐石屏	Melody Stone Screen (Guangxi)
殷墟遗址	Yinxu Ruin (the capital city in the late Shang Dynasty) (He'nan)
银婚	silver wedding (the 25th anniversary of marriage)
银肯响沙湾	Yinken Resonant Sand Bay (Inner Mongolia)
银矿湾泳滩	Silver Mine Bay Beach (Hong Kong)
银雀山汉墓竹简博物馆	Museum of Bamboo Slips at Yinque Mountain (Shandong)
银鹊树	〈植〉*Tapiscia sinensis*; silver magpie tree
银线湾泳滩	Silver Strand Beach (Hong Kong)
银子岩景区	Yinziyan Scenic Area; Silver Rock Scenic Spot (Guangxi)
银子岩溶洞	Yinziyan Karst Cave; Silver Rock Cave (Guangxi)
引静桥	Yinjing Bridge (Jiangsu) →三步桥
引路幡	〈丧〉road guider for the deceased
引滦入津工程纪念碑	Monument of Water Diversion Project from Luanhe River to Tianjin
饮食之礼	etiquette of eating
隐棒花	〈植〉*Cryptocoryne crispatula*
隐屏峰	(of Mount Wuyi) Hidden Screen Peak; Cloud-Covered Peak
隐仙岩	(of Mount Wudang) Hermit Immortal Rock
隐序南星	〈植〉*Arisaema wardii*
隐岳寺	Yinyue Temple (Zhejiang)
印台山公园	Yintai Mountain Park; Ink Pad Mountain Park (Hubei)
莺啭乔木	(of Chengde Mountain Resort) Warblers Twittering in Arbores
婴儿出窠	〈习俗〉to bring a baby to visit relatives (when he/she is one month old)

樱园	Sakura Garden; Cherry Blossom Garden (Hubei)
鹦哥岭树蛙	〈动〉*Rhacophorus yinggelingensis*
鹦鹉山	Parrot Mountain (Yunnan)
鹦鹉峡	Yingwu Gorge (Hubei)
鹰爪洞	(of Jiuzhai Valley) Eagle Claw Cave
鹰爪拳	〈武术〉Hawk's Claw Boxing
鹰嘴峰	eagle's beak peak
鹰嘴岩	Eagle Beak Rock (Fujian)
迎宾池	(of Huanglong Valley) Guest Welcoming Ponds
迎客松	(of Mount Huangshan) Guest-Greeting Pine
迎老爷	〈民俗〉(of Chaozhou and Shantou) to invite the local god; to worship the local god
迎亲书	〈婚〉wedding letter →三书
迎娶	〈婚〉to go to the bride's home to escort bride
迎三	→接三 [迎三]
萤火虫水洞	Firefly Water Cave (Guizhou)
营盘古墓	Ancient Tombs of Yingpan (Xinjiang)
营盘山	Yingpan Mountain (Yunnan)
楹联	yinglian; pillar couplets; couplets hung on the columns of a hall
瀛洲飞瀑	Yingzhou Waterfall (Zhejiang)
应县木塔	Wood Tower of Yingxian County (Shanxi)
映霞壁	Yingxia Cliff; Cliff Mirroring Rosy Clouds (Fujian)
雍布拉康	Yungbu Lakang Palace (Tibet)
雍和宫	Yonghe Lamasery (Beijing)
雍剑秋旧居	Former Residence of Yong Jianqiu (Tianjin)
永瓣藤	〈植〉*Monimopetalum chinense*
永昌钟鼓楼	Yongchang Bell and Drum Tower (Gansu)
永春牛姆林生态旅游区	Niumu Forest Ecotourist Zone of Yongchun (Fujian)
永德雪山	Yongde Snow Mountain (Yunnan)
永定门	Yongding Gate (Beijing)
永定土楼	Yongding Tulou; Yongding Earth Building (Fujian)

永和宫	(of Imperial Palace) Yongle Temple; Palace of Eternal Harmony
永乐禅寺	Eternal Happiness Temple (Fujian)
永乐大钟	Yongle Bell
永利街	Wing Lee Street (Hong Kong)
永年广府古城	Guangfu Ancient City in Yongnian County (Hebei)
永寿宫	(of Imperial Palace) Palace of Eternal Life
永恬居	(of Chengde Mountain Resort) Residence with Everlasting Tranquility
永兴岛	Yongxing Island; Woody Island (Hai'nan)
咏春拳	〈武术〉Yongchun Quan; Yongchun Boxing
涌翠岩	(of Chengde Mountain Resort) Emerald-Water-Pouring Rocks
涌泉寺	Yongquan Temple; Temple of Surging Fountain (Fujian)
优婆离	〈佛〉Upali (one of the ten disciples of the Buddha, best-known for his disciplinary)
优秀旅游城市	excellent tourism city
幽灵蜘蛛	〈动〉*Pholcus opilionoides*
尤尔都斯盆地	Yulduz Basin; Yulduz Depression (Xinjiang)
油菜花海	cole flower sea
油茶	〈植〉*Camellia oleifera*; tea-oil camellia
油饭	〈烹饪〉Glutinous Oil Rice (a Taiwan cuisine)
油麦吊云杉	〈植〉*Picea brachytyla*; sargent spruce
油桐树	〈植〉*Vernicia fordii*; tung tree; Chinese varnish tree
油樟	〈植〉*Cinnamomum longipaniculatum*
疣刺齿蟾	〈动〉*Oreolalax rugosus*; warty toothed toad
疣刺齿突蟾	〈动〉*Scutiger spinosus*
疣棘溪蟾	〈动〉*Torrentophryne tuberospinius*
游方节	〈苗族〉Youfang Festival
友谊大桥	Friendship Bridge (Ponte de Amizade) (Macao)
友谊峰	Youyi Peak; Friendship Peak (Xinjiang)

酉并酒	〈黎族〉You Biang wine
右单鞭	〈武术〉(of Tai Chi) Right single whip
右蹬脚	〈武术〉(of Tai Chi) Kicking with right heel
右分脚	〈武术〉(of Tai Chi) Right parting kick
右揽雀尾	〈武术〉(of Tai Chi) Grasping the peacock's tail on right side
右下独立式	〈武术〉(of Tai Chi) Pushing down and stand on right
盂兰(盆)节	〈佛〉Yulan Festival; Obon Festival (on the 15th of the 7th lunar month)
鱼梁洲蓝调薰衣草庄园	Blue Lavender Manor on Yuliangzhou Island (Hubei)
鱼梁洲中央生态公园	Yuliang Zhou Central Ecopark (Hubei)
鱼米之乡	land of abundance; land abundant in fish and rice
鱼跃龙门	〈成〉a carp leaping over the dragon gate (a metaphor for success or promotion)
鱼沼飞梁	(of Jinci Temple) Bridge over the Fish Pond
鱼嘴分水堤	Fish Mouth-Shaped Diversion Dike (Sichuan)
竽	〈乐〉yu (an ancient 36-reed windpipe)
俞伯牙台	Yu Boya Pavilion (Hubei) →古琴台
俞氏宗祠	Ancestral Temple of the Yu family (Jiangxi)
渔村夕照	Fishing Village at Sunset (one of Eight Views of Xiaoxiang) (Hu'nan)
渔村烟雨	Fog and Water in Fishing Village (Zhejiang)
渔家乐	fishing resort; fishery & resort
渔民文化村	Fisherfolk's Village (Hong Kong)
渔人码头	Fisherman's Wharf (Guangdong)
渔潭会	〈白族〉Yutan Fair (from the 15th day to the 21st day of the 8th lunar month)
渝中半岛	Yuzhong Peninsular (Chongqing)
榆林窟	Yulin Grottoes (Gansu)
虞山城墙秋游园灯会	Mid-Autumn Lantern Fair at Yushan City Wall (Jiangsu)
虞山景区	Yushan Scenic Area (Jiangsu)

虞山森林公园	Yushan Forest Park (Jiangsu)
与人共食,慎莫先尝	〈礼〉don't take a bite before the host asks you to eat
与人同饮,莫先起觞	〈礼〉don't pick up your cup before the host asks you to drink
与谁同坐轩	(of Humble Administrator's Garden) Pavilion of Sitting with Whom
雨儿胡同	Yu'er Hutong (Beijing)
雨花台	Rain Flower Terrace; Terrace of the Raining Flowers (Nanjing)
雨花台景区	Yuhuatai Scenic Area; Rain Flower Terrace (Jiangsu)
雨水	〈节气〉Rain Water (the 2nd solar term)
禹山贵族墓地	Aristocrat Graveyard at Yushan Mountain (Jilin)
禹王碑	King Yu's Stele (Hu'nan)
禹王宫[庙]	〈道〉Temple of King Yu (Anhui)
禹王山	Yuwang Mountain (He'nan)
玉翠亭	(of Imperial Palace) Green Jade Pavilion
玉带桥	Jade-Belt Bridge (Beijing)
玉笛	〈乐〉jade flute
玉峰寺	Yufeng Temple (Yunnan)
玉佛禅寺	Jade Buddha Temple (Shanghai)
玉佛殿	(of Wanfo Garden) Jade Buddha Hall
玉佛阁	jade Buddha palace
玉佛楼	jade Buddha chamber
玉佛苑	Jade Buddha Garden (Liaoning)
玉华宫	Yuhua Palace (Shaanxi)
玉皇大帝	(of Chinese legend) Jade Emperor; Emperor/God of the Heaven (supreme ruler of the pantheon world)
玉皇殿	〈道〉Jade Emperor Pagoda; Jade Emperor Hall
玉皇顶	(of Mount Taishan) Jade Emperor Peak; Peak of the Heavenly Emperor
玉皇洞	(of Zhangjiajie) Jade Emperor's Grottoes
玉皇飞云	(of West Lake) Scud over Yuhuang; Clouds Scurrying over Yuhuang Hill; Flying Clouds over Jade Emperor Hill

玉皇阁	yuhuang pavilion; jade emperor pavilion
玉皇阁公园	Yuhuang Pavilion Park; Jade Emperor Pavilion Park (Ningxia)
玉皇行宫	〈道〉Temporary Palace of Jade Emperor
玉京峰	(of Mount Sanqing) Yujing Peak
玉兰	〈植〉*Magnolia denudata*; Yulania denudate; yulan magnolia; yulan
玉澜堂	(of Summer Palace) Hall of Jade Billows
玉龙喀什河	Yurun-Kash; Yurungkash River (Qinghai) →白玉河
玉龙沙湖旅游度假区	Yulong Sand Lake Tourist Zone; Sand Lake Tourist Zone of Yulong (Inner Mongolia)
玉龙雪山	Yulong Snow Mountain; Jade Dragon Snow Mountain (Yunnan)
玉露	〈植〉*Haworthia cooperi*; jade dew
玉门关	Yumen Pass; Jade Gate Pass (Gansu)
玉女穿梭	〈武术〉(of Tai Chi) Fair lady working at the shuttle
玉女峰	(of Mount Wuyi and Huashan) Yunü Peak; Jade Maiden Peak
玉女潭景区	Yunü Pond Scenic Spot (Jiangsu)
玉屏峰	(of Mount Huangshan) Jade Screen Peak
玉琴轩	(of Chengde Mountain Resort) House of Jade Zither-Sounding Stream
玉泉山	(of Yuanming Garden) Yuquan Hill; Jade Spring
玉泉寺	Yuquan Temple; Jade Spring Temple (Hubei)
玉山寺石窟	Yushan Temple Grottos (Gansu)
玉笥山	Yusi Mountain (Hu'nan, Jiangxi)
玉笋河	Yusun River; Jade Stalagmite River (Yunnan)
玉笋岩	(of Huanglong Valley) Yusun Cliff; Bamboo Shoot Cliff
玉泰盐铺原址	Site of the Yutai Salt Shop (Zhejiang)
玉溪汇龙生态园	Yuxi Huilong Ecology Garden (Yunnan)
玉溪溶洞	Yuxi Karst Cave (Yunnan)
玉虚宫	(of Mount Wudang) Yuxu Palace
玉虚岩	(of Mount Wudang) Yuxu Peak

玉印岩	Yuyin Rock (Hubei)
玉渊潭公园	Yuyuan Tan Park; Yuyuan Pond Park (Beijing)
玉柱擎天	(of Yulong Snow Mountain) Jade Pillar Supporting the Sky
郁灵山	Yuling Mountain (Liaoning)
浴德堂	(of Imperial Palace) Hall of Bathing in Virtue (which means bathing the body and cleansing virtue, or improving oneself by meditation); Hall of Virtue Cultivation
浴佛节	Buddha Bathing Festival (on the 8th day of the 4th lunar month) →佛诞日
遇林亭	(of Mount Wuyi) Yulin Pavilion; Lins-Encountering Pavilion
遇林亭窑址	(of Mount Wuyi) Kiln Site at Yulin Pavilion (a pottery kiln of the Song Dynasty)
遇仙桥	Immortal-Meeting Bridge (Hu'nan)
遇仙寺	(of Mount Emei) Immortal Encountering Temple
遇真宫	(of Mount Wudang) Yuzhen Palace; Sage-Encounter Palace
御碑亭	(of Mount Lushan) Yubei Pavilion; Imperial Stele Pavilion
御笔峰	(of Zhangjiajie) Peak of Imperial Writing Brushes
御道	(of Imperial Palace) Imperial Avenue
御花园	(of Imperial Palace) Imperial Garden; Royal Garden
御景亭	(of Imperial Palace) Imperial View Pavilion
御书房	(of Imperial Palace) Imperial Study
御窑厂	imperial kiln plant
御竹林	(of Hongluo Temple) Imperial Bamboo Forest
裕固族	Yugur ethnic group; Yugur
裕陵	Yuling Mausoleum; Mausoleum of the Emperor Kien Lung (Hebei)
愈乔二公祠	Yu Kiu Ancestral Hall (declared monuments of Hong Kong)

毓园	Yuyuan Garden (for the memory of Dr. Lin Qiaozhi) (Fujian)
豫西百草园景区	Baicao Garden Scenic Area of Western-He'nan
豫园	Yuyuan Garden (Shanghai)
豫园寺	Yuyuan Temple (Shanghai)
豫章合省会馆	〈古〉Yuzhang Guild Hall (now, "Yuzhang" refers to Jiangxi) (Guizhou) →石阡万寿宫
鸳鸯	〈动〉*Aix galericulata*; yuanyang; mandarin duck
鸳鸯岛	Yuanyang Island; Mandarin Duck Island (Hu'nan)
鸳鸯湖	Yuanyang Lake; Mandarin Duck Lake (Zhejiang)
鸳鸯瀑布	(of Zhangjiajie) Yanyang Waterfalls; Mandarin Duck Waterfalls
鸳鸯泉	(of Zhangjiajie) Yanyang Springs; Mandarin Duck Springs
鸳鸯溪	Yuanyang Stream; Mandarin Duck Stream (Fujian)
元大都	〈古〉Capital of the Yuan Dynasty (present Beijing)
元大都城垣遗址公园	City Wall Relics Park of the Yuan Dynasty Capital (Beijing)
元代龙兴寺遗址	Site of Longxing Temple of the Yuan Dynasty (Inner Mongolia)
元和宫	(of Mount Wudang) Yuanhe Temple
元亨	〈易〉Yen-hun (supreme sacrificial ceremony)
元江	Yuanjiang River (Yunnan)
元朗公园	Yuen Long Park (Hong Kong)
元龙阁	Yuanlong Pavilion (Yunnan)
元谋土林	Yuanmou Soil Forest (Yunnan)
元清阁	Yuen Ching Kwok (Hong Kong)
元上都	Xanadu of the Yuan Dynasty; Shangdu of the Yuan Dynasty; Upper Capital of the Yuan Dynasty (Inner Mongolia)
元上都遗址	Site of the Yuan Dynasty Upper Capital); Site of Xanadu of the Yuan Dynasty (Inner Mongolia)
元宵	yuanxiao; sweet dumplings (made of glutinous rice flour)

元宵节	Lantern Festival (on the 15th day of the 1st lunar month) →上元节
元宵节庆典	Lantern Festival celebration; a ceremony to celebrate Lantern Festival
芫菁	〈动〉*Lytta caragana Pallas*; cantharid; blister beetle
芫茜	〈植〉*Coriandrum sativum*
园恩寺胡同	Yuan'en Temple Hutong (Beijing)
园圃街雀鸟花园	Bird Garden of Yuen Po Street (Hong Kong)
原天麻	〈植〉*Gastrodia angusta*
原髭蟾	〈动〉*Vibrissaphora promustache*
圆明宫	(of Mount Qingcheng) Yuanming Palace
圆明新园	New Yuanming Yuan Garden (Guangdong)
圆明园	YuanmingYuan; Yuanming Garden; Old Summer Palace (Beijing) →圆明园皇家花园
圆明园皇家花园	Yuanming Yuan Imperial Garden (Beijing) →圆明园
圆明园遗址	Ruins of the Yuanming Yuan Imperial Garden; Ruins of the Old Summer Palace (Beijing)
圆明园遗址公园	Ruins of Yuanming Imperial Garden (Beijing)
圆通殿	〈佛〉Hall of Universal Understanding; Harmony and Understanding Hall
圆玄学园	Yuan Xian Academy (Hong Kong)
圆叶舌蕨	〈植〉*Elaphoglossum sinii*
圆疣蟾蜍	〈动〉*Bufo tuberculatus*; round-warted toad
圆疣齿突蟾	〈动〉*Scutiger tuberculatus*; round-tubercled cat-eyed toad
圆缘民俗园	Yuanyuan Folk Culture Park (Zhejiang)
圆洲角公园	Yuen Chau Kok Park (Hong Kong)
圆籽荷	〈植〉*Apterosperma oblata*
鼋头渚公园	Turtle Head Islet Park (Jiangsu)
源影寺塔	Yuanying Temple Pagoda (Hebei)
远东刺猬	→东北[远东]刺猬
远近泉声	(of Chengde Mountain Resort) Murmuring of the Far-and-Near Stream Flows

远香堂	(of Humble Administrator's Garden) Yuanxiang Hall; Drifting Fragrance Hall
院曲风荷	(of West Lake) Lotus in the Breeze at Crooked Courtyard
月饼	moon cake; mooncake
月到风来亭	(of Master-of-Nets Garden) Pavilion of Moon with Breeze
月光菩萨	Moonlight Bodhisattva
月湖雕塑公园	Moon Lake Sculpture Park (Shanghai)
月湖桥	Yuehu Bridge (Hubei)
月季	〈植〉*Rosa chinensis*; Chinese rose
月亮广场	Moon Square (Zhejiang)
月亮节	〈拉祜族〉Moon Festival (on the 15th day of the 8th lunar month)
月琴	〈乐〉yueqin; yukin (a four-stringed plucked instrument with a full-moon-shaped sound box)
月台子景区	(of Guanmen Mountain) Yuetaizi Scenic Area
月坨岛	Yuetuo Island (Hebei)
月牙泉	Crescent Moon Lake (Gansu)
月牙湾公园	Crescent Bay Park (Shandong)
月沼	Moon Pond (Anhui)
岳飞庙	Yue Fei Temple (He'nan)
岳桦林景观带	Birch Forest Landscape (Jilin)
岳麓山	Mount Yuelu; Yuelu Mountain (Hu'nan)
岳墓栖霞	Yue Fei's Tomb in Dwelling Sunglow (one of Ten Views of the West Lake)
岳王庙	Yuewang Temple; Memorial Temple to Yue Fei (Zhejiang)
岳王墓庙	(of West Lake) Yuewang Tomb Temple
岳阳楼	Yueyang Tower (Hu'nan)
阅微草堂	Yuewei Humble Cottage (Beijing) →纪晓岚故居
越城岭	Yuecheng Mountain Ridge (Guangxi, Hu'nan)
越剧	〈戏〉Yue Opera →绍兴戏
越文化发祥地	birthplace of Yue Culture

越秀公园	Yuexiu Park (Guangdong)
粤菜	Guangdong cuisine; Cantonese cuisine
粤剧	Yueju Opera; Cantonese Opera; Guangdong Opera
粤剧演员	Cantonese Opera performer
粤式点心	Cantonese dim sum
粤紫萁	〈植〉*Osmunda mildei*
云帆月舫	(of Chengde Mountain Resort) Sailing Boat in Clouds and to the Moon
云峰湖景区	Yunfeng Lake Scenic Area (Jilin)
云峰山景区	Yunfeng Mountain Scenic Area (Beijing)
云峰峡谷	Yunfeng Canyon (Anhui)
云冈石窟	Yungang Grottoes (Shanxi)
云冈西部万佛洞	Cave of Ten Thousand Buddhas of Western Yungang (Shanxi)
云谷寺	(of Mount Huangshan) Cloud Valley Temple
云光洞	Yunguang Cave (Shandong)
云贵高原	Yunnan-Guizhou Plateau
云海佛光	Buddha halo shining over cloud-sea
云华山	Yunhua Mountain (Yunnan)
云窟月洞门	(of Master-of-Nets Garden) Moon Gate in Cloud Hollow
云岭山(脉)	Yunling Mountain (Range) (Yunnan)
云龙河地缝	Yunlong River Ground Fissure (Hubei)
云龙湖	Yunlong Lake (Jiangsu)
云麓宫	Yunlu Palace (Hu'nan)
云蒙山	Yunmeng Mountain (Beijing)
云蒙山森林公园	Yunmeng Mountain Forest Park (Beijing)
云梦山	Yunmeng Mountain (Hebei, He'nan)
云梦县桂花潭	Guihua Pond of Yunmeng County (Hubei)
云南闭壳龟	〈动〉*Cuora yunnanensis*; Yunnan box turtle
云南蓝果树	〈植〉*Nyssa yunnanensis*; Yunnan tupelo
云南链荚豆	〈植〉*Alysicarpus yunnanensis*; Yunnan alyce clover

云南陆军讲武堂	〈旧〉Yunnan Land Force Lecture Academy
云南民族村	Yunnan Ethnic Villages
云南拟单性木兰	〈植〉*Parakmeria yunnanensis*
云南三江并流保护区	Three Parallel Rivers of Yunnan Protected Areas; Protection Zone of Three Parallel Rivers in Yunnan
云南十八怪	Eighteen Wonders in Yunnan
云南石林	Yunnan Stone Forest
云瀑	cloud waterfall
云栖竹径	(of West Lake) Cloud Dwelling and Bamboo Path; Bamboo-Lined Path at Yunqi
云墙	(of Garden of Harmony) Cloud Wall
云泉寺	Yunquan Temple; Temple of Clouds and Spring (Hebei)
云泉仙馆	Yunquan Immortal Temple (Guangdong)
云雀	〈动〉*Alauda arvensis*; skylark
云容水态	(of Chengde Mountain Resort) Cloud Forms and Water looks
云山胜地	(of Chengde Mountain Resort) Pavilion with a View of Mountains in Clouds
云杉坪	Yunshan Plateau; Spruce Plateau (Yunnan)
云手	(of Tai Chi) Cloud hands; Waving hands like clouds
云水谣古镇	Yunshui Yao Ancient Town (Fujian)
云台峰	(of Mount Huashan) Yuntai Peak; Cloud Terrace Peak →北峰
云台石阁	→居庸关云台
云天石廊	Stone Corridor in Cloud Sky (Fujian)
云窝	(of Mount Wuyi) Cumulus Cloud Caves
云雾瘰螈	〈动〉*Paramesotriton yunwuensis*; Yunwu warty newts
云崖撒珠	(of Xingtai Canyon group) Cloud Cliff Scattering Pearls
云崖寺	Yunya Temple (Gansu)

云烟之乡	Hometown of Yunnan Tobacco (referring to Yuxi, Yunnan)
云月湖	Cloud and Moon Lake (Hai'nan)
郧西县王家坪烈士陵园	Wangjia Ping Martyrs Cemetery of Yunxi County (Hubei)
郧阳湖湿地公园	Yunyang Lake Wetland Park (Hubei)
浕水湿地公园	Yunshui Wetland Park (Hubei)
运木古井	Ancient Wood-Transport Well (Zhejiang)

Z

咂酒	〈羌族、苗族〉zajiu; zajiu wine (especially drunk on the 1st day of the 10th lunar month)
杂技民俗风情园	(of Wuqiao Acrobatics World) Acrobatic Folk Customs Garden
杂技奇观宫	Palace of Acrobatic spectacles
杂联	miscellaneous couplets (including humorous couplets)
栽秧会	〈白族〉Rice-Transplanting Festival
载酒堂	(of Couple's Retreat Garden) Carrying Wine Hall; Wine Carrying Hall
宰牲亭	(of Temple of Heaven) Butcher Pavilion
再拜	〈礼〉to bow twice (courteous expression in writing letters)
赞字碑	(of Huanglong Valley) Praise-Inscription Stele
藏獒	〈动〉Tibetan mastiff
藏北草原	Northern Tibetan Grassland
藏仓鼠	〈动〉*Cricetulus kamensis*; Tibetan hamster
藏传佛教	Tibetan Buddhism; Vajrayana Buddhist →喇嘛教
藏传佛教寺院	Tibetan Buddhism temple
藏刀	Tibetan knife
藏狐	〈动〉*Vulpes ferrilata*; Tibetan fox
藏历新年	Tibetan New Year (from the 1st to the 15th day of January in Tibetan calendar)
藏羚羊	〈动〉*Pantholops hodgsonii*; chiru (in Tibet); Tibetan antelope
藏马鸡	〈动〉*Crossoptilon harmani*; Tibetan eared-pheasant

藏缅语族	Tibeto-Burman languages
藏羌碉楼与村寨	barbican and (stockaded) villages for Tibetan and Qiang ethnic groups (a cultural landscape heritage in southwest China)
藏酋猴	〈动〉*Macaca thibetana*; Tibetan macaque
藏式门	Tibetan-styled door
藏饰	Tibet ornaments
藏鼠兔	〈动〉*Ochotona thibetana*; moupin pika
藏王墓	Tomb of Early Tibetan Kings; tombs of the Tibetan kings (Tibet)
藏雪鸡	〈动〉*Tetraogallus tibetanus*; Tibetan snowcock
藏原羚	〈动〉*Procapra picticaudata*; Tibetan gazelle; goa
藏族	Tibetan ethnic group; Tibetan
早生贵子	(of wedding) wish to have a lovely baby early (with 红枣 (Chinese date) being homophonic with early, 花生 (peanut) with giving birth, 桂圆 (longan) with lovely and 栗子 (chestnut) with baby)
枣树	〈植〉*Ziziphus jujuba*; Chinese jujube
枣阳汉城影视基地	Hancheng Film and Television Base in Zaoyang; Zaoyang Film and Television Base of Ancient Han City (Hubei)
枣园革命旧址	Zaoyuan Revolutionary Site (Shaanxi)
澡塘会	〈傈僳族〉Hot Spring Day (from the 1st day to the 3rd day of the 1st lunar month)
则查洼沟景区	(of Jiuzhai Valley) Zechawa Gully tour route
则查洼沟区段	(of Jiuzhai Valley) Zechawa Gully
择吉地	(of Fengshui) to select an auspicious graveyard
择吉日	(of Fengshui) to select an auspicious day
鲗鱼涌公园	Quarry Bay Park (Hong Kong)
曾大屋	Tsang Tai Uk (Hong Kong)
曾侯乙编钟	〈乐〉Zenghouyi bianzhong; Zenghouyi chime bells (a set of large-scale ritual and musical instruments in the early Warring States period)
扎尕那自然保护区	Gahai-Zecha Nature Reserve (Gansu)

扎陵湖	Zhaling Lake; Gyaring Lake (Qinghai)
扎龙自然保护区	Zhalong Nature Reserve (Heilongjiang)
扎染	tie-dyeing; bandhnu (a traditional and unique dyeing process of the Han nationality)
扎如沟风景线	(of Jiuzhai Valley) Zharu Gully tour route
扎如马道	(of Jiuzhai Valley) Zharu Horse Trail
扎如桥	(of Jiuzhai Valley) Zharu Bridge
扎如寺	(of Jiuzhai Valley) Zharu Temple
扎什伦布寺	Tashilhunpo Monastery (Tibet)
扎西多半岛纳木湖	Zhaxiduo Peninsula Namu Lake (Tibet)
扎叶巴寺展佛节	〈藏族〉Drak Yerpa Thangka Festival (on the 10th July of the Tibetan calendar)
扎依扎嘎神山	(of Jiuzhai Valley) Zhayizhaga Holy Mountain
斋宫	(of Summer Palace and Temple of Heaven) Hall of Abstinence; Palace for Abstinence
斋戒铜人石亭	Pavilion of Bronze Statue (Beijing)
摘星台	(of Zhangjiajie) Star Picking Stand
瞻园	Zhanyuan Garden (Jiangsu)
斩衰［缞］	〈丧〉zhancui; garb of unhemmed sackcloth (the most solemn of five types of dressing for grieving over the deceased) →五服
战国采菱城遗址	Site of Cailing City in the Warring States Period (Hu'nan)
湛山寺	Zhanshan Temple (Shandong)
张大千纪念馆	Memorial Hall of Zhang Daqian (Sichuan, Taiwan)
张果老	(of Chinese legend) Elder Zhang Guo; Zhang Guolao (one of the Eight Immortals)
张果老桥	Zhang Guolao Bridge (Liaoning)
张果老山	Zhang Guolao Mountain (Hebei)
张家墩古文化遗址	Site of Zhangjia Dun Ancient Culture (Hubei)
张家湖湿地公园	Zhangjia Lake Wetland Park (Hubei)
张家界	Zhangjiajie (Hu'nan)
张家界国家森林公园	Zhangjiajie National Forest Park (Hu'nan)

张家界景区	Zhangjiajie Scenic Area (Hu'nan)
张家界森林公园	Zhangjiajie Forest Park (Hu'nan)
张家咀湿地公园	Zhangjiazui Wetland Park (Hubei)
张良庙	Zhang Liang Temple (Shaanxi)
张氏肥螈	〈动〉*Pachytriton changi*; Zhang's paddle-tail newts
张氏异角蟾	〈动〉*Xenophrys zhangi*; Zhang's horned toad; Zhang's spadefoot toad
张学铭旧居	Former Residence of Zhang Xueming (Tianjin)
张勋故居	Former Residence of Zhang Xun (Tianjin)
张掖丹霞地貌	Zhangye Danxia Landform (Gansu)
张载祠	Zhangzai Memorial Temple; Memorial Temple of Zhangzai (Shaanxi)
獐	〈动〉*Hydropotes inermis*; Chinese water deer; river deer
漳河源自然保护区	Natural Protection Zone of Zhanghe River Source (Hubei)
漳州土楼	Zhangzhou Tulou; Zhangzhou Earth House (Fujian)
掌肉待客节	〈瑶族〉Festival of Guest-Entertaining (with Large Pieces of Meat) (on the 29th day of the 5th lunar month)
掌叶木	〈植〉*Handeliodendron bodinieri*
障山大峡谷	Zhangshan Grand Canyon (Anhui)
嶂石岩国家公园	Zhangshiyan National Forest Park (Hebei)
嶂石岩景区	Zhangshiyan Scenic Area (Hebei)
招兵节	〈畲族〉Soldier-Recruitment Festival (a religious festival of the She ethnic group to commemorate their ancestors)
招魂	〈表〉to call back the spirit of the deceased
昭德门	(of Imperial Palace) Gate of Manifest Virtue
昭怙厘大寺遗址	Grand Zhaohuli Temple Ruins (Xinjiang)
昭化寺	Zhaohua Temple (Hebei)
昭君岛	Zhaojun Island (Inner Mongolia)

昭君墓	Zhaojun Tomb (Inner Mongolia)
昭陵	Zhaoling Mausoleum (Beijing)
昭平雨蛙	〈动〉*Hyla zhaopingensis*; Zhaoping tree frog
昭苏草原	Zhaosu Grassland (Xinjiang)
昭西陵	Zhaoxi Mausoleum (Hebei)
召稼楼	Zhaojia Lou; Grain Calling Masion (Shanghai)
诏安土楼	Zhao'an Earth Building (Fujian)
赵家棚抗日烈士陵园	Zhaojia Peng Anti-Japanese Martyrs Cemetery (Hubei)
赵一曼纪念馆	Memorial Hall of Zhao Yiman (Sichuan)
赵州桥	Zhaozhou Bridge (Hebei)
肇庆七星岩公园	Seven-Star Crags Park of Zhaoqing (Guangdong)
肇兴侗寨	Zhaoxing Dong Village (Guizhou)
肇周圣祖牌坊	Zhaozhou Ancestor Paifang; Memorial Arch of Zhaozhou Ancestor (Gansu)
遮打花园	Chater Garden (Hong Kong)
遮虏障	→居延文化遗址
遮阳山	Zheyang Mountain; Sunshade Mountain (Gansu)
折子戏	〈戏〉Opera Highlights
哲蚌寺	Drepung Monastery (Tibet)
哲人峰	(of Tiantang Zhai) Philosopher Peak
赭山公园	Zheshan Mountain Park (Anhui)
赭塔晴岚	Reddish Brown Tower in Clear Haze (Anhui)
柘林瀑	Zhelin Waterfall (Zhejiang)
浙(江)菜	Zhejiang cuisine
浙东大峡谷	Grand Valley of Eastern Zhejiang
浙江金线兰	〈植〉*Anoectochilus zhejiangensis*
浙江昆曲剧团	Zhejiang Kunqu Opera Troupe
浙门峡	Zhemen Valley (Zhejiang)
浙西大峡谷	Grand Valley of Western Zhejiang
贞女祠	→孟姜女庙
贞女寺	Meng Jiangnü Temple (Hebei)
贞顺门	(of Imperial Palace) Gate of Loyalty and Obedience

针叶火绒草	〈植〉*Leontopodium leontopodioides*
珍宝岛	Zhenbao Island; Treasure Island (Heilongjiang)
珍宝王国	Jumbo Kingdom (Hong Kong)
珍妃井	(of Imperial Palace) Zhenfei Well; Well of Imperial Concubine Zhen
珍珠矮	〈植〉*Cymbidium nanulum*
珍珠婚	pearl wedding (the 30th anniversary of marriage)
珍珠乐园	Pearl Land Amusement Park (Guangdong)
珍珠瀑	Pearl Waterfall (Beijing)
珍珠滩	(of Jiuzhai Valley) Pearl Shoal
珍珠滩瀑布	(of Jiuzhai Valley) Pearl Shoal Waterfall
真觉寺	〈旧〉Zhenjue Temple (Beijing) →北京石刻艺术博物馆
真君庙	Chun Kwan Temple; Zhenjun Temple (Hong Kong)
真君石殿	Zhenjun Stone Temple (Hubei)
真庆道院	Zhenqing Taoist Temple (Jiangsu)
真趣亭	(of Lion Forest Garden) True Delight Pavilion
真武殿	(of Mount Huashan) Zhenwu Hall
真意门	(of Master-of-Nets Garden) True Feeling Gate
震旦鸦雀	〈动〉*Paradoxornis heudei*; reed parrotbill
镇北堡西部影视城	West Movie-TV Program Tourism Town in Zhenbei Bu (Ningxia)
镇北台	Zhenbei Tower; Zhenbei Fortress (Shaanxi)
镇国寺	Zhenguo Monastery (Shanxi)
镇海棘螈	〈动〉*Echinotriton chinhaiensis*; Chinhai spiny newt
镇海塔公园	Zhenhai Tower Park (Hong Kong)
镇江焦山	Zhenjiang Jiaoshan Mountain (Jiangsu)
镇山民族文化村	Zhenshan Ethnic Culture Village (Guizhou)
镇山之宝	top treasure of a mountain
镇远古城	Zhenyuan Ancient City (Guizhou)
正对	couplets parallel in meaning
正净	〈戏〉(of Beijing Opera) Zhengjing (usually a positive character with upright personality, whose performance is mainly based on singing) →铜锤

正觉寺	(of Yuanming Garden) Zhengjue (Enlightenment) Temple
正踢腿	〈武术〉Forward front kick
正阳草原	Zhengyang Grassland (Shaanxi)
正月	the first month of the lunar calendar; the first lunar month
郑成功纪念馆	Memorial Hall of Koxinga; Memorial Hall of Zheng Chenggong (Fujian)
郑成功祖庙	Koxinga Ancestral Shrine; Ancestral Temple of Zheng Chenggong (Taiwan)
郑家大屋	Mandarin's House; Family House of Zheng Guanying (Macao)
郑家大院	Courtyard of the Zheng Family (Tianjin, Sichuan)
郑州孔庙	Zhengzhou Confucius Temple (He'nan)
支祠	branch ancestral hall
芝径云堤	(of Chengde Mountain Resort) Tortuous Track and Clouded Causeway
知鱼矶	(of Chengde Mountain Resort) Rocky Ledge of Joy to Understand Fish
织金瘰螈	〈动〉*Paramesotriton zhijinensis*
执绋	〈丧〉to take part in a funeral procession; to attend a funeral
执剑礼	〈武术〉salute with sword
直瓣苣苔	〈植〉*Ancylostemon saxatilis*; straight chicory
直贡梯寺	Drigung Thel Kloser; Drigung Thel Monastery (Tibet)
直贡提寺跳神	〈藏族〉Cham in Drigung Thel Kloser; Lama Dancing in Drigung-til Monastery
直隶总督署	〈旧〉Zhili Govern-General's Office; Zhili Provincial Governor's Office (Hebei)
植树节	Tree-Planting Day; China's Arbor Day (on the 12th March)
指柏轩	(of Lion Forest Garden) Pavilion Facing Cypress
纸婚	paper wedding (the 1st anniversary of marriage)

枳	〈植〉*Poncirus trifoliata*; trifoliate orange
至圣林	→孔林
至圣庙坊	Archway of Ultimate Sage Temple (Shandong)
志莲净苑	Chi Lin Nunnery (Hong Kong)
治丧	to take care of the funeral rites; to make funeral arrangements; funeral service
智慧海	(of Summer Palace) Sea of Wisdom (a religious building in the Summer Palace)
智取华山路	Circumventing Road to Huashan Mountain
智者大师纪念塔	Master Zhizhe Memorial Pagoda; Memorial Pagoda of Master Zhizhe (Zhejiang)
雉鸡	→环颈雉
中部平原解放地区	〈旧〉Central Plain liberated area
中都游牧源	Zhongdu Nomadic Land (Hebei)
中俄边界	Sino-Russian boundary
中俄旅游年	Sino-Russia Tourism Year; China-Russia Tourism Year
中峰寺	(of Mount Emei) Central Peak Temple
中共一大会址	Site of the First National Congress of the Communist Party of China (Shanghai)
中共一大纪念馆	Memorial Hall of First National Congress of CPC (Shanghai)
中国白酒文化	Chinese baijiu culture
中国北部边境省	China's Northern frontier provinces
中国北方瓷都	Capital of Ceramics in Northern China (referring to Tangshan, Hebei)
中国边境城市	Chinese border cities
中国边境城镇	Chinese border towns
中国茶文化	Chinese tea culture
中国禅佛文化研究中心	China Zen-Buddhist Culture Research Centre
中国常熟服装城	China Changshu Garment City (Jiangsu)
中国除夕夜	Chinese New Year's Eve; Chinese Spring Festival's Eve (the last day of the 12th lunar month)
中国传统成人礼	Chinese traditional adulthood ceremony; traditional Chinese adulthood ceremony

中国传统工艺	traditional Chinese arts and crafts; traditional Chinese craftsmanship
中国传统画	traditional Chinese paintings
中国传统婚礼	traditional Chinese wedding
中国传统婚俗	traditional Chinese wedding custom
中国传统家庭观念	traditional Chinese family concept
中国传统乐器	traditional Chinese (musical) instruments
中国传统历法	traditional Chinese calendar
中国传统美食	traditional Chinese food
中国传统民间艺术	traditional Chinese folk art
中国传统烹饪	traditional Chinese cooking
中国传统武术	traditional Chinese martial arts; traditional Chinese Wushu
中国传统葬礼	traditional Chinese funeral
中国春节	China's Spring Festival; Chinese Spring Festival (on the 1st day of the 1st lunar month) →中国新年
中国春运	Chinese Spring Festival travel season; China's Spring Festival travel rush
中国瓷都	Porcelain Capital of China (referring to Jingdezhen in Jiangxi)
中国慈善日	Charity Day of China (January 25th)
中国大鲵	〈动〉*Andrias davidianus*; Chinese giant salamander
中国大运河	China's Grand Canal
中国丹霞地貌	Danxia landform of China; China's Danxia landform
中国灯笼	Chinese lantern
中国电影节	China's Film Festival; Chinese Film Festival
中国电影周	Chinese Film Week
中国钓鱼岛	China's Diaoyu Island (East China Sea)
中国东北边境	China's Northeast border
中国东海	East China Sea
中国东海岸	east coast of China; China's east coast
中国—菲律宾传统文化节	China/Sino-Philippines Traditional Cultural Festival

中国港口城市	Chinese port city
中国歌剧舞剧院	China National Opera & Dance Drama Theatre (Beijing)
中国革命博物馆	〈旧〉Museum of Chinese Revolution (Beijing) →中国革命历史博物馆
中国革命历史博物馆	〈旧〉China Revolutionary History Museum; Museum of Chinese Revolution and History (Beijing) →中国革命博物馆, 中国历史博物馆, 中国国家博物馆
中国工艺美术馆	China National Arts and Crafts Museum (Beijing)
中国共产党成立[诞生]纪念日	Anniversary of the Foundation of Chinese Communist Party (July 1st)
中国古典园林	classical Chinese gardens
中国古都	ancient Chinese capital; ancient capital of China
中国馆	(of World Expo) China Pavilion (Shanghai)
中国国际动漫节	China Inter Comics/Cartoon Festival; CICF
中国国际马戏节	China Inter Circus Festival
中国国际青年艺术周	China International Youth Art Week
中国国家博物馆	National Museum of China (Beijing)
中国国庆日	Chinese National Day (October 1st)
中国航海博物馆	China Maritime Museum (Shanghai)
中国红	China red; Chinese red
中国红石公园	China Red Stone Park (Guangdong)
中国画里的乡村	A Village in Chinese Painting (referring to Hongcun, Anhui)
中国皇家花园	Chinese imperial garden
中国黄山国际旅游节	China Huangshan Mountain International Tourism Festival
中国记者节	China's Journalists' Day (on the 8th November)
中国建军节	China Army Day (on the 1st August)
中国(常熟)江南文化节	China (Changshu) Jiangnan Culture Festival
中国江苏(常熟)服装服饰博览会	China Jiangsu (Changshu) Fashion Fair; China Jiangsu (Changshu) Clothing and Accessories Fair

中国教师节	China's Teachers' Day (on the 10th September)
中国节气	Chinese solar term
中国结	Chinese knot
中国结婚仪式	Chinese wedding ceremony
中国景区	scenic resort and historic site in China
中国酒	Chinese alcoholic drinks; Chinese liquor; Chinese wine
中国科学技术馆	China Science and Technology Museum (Beijing)
中国科学院紫金山天文台	Purple Mountain Observatory of Chinese Academy of Sciences (Jiangsu)
中国老字号品牌	Chinese time-honored brand
中国历史博物馆	〈旧〉China History Museum; Museum of Chinese History (Beijing) →中国革命历史博物馆
中国莲	〈植〉*Nelumbo nucifera*
中国瘰螈	〈动〉*Paramesotriton chinensis*; Chinese warty newt
中国洛阳牡丹文化节	Peony Culture Festival of Luoyang China (around April 5th to May 5th every year)
中国马术节	China equestrian festival
中国美食节	Chinese Food Festival; China Food Festival (from the 1st to 8th November)
中国美术馆	National Art Museum of China (Beijing)
中国民歌	Chinese folk song
中国民间故事	Chinese folk tale
中国民间文学	Chinese folk literature
中国民间舞蹈	Chinese folk dance
中国民间艺术节	China Folk Art Festival; Chinese Folk Art Festival
中国民间音乐	Chinese folk music
中国民俗文化	Chinese folk culture
中国民俗文化村	China Folk Cultural Village (Guangdong)
中国民族史	Chinese national history
中国民族文化	Chinese national culture
中国民族意识	Chinese national consciousness

中国民族主义	Chinese nationalism
中国木偶(艺术)剧院	China Puppet Theatre (Beijing)
中国男性健康日	Chinese Men's Health Day (October 28th)
中国南海	South China Sea
中国脑健康日	Chinese Brain Health Day (September 16th)
中国内地	Chinese mainland
中国农历	Chinese calendar; Chinese lunar calendar
中国农民丰收节	Chinese Farmers' Harvest Festival (in Autumn Equinox)
中国农业博物馆	China Agricultural Museum (Beijing)
中国票号博物馆	Chinese Draft Bank Museum (Shanxi)
中国普洱茶节	China Pu'er Tea Festival (in April or May)
中国青年节	Chinese Youth Day (May 4th) →五四青年节
中国人民革命军事博物馆	Military Museum of the Chinese People's Revolution (Beijing)
中国人民抗日战争纪念日	Anniversary of the Chinese People's War of Resistance against Japanese Aggression (September 3rd)
中国榕树之王	king of banian trees in China
中国山水画的摇篮	cradle of Chinese landscape painting
中国扇博物馆	China Fan Museum (Zhejiang)
中国(常熟)尚湖国际文化节	China (Changshu) Shanghu Lake International Culture Festival
中国尚湖牡丹花会	China Peony Fair at Shanghu Lake
中国少数民族	China's ethnic group; Chinese ethnic minority
中国死海	China's Dead Sea (Sichuan) →大英死海
中国五岳	Five Sacred Mountains of China (Mount Taishan, Mount Huashan, Southern Mount Hengshan, Northern Mount Hengshan and Mount Songshan)
中国西北边陲	border areas of northwest China
中国习俗	China's customs; Chinese customs
中国象棋	Chinese chess

中国小鲵	〈动〉*Hynobius chinensis*; Chinese salamander
中国新年	China's New Year; Chinese New Year →中国春节
中国岩溶百科全书	Encyclopedia of Karst in China (referring to Jiudongtian Cave, Guizhou)
中国银行大厦	Bank of China Tower (Hong Kong)
中国印	(of Beijing Olympics) Chinese Seal
中国雨蛙	〈动〉*Hyla chinensis*; Chinese tree toad
中国藏族地区	ethnic Tibetan area of China; China's ethnic Tibetan area
中国藏族聚居区	China's Tibetan-Inhabited areas
中国藏族文化艺术彩绘大观	Magnificent Spectacle of Color Paintings about Chinese Tibetan Culture and Arts
中国雉	〈动〉*Phasiaus colchicus*; Chinese pheasant
中国紫檀博物馆	China Red Sandalwood Museum (Beijing)
中和殿	(of Imperial Palace) Hall of Central Harmony
中和节	Zhonghe Festival (on the 2nd of the 2nd lunar month)
中华白海豚	〈动〉*Sousa chinensis*; Chinese white dolphin
中华传统文化	Chinese traditional culture
中华传统五礼	Traditional Chinese Five Rites and Rituals (Rite of Ji, Xiong, Jun, Bin and Jia)
中华大熊猫苑	China Giant Panda Garden (Sichuan)
中华鳄	〈动〉*Alligator sinensis*; Chinese alligator
中华肝吸虫	〈动〉*Clonorchis sinensis*; Chinese liver fluke
中华虎凤蝶	〈动〉*Luehdorfia chinensis*; Chinese luehdorfia butterfly
中华回乡文化园	Customs and Culture Park of the Chinese Hui Homeland (Ningxia)
中华卷瓣兰	〈植〉*Bulbophyllum chinense*
中华恐龙园	China Dinosaur Park/Land (Jiangsu) →东方侏罗纪
中华鬣羚	〈动〉*Capricornis milneedwardsii*; Chinese serow
中华门	(of Imperial Palace) Zhonghua Gate; China Gate
中华民族	Chinese nation; Chinese ethnic group
中华民族园	China Ethnic Culture Park (Beijing)

中华蚖蠊	〈动〉*Galloisiana sinensis*
中华曲苑	Zhonghua Quyuan; Chinese Cross-talk Assembly Hall (Tianjin)
中华人民共和国国庆节	National Day of the People's Republic of China (on the 1st October)
中华绒螯蟹	〈动〉*Eriocheir sinensis*; Chinese mitten crab
中华三祖堂	China Sanzutang; Three Ancestors' Hall of China (Hebei)
中华世纪坛	China Millennium Monument (Beijing)
中华曙猿馆	China Ape Hall (Jiangsu)
中华水韭	〈植〉*Isoetes sinensis*
中华台北	Chinese Taipei
中华坛花兰	〈植〉*Acanthephippium sinense*
中华蚊母(树)	〈植〉*Distylium chinense*; Chinese winter-hazel
中华鲟	〈动〉*Acipenser sinsensis*; Chinese sturgeon
中环广场	Central Plaza (Hong Kong)
中环海滨长廊	Central Waterfront Promenade (Hong Kong)
中环码头	Central Pier (Hong Kong)
中葵涌公园	Central Kwai Chung Park (Hong Kong)
中南海	Zhong Nan Hai (Beijing)
中秋节	Mid-autumn Festival; Moon Festival; Mooncake Festival (on the 15th day of the 8th lunar month)
中沙群岛	(of South China Sea) Chungsha Archipelago; Zhongsha Islands
中山公园	Zhongshan Park (Beijing)
中山公园革命烈士纪念碑	Revolutionary Martyrs Memorial Monument in Zhongshan Park (Ningxia)
中山公园音乐堂	Zhongshan Park Music Hall; Forbidden City Concert Hall (Beijing)
中山故居	Former Residence of Sun Yat-sen
中山国遗址	Site of the Zhongshan State (Hebei)
中山湖景区	Zhongshan Lake Scenic Area (Hebei)
中山纪念碑	Monument to Dr. Sun Yat-sen (Guangdong)
中山纪念堂	Sun Yat-sen Memorial Hall; Zhongshan Memorial Hall (Guangdong)

中山陵	Sun Yat-sen Mausoleum (Jiangsu)
中山书院	Sun Yat-sen Academy (Jiangsu)
中山堂	(of Zhongshan Park) Memorial Hall of Sun Yat-sen
中山植物园	Zhongshan Botanical Garden (Jiangsu)
中式风格	Chinese style
中天门	(of Mount Taishan) Midway Gate to Heaven
中晚籼稻	middle and late indica rice
中央大街	Central Street (Helongjiang)
中央电视塔	Central Television Tower (Beijing)
中央电视台建筑群	Central Television Complex (Beijing)
中央电视台无锡影视基地	CCTV Wuxi Movie and Television Base (Jiangsu)
中央山脉	Central Mountain Range (Taiwan)
中元节	Zhongyuan Festival (on the 15th day of the 7th lunar month) →七月半, 鬼节
中原	Central Plains (comprising the middle and lower reaches of the Huanghe River)
中原军区旧址	Site of the Military Region on Central Plains (Hubei)
中原绿色庄园	Zhongyuan Green Park (He'nan)
中原文化	China Central Plains culture
中岳庙	(of Shaolin Temple) Zhongyue Temple
中岳庙景区	Zhongyue Temple Scenic Area (He'nan)
中岳嵩山	Mount Songshan; Songshan Mountain (as the Central One of the Five Sacred Mountains in China) (He'nan)
中正殿	(of Imperial Palace) Hall of Rectitude
中座为尊	〈礼〉(of table etiquette) to take the middle seats as superiority
忠堡大捷纪念公园	Zhongbao Dajie Memorial Park; Memorial Park of Great Victory at Zhongbao (Hubei)
忠孝节	〈伊斯兰〉→古尔邦节
忠孝仁义	honest, piety, faithfulness and righteousness
终南山	Zhongnan Mountain (Shaanxi) →太乙山

钟表馆	Museum of Clocks (Beijing)
钟翠宫	(of Imperial Palace) Palace of Accumulated Purity
钟鼎文	→金文
钟鼓楼	bell and drum tower
钟楼	Bell Tower; Clock Tower (Shaanxi, Hebei)
钟乳石洞	stalactites cave
钟乳悬匾	(of Swallow Cave) Hanging Plaques on Stalactites
钟山景区	Zhongshan Mountain Scenic Area; Bell Mountain Scenic Area (Jiangsu)
钟亭	bell pavilion
众坊街	Public Square Street (Hong Kong)
众神诞节	〈壮族〉Birthday of All Lords (on the 2nd day of the 8th lunar month)
重殓厚葬	to attach a great importance to funerals
重要药用植物	important medicinal plant
舟	〈古〉zhou (boat)
舟山群岛	Zhoushan Islands; Zhoushan Archipelago (Zhejiang)
州桥老街	Zhouqiao Old Street (Shanghai)
周恩来邓颖超纪念馆	Memorial Hall of Zhou Enlai and Deng Yingchao (Tianjin)
周恩来故居	Former Residence of Zhou Enlai (Shanghai)
周公馆	Residence of Zhou Enlai (Shanghai)
周公庙	Zhougong Temple (Shaanxi)
周口店北京人遗址	Peking Man Site at Zhoukoudian (Beijing)
周口店北京人遗址博物馆	Zhoukoudian Peking Man Relics Museum (Beijing)
周口店龙骨山	Dragon Bone Hill of Zhoukoudian (Beijing)
周口店遗址博物馆	Zhoukoudian Site Museum (Beijing)
周明泰旧宅	Old House of Zhou Mingtai (Tianjin)
周原遗址	Zhouyuan Site (large ancient ruins from the 11th century to the 8th century B.C.) (Shaanxi)
周庄古镇	Zhouzhuang Ancient Town (Jiangsu)

周祖碑亭	Zhouzu Stele Pavilion (Gansu)
周祖陵森林公园	Zhouzu Ling National Forest Park (Gansu)
周祖陵亭	Zhouzu Mausoleum Pavilion (Gansu)
肘底捶	〈武术〉(of Tai Chi) Fist under elbow
朱碑亭	Tablet Pavilion of Zhu De; Zhu De's Tablet Pavilion (Hubei)
朱德旧居	Former Residence of Zhu De
朱鹮	〈动〉*Nipponia nippon*; Crested ibis; Asian Crested Ibis
朱家花园	Private Garden of the Zhu Family (Yunnan)
朱家尖岛	Zhujiajian Island (Zhejiang)
朱家角放生桥	Zhujiajiao Life-Free Bridge (Shanghai)
朱家角课植园	Zhujiajiao After-Class Plantation (Shanghai)
朱家角镇	Zhujiajiao Town (Shanghai)
朱槿	〈植〉*Hibiscus rosa-sinensis*; China rose; Chinese hibiscus →扶桑
朱开沟文化	〈古〉Zhukaigou Culture (2200–1500 B.C., in Ordos Region) →朱开沟遗址
朱开沟遗址	Ancient Ruins of Zhukaigou (archaeological Culture in the Xia and Shang Dynasties) (Inner Mongolia) →朱开沟文化
朱启钤旧居	Former Residence of Zhu Qiqian (Tianjin)
朱雀森林公园	Zhuque Forest Park (Shaanxi)
朱雀山森林公园	Zhuque Mountain Forest Park (Jilin)
朱熹故居	Former Residence of Zhu Xi (Fujian)
珠峰大本营	→珠穆朗玛峰大本营
珠海渔女	Statue of Zhuhai Fisher Girl (Guangdong)
珠江	Zhujiang River; Pearl River
珠江口	Pearl River Estuary; Mouth of the Zhujiang River (Guangdong)
珠江口盆地	Pearl River Mouth Basin
珠江流域	Zhujiang River Basin; Pearl River Basin
珠江三角洲	Zhujiang River Delta; Pearl River Delta
珠江源	Source of Zhujiang River; Head waters of the Pearl River (Yunnan)

珠帘瀑布	pearl-curtain waterfall
珠穆朗玛峰	Mount Qomolangma (Tibet)
珠穆朗玛峰大本营	Qomolangma Base Camp (Tibet)
珠日河草原旅游区	Zhurihe Grassland Tour Zone (Inner Mongolia)
珠三角	→珠江三角洲
珠三角城市	Pearl River Delta city
珠三角经济区	Pearl River Delta Economic Zone
珠算	reckoning by the abacus; calculation with an abacus
诸葛菜	〈植〉*Orychophragmus violaceus*; Chinese violet cress
诸葛—长乐村民居	Local-Style Dwelling Houses of Zhuge and Changle Villages (Zhejiang)
诸葛亮故里纪念馆	Memorial Hall of Zhuge Liang's Home Village (Shandong)
诸葛铜鼓	Zhuge Bronze Drum
诸罗树蛙	〈动〉*Rhacophorus arvalis*; *Zhangixalus arvalis*; farmland green treefrog
猪笼草	〈植〉*Nepenthes*; pitcher plant
猪年	Year of the Pig (one of 12 zodiac signs)
猪尾鼠	〈动〉*Typhlomys cinereus*; Chinese pygmy dormouse
猪血木	〈植〉*Euryodendron excelsum*
竹板快书	→山东[竹板]快书
竹蛏	〈动〉*Solen strictus*; razor clam
竹笛	〈乐〉bamboo flute
竹峰栈道	Zhufeng Plank Road (Zhejiang)
竹管	〈乐〉bamboo pipe
竹(筒)酒	〈独龙族〉bamboo wine (a medicinal diet with liquor, gardenia, amomum and honey as the main ingredients, which are put in the bamboo when it is still bamboo shoot seedling)
竹林寺	Zhulin Temple; Bamboo Forest Monastery (Jiangsu)

竹山石佛寺	Zhushan Stone Buddha Temple (Hubei)
竹荪［笙］	〈植〉*Dictyophora indusiata*; bamboo fungus
竹筒	bamboo tube
竹湾海滩	Cheoc Van Beach (Macao)
竹文化博物馆	Bamboo Culture Museum (Jiangsu)
竹子	〈植〉*Bambusoideae*; bamboo
竹子湖景区	Bamboo Lake Scenic Spot (Taiwan)
主题馆	(of World Expo) theme pavilion
抓髻娃娃	zhuaji wawa (kid); zhuaji moppet (a folk paper cutting art)
抓周	〈习俗〉Zhuazhou; One-Year-Old Catch
砖窑洞	Cave Dwelling Made of Bricks
转身摆莲	〈武术〉(of Tai Chi) Spinning lotus kick; Turning the body with lotus kick
转身搬拦捶	〈武术〉(of Tai Chi) Turning body, moving, parrying and punching
转身大捋	〈武术〉(of Tai Chi) Turning the body and deflecting opponent's arm
转身拍脚	〈武术〉(of Tai Chi) Turning the body and smacking foot
转身推掌	〈武术〉Turning the body and pushing palm
转身左蹬脚	〈武术〉(of Tai Chi) Turning the body and kicking with left heel
转轮藏	1 (of Summer Palace) Prayer Wheel Repository 2 〈佛〉Revolving Archives; Revolving Buddhist Scripture Repository
转轮藏阁	〈佛〉Revolving Archives' Pavilion; Pavilion of Revolving Buddhist Scripture Repository
转山会	〈藏族〉Festival of Worship to Mountain (on the 8th day of the 4th lunar month)
转山节	→朝［转］山节
转转酒	〈彝族〉Zhuanzhuan wine (a glass of wine, which is passed from hand to hand, and drunk by everyone); wine-drinking in a circle turn

转花池	(of Huánglong Valley) Revolving Flower Pond
装饰联	decorative couplets
壮乡铁角蕨	〈植〉*Asplenium cornutissimum*
壮行酒	farewell wine
壮族	Zhuang ethnic group; Zhuang
壮族春节	Zhuang Festival (on the 30th of the 11th lunar month) →壮族新年
壮族新年	Zhuang New Year (on the 30th day of the 11th lunar month)
状元阁	Zhuangyuan Pavilion (Jiangsu)
追悼会	memorial ceremony; funeral ceremony
锥子山森林公园	Zhuizi Mountain Forest Park (Anhui)
准噶尔盆地	Junggar Basin (Xinjiang)
拙政园	Humble Administrator's Garden (Jiangsu)
捉蚂蚱节	〈哈尼族〉Grasshopper-Catching Day (in the 6th lunar month)
捉迷藏	hide-and-seek game →躲猫猫
桌子山岩画	Rock /Cliff Paintings on Zhuozi Mountain (Inner Mongolia)
卓刀泉	Zhuodao Spring (Hubei)
卓克基土司官寨	Chieftain Official Stronghold of Zhuokeji (Sichuan)
卓玛	〈藏族〉Drolma (a goodness)
濯水古镇	Zhuoshui Ancient Town (Chongqing)
齐衰[缞]	〈丧〉gown of gunnysack (one of five funeral garments) →五服
资江漂流	Zijiang River drift (Guangxi)
资丘七十七烈士纪念碑	Monument to the Seventy-seven Martyrs of Ziqiu (Hubei)
资中文庙	Zizhong Confucius Temple; Confucious Temple of Zizhong County (Sichuan)
子贡庐墓处	Zigong's Shelter for Keeping Watch on the Tomb (Shandong)
梓叶槭	〈植〉*Acer catalpifolium*

紫背鹿蹄草	〈植〉*Pyrola atropurpurea*
紫海鹭缘浪漫庄园	Purple Sea Heron Romantic Manor (Shanghai)
紫花地丁	〈植〉*Viola philippica*; Chinese Violet; Viola Yedoensis
紫金山	Zijin Mountain; Purple-Gold Mountain (Jiangsu)
紫金山天文台	Zijin Mountain Observatory; Purple Mountain Astronomical Observatory (Jiangsu)
紫禁城	〈旧〉Forbidden City (Beijing) →故宫
紫荆关	Zijingguan; Zijing Pass (Hebei)
紫菊	〈植〉*Notoseris psilolepis*; purple chrysanthemum
紫米酒	〈哈尼族〉purple rice wine
紫伞芹	〈植〉*Melanosciadium pimpinelloidium*; purple umbrella-shaped celery
紫砂艺术博物馆	Purple Clay Art Museum (Shanghai)
紫藤	〈植〉*Wisteria sinensis*; Chinese wisteria
紫藤寄松	(of Hongluo Temple) Pines Entangled with Chinese Wisteria
紫溪山森林公园	Zixi Mountain Forest Park (Yunnan)
紫霞洞	Purple Glow Cave (Hu'nan)
紫霄宫	(of Mount Wudang) Zixiao Palace; Purple Heaven Palace
紫云山景区	Purple Cloud Mountain Scenic Spot (He'nan)
紫云山自然景区	Ziyun Mountain Natural Scenic Spot (He'nan, Beijing)
紫云英	〈植〉*Astragalus sinicus*; Chinese milk vetch
紫竹林教堂	Zizhulin Church (Tianjin)
紫竹院公园	Purple Bamboo Park; Black Bamboo Park (Beijing)
紫棕掌突蟾	〈动〉*Paramegophrys purpura*
自然村	natural village; unincorporated village
自然资源保护区	natural resource protection area
自由行	self-guided tour
宗喀巴大师	Master Tsongkhapa
宗喀巴纪念塔	Tsongkhapa Memorial Pagoda (Qinghai)

棕点湍蛙	〈动〉*Amolops loloensis*; lolokou sucker frog; rufous-spotted torrent frog
棕黑疣螈	〈动〉*Tylototriton verrucosus*
棕熊	〈动〉*Ursus arctos*; brown bear
粽粑节	〈侗族〉Zongba Festival (on the 5th day of the 5th lunar month)
粽子	zongzi; sticky rice dumpling; traditional Chinese rice-pudding
邹人	Tsou people; Tsou
走百病	〈满族〉Walking for All Diseases Elimination (on the 15th or 16th day of the 1st lunar month)
走马楼	zouma building (with corridors all around)
走牲道	(of Temple of Heaven) Cattle's Tunnel
族徽	clan emblem
族长	patriarch; clan elder; head of a clan
祖庙	ancestral temple
祖山景区	Zushan Mountain Scenic Area (Hebei)
祖师殿	(of Mount Qingcheng) Founding Master Palace; Hall of Patriarch
祖堂山	Zutang Mountain (Jiangsu)
钻石婚	diamond wedding (the 18th anniversary of marriage)
醉罗汉	(of Zhangjiajie) Drunken Arhat
醉拳	〈武术〉Drunken Boxing; Drunker-Style Boxing
醉石	(of Mount Lushan) Rock of Drunken Man; Drunken Rock
醉翁亭	(of Mount Langya) Zuiweng Pavilion; Pavilion of Old Drunkard
遵化汤泉	Zunhua Hot Spring (Hebei)
遵义会议会址	Site of Zunyi Conference (Guizhou)
樽	〈古〉zun (wine vessel)
左单鞭	〈武术〉(of Tai Chi) Left single whip
左分脚	〈武术〉(of Tai Chi) Left parting kick
左揽雀尾	〈武术〉(of Tai Chi) Grasping the peacock's tail on left side

左下独立式	〈武术〉(of Tai Chi) Pushing down and stand on left leg
左右穿梭	〈武术〉(of Tai Chi) Working at shuttles on both sides
左右蹬脚	〈武术〉(of Tai Chi) Left and right heel kick; Kicking with both two heels
左右搂膝拗步	〈武术〉(of Tai Chi) Brushing knee and twisting step on both sides
左右野马分鬃	〈武术〉(of Tai Chi) Parting the wild horse's mane on both sides
佐敦谷公园	Jordan Valley Park (Hong Kong)
作揖	〈古〉to make a bow with hands folded in front → 拱手礼
作揖礼	〈礼〉to make a bow with hands folded in front
坐北朝南	(of house) to face south
坐春望月楼	(of Garden of Quiet Meditation) Moon-Watching Tower
坐盘	〈武术〉Cross-legged sitting stance
坐月子	〈习俗〉sitting the month; confinement in childbirth
做华周	〈习俗〉to celebrate one-year-old birthday
做七	〈丧〉to sacrifice to the deceased every seven days for seven repetitions
做三朝	〈习俗〉to celebrate on the third day of a new birth (for Hakka)

附录一 国家 AAAA 级旅游景区

阿克陶县奥依塔克冰川公园景区	Oitak Glacier Park Scenic Area of Aketao County (Xinjiang)
阿克陶县克州冰川公园	Kezhou Glacier Park of Aketao County (Xinjiang)
艾提尕民俗文化旅游风景区	Etgal/Atigar Folk Culture Tourist Area (Xinjiang)
安徽博物馆	Anhui Museum
安徽名人馆	Anhui Museum of Historical Notables; Anhui's Celebrities Museum
安康瀛湖旅游景区	Ankang Yinghu Lake Tourist Area (Shaanxi)
安陆白兆山李白文化旅游区	Li Bai Cultural Tourism Zone of Baizhao Mountain in Anlu (Hubei)
安庆白马潭景区	Anqing Baimatan Scenic Area; White Horse Pond Scenic Area in Anqing (Anhui)
安庆市菱湖风景区	Linghu Lake Scenic Area in Anqing (Anhui)
安丘青云山民俗游乐园	Qingyun Mountain Folk Amusement Park of Anqiu (Shandong)
安丘市景芝酒之城［博物馆］	Anqiu Jingzhi Wine City; Jingzhi Wine Culture Museum of Anqiu (Shandong)
安溪清水岩旅游区	Clear Water Rock Tourist Area of Anxi County (Fujian)
安阳殷墟旅游景区	Anyang Yinxu Ruin Tourist Attraction (He'nan)
安阳羑里城旅游景区	Youli City Tourist Area in Anyang (He'nan)
安义古村风景名胜区	Anyi Ancient Village Scenic Area
鞍山千山国家风景名胜区	Qianshan National Scenic Area in Anshan (Liaoning)
鞍山玉佛苑	Anshan Jade Buddha Park (Liaoning)
奥林匹克水上公园	Olympic Water Park; Beijing Olympic Rowing-Canoeing Park (Beijing)

八达岭水关长城景区	Badaling Shuiguan Great Wall Scenic Area; Shuiguan Great Wall Scenic Area at Badaling; Water Pass Great Wall Scenic Area at Badaling (Beijing)
八大处公园	Badachu Park; Eight Great Sites Park (Beijing)
八台山风景区	Batai Mountain Scenic Area (Sichuan)
八仙过海旅游景区	Eight Immortals Crossing the Sea Tourist Spot; Tourist Spot of Eight Immortals Crossing the Sea (Shandong)
白山望天鹅风景区	Baishan Wang Tian'e (Swan Lookout) Scenic Area; Scenic Area of Looking at the Swan (Jilin)
百色乐业大石围天坑群景区	Dashiwei Tiankeng Group Scenic Area of Leye County in Baise; Scenic Spot of Dashiwei Karst Doline and Cave Cluster of Leye County in Baise (Guangxi)
百色通灵大峡谷	Baise Tongling Grand Canyon (Guangxi)
包头南海湿地公园	Baotou Nanhai Wetland Park (Inner Mongolia)
包头市北方兵器城	Baotou Northern Weaponry City (Inner Mongolia)
包头五当召旅游景区	Baotou Wudang Lamasery Tourist Attraction (Inner Mongolia)
宝鸡大水川风景区	Baoji Dashui Plain Scenic Area (Shaanxi)
宝鸡市凤县凤凰湖景区	Baoji Phoenix Lake Scenic Area (Shaanxi)
宝山国际民间艺术博览馆	Baoshan International Folk Art Exhibition Hall (Shanghai)
宝天曼峡谷漂流景区	Baotianman Valley Rafting Scenic Spot (He'nan)
保定阜平晋察冀边区革命纪念馆	Jin-Cha-Ji Border Area Revolutionary Memorial Hall in Fuping County (Hebei)
保定虎山风景区	Baoding Hushan Mountain Scenic Area (Hebei)
保定易县狼牙山风景区	Langya Mountain Scenic Area in Baoding (Hebei)
保定易县清西陵	Baoding Western Qing Mausoleum in Yi County (Hebei)

保定直隶总督署	Baoding Zhili Govern-General's Office; Baoding Zhili General Governor's Mansion (Hebei)
北川老县城地震遗址	Earthquake Ruins of Beichuan Old County (Sichuan)
北川药王谷风景区	Medicine King Valley Scenic Area in Beichuan (Sichuan)
北戴河联峰山景区	Beidaihe Lianfeng Mountain Scenic Area (Hebei)
北宫国家森林公园	Beigong National Forest Park (Beijing)
北海公园旅游景区	Beihai Park Tourist Area (Beijing)
北海银滩旅游区	Beihai Silver Beach Tourist Area (Guangxi)
北京动物园	Peking Zoo; Beijing Zoo
北京海洋馆	Beijing Aquarium
北京欢乐谷旅游	Beijing Happy Valley Scenic Area
北京千灵山风景区	Beijing Qianling Mountain Scenic Area
北京十渡风景名胜区	Beijing Shidu Scenic Area
北京石花洞国家地质公园	Beijing Shihua Cave National Geopark
北京世界公园	Beijing World Park
北京市规划展览馆	Beijing Planning Exhibition Hall
北京市植物园	Beijing Botanical Garden
北京野生动物园	Beijing Wildlife Park
北武当山风景区	Mount Beiwudang Scenic Area (Shanxi)
北岳恒山旅游景区	Northern Mount Hengshan Tourist Area (Shanxi)
北岳庙旅游景区	Beiyue Temple Tourist Area (Hebei)
本溪水洞风景区	Benxi Water Cave Scenic Area (Liaoning)
蚌埠市龙子湖风景区	Longzi Lake Scenic Area in Bengbu; Dragon Son Lake Scenic Area in Bengbu (Anhui)
比干庙景区	Bigan Temple Scenic Area (He'nan)
笔架山旅游景区	Bijia Mountain Tourist Area (Liaoning)
碧海金沙水上乐园	Bihai Jinsha Water Park (Shanghai)
宾县二龙山旅游风景区	Erlong Mountain Scenic Area of Bingxian County (Heilongjiang)
渤海国上京龙泉府遗址	Shangjing Longquanfu Ruins of Bohai State; Site of the Upper Capital of Bohai State (Heilongjiang)

布尔津县喀纳斯风景名胜区	Kanas Scenic Area of Burjin County (Xinjiang)
沧州吴桥杂技大世界	Wuqiao Acrobatics World in Cangzhou (Hebei)
曹州牡丹园景区	Caozhou Peony Garden Scenic Area (Shandong)
嵖岈山风景区	Chaya Mountain Scenic Area (He'nan)
察布查尔县锡伯民俗风情园	Xibo Nationality Folklore Park of Chabuchar (Qapqal) County (Xinjiang)
昌吉杜氏旅游景区	Du Famliy Tourist Resort in Changji (Xinjiang)
昌平温都水城	Wendu Hot Spring Leisure Town of Changping (Beijing)
昌邑绿博园	Changyi Green Expo Garden (Shandong)
长白山国家级自然保护区	Changbai Mountain National Nature Reserve (Jilin)
长春世界雕塑公园	Changchun World Sculpture Park (Jilin)
长春市莲花山滑雪场	Changchun Lianhua (Lotus) Mountain Skiing Resort (Jilin)
长春伪满皇宫博物院	Museum of the Imperial Palace of "Manchu State"; Puppet Emperor's Imperial Palace in Changchun (Jilin)
长江三峡工程坛子岭旅游区	Tanziling Tourist Area of the Three Gorges Project of the Yangtze River (Hubei)
长沙大围山国家森林公园	Dawei Mountain National Forest Park in Changsha (Hu'nan)
长沙海底世界	Changsha Undersea World (Hu'nan)
长沙胡耀邦故里旅游区	Hu Yaobang's Hometown Tourist Area in Changsha; Tourist Area of Hu Yaobang's Hometown in Changsha (Hu'nan)
长沙靖港古镇景区	Jinggang Ancient Town Scenic Area in Changsha (Hu'nan)
长沙世界之窗	Window of the World in Changsha (Hu'nan)
长沙市雷锋纪念馆	Changsha Leifeng Memorial Hall (Hu'nan)
长沙天心阁	Changsha Tianxin Pavilion (Hu'nan)
长沙沩山风景名胜区	Weishan Mountain Scenic Area in Changsha (Hu'nan)

长沙杨开慧纪念馆	Yang Kaihui Memorial Hall in Changsha (Hu'nan)
长寿湖风景名胜区	Changshou Lake Scenic Area; Longevity Lake Scenic Area (Chongqing)
常德市清水湖旅游区	Qingshui Lake Scenic Area in Changde (Hu'nan)
常熟蒋巷村旅游景区	Changshu Jiangxiang Village Tourist Attraction (Jiangsu)
常熟虞山—尚湖风景区	Yushan Mountain—Shanghu Lake Scenic Area in Changshu (Jiangsu)
常州天宁寺	Changzhou Tianning Temple (Jiangsu)
巢湖市金孔雀温泉旅游度假村	Golden Peacock Spa Resort in Chaohu; Golden Peacock Hot Spring Resort in Chaohu (Anhui)
朝阳凤凰山国家森林公园	Phoenix Mountain National Forest Park in Chaoyang (Liaoning)
朝阳公园	Chaoyang Park (Beijing)
朝阳鸟化石国家地质公园	Chaoyang Bird Fossil National Geopark (Liaoning)
郴州汝城温泉·福泉山庄	Chenzhou Rucheng Hot Spring—Fuquan Holiday Resort (Hu'nan)
郴州市龙女景区	Scenic Area of the Dragon King's Daughter in Chenzhou (Hu'nan)
郴州苏仙岭风景名胜区	Suxianling Scenic Area of Chenzhou; Suxian Fairy Mountain Scenic Area of Chenzhou (Hu'nan)
郴州天堂温泉	Chenzhou Paradise Hot Spring Resort (Hu'nan)
陈巴尔虎旗呼和诺尔旅游景区	Huhe Noer Tourist Attraction of Chenbarhu Banner (Inner Mongolia)
陈云故居暨青浦革命历史纪念馆	Former Residence of Chen Yun and Qingpu Revolutionary History Memorial Hal in Shanghai; Chen Yun Memorial Hall in Shanghai
成都国色天乡乐园	Guose Tianxiang Paradise in Chengdu; Floraland Amusement Park in Chengdu (Sichuan)
成都金沙遗址博物馆	Jinsha Site Museum in Chengdu (Sichuan)

成都市建川博物馆聚落	Jianchuan Museum Cluster in Chengdu (Sichuan)
成都武侯祠博物馆	Wuhou Temple Museum in Chengdu (Sichuan)
成县《西峡颂》风景区	Xixiasong (Ode to Xixia) Scenic Area of Chengxian County (Gansu)
承德普陀宗乘之庙	Putuo Zongcheng Temple in Chengde; Temple of the Potaraka Doctrine in Chengde (Hebei)
承德市普宁寺	Chengde Puning Temple (Hebei)
承德双塔山风景区	Chengde Twin Peak Scenic Area (Hebei)
澄城县尧头窑文化旅游生态园区	Yaotou Kiln Culture Eco-park Tourist Area of Chengcheng County (Shaanxi)
池州牯牛降风景区	Chizhou Guniujiang Scenic Area (Anhui)
池州市大王洞景区	Dawang (King) Cave Scenic Area in Chizhou (Anhui)
池州市杏花村景区	Xinhua Village Scenic Area in Chizhou City (Anhui)
赤壁龙佑温泉度假区	Longyou Hot Spring Holiday Resort in Chibi (Hubei)
赤壁陆水湖风景区	Lushui Lake Scenic Area in Chibi (Hubei)
赤峰喀喇沁亲王府	Chifeng Prince Kharqin's Mansion (Inner Mongolia)
赤山风景名胜区	Chishan Mountain Scenic Area (Shandong)
重庆巴国城	Chongqing Baguo City
重庆动物园	Chongqing Zoo
重庆湖广会馆	Hu-Guang Guild Hall in Chongqing
重庆科技馆	Chongqing Science and Technology Museum
重庆南山风景区	Chongqing Nanshan Mountain Scenic Spot
重庆人民大礼堂及人民广场	Chongqing People's Auditorium and People's Square; Chongqing People's Great Hall and People's Square
重庆市北温泉风景区	North Hot Spring Scenic Area in Chongqing
重庆市贝迪颐园温泉	Beidi Yiyuan Hot Spring in Chongqing
重庆市磁器口古镇	Ciqikou Ancient Town in Chongqing
重庆市规划展览馆	Chongqing Planning Exhibition Gallery

重庆市湖广会馆	Hu-Guang Guild Hall in Chongqing
重庆市南山植物园	Chongqing Nanshan Botanical Garden; South Mountain Botanical Garden of Chongqing
重庆市聂荣臻元帅陈列馆	Marshal Nie Rongzhen Museum in Chongqing
重庆市统景温泉风景区	Tongjing Hot Spring Scenic Area in Chongqing
重庆市颐尚温泉	Chongqing Yishang Hot Spring
重庆野生动物世界	Chongqing Wildlife Park
重庆中国三峡博物馆	China Three Gorges Museum in Chongqing
崇信县龙泉寺景区	Chongxin Longquan Temple Scenic Area (Gansu)
崇义县阳岭国家森林公园	Chongyi Yangling National Forest Park (Jiangxi)
滁州琅琊山旅游区	Chuzhou Langya Mountain Tourist Area (Anhui)
川鸡足山景区	Jizu Mountain Scenic Area of Binchuan County (Yunnan)
串场河海盐历史文化风貌区	Sea-Salt Historical and Cultural Scenic Area of Chuanchang River (Jiangsu)
慈溪雅戈尔达蓬山景区	Yage'er Dapeng Mountain Scenic Area in Cixi (Zhejiang)
翠华山风景区	Cuihua Mountain Scenic Spot (Shaanxi)
达里诺尔湖风景区	Dali Nuoer Lake Scenic Area (Inner Mongolia)
大报恩寺遗址公园	Dabao'en Temple Ruins Park (Jiangsu)
大别山彩虹瀑布风景区	Rainbow Waterfall Scenic Area at Dabie Mountain (Anhui)
大丰麋鹿国家级自然保护区	Dafeng Milu National Nature Reserve (Jiangsu)
大觉山自然景区	Dajue Mountain Natural Scenic Area (Jiangxi)
大理古城	Dali Ancient/Old City (Yunnan)
大理南诏风情岛	Nanzhao Customs Island in Dali (Yunnan)
大荔县同州湖景区	Tongzhou Lake Scenic Area of Dali County (Shaanxi)
大连冰峪旅游度假区	Dalian Ice Valley Holiday Resort (Liaoning)
大连森林动物园	Dalian Forest Zoo (Liaoning)
大连圣亚海洋世界	Dalian Sun-Asia Ocean World (Liaoning)
大连世界和平公园	Dalian World Peace Park (Liaoning)

大青沟生态旅游区	Daqinggou (Valley) Ecological Tourism Zone (Inner Mongolia)
大庆市北国温泉养生休闲旅游区	Beiguo Hot Spring Health-Preserving and Leisure Tourist Area in Daqing (Heilongjiang)
大庆市连环湖景区	Lianhuan Lake Scenic Area in Daqing (Heilongjiang)
大庆铁人王进喜纪念馆	Memorial Hall of the Iron Man Wang Jinxi in Daqing (Heilongjiang)
大庆油田历史陈列馆	Historical Exhibition Hall of Daqing Oil Field (Heilongjiang)
大石围天坑群风景区	Dashiwei Tiankeng Group Scenic Area; Dashiwei Karst Dolines Scenic Area (Guangxi)
大通县老爷山风景名胜区	Laoye/Master Mountain Scenic Area of Datong County (Qinghai)
大同华严寺旅游景区	Datong Huayan Temple Tourist Attraction (Shanxi)
大围山国家森林公园	Dawei Mountain National Forest Park (Hu'nan)
大冶雷山风景区	Daye Leishan Mountain Scenic Area (Hubei)
大邑刘氏庄园博物馆	Dayi Liu's Manor Museum; Dayi Liu Family Manorial Museum (Sichuan)
大英死海旅游景区	Daying Dead Sea Tourist Attraction (Sichuan)
大余丫山景区	Yashan Mountain Scenic Area of Dayu County (Jiangxi)
大禹文化旅游区	Dayu Cultural Tourism Area of Wenchuan County (Sichuan)
丹东虎山长城旅游景区	Tourist Attraction of Dandong Hushan Great Wall (Liaoning)
丹东青山沟风景区	Dandong Qingshan Valley Scenic Area (Liaoning)
丹东鸭绿江风景名胜区	Dandong Yalu River Scenic Area (Liaoning)
丹江漂流景区	Danjiang River Rafting Scenic Spot (Shaanxi)
当阳玉泉寺景区	Dangyang Yuquan Temple Scenic Area (Hubei)
德格印经院	Dege Sutra-Printing House (Sichuan)
德宏芒市勐巴娜西珍奇园	Mengbanaxi Exotic Garden in Mangshi (Yunnan)

德清莫干山风景区	Deqing Mogan Mountain Scenic Area (Zhejiang)
德州董子文化园	Dezhou Dongzi Cultural Park (Shandong)
德州齐河泉城海洋极地世界	Qihe Quancheng Ocean and Polar World in Dezhou (Shandong)
德州庆云海岛金山寺景区	Jinshan Temple Scenic Area of Qingyun Island in Dezhou (Shandong)
德州夏津黄河故道森林公园	Deahou-Xiajin Yellow River Original Course Forest Park (Shandong)
德州中国太阳谷	Dezhou Chinese Sun Valley (Shandong)
迪庆梅里雪山景区	Meili Snow Mountain Scenic Area in Diqing (Yunnan)
定南县九曲度假村	Jiuqu Holiday Resort of Dingnan County (Jiangxi)
东城龙潭公园	Dongcheng Longtan Tourist Park (Beijing)
东川红土地旅游景区	Dongchuan Red Land Tourist Attraction (Yunnan)
东莞欢笑天地旅游区	Dongguan Happy World Tourist Attraction (Guangdong)
东莞市观音山国家森林公园	Guanyin Mountain National Forest Park in Dongguan (Guangdong)
东莞市鸦片战争博物馆	Dongguan Opium War Museum (Guangdong)
东南花都花博园景区	Southeast Flower Capital Scenic Area; Southeast Flower Expo Garden (Fujian)
东宁要塞遗址	Dongning Fortress Site (Heilongjiang)
东平湖风景区	Dongping Lake Scenic Area (Shandong)
东山风动石景区	Dongshan Fengdong Rock Scenic Area; Dongshan Wind-Swaying Rock Scenic Area (Fujian)
东阳横店红色旅游城	Dongyang Hengdian Red Tourism Town (Zhejiang)
东至县南溪古寨景区	Dongzhi Nanxi Ancient Village Scenic Area (Anhui)
东至县升金湖湿地景区	Dongzhi Shengjin Lake Wetland Scenic Area (Anhui)

都匀斗篷山—剑江风景名胜区	Doupeng Mountain—Jianjiang River Scenic Area in Duyun (Guizhou)
独龙江风景区	Dulong River Scenic Area (Yunnan)
敦煌雅丹国家地质公园	Dunhuang Yadan National Geopark (Gansu)
敦煌阳关文物景区	Yangguan Pass Cultural Heritage Scenic Area of Dunhuang County (Gansu)
鄂尔多斯市察罕苏力德游牧生态旅游区	Chahan Sulide Nomadic Ecotourism Area in Ordos (Inner Mongolia)
鄂尔多斯市秦直道旅游区	Qinzhi Road Tourist Area in Ordos (Inner Mongolia)
鄂尔多斯市释尼召旅游景区	Shi Nizhao Tourist Attraction in Ordos (Inner Mongolia)
鄂尔多斯文化旅游村	Ordos Cultural Tourist Village (Inner Mongolia)
鄂豫皖苏区首府革命博物馆	Revolutionary Museum of the Capital of Hubei-He'nan-Anhui Soviet Area (He'nan)
恩格贝生态旅游区	Engebei Ecological Tourist Area (Inner Mongolia)
恩平锦江温泉旅游度假区	Jinjiang Hot Spring Tourist Resort in Enping (Guangdong)
恩施利川佛宝山大峡谷漂流景区	Fobaoshan Grand Canyon Drifting Area in Enshi (Hubei)
恩施唐崖河旅游景区	Enshi Tangya River Scenic Area (Hubei)
二连浩特市恐龙地质公园	Erenhot Dinosaur Geopark (Inner Mongolia)
二七区樱桃沟景区	Cherry Valley Scenic Area of Erqi District (He'nan)
二滩国家森林公园	Ertan National Forest Park in Panzhihua (Sichuan)
房山云居寺	Fangshan Yunju Temple (Beijing)
飞渡峡·黄安坝景区	Feidu Gorge-Huang'an Dam Scenic Area (Shaanxi)
飞来峡水利枢纽风景区	Feilaixia Water Conservancy Pivotal Scenic Area; Feilai Gorge Water Control Project Scenic Area (Guangdong)
丰都鬼城旅游区	Fengdu Ghost City Tourist Attraction (Chongqing)

丰都名山风景区	Fengdu Mingshan Mountain Scenic Area (Chongqing)
丰都雪玉洞	Fengdu Snow Jade Cave in Chongqing (Chongqing)
丰宁大汗行宫风景区	Scenic Area of Fengning Khan Temporary Palace (Hebei)
枫泾古镇旅游景区	Fengjing Ancient Town Tourist Attraction (Shanghai)
凤城凤凰山国家风景名胜区	Fengcheng Phoenix Mountain National Scenic Area (Liaoning)
凤凰沟风景区	Fenghuang Vale Scenic Spot; Phoenix Vale Scenic Spot (Jiangxi)
凤凰古城旅游区	Fenghuang Ancient Town Scenic Area; Phoenix Ancient Town Scenic Area (Hu'nan)
凤凰岭自然风景区	Fenghuangling Natural Scenic Area; Phoenix Hill Natural Scenic Area (Beijing)
凤县通天河景区	Tongtian River Scenic Area of Fengxian County (Shaanxi)
佛坪熊猫谷景区	Foping Panda Valley Scenic Area (Shaanxi)
佛山清晖园景区	Foshan Chinghui Garden Scenic Area (Guangdong)
佛山市长鹿旅游休博园	Changlu Leisure Expo Garden in Foshan (Guangdong)
佛山市三水荷花世界	Foshan Sanshui Lotus World (Guangdong)
佛山市三水森林公园	Foshan Sanshui Forest Park (Guangdong)
佛山市西樵山风景名胜区	Xiqiao Mountain Scenic Area in Foshan (Guangdong)
佛山祖庙旅游景区	Foshan Ancestral Temple Tourist Area (Guangdong)
福清市石竹山风景名胜区	Shizhu Mountain Scenic Area in Fuqing (Fujian)
福如东海文化园	Furu Donghai Happy Cultural Park; Cultural Park of Happiness as the Eastern Sea (Shandong)
福州国家森林公园	Fuzhou National Forest Park (Fujian)

抚州名人雕塑园	Fuzhou Celebrity Sculpture Park (Jiangxi)
阜阳市生态乐园	Fuyang Ecological Park; Fuyang Ecological Paradise (Anhui)
甘谷大象山风景区	Gangu Daxiang Mountain Scenic Area (Gansu)
赣县客家文化城	Ganxian Hakka Culture City (Jiangxi)
赣州汉仙岩风景区	Hanxian Rock Scenic Area in Ganzhou (Jiangxi)
赣州市宝葫芦农庄	Ganzhou Baohulu Farm; Treasure Calabash Farm in Ganzhou (Jiangxi)
赣州市宁都翠微峰景区	Cuiwei Peak Scenic Area of Ningdu County in Ganzhou (Jiangxi)
赣州通天岩风景名胜区	Tongtian Rock Scenic Area in Ganzhou (Jiangxi)
歌乐山烈士陵园	Gele Mountain Martyrs Cemetery (Chongqing)
格尔木昆仑旅游区	Golmud Kunlun Tourist Scenic Area (Qinghai)
格根塔拉草原旅游区	Gegentala Grassland Tourist Area (Inner Mongolia)
巩义康百万庄园	Kang Baiwan Manor in Gongyi; Millionaire Kang's Manor in Gongyi (He'nan)
共青城富华山景区	Fuhua Mountain Scenic Area of Gongqing City; Fuhua Mountain Scenic Area of Communist Youth City (Jiangxi)
沽源沽水福源度假村	Gushuiyuan Holiday Resort in Guyuan County (Hebei)
沽源塞外庄园	Saiwai Holiday Resort in Guyuan County; Guyuan Holiday Resort beyond the Great Wall in Guyuan County (Hebei)
沽源天鹅湖	Guyuan Swan Lake (Hebei)
古县牡丹文化旅游区	Peony Culture Tourist Area of Guxian County (Shanxi)
关门山国家森林公园	Guanmen Mountain National Forest Park (Liaoning)
关山草原风景名胜区	Guanshan Grassland Scenic Area (Shaanxi)
关山国家地质公园	Guanshan Mountain National Geopark (He'nan)
观音桥商圈都市旅游区	Urban Tourism Area of Guanyin Bridge Business District in Chongqing (Chongqing)

冠世榴园生态文化旅游区	Guanshi Pomegranate Garden Eco-cultural Tourist Area; World Crown Liuyuan Eco-cultural Tourism Zone (Shandong)
鹳河漂流风景区	Guanhe/Stork River Rafting Scenic Area (He'nan)
广德太极洞风景区	Tai Chi Cave Scenic Area of Guangde (Anhui)
广东美术馆	Guangdong Museum of Art (Guangdong)
广汉三星堆博物馆	Sanxingdui Museum in Guanghan (Sichuan)
广西科学技术馆	Guangxi Science and Technology Museum (Guangxi)
广元曾家山风景区	Zengjia Mountain Scenic Area in Guangyuan (Sichuan)
广元翠云廊	Cuiyun Corridor in Guangyuan (Sichuan)
广元东河口地震遗址公园	Donghekou Earthquake Relics Park in Guangyuan (Sichuan)
广元红军渡	Red Army's Ferry Crossing in Guangyuan (Sichuan)
广元皇泽寺	Huangze Temple in Guangyuan (Sichuan)
广元明月峡	Bright Moon Gorge in Guangyuan (Sichuan)
广元七里峡鼓城山	Qilixia Gucheng Mountain in Guangyuan (Sichuan)
广元千佛崖	Qianfo Cliff in Guangyuan; Thousand Buddhas Cliff in Guangyuan (Sichuan)
广元唐家河景区	Tangjia River Scenic Area in Guangyuan (Sichuan)
广元昭化古城	Zhaohua Ancient City in Guangyuan (Sichuan)
广州陈家祠旅游景区	Chen Clan Academy Tourist Attraction in Guangzhou (Guangdong)
广州番禺宝墨园	Panyu Baomo Garden in Guangzhou (Guangdong)
广州黄花岗公园	Guangzhou Huanghuagang Park (Guangdong)
广州莲花山旅游区	Lotus Mountain Tourist Area in Guangzhou (Guangdong)

广州市从化碧水湾温泉度假村	Conghua Bishuiwan Hot Spring Holiday Resort in Guangzhou (Guangdong)
广州西汉南越王博物馆	Museum of the Western Han Dynasty Mausoleum of the Nanyue King (Guangdong)
广州香江野生动物世界	Guangzhou Xiangjiang Safari Park (Guangdong)
广州越秀公园	Guangzhou Yuexiu Park (Guangdong)
广州中山纪念堂	Guangzhou Sun Yat-sen Memorial Hall (Guangdong)
归园·赛金花故居	Guiyuan Park-Sai Jinhua's Former Residence (Anhui)
贵阳黔灵山公园	Guiyang Qianling Mountain Park (Guizhou)
贵阳市黔灵山公园	Qianling Mountain Park in Guiyang (Guizhou)
桂林穿山景区	Guilin Chuanshan Hill Scenic Area (Guangxi)
桂林龙胜温泉旅游度假区	Guilin Longsheng Hot Spring Tourism Resort (Guangxi)
桂林芦笛景区	Reed Flute Scenic Area in Guilin (Guangxi)
桂林芦笛岩风景区	Scenic Area of Guilin Reed Flute Cave (Guangxi)
桂林七星景区	Seven Star Scenic Area/Spot in Guilin (Guangxi)
桂林世外桃源旅游区	Guilin Xanadu Tourist Area (Guangxi)
哈尔滨东北虎林园	Harbin Siberian Tiger Park (Heilongjiang)
哈尔滨黑龙江电视塔[龙塔]旅游区	Heilongjiang TV Tower (Dragon Tower) Tourist Area in Harbin (Heilongjiang)
哈尔滨金源文化旅游区	Jin Yuan Cultural Tourist Area in Harbin (Heilongjiang)
哈尔滨圣索非亚教堂景区	Saint Sophia Cathedral Scenic Area in Harbin (Heilongjiang)
海兰云天温泉度假区	Hailan Yuntian Hot Springs Resort (Chongqing)
海螺沟冰川森林公园	Hailuo Gully Glaciers Forest Park in Luding (Sichuan)
海南热带野生动植物园	Hai'nan Tropical Wildlife Park and Botanical Garden (Hai'nan)
邯郸武安京娘湖风景区	Jingniang Lake Scenic Area in Handan (Hebei)
函谷关历史文化旅游区	Hangu Pass Historical and Cultural Tourist Area (He'nan)

韩城市党家村景区	Hancheng Dangjia Village Scenic Area (Shaanxi)
韩城市司马迁祠	Sima Qian Memorial Temple in Hancheng (Shaanxi)
汉诺庄园旅游景区	Hanover Manor; Hannuo Manor Tourism Attraction (Shandong)
汉中石门栈道景区	Shimen Plank Road Scenic Area in Hanzhong (Shaanxi)
杭州柳溪江风景区	Liuxi River Scenic Area in Hangzhou (Zhejiang)
杭州宋城旅游景区	Song Cheng City Tourist Area in Hangzhou (Zhejiang)
杭州湘湖风景区	Xianghu Lake Scenic Area in Hangzhou (Zhejiang)
杭州野生动物世界	Hangzhou Safari Park; Hangzhou Wildlife Park (Zhejiang)
合肥包公园旅游景区	Hefei Baogong Garden Tourist Area (Anhui)
合肥渡江战役纪念馆	Hegei Memorial of Crossing-the-Yangtze-River Campaign (Anhui)
合肥市徽园	Hefei Huiyuan Park; Hefei Emblem Park (Anhui)
合肥市李鸿章故居	Former Residence of Li Hongzhang in Hefei; Li Hongzhang's Former Residence in Hefei (Anhui)
合肥市三河古镇旅游景区	Sanhe Ancient Town Tourist Area in Hefei (Anhui)
合阳洽川风景区	Heyang Hechuan Scenic Area (Shaanxi)
和硕县金沙滩旅游景区	Jinsha Beach Tourist Area of Hoxud County (Xinjiang)
河南大苏山国家森林公园	Dasu Mountain National Forest Park in He'nan (He'nan)
河源市新丰江国家森林公园	Xinfengjiang National Forest Park in Heyuan (Guangdong)
贺兰山南寺生态旅游区	Helan Mountain South Monastery Ecotourism Area (Ningxia)
贺兰山苏峪口国家森林公园	Suyukou National Forest Park of Helan Mountain (Ningxia)
贺兰山岩画	Helan Mountain Rock Paintings (Ningxia)

鹤壁市大伾山旅游风景区	Dapi Mountain Tourist Area in Hebi (He'nan)
鹤壁云梦山风景区	Yunmeng Mountain Scenic Area in Hebi (He'nan)
鹤岗市萝北名山景区	Luobei Mingshan Scenic Area in Hegang (Heilongjiang)
黑龙江科学技术馆	Heilongjiang Science and Technology Museum (Heilongjiang)
黑龙江扎龙国家级自然保护区	Zhalong National Nature Reserve in Heilongjiang (Heilongjiang)
黑龙潭旅游区	Heilong Pool Tourist Area; Black Dragon Pool Tourist Area (Beijing)
衡水市武强年画博物馆	Hengshui Museum of Wuqiang New Year Pictures (Hebei)
衡阳市罗荣桓故居纪念馆	Memorial Hall of the Former Residence of Marshal Luo Ronghuan in Hengyang (Hu'nan)
红枫湖景区	Hongfeng Lake Scenic Area; Red Maple Lake Scenic Area (Guizhou)
红螺寺旅游景区	Hongluo Temple Tourist Attraction (Beijing)
红岩革命纪念馆	Hongyan Revolution Memorial Hall; Red Rock Revolution Memorial Hall (Chongqing)
洪崖洞民俗风貌区	Hongyadong Folk Custom Area (Chongqing)
呼和浩特市神泉生态旅游景区	Hohhot Shenquan Ecotourist Attraction (Inner Mongolia)
呼伦贝尔市海拉尔农业发展园区	Hailaer Agricultural Development Park in Hulun Buir (Inner Mongolia)
胡里山炮台旅游景区	Hulishan Fortress Tourist Attraction (Fujian)
葫芦岛葫芦山庄	Hulu Mountain Villa in Huludao (Liaoning)
葫芦岛兴城海滨风景区	Xingcheng Seaside Scenic Area in Huludao
湖北省博物馆	Hubei Provincial Museum; Museum of Hubei Province
湖南省博物馆	Hu'nan Provincial Museum; Museum of Hu'nan Province
湖南省森林植物园	Hu'nan Forest Botanical Garden
虎跳峡旅游景区	Tiger Leaping Gorge Tourist Attraction (Yunnan)
花溪天河潭景区	Huaxi Tianhe Pool Scenic Area (Guizhou)

华岩—龙门阵旅游区	Huayan—Longmenzhen Tourist Area; Huayan—Dragon Gate Array Tourist Area (Chongqing)
画眉谷生态旅游区	Thrush Valley Ecological Tourist Area (He'nan)
怀柔慕田峪风景区	Huairou Mutian Valley Scenic Area (Beijing)
淮安市周恩来故居	Zhou Enlai's Former Residence in Huai'an (Jiangsu)
淮北相山公园	Xiangshan Mountain Park in Huaibei (Anhui)
淮河蚌埠闸水利风景区	Bengbu Sluice Water Conservancy Scenic Spot of Huaihe River (Anhui)
淮阳县太昊陵景区	Taihao Mausoleum Scenic Spot of Huaiyang County (He'nan)
黄陂锦里沟土家风情谷旅游区	Jinligou Tujia Valley Scenic Resort in Huangpi District (Hubei)
黄冈李先念故居纪念园	Li Xiannian's Former Residence in Huanggang (Hubei)
黄河风景名胜区	Yellow River Scenic Area (He'nan)
黄河富景生态世界	Yellow River Landscape Ecological World (He'nan)
黄河三峡风景名胜区	Three Gorges Scenic Area of the Yellow River (He'nan)
黄河小浪底风景区	Xiaolangdi Dam Scenic Area of Yellow River (He'nan)
黄陵国家森林公园	Huangling National Forest Park; National Forest Park of the Yellow Emperor's Mausoleum (Shaanxi)
黄麻起义和鄂豫皖苏区革命烈士陵园	Huang'an-Macheng Uprising and Cemetery of Revolutionary Martyrs' of the Hubei, He'nan and Anhui Soviet Areas (Hubei)
黄沙古渡生态旅游区	Huangsha Ancient Ferry Ecotourism Area (Ningxia)
黄山翡翠谷[情人谷]风景区	Emerald Valley Scenic Area in Huangshan Mountain; Lover's Valley Scenic Area in Huangshan Mountain (Anhui)

黄山市花山谜窟—渐江风景区	Huashan Mystery Grottoes—Jianjiang River Scenic Area in Huangshan (Anhui)
黄山市徽州古城	Huizhou Ancient Town in Huangshan (Anhui)
黄山市太平湖风景区	Taiping Lake Scenic Area in Huangshan (Anhui)
黄山市唐模景区	Tang Mo Scenic Area in Hunagshan (Anhui)
黄山市屯溪区醉温泉景区	Tunxi Ravishing Hot Spring Scenic Area in Huangshan (Anhui)
黄石国家矿山公园	Huangshi National Mine Park (Hubei)
辉南县龙湾群国家森林公园	Dragon Bay National Forest Park of Huinan County (Jilin)
惠安崇武古城风景区	Chongwu Ancient City Scenic Area of Hui'an County (Fujian)
惠州市龙门南昆山生态旅游区温泉旅游大观园	South Kunshan Ecotourism Area of Hot Spring Tourism Grand View Park in Huizhou (Guangdong)
惠州市龙门温泉旅游度假区	Longmen Hot Spring Tourist Resort in Huizhou (Guangdong)
惠州市南昆山大观园生态度假区	Ecotourism Area of South Kunshan Grand View Garden in Huizhou (Guangdong)
惠州市西湖风景名胜区	Huizhou West Lake Scenic Area (Guangdong)
浑源恒山旅游区	Hengshan Mountain Tourist Area in Huanyuan County (Shanxi)
霍邱临淮岗风景区	Linhuaigang Scenic Area of Huoqiu County; Linhuai Mound Scenic Area of Huoqiu County (Anhui)
鸡西兴凯湖风景区	Jixi Khanka Lake Scenic Area (Heilongjiang)
吉安庐陵文化生态园	Ji'an Luling Cultural Ecological Park (Jiangxi)
吉安市渼陂古村	Ji'an Meibei Ancient Village (Jiangxi)
吉安天祥景区	Wen Tianxiang (a national hero in late Song Dynasty) Scenic Area in Ji'an (Jiangxi)
吉林市博物馆	Jilin Municipal Museum; Jilin Meteorite Museum
吉林松花湖风景名胜区	Songhua Lake Scenic Area in Jilin (Jilin)
吉首市乾州古城景区	Qianzhou Ancient Town Scenic Area of Jishou County (Hu'nan)

集安市高句丽文物古迹旅游景区	Koguryo Cultural Relic Scenic Area in Ji'an (Jilin)
济南大明湖	Jinan Daming Lake (Shandong)
济南灵岩寺旅游区	Jinan Lingyan Temple Tourist Area (Shandong)
济南跑马岭旅游区	Jinan Paomaling Tourist Area (Shandong)
济南千佛山风景区	Jinan Qianfo Mountain Scenic Area (Shandong)
济源王屋山风景区	Wangwu Mountain Scenic Area in Jiyuan (He'nan)
绩溪县龙川景区	Longchuan Scenic Area of Jixi County (Anhui)
蓟州独乐寺旅游景区	Jizhou Dule Temple Tourist Area (Tianjin)
加勒比海水世界景区	Caribbean Sea World Scenic Area (Chongqing)
夹江天福观光茶园	Tianfu Tourism Tea Garden of Jiajiang County (Sichuan)
建始野三河旅游区	Jianshi Yesan River Tourist Area in Enshi (Hubei)
建水燕子洞风景名胜区	Jianshui Swallow Cave Scenic Area (Yunnan)
江门市圭峰山风景名胜区	Guifeng Mountain Scenic Area in Jiangmen (Guangdong)
江门市金山温泉旅游度假区	Jinshan Hot Spring Tourist Resort in Jiangmen (Guangdong)
江门市开平立园	Kaiping Liyuan Garden in Jiangmen (Guangdong)
江门市新会古兜温泉旅游度假村	Xinhui Gudou Hot Spring Holiday Resort in Jiangmen (Guangdong)
江油窦圌山风景区	Jiangyou Douchui MountainScenic Area (Sichuan)
江油李白纪念馆景区	Libai Memorial Hall Scenic Area in Jiangyou (Sichuan)
交城县卦山天宁寺	Guashan Mountain Tianning Monastery of Jiaocheng County (Shanxi)
交城县石壁玄中寺	Shibi Xuanzhong Monastery of Jiaocheng County (Shanxi)
蛟河拉法山国家森林公园	Jiaohe Lafa Mountain National Forest Park (Jilin)
介休市绵山风景名胜区	Jiexiu Mianshan Mountain Scenic Area (Shanxi)

金刚台猫耳峰旅游区	Cat's Ear Peak Tourist Area of Jingangtai (He'nan)
金海湖风景区	Jinhai Lake Scenic Area (Beijing)
金华双龙风景旅游区	Jinhua Shuanglong Tourist Area; Double Dragon Tourist Area in Jinhua (Zhejiang)
金沙遗址博物馆	Jinsha Site Museum (Sichuan)
金源方特科幻公园	Jinyuan Fangte Science Fiction Park (Chongqing)
金寨县燕子河大峡谷景区	Jinzhai Swallow River Grand Canyon Scenic Area (Anhui)
津南宝成奇石园旅游景区	Jinnan Tourist Area of Baocheng Alpine Garden (Tianjin)
晋中市平遥日升昌——中国票号博物馆	Museum of China's Currency Exchange Shop—Rishengchang in Jinzhong (Shanxi)
缙云鼎湖峰风景名胜区	Jinyun Dinghu Peak Scenic Area (Zhejiang)
缙云山国家级自然保护区	Jinyun Mountain National Nature Reserve (Chongqing)
缙云仙都风景名胜区	Jinyun Xiandu Scenic Area (Zhejiang)
缙云仙都黄龙景区	Xiandu Huanglong Scenic Area; Xiandu Yellow Dragon Scenic Area (Zhejiang)
京东大溶洞	Jingdong Grand Karst Cave; Jingdong Great Limestone Cave (Beijing)
京东大峡谷旅游区	Jingdong Grand Canyon Tourist Area (Beijing)
京东石林峡风景区	Jingdong Shilinxia Scenic Area; Jingdong Stone Forest Gorge Scenic Area; Stone Forest Gorge Scenic Area in East Beijing (Beijing)
京杭大运河杭州段	Hangzhou Scenic Area of Beijing-Hangzhou (Zhejiang)
泾县云岭新四军军部旧址纪念馆	Yunling Memorial Hall of the New Fourth Army Headquarters in Jingxian County (Anhui)
荆州博物馆	Jingzhou Museum (Hubei)
旌德县江村风景区	Jingde Jiangcun Village Scenic Area in Xuancheng (Anhui)
井陉苍岩山风景区	Jingxing Cangyan Mountain Scenic Area (Hebei)

景德镇浮梁古县衙	Fuliang Ancient County Government in Jingdezhen (Jiangxi)
景德镇市得雨生态园	Jingdezhen Deyu Ecological Park (Jiangxi)
景德镇市浮梁古县衙景区	Fuliang Ancient Yamen Scenic Area in Jingdezhen; The Fuliang Ancient County Government in Jingdezhen (Jiangxi)
景德镇市高岭—瑶里风景名胜区	Jingdezhen Kaolin—Yaoli Ancient Town Scenic Area (Jiangxi)
景德镇市洪岩仙境风景区	Jingdezhen Hongyan Fairyland Scenic Area (Jiangxi)
景德镇陶瓷历史博览区	Jingdezhen Ceramic Historical Expo Area; Jingdezhen Ceramic History Museum (Jiangxi)
景宁大均中国畲乡之窗景区	Window of Chinese She Culture Scenic Area (Zhejiang)
景宁云中大漈景区	Yunzhong Daji Scenic Area of Jingning; Cloud-Capped Daji Scenic Area of Jingning (Zhejiang)
景山公园旅游景区	Jingshan Park Tourist Attraction (Beijing)
景泰黄河石林风景旅游区	Yellow Rive Stone Forest Scenic Spot of Jingtai County (Gansu)
靖西县古龙山峡谷群生态旅游景区	Gulong Mountain Canyons Ecotourism Area of Jingxi County (Guangxi)
九成宫碑亭景区	Jiucheng Palace Stele Pavilion Scenic Area (Shaanxi)
九洞天国家级风景名胜区	Jiudongtian National Scenic Area (Guizhou)
九华天池旅游景区	Jiuhua Tianchi Scenic Resort; Jiuhua Heavenly Lake Scenic Resort (Anhui)
九江湖口石钟山	Hukou Shizhong/Stone Bell Mountain in Jiujiang (Jiangxi)
九仙山风景区	Jiuxian Mountain Scenic Area (Fujian)
九嶷山舜帝陵景区	Emperor Shun's Mausoleum Scenic Area of Jiuyi Mountain (Hu'nan)
居庸关长城风景区	Scenic Area of Juyong Pass Great Wall (Beijing)
鄄城县孙膑旅游城·亿城寺景区	Sun Bin Tourist City and Yicheng Temple Scenic Area of Juancheng County (Shandong)

开封包公祠旅游景区	Kaifeng Baogong Temple Tourist Area; Memorial Temple of Lord Bao in Kaifeng (He'nan)
开封大相国寺旅游景区	Tourist Attraction of Grand Xiangguo Temple in Kaifeng (He'nan)
开封府旅游景区	Kaifeng Prefecture Tourist Attraction; Kaifeng Government Office Tourist Attraction (He'nan)
开封龙亭风景区	Dragon Pavilion Scenic Area in Kaifeng (He'nan)
开封铁塔公园	Kaifeng Iron Tower Park (He'nan)
开滦国家矿山公园	Kailuan National Mine Park (Hebei)
开县刘伯承同志纪念馆	Kaixian Liu Bocheng Memorial Hall (Chongqing)
开阳南江大峡谷景区	Nanjiang Grand Canyon Scenic Area of Kaiyang County (Guizhou)
坎布拉国家森林公园	Kanbula National Forest Park (Qinghai)
康定木格措风景区	Kangding Mugecuo Scenic Area (Sichuan)
康定情歌风景区	Kangding Love Song Scenic Area (Sichuan)
康定野人海景区	Kangding Savage Lake Scenic Area (Sichuan)
康县阳坝自然风景区	Yangba Natural Scenic Area of Kangxian County (Gansu)
抗美援朝纪念馆	Chinese Memorial Hall of the War to Resist US Aggression and Aid Korea (Liaoning)
克什克腾世界地质公园	Hexigten Global Geopark (Inner Mongolia)
客家博物馆	Hakka Museum (Guangdong)
崆山白云洞景区	White Cloud Cave Scenic Area of Kongshan Mountain (Hebei)
孔庙和国子监博物馆	Confucian Temple and Imperial College Museum (Beijing)
库车王府	Kuqa Palace of Prince; Kuqa Prince's Residence (Xinjiang)
库车县龟兹绿洲生态园	Quici Oasis Ecopark of Kuqa County (Xinjiang)
昆明官渡古镇	Guandu Ancient Town in Kunming (Yunnan)
昆明金殿旅游景区	Kunming Golden Palace/Temple Tourist Attraction (Yunnan)
昆明民族村旅游景区	Nationalities Village Tourist Attraction in Kunming (Yunnan)

昆明石林风景名胜区	Kunming Stone Forest Scenic Area (Yunnan)
昆明市大观公园	Kunming Daguan Park; Kunming Grand View Park (Yunnan)
昆明市西山森林公园	Xishan Mountain Forest Park in Kunming (Yunnan)
拉卜楞寺旅游景区	Labrang Monastery Tourist Attraction; Labuleng Lamasery Tourist Attraction (Gansu)
拉法山国家森林公园	Lafa Mountain National Forest Park (Jilin)
拉萨罗布林卡旅游景区	Norbulingka Palace Tourist Attraction in Lhasa (Tibet)
兰溪诸葛八卦村	Zhuge's Village of Eight Diagram in Lanxi County (Zhejiang)
兰州水车博览园	Lanzhou Waterwheel Expo Park (Gansu)
岚皋南宫山景区	Nangong Mountain Scenic Area of Langao County (Shaanxi)
乐山东方佛都旅游景区	Tourist Area of Leshan Oriental Buddha Park (Sichuan)
雷山西江千户苗寨	Xijiang Qianhu Miao Village of Leishan County; Xijiang Thousand Miao's Village of Leishan County (Guizhou)
骊山风景名胜区	Lishan Scenic Area (Shaanxi)
梨木台自然风景区	Limutai Natural Scenic Area (Tianjin)
黎平侗乡风景名胜区	Liping Dong Villages Scenic Area (Guizhou)
礼泉袁家村—关中印象体验地景区	Yuan Family Village—Guanzhong Ecosystem Life Experience Scenic Area of Liquan County (Shaanxi)
丽江古城景区	Lijiang Old Town Scenic Area; Lijiang Ancient City Scenic Spot (Yunnan)
丽江木府旅游景区	Lijiang Mufu Mansion Tourist Attraction (Yunnan)
丽江束河古镇	Shuhe Ancient Town in Lijiang (Yunnan)
丽江玉水寨景区	Jade Water Village Scenic Area in Lijiang (Yunnan)

丽水莲都东西岩景区	Liandu Dongxi Rock Scenic Area; Liandu East-West Rock Scenic Resort (Zhejiang)
丽水龙泉山景区	Longquan Mountain Scenic Area (Zhejiang)
丽水遂昌金矿国家矿山公园	Suichang National Gold Mine Park in Lishui (Zhejiang)
利川腾龙洞风景旅游区	Lichuan Tenglong Cave Scenic Area in Enshi; Lichuan Soaring Dragon Cave Scenic Area (Hubei)
荔波小七孔景区	Xiaoqikong Scenic Area of Libo County; Small Seven-Hole Bridge Scenic Area of Libo County (Guizhou)
荔浦丰鱼岩田园旅游度假区	Fengyu Cave Rual Tourism Resort of Lipu County (Guangxi)
连城冠豸山风景区	Liancheng Guanzhi Mountain Scenic Area (Fujian)
连云港花果山风景区	Huaguo Mountain Scenic Area in Lianyungang; Flower and Fruit Mountain Scenic Area in Lianyungang (Jiangsu)
连云港孔望山风景区	Kongwang Mountain Scenic Area in Lianyungang (Jiangsu)
连云港连岛旅游度假区	Liandao Island Tourist Area in Lianyungang (Jiangsu)
连云港渔湾风景区	Fishing Bay Scenic Area in Lianyungang (Jiangsu)
梁河南甸宣抚司署	Nandian Xuanfu Ancient Chieftain Office of Lianghe County (Yunnan)
林芝鲁朗林海景区	Lulang Forest Sea in Nyingchi (Tibet)
临汾市尧庙—华门旅游区	Yao Temple—Huamen Gate Tourist Area in Linfen (Shanxi)
临沂蒙山风景区	Mengshan Mountain Scenic Area in Linyi (Shandong)
临沂麒麟山风景区	Linyi Kirin Mountain Scenic Area (Heilongjiang)
临沂沂水地下荧光湖旅游区	Yishui Underground Fluorescent Lake Tourist Area in Linyi (Shandong)

临沂沂水天上王城景区	Yishui Sky City Scenic Spot in Linyi (Shandong)
临沂沂水雪山彩虹谷风景区	Yishui Snow Mountain Rainbow Valley in Linyi (Shandong)
灵龙湖生态文化旅游区	Linglong Lake Eco-cultural Tourist Area (He'nan)
灵石王家大院旅游景区	Wang Family Compound Tourist Attraction in Lingshi County (Shanxi)
刘少奇同志纪念馆	Comrade Liu Shaoqi Memorial Hall (Hu'nan) (Hu'nan)
柳州大龙潭风景区	Liuzhou Dalongtan (Grand Dragon Pond) Scenic Area (Guangxi)
柳州立鱼峰风景区	Liuzhou Liyu Peak Scenic Area (Guangxi)
六安市金安区东石笋景区	Jin'an Dongshisun Scenic Area in Lu'an; Jin'an East Stalagmite Scenic Area in Lu'an (Anhui)
六安市万佛湖风景区	Lu'an Wanfo Lake Scenic Area; Scenic Area of Ten Thousand Buddhas Lake in Lu'an (Anhui)
六盘山国家森林公园	Liupan Mountain National Forest Park (Ningxia)
龙脉温泉度假村	Longmai Hot Spring Holiday Village (Beijing)
龙庆峡旅游区	Longqing Gorge Tourist Area (Beijing)
龙湾群国家森林公园	Longwanqun National Forest Park (Jilin)
龙岩龙硿洞风景名胜区	Longkong Cavc Scenic Area in Longyan (Fujian)
陇南市万象洞风景区	Wangxiang Cave Scenic Area in Longnan (Gansu)
娄底市紫鹊界梯田景区	Ziquejie Terrace Scenic Area in Loudi (Hu'nan)
庐山龙湾温泉度假村	Lushan Longwan Hot Spring Resort; Longwan Hot Spring Holiday Resort of Lushan Mountain (Jiangxi)
庐山天沐温泉度假村	Lushan Tianmu Hot Spring Resort; Tianmu Hot Spring Resort of Lushan Mountain (Jiangxi)
庐阳三十岗乡生态农业旅游区	Luyang Sanshigang Eco-agricultural Tourist Area (Anhui)
泸沽湖旅游景区	Lugu Lake Tourist Area in Liangshan (Sichuan)
泸西阿庐古洞景区	Alu Ancient Cave Scenic Area of Luxi County (Yunnan)

泸州古蔺黄荆景区	Gulin Huangjing Scenic Area in Luzhou (Sichuan)
泸州国宝窖池景区	Guobao Pit Scenic Area in Luzhou; National Treasure Pit Scenic Area in Luzhou (Sichuan)
泸州太平古镇景区	Taiping Ancient Town Scenic Area in Luzhou (Sichuan)
鲁南水城·枣庄老街	Lunan Shuicheng-Zaozhuang Old Street; Lunan City of Rivers-Zaozhuang Old Street (Shandong)
陆良彩色沙林景区	Luliang Colorful Sand Forest Scenic Area (Yunnan)
鹿回头山顶公园	Luhuitou Mountain Park (Hai'nan)
鹿邑太清宫景区	Taiqing Palace Scenic Area of Luyi County (He'nan)
鹿邑县老子故里景区	Laozi's Hometown Scenic Area of Luyi County (He'nan)
栾川重渡沟风景名胜区	Chongdu Vale Scenic Area in Luanchuan; Re-ferrying Journey Vale Scenic Area in Luanchuan (He'nan)
栾川养子沟风景区	Yangzi Vale Scenic Area of Luanchuan County; Scenic Area of Bringing-up-Sons Vale in Luanchuan (He'nan)
罗平九龙瀑布群风景区	Jiulong Waterfalls Scenic Area of Luoping County (Yunnan)
罗田天堂寨风景区	Luotian Tiantangzhai Scenic Area; Luotian Heaven Village Scenic Spot (Hubei)
洛阳白马寺旅游景区	White Horse Temple Tourist Attraction in Luoyang (He'nan)
洛阳关林庙旅游景区	Luoyang Guanlin Temple Tourist Attraction (He'nan)
洛阳灵山寺旅游景区	Lingshan Mountain Temple Tourist Attraction in Luoyang (He'nan)
洛阳青要山景区	Qingyao Mountain Scenic Area in Luoyang (He'nan)

洛阳天河大峡谷景区	Tianhe Grand Canyon Scenic Area in Luoyang (He'nan)
漯河开源金凤凰鸟文化乐园	Kaiyuan Golden Phoenix Culture Park in Luohe (He'nan)
漯河开源森林公园	Luohe Kaiyuan Forest Park (He'nan)
漯河南街村景区	Nanjie Village Scenic Area in Luohe (He'nan)
吕梁市汾阳汾酒文化景区	Fenjiu Liquor Culture Scenic Spot of Fenyang in Lüliang (Shanxi)
麻城龟峰山风景区	Macheng Guifeng Mountain Scenic Area; Macheng Turtle Peak Mountain Scenic Area (Hubei)
麻城烈士陵园	Macheng Martyrs' Cemetery (Hubei)
马鞍山采石风景名胜区	Ma'an Mountain Quarry Scenic Area (Anhui)
马栏革命旧址景区	Malan Revolutionary Site Scenic Area (Shaanxi)
马仁奇峰风景区	Maren Striking Peak Scenic Area (Anhui)
玛多鄂陵湖风景区	Madoi Ngoring Lake Scenic Area (Qinghai)
满洲里俄罗斯套娃广场	Matryoshka Doll Plaza in Manchuria (Inner Mongolia)
满洲里国门景区	Manchuria National Gate Scenic Area (Inner Mongolia)
满洲里中俄互市贸易旅游区	Manchuria Sino-Russian Trade and Tourist Area (Inner Mongolia)
漫川古镇景区	Manchuan Ancient Town Scenic Spot (Shaanxi)
茂陵博物馆	Maoling Mausoleum Museum (Shaanxi)
梅州华银雁鸣湖旅游度假区	Huayin Yanming Lake Tourist Resort in Meizhou (Guangdong)
梅州市蕉岭县长潭旅游区	Jiaoling Changtan Tourism Area in Meizhou (Guangdong)
梅州市客天下景区	Meizhou Hakka Scenic Area (Guangdong)
梅州市灵光寺旅游区	Ling Guang Temple Tourist Area in Meizhou (Guangdong)
梅州市雁鸣湖风景区	Yanming Lake Scenic Area in Meizhou (Guangdong)

梅州市雁南飞茶田度假村	Yan-Nan-Fei Tea plantation Resort in Meizhou; Yearning Tea Plantation Holiday Village in Meizhou (Guangdong)
湄州岛国家旅游度假区	Meizhou Island National Holiday Resort (Fujian)
门头沟戒台寺	Mentougou Jietai Temple Scenic Area (Beijing)
米林南伊沟旅游景区	Nanyi Vale Tourist Area of Milin County (Tibet)
泌阳铜山风景区	Biyang Tongshan (Copper) Mountain Scenic Area (He'nan)
勉县武侯墓景区	Wuhou Tomb Scenic Area of Mianxian County (Shaanxi)
明城墙遗址公园	City Wall Relics Park of Ming Dynasty (Beijing)
明月山天沐温泉度假村	Mingyue Mountain Tianmu Hot Spring Resort; Tianmu Hot Spring Resort of the Clear Moon Mountain (Jiangxi)
鸣翠湖国家湿地公园	Mingcui Lake National Wetland Park (Ningxia)
摩天岭生态旅游区	Motianling Ecotourism Area; Cloud-Capped Mountain Ecotourism Area (Shandong)
莫莫格国家级自然保护区	Momogo National Natural Preserve (Jilin)
牡丹江市紫菱湖旅游区	Ziling Lake Tourist Area in Mudanjiang (Heilongjiang)
木渎古镇旅游景区	Mudu Ancient Town Tourist Attraction (Jiangsu)
那拉提旅游风景区	Xinjiang Naraty Tourist Area (Xinjiang)
南昌梅岭狮子峰	Lion Peak of Meiling Mountain in Nanchang (Jiangxi)
南昌市八一起义纪念馆	Nanchang August 1st Uprising Memorial Hall (Jiangxi)
南昌市天香园景区	Tianxiang Garden Scenic Area in Nanchang (Jiangxi)
南充市凌云山景区	Lingyun Mountain Scenic Area in Nanchong (Sichuan)
南充西山风景区	Xishan Mountain Scenic Area in Nanchong (Sichuan)
南宫旅游景区	Nangong Tourist Area (Beijing)

南海禅寺旅游景区	Nanhai-Buddhist Temple Tourist Attraction (He'nan)
南迦巴瓦峰旅游景区	Namcha Barwa Peak Tourist Attraction (Tibet)
南江光雾山风景区	Nanjiang Guangwu Mountain Scenic Area (Sichuan)
南江峡谷风景区	Nanjiang Canyon Scenic Area (Guizhou)
南京莫愁湖风景区	Nanjing Mochou Lake Scenic Area (Jiangsu)
南京牛首山风景区	Nanjing Niushou Mountain Scenic (Jiangsu)
南京栖霞山风景区	Nanjing Qixia Mountain Scenic Area (Jiangsu)
南京雨花台风景名胜区	Rain Flower Terrace Scenic Area in Nanjing (Jiangsu)
南京总统府旅游景区	Nanjing Presidential Palace Tourist Attraction (Jiangsu)
南昆山国家森林公园	Nankun Mountain National Forest Park (Guangdong)
南宁八桂田园景区	Bagui Rural Scenic Resort in Nanning; Nanning Bagui Farmland Scenic Area (Guangxi)
南宁嘉和城景区	Jiahe City Scenic Area in Nanning (Guangxi)
南通博物苑	Nantong Museum (Jiangsu)
南通中国珠算博物馆	Chinese Abacuses Museum in Nantong (Jiangsu)
南湾猴岛旅游景区	Nanwan Monkey Island Tourist Attraction (Hai'nan)
南湾猴岛生态景区	Ecological Scenic Spot of Nanwan Monkey Island (Hai'nan)
南湾湖风景区	Nanwan lake Scenic Area (He'nan)
南阳市西峡恐龙遗址园	Xixia Dinosaur Relics Park in Nanyang (He'nan)
南阳卧龙岗武侯祠	Wolong Gang Wuhou Temple in Nanyang; Wuhou Temple on Lying Dragon Hill in Nanyang (He'nan)
内蒙古格根塔拉草原旅游中心	Gegentala Grassland Tourism Center in Inner Mongolia (Inner Mongolia)
内乡县衙旅游景区	Tourist Attraction of Ancient Neixiang County's Yamen (He'nan)

宁安市火山口国家森林公园	Ning'an Volcanic Vent National Forest Park (Heilongjiang)
宁波保国寺旅游景区	Ningbo Baoguo Temple Tourist Area (Zhejiang)
宁波博物馆	Ningbo Museum (Zhejiang)
宁波大桥生态农庄旅游区	Ningbo Bridge Ecological Farm Tourist Area (Zhejiang)
宁波凤凰山主题乐园	Ningbo Harborland Theme Park; Ningbo Phoenix Mountain Theme Park (Zhejiang)
宁波九龙湖旅游区	Ningbo Jiulong Lake Tourist Area (Zhejiang)
宁波市镇海区招宝山旅游风景区	Zhenhai Zhaobao Mountain Tourist Spot in Ningbo (Zhejiang)
宁波镇海郑氏十七房	Zhenghai Zheng's Seventeen Rooms in Ningbo (Zhejiang)
宁国市恩龙山庄生态旅游度假区	Enlong Mountain Villa Ecotourism Resort in Ningguo (Anhui)
宁夏固原博物馆	Guyuan Museum of Ningxia
牛背梁国家森林公园	Niubeiliang National Forest Park (Shaanxi)
攀西大裂谷格萨拉生态旅游区	Gesala Eco-tourism Area of Panxi Great Rift Valley in Panzhihua (Sichuan)
盘龙峡生态旅游区	Panlong Gorge Eco-tourism Region (Guangdong)
蓬安县嘉陵第一桑梓	Jialing First Hometown of Peng'an County in Nanchong (Sichuan)
蓬莱海洋极地世界	Penglai Polar Ocean World (Shandong)
平谷青龙山旅游区	Pinggu Qinglong Mountain Scenic Area (Beijing)
平江石牛寨景区	Pingjiang Shiniuzhai Scenic Area (Hu'nan)
平利天书峡景区	Pingli Tianshu Gorge Scenic Area (Shaanxi)
平塘风景名胜区	Pingtang Scenic Area (Guizhou)
平武报恩寺	Bao'en Temple of Pingwu County; Pingwu Thanksgiving Temple (Sichuan)
平遥双林寺彩塑艺术馆	Pingyao Art Museum of Shuanglin Temple Painted Sculpture (Shanxi)
平遥双林寺旅游景区	Pingyao Shuanglin Temple Tourist Attraction (Shanxi)

平遥文庙学宫博物馆	Pingyao Museum of Confucius Temple Academy (Shanxi)
平遥县城隍庙财神庙	Wealth Temple and City God Temple of Pingyao County (Shanxi)
平遥县协同庆钱庄博物馆	Xietongqing Ancient Bank Museum in Pingyao County (Shanxi)
平遥县衙博物馆	Museum of Pingyao Ancient Government Office in Jinzhong; County Yamen Museum of Pingyao (Shanxi)
平遥县镇国寺	Zhenguo Temple in Pingyao County (Shanxi)
鄱阳湖生态湿地公园	Poyang Lake Ecological Wetland Park (Jiangxi)
濮上园景区	Pushang Park Scenic Area (He'nan)
濮阳绿色庄园景区	Puyang Green Manor Scenic Area (He'nan)
普兰冈仁波齐峰风景区	Pulan Kailash Mountain Scenic Area (Tibet)
普陀长风公园	Putuo Changfeng Park (Shanghai)
七星湖沙漠生态旅游区	Seven-Star Lake Desert Ecotourism Area (Inner Mongolia)
戚城文物景区	Qicheng City Cultural Relics Scenic Spot (He'nan)
齐齐哈尔市龙沙公园	Qiqihar Longsha Park (Heilongjiang)
齐齐哈尔市明月岛景区	Mingyue Island Scenic Area in Qiqihar; Clear Moon Island Scenic Area in Qiqihar (Heilongjiang)
齐云山风景名胜区	Qiyun Mountain Scenic Area (Anhui)
祁门县牯牛降景区	Guniujiang Scenic Area of Qimen County (Anhui)
祁县乔家大院旅游区	Qiao Family Compound Tourist Attraction; Qiao Family Courtyard; Qiao Family Grand Courtyard (Shanxi)
淇县古灵山风景区	Ancient Lingshan Mountain Scenic Area of Qixian County (He'nan)
綦江古剑山风景区	Gujian Mountain Scenic Area of Qijiang District (Chongqing)

千唐志斋博物馆	Qiantang Zhizhai Museum; Qiantang Epigraph Museum (He'nan)
前南峪国家森林公园	Qiannanyu National Forest Park in Xingtai (Hebei)
乾陵博物馆	Qianling Mausoleum Museum (Shaanxi)
黔江小南海风景区	Scenic Area of Qianjiang Lesser South China Sea (Chongqing)
钦州八寨沟旅游景区	Bazhai Vale Scenic Area in Qinzhou (Guangxi)
秦安凤山风景区	Qin'an Fengshan Mountain Scenic Area (Gansu)
秦皇岛北戴河景区	Qinhuangdao Beidaihe Scenic Area (Hebei)
秦皇岛新澳海底世界	Qinhuangdao Xin'ao Marine World (Hebei)
秦皇岛燕塞湖景区	Qinhuangdao Yansai Lake Scenic Area (Hebei)
秦皇岛野生动物园	Qinhuangdao Wildlife Park (Hebei)
秦岭野生动物园	Qinling Wildlife Park (Shaanxi)
秦始皇陵景区	Qin Shihuang's Mausoleum Scenic Area; Mausoleum of the First Qin Emperor (Shaanxi)
青岛海滨风景区	Qingdao Seaside Scenic Area (Shandong)
青岛海底世界	Qingdao Underwater World (Shandong)
青岛天泰温泉度假区	Qingdao Tiantai Hot Spring Holiday Resort (Shandong)
青海金银滩景区	Jinyintan Scenic Area in Qinghai
青海省博物馆	Qinghai Provincial Museum
青海藏医药文化博物馆	Qinghai Tibetan Medicine Culture Museum
青龙峡旅游度假区	Qinglongxia Tourist Resort; Qinglong Gorge Tourist Resort (Beijing)
青田石门洞景区	Qingtian Shimen Cave Scenic Area; Qingtian Stone Gate Cave Scenic Areai (Zhejiang)
青田中国石雕文化旅游区	Qingtian Stone Carving Cultural Tourist Area of China; Chinese Stone Carving Cultural Tourism Area of Qingtian (Zhejiang)
青铜峡黄河大峡谷旅游区	Tourist Area of Qingtongxia Yellow River Canyon (Ningxia)
青阳县九子岩景区	Jiuziyan Scenic Area of Qingyang County; Nine Rocks Scenic Area of Qingyang County (Anhui)

青阳县莲峰云海景区	Qingyang Lianfeng Cloud Sea Scenic Area (Anhui)
青州泰和山风景区	Qingzhou Taihe Mountain Scenic Area (Shandong)
青州仰天山国家森林公园	Qingzhou Yangtian Mountain National Forest Park (Shandong)
青州云门山风景区	Qingzhou Yunmen Mountain Scenic Area (Shandong)
清远市碧桂园假日半岛故乡里旅游度假区	Biguiyuan Holiday Peninsula Hometown Tourist Resort in Qingyuan; Hometown Tourist Resort of Country Garden Holiday Peninsula (Guangdong)
清远市黄藤峡生态旅游区	Huangteng Gorge Ecotourism Area in Qingyuan (Guangdong)
清远市连州地下河	Lianzhou Underground River in Qingyuan (Guangdong)
清远市清新温矿泉旅游度假区	Qingxin Hot Spring Holiday Resort in Qingyuan; Refreshing Hot Spring Holiday Resort in Qingyuan (Guangdong)
清远市玄真古洞生态旅游区	Xuanzhen Ancient Cave Ecotourism Area in Qingyuan (Guangdong)
邛崃天台山旅游景区	Tiantai Mountain Tourist Area in Qionglai (Sichuan)
邛崃市平乐古镇	Pingle Ancient Town in Qionglai (Sichuan)
衢州江郎山风景区	Jianglang Mountain Scenic Area in Quzhou (Zhejiang)
衢州天脊龙门［龙门峡谷］	Quzhou Tianji Dragon Gate; Longmen (Dragon's Gate) Canyon (Zhejiang)
曲阜市孔子精华园·六艺城	Qufu Confucius Essence Garden—Six Arts City (Shandong)
曲江海洋极地公园	Qujiang Polar Ocean Park (Shaanxi)
曲靖师宗凤凰谷生命文化主题公园	Life Culture Theme Park of Shizong Phoenix Valley in Qujing (Yunnan)
泉州开元寺	Kaiyuan Temple of Quanzhou; Quanzhou Kaiyuan Temple (Fujian)

确山金顶山风景区	Queshan Jinding Mountain Scenic Area (He'nan)
日照海滨国家森林公园	Rizhao Seashore National Forest Park (Shandong)
日照刘家湾赶海园	Rizhao Liujiawan Beachcombing Park (Shandong)
日照汤谷太阳文化源风景区	Tanggu Sun Culture Origin Scenic Area (Shandong)
日照五莲山风景区	Rizhao Wulian Mountain Scenic Area (Shandong)
日照竹洞天风景区	Rizhao Bamboo Cave Scenic Area (Shandong)
荣县大佛寺	Grand Buddha Temple of Rongxian County (Sichuan)
榕江苗山侗水风景名胜区	Miaoshan and Dongshui Scenic Area of Rongjiang County; Scenic Area of Miao Mountain and Dong River in Rongjiang (Guizhou)
如皋水绘园景区	Rugao Shuihui Garden Scenic Area; Rugao Water Reflection Park (Jiangsu)
汝州风穴寺旅游景区	Ruzhou Fengxue Temple Tourist Area (He'nan)
瑞金叶坪红色旅游景区	Yeping Red Tourist Attraction of Ruijin County (Jiangxi)
瑞丽莫里热带雨林景区	Mori Tropical Rainforest Scenic Area of Ruili County (Yunnan)
三江丹洲风景区	Sanjiang Danzhou Scenic Area (Guangxi)
三僚风水文化景区	Sanliao Fengshui Cultural Scenic Spot; Sanliao Geomantic Omen Cultural Tourist Area (Jiangxi)
三门峡虢国博物馆	Guo State Museum in Sanmenxia (He'nan)
三明格氏栲国家森林公园	Geshikao National Forest Park in Sanming (Fujian)
三明梅列瑞云山旅游区	Meilie Ruiyun Mountain Tourist Area in Sanming (Fujian)
三清山田园牧歌乡村旅游区	Pastoral Rural Tourism Area of Sanqing Mountain (Jiangxi)
三爪仑国家森林公园	Sanzhaolun National Forest Park (Jiangxi)

森工平山旅游区	Pingshan Scenic Area of Longjiang Forest Industry (Heilongjiang)
沙澧河风景区	Shali River Scenic Area (He'nan)
沙市春秋阁风景区	Shashi Spring and Autumn Pavilion Scenic Area (Hubei)
山南地区桑耶寺	Samye Monastery in Shannan Region (Tibet)
陕西黎坪国家森林公园	Liping National Forest Park in Shaanxi (Shaanxi)
陕西历史博物馆	Shaanxi History Museum (Shaanxi)
陕西张裕瑞那城堡酒庄景区	Changyu Rena Chateau Scenic Area in Shaanxi (Shaanxi)
陕西自然博物馆	Shaanxi Natural Science Museum (Shaanxi)
陕州地坑院景区	Shanzhou Silo-Cave Scenic Area (He'nan)
汕头南澳生态旅游区	Nanao Ecotourism Area in Shantou (Guangdong)
汕头市礐石风景名胜区	Shantou Queshi Scenic Area (Guangdong)
汕头市中信高尔夫海滨旅游度假区	CITIC Golf Seaside Holiday Resort in Shantou (Guangdong)
汕尾市玄武山旅游区	Xuanwu Mountain Tourist Area in Shanwei (Guangdong)
商丘古文化旅游区	Shangqiu Ancient Culture Tourist Area (He'nan)
商丘日月湖景区	Sun-Moon Lake Scenic Area in Shangqiu (He'nan)
上邦温泉旅游区	Shangbang Hot Spring Tourist Area (Chongqing)
上海博物馆	Shanghai Museum
上海城市规划展示馆	Shanghai Urban Planning Exhibition Hall
上海大观园	Shanghai Grand View Garden
上海东平国家森林公园	Dongping National Forest Park in Shanghai
上海共青森林公园	Shanghai Gongqing Forest Park
上海古猗园	Shanghai Ancient Yiyuan Garden
上海海湾国家森林公园	Haiwan National Forest Park in Shanghai; Shanghai Bay National Forest Park
上海金茂大厦 88 层观光厅	the 88th Sightseeing Hall of Jinmao Tower in Shanghai; Observation Deck of the 88-Story Jinmao Tower in Shanghai
上海金山城市沙滩	Jinshan City Beach in Shanghai

上海科技馆	Shanghai Science & Technology Museum
上海佘山国家森林公园	Sheshan Mountain National Forest Park in Shanghai
上海世纪公园	Shanghai Century Park; Pudong Century Park in Shanghai
上海市动物园	Shanghai Zoo
上海市青少年校外活动营地—东方绿舟	Shanghai Youth Campsite for off-Campus Activities-Shanghai Oriental Green Boat Campsite
上海太阳岛旅游度假区	Shanghai Taiyang (Sun) Island Tourist Resort
上海野生动物园	Shanghai Wild Animal Park; Shanghai Wildlife Park
上海豫园	Shanghai Yuyuan Garden
上饶集中营	Relic of Shangrao Concentration Camp (Jiangxi)
韶关市曹溪温泉假日度假村	Caoxi Hot Spring Holiday Resort in Shaoguan (Guangdong)
韶关市丹霞山风景名胜区	Danxia Mountain Scenic Area in Shaoguan (Guangdong)
绍兴柯岩风景区	Shaoxing Keyan Scenic Area (Zhejiang)
绍兴兰亭风景区	Shaoxing Orchid Pavilion Scenic Area (Zhejiang)
歙县棠樾牌坊群·鲍家花园景区	Tangyue Archway Group—Bao Family Garden Scenic Area of Shexian County (Anhui)
歙县新安江山水画廊风景区	Xin'an River Landscape Gallery Scenic Area of Shexian County (Anhui)
深圳观澜湖高尔夫球会	Shenzhen Mission Hills Golf Club (Guangdong)
深圳市仙湖植物园	Shenzhen Xianhu Botanical Garden; Shenzhen Fairy Lake Botanical Garden (Guangdong)
深圳梧桐山风景名胜区	Shenzhen Wutong Mountain Scenic Area (Guangdong)
深圳梧桐山国家公园	Shenzhen Wutong Mountain National Park (Guangdong)
沈阳故宫博物馆	Shenyang Palace Museum; Shengyang Imperial Palace Museum (Liaoning)
沈阳棋盘山风景区	Shenyang Chessboard Mountain Scenic Area (Liaoning)

沈阳棋盘山国际风景旅游开发区	Qipanshan International Tourism Development Zone in Shengyang; International Tourism Development Zone of Qipan Mountain Scenic Spot in Shengyang (Liaoning)
圣莲山旅游度假区	Shenglian Mountain Tourist Resort (Beijing)
什刹海风景区	Shichahai Scenic Area (Beijing)
十堰黄龙滩旅游区	Shiyan Huanglongtan Tourist Area; Shiyan Huanglong Beach Tourist Resort (Hubei)
十堰赛武当景区	Shiyan Saiwudang (Fulong Mountain) Scenic Area (Hubei)
十堰上津古镇旅游文化区	Shangjin Ancient Town Cultural Tourist Area in Shiyan (Hubei)
十堰郧西天河旅游区	Yunxi Tianhe Tourist Area in Shiyan (Hubei)
石城通天寨景区	Shicheng Tongtian Mountain Scenic Area (Jiangxi)
石家庄抱犊寨景区	Baoduzhai Scenic Area in Shijiazhuang (Hebei)
石家庄市灵寿秋山景区	Qiushan Mountain Scenic Area in Lingshou County; Autumn Mountain Scenic Area in Lingshou County (Hebei)
石家庄市平山县黑山大峡谷景区	Heishan Grand Canyon Scenic Area in Pingshan County (Hebei)
石家庄天桂山景区	Tiangui Mountain Scenic Area in Shijiazhuang (Hebei)
石景山游乐园	Shijingshan Amusement Park (Beijing)
石漫滩国家森林公园	Shiman Beach National Park (He'nan)
石阡温泉群风景名胜区	Shiqian Hot Springs Scenic Area (Guizhou)
石泉古城景区	Shiquan Ancient City Scenic Area (Shaanxi)
石泉县中坝大峡谷景区	Zhongba Grand Canyon Scenic Area of Shiquan County (Shaanxi)
石泉燕翔洞景区	Yanxiang Cave Scenic Area of Shiquan County (Shaanxi)
石山火山群国家地质公园	National Geological Park of Shishan Mountain Crater Cluster (Hai'nan)
石台县牯牛降景区	Guniujiang Scenic Area of Shitai County (Anhui)

石台县怪潭景区	Guaitan Lake Scenic Area of Shitai County (Anhui)
石柱县大风堡景区	Dafengbao Scenic Area of Shizhu County (Chongqing)
世界花卉大观园	Beijing World Flower Garden; Beijing Garden of World's Flowers (Beijing)
世界园艺博览园	World Horticultural Expo Garden in Kunming (Yunnan)
首都博物馆	Capital Museum (Beijing)
寿县八公山风景区	Shouxian Bagong Mountain Scenic Area (Anhui)
舒城县万佛山风景区	Shucheng Wanfo Mountain Scenic Area (Anhui)
双流县黄龙溪旅游区	Huanglongxi Tourist Area of Shuangliu County (Sichuan)
双龙生态旅游景区	Double Dragons Ecotourism Area (Shaanxi)
双牌阳明山旅游区	Yangming Mountain Scenic Area of Shuangpai County (Hu'nan)
水泊梁山风景区	Shuipo Liangshan Scenic Area; Water Margin Liangshan Mountain Scenic Area (Shandong)
水富西部大峡谷景区	Western Grand Canyon Scenic Area of Shuifu County (Yunnan)
水磨沟风景区	Shuimo Valley Scenic Area; Watermill Valley Scenic Area (Xinjiang)
司马台长城景区	Simatai Great Wall Scenic Area (Beijing)
四姑娘山风景区	Four Maiden's Mountain Scenic Area (Sichuan)
松江方塔园风景区	Songjiang Fangta Garden Scenic Area (Shanghai)
松鸣岩风景名胜区	Songming Rock Scenic Area (Gansu)
松原市查干湖旅游度假区	Chagan Lake Holiday Resort in Songyuan (Jilin)
嵩山中岳庙	Zhongyue Temple of Songshan Mountain (He'nan)
嵩阳书院	Songyang Academy (He'nan)
苏州寒山寺旅游景区	Suzhou Hanshan Temple Tourist Area (Jiangsu)
苏州乐园	Suzhou Amusement Land (Jiangsu)

苏州甪直古镇旅游区	Luzhi Ancient Town Tourist Area in Suzhou (Jiangsu)
苏州市平江历史街区	Pingjiang Historic District of Suzhou (Jiangsu)
苏州市七里山塘景区	Seven-Mile Shantang Street Scenic Area in Suzhou (Jiangsu)
苏州同里古镇旅游区	Tongli Ancient Town Tourist Area in Suzhou (Jiangsu)
肃南马蹄寺风景名胜区	Sunan Mati Temple Scenic Area (Gansu)
宿迁湖滨公园	Suqian Hubin Park; Suqian Lakeside Park (Jiangsu)
宿迁雪枫公园	Suqian Peng Xuefeng Park (Jiangsu)
随州大洪山风景区	Dahong Mountain Scenic Area in Suizhou; National Scenic Area of Dahong Mountain in Suizhou (Hubei)
遂昌千佛山景区	Suichang Qianfo Hill Scenic Area; Suichang Thousand-Buddha Mountain Scenic Area (Zhejiang)
遂昌县南尖岩景区	Nanjian Rock Scenic Spot (Zhejiang)
遂昌县神龙飞瀑景区	Shenlong Waterfalls Scenic Area of Suichang; Dragon Valley Waterfall Scenic Area of Suichang (Zhejiang)
遂宁市中国观音故里旅游区	China's Hometown of Kwan-yin in Suining (Sichuan)
孙中山故居	Sun Yat-sen's Former Residence (Guangdong)
塔尔寺旅游区	Ta'er Lamasery Tourist Area (Qinghai)
台儿庄大战纪念馆	Memorial Hall of Taierzhuang Campaign (Shandong)
台儿庄古城	Taierzhuang Ancient Town (Shandong)
太行九莲山景区	Jiulian Mountain Scenic Area of Taihang Ridge (He'nan)
太行山大峡谷风景区	Taihang Grand Canyon Scenic Area (Shanxi)
太极峡风景区	Tai Chi George Scenic Area (Hubei)
太原东湖醋园	Donghu Vinegar Culture Museum in Taiyuan (Shanxi)

太原晋祠旅游景区	Taiyuan Jinci Temple Tourist Attraction (Shanxi)
太原清徐宝源老醋坊	Qingxu Baoyuan Old Vinegar Workshop in Taiyuan (Shanxi)
太原市晋祠旅游风景区	Jinci Temple Tourist Area in Taiyuan ; Jin Ancestral Temple Tourist Area in Taiyuan (Shanxi)
太原中国煤炭博物馆	China Coal Museum in Taiyuan City (Shanxi)
潭柘寺旅游景区	Tanzhe Temple Tourist Attraction (Beijing)
汤阴县岳飞庙景区	Yue Fei Temple Scenic Area of Tangyin County (He'nan)
唐山南湖城市中央生态公园	Nanhu Lake Central Eco-park in Tangshan (Hebei)
塘沽大沽炮台遗址	Tanggu Dagu Fort Site (Tianjin)
桃源仙谷自然风景区	Taoyuan Xiangu Natural Scenic Area; Taoyuan Fairy Valley Scenic Area (Beijing)
陶然亭公园	Taoranting Park; Joyous Pavilion Park (Beijing)
腾冲和顺古镇	Heshun Ancient Town in Tengchong (Yunnan)
滕州盈泰生态温泉度假村	Tengzhou Yingtai Hot Spring Holiday Resort (Shandong)
天池山风景区	Tianchi Mountain Scenic Spot (Jiangsu, He'nan)
天鹅湖国家城市湿地公园	National Urban Wetland Park of Swan Lake (He'nan)
天福茶博物院景区	Tianfu Tea Museum Scenic Area (Fujian)
天津宝成博物苑	Tianjin Baocheng Museum (a strange stone park)
天津滨海航母主题公园	Binhai Aircraft Carrier Theme Park in Tianjin
天津海滨旅游度假区	Tianjin Seashore Holiday Resort
天津黄崖关长城风景游览区	Huangyaguan Great Wall Scenic Area in Tianjin
天津蓟县独乐寺	Dule Temple in Tianjin
天津盘山风景区	Panshan Mountain Scenic Area in Tianjin
天津热带植物观光园	Tianjin Tropical Botanical Garden
天津水上乐园	Tianjin Water Park
天津天塔湖风景区	Tianta Lake Scenic Area in Tianjin

天津杨柳青博物馆［石家大院］	Yangliuqing Museum (Shi Family Compound/Manor) in Tianjin
天龙源温泉度假村	Tianlongyuan Hot Spring Holiday Resort (Beijing)
天涯海角风景区	Tianya-Haijiao Scenic Area; Scenic Area of the End of the Earth (Hai'nan)
天婴山国家森林公园	Tianzhao Mountain National Forest Park (Sichuan)
天竺山国家森林公园	Tianzhu Mountain National Forest Park (Shaanxi)
通海秀山历史文化公园	Xiushan Historical and Cultural Park of Tonghai County (Yunnan)
通化市杨靖宇烈士陵园	Tonghua Yang Jingyu Martyrs Cemetery (Jilin)
通辽市库伦三大寺	Kulun Three Major Monasteries in Tongliao (Inner Mongolia)
通山九宫山风景名胜区	Jiugong Mountain Scenic Area of Tongshan County (Hubei)
通山隐水洞地质公园	Tongshan Yinshui Cave Geopark (Hubei)
通山隐水洞风景区	Tongshan Yinshui Cave Scenic Area; Hidden River Cave Scenic Area of Tongshan County (Hubei)
通榆县向海国家级自然保护区	Xianghai National Nature Reserve of Tongyu County (Jilin)
桐城市孔城老街景区	Kongcheng Old Street Scenic Area in Tongcheng (Anhui)
桐城市嬉子湖生态旅游区	Xizi Lake Ecotourism Area in Tongcheng (Anhui)
铜川市药王山景区	Yaowang Mountain Scenic Area in Tongchuan (Shaanxi)
铜川市玉华宫风景名胜区	Yuhua Palace Scenic Area in Tongchuan (Shaanxi)
铜川照金—香山景区	Zhaojin Revolutionary Site-Xiangshan Temple Scenic Area in Tongchuan (Shaanxi)
铜陵天井湖风景区	Tianjing Lake Scenic Area in Tongling (Anhui)
铜仁市九龙洞风景区	Tongren Nine-Dragon Cave Scenic Area (Guizhou)

潼南县杨闇公故里	Tongnan Yang An-Gong's Former Residence (Chongqing)
筒车湾休闲景区	Tongche Riverbend Leisure Scenic Area (Shaanxi)
吐鲁番库木塔格沙漠风景区	Turpan Kumtag Desert Scenic Area (Xinjiang)
吐鲁沟国家森林公园	Tulu Gully National Forest Park (Gansu)
万寿山景区	Longevity Mountain Scenic Area (Beijing)
万仙山风景名胜区	Wanxian Mountain Scenic Area; Scenic Area of Ten Thousand Fairies' Mountain (He'nan)
万州大瀑布群旅游区	Wanzhou Great Waterfalls Tourist Area (Chongqing)
威海成山头风景区	Weihai Chengshantou Scenic Area; Weihai Chengshan Hilltop Scenic Area (Shandong)
威海华夏城景区	Weihai Huaxia City Scenic Area (Shandong)
威海乳山银滩旅游度假区	Rushan Silver Beach Tourist Resort in Weihai (Shandong)
微山湖湿地红荷旅游区	Weishan Lake Wetland Red Lotus Tourist Area; Wetland Red Lotus Tourist Area of Weishan Lake (Shandong)
潍坊金宝乐园	Weifang Jinbao Amusement Park (Shandong)
渭南卤阳湖景区	Weinan Luyang Lake Scenic Area (Shaanxi)
渭南葡萄产业园	Weinan Grape Industrial Park (Shaanxi)
渭南市富平陶艺村景区	Fuping Pottery Art Village Scenic Area in Weinan (Shaanxi)
渭南市少华山国家森林公园	Shaohua Mountain National Forest Park in Weinan (Shaanxi)
温宿县天山神木园景区	Tianshan Mountain Shenmu Garden of Wensu County (Xinjiang)
汶川大禹农庄	Wenchuan Dayu Farm Houses (Sichuan)
汶川水磨古镇	Wenchuan Shuimo Ancient Town; Watermill Ancient Town of Wenchuan County (Sichuan)
汶上宝相寺旅游景区	Wenhang Baoxiang Temple Tourist Area (Shandong)
瓮安江界河国家级风景名胜区	Jiangjie River National Scenic Area of Weng'an County (Guizhou)

乌兰布统草原将军泡子	Jiangjun Lake Wetland of Ulan Butong Grassland (Inner Mongolia)
乌鲁木齐市红山公园景区	Mount Hongshan Park Scenic Area in Urumqi (Xinjiang)
巫溪红池坝森林旅游景区	Forest Tourism Scenic Area of Wuxi Red Pool Dam (Chongqing)
无锡博物院	Wuxi Museum (Jiangsu)
无锡锡惠公园旅游景区	Wuxi Xihui Park Tourist Attraction (Jiangsu)
芜湖鸠兹风景区	Wuhu Jiuzi Scenic Area (Anhui)
芜湖市马仁奇峰森林风景旅游区	Maren Grotesque Peak Forest Scenic Area in Wuhu (Anhui)
芜湖市王稼祥纪念园	Wang Jiaxiang Memorial Garden in Wuhu (Anhui)
芜湖市赭山风景区	Wuhu Zheshan Mountain Scenic Area (Zheshan Park, Guangji Temple, Jiuhua Square) (Anhui)
芜湖天井山国家森林公园	Tianjing Mountain National Forest Park in Wuhu (Anhui)
芜湖丫山风景区	Yashan Mountain Scenic Area in Wuhu (Anhui)
吴桥杂技大世界	Wuqiao Acrobatic Grand World (Hebei)
梧州市骑楼城·龙母庙景区	Qilou Street Town-Longmu Temple Scenic Area in Wuzhou; Wuzhou Arcade City-Longmu Temple Scenic Area (Guangxi)
五彩大地观光休闲旅游区	Colorful Farmland Sightseeing and Leisure Tourist Area (He'nan)
五龙洞国家森林公园	Wulongdong National Forest Park (He'nan)
五龙口风景名胜区	Wulongkou Scenic Area (He'nan)
五女峰国家森林公园	Wunüfeng (Peak) National Forest Park (Jilin)
武安东山文化博艺园	Dongshan Cultural Fair Park in Handan (Hebei)
武昌首义文化旅游区	Wuchang Shouyi Cultural Tourist Area (Hubei)
武当山静乐宫景区	Jingle Palace Scenic Area of Wudang Mountain (Hubei)
武汉东湖风景区	Wuhan East Lake Scenic Area (Hubei)
武汉革命博物馆	Wuhan Revolutionary Museum (Hubei)
武汉归元禅寺	Wuhan Guiyuan Temple (Hubei)

武汉黄陂木兰山	Huangpi Mulan Mountain in Wuhan (Hubei)
武汉科技馆	Wuhan Science and Technology Museum (Hubei)
武汉木兰清凉寨旅游区	Mulan Qingliangzhai Tourist Area in Wuhan; Mulan Cool and Refreshing Village Resort in Wuhan (Hubei)
武汉木兰天池旅游区	Tianchi Scenic Area of Mulan Mountain in Wuhan (Hubei)
武汉木兰云雾山	Mulan Yunwu Mountain in Wuhan; Cloud-Capped Mountain in Wuhan (Hubei)
武汉市博物馆	Wuhan Museum (Hubei)
武山水帘洞旅游景区	Tourist Attraction of Wushan Water Curtain Cave (Gansu)
武威沙漠公园	Wuwei Desert Park (Gansu)
武威神州荒漠野生动物园	Shenzhou Desert Wildlife Park in Wuwei (Gansu)
武威市雷台公园	Leitai Park of Wuwei (Gansu)
武威文庙	Wuwei Confucius Temple (Gansu)
武陟县嘉应观景区	Jiaying Temple Scenic Area of Wuzhi County; Taoist Temple of Good Response of Wuzhi County (He'nan)
舞阳河风景名胜区	Wuyang River Scenic Area (Guizhou)
婺源李坑旅游景区	Wuyuan Likeng Tourist Attraction (Jiangxi)
婺源汪口旅游区	Wuyuan Wangkou Tourist Area (Jiangxi)
婺源文公山景区	Wuyuan Wengong Mountain Scenic Area (Jiangxi)
婺源县大鄣山卧龙谷旅游区	Wolong Valley Tourist Area of Dazhang Mountain in Wuyuan County; Lying-Dragon Valley Tourist Area of Wuyuan Dazhang Mountain (Jiangxi)
婺源县灵岩洞旅游区	Lingyan (Karst) Cave Tourist Attraction of Wuyuan County (Jiangxi)
婺源鸳鸯湖景区	Wuyuan Yuanyang Lake Scenic Area (Jiangxi)
西安白鹿原影视城景区	Bailuyuan Film and Television City; White Deer Plain Film and Television City (Shaanxi)
西安半坡博物馆	Banpo Museum in Xi'an (Shaanxi)

西安碑林博物馆	Xi'an Beilin Museum; Forest of Stone Steles Museum in Xi'an (Shaanxi)
西安博物院	Xi'an Museum (Shaanxi)
西安浐灞国家湿地公园	Xi'an Chanba National Wetland Park (Shaanxi)
西安城墙景区	Xi'an City Wall Scenic Area (Shaanxi)
西安大唐西市	Xi'an Datang West City (Shaanxi)
西安沣东现代都市农业示范园[博览园]	Fengdong Modern Urban Agriculture Demonstration Park in Xi'an (Shaanxi)
西安关中民俗艺术博物院	Guanzhong Folk Art Museum in Xi'an (Shaanxi)
西安汉城湖国家水利风景区	National Water Conservancy Scenic Area of Hancheng Lake in Xi'an (Shaanxi)
西安金龙峡风景区	Jinlong Gorge Scenic Area in Xi'an (Shaanxi)
西安楼观台	Xi'an Louguantai Daoist Temple (Shaanxi)
西安楼观中国道文化展示区	Chinese Taoism Culture Exhibition Area of Xi'an Louguan Town (Shaanxi)
西安世博园	Xi'an World Expo Garden (Shaanxi)
西安市黑河旅游景区	Heihe River Tourist Area in Xi'an (Shaanxi)
西安市王顺山景区	Wangshun Mountain Scenic Area in Xi'an (Shaanxi)
西安太平国家森林公园	Xi'an Taiping National Forest Park (Shaanxi)
西北农林科技大学博览园	Expo Park of Northwest Agriculture and Forestry University (Shaanxi)
西递古民居景区	Xidi Ancient Residential Scenic Area (Anhui)
西汉酒泉胜迹	Jiuquan Historical Site of the Western Han Dynasty (Gansu)
西和晚霞湖景区	Xihe Sunset Lake Scenic Area (Gansu)
西九华山风景区	West Jiuhua Mountain Scenic Area (He'nan)
西双版纳傣族园	Xishuangbanna Dai Nationality Garden (Yunnan)
西双版纳热带花卉园	Xishuangbanna Tropical Flower Garden (Yunnan)
西双版纳望天树景区	Wangtian Tree Scenic Area in Xishuang Banna; Wantianshu Scenic Area in Xishuang Banna (Yunnan)

西双版纳野象谷景区	Wild Elephant Valley Scenic Area in Xishuangbanna (Yunnan)
西双版纳原始森林公园	Xishuangbanna Virgin Forest Park (Yunnan)
西狭颂风景名胜区	Xixia Song Scenic Spot (Gansu)
西夏王陵	Western Xia Imperial Tombs; Mausoleum of Western Xia Dynasty (Ningxia)
西藏博物馆	Tibet Museum (Tibet)
浠水三角山旅游风景区	Xishui Triangle Mountain Scenic Area (Hubei)
淅川县香严寺景区	Xiangyan Temple Scenic Area of Xichuan County (He'nan)
锡林郭勒盟多伦湖旅游区	Duolun Lake Tourist Area in Xilingol League (Inner Mongolia)
锡林浩特贝子庙旅游景区	Xilinhot Beizi Temple Scenic Area (Inner Mongolia)
厦门北辰山风景区	Xiamen Beichen Mountain Scenic Area (Fujian)
厦门梵天寺旅游景区	Xiamen Fantian Temple Tourist Attraction (Fujian)
厦门海沧大桥旅游区	Xiamen Haicang Bridge Tourist Area (Fujian)
厦门集美嘉庚公园	Jimei Jiageng Park in Xiamen (Fujian)
厦门日月谷温泉主题公园	Riyuegu Hot Springs Theme Park in Xiamen; Hot Spring Theme Park of Sun-Moon Valley in Xiamen (Fujian)
厦门园林植物园	Xiamen Botanical Garden (Fujian)
仙人台风景区	Xianren Tai Scenic Spot; Immortal Summit Scenic Spot (Liaoning, Hubei)
咸阳汉阳陵博物馆	Hanyang Mausoleum Museum in Xianyang (Shaanxi)
香山公园风景区	Xiangshan Park Scenic Area (Beijing)
香溪洞风景区	Xiangxi Cave Scenic Area (Shaanxi)
湘潭彭德怀纪念馆	Peng Dehuai Memorial Hall in Xiangtan (Hu'nan)
湘潭市湘乡东山书院旅游区	Dongshan Academy Tourist Area of Xiangxiang County in Xiangtan (Hu'nan)
湘西州凤凰奇梁洞景区	Qiliang Cave Scenic Spot of Phoenix Ancient Town in Xiangxi (Hu'nan)

湘西州芙蓉镇景区	Furong Town Scenic Area in Xiangxi; Hibiscus Town Scenic Area in Xiangxi (Hu'nan)
湘西州猛洞河漂流景区	Mengdong River Rafting Scenic Area in Xiangxi (Hu'nan)
襄阳凤凰温泉旅游区	Xiangyang Phoenix Hot Spring Resort (Hubei)
消灾寺景区	Xiaozai Temple Scenic Area; Disaster Avoidance Temple Scenic Area (Shaanxi)
萧县皇藏峪国家森林公园	Huangcangyu National Forest Park of Xiaoxian County; Emperor Hidden Valley-National Forest Park of Xiaoxian County (Anhui)
小汤山现代农业示范园区	Xiaotangshan Modern Agricultural Science Demonstration Park; Xiaotangshan Modern Agricultural Area (Beijing)
小雁塔景区	Xiaoyan Pagoda Scenic Area (Shaanxi)
孝感双峰山旅游度假	Shuangfeng Mountain Tourism Resort in Xiaogan (Hubei)
蟹岛绿色生态农庄	Crab Island Green Eco-farm (Beijing)
辛亥革命武昌起义纪念馆	Memorial Museum of Wuchang Uprising of 1911 Revolution (Hubei)
新昌大佛寺风景名胜区	Dafo Temple Scenic Area of Xinchang County; Grand Buddha Temple Scenic Area of Xinchang County (Zhejiang)
新疆民街民俗博物馆	Xinjiang Folk Street and Custom Museum (Xinjiang)
新疆维吾尔自治区博物馆	Museum of Xinjiang Uyghur Autonomous Region (Xinjiang)
新密市红石林景区	Red Stone Forest Scenic Spot of Xinmi (He'nan)
新宁崀山旅游区	Xinning Langshan Mountain Tourist Area (Hu'nan)
新乡京华园景区	Jinghua Garden Scenic Area in Xinxiang (He'nan)
新余市仙女湖风景旅游区	Fairy Lake Tourist Area in Xinyu; Fairy Lake Scenic Resort in Xinyu (Jiangxi)

新郑黄帝故里	Huangdi's Hometown in Xinzheng; Yellow Emperor's Hometown in Xinzheng (He'nan)
兴隆热带植物园	Xinglong Tropical Botanical Garden (Hai'nan)
兴隆山国家级自然保护区	Xinglong Mountain National Nature Reserve (Gansu)
兴平马嵬驿民俗文化体验园	Maweiyi Folk Culture Experience Park in Xingping; Folk Culture Experience Park of Ancien Mawei Posthouse in Xingping (Shaanxi)
兴业鹿峰山风景区	Lufeng Mountain Scenic Area of Xingye County (Guangxi)
兴义市马岭河峡谷旅游景区	Maling River Canyon Scenic Area of Xingyi County (Guizhou)
兴义市万峰林景区	Wanfeng Peak Forest Scenic Area in Xingyi; Scenic Area of Ten Thousand Peaks Scenic Area in Xingyi (Guizhou)
邢台扁鹊庙	Xingtai Bianque Temple (Hebei)
邢台大峡谷景区	Xingtai Grand Canyon Scenic Area (Hebei)
邢台丰乐园景区	Xingtai Fengle Garden Scenic Area (Hebei)
邢台崆山白云洞	Xingtai White Cloud Cave of Kongshan Mountain (Hebei)
邢台前南峪生态观光旅游区	Qiannanyu Ecological Tourist Area in Xingtai (Hebei)
邢台天河山	Xingtai Tianhe Mountain (Chinese Love Mountain) (Hebei)
邢台峡谷群景区	Xingtai Canyon Group Scenic Area (Hebei)
邢台云梦山景区	Xingtai Yunmeng Mountain Scenic Area (Hebei)
休宁县齐云山风景名胜区	Qiyun Mountain Scenic Area in Xiuning County (Anhui)
盱眙黄花塘新四军军部纪念馆	Huanghuatang Memorial Hall of the New Fourth Army Headquarters in Xuyi County (Jiangsu)
盱眙明祖陵旅游景区	Ming Ancestors' Mausoleum Tourist Attraction in Xuyi (Jiangsu)
盱眙县铁山寺国家森林公园	Tieshan Temple National Forest Park of Xuyi County (Jiangsu)

须弥山石窟风景名胜区	Grottoes Scenic Area of Xumi Mountain (Ningxia)
徐州淮海战役烈士纪念塔园林	Huaihai Campaign Martyrs Memorial Monument Park in Xuzhou (Jiangsu)
徐州市云龙湖风景区	Yunlong Lake Scenic Area in Xuzhou (Jiangsu)
许昌灞陵桥景区	Xuchang Baling Bridge Scenic Area (He'nan)
玄武湖旅游景区	Xuanwu Lake Tourist Attraction (Jiangsu)
循化撒拉族绿色家园	Salar Nationality Green Home of Xunhua County (Qinghai)
雅鲁藏布大峡谷旅游景区	Tourist Area of Yarlong Tsangpo Grand Canyon (Tibet)
亚布力滑雪旅游度假区	Yabuli Skiing Holiday Resort (Heilongjiang)
亚龙湾国家旅游度假区	Yalong Bay National Tourism Resort (Hai'nan)
烟台南山旅游区	Yantai Nanshan Mountain Tourist Area; Yantai Southern Mountain Tourist Area (Shandong)
烟台市牟氏庄园	Mou Family Manor in Yantai (Shandong)
烟台天街广场·金沙滩景区	Yantai Paradise Walking Square—Golden Sand Beach Scenic Area (Shandong)
烟台张裕酒文化博物馆	Yantai Changyu Wine Culture Museum (Shandong)
焉支山森林公园	Yanzhi Mountain Forest Park (Gansu)
鄢陵国家花木博览园	Yanling National Flower and Wood Expo Garden (He'nan)
延安宝塔山旅游景区	Yan'an Baota Mountain Tourist Area (Shaanxi)
延安革命纪念馆	Yan'an Revolutionary Memorial Hall (Shaanxi)
延安枣园革命旧址	Yan'an Zaoyuan Revolutionary Site (Shaanxi)
延川黄河乾坤湾景区	Yanchuan Qiankun Bend of the Yellow River Scenic Area (Shaanxi)
延庆百里山水画廊景区	Scenic Area of Yanqing Baili Landscape Gallery (Beijing)
沿河乌江山峡风景名胜区	Wujiang River Gorge Scenic Area of Yanhe County (Guizhou)
盐城大纵湖旅游景区	Dazong Lake Tourist Area in Yancheng (Jiangsu)
盐城新四军纪念馆	Memorial Hall of the New Fourth Army in Yancheng (Jiangsu)

雁栖湖旅游区	Yanqi Lake Tourist Area (Beijing)
燕山塔陵旅游景区	Tourist Attraction of Tower-Shaped Mausoleum at Yanshan Mountain (Hebei)
扬州博物馆	Yangzhou Museum & China Block Printing Museum (Jiangsu)
扬州大明寺	Yangzhou Daming Temple (Jiangsu)
扬州何园旅游景区	Ho Family Garden Tourist Attraction (Jiangsu)
扬州京华城休闲旅游区	Jinghua City Leisure Tourist Area in Yangzhou (Jiangsu)
扬州市个园	Yangzhou Geyuan Garden (Jiangsu)
阳泉翠枫山自然风景区	Cuifeng Mountain Natural Scenic Area (Shanxi)
阳新仙岛湖生态旅游风景区	Yangxin Xiandao Lake Ecological Tourism Scenic Area (Hubei)
杨凌农林博览园	Yangling Agriculture and Forestry Expo Park (Shaanxi)
洋县华阳景区	Huayang Scenic Area of Yangxian County (Shaanxi)
洋县朱鹮梨园景区	Crested Ibis and Pear Orchard Scenic Spot of Yangxian County (Shaanxi)
养马岛旅游度假区	Yangma Island Tourist Resort (Shandong)
冶力关风景区	Yeli Pass Scenic Area (Gansu)
叶剑英故居	Ye Jianying's Former Residence (Guangdong)
伊川县二程文化园	Ercheng Cultural Park of Yichuan County (He'nan)
伊春市嘉荫恐龙国家地质公园	Jiayin Dinosaur National Geopark in Yichun (Heilongjiang)
伊春市小兴安岭桃山景区	Taoshan Scenic Area of Lesser Khingan Mountains in Yichun (Heilongjiang)
伊春五营国家森林公园	Wuying National Forest Park in Yichun (Heilongjiang)
沂山风景区	Yishan Mountain Scenic Area (Shandong)
沂水东方瑞海国际温泉度假村	Oriental Rihigh International Hot Spring Holiday Resort of Yishui County (Shandong)
沂水天然地下画廊	Yishui Natural Underground Gallery (Shandong)
宜宾李庄古镇	Lizhuang Ancient Town in Yibin (Sichuan)

宜宾蜀南竹海风景名胜区	Shu'nan Zhuhai Scenic Area in Yibin; Bamboo Sea Scenic Area of South Sichuan in Yibin (Sichuan)
宜昌白马洞旅游	White Horse Cave Tourist Attraction in Yichang (Hubei)
宜昌百里荒草原风景区	Alpine Grassland Tourist Area of Baili Huang in Yichang (Hubei)
宜昌柴埠溪峡谷风景区	Chaibuxi Canyon Scenic Area in Yichang (Hubei)
宜昌车溪民俗风景区	Chexi Folk Custom Scenic Area in Yichang (Hubei)
宜昌九畹溪风景区	Jiuwan Stream Scenic Area in Yichang (Hubei)
宜昌清江画廊度假风景区	Qingjiang River Gallery Scenic Resort in Yichang (Hubei)
宜昌三峡石牌要塞旅游区	Stone Fortress Scenic Area of The Three Gorges in Yichang (Hubei)
宜昌三游洞风景区	Sanyou Cave Scenic Area in Yichang; Three Visitors Cave Scenic Area in Yichang (Hubei)
宜昌西陵峡口风景名胜区	Xiling Gorge Scenic Area in Yichang (Hubei)
宜昌晓峰风景区	Xiaofeng Peak Scenic Area in Yichang (Hubei)
宜春靖安中部梦幻城	Jing'an Central Dreamland in Yichun (Jiangxi)
宜春明月山温泉风景名胜区	Mingyue Mountain Hot Spring Scenic Spot in Yichun; Hot Spring Scenic Spot of the Clear Moon Mountain in Yichun (Jiangxi)
宜良九乡风景名胜区	Yiliang Jiuxiang Scenic Area (Yunnan)
宜兴善卷洞风景区	Shanjuan Cave Scenic Area in Yixing (Jiangsu)
宜兴竹海风景区	Bamboo Sea Scenic Area in Yixing (Jiangsu)
义乌中国国际商贸城购物旅游区	Yiwu International Trade City Tourist Area; Yiwu International Trade Center (Zhejiang)
益阳奥林匹克公园	Yiyang Olympic Sports Park (Hu'nan)
益阳山乡巨变第一村旅游区	Scenic Area of Great Changes in a Mountain Village (Hu'nan)
益阳市安化茶马古道风景区	Ancient Tea-Horse Road Scenic Area of Anhua County in Yiyang (Hu'nan)
银山塔林风景区	Yinshan Talin Scenic Area (Beijing)

英山县桃花冲风景区	Taohua Chong Scenic Area of Yingshan County; Peach Blossom Valley Scenic Area of Yingshan County (Hubei)
英山县吴家山[大别山主峰]风景区	Yingshan Wujia Mountain (Main Peak of Dabie Mountain) Scenic Area in Huanggang (Hubei)
颍上县八里河风景区	Bali River Scenic Area of Yingshang County (Anhui)
颍上县迪沟生态旅游风景区	Yingshang Digou Ecotourism Scenic Area in Fuyang (Anhui)
应县木塔景区	Yingxian Wooden Pagoda Scenic Area in Shanxi (Shanxi)
永安桃源洞旅游区	Yong'an Taoyuan Cave Tourist Area (Fujian)
永城市芒砀山文物旅游区	Mangdang Mountain Heritage Tourism Area in Yongcheng (He'nan)
永春牛姆林生态旅游区	Yongchun Niumulin Ecological Tourism Area (Fujian)
永吉北大湖滑雪场	Yongji Beidahu Ski Resort/Area (Jilin)
永济普救寺旅游区	Pujiu Temple Tourist Area in Yongji (Shanxi)
永济五老峰风景名胜区	Yongji Wulaofeng (Five Peaks) Scenic Area in Yuncheng (Shanxi)
永嘉楠溪江风景区	Yongjia Nanxi River Scenic Area (Zhejiang)
永泰青云山风景名胜区	Qingyun Mountain Scenic Spot of Yongtai County (Fujian)
永州浯溪碑林景区	Wuxi Steles Forest Scenic Area in Yongzhou (Hu'nan)
酉阳龚滩古镇	Youyang Gongtan Ancient Town (Chongqing)
酉阳龙潭古镇景区	Longtan Ancient Town Scenic Area of Youyang County (Chongqing)
榆次常家庄园	Chang Family Compound in Yuci County; Chang Family Manor in Yuci County (Shanxi)
榆林佳县白云山景区	Jiaxian Baiyun Mountain Scenic Area in Yulin (Shaanxi)
榆林神木二郎山景区	Shenmu Erlang Mountain Scenic Area in Yulin (Shaanxi)

榆林神木红碱淖景区	Shenmu Hongjiannao Lake Scenic Area in Yulin; Hongjian Lake Wetland Scenic Area in Yulin (Shaanxi)
榆阳黑龙潭景区	Yuyang Black Dragon Pool Scenic Area (Shaanxi)
玉溪抚仙湖风景区	Yuxi Fuxian Lake Scenic Area (Yunnan)
玉溪汇龙生态园	Huilong Ecological Park in Yuxi (Yunnan)
玉溪映月潭休闲文化中心	Yingyue Lake Leisure Culture Center in Yuxi; Leisure Culture Center of Moon Image Lake in Yuxi (Yunnan)
玉渊潭公园	Yuyuantan Park; Yuyuan Pond Park (Beijing)
豫西百草园景区	Hundred Herbs Garden Scenic Area in Western He'nan (He'nan)
豫西大峡谷风景区	Grand Canyon of Western-He'nan Scenic Area (He'nan)
元大都城垣遗址公园	Capital City Wall Site Park of Yuan Dynasty (Beijing)
圆明园遗址公园	Yuanmingyuan Relic Park (Beijing)
远安鸣凤山风景区	Yuan'an Mingfeng Mountain Scenic Area (Hubei)
岳西明堂山风景区	Mingtang Mountain Scenic Area of Yuexi County (Anhui)
岳西县天峡风景区	Tianxia Valley Scenic Area of Yuexi County (Anhui)
岳阳市任弼时纪念馆	Ren Bishi Memorial Hall in Yueyang (Hu'nan)
岳阳市张谷英旅游景区	Zhang Guying Village Tourist Area in Yueyang (Hu'nan)
云和湖仙宫景区	Yunhe Lake—Fairy Palace Scenic Area (Zhejiang)
云和梯田景区	Yunhe Terrace Scenic Area (Zhejiang)
郧西五龙河旅游区	Yunxi Wulong River Tourist Area (Hubei)
郧县九龙瀑旅游区	Shiyan Jiulong Waterfall Tourist Spot of Yunxian County; Yunxian Nine Dragons Waterfall (Hubei)
运城市解州关帝庙旅游区	Xiezhou Guan Yu Temple Tourist Area in Yuncheng (Shanxi)

运城市芮城县永乐宫旅游区	Ruicheng Yongle Palace Tourist Area in Yuncheng (Shanxi)
枣阳汉城影视基地	Hancheng Film and Television Base in Zaoyang; Zaoyang Film and Television Base of Ancient Han City (Hubei)
枣庄抱犊崮国家森林公园	Baodugu National Forest Park in Zaozhuang (Shandong)
扎兰屯吊桥景区	Zhalantun Suspension Bridge Scenic Area (Inner Mongolia)
柞水溶洞景区	Zhashui Karst Cave Scenic Area (Shaanxi)
沾益县珠江源旅游景区	Pearl River Source Tourist Attraction of Zhanyi County (Yunnan)
湛江蓝月湾温泉度假邨	Lanyuewan Hot Spring Holiday Resort in Zhanjiang (Guangdong)
湛江市湖光岩风景名胜区	Zhanjiang Huguangyan Scenic Area; Huguangyan National Scenic Area in Zhanjiang (Guangdong)
张家港市凤凰山风景区	Fenghuang (Phoenix) Mountain Scenic Area in Zhangjiagang (Jiangsu)
张家界宝峰湖风景名胜区	Zhangjiajie Baofeng Lake Scenic Area (Hu'nan)
张家界大峡谷风景区	Zhangjiajie Grand Canyon Scenic Area (Hu'nan)
张家界黄龙洞旅游区	Zhangjiajie Huanglong Cave Tourist Area; Yellow Dragon Cave Tourist Area of Zhangjiajie (Hu'nan)
张家界江垭温泉度假村	Zhangjiajie Jiangya Hot Spring Resort (Hu'nan)
张家界龙王洞旅游区	Dragon King Cave Tourist Area of Zhangjiajie (Hu'nan)
张家界茅岩河—九天洞旅游区	Zhangjiajie Maoyan River-Jiutian Cave Tourist Area (Hu'nan)
张家界市大庸府城	Zhangjiajie Dayongfu City (Hu'nan)
张家界市贺龙纪念馆	He Long Memorial Hall in Zhangjiajie (Hu'nan)
张家界土家风情园	Zhangjiajie Tujia Folk Customs Park (Hu'nan)
张家界万福温泉国际旅游度假区	Wanfu Hot Spring International Tourism Resort of Zhangjiajie (Hu'nan)

张家口市沽源县天鹅湖景区	Swan Lake Scenic Area in Zhangjiakou (Hebei)
张家口市下花园鸡鸣山景区	Jiming Mountain Scenic Area in Zhangjiakou (Hebei)
张良庙—紫柏山风景名胜区	Zhangliang Temple—Zibai Mountain Scenic Area in Hanzhong (Shaanxi)
张掖大佛寺	Zhangye Buddhist Temple (Gansu)
张掖丹霞国家地质公园	Zhangye Danxia National Geological Park (Gansu)
张裕爱菲堡国际酒庄	Chateau Changyu AFIP Global (Beijing)
漳县贵清山·遮阳山旅游风景区	Guiqing Mountain—Zheyang Mountain Tourist Area of Zhangxian County (Gansu)
漳州平和三平风景区	Sanping Scenic Resort of Pinghe County in Zhangzhou (Fujian)
障山大峡谷自然保护区	Zhangshan Grand Canyon Nature Reserve (Anhui)
嶂石岩风景区	Zhangshiyan Tourism Scenic Area (Hebei)
赵县赵州桥	Zhaozhou Bridge of Zhaoxian County (Hebei)
肇庆市星湖风景名胜区	Zhaoqing Star Lake Scenic Area; Xinghu Lake Scenic Area in Zhaoqing (Guangdong)
震源映秀	Memorial Site of Earthquake Epicenter Yingxiu (Sichuan)
镇安塔云山景区	Zhen'an Tayun Mountain Scenic Area (Shaanxi)
镇江茅山风景区	Maoshan Mountain Scenic Area in Zhenjiang (Jiangsu)
镇江市金山公园	Zhenjiang Jinshan Hill Park (Jiangsu)
镇赉县莫莫格国家自然保护区	Momoge National Nature Reserve of Zhenhai County (Jilin)
正定隆兴寺	Longxing Temple in Zhengding (Hebei)
正定隆兴寺旅游景区	Zhengding Longxing Temple Tourist Attraction (Hebei)
郑州绿博园	Zhengzhou Green Expo Garden (He'nan)
芷江抗战受降纪念旧址	Anti-Japanese War Victory and Surrender Acceptance Museum; Former Site of Japanese Surrender upon the Victory in the War of Resistance against Japan (Hu'nan)

中国地质大学逸夫博物馆	Yifu Museum of China University of Geosciences (Heilongjiang)
中国海盐博物馆	China Sea-Salt Museum (Jiangsu)
中国翰园碑林	China Hanyuan Stele Forest Park (He'nan)
中国航海博物馆	China Maritime Museum (Shanghai)
中国航空博物馆	China Aviation Museum (Beijing)
中国科学技术馆	China Science and Technology Museum (Beijing)
中国科学院武汉植物园	Wuhan Botanical Garden of Chinese Academy of Sciences (Hubei)
中国人民抗日战争纪念馆	Museum of the War of Chinese People's Resistance Against Japanese Aggression (Beijing)
中国紫檀博物馆	China Red Sandalwood Museum (Beijing)
中华黄河坛旅游区	Tourist Area of Chinese Yellow River Altar (Ningxia)
中华回乡文化园	Park of Customs and Culture in the Homeland of Chinese Hui People (Ningxia)
中华麋鹿园	Chinese Milu Park (Jiangsu)
中华民族园	Chinese Ethnic Culture Park (Beijing)
中华石鼓园景区	Chinese Shigu Garden Scenic Area; Chinese Stone Drum Garden Scenic Area (Shaanxi)
中山公园	Zhongshan Park (Beijing)
中山詹园旅游景区	Zhongshan Zhanyuan Park Tourist Attraction (Guangdong)
中信国安第一城	CITIC Guoan Grand Epoch City (Hebei)
中央广播电视塔	China Central Radio and Television Tower (Beijing)
忠县石宝寨	Shibao Mountain Fastness of Zhongxian County (Chongqing)
终南山旅游景区	Zhongnan Mountain Tourist Attraction (Shaanxi)
钟祥黄仙洞	Zhongxiang Huangxian Cave; Zhongxiang Yellow Fairy (Hubei)
钟祥明显陵旅游景区	Xianling Tomb of the Ming Dynasty in Zhongxiang (Hubei)
舟山桃花岛	Zhoushan Peach Blossom Island (Zhejiang)

周恩来邓颖超纪念馆	Memorial Hall of Zhou Enlai and Deng Yingchao (Tianjin)
周公庙风景名胜区	Zhougong Temple Scenic Area (Shaanxi)
周口店龙骨山	Dragon Bone Hill of Zhoukoudian (Beijing)
周口店遗址博物馆	Zhoukoudian Site Museum; Peking Man Museum; Peking Man Site at Zhoukoudian (Beijing)
周至水街沙沙河景区	Zhouzhi Water Street-Shasha River Scenic Area (Shaanxi)
周祖陵森林公园	Zhouzu Ling National Forest Park (Gansu)
朱家尖大青山旅游景区	Zhujiajian Daqing Mountain Tourist Area (Zhejiang)
朱家角古镇旅游区	Zhujiajiao Ancient Town Tourist Area (Shanghai)
朱雀国家森林公园	Zhuque National Forest Park (Shaanxi)
珠海市农科奇观景区	Marvelous Spectacle in Agriculture Science in Zhuhai (Guangdong)
珠海市圆明新园	Zhuhai New Yuanming Palace; Zhuhai New Yuanmingyuan Park (Guangdong)
珠穆朗玛峰国家级自然保护区	National Nature Reserve of Mount Qomolangma (Tibet)
株洲茶陵云阳山景区	Chaling Yunyang Mountain Scenic Area in Zhuzhou (Hu'nan)
株洲神农谷国家森林公园	Shennong Valley National Forest Park in Zhuzhou (Hu'nan)
株洲市方特欢乐世界	Fantawild Adventure Amusement Park in Zhuzhou (Hu'nan)
株洲市神农城炎帝文化主题公园	Yandi Cultural Theme Park of Shengnong City in Zhuzhou (Hu'nan)
株洲炎帝陵旅游区	Yandi Mausoleum Scenic Area in Zhuzhou; Emperor Yan's Mausoleum Scenic Area in Zhuzhou (Hu'nan)
诸城常山文化博物苑	Museum of Changshan Mountain Culture of Zhucheng (Shandong)
诸城恐龙博物馆	Zhucheng Dinosaur Museum (Shandong)

诸城恐龙文化旅游区	Zhucheng Dinosaur Culture Tourist Area (Shandong)
诸城潍河国家水利风景区[诸城潍河公园]	Weihe National Water Conservancy Scenic Area of Zhucheng; Zhucheng Weihe River Park (Shandong)
庄浪云崖寺旅游景区	Zhuanglang Yunya Temple Tourist Attraction (Gansu)
卓尼县大峪沟景区	Dayugou Valley Scenic Area of Zhuoni County (Gansu)
梓潼七曲山大庙	Qiqu Mountain Temple of Zitong County (Sichuan)
梓潼七曲山风景区	Zitong Qiqu Mountain Scenic Area (Sichuan)
紫云格凸河风景名胜区	Getu River Scenic Area of Ziyun County (Guizhou)
紫竹院公园	Zizhuyuan Park; Purple Bamboo Park (Beijing)
自贡恐龙博物馆	Zigong Dinosaur Museum (Sichuan)
邹城孟府孟庙景区	Zoucheng Meng Mansion and Meng Temple Scenic Area (Shandong)
邹城市峄山风景旅游区	Zoucheng Yishan Mountain Scenic Area (Shandong)
遵化万佛园旅游景区	Tourist Attraction of Zunhua Ten-Thousand Buddha Park (Hebei)

附录二　国家 AAAAA 级旅游景区

阿坝藏族羌族自治州九寨沟旅游景区	Jiuzhaigou Tourist Area in Aba Prefecture (Sichuan)
阿坝州黄龙景区	Huanglong Scenic Area in Aba Prefecture (Sichuan)
阿坝州汶川特别旅游区	Wenchuan Special Tourist Area in Aba Prefecture (Sichuan)
阿尔山·柴河旅游景区	Mount Arxan and Chaihe River Scenic Area (Inner Mongolia)
阿拉善盟胡杨林旅游区	Huyanglin Tourist Area of Alxa League (Inner Mongolia)
阿勒泰地区富蕴可可托海景区	Ocoa Sea Breeze Scenic Area in Altay Préfecture (Xinjiang)
阿勒泰地区喀纳斯景区	Kanas Scenic Area in Altay Autonomous Prefecture (Xinjiang)
阿咪东索风景区	Ami Dongsuo Scenic Area (Qinghai)
安庆市天柱山风景区	Mount Tianzhu Scenic Spot in Anqing; Tianzhu Mountain Scenic Area in Anqing (Anhui)
安顺市黄果树大瀑布景区	Anshun Huangguoshu Waterfall Scenic Area (Guizhou)
安顺市龙宫景区	Anshun Longgong National Park Scenic Area (Guizhou)
安图长白山风景区	Antu Changbai Mountain Scenic Area (Jilin)
安阳殷墟景区	Anyang Yinxu Scenic Area (He'nan)
鞍山市千山景区	Qianshan Mountain Scenic Area in Anshan (Liaoning)
八达岭风景区	Badaling Scenic Area (Beijing)
巴音郭楞蒙古自治州博斯腾湖景区	Bosten Lake Scenic Area in Bayingolin Mongolian Autonomous Prefecture (Xinjiang)

巴音郭楞州巴音布鲁克景区	Bayinbluk Grassland Scenic Area in Bayingol (Xinjiang)
百色起义纪念园风景区	Scenic Area of Baise Uprising Memorial Park (Guangxi)
宝鸡市法门寺佛文化景区	Famen Temple Buddhist Culture Scenic Area in Baoji; Buddhist Culture Scenic Spot of Famen Temple in Baoji (Shaanxi)
宝鸡市太白山旅游景区	Taibai Mountain Scenic Spot in Baoji (Shaanxi)
保定市安新白洋淀景区	Anxin Baiyang Lake Scenic Area in Baoding (Hebei)
保定市白石山景区	Baishishan Scenic Spot in Baoding; Whitestone Mountain Scenic Area in Baoding (Hebei)
保定市清西陵景区	Baoding West Qing Tombs Scenic Spot (Hebei)
保山市腾冲火山热海旅游区	Tengchong Volcano & Hot Sea Tourism Area in Baoshan (Yunnan)
北海涠洲岛南湾鳄鱼山景区	Nanwan Crocodile Mountain Scenic Area of Weizhou Island Beihai (Guangxi)
北京奥林匹克公园	Beijing Olympic Park; Beijing Olympic Sport Park
本溪市本溪水洞景区	Benxi Water Cave Scenic Area (Liaoning)
毕节市百里杜鹃景区	Baili Azalea Scenic Area in Bijie (Guizhou)
毕节市织金洞景区	Zhijin Cave Scenic Area in Bijie (Guizhou)
槟榔谷黎苗文化旅游区	Binglang Valley and Li & Miao Cultural Heritage Park in Hai'nan; Betelnut Valley and Li & Miao Cultural Tourist Area (Hai'nan)
炳灵寺世界文化遗产旅游区	Tourist Area of Bingling Temple World Cultural Heritage (Gansu)
长春净月潭景区	Jingyuetan Scenic Area in Changchun (Jilin)
长春市长影世纪城	Changchun Movie Wonderland; Changying Century City in Changchun (Jilin)
长春市世界雕塑公园旅游景区	Changchun World Sculpture Park (Jilin)
长春市伪满皇宫博物院	Museum of the Imperial Palace of Manchukuo in Changchun (Jilin)

长江采石矶文化生态旅游区	Caishiji Cultural and Ecotourism Area of the Yangtze River (Anhui)
长沙市花明楼景区	Huaminglou Scenic Area in Changsha (Hu'nan)
长沙市岳麓山·橘子洲旅游区	Changsha Yuelu Mountain and Orange Island Tourist Area (Hu'nan)
长治市壶关太行山大峡谷八泉峡景区	Baquan Gorge Scenic Area of Huguan Taihang Mountain Grand Canyon of Changzhi (Shanxi)
常德桃花源旅游区	Peach Bloom Garden Tourist Area in Changde (Hu'nan)
常州市环球恐龙城休闲旅游区	Changzhou Universal Dinosaur City (Jiangsu)
常州市天目湖景区	Tianmu Lake Scenic Area in Changzhou (Jiangsu)
常州市中国春秋淹城旅游区	Chunqiu Yancheng Tourist Area in Changzhou; China Spring and Autumn Yancheng Scenic Area in Changzhou (Jiangsu)
郴州市东江湖旅游区	Dongjiang Lake Tourist Area in Chengzhou (Hu'nan)
成都市安仁古镇景区	Anren Ancient Town Scenic Area in Chendgu (Sichuan)
成都市青城山—都江堰旅游景区	Qingcheng Mountain and Dujiangyan Tourist Scenic Spot in Chengdu (Sichuan)
承德避暑山庄及周围寺庙景区	Chengde Mountain (Summer) Resort and the Surrounding Temples (Hebei)
池州市九华山风景区	Chizhou Mount Jiuhua Scenic Area (Anhui)
赤峰市阿斯哈图石阵旅游区	Asihatu Stone Forest in Chifeng of Inner Mongolia; Asihatu Shilin in Chifeng (Inner Mongolia)
赤水丹霞旅游区	Chishui Danxia Tourist Area (Guizhou)
崇左市德天跨国瀑布景区	Detian Transnational Waterfall Scenic Spot in Chongzuo; Detian Cross-border Waterfall in Chongzuo (Guangxi)
大报恩寺琉璃宝塔	Glazed Pagoda of Dabao'en Temple; Porcelain Tower of Dabao'en Temple (Jiangsu)
大丰中华麋鹿园景区	Dafeng Chinese Milu Nature Reserve (Jiangsu)

大理市崇圣寺三塔文化旅游区	Three Pagodas Cultural Tourist Area of Chongsheng Temple in Dali; Chongsheng Temple & Three-pagoda Cultural Tourist Area in Dali (Yunnan)
大连老虎滩海洋公园	Tiger Beach Ocean Park in Dalian (Liaoning)
大连老虎滩极地馆	Tiger Beach Polar Museum in Dalian (Liaoning)
大明宫国家遗址公园	Daming Palace National Heritage Park (Shaanxi)
大同云冈石窟	Yungang Grottoes in Datong (Shanxi)
大足石刻景区	Dazu Rock Carvings Scenic Area (Chongqing)
稻城亚丁景区	Daocheng Aden Scenic Area (Sichuan)
登封市嵩山少林景区	Songshan Shaolin Scenic Area in Dengfeng; Mount Songshan and Shaolin Monastery Scenic Area in Dengfeng (He'nan)
迪庆州香格里拉普达措景区	Shangri-La Pudacuo Scenic Area in Diqing; Shangri-La Pudacuo National Park in Diqing (Yunnan)
东方明珠广播电视塔	Oriental Pearl Radio & TV Tower
东平水浒城影视城	Water Margin Town (Jiangsu)
东营市黄河口生态旅游区	Ecological Tourism Zone of Yellow River Delta in Dongying (Shandong)
敦化市六鼎山文化旅游区	Liuding Mountain Cultural Tourist Area in Dunhua (Jilin)
敦煌鸣沙山月牙泉景区	Echoing-sand Mountain and Crescent Moon Spring in Dunhuang (Gansu)
鄂尔多斯成吉思汗陵旅游区	Tourist Area of Ordos Mausoleum of Genghis Khan (Inner Mongolia)
鄂尔多斯响沙湾旅游景区	Ordos Xiangshawan Tourist Area (Inner Mongolia)
恩施州恩施大峡谷景区	Grand Canyon Scenic Spot in Enshi; Enshi Grand Canyon Scenic Spot (Hubei)
恩施州神龙溪纤夫文化旅游区	Boat Tracker Culture of Shenlong Stream in Enshi (Hubei)
分界洲岛旅游区	Demarcation Islet Ecological and Cultural Tourism Resort (Hai'nan)

奉节白帝城·瞿塘峡景区	Fengjie Baidi City-Qutang Gorge Sceic Area (Chongqing)
佛山市长鹿旅游休博园	Chuanlord Tourism & Leisure EXPO Park in Foshan (Guangdong)
佛山市西樵山景区	Xiqiao Mountain Scenic Spot in Foshan (Guangdong)
福州市三坊七巷景区	Sanfang Qixiang Scenic Area in Fuzhou; Three Lanes and Seven Alleys Scenic Area in Fuzhou (Fujian)
抚州市大觉山景区	Dajue Mountain Scenic Area in Fuzhou (Jiangxi)
阜阳市颖上八里河景区	Yingshang Bali River Scenic Area in Fuyang (Anhui)
甘肃天水麦积山景区	Tianshui Maiji Mountain Scenic Area in Gansu
甘孜州海螺沟景区	Ganzi Hailuo Valley Scenic Area (Shaanxi)
赣州市三百山景区	Sanbai Mountain Scenic Area in Ganzhou (Jiangxi)
恭王府景区	Prince Gong's Mansion (Beijing)
故宫博物院	Palace Museum (Beijing)
光雾山风景名胜区	Guangwu Mountain Scenic Area (Sichuan)
广安市邓小平故里旅游区	Deng Xiaoping Hometown Tourism Area in Guang'an (Sichuan)
广元剑门关风景区	Jianmen Pass Scenic Area in Guangyuan (Sichuan)
广州市白云山风景区	Guangzhou Baiyun Mountain Scenic Area (Guangdong)
广州市长隆旅游度假区	Guangzhou Chimelong Tourist Resort (Guangdong)
贵阳市花溪青岩古镇景区	Qingyan Ancient Town of Huaxi District in Guiyang (Guizhou)
桂林叠彩山	Guilin Diecai Hill; Guilin Piled Silk Hill; Guilin Folded Brocade Hill (Guangxi)
桂林伏波山景区	Guilin Fubo Mountain Scenic Area (Guangxi)
桂林市独秀峰—王城景区	Guilin Solitary Beauty Peak and Prince City Scenic Area (Guangxi)

桂林市乐满地度假世界	Guilin Merryland Vacation World (Guangxi)
桂林市漓江景区	Guilin Lijiang River Scenic Area (Guangxi)
桂林市两江四湖·象山景区	Liangjiang Sihu and Xiangshan Scenic Area; Two Rivers and Four Lakes— Elephant Trunk Hill Scenic Area (Guangxi)
桂林象山景区	Elephant Trunk Hill Scenic Spot in Guilin (Guangxi)
哈尔滨市太阳岛景区	Sun Island Scenic Area in Harbin (Heilongjiang)
海淀区圆明园景区	Yuanming Garden Scenic Area of Haidian District (Beijing)
海东市互助土族故土园景区	Huzhu Tu Homeland Park Scenic Area in Haidong of Qinghai
邯郸市广府古城景区	Scenic Area of Guangfu Ancient City in Handan (Hebei)
邯郸市娲皇宫景区	Nüwa Imperial Palace in Handan; Wahuang Palace in Handan (Hebei)
杭州市千岛湖风景名胜区	Hangzhou Qiandao Lake Scenic Area (Zhejiang)
杭州市西湖风景名胜区	Hangzhou West Lake Scenic Area (Zhejiang)
杭州西溪湿地旅游区	Hangzhou Xixi Wetland Tourist Area; Hangzhou Xixi National Wetland Park (Zhejiang)
合肥市三河古镇景区	Sanhe Ancient Town Scenic Area in Hefei (Anhui)
贺州市黄姚古镇景区	Huangyao Ancient Town Scenic Area in Hezhou (Guangxi)
黑河五大连池景区	Heihe Wudalianchi Scenic Area (Heilongjiang)
衡阳市南岳衡山旅游区	South Mount Hengshan Tourist Area in Hengyang (Hu'nan)
红旗渠·太行大峡谷	Red Flag Canal and Taihang Grand Canyon (He'nan)
洪泽湖湿地景区	Hongze Lake Wetland Park (Jiangsu)
湖州市南浔古镇景区	Huzhou Nanxun Old Town (Zhejiang)
虎林市虎头旅游景区	Hutou Scenic Area in Hulin (Heilongjiang)
黄河壶口瀑布风景区	Scenic Area of Hukou Waterfall at Huanghe/Yellow River (Shaanxi, Shanxi)

黄山市古徽州文化旅游区	Ancient Huizhou Cultural Tourism Zone in Huangshan (Anhui)
黄山市黄山风景区	Mount Huangshan Scenic Area; Huangshan Mountain Scenic Area
黄山市皖南古村落—西递宏村	Ancient Villages in Southern Anhui—Xidi and Hongcun (Anhui)
惠州市惠州西湖旅游景区	Huizhou West Lake Scenic Area (Guangdong)
惠州市罗浮山景区	Luofu Mountain Scenic Area in Huizhou (Guangdong)
鸡公山风景区	Jigong Mountain Scenic Area; Rooster Mountain Scenic Area (He'nan)
吉安市井冈山风景旅游区	Jinggang Mountain Scenic Area in Ji'an (Jiangxi)
济南市天下第一泉景区	The World's Best Spring Scenic Spot in Jinan; Jinan Baotu Spring Scenic Spot (Shandong)
济南五龙潭公园	Jinan Five-Dragon Pool Park (Shandong)
济宁市曲阜明故城（三孔）旅游区	Tourist Area of Qufu Old City in Ming Dynasty; the Temple and Cemetery of Confucius and the Kong Family Mansion in Qufu (Shandong)
济宁市微山湖旅游区	Weishan Lake Tourist Area in Jining (Shandong)
嘉兴市南湖旅游区	Jiaxing South Lake Tourist Area (Zhejiang)
嘉兴市桐乡乌镇古镇旅游区	Tongxiang Wuzhen Ancient Town Tourist Area in Jiaxing (Zhejiang)
嘉兴市西塘古镇旅游景区	Ancient Town of Xitang in Jaxing; Xitang Ancient Town Tourist Scenic Spot (Zhejiang)
嘉峪关文物景区	Jiayuguan Cultural Relics Scenic Spot; Jiayu Pass Cultural Relics Scenic Spot (Gansu)
江布拉克景区	Jiangbulake Scenic Area (Xinjiang)
江津四面山景区	Jiangjin Simian Mountain Scenic Area (Chongqing)
姜堰溱湖旅游景区	Jiangyan Qinhu Lake Scenic Area in Taizhou (Jiangsu)
焦作市云台山—神农山·青天河景区	Yuntai—Shennong Mountain and Qingtian River Scenic Area in Jiaozuo (He'nan)

金华市东阳横店影视城景区	Dongyang Hengdian Film and Television City in Jinghua; Dongyang Hengdian World Studios in Jinhua (Zhejiang)
金山岭长城旅游区	Great Wall Tourism Area at Jinshan Mountain (Hebei)
晋城皇城相府生态文化旅游区	Eco-cultural Tourist Area of the Huangcheng Chancellor's House (Shanxi)
晋中市介休绵山景区	Mianshan Mountain Scenic Area in Jinzhong (Shanxi)
晋中市平遥古城景区	Scenic Area of Pingyao Ancient City in Jinzhong; Ancient City Scenic Area of Pingyao in Jinzhong (Shanxi)
景德镇古窑民俗博览区	Jingdezhen Ancient Kiln Folk Customs Museum (Jiangxi)
喀什地区喀什噶尔老城景区	Kashgar Old Town Scenic Area in Kashgar (Xinjiang)
喀什地区帕米尔旅游区	Pamir Tourist Attraction in Kashgar (Xinjiang)
喀什地区泽普金湖杨景区	Jinhu Yang Scenic Area in Kashgar (Xinjiang)
开封清明上河园	Kaifeng Qingming Riverside Landscape Garden (He'nan)
开平碉楼文化旅游区	Kaiping Diaolou Culture Tourist Area (Guangdong)
克拉玛依世界魔鬼城景区	World Ghost Town of Karamay (Xinjiang)
昆明市昆明世博园景区	Kunming World Horticultural Expo Garden (Yunnan)
昆明市石林风景区	Kunming Shilin Scenic Area; Kunming Stone Forest Scenic Area (Yunnan)
拉萨布达拉宫景区	Lhasa Potala Palace (Tibet)
拉萨大昭寺	Jokhang Temple in Lhasa (Tibet)
乐山市峨眉山景区	Mount Emei Scenic Area in Leshan (Sichuan)
乐山市乐山大佛景区	Leshan Giant Buddha Scenic Spot (Sichuan)
丽江市丽江古城景区	Lijiang Ancient Town Scenic Spot (Yunnan)
丽江市玉龙雪山景区	Yulong Snow Mountain Scenic Area in Lijiang (Yunnan)

丽水市缙云仙都景区	Jinyun Xiandu Scenic Area in Lishui (Zhejiang)
连云港花果山景区	Lianyungang Mount Huaguo Scenic Spot; Lianyungang Huaguo Maintain Scenic Spot (Jiangsu)
辽宁大连金石滩景区	Golden Pebble Beach Scenic Area in Dalian of Liaoning
林芝巴松措景区	Nyingchi Tsozong Gongba Monastery (Tibet)
临汾市洪洞大槐树寻根祭祖园景区	Hongtong Dahuaishu Ancestor Memorial Garden in Linfen of Shanxi; Hongtong Sophora Japonica Tree Root Search and Ancestral Garden Scenic Area (Shanxi)
临沂市萤火虫水洞·地下大峡谷旅游区	Firefly Water Cave and Underground Grand Canyon Tourist Area in Linyi (Shandong)
临汾市云丘山景区	Yunqiu Mountain Scenic Area in Linfen (Shanxi)
六安市天堂寨旅游景区	Lu'an Tiantangzhai Tourist Area (Anhui)
六安市万佛湖景区	Wanfo Lake Scenic Area in Lu'an (Anhui)
龙岩市古田旅游区	Gutian Tourist Area in Longyan (Fujian)
陇南市官鹅沟景区	Guan'e Valley Scenic Area in Longnan (Gansu)
庐山风景名胜区	Mount Lushan Scenic Area in Jiangxi; Lushan Mountain Scenic Area (Jiangxi)
庐山西海风景名胜区	Lushan West Sea Scenic Area (Jiangxi)
洛阳白云山景区	Luoyang Baiyun Mountain Scenic Area (He'nan)
洛阳栾川老君山·鸡冠洞旅游区	Luanchuan Laojun Mountain and Jiguan Cave Tourist Area in Luoyang (He'nan)
洛阳市龙门石窟景区	Luoyang Longmen Grottoes Scenic Area (He'nan)
洛阳市龙潭大峡谷景区	Longtan Grand Canyon Scenic Area in Luoyang (He'nan)
满洲里市中俄边境旅游区	Sino-Russian Border Tourism Area in Manchuria (Inner Mongolia)
梅州市雁南飞茶田景区	Yearning Tea Plantation Tourist Attraction in Meizhou (Guangdong)
湄洲岛妈祖文化旅游区	Mazu Cultural Tourism Area of Meizhou Island (Fujian)
绵阳市北川羌城旅游区	Beichuan Qiangcheng Tourism Area in Mianyang (Sichuan)

明十三陵景区	Ming Tombs Scenic Area (Beijing)
漠河北极村旅游区	Mohe Arctic Village Tourism Attraction (Heilongjiang)
牡丹江镜泊湖景区	Jingpo Lake Scenic Area in Mudanjiang (Heilongjiang)
慕田峪长城	Mutianyu Great Wall; Mutian Valley Great Wall (Beijing)
南昌市滕王阁旅游区	Nanchang Tengwang Pavilion Tourist Area (Jiangxi)
南充市阆中古城旅游区	Langzhong Ancient City Tourist Area in Nanchong (Sichuan)
南充市仪陇朱德故里景区	Yilong Zhu De Hometown Scenic Area in Nanchong (Sichuan)
南川金佛山景区	Nanchuan Jinfo Mountain Scenic Area (Chongqing)
南京市夫子庙—秦淮风光带景区	Nanjing Fuzimiao Qinhuai Scenic area; Nanjing Confucius Temple and Qinhuai River Scenic Area (Jiangsu)
南京市钟山风景名胜区—中山陵园风景区	Nanjing Zhongshan Mountain and Sun Yat-sen Mausoleum Scenic Area (Jiangsu)
南宁青秀山风景旅游区	Qingxiu Mountain Scenic Area in Nanning (Guangxi)
南平市武夷山风景名胜区	Nanping Wuyi Mountains Scenic Area (Fujian)
南通市濠河景区	Nantong Haohe River Scenic Area (Jiangsu)
南阳市西峡伏牛山老界岭·恐龙遗址园旅游区	Xixia Funiu Mountain and Dinosaur Relics Park in Nanyang (He'nan)
宁波市奉化溪口·滕头旅游景区	Fenghua Xikou—Tengtou Tourist Area in Ningbo (Zhejiang)
宁波市天一阁·月湖景区	Ningbo Tianyi Pavilion and Moon Lake Scenic Area (Zhejiang)
宁德市白水洋—鸳鸯溪旅游区	Baishuiyang and Yuanyangxi Tourist Area in Ningde (Fujian)
宁德市福鼎太姥山旅游区	Fuding Taimu Mountain Tourist Area in Ningde (Fujian)

盘锦市红海滩风景廊道景区	Red Beach Scenic Corridor in Panjin (Liaoning)
彭水县阿依河景区	Ayi River Scenic Area of Pengshui (Chongqing)
平顶山市尧山—中原大佛景区	Yaoshan Mountain and Spring Temple Buddha Scenic Area in Pingdingshan (He'nan)
平凉市崆峒山风景名胜区	Jiayuguan Cultural Relics Scenic Spot; Jiayu Pass Cultural Relics Scenic Spot (Gansu)
萍乡市武功山景区	Wugong Mountain Scenic Area in Pingxiang (Jiangxi)
黔东南州镇远古城旅游景区	Zhenyuan Ancient Town Tourist Attraction in Qiandongnan Miao and Dong Autonomous Prefecture (Guizhou)
黔江区濯水景区	Zhuoshui Scenic Area of Qianjiang District (Chongqing)
黔南州荔波樟江风景区	Libo Zhangjiang River Scenic Area in Qiannan
秦皇岛山海关景区	Shanhai Pass Scenic Area in Qinghuangdao
秦始皇帝陵博物院	Museum of Emperor Qin Shihuang's Mausoleum Site
青岛崂山景区	Qingdao Laoshan Mountain Scenic Spot (Shandong)
青海湖景区	Qinghai Lake Scenic Area (Gansu)
清远市连州地下河旅游景区	Lianzhou Subterranean River in Qingyuan (Guangdong)
衢州市江郎山·廿八都景区	Mount Jianglang and Nianba Ancient Town Scenic Area in Quzhou (Zhejiang)
衢州市开化根宫佛国文化旅游景区	Kaihua Root Palace Buddhist Cultural Tourism Zone in Quzhou (Zhejiang)
泉州市清源山景区	Quanzhou Qingyuan Mountain Scenic Area (Fujian)
日喀则扎什伦布寺景区	Shigatse Tashi Lhunpo Monastery (Tibet)
瑞金市共和国摇篮旅游区	Cradle of the People's Republic of China in Ruijin (Jiangxi)
赛里木湖风景名胜区	Sayram Lake Scenic Area (Xinjiang)
三明市泰宁风景旅游区	Taining Scenic Area in Sanming (Fujian)

三亚市南山大小洞天旅游区	Sanya Nanshan Cave Tourist Area; Sanya Nanshan Dongtian Park (Hai'nan)
三亚市南山文化旅游区	Sanya Nanshan Buddhism Cultural Zone (Hai'nan)
三亚市蜈支洲岛旅游区	Sanya Wuzhizhou Island Tourist Attraction (Hai'nan)
商洛市金丝峡景区	Jinsi Gorge Scenic Spot in Shangluo; Golden Silk Gorge Scenic Spot in Shangluo (Shaanxi)
上海科技馆	Shanghai Science & Technology Museum
上海野生动物园	Shanghai Wild Animal Park; Shanghai Wildlife Park
上饶市龟峰景区	Wuyuan Guifeng Peak Scenic Area in Shangrao (Jiangxi)
上饶市三清山旅游景区	Sanqing Mountain Tourist Scenic Spot in Shangrao (Jiangxi)
上饶市婺源江湾景区	Jiangwan Scenic Area in Shangrao (Jiangxi)
韶关市丹霞山景区	Mount Danxia Scenic Area in Shaoguan; Shaoguan Danxia Landform Scenic Area (Guangdong)
邵阳市崀山景区	Nangshan Mountain Scenic Area in Shaoyang (Hu'nan)
绍兴市鲁迅故里沈园景区	Shaoxing Lu Xun's Residence in Shen Garden Scenic Area (Zhejiang)
深圳华侨城旅游度假区	Shenzhen Overseas Chinese Town Tourist Resort (Guangdong)
深圳市观澜湖休闲旅游区	Shenzhen Guanlan Lake Leisure Tourism Area (Guangdong)
神农架旅游区	Shennongjia Tourist Attraction; Shennongjia Scenic Area (Hubei)
沈阳市植物园	Shenyang Botanical Garden (Liaoning)
十堰市武当山风景区	Shiyan Wudang Mountain Scenic Spot (Hubei)
石家庄市西柏坡景区	Xibaipo Scenic Spot in Shijiazhuang (Hebei)
石嘴山市沙湖旅游景区	Shahu Tourist Attractions in Shizuishan (Ningxia)

苏州市姑苏区苏州园林（拙政园、虎丘山、留园）	Gusu Classical Gardens of Suzhou (Humble Administrator's Garden, Tiger Hill, Lingering Garden) (Jiangsu)
苏州市金鸡湖景区	Suzhou Jinji Lake Scenic Area (Jiangsu)
苏州市沙家浜·虞山尚湖旅游区	Shajiabang Yushan—Shanghu Tourism Area in Suzhou (Jiangsu)
苏州市同里古镇景区	Suzhou Tongli Ancient Town Scenic Area (Jiangsu)
苏州市吴中太湖旅游区	Wuzhong Taihu Lake Tourist Area in Suzhou; Tourist Area of Wuzhong Taihu Lake in Suzhou (Jiangsu)
苏州市周庄古镇景区	Zhouzhuang Ancient Town Scenic Area in Suzhou (Jiangsu)
塔克拉玛干·三五九旅文化旅游区	Taklimakan Cultural Tourism Area of 359th Brigade (Xinjiang)
台州市台州府城文化旅游区	Tourist Area of the Ancient City Of Taizhou (Zhejiang)
台州市神仙居景区	Shenxianju Scenic Area in Taizhou
台州市天台山景区	Tiantai Mountain Scenic Area in Taizhou (Zhejiang)
泰安市泰山景区	Tai'an Taishan Mountain Scenic Area (Shandong)
腾龙洞风景区	Tenglong Cave Scenic Area (Hubei)
天津古文化街旅游区	Tianjin Ancient Culture Street; Tourist Area of Tianjin Ancient Culture Street
天津盘山风景名胜区	Panshan Mountain Scenic Area in Tianjin
天山天池风景名胜区	Tianshan Tianchi Scenic Spot in Xingjiang
天坛公园	Temple of Heaven (Beijing)
通化市高句丽文物古迹旅游景区	Koguryo Cultural Relics and Tourist Sites in Tonghua (Jilin)
铜仁市梵净山旅游区	Fanjing Mountain Tourism Area in Tongren (Guizhou)
土楼（永定·南靖）旅游区	(Yongding—Nanjing) Tulou Tourism Attraction; Earth Building Tourism Attraction (Fujian)
吐鲁番市葡萄沟风景区	Turpan Grape Valley Scenic Area (Xinjiang)

万盛经开区黑山谷景区	Black Valley Scenic Area in Wansheng Economic and Development Zone (Chongqing)
威海刘公岛景区	Weihai Liugong Island Scenic Area in (Shandong)
威海市华夏城旅游景区	Weihai Huaxiacheng Scenic Area (Shandong)
潍坊市青州古城旅游区	Qingzhou Ancient City in Weifang (Shandong)
渭南华山景区	Mount Huashan Scenic Area in Weinan; Huashan Mountain Scenic Area in Weinan (Shaanxi)
温州刘伯温故里景区	Liu Bowen's Hometown Scenic Area in Wenzhou (Zhejiang)
温州市雁荡山风景名胜区	Wenzhou Yandang Mountain Scenic Area (Zhejiang)
文山州丘北普者黑景区	Qiubei Puzhehei Scenic Area in Wenshan (Yunnan)
乌鲁木齐天山大峡谷景区	Urumqi Tianshan Grand Canyon Scenic Spot (Xinjiang)
巫山小三峡—小小三峡	Wushan Lesser Three Gorges—Mini Three Gorges (Chongqing)
无锡市惠山古镇景区	Scenic Spot of Huishan Ancient Town in Wuxi (Jiangsu)
无锡市灵山景区	Wuxi Lingshan Mountain Scenic Area; Wuxi Lingshan Grand Buddha Scenic Area (Jiangsu)
无锡市鼋头渚景区	Wuxi Yuantouzhu Scenic Area (Jiangsu)
芜湖市方特旅游区	Wuhu Fante Tourist Area in Anhui; Wuhu Fanta Wild Adventure in Anhui (Anhui)
武汉黄鹤楼景区	Yellow Crane Tower Scenic Area in Wuhan (Hubei)
武汉市东湖景区	Wuhan East Lake Scenic Area (Hubei)
武汉市黄陂木兰文化生态旅游区	Huangpi Mulan Cultural and Ecological Tourism Zone in Wuhan
武隆喀斯特旅游区(天生三桥·仙女山·芙蓉洞)	Wulong Karst Tourist Area (Three Natural Bridges—The Fairy Mountain—Furong Cave) (Chongqing)
西安大雁塔·大唐芙蓉园景区	Dayan Pagoda and Tang Paradise in Xi'an (Shaanxi)

西安市城墙·碑林历史文化景区	Xi'an City Wall and Steles Forest Museum (Shaanxi)
西安市华清池景区	Huaqing Palace Heritage Site in Xi'an (Shaanxi)
西安市秦始皇兵马俑博物馆	Xi'an Emperor Qinshihuang's Terracotta Warriors and Horses Museum; Museum of Terracotta Warriors and Horses of Emperor Qinshihuang in Xi'an (Shaanxi)
西宁市塔尔寺景区	Xining Kumbum Monastery Scenic Area (Qinghai)
厦门市鼓浪屿风景名胜区	Xiamen Gulangyu Scenic Area (Fujian)
咸宁市三国赤壁古战场景区	Chibi Ancient Battlefield of Three Kingdoms in Xianning (Hubei)
湘潭市韶山旅游区	Shaoshan Tourist Area in Xiangtan (Hu'nan)
湘西土家族苗族自治州矮寨·十八洞·德夯大峡谷景区	Aizhai·Eighteen Cave·Dehang Grand Canyou Scenic Area (Hunan)
襄阳市古隆中景区	Ancient Longzhong Scenic Area in Xiangyang (Hubei)
忻州市五台山风景名胜区	Wutai Mountain Scenic Area in Xinzhou (Shanxi)
忻州市雁门关景区	Yanmen Pass Scenic Area in Xinzhou (Shanxi)
新疆生产建设兵团第十师白沙湖景区	Baisha Lake Scenic Area in Xinjiang Uygur Autonomous Region
新乡市八里沟景区	Baligou Scenic Area in Xinxiang (He'nan)
徐州市云龙湖景区	Xuzhou Yunlong Lake Scenic Area (Jiangsu)
宣城市绩溪龙川景区	Jixi Longchuan Scenic Area in Xuancheng (Anhui)
雅安市碧峰峡旅游景区	Bifeng Valley Tourist Scenic Area in Ya'an (Sichuan)
雅鲁藏布大峡谷旅游景区	Tourist Attractions of Yarlung Zangbo Grand Canyon (Tibet)
呀诺达雨林文化旅游区	Yanoda Rainforest Cultural Tourism Zone (Hai'nan)
烟台龙口南山景区	Longkou Nanshan Scenic Spot in Yantai (Shandong)

烟台市蓬莱阁旅游区(三仙山—八仙过海)	Yantai Penglai Pavilion Tourist Area (Sanxian Mountain and The Eight Immortals Crossing the Sea) (Shandong)
延安市黄帝陵景区	Jiayuguan Cultural Relics Scenic Spot; Jiayu Pass Cultural Relics Scenic Spot (Shaanxi)
延安市延安革命纪念地景区	Yan'an Revolution Memorial Scenic Area in Yan'an (Shaanxi)
扬州市瘦西湖风景区	Yangzhou Slender West Lake Scenic Area (Jiangsu)
阳江市海陵岛大角湾海上丝路旅游区	Hailing Island Dajiao Bay & Maritime Silk Road in Yangjiang (Guangdong)
野三坡风景名胜区	Yesanpo Nature Scenic Area (Hebei)
伊春市汤旺河林海奇石景区	Tangwanhe Stone Forest Scenic Area in Yichun (Heilongjiang)
伊犁那拉提旅游风景区	Nalati Scenic Spot of Yili in Xinjiang
伊犁州喀拉峻景区	Kalajun Grassland Scenic Area in Yili (Xinjiang)
沂蒙山旅游区	Linyi Yimeng Mountain Tourist Area (Shandong)
宜昌市长阳清江画廊景区	Changyang Qingjiang Gallery Scenic Area in Yichang (Hubei)
宜昌市三峡大坝—屈原故里旅游区	Yichang Three Gorges Dam and Qu Yuan's Hometown Tourist Area (Hubei)
宜昌市三峡大瀑布风景区	Grand Waterfall Scenic Area of the Three Gorges (Hubei)
宜昌市三峡人家风景区	Three Gorges Tribe Scenic Spot in Yichang (Hubei)
宜春市明月山旅游区	Yichun Mingyue Mountain Tourist Area (Jiangxi)
颐和园	Summer Palace (Beijing)
银川市灵武水洞沟旅游区	Lingwu Shuidonggou Tourism Area in Yinchuan (Ningxia)
银川镇北堡西部影视城	Zhenbeibu China West Film Studio in Yinchuan (Ningxia)
鹰潭市龙虎山旅游景区	Yingtan Longhu Mountain Scenic Spot (Jiangxi)
永城市芒砀山汉文化旅游景区	Han Culture Tourism Scenic Spot of Mount Mangdang in Yongcheng (He'nan)

西阳桃花源旅游景区	Youyang Taohuayuan Scenic Area (Chongqing)
岳阳市岳阳楼—君山岛景区	Yueyang Tower—Junshan Island Scenic Spot
云阳龙缸景区	Yunyang Longgang Scenic Area (Chongqing)
枣庄市台儿庄古城景区	Taierzhuang Ancient Town Scenic Area in Zaozhuang (Shandong)
张家界武陵源—天门山风景区	Zhangjiajie Wulingyuan and Tianmen Mountain Scenic Area (Hu'nan)
张掖市七彩丹霞景区	Colorful Danxia Scenic Spot in Zhangye (Gansu)
肇庆市星湖旅游景区	Seven Star Crags and Dinghu Mountain Tourist Attraction in Zhaoqing (Guangdong)
镇江市金山·焦山·北固山旅游景区	Three Mountains of Zhenjiang (Jinshan, Jiaoshan and Beigushan) Tourist Area (Jiangsu)
镇江市句容茅山景区	Jurong Maoshan Mountain Scenic Area in Zhenjiang (Jiangsu)
中国共产党一大·二大·四大纪念馆景区	Memorial Halls of First-Second-Fourth National Congress of Communist Party of China (Shanghai)
中国科学院西双版纳热带植物园	Xishuangbanna Tropical Botanical Garden of Chinese Academy of Sciences (Yunnan)
中山市孙中山故里旅游区	Tourism Area of Sun Yat-sen Hometown in Zhongshan; Hometown of Sun Yat-sen in Zhongshan (Guangdong)
中卫市沙坡头旅游景区	Shapotou Tourist Area in Zhongwei (Ningxia)
中央电视台无锡影视基地三国水浒景区	CCTV Wuxi Movie/TV Base—Three-Kingdom and Water Margin Scenic Area (Jiangsu)
舟山市普陀山风景名胜区	Zhoushan Mount Putuo Scenic Area (Zhejiang)
周恩来淮安故里旅游景区	Huai'an Former Residence of Zhou Enlai (Jiangsu)
株洲市炎帝陵景区	Scenic Spot of Emperor Yan's Mausoleum in Zhuzhou (Hu'nan)
驻马店市嵖岈山旅游景区	Chaya Mountain Tourist Area in Zhumadian (He'nan)
遵化市清东陵景区	Eastern Royal Tombs of the Qing Dynasty in Zunhua (Hebei)

附录三　中国国家森林公园

阿尔山国家森林公园	Aer Mountain National Forest Park (Inner Mongolia)
阿尔泰山温泉国家森林公园	Altai Mountain Hot Spring National Forest Park (Xinjiang)
阿里河国家森林公园	Ali River National Forest Park (Inner Mongolia)
矮寨国家森林公园	Aizhai National Forest Park (Hu'nan)
艾山国家森林公园	Aishan Mountain National Forest Park (Shandong)
安陆古银杏国家森林公园	Anlu Ancient Ginkgo National Forest Park (Hubei)
安源国家森林公园	Anyuan National Forest Park (Jiangxi)
安泽国家森林公园	Anze National Forest Park (Shanxi)
八达岭国家森林公园	Badaling National Forest Park (Beijing)
八公山国家森林公园	Bagong Mountain National Forest Park (Anhui)
八角寨国家森林公园	Bajiaozhai National Forest Park (Guangxi)
八里湾国家森林公园	Bali Bay National Forest Park (Heilongjiang)
八岭山国家森林公园	Baling Mountain National Forest Park (Hubei)
巴楚胡杨林国家森林公园	Bachu Populus euphratica Forest National Forest Park (Xinjiang)
巴松措国家森林公园	Basum Lake National Forest Park (Tibet)
坝上沽源国家森林公园	Bashang Guyuan National Forest Park (Hebei)
霸王岭国家森林公园	Bawang Ridge National Forest Park (Hai'nan)
白草洼国家森林公园	Baicaowa National Forest Park (Hebei)
白哈巴国家森林公园	Baihaba National Forest Park (Xinjiang)
白鸡腰国家森林公园	Baijiyao National Forest Park (Jilin)
白石山国家森林公园	Baishi Mountain National Forest Park (Hebei, Jilin)
白水河国家森林公园	Baishui River National Forest Park (Sichuan)

白云山国家森林公园	Baiyun Mountain National Forest Park (He'nan)
白竹园寺国家森林公园	Baizhuyuansi National Forest Park (Hubei)
百里杜鹃国家森林公园	Baili (Hundred-Li) Azaleas National Forest Park (Guizhou)
百里龙山国家森林公园	National Forest Park of Baili Longshan Mountain (Hu'nan)
班公湖国家森林公园	Banggong Lake National Forest Park (Tibet)
半拉山国家森林公园	Banla Mountain National Forest Park (Jilin)
薄山国家森林公园	Boshan Mountain National Forest Park (He'nan)
宝格达乌拉国家森林公园	Baogedaula National Forest Park (Inner Mongolia)
宝华山国家森林公园	Jiangsu Baohuashan National Forest Park (Jiangsu)
宝华山国家森林公园	Baohua Mountain National Forest Park (Shanghai)
宝台山国家森林公园	Baotai Mountain National Forest Park (Yunnan)
抱犊崮国家森林公园	Baodugu National Forest Park (Shandong)
北川国家森林公园	Beichuan National Forest Park (Sichuan)
北大山石海森林公园	Shihai Forest Park in Beida Mountain (Hebei)
北峰山国家森林公园	Beifeng Mountain National Forest Park (Guangdong)
北宫国家森林公园	Beigong National Forest Park (Beijing)
北极村国家森林公园	Arctic Village National Forest Park (Heilongjiang)
北罗霄国家森林公园	Beiluoxiao National Forest Park (Hu'nan)
北山国家森林公园	North Mountain National Forest Park (Qinghai)
本溪国家森林公园	Benxi National Forest Park (Liaoning)
本溪环城国家森林公园	Benxi Round-the-City National Forest Park (Liaoning)
比日神山国家森林公园	Biri Shenshan National Forest Park (Tibet)
毕节国家森林公园	Bijie National Forest Park (Guizhou)
碧湖潭国家森林公园	Bihutan National Forest Park (Jiangxi)
冰砬山国家森林公园	Bingla Mountain National Forest Park (Liaoning)
勃利国家森林公园	Boli National Forest Park (Heilongjiang)

不二门国家森林公园	Bu'ermen National Forest Park (Hu'nan)
苍溪国家森林公园	Cangxi National Forest Park (Sichuan)
沧浪山国家森林公园	Canglangshan National Forest Park (Hubei)
岑山国家森林公园	Censhan National Forest Park (Jiangxi)
茶山竹海国家森林公园	Chashan Mountain Zhuhai National Forest Park (Chongqing)
嵖岈山国家森林公园	Chaya Mountain National Forest Park (He'nan)
槎山国家森林公园	Chashan Mountain National Forest Park (Shandong)
察尔森国家森林公园	Qarsan National Forest Park (Inner Mongolia)
柴埠溪国家森林公园	Chaibu Stream National Forest Park (Hubei)
长白国家森林公园	Changbai National Forest Park (Jilin)
长白山北坡国家森林公园	Changbai Mountain North Slope National Forest Park (Jilin)
长岛国家森林公园	Changdao National Forest Park (Shandong)
长乐国家森林公园	Changle National Forest Park (Fujian)
长坡岭国家森林公园	Changpo Ridge National Forest Park (Guizhou)
长沙黑麋峰国家森林公园	Changsha Heimifeng National Forest Park (Hu'nan)
长山群岛国家森林公园	Changshan Isles National Forest Park (Liaoning)
长寿国家森林公园	Longevity National Forest Park (Heilongjiang)
长寿山国家森林公园	Changshou Mountain National Forest Park (Hebei)
绰尔大峡谷国家森林公园	Chuoer Grand Canyon National Forest Park (Inner Mongolia)
绰源国家森林公园	Chuoyuan National Forest Park (Inner Mongolia)
车师古道国家森林公园	Cheshigu Road National Forest Park (Xinjiang)
成吉思汗国家森林公园	Genghis Khan National Forest Park (Inner Mongolia)
茌平国家森林公园	Chiping National Forest Park (Shandong)
赤水竹海国家森林公园	Chishui Zhuhai National Forest Park (Guizhou)
重庆南山国家森林公园	South Mountain National Forest Park of Chongqing (Chongqing)

崇阳国家森林公园	Chongyang National Forest Park (Hubei)
徂徕山国家森林公园	Culai Mountain National Forest Park (Shandong)
翠微峰国家森林公园	Cuiwei Peak National Forest Park (Jiangxi)
措普国家森林公园	Cuopu National Forest Park (Sichuan)
达尔滨湖国家森林公园	Darbin Lake National Forest Park (Inner Mongolia)
大安国家森林公园	Da'an National Forest Park (Jilin)
大板水国家森林公园	Dabanshui National Forest Park (Guizhou)
大北山国家森林公园	Dabei Mountain National Forest Park (Guangdong)
大别山国家森林公园	Dabie Mountain National Forest Park (Hubei)
大孤山国家森林公园	Dagu Mountain National Forest Park (Liaoning)
大桂山国家森林公园	Dagui Mountain National Forest Park (Guangxi)
大河坝国家森林公园	Daheba National Forest Park (Gansu)
大黑山国家森林公园	Dahei Mountain National Forest Park (Liaoning)
大洪山国家森林公园	Dahongshan National Forest Park (Hubei)
大鸿寨国家森林公园	Dahongzhai National Forest Park (He'nan)
大口国家森林公园	Dakou National Forest Park (Hubei)
大老岭国家森林公园	Dalao Ridge National Forest Park (Hubei)
大连大赫山国家森林公园	Dalian Daheshan National Forest Park (Liaoning)
大连国家森林公园	Dalian National Forest Park (Liaoning)
大连天门山国家森林公园	Tianmen Mountain National Forest Park in Dalian (Liaoning)
大连西郊国家森林公园	Dalian Xijiao National Forest Park (Liaoning)
大连银石滩国家森林公园	Yinshitan National Forest Park in Dalian (Liaoning)
大亮子河国家森林公园	Daliangzi River National Forest Park (Heilongjiang)
大龙山国家森林公园	Dalong Mountain National Forest Park (Anhui)
大茂山国家森林公园	Damao Mountain National Forest Park (Hebei)
大奇山国家森林公园	Daqi Mountain National Forest Park (Zhejiang)
大青观国家森林公园	Daqingguan National Forest Park (Heilongjiang)
大青山国家森林公园	Daqingshan National Forest Park (Hebei)
大庆国家森林公园	Daqing National Forest Park (Heilongjiang)

大容山国家森林公园	Darong Mountain National Forest Park (Guangxi)
大苏山国家森林公园	Dasushan National Forest Park (He'nan)
大通国家森林公园	Datong National Forest Park (Qinghai)
大王山国家森林公园	Daiwang Mountain National Forest Park (Guangdong)
大围山国家森林公园	Dawei Mountain National Forest Park (Hu'nan)
大溪国家森林公园	Daxi National Forest Park (Zhejiang)
大峡沟国家森林公园	Daxiagou/Daxia Valley National Forest Park (Gansu)
大兴古桑国家森林公园	Daxing Old-Mulberry National Forest Park (Beijing)
大熊山国家森林公园	Daxiong Mountain National Forest Park (Hu'nan)
大阳山国家森林公园	Jiangsu Dayangshan National Forest Park (Jiangsu)
大杨山国家森林公园	Dayang Mountain National Forest Park (Beijing)
大瑶山国家森林公园	Dayao Mountain National Forest Park (Guangxi)
大峪国家森林公园	Dayu Valley National Forest Park (Gansu)
大园洞国家森林公园	Dayuan Cave National Forest Park (Chongqing)
大云山国家森林公园	Dayun Mountain National Forest Park (Hu'nan)
大沾河国家森林公园	Dazhan River National Forest Park (Heilongjiang)
大竹海国家森林公园	Dazhuhai National Forest Park (Zhejiang)
丹江口国家森林公园	Danjiangkou National Forest Park (Hubei)
丹清河国家森林公园	Danqing River National Forest Park (Heilongjiang)
德化石牛山国家森林公园	Dehua Shiniu Mountain National Forest Park (Fujian)
第一山国家森林公园	Diyi Mountain National Forest Park (Shanghai)
吊罗山国家森林公园	Diaoluo Mountain National Forest Park (Hai'nan)
吊水壶国家森林公园	Diaoshuihu National Forest Park (Jilin)
东阿黄河国家森林公园	Dong'a Yellow River National Forest Park (Shandong)

东海岛国家森林公园	Donghai Island National Forest Park (Guangdong)
东平国家森林公园	Dongping National Forest Park (Shanghai)
东山国家森林公园	Dongshan National Forest Park (Fujian)
东山国家森林公园	Dongshan National Forest Park (Yunnan)
东台山国家森林公园	Dongtai Mountain National Forest Park (Hu'nan)
东吴国家森林公园	Jiangsu Soochow/Dongwu National Forest Park (Jiangsu)
陡水湖国家森林公园	Doushui Lake National Forest Park (Jiangxi)
都江堰国家森林公园	Dujiang Weir National Forest Park (Sichuan)
峨庄古村落国家森林公园	Ezhuang Ancient Village National Forest Park (Shandong)
鹅湖山国家森林公园	Ehu Mountain National Forest Park (Jiangxi)
额济纳胡杨国家森林公园	Ejina/Ejin National Forest Park of Populus Euphratica (Inner Mongolia)
二郎山国家森林公园	Erlang Mountain National Forest Park (Sichuan)
二龙什台国家森林公园	Erlong Shitai National Forest Park (Inner Mongolia)
二滩国家森林公园	Ertan National Forest Park (Sichuan)
方山国家森林公园	Fangshan Mountain National Forest Park (Shanxi)
方正龙山国家森林公园	National Forest Park of Fangzheng Longshan Mountain (Heilongjiang)
飞来寺国家森林公园	Feilai Temple National Forest Park (Yunnan)
飞龙湖国家森林公园	Feilong Lake National Forest Park (Guangxi)
风穴寺国家森林公园	Fengxue Temple National Forest Park (He'nan)
峰峦溪国家森林公园	Fengluanxi National Forest Park (Hu'nan)
峰山国家森林公园	Fengshan National Forest Park (Jiangxi)
凤凰山国家森林公园	Fenghuang (Phoenix) Mountain National Forest Park (Heilongjiang, Guizhou, Liaoning)
凤山根旦国家森林公园	Fengshan Gandan National Forest Park (Hai'nan)
佛手山国家森林公园	Foshou Mountain National Forest Park (Heilongjiang)
浮山国家森林公园	Fushan Mountain National Forest Park (Anhui)

福宝国家森林公园	Fubao National Forest Park (Sichuan)
福音山国家森林公园	Gospel Mountain National Forest Park (Hu'nan)
福州国家森林公园	Fuzhou National Forest Park (Fujian)
富春江国家森林公园	Fuchun River National Forest Park (Zhejiang)
盖州国家森林公园	Gaizhou National Forest Park (Liaoning)
甘山国家森林公园	Ganshan Mountain National Forest Park (He'nan)
甘溪国家森林公园	Ganxi National Forest Park (Guizhou)
赣州阳明湖国家森林公园	Ganzhou Yangming Lake National Forest Park (Jiangxi)
冈仁波齐国家森林公园	Gangren Boqi National Forest Park (Tibet)
高山国家森林公园	Gaoshan Mountain National Forest Park (Sichuan)
歌乐山国家森林公园	Gele Mountain National Forest Park (Chongqing)
阁皂山国家森林公园	Gezaoshan National Forest Park (Jiangxi)
巩留恰西国家森林公园	Gongliuchaxi National Forest Park (Xinjiang)
巩乃斯国家森林公园	Künes National Forest Park (Xinjiang)
共青国家森林公园	National Forest Park of Communist Youth (Shanghai)
岣嵝峰国家森林公园	Yiloufeng National Forest Park (Hu'nan)
姑婆山国家森林公园	Gupo Mountain National Forest Park (Guangxi)
古北岳国家森林公园	Gubeiyue National Forest Park (Hebei)
关帝山国家森林公园	Guandi Mountain National Forest Park (Shanxi)
观山国家地质公园	Guanshan Mountain National Geopark (He'nan)
观音山国家森林公园	Guanyin Mountain National Forest Park (Guangdong)
观音峡国家森林公园	Guanyin Valley National Forest Park (Chongqing)
官鹅沟国家森林公园	Guanegou National Forest Park (Gansu)
官马莲花山国家森林公园	Guanma Lianhua Mountain National Forest Park (Jilin)
管涔山国家森林公园	Guancen Mountain National Forest Park (Shanxi)
广宁竹海国家森林公园	Bamboo Sea National Forest Park of Guangning (Guangdong)

广元天台国家森林公园	Guangyuan Tiantai National Forest Park (Sichuan)
圭峰山国家森林公园	Guifeng Mountain National Forest Park (Guangdong)
圭山国家森林公园	Guishan Mountain National Forest Park (Yunnan)
龟峰国家森林公园	Guifeng Peak National Forest Park (Jiangxi)
鬼谷岭国家森林公园	Guigu Valley National Forest Park; Ghost Valley National Forest Park (Shaanxi)
贵清山国家森林公园	Guiqingshan National Forest Park (Gansu)
贵清山国家森林公园	Guiqing Mountain National Forest Park (Gansu)
桂林国家森林公园	Guilin National Forest Park (Guangxi)
哈巴河白桦国家森林公园	Haba River White Birch National Forest Park (Xinjiang)
哈达门国家森林公园	Hadamen National Forest Park (Inner Mongolia)
哈尔滨国家森林公园	Harbin National Forest Park (Heilongjiang)
哈里哈图国家森林公园	Halihatu National Forest Park (Qinghai)
哈密天山国家森林公园	Hami Tianshan National Forest Park (Xinjiang)
哈日图热格国家森林公园	Haritureg National Forest Park (Xinjiang)
海滨国家森林公园	Coastal National Forest Park (Hebei)
海口火山国家森林公园	Haikou Volcano National Forest Park (Hai'nan)
海拉尔国家森林公园	Hailar National Forest Park (Inner Mongolia)
海螺沟国家森林公园	Hailuo Valley National Forest Park (Sichuan)
海上国家森林公园	Coastal National Forest Park (Hai'nan)
海棠山国家森林公园	Haitang Mountain National Forest Park (Liaoning)
海湾国家森林公园	Gulf National Forest Park (Shanghai)
寒葱顶国家森林公园	Hancongding National Forest Park (Jilin)
汉江瀑布群国家森林公园	Hanjiang waterfall Group National Forest Park (Hubei)
汉寿竹海国家森林公园	Hanshou Zhuhai National Forest Park (Hu'nan)
汉阴凤凰山国家森林公园	Hanyin Fenghuangshan National Forest Park (Shaanxi)

汉中天台国家森林公园	Tiantai National Forest Park in Hanzhong (Shaanxi)
杭州半山国家森林公园	Hangzhou Banshan National Forest Park (Zhejiang)
杭州西山国家森林公园	Hangzhou Xishan National Forest Park (Zhejiang)
好森沟国家森林公园	Haosen Gully National Forest Park (Inner Mongolia)
合肥滨湖国家森林公园	Hefei Binhu National Forest Park (Anhui)
合肥大蜀山国家森林公园	Hefei Dashushan National Forest Park (Anhui)
和睦国家森林公园	Harmony National Forest Park (Liaoning)
河伏国家森林公园	Hefu National Forest Park (Hu'nan)
河套国家森林公园	Hetao National Forest Park (Inner Mongolia)
荷花海国家森林公园	Hehuahai National Forest Park (Sichuan)
贺兰山国家森林公园	Helan Mountain National Forest Park (Ningxia, Inner Mongolia)
赫章夜郎国家森林公园	Hezhang Yelang National Forest Park (Guizhou)
鹤伴山国家森林公园	Heban Mountain National Forest Park (Shandong)
鹤岗国家森林公园	Hegang National Forest Park (Heilongjiang)
黑大门国家森林公园	Heidamen National Forest Park (Inner Mongolia)
黑河国家森林公园	Heihe National Forest Park (Shaanxi)
黑龙山国家森林公园	Heilongshan National Forest Park (Hebei)
黑山国家森林公园	Heishan Mountain National Forest Park (Chongqing)
黑竹沟国家森林公园	Heizhu Valley National Forest Park (Sichuan)
恒山国家森林公园	Hengshan Mountain National Forest Park (Shanxi)
横山国家森林公园	Hengshan Mountain National Forest Park (Anhui)
红安天台山国家森林公园	Hongan Tiantai Mountain National Forest Park (Hubei)
红茶沟国家森林公园	Hongcha Valley National Forest Park (Guangxi)
红池坝国家森林公园	Hongchiba National Forest Park (Chongqing)

红花尔基樟子松国家森林公园	Honghua'erji National Forest Park of Mongolian Pine (Inner Mongolia)
红山国家森林公园	Hongshan Mountain National Forest Park (Inner Mongolia)
红石国家森林公园	Hongshi National Forest Park (Jilin)
红松林国家森林公园	Korean Pine Forest National Forest Park (Heilongjiang)
红叶岭国家森林公园	Hongyeling National Forest Park (Jilin)
洪庆山国家森林公园	Hongqingshan National Forest Park (Shaanxi)
洪岩国家森林公园	Hongyan National Forest Park (Jiangxi)
猴石国家森林公园	Houshi National Forest Park (Liaoning)
呼兰国家森林公园	Hulan National Forest Park (Heilongjiang)
呼中国家森林公园	Huzhong National Forest Park (Heilongjiang)
虎爪山国家森林公园	Tiger claw Mountain National Forest Park (Hubei)
花果山国家森林公园	Huaguo Mountain National Forest Park (He'nan)
花马寺国家森林公园	Huama Temple National Forest Park (Ningxia)
花山国家森林公园	Huashan Mountain National Forest Park (Jilin)
花岩国家森林公园	Huayan National Forest Park (Zhejiang)
花岩溪国家森林公园	Huayan Stream National Forest Park (Hu'nan)
花鱼洞国家森林公园	Huayudong National Forest Park (Yunnan)
花鱼洞国家森林公园	Huayu Cave National Forest Park (Yunnan)
华安国家森林公园	Hua'an National Forest Park (Fujian)
华顶国家森林公园	Huading Mountain National Forest Park (Zhejiang)
华夏东极国家森林公园	Huaxia East pole National Forest Park (Heilongjiang)
华蓥山国家森林公园	Huaying Mountain National Forest Park (Sichuan)
桦川国家森林公园	Huachuan National Forest Park (Heilongjiang)
桦木沟国家森林公园	Huamu Valley National Forest Park (Inner Mongolia)
怀玉山国家森林公园	Huaiyushan National Forest Park (Jiangxi)
淮河源国家森林公园	National Forest Park at Huaihe River Headwaters (He'nan)

桓仁国家森林公园	Huanren National Forest Park (Liaoning)
皇甫山国家森林公园	Huangfu Mountain National Forest Park (Anhui)
皇藏峪国家森林公园	Huangzang Valley National Forest Park (Anhui)
黄柏山国家森林公园	Huangbaishan National Forest Park (He'nan)
黄岗梁国家森林公园	Huanggang Ridge National Forest Park (Inner Mongolia)
黄果树瀑布源国家森林公园	Huangguoshu Waterfall Source National Forest Park (Guizhou)
黄海海滨国家森林公园	Jiangsu Huanghai Seashore National Forest Park (Jiangsu)
黄河故道国家森林公园	Old Course National Forest Park of Yellow River (He'nan)
黄河口国家森林公园	Yellow River Estuary National Forest Park (Shandong)
黄猄洞天坑国家森林公园	National Forest Park at Huangjing Cave and Cenote (Guangxi)
黄陵国家森林公园	Huangling National Forest Park (Shaanxi)
黄龙山国家森林公园	Huanglongshan National Forest Park (Shaanxi)
黄山国家森林公园	Huangshan Mountain National Forest Park (Anhui)
黄山头国家森林公园	Huangshantou National Forest Park (Hu'nan)
黄水国家森林公园	Huangshui National Forest Park (Chongqing)
黄松峪国家森林公园	Huangsong Valley National Forest Park (Beijing)
黄崖洞国家森林公园	Huangya Cave National Forest Park (Shanxi)
黄羊山国家森林公园	Huangyang Mountain National Forest Park (Hebei)
徽州国家森林公园	Huizhou National Forest Park (Anhui)
回龙湾国家森林公园	Huilong Bay National Forest Park (Heilongjiang)
廻龙湾国家森林公园	Jialongwan National Forest Park (Heilongjiang)
会昌山国家森林公园	Huichang Mountain National Forest Park (Jiangxi)
惠山国家森林公园	Jiangsu Huishan National Forest Park (Jiangsu)
火山口国家森林公园	Crater National Forest Park (Heilongjiang)
火石寨国家森林公园	Huoshizhai National Forest Park (Ningxia)

鸡峰山国家森林公园	Jifeng Mountain National Forest Park (Gansu)
鸡笼山国家森林公园	Jilong Mountain National Forest Park (Anhui)
加格达奇国家森林公园	Gagdachi National Forest Park (Heilongjiang)
嘉禾国家森林公园	Jiahe National Forest Park (Hu'nan)
嘉山国家森林公园	Jiashan National Forest Park (Hu'nan)
夹金山国家森林公园	Jiajin Mountain National Forest Park (Sichuan)
夹皮沟国家森林公园	Jiapigou National Forest Park (Heilongjiang)
夹山寺国家森林公园	Jiashan Temple National Forest Park (Hu'nan)
贾登峪国家森林公园	Jiadengyu National Forest Park (Xinjiang)
尖峰岭国家森林公园	Jianfeng Ridge National Forest Park (Hai'nan)
剑门关国家森林公园	Jianmen Pass National Forest Park (Sichuan)
江布拉克国家森林公园	Jiangbulake National Forest Park (Xinjiang)
江源国家森林公园	Jiangyuan National Forest Park (Jilin)
将乐天阶山国家森林公园	Tianjie Mountain National Forest Park of Jiangle (Fujian)
交城山国家森林公园	Jiaocheng Mountain National Forest Park (Shanxi)
街津山国家森林公园	Jiejin Mountain National Forest Park (Heilongjiang)
姐德秀国家森林公园	Jiedexiu National Forest Park (Tibet)
金殿国家森林公园	Jindian National Forest Park (Yunnan)
金顶山国家森林公园	Jindingshan National Forest Park (He'nan)
金洞国家森林公园	Jindong National Forest Park (Hu'nan)
金佛山国家森林公园	Jinfo Mountain National Forest Park (Chongqing)
金河口森林公园	Jinhekou Valley Forest Park (Hebei)
金湖杨国家森林公园	Jinhuyang National Forest Park (Xinjiang)
金兰山国家森林公园	Jinlan Mountain National Forest Park (He'nan)
金龙寺国家森林公园	Jinlong Temple National Forest Park (Liaoning)
金盆山国家森林公园	Jinpenshan National Forest Park (Jiangxi)
金泉国家森林公园	Jinquan National Forest Park (Heilongjiang)
金山国家森林公园	Jinshan Mountain National Forest Park (Heilongjiang)
金丝大峡谷国家森林公园	Jinsi Grand Canyon National Forest Park (Shaanxi)

金银滩国家森林公园	Jinyin Beach National Forest Park (Hebei)
景德镇国家森林公园	Jingdezhen National Forest Park (Jiangxi)
径山(山沟沟)国家森林公园	Jingshan (Mountain Gully) National Forest Park (Zhejiang)
净月潭国家森林公园	Jingyue Lake National Forest Park (Jilin)
敬亭山国家森林公园	Jingting Mountain National Forest Park (Anhui)
靖州国家森林公园	Jingzhou National Forest Park (Hu'nan)
镜泊湖国家森林公园	Jingpo Lake National Forest Park (Heilongjiang)
九重山国家森林公园	Jiuchong Mountain National Forest Park (Chongqing)
九道水国家森林公园	Jiudaoshui National Forest Park (Guizhou)
九峰国家森林公园	Jiufeng National Forest Park (Hubei)
九华山国家森林公园	Jiuhua Mountain National Forest Park (Anhui)
九连山国家森林公园	Jiulian Mountain National Forest Park (Jiangxi)
九岭山国家森林公园	Jiulingshan National Forest Park (Jiangxi)
九龙谷国家森林公园	Kowloon Valley National Forest Park (Fujian)
九龙江国家森林公园	Jiulongjiang National Forest Park (Hu'nan)
九龙瀑布群国家森林公园	National Forest Park of Jiulong River Waterfalls (Guangxi)
九龙山国家森林公园	Jiulong Mountain National Forest Park (Tianjin, Zhejiang, Guizhou)
九龙竹海国家森林公园	Kowloon Zhuhai National Forest Park (Fujian)
九女峰国家森林公园	Jiunüfeng National Forest Park (Hubei)
九嶷山国家森林公园	Jiuyi Mountain National Forest Park (Hu'nan)
九寨国家森林公园	Jiuzhai National Forest Park (Sichuan)
韭山国家森林公园	Jiushan Mountain National Forest Park (Anhui)
鹫峰国家森林公园	Jiufeng National Forest Park (Beijing)
岠嵎山国家森林公园	Juyu Mountain National Forest Park (Shandong)
军峰山国家森林公园	Junfeng Mountain National Forest Park (Jiangxi)
开封国家森林公园	Kaifeng National Forest Park (He'nan)
坎布拉国家森林公园	Kanbula National Forest Park (Qinghai)
康禾温泉国家森林公园	Kanghe Hot Spring National Forest Park (Guangdong)
科桑溶洞国家森林公园	Kesang Karst Cave National Forest Park (Xinjiang)

空山国家森林公园	Kongshan Mountain National Forest Park (Sichuan)
库区国家森林公园	Reservoir Area National Forest Park (Liaoning)
匡山国家森林公园	Kuangshan National Forest Park (Fujian)
昆嵛山国家森林公园	Kunyu Mountain National Forest Park (Shandong)
括苍山国家森林公园	Kuocang Mountain National Forest Park (Zhejiang)
拉法山国家森林公园	Lafa Mountain National Forest Park (Jilin)
拉提国家森林公园	Narati National Forest Park (Xinjiang)
喇叭沟门国家森林公园	Labagoumen National Forest Park (Beijing)
喇嘛山国家森林公园	Lamashan National Forest Park (Inner Mongolia)
腊山国家森林公园	Lashan Mountain National Forest Park (Shandong)
腊子口国家森林公园	Lazikou National Forest Park (Gansu)
来凤山国家森林公园	Laifeng Mountain National Forest Park (Yunnan)
莱芜华山国家森林公园	National Forest Park of Laiwu Huashan Mountain (Shandong)
兰家大峡谷国家森林公园	Lanjia Grand Canyon National Forest Park (Jilin)
兰亭国家森林公园	Lanting National Forest Park (Zhejiang)
蓝洋温泉国家森林公园	Lanyang Hot-Spring National Forest Park (Hai'nan)
狼牙山国家森林公园	Langya Mountain National Forest Park (Hebei)
阆中国家森林公园	Langzhong National Forest Park (Sichuan)
琅琊山国家森林公园	Langya Mountain National Forest Park (Anhui)
劳山国家森林公园	Laoshan Mountain National Forest Park (Shaanxi)
崂山国家森林公园	Laoshan Mountain National Forest Park (Shandong)
老顶山国家森林公园	Laoding Mountain National Forest Park (Shanxi)
老嘉山国家森林公园	Laojiashan National Forest Park (Anhui)
雷公山国家森林公园	Leigong Mountain National Forest Park (Guizhou)
骊山国家森林公园	Lishan Mountain National Forest Park (Shaanxi)
黎母山国家森林公园	Limu Mountain National Forest Park (Hai'nan)

黎平国家森林公园	Liping National Forest Park (Guizhou)
黎坪国家森林公园	Liping National Forest Park (Shaanxi)
丽水白云国家森林公园	Lishui Baiyun National Forest Park (Zhejiang)
莲花国家森林公园	Lianhua National Forest Park (Fujian)
莲花山国家森林公园	Lianhua Mountain National Forest Park (Gansu)
良凤江国家森林公园	Liangfeng River National Forest Park (Guangxi)
梁化国家森林公园	Lianghua National Forest Park (Guangdong)
梁平东山国家森林公园	National Forest Park of Liangping East Mountain (Chongqing)
梁希国家森林公园	Liangxi National Forest Park (Zhejiang)
两江峡谷国家森林公园	Liangjiang Canyon National Forest Park (Hu'nan)
辽河源国家森林公园	National Forest Park of Liaohe River Headwaters (Hebei)
临江国家森林公园	Linjiang National Forest Park (Jilin)
临江瀑布群国家森林公园	Linjiang waterfall Group National Forest Park (Jilin)
灵宝山国家森林公园	Lingbao Mountain National Forest Park (Yunnan)
灵山湾国家森林公园	Lingshan Bay National Forest Park (Shandong)
灵石山国家森林公园	Lingshi Mountain National Forest Park (Fujian)
灵岩洞国家森林公园	Lingyan Cave National Forest Park (Jiangxi)
凌云山国家森林公园	Lingyun Mountain National Forest Park (Sichuan)
刘公岛国家森林公园	Liugong Island National Forest Park (Shandong)
留山古火山国家森林公园	Liushan ancient Volcano National Forest Park (Shandong)
流溪河国家森林公园	Liuxi River National Forest Park (Guangdong)
柳埠国家森林公园	Liubu National Forest Park (Shandong)
六峰山国家森林公园	Liufeng Mountain National Forest Park (Heilongjiang)
六里坪国家森林公园	Liuliping National Forest Park (Hebei)
六盘山国家森林公园	Liupan Mountain National Forest Park (Ningxia)
龙苍沟国家森林公园	Longcanggou National Forest Park (Sichuan)
龙池国家森林公园	Longchi National Forest Park (Sichuan)

龙凤国家森林公园	Longfeng National Forest Park (Heilongjiang)
龙架山国家森林公园	Longjiashan National Forest Park (Guizhou)
龙江三峡国家森林公园	National Forest Park of Longjiang River Three Gorges (Heilongjiang)
龙口南山国家森林公园	National Forest Park of Longkou South Mountain (Shandong)
龙门河国家森林公园	Longmen River National Forest Park (Hubei)
龙泉国家森林公园	Longquan National Forest Park (Shanxi, Yunan)
龙山湖国家森林公园	Longshan Lake National Forest Park (Jilin)
龙胜国家森林公园	Longsheng National Forest Park (Inner Mongolia)
龙胜温泉国家森林公园	National Forest Park of Longsheng Hot Spring (Guangxi)
龙滩大峡谷国家森林公园	Longtan Grand Canyon National Forest Park (Guangxi)
龙潭国家森林公园	Longtan National Forest Park (Guangxi)
龙湾群国家森林公园	Longwan-Bay Cluster National Forest Park (Jilin)
龙湾潭国家森林公园	Longwan Pond National Forest Park (Zhejiang)
龙峡山国家森林公园	Longxiashan National Forest Park (Guangxi)
龙岩国家森林公园	Longyan National Forest Park (Fujian)
龙峪湾国家森林公园	Longyu Bay National Forest Park (He'nan)
楼观台国家森林公园	Louguantai National Forest Park (Shaanxi)
庐山山南国家森林公园	National Forest Park of Lushan South Mountainside (Jiangxi)
鲁布格国家森林公园	Lubuge National Forest Park (Yunnan)
鲁山国家森林公园	Lushan Mountain National Forest Park (Shandong)
鹿门寺国家森林公园	Lumensi National Forest Park (Hubei)
露水河国家森林公园	Lushuihe National Forest Park (Jilin)
轮台胡杨林森林公园	Luntai Poplar Forest Park (Xinjiang)
罗山国家森林公园	Luoshan Mountain National Forest Park (Shandong)
罗霄山大峡谷国家森林公园	Luoxiao Mountain Grand Canyon National Forest Park (Jiangxi)

旅顺口国家森林公园	Lüshunkou National Forest Park (Liaoning)
马鞍山国家森林公园	Ma'an Mountain National Forest Park (Inner Mongolia)
马家溪国家森林公园	Majiaxi National Forest Park (Anhui)
马祖山国家森林公园	Mazu Mountain National Forest Park (Jiangxi)
玛旁雍措国家森林公园	Manasarovar Lake National Forest Park (Tibet)
麦积国家森林公园	Maiji National Forest Park (Gansu)
麦秀国家森林公园	Maixiu National Forest Park (Qinghai)
满天星国家森林公园	Mantianxing National Forest Park (Jilin)
莽山国家森林公园	Mangshan Mountain National Forest Park (Hu'nan)
蟒山国家森林公园	Mangshan National Forest Park; Python Mountain National Forest Park (Beijing)
蟒头山国家森林公园	Mangtou Mountain National Forest Park (Shaanxi)
猫儿山国家森林公园	Mao'er Mountain National Forest Park (Fujian)
茅荆坝国家森林公园	Maojingba National Forest Park (Hebei)
茅兰沟国家森林公园	Maolan Valley National Forest Park (Heilongjiang)
茂云山国家森林公园	Maoyun Mountain National Forest Park (Chongqing)
帽儿山国家森林公园	Mao'er Mountain National Forest Park (Jilin)
梅关国家森林公园	Meiguan National Forest Park (Jiangxi)
梅花山国家森林公园	Meihua Mountain National Forest Park (Heilongjiang)
梅岭国家森林公园	Meiling Ridge National Forest Park (Jiangxi)
美女峰国家森林公园	Meinü Peak National Forest Park (Sichuan)
蒙山国家森林公园	Mengshan Mountain National Forest Park (Shandong)
孟良崮国家森林公园	Menglianggu National Forest Park (Shandong)
米仓山国家森林公园	Micang Mountain National Forest Park (Sichuan)
密州国家森林公园	Mizhou National Forest Park (Shandong)
妙道山国家森林公园	Miaodao Mountain National Forest Park (Anhui)
闽江源国家森林公园	Minjiangyuan National Forest Park (Fujian)

明月山国家森林公园	Mingyue Mountain National Forest Park (Jiangxi)
莫尔道嘎国家森林公园	Moridaga National Forest Park (Inner Mongolia)
磨盘山国家森林公园	Mopan Mountain National Forest Park (Yunnan)
牡丹峰国家森林公园	Mudan Peak National Forest Park (Heilongjiang)
木兰围场国家森林公园	Mulan National Forest Park of Enclosed Imperial Hunting Ground (Hebei)
木王国家森林公园	Muwang National Forest Park (Shaanxi)
沐川国家森林公园	Muchuan National Forest Park (Sichuan)
幕阜山国家森林公园	Mufu Mountain National Forest Park (Hu'nan)
那拉提国家森林公园	Narati National Forest Park (Xinjiang)
	Nuoxi National Forest Park (Hu'nan)
南澳海岛国家森林公园	Nan'ao Island National Forest Park (Guangdong)
南澳海岛国家森林公园	National Forest Park of Nan'ao Sea Island (Guangdong)
南宫山国家森林公园	Nangong Mountain National Forest Park (Shaanxi)
南华山国家森林公园	Nanhua Mountain National Forest Park (Hu'nan)
南京老山国家森林公园	Nanjing Laoshan National Forest Park (Jiangsu)
南京栖霞山国家森林公园	Nanjing Qixia Mountain National Forest Park (Jiangsu)
南京无想山国家森林公园	Nanjing Wuxiangshan National Forest Park (Jiangsu)
南京紫金山国家森林公园	Nanjing Zijinshan National Forest Park (Jiangsu)
南靖土楼国家森林公园	Nanjing Tulou National Forest Park (Fujian)
南昆山国家森林公园	Nankun Mountain National Forest Park (Guangdong)
南岭国家森林公园	Nanling Mountain National Forest Park (Guangdong)
南山国家森林公园	Nanshan National Forest Park (Chongqing, Jiangsu)
南山湖国家森林公园	Nanshan Lake National Forest Park (Zhejiang)
南台山国家森林公园	Nantai Mountain National Forest Park (Guangdong)
南湾国家森林公园	South Bay National Forest Park (He'nan)
尼木国家森林公园	Nimu National Forest Park (Tibet)

尼山国家森林公园	Nishan Mountain National Forest Park (Shandong)
宁乡香山国家森林公园	Ningxiang Xiangshan National Forest Park (Hu'nan)
牛背梁国家森林公园	Niubeiliang National Forest Park (Shaanxi)
牛山国家森林公园	Niushan Mountain National Forest Park (Shandong)
牛头山国家森林公园	Niutou Mountain National Forest Park (Hubei, Zhejiang)
蟠龙山国家森林公园	Panlongshan National Forest Park (Shandong)
彭泽国家森林公园	Pengze National Forest Park (Jiangxi)
偏头山国家森林公园	Piantoushan National Forest Park (Hubei)
平坛海岛国家森林公园	Pingtan National Forest Park of Sea Island (Fujian)
平潭海岛国家森林公园	Pingtan Island National Forest Park (Fujian)
平天山国家森林公园	Pingtian Mountain National Forest Park (Guangxi)
坪坝营国家森林公园	Pingbaying National Forest Park (Hubei)
鄱阳湖国家森林公园	Poyang Lake National Forest Park (Jiangxi)
鄱阳湖口国家森林公园	Poyang Hukou National Forest Park (Jiangxi)
鄱阳莲花山国家森林公园	Poyang Lianhua Mountain National Forest Park (Jiangxi)
普兰店国家森林公园	Pulandian National Forest Park (Liaoning)
七曲山国家森林公园	Qiqu Mountain National Forest Park (Sichuan)
七仙岭温泉国家森林公园	National Forest Park of Qixian-Peak Hot Spring (Hai'nan)
七星峰国家森林公园	Qixingfeng National Forest Park (Heilongjiang)
七星山国家森林公园	Qixingshan National Forest Park (Heilongjiang)
齐齐哈尔国家森林公园	Qiqihar National Forest Park (Heilongjiang)
齐云峰国家森林公园	Qiyunfeng National Forest Park (Hu'nan)
齐云山国家森林公园	Qiyun Mountain National Forest Park (Anhui)
岐山国家森林公园	Qishan National Forest Park (Hu'nan)
崎峰山国家森林公园	Qifeng Mountain National Forest Park (Beijing)
棋盘山国家森林公园	Qipan Mountain National Forest Park (Yunnan)
棋山幽峡国家森林公园	Qishan Youxia National Forest Park (Shandong)
棋子山国家森林公园	Qizishan National Forest Park (Shanxi)

旗山国家森林公园	Qishan Mountain National Forest Park (Fujian)
千岛湖国家森林公园	Thousand-Island Lake National Forest Park (Zhejiang)
千佛洞国家森林公园	Qianfo (Thousand Buddhas) Cave National Forest Park (Hubei)
千佛山国家森林公园	Qianfo Mountain National Forest Park (Sichuan)
千家峒国家森林公园	Qianjiadong National Forest Park (Hu'nan)
千家坪国家森林公园	Qianjiaping National Forest Park (Shaanxi)
千山仙人台国家森林公园	National Forest Park of Qianshan Mountain Fairy Terrace (Liaoning)
前南峪国家森林公园	Qiannanyu National Forest Park (Hebei)
钱江源国家森林公园	Qianjiangyuan National Forest Park (Zhejiang)
钱江源国家森林公园	National Forest Park of Qianjiang River Headwaters (Zhejiang)
潜山国家森林公园	Qianshan Mountain National Forest Park (Hubei)
黔江国家森林公园	Qianjiang River National Forest Park (Chongqing)
桥口坝国家森林公园	Qiaokouba National Forest Park (Chongqing)
秦皇岛海滨国家森林公园	Qinghuangdao Seaside National Forest Park (Hebei)
青峰峡国家森林公园	Qingfengxia National Forest Park (Shaanxi)
青龙湖国家森林公园	Qinglong Lake National Forest Park (Chongqing)
青龙湾国家森林公园	Qinglongwan National Forest Park (Anhui)
青山国家森林公园	Qingshan Mountain National Forest Park (Heilongjiang)
青山湖国家森林公园	Qingshan Lake National Forest Park (Zhejiang)
青羊湖国家森林公园	Qingyang Lake National Forest Park (Hu'nan)
青云湖国家森林公园	Qingyun Lake National Forest Park (Guizhou)
清东陵国家森林公园	National Forest Park of Eastern Qing Tombs (Hebei)
清华洞国家森林公园	Qinghua Cave National Forest Park (Yunnan)
清江国家森林公园	Qingjiang River National Forest Park (Hubei)
清凉山国家森林公园	Qingliangshan National Forest Park (Jiangxi)
清原红河谷国家森林公园	National Forest Park of Qingyan Honghe River Valley (Liaoning)

庆元国家森林公园	Qingyuan National Forest Park (Zhejiang)
磬棰峰国家森林公园	Qingchui Peak National Forest Park (Hebei)
磬槌峰国家森林公园	Qingchuifeng National Forest Park (Hebei)
泉林国家森林公园	Quanlin National Forest Park (Shandong)
泉阳泉国家森林公园	Quanyangquan National Forest Park (Jilin)
群加国家森林公园	Qunja National Forest Park (Qinghai)
然乌湖国家森林公园	Rawok Lake National Forest Park (Tibet)
热振国家森林公园	Razheng National Forest Park (Tibet)
日月峡国家森林公园	Sun-Moon Canyon National Forest Park (Heilongjiang)
日照国家森林公园	Rizhao National Forest Park (Shandong)
日照海滨国家森林公园	Rizhao seaside National Forest Park (Shandong)
汝州国家森林公园	Ruzhou National Forest Park (He'nan)
塞罕坝国家森林公园	Saihanba National Forest Park (Hebei)
三百山国家森林公园	Sanbai Mountain National Forest Park (Jiangxi)
三道关国家森林公园	Sandaoguan (Three Passes) National Forest Park (Heilongjiang)
三叠泉国家森林公园	Three-Step Cascades National Forest Park (Jiangxi)
三瓜仑国家森林公园	Sangualun National Forest Park (Jiangxi)
三角山国家森林公园	Sanjiao Mountain National Forest Park (Hubei)
三块石国家森林公园	Three Stones National Forest Park (Liaoning)
三岭山国家森林公园	Sanling Mountain National Forest Park (Guangdong)
三门江国家森林公园	Sanmen River National Forest Park (Guangxi)
三明仙人谷国家森林公园	Sanming Xianren Valley National Forest Park (Fujian)
三衢国家森林公园	Sanqu National Forest Park (Zhejiang)
三台山国家森林公园	Jiangsu Santai Mountain National Forest Park (Jiangsu)
三湾国家森林公园	Sanwan National Forest Park (Jiangxi)
三仙夹国家森林公园	San-Xian-Jia National Forest Park (Jilin)
三元国家森林公园	Sanyuan National Forest Park (Fujian)
三爪仑国家森林公园	Sanjialun National Forest Park (Jiangxi)

色季拉国家森林公园	Sejila National Forest Park (Tibet)
沙滩国家森林公园	Shatan National Forest Park (Gansu)
山海关国家森林公园	Shanhaiguan National Forest Park (Hebei)
上坝河国家森林公园	Shangbahe National Forest Park (Shaanxi)
上方山国家森林公园	Shangfang Mountain National Forest Park (Jiangsu, Beijing)
上海东平国家森林公园	Dongping National Forest Park (Shanghai)
上海海湾国家森林公园	Shanghai Bay National Forest Park
上杭国家森林公园	Shanghang National Forest Park (Fujian)
上清国家森林公园	Shangqing National Forest Park (Jiangxi)
上窑国家森林公园	Shangyao National Forest Park (Anhui)
韶关国家森林公园	Shaoguan National Forest Park (Guangdong)
绍兴会稽山国家森林公园	Shaoxing Kuaijishan National Forest Park (Zhejiang)
少华山国家森林公园	Shaohuashan National Forest Park (Shaanxi)
佘山国家森林公园	Sheshan Mountain National Forest Park (Shanghai)
神洞山国家森林公园	Shendong Mountain National Forest Park (Heilongjiang)
神光山国家森林公园	Shenguang Mountain National Forest Park (Guangdong)
神灵寨国家森林公园	Shenlingzhai National Forest Park (He'nan)
神农谷国家森林公园	Shennong Valley National Forest Park (Hu'nan)
神农架国家森林公园	Shennongjia National Forest Park (Hubei)
神山国家森林公园	Shenshan Mountain National Forest Park (Anhui, Inner Mongolia)
沈阳国家森林公园	Shenyang National Forest Park (Liaoning)
圣水堂国家森林公园	Shengshuitang National Forest Park (Jiangxi)
胜山要塞国家森林公园	Shengshan Mountain National Forest Park (Heilongjiang)
诗经源国家森林公园	Shijingyuan National Forest Park (Hubei)
狮子山国家森林公园	Lion Mountain National Forest Park (Guangxi)
十八连山国家森林公园	Shibalian Mountain National Forest Park (Yunnan)

十三陵国家森林公园	Ming Tombs National Forest Park (Beijing)
十万大山国家森林公园	National Forest Park of Shiwan Grand Mountains (Guangxi)
石佛沟国家森林公园	Shifo Gully National Forest Park (Gansu)
石佛国家森林公园	Stone Buddha National Forest Park (Hebei)
石湖国家森林公园	Shihu Lake National Forest Park (Jilin)
石莲洞国家森林公园	Shiliandong National Forest Park (Anhui)
石龙山国家森林公园	Shilong Mountain National Forest Park (Heilongjiang)
石漫滩国家森林公园	Shiman Beach National Forest Park (He'nan)
石门洞国家森林公园	Shimen Cave National Forest Park (Zhejiang)
石门国家森林公园	Shimen National Forest Park (Guangdong)
石牛山国家森林公园	Shiniu Mountain National Forest Park (Fujian)
始祖山国家森林公园	Shizu Mountain National Forest Park (He'nan)
首山国家森林公园	Shoushan Mountain National Forest Park (Liaoning)
寿鹿山国家森林公园	Shoulu Mountain National Forest Park (Gansu)
蜀山国家森林公园	Shushan National Forest Park (Anhui)
双岛国家森林公园	Shuangdao (Twin Islands) National Forest Park (Shandong)
双峰国家森林公园	Shuangfeng (Twin Peaks) National Forest Park (Zhejiang)
双峰山国家森林公园	Shuangfeng (Twin Peaks) Mountain National Forest Park (Hubei)
双桂山国家森林公园	Shuanggui Mountain National Forest Park (Chongqing)
双江古茶山国家森林公园	Shuangjiang Ancient Tea Mountain National Forest Park (Yunnan)
双龙洞国家森林公园	Shuanglong Cave National Forest Park (Zhejiang)
水西国家森林公园	Shuixi National Forest Park (Anhui)
舜耕山国家森林公园	Shungeng Mountain National Forest Park (Anhui)

舜皇山国家森林公园	Shunhuang Mountain National Forest Park (Hu'nan)
四明山国家森林公园	Siming Mountain National Forest Park (Hu'nan, Zhejiang)
寺山国家森林公园	Sishan Mountain National Forest Park (He'nan)
松鸣岩国家森林公园	Songming Rock National Forest Park (Gansu)
松阳卯山国家森林公园	Maoshan Mountain National Forest Park in Songyang (Zhejiang)
嵩山国家森林公园	Songshan Mountain National Forest Park (He'nan)
苏峪口国家森林公园	Suyukou National Forest Park (Ningxia)
绥芬河国家森林公园	Suifen River National Forest Park (Heilongjiang)
绥中长城国家森林公园	Suizhong Great Wall National Forest Park (Liaoning)
遂昌国家森林公园	Suichang National Forest Park (Zhejiang)
塔川国家森林公园	Tachuan National Forest Park (Anhui)
塔西河国家森林公园	Tashi River National Forest Park (Xinjiang)
台江国家森林公园	Taijiang National Forest Park (Guizhou)
太白山国家森林公园	Taibai Mountain National Forest Park (Shaanxi)
太行洪谷国家森林公园	Taihang Honggu National Forest Park (Shanxi)
太行峡谷国家森林公园	Taihang Canyon National Forest Park (Shanxi)
太湖山国家森林公园	Taihu Mountain National Forest Park (Anhui)
太平国家森林公园	Taiping National Forest Park (Shaanxi)
太平狮山国家森林公园	Shishan Mountain National Forest Park of Taiping (Guangxi)
太阳河国家森林公园	Sun River National Forest Park (Yunnan)
太岳山国家森林公园	Taiyue Mountain National Forest Park (Shanxi)
太子山国家森林公园	Taizi Mountain National Forest Park (Hubei)
泰和国家森林公园	Taihe National Forest Park (Jiangxi)
泰山国家森林公园	Taishan Mountain National Forest Park (Shandong)
唐布拉国家森林公园	Tangbula National Forest Park (Xinjiang)
棠溪源国家森林公园	Tangxiyuan National Forest Park (He'nan)
桃花江国家森林公园	Taohuajiang National Forest Park (Hu'nan)
桃花源国家森林公园	Taohuayuan National Forest Park (Hu'nan)

桃山国家森林公园	Taoshan Mountain National Forest Park (Heilongjiang)
腾云岭国家森林公园	Tengyunling National Forest Park (Hu'nan)
滕州墨子国家森林公园	Tengzhou Mozi National Forest Park (Shandong)
天池国家森林公园	Tianchi Lake National Forest Park (Xingjiang, Gansu)
天池山国家森林公园	Tianchi Mountain National Forest Park (He'nan, Chongqing)
天鹅山国家森林公园	Tian'e Mountain National Forest Park (Hu'nan)
天花井国家森林公园	Tianhuajing National Forest Park (Jiangxi)
天华山国家森林公园	Tianhua Mountain National Forest Park (Shaanxi)
天际岭国家森林公园	Tianji Ridge National Forest Park (Hu'nan)
天井山国家森林公园	Tianjingshan Mountain National Forest Park (Guangdong)
天井山国家森林公园	Tianjing Mountain National Forest Park (Anhui)
天龙山国家森林公园	Tianlong Mountain National Forest Park (Shanxi)
天马山国家森林公园	Tianma Mountain National Forest Park (Sichuan)
天门山国家森林公园	Tianmen Mountain National Forest Park (Hu'nan, Beijing)
天目湖国家森林公园	Jiangsu Tianmu Lake National Forest Park (Jiangsu)
天目山国家森林公园	Tianmu Mountain National Forest Park (He'nan)
天桥沟国家森林公园	Tianqiao Valley National Forest Park (Liaoning)
天泉山国家森林公园	Tianquan Mountain National Forest Park (Hu'nan)
天山大峡谷国家森林公园	Tianshan Grand Canyon National Forest Park (Xinjiang)
天生桥国家森林公园	Natural Bridge National Forest Park (Hebei)
天台山国家森林公园	Tiantai Mountain National Forest Park (Hubei, Sichuan, Shaanxi)
天堂山国家森林公园	Paradise Mountain National Forest Park (Hu'nan)
天堂寨国家森林公园	Tiantangzhai National Forest Park (Anhui)

天童国家森林公园	Tiantong National Forest Park (Zhejiang)
天星国家森林公园	Tianxing National Forest Park (Yunnan)
天星山国家森林公园	Tianxing Mountain National Forest Park (Fujian)
天罩山国家森林公园	Tianzhaoshan National Forest Park (Sichuan)
天竺山国家森林公园	Tianzhu Mountain National Forest Park (Shaanxi)
天柱峰国家森林公园	Tianzhu Peak National Forest Park (Jiangxi)
天柱山国家森林公园	Tianzhu Mountain National Forest Park (Anhui, Fujian)
天祝三峡国家森林公园	Three-Valley National Forest Park of Tianzhu (Gansu)
铁峰山国家森林公园	Tiefeng Mountain National Forest Park (Chongqing)
铁岭麒麟湖国家森林公园	Tieling Qilin Lake National Forest Park (Liaoning)
铁山国家森林公园	Tieshan National Forest Park (Sichuan)
铁山寺国家森林公园	Tieshan Temple National Forest Park (Shanghai)
通化石湖国家森林公园	Tonghua Shihu National Forest Park (Jilin)
通天河国家森林公园	Tongtian River National Forest Park (Shaanxi)
桐庐瑶琳国家森林公园	Tonglu Yaolin National Forest Park (Zhejiang)
铜钹山国家森林公园	Tongbo Mountain National Forest Park (Jiangxi)
铜铃山国家森林公园	Tongling Mountain National Forest Park (Zhejiang)
铜锣坝国家森林公园	Tongluo Dam National Forest Park (Yunnan)
铜山湖国家森林公园	Tongshan Lake National Forest Park (He'nan)
图博勒国家森林公园	Tubole National Forest Park (Inner Mongolia)
图们江国家森林公园	Tumen River National Forest Park (Jilin)
图们江源国家森林公园	National Forest Park of Tumen River Headwaters (Jilin)
吐鲁沟国家森林公园	Tulu Gully National Forest Park (Gansu)
驼梁山国家森林公园	Tuoliangshan National Forest Park (Hebei)
瓦屋山国家森林公园	Wawu Mountain National Forest Park (Sichuan)
湾沟国家森林公园	Wangou National Forest Park (Jilin)
完达山国家森林公园	Wanda Mountain National Forest Park (Heilongjiang)

万安国家森林公园	Wan'an National Forest Park (Jiangxi)
万佛山国家森林公园	Wanfo Mountain National Forest Park (Anhui)
万有国家森林公园	Wanyou National Forest Park (Guangdong)
王寿山国家森林公园	Wangshou Mountain National Forest Park (Fujian)
王顺山国家森林公园	Wangshun Mountain National Forest Park (Shaanxi)
旺业甸国家森林公园	Wangyedian National Forest Park (Inner Mongolia)
望龙山国家森林公园	Wanglong Mountain National Forest Park (Heilongjiang)
威虎山国家森林公园	Weihu Mountain National Forest Park (Heilongjiang)
巍宝山国家森林公园	Weibao Mountain National Forest Park (Yunnan)
浠水国家森林公园	Weishui Dam National Forest Park (Hubei)
伟德山国家森林公园	Weide Mountain National Forest Park (Shandong)
渭河源国家森林公园	National Forest Park of Weihe River Headwaters (Gansu)
文县天池国家森林公园	Wenxian Tianchi National Forest Park (Gansu)
乌尔旗汉国家森林公园	Orqohan National Forest Park (Inner Mongolia)
乌金山国家森林公园	Wujin Mountain National Forest Park (Shanxi)
乌拉山国家森林公园	Ula Mountain National Forest Park (Inner Mongolia)
乌龙国家森林公园	Wulong National Forest Park (Heilongjiang)
乌鲁木齐天山国家森林公园	Urumqi Tianshan National Forest Park (Xinjiang)
乌马河国家森林公园	Wumahe National Forest Park (Heilongjiang)
乌山国家森林公园	Wushan Mountain National Forest Park (Fujian)
乌苏佛山国家森林公园	Wusu Foshan National Forest Park (Xinjiang)
乌苏里江国家森林公园	Usuli River National Forest Park (Heilongjiang)
乌素图国家森林公园	Usutu National Forest Park (Inner Mongolia)
吴家山国家森林公园	Wujia Mountain National Forest Park (Hubei)

梧桐山国家森林公园	Wutong Mountain National Forest Park (Guangdong)
五大连池国家森林公园	Wudalianchi (Five Lotus Ponds) National Forest Park (Heilongjiang)
五当召国家森林公园	Wudang Temple National Forest Park (Inner Mongolia)
五顶山国家森林公园	Wuding Mountain National Forest Park (Heilongjiang)
五峰山国家森林公园	Wufeng Mountain National Forest Park (Sichuan, Yunnan)
五府山国家森林公园	Wufushan National Forest Park (Jiangxi)
五虎山国家森林公园	Wuhushan National Forest Park (Fujian)
五尖山国家森林公园	Wujianshan National Forest Park (Hu'nan)
五老峰国家森林公园	Wulao Peak National Forest Park (Shanxi)
五老山国家森林公园	Wulao Mountain National Forest Park (Yunnan)
五莲山国家森林公园	Wulian Mountain National Forest Park (Shandong)
五龙洞国家森林公园	Wulong Cave National Forest Park (He'nan, Shaanxi)
五脑山国家森林公园	Wunaoshan National Forest Park (Hubei)
五女峰国家森林公园	Wunü Peak National Forest Park (Jilin)
五台山国家森林公园	Wutai Mountain National Forest Park (Shanxi)
五泄国家森林公园	Wuxie National Forest Park (Zhejiang)
五营国家森林公园	Wuying National Forest Park (Heilongjiang)
五岳寨国家森林公园	Wuyuezhai National Forest Park (Hebei)
五指峰国家森林公园	Wuzhi (Five Fingers) Peaks National Forest Park (Jiangxi)
午潮山国家森林公园	Wuchao Mountain National Forest Park (Zhejiang)
武安国家森林公园	Wu'an National Forest Park (Hebei)
武功山国家森林公园	Wugong Mountain National Forest Park (Jiangxi)
武陵山国家森林公园	Wuling Mountain National Forest Park (Chongqing)
武夷山国家森林公园	Wuyi Mountain National Forest Park (Fujian)

武夷天池国家森林公园	Wuyi Tianchi National Forest Park (Fujian)
潕阳湖国家森林公园	Wuyang Lake National Forest Park (Guizhou)
潕阳湖国家森林公园	Fuyang Lake National Forest Park (Guizhou)
西口古道国家森林公园	Xikou Ancient Road National Forest Park (Shanxi)
西岭国家森林公园	Xiling Ridge National Forest Park (Sichuan)
西樵山国家森林公园	Xiqiao Mountain National Forest Park (Guangdong)
西塞国家森林公园	Western Cyprus National Forest Park (Hubei)
西山国家森林公园	Xishan National Forest Park; West Mountain National Park (Beijing, Jiangsu)
西双版纳国家森林公园	Xishuang Banna National Forest Park (Yunnan)
西瑶绿谷国家森林公园	Xiyao Green Valley National Forest Park (Hu'nan)
溪口国家森林公园	Xikou National Forest Park (Zhejiang)
溪水国家森林公园	Xishui Stream National Forest Park (Heilongjiang)
习水国家森林公园	Xishui National Forest Park (Guizhou)
霞云岭国家森林公园	Xiayun Ridge National Forest Park (Beijing)
夏津黄河故道国家森林公园	Xiajin Yellow River National Forest Park (Shandong)
夏塔古道国家森林公园	Xiata Ancient Road National Forest Park (Xinjiang)
厦门莲花国家森林公园	Xiamen Lotus National Forest Park (Fujian)
仙鹤坪国家森林公园	Xianheping National Forest Park (Guizhou)
仙居国家森林公园	Xianju National Forest Park (Zhejiang)
仙米国家森林公园	Xianmi National Forest Park (Qinghai)
仙女国家森林公园	Xiannü (Fairy Maiden) National Forest Park (Chongqing)
仙女山国家森林公园	Fairy Mountain National Forest Park (Chongqing)
仙人洞国家森林公园	Fairy Cave National Forest Park (Liaoning)
仙人谷国家森林公园	Fairy Valley National Forest Park (Fujian)
仙人台国家森林公园	Xianrentai National Forest Park (Liaoning)
仙堂山国家森林公园	Xiantang Mountain National Forest Park (Shanxi)
仙翁山国家森林公园	Xianweng Mountain National Forest Park (Heilongjiang)

仙霞国家森林公园	Xianxia National Forest Park (Zhejiang)
岘山国家森林公园	Danshan National Forest Park (Hubei)
相山国家森林公园	Xiangshan National Forest Park (Anhui)
香格里拉普达措国家森林公园	Shangri-La Potatso National Forest Park (Yunnan)
香炉山国家森林公园	Xianglu Mountain National Forest Park (Heilongjiang)
湘江源国家森林公园	Xiangjiangyuan National Forest Park (Hu'nan)
翔云岛国家森林公园	Xiangyun Island National Forest Park (Hebei)
响堂山国家森林公园	Xiangtang Mountain National Forest Park (Hebei)
小白龙国家森林公园	Xiaobailong (Little White Dragon) National Forest Park (Yunnan)
小坑国家森林公园	Xiaokeng National Forest Park (Guangdong)
小龙门国家森林公园	Xiaolongmen National Forest Park (Beijing)
小陇山国家森林公园	Xiaolong Mountain National Forest Park (Gansu)
小三峡国家森林公园	Lesser Three Gorges National Forest Park (Chongqing)
小兴安岭红松林国家森林公园	Xiaoxing'anling Korean Pine Forest National Forest Park (Heilongjiang)
小兴安岭石林国家森林公园	Stone Forest National Forest Park of Lesser Khingan Mountain (Heilongjiang)
蝎子沟国家森林公园	Scorpion ditch National Forest Park (Hebei)
薤山国家森林公园	Xieshan Mountain National Forest Park (Hubei)
新丰江国家森林公园	Xinfeng River National Forest Park (Guangdong)
新生桥国家森林公园	Xinshengqiao National Forest Park (Yunnan)
新泰莲花山国家森林公园	Lianhua (Lotus) Mountain National Forest Park of Xintai (Shandong)
兴安国家森林公园	Xing'an National Forest Park (Inner Mongolia, Heilongjiang)
兴隆国家森林公园	Xinglong National Forest Park (Inner Mongolia, Heilongjiang)
兴隆侨乡国家森林公园	Xinglong Qiaoxiang National Forest Park (Hai'nan)

熊峰山国家森林公园	Xiongfeng Mountain National Forest Park (Hu'nan)
盱眙第一山国家森林公园	Jiangsu Xuyi First Mountain National Forest Park (Jiangsu)
徐家山国家森林公园	Xujia Mountain National Forest Park (Gansu)
徐州环城国家森林公园	Xuzhou Round-the-City National Forest Park (Shanghai)
溆浦国家森林公园	Xupu National Forest Park (Hu'nan)
宣汉国家森林公园	Xuanhan National Forest Park (Sichuan)
萱洲国家森林公园	Xuanzhou National Forest Park (Hu'nan)
雪宝山国家森林公园	Xuebao Mountain National Forest Park (Chongqing)
雪峰山国家森林公园	Xuefeng Mountain National Forest Park (Hu'nan)
雪乡国家森林公园	Xuexiang (Snowy Countryside) National Forest Park (Heilongjiang)
岣嵝峰国家森林公园	Goulou Peak National Forest Park (Hu'nan)
牙山国家森林公园	Yashan Mountain National Forest Park (Shandong)
雅克夏国家森林公园	Yaksha National Forest Park (Sichuan)
亚布力国家森林公园	Yabuli National Forest Park (Heilongjiang)
亚武山国家森林公园	Yawu Mountain National Forest Park (He'nan)
延安国家森林公园	Yan'an National Forest Park (Shaanxi)
延边仙峰国家森林公园	Xianfeng National Forest Park in Yanbian (Jilin)
岩泉国家森林公园	Yanquan National Forest Park (Jiangxi)
雁荡山国家森林公园	Yandang Mountain National Forest Park (Zhejiang)
燕子山国家森林公园	Yanzi Mountain National Forest Park (He'nan)
燕子岩国家森林公园	Yanzi Rock National Forest Park (Guizhou)
阳岭国家森林公园	Yangling Hill National Forest Park (Jiangxi)
阳明山国家森林公园	Yangming Mountain National Forest Park (Hu'nan)
阳朔国家森林公园	Yangshuo National Forest Park (Guangxi)
杨梅洲峡谷国家森林公园	Yangmeizhou Canyon National Forest Park (Fujian)

仰天山国家森林公园	Yangtian Mountain National Forest Park (Shandong)
尧人山国家森林公园	Yaorenshan National Forest Park (Guizhou)
瑶里国家森林公园	Yaoli National Forest Park (Jiangxi)
瑶人山国家森林公园	Yaoren Mountain National Forest Park (Guizhou)
药乡国家森林公园	Medicine Hometown National Forest Park (Shandong)
冶父山国家森林公园	Yefu Mountain National Forest Park (Anhui)
冶力关国家森林公园	Yeli Pass National Forest Park (Gansu)
野三坡国家森林公园	Yeshanpo National Forest Park (Hebei)
一面坡国家森林公园	Yimianpo National Forest Park (Heilongjiang)
伊春兴安国家森林公园	Yichun Xing'an National Forest Park (Heilongjiang)
医巫闾山国家森林公园	Yiwulu Mountain National Forest Park (Liaoning)
沂山国家森林公园	Yishan Mountain National Forest Park (Shandong)
宜兴国家森林公园	Yixing National Forest Park (Shanghai)
易州国家森林公园	Yizhou National Forest Park (Hebei)
峄城古石榴国家森林公园	Yicheng Ancient Pomegranate National Forest Park (Shandong)
峄山国家森林公园	Yishan National Forest Park (Shandong)
驿马山国家森林公园	Yima Mountain National Forest Park (Heilongjiang)
阴那山国家森林公园	Yinnashan National Forest Park (Guangdong)
英德国家森林公园	Yingde National Forest Park (Guangdong)
永丰国家森林公园	Yongfeng National Forest Park (Jiangxi)
永兴丹霞国家森林公园	Yongxing Danxia National Forest Park (Hu'nan)
攸州国家森林公园	Youzhou National Forest Park (Hu'nan)
油杉河大峡谷国家森林公园	Yashanhe Grand Canyon National Forest Park (Guizhou)
游子山国家森林公园	Jiangsu Youzishan National Forest Park (Jiangsu)
酉阳桃花源国家森林公园	Youyang Taohuayuan National Forest Park (Chongqing)

榆林沙漠国家森林公园	Yulin Desert National Forest Park (Shaanxi)
虞山国家森林公园	Yushan Mountain National Forest Park (Shanghai)
禹王洞国家森林公园	Yuwang Cave National Forest Park (Shanxi)
玉苍山国家森林公园	Yucang Mountain National Forest Park (Zhejiang)
玉华宫国家森林公园	Yuhua Palace National Forest Park (Shaanxi)
玉皇山国家森林公园	Yuhuang Mountain National Forest Park (He'nan)
玉龙山国家森林公园	Yulong Mountain National Forest Park (Chongqing)
玉泉寺国家森林公园	Yuquan Temple National Forest Park (Hubei)
玉舍国家森林公园	Yushe National Forest Park (Guizhou)
郁山国家森林公园	Yushan Mountain National Forest Park (He'nan)
御景峰国家森林公园	Yujing Peak National Forest Park (Guangdong)
毓青山国家森林公园	Yuqingshan National Forest Park (Chongqing)
元宝山国家森林公园	Yuanbao Mountain National Forest Park (Guangxi)
元帅林国家森林公园	Marshal Forest National Forest Park (Liaoning)
沅陵国家森林公园	Yuanling National Forest Park (Hu'nan)
原山国家森林公园	Yuanshan Mountain National Forest Park (Shandong)
月岩国家森林公园	Yueyan National Forest Park (Hu'nan)
云碧峰国家森林公园	Yunbi Peak National Forest Park (Jiangxi)
云冈国家森林公园	Yungang National Forest Park (Shanxi)
云湖国家森林公园	Yunhu Lake National Forest Park (Sichuan)
云蒙山国家森林公园	Yunmeng Mountain National Forest Park (Beijing)
云梦山国家森林公园	Yunmengshan National Forest Park (He'nan)
云山国家森林公园	Yunshan Mountain National Forest Park (Hu'nan)
云台山国家森林公园	Yuntai Mountain National Forest Park (He'nan)
云台山国家森林公园	Yuntai Mountain National Forest Park (Jiangsu)
云崖寺国家森林公园	Yunya Temple National Forest Park (Gansu)
云阳国家森林公园	Yunyang National Forest Park (Hu'nan)

陨石山国家森林公园	Meteorite Mountain National Forest Park (Liaoning)
皂阁山国家森林公园	Zaoge Mountain National Forest Park (Jiangxi)
张家界国家森林公园	Zhangjiajie National Forest Park (Hu'nan)
章凤国家森林公园	Zhangfeng National Forest Park (Yunnan)
章古台沙地国家森林公园	Sandy Land National Forest Park of Zhanggutai (Liaoning)
章丘国家森林公园	Zhangqiu National Forest Park (Shandong)
漳平天台国家森林公园	Zhangping Tiantai National Forest Park (Fujian)
招虎山国家森林公园	Zhaohu Mountain National Forest Park (Shandong)
赵杲观国家森林公园	Zhaogao Temple National Forest Park (Shanxi)
照壁山国家森林公园	Zhaobi Mountain National Forest Park (Xinjiang)
肇大鸡山国家森林公园	Zhaodaji Mountain National Forest Park (Jilin)
柘林湖国家森林公园	Zhelin Lake National Forest Park (Jiangxi)
柘溪国家森林公园	Zhexi National Forest Park (Hu'nan)
珍宝岛国家森林公园	Zhenbaodao/Treasure Island National Forest Park (Heilongjiang)
镇江南山国家森林公园	Zhenjiang National Forest Park of South Mountain (Shanghai)
镇龙山国家森林公园	Zhenlong Mountain National Forest Park (Sichuan)
镇山国家森林公园	Zhenshan National Forest Park (Guangdong)
郑州国家森林公园	Zhengzhou National Forest Park (He'nan)
支提山国家森林公园	Zhiti Mountain National Forest Park (Fujian)
中华山国家森林公园	Zhonghua Mountain National Forest Park (Hubei)
中坡国家森林公园	Zhongpo National Forest Park (Hu'nan)
中山国家森林公园	Zhongshan National Forest Park (Guangdong)
中条山国家森林公园	Zhongtiao Mountain National Forest Park (Shanxi)
终南山国家森林公园	Zhongnanshan National Forest Park (Shaanxi)
钟灵山国家森林公园	Zhongling Mountain National Forest Park (Yunnan)

周祖陵国家森林公园	Zhouzu Mausoleum National Forest Park (Gansu)
朱家山国家森林公园	Zhujia Mountain National Forest Park (Guizhou)
朱雀国家森林公园	Zhuque National Forest Park (Shaanxi)
朱雀山国家森林公园	Zhuque Mountain National Forest Park (Jilin)
珠江源国家森林公园	Pearl-River Headwaters National Forest Park (Yunnan)
珠山国家森林公园	Zhushan Mountain National Forest Park (Shandong)
诸暨香榧国家森林公园	Zhuji Torreya Grandis National Forest Park (Zhejiang)
竹海国家森林公园	Bamboo Sea National Forest Park (Guizhou)
竹乡国家森林公园	Bamboo Home National Forest Park (Zhejiang)
子午岭国家森林公园	Ziwuling National Forest Park (Gansu)
紫柏山国家森林公园	Zibaishan National Forest Park (Shaanxi)
紫金山国家森林公园	Zijin Mountain National Forest Park (Yunnan)
紫林山国家森林公园	Zilin Mountain National Forest Park (Guizhou)
紫蓬山国家森林公园	Zipeng Mountain National Forest Park (Anhui)
紫微山国家森林公园	Ziwei Mountain National Forest Park (Zhejiang)
坐龙峡国家森林公园	Sitting Dragon Gorge National Forest Park (Hu'nan)

附录四　中国国家地质公园、中国国家矿山公园

阿尔山国家地质公园	Arxan (Mountain) National Geopark (Inner Mongolia)
阿拉善沙漠国家地质公园	Alxa Desert National Geopark (Inner Mongolia)
白山板石国家矿山公园	Banshi National Mine Park in Baishan (Jilin)
白银火焰山国家矿山公园	Flaming Mountain National Mine Park in Baiyin (Gansu)
百色乐业大石围天坑群国家地质公园	Leye National Geopark of Dashiwei Karst Cenote in Baise (Guangxi)
北海涠洲岛火山国家地质公园	Weizhou Isle Volcano National Geopark in Beihai (Guangxi)
北京十渡国家地质公园	Beijing Shidu National Geopark
北京石花洞国家地质公园	Beijing Shihua Cave National Geopark
北京延庆硅化木国家地质公园	Yanqing Silicified Wood National Geopark in Beijing
本溪国家地质公园	Benxi National Geopark (Liaoning)
布尔津喀纳斯湖国家地质公园	Kanas Lake National Geopark of Burqin (Xinjiang)
嵖岈山国家地质公园	Chaya Mountain National Geopark (He'nan)
长江三峡国家地质公园	Three Gorges National Geopark of Yangtze River (Hubei, Chongqing)
长山列岛国家地质公园	Changshan Islands National Geopark (Shandong)
常山国家地质公园	Changshan National Geopark (Zhejiang)
朝阳古生物化石国家地质公园	Chaoyang Palaeontological Fossil National Geopark (Liaoning)

朝阳鸟化石国家地质公园	Chaoyang Bird Fossil National Geopark (Liaoning)
郴州飞天山国家地质公园	Feitian Mountain National Geopark in Chenzhou (Hu'nan)
澄江国家地质公园	Chenjiang Ancient Fauna National Geopark (Yunnan)
赤峰巴林石国家矿山公园	Bailin Stone National Mine Park of Chifeng (Inner Mongolia)
崇明岛国家地质公园	Chongming Island National Geopark (Shanghai)
翠华山国家地质公园	Cuihuas Mountain National Geopark (Shaanxi)
大别山国家地质公园	Dabie Mountain National Geopark (Hubei, Anhui)
大渡河峡谷国家地质公园	Dadu River Canyon National Geopark (Sichuan)
大金湖国家地质公园	Dajin Lake National Geopark (Fujian)
大理苍山国家地质公园	Cangshan Mountain National Geopark in Dali (Yunnan)
大连滨海国家地质公园	Dalian Coastal National Geopark (Liaoning)
大连冰峪沟国家地质公园	Dalian Bingyu Walley National Geopark (Liaoning)
大同晋华宫矿国家矿山公园	Jinhuagong Mine National Mine Park in Datong (Shanxi)
丹巴白云母国家矿山公园	Danba Muscovite National Mine Park (Sichuan)
丹霞山世界地质公园	Danxia Mountain National Geopark (Guangdong)
德化石牛山国家地质公园	Dehua Shiniu Mountain National Geopark (Fujian)
东营黄河三角洲国家地质公园	Yellow River Delta National Geopark in Dongying (Shandong)
敦煌雅丹国家地质公园	Dunhuang Yardang National Geopark (Gansu)
恩平地热国家地质公园	Enping Geotherm National Geopark (Guangdong)
封开国家地质公园	Fengkai National Geopark (Guangdong)
凤凰国家地质公园	Fenghuang National Geopark (Hu'nan)

凤山岩溶国家地质公园	Fengshan Mountain Karst National Geopark (Guangxi)
佛山西樵山国家地质公园	Xiqiao Mountain National Geopark in Foshan (Guangdong)
浮山国家地质公园	Fushan Mountain National Geopark (Anhui)
福鼎太姥山国家地质公园	Fuding Taimu Mountain National Geopark (Fujian)
阜平天生桥国家地质公园	Fuping Natural Bridge National Geopark (Hebei)
阜新海州露天矿国家矿山公园	Fuxin National Mine Park of Haizhou Open-Pit Mine (Liaoning)
富蕴可可托海国家地质公园	Koktokay National Geopark of Fuyun (Xinjiang)
格尔木察尔汗盐湖国家矿山公园	Qarham Salt-Lake National Mine Park of Golmud (Qinghai)
格尔木昆仑山国家地质公园	Kunlun Mountain National Geopark of Golmud (Qinghai)
古丈红石林国家地质公园	Guzhang National Geopark of Red Carbonate-Rock Stone Forest (Hu'nan)
关岭化石群国家地质公园	Guanling Fossil Cluster National Geopark (Guizhou)
关山国家地质公园	Guanshan Mountain National Geopark (He'nan)
海口石山火山群国家地质公园	Shishan Mountain National Geopark of Volcano Cluster in Haikou (Hai'nan)
海螺沟国家地质公园	Hailuo Valley National Geopark (Sichuan)
鹤岗市国家矿山公园	Hegang National Mine Park (Heilongjiang)
壶关峡谷国家地质公园	Huguan Canyon National Geopark (Shanxi)
互助北山国家地质公园	Beishan Mountain National Geopark of Huzhu (Qinghai)
华蓥山国家地质公园	Huaying Mountain National Geopark (Sichuan)
淮北国家矿山公园	Huaibei National Mine Park (Anhui)
黄河壶口瀑布国家地质公园	Hukou Falls National Geopark of Yellow River (Shaanxi, Shanxi)
黄龙国家地质公园	Huanglong National Geopark (Sichuan)
黄山世界地质公园	Huangshan Mountain National Geopark (Anhui)

黄石国家矿山公园	Huangshi National Mine Park (Hubei)
黄松峪国家地质公园	Huangsong Valley National Geopark (Beijing)
鸡西恒山国家矿山公园	Hengshan Mountain National Mine Park in Jixi (Heilongjiang)
蓟县国家地质公园	Jixian National Geopark (Tianjin)
嘉荫恐龙国家地质公园	Jiayin Dinosaur National Geopark (Heilongjiang)
嘉荫乌拉嘎国家矿山公园	Wulaga National Mine Park of Jiayin (Heilongjiang)
尖扎坎布拉国家地质公园	Kanbula National Geopark of Jianzha (Qinghai)
江油国家地质公园	Jiangyou National Geopark (Sichuan)
晋江深沪湾国家地质公园	Jinjiang Shenhu Bay National Geopark (Fujian)
景德镇高岭国家矿山公园	Gaoling National Mine Park in Jingdezhen (Jiangxi)
景泰黄河石石林国家地质公园	Stone Forest National Geopark at Yellow River in Jingtai (Gansu)
靖宇火山矿泉群国家地质公园	Jingyu National Geopark of Volcano and Warm Mineral Spring Cluster (Jilin)
镜泊湖国家地质公园	Jingpo Lake National Geopark (Heilongjiang)
九寨沟国家地质公园	Jiuzhai Valley National Geopark (Sichuan)
久治年宝玉则国家地质公园	Nyanboyeshizer National Geopark of Jigzhi (Qinghai)
酒埠江国家地质公园	Jiubu River National Geopark (Hu'nan)
开滦国家矿山公园	Kailuan Coal Mine National Park (Hebai)
克什克腾国家地质公园	Hexigten National Geopark (Inner Mongolia)
涞水野三坡国家地质公园	Yeshanpo National Geopark of Laishui (Hebei)
涞源白石山国家地质公园	White Stone Mountain National Geopark of Laiyuan (Hebei)
崀山国家地质公园	Langshan Mountain National Geopark (Hu'nan)
临城国家地质公园	Lincheng National Geopark (Hebei)
临海国家地质公园	Linhai National Geopark (Zhejiang)
刘家峡恐龙国家地质公园	Liujia Gorge Dinosaur National Park (Gansu)
六合国家地质公园	Liuhe National Geopark (Jiangsu)
六盘水乌蒙山国家地质公园	Wumeng Mountain National Geopark in Liupanshui (Guizhou)

龙虎山国家地质公园	Danxia Geomorphy National Geopark of Longhu Mountain (Jiangxi)
龙门山国家地质公园	Longmen Mountain Geostructure National Geopark (Sichuan)
庐山世界地质公园	Quaternary Glaciation National Geopark of Lushan Mountain (Jiangxi)
鹿寨香桥岩溶国家地质公园	Xiangqiao Karst National Geopark of Luzhai (Guangxi)
禄丰恐龙国家地质公园	Lufeng Dinosaur National Geopark (Yunnan)
洛川黄土国家地质公园	Luochuan Loess National Geopark (Shaanxi)
洛宁神灵寨国家地质公园	Shenlingzhai National Geopark of Luoning (He'nan)
洛阳黛眉山国家地质公园	Daimei Mountain National Geopark in Luoyang (He'nan)
满洲里市扎赉诺尔国家矿山公园	Jalai Nur National Mine Park in Manzhouli (Inner Mongolia)
南淮八公山国家地质公园	Bagong Mountain National Geopark in Huainan (Anhui)
南阳独山玉国家矿山公园	Dushan Jade National Mine Park in Nanyang (He'nan)
内乡宝天幔国家地质公园	Neixiang Baotianman National Geopark (He'nan)
宁化天鹅洞群国家地质公园	Ninghua Tian'e Caves National Geopark (Fujian)
宁武冰洞国家地质公园	Ningwu Ice Cave National Geopark (Shanxi)
平谷黄松峪国家矿山公园	Huangsongyu National Mine Park of Pinggu (Beijing)
平凉崆峒山国家地质公园	Kongtong Mountain National Geopark of Pingliang (Gansu)
平塘国家地质公园	Pingtang National Geopark (Guizhou)
屏南白水洋国家地质公园	Pingnan Baishuiyang National Geopark (Fujian)
齐云山国家地质公园	Qiyun Mountain National Geopark (Anhui)
祁门牯牛降国家地质公园	Guniujiang National Geopark of Qimen (Anhui)
奇台硅化木恐龙国家地质公园	Qitai Silicified Wood-Dinosaur National Geopark (Xinjiang)

黔江小南海国家地质公园	Xiaonanhai (Lake) National Geopark of Qianjiang (Chongqing)
秦皇岛柳江国家地质公园	Liujiang National Geopark in Qinhuangdao (Hebei)
任丘华北油田国家矿山公园	Renqiu National Mine Park of North China Oil Field (Hebai)
三清山国家地质公园	Sanqing Mountain National Geopark (Jiangxi)
山旺国家地质公园	Shanwang National Geopark (Shandong)
上杭紫金山国家矿山公园	Zijin Mountain National Mine Park of Shanghang (Fujian)
韶关芙蓉山国家矿山公园	Furong Mountain National Mine Park in Shaoguan (Guangdong)
射洪硅化木国家地质公园	Shehong Silicified Wood National Geopark (Sichuan)
深圳大鹏半岛国家地质公园	Dapeng Peninsula National Park in Shenzhen (Guangdong)
深圳凤凰山国家矿山公园	Fenghuang Mountain National Mine Park in Shenzhen (Guangdong)
深圳鹏茜国家矿山公园	Pengxi National Mine Park in Shenzhen (Guangdong)
神农架国家地质公园	Shennongjia National Geopark (Hubei)
石林世界地质公园	Shilin National Geopark of Karst Peak Forest (Yunnan)
寿山国家矿山公园	Shoushan Mountain National Mine Park (Fujian)
四姑娘山国家地质公园	Siguniang (Four Girls) Mountain National Geopark (Sichuan)
嵩山地层构造国家地质公园	Stratigraphic Structure National Geopark of Songshan Mountain (He'nan)
苏州太湖西山国家地质公园	West Mountain National Geopark at Taihu Lake in Suzhou (Jiangsu)
绥阳双河洞国家地质公园	Shuanghe Cave National Geopark of Suiyang (Guizhou)
遂昌金矿国家矿山公园	Suichang Gold National Mine Park (Zhejiang)

泰山国家地质公园	Taishan Mountain National Geopark (Shandong)
腾冲国家地质公园	Tengchong Volcano and Geotherm National Geopark (Yunnan)
天柱山国家地质公园	Tianzhu Mountain National Geopark (Anhui)
万山汞矿国家矿山公园	Wanshan Mercury National Mine Park (Guizhou)
王屋山国家地质公园	Wangwu Mountain National Geopark (He'nan)
五大连池世界地质公园	Wudalianchi Global Geopark (Heilongjiang)
五台山国家地质公园	Wutai Mountain National Geopark (Shanxi)
武安国家地质公园	Wu'an National Geopark (Hebei)
武安西石门铁矿国家矿山公园	Wu'an National Mine Park of Xishimen Iron Mine (Hebei)
武功山国家地质公园	Wugong Mountain National Geopark (Jiangxi)
武汉木兰山国家地质公园	Mulan Mountain National Park in Wuhan (Hubei)
武隆岩溶国家地质公园	Wulong Karst National Geopark (Chongqing)
西吉火石寨国家地质公园	Xiji Huoshizhai National Geopark (Ningxia)
西峡伏牛山国家地质公园	Xixia Funiu Mountain National Geopark (He'nan)
县安国家地质公园	Anxian Bioherm National Geopark (Sichuan)
新昌硅化木国家地质公园	Xinchang Silicified Wood National Geopark (Zhejiang)
信阳金岗台国家地质公园	Xinyang Jingangtai National Geopark (He'nan)
兴凯湖国家地质公园	Xingkai Lake National Geopark (Heilongjiang)
兴文石海国家地质公园	Xingwen Stone Forest National Geopark (Sichuan)
兴义国家地质公园	Xingyi National Geopark (Guizhou)
盱眙象山国家矿山公园	Xiangshan Mountain National Mine Park of Xuyi (Jiangsu)
延川黄河蛇曲国家地质公园	Meander Bends National Geopark of Yellow River in Yanchuan (Shaanxi)
雁荡山国家地质公园	Yandang Mountain National Geopark (Zhejiang)
阳春凌霄岩国家地质公园	Lingxiao Rock National Geopark of Yangchun (Guangdong)
伊春花岗岩石林国家地质公园	Yichun Granite Stone-Forest National Geopark (Heilongjiang)

沂蒙山国家地质公园	Yimeng Mountain National Geopark (Shandong)
沂蒙钻石国家矿山公园	Yimeng Diamond National Mine Park (Shandong)
易贡国家地质公园	Yigong National Geopark (Tibet)
永安国家地质公园	Yong'an National Geopark (Fujian)
玉龙黎明—老君山国家地质公园	Liming—Laojun Mountain National Geopark of Yulong (Yunnan)
云台山国家地质公园	Yuntai Mountain National Geopark (He'nan)
云阳龙缸国家地质公园	Yunyang Longgang National Geopark (Chongqing)
郧县恐龙蛋化石群国家地质公园	Yunxian National Geopark of Dinosaur-Egg Fossil Cluster (Hubei)
赞皇嶂石岩国家地质公园	Zhangshi Rock National Geopark of Zanhuang (Hebei)
枣庄熊耳山国家地质公园	Xiong'er Mountain National Geopark in Zaozhuang (Shandong)
札达土林国家地质公园	Zhada Clay Forest National Geopark (Tibet)
湛江湖光岩国家地质公园	Huguang Rock National Geopark in Zhanjiang (Guangdong)
张家界沙石峰国家地质公园	Sandstone Peak Forest National Geopark of Zhangjiajie (Hu'nan)
漳州滨海火山国家地质公园	Zhangzhou National Geopark of Littoral Volcanic Geomorphy (Fujian)
漳州国家地质公园	Zhangzhou National Geopark (Fujian)
郑州黄河国家地质公园	Yellow River National Geopark in Zhengzhou (He'nan)
织金洞国家地质公园	Zhijin Cave National Geopark (Guizhou)
资源国家地质公园	Ziyuan National Geopark (Guangxi)
自贡恐龙国家地质公园	Zigong National Geopark of Dinosaur and Ancient Organism (Sichuan)

附录五　国家级自然保护区

阿尔金山国家自然保护区	Altun Mountains National Nature Reserve (Xinjiang)
阿鲁科尔沁草原国家自然保护区	Ar Horqin Grassland National Nature Reserve (Inner Mongolia)
哀牢山国家自然保护区	Ailao Mountain National Nature Reserve (Yunnan)
安南坝野骆驼国家自然保护区	Annanba National Nature Reserve for Bactrian Camel (Gansu)
安西极旱荒漠国家自然保护区	Anxi National Nature Reserve of Extreme-Arid Desert (Gansu)
八岔岛国家自然保护区	Bacha Isle National Nature Reserve (Heilongjiang)
八大公山国家自然保护区	Badagong Mountain National Nature Reserve (Hu'nan)
八仙山国家自然保护区	Baxian Mountain National Nature Reserve (Tianjin)
巴东金丝猴国家自然保护区	Golden Monkey National Nature Reserve of Badong (Hubei)
巴音布鲁克国家自然保护区	Bayanbulak National Nature Reserve (Xinjiang)
霸王岭国家自然保护区	Bawang Ridge National Nature Reserve (Hai'nan)
白芨滩国家自然保护区	Baijitan National Nature Reserve (Ningxia)
白马雪山国家自然保护区	National Nature Reserve of Baima Snow Mountains (Yunnan)
白石砬子国家自然保护区	Baishi Lazi National Nature Reserve (Liaoning)
白水河国家自然保护区	Baishuihe National Nature Reserve (Sichuan)
白音敖包国家自然保护区	Bayan Obo National Nature Reserve (Inner Mongolia)

白音锡勒草原国家自然保护区	Baiyinxile Grassland National Nature Reserve (Inner Mongolia)
宝天曼国家自然保护区	Baotianman National Nature Reserve (He'nan)
北仑河口海洋国家自然保护区	National Nature Reserve of Beilun River Estuary (Guangxi)
北票鸟化石群国家自然保护区	Beipiao National Nature Reserve for Bird Fossil (Liaoning)
崩尖子国家自然保护区	Bengjianzi National Nature Reserve (Hubei)
滨州贝壳堤岛与湿地国家自然保护区	Binzhou Shell-Dyke Island and Marsh National Nature Reserve (Shandong)
苍山洱海国家自然保护区	National Nature Reserve of Cangshan Mountains and Erhai Lake (Yunnan)
草海国家自然保护区	Grass Lake National Nature Reserve (Guizhou)
查干湖国家自然保护区	Chagan Lake National Nature Reserve (Jilin)
察青松多白唇鹿国家自然保护区	Chugqênsumdo National Nature Reserve White-Lipped Deer (Sichuan)
察隅慈巴沟国家自然保护区	Ciba Gully National Nature Reserve of Zayu (Tibet)
昌黎黄金海岸国家自然保护区	Gold Coast National Nature Reserve of Changli (Hebei)
长白山国家自然保护区	Changbai Mountain National Nature Reserve (Jilin)
长岛国家自然保护区	Changdao Isle National Nature Reserve (Shandong)
长江合江—雷波段珍稀鱼类国家自然保护区	National Nature Reserve for Precious and Rare Fish Species at Hejiang—Leibo Section of Yangtze River (Sichuan)
长江天鹅洲白鱀豚国家自然保护区	Yangtze River National Nature Reserve for Chinese White Dolphin at Swan Islet (Hubei)
长江新螺段白鱀豚国家自然保护区	National Nature Reserve for Chinese White Dolphin at Xinluo Section of Yangtze River (Hubei)
长宁竹海国家自然保护区	Changning National Nature Reserve for Bamboo Sea (Sichuan)
长青国家自然保护区	Changqing National Nature Reserve (Shaanxi)

长兴地质遗迹国家自然保护区	Changxing National Nature Reserve for Geologic Relic (Zhejiang)
车八岭国家自然保护区	Cheba Mountain National Nature Reserve (Guangdong)
城山头海滨地貌国家自然保护区	Coastal Geomorphy National Nature Reserve of Chengshantou (Liaoning)
赤水桫椤国家自然保护区	Chishui River National Nature Reserve for Spinulose Tree Fern (Guizhou)
崇明东滩鸟类国家自然保护区	Bird National Nature Reserve at Chongming East Tidalflat (Shanghai)
达赉湖国家自然保护区	Dalai Lake National Nature Reserve (Inner Mongolia)
达里诺尔鸟类国家自然保护区	Dali Nur National Nature Reserve for Birds (Inner Mongolia)
大巴山国家自然保护区	Daba Mountain National Nature Reserve (Chongqing)
大布苏国家自然保护区	Dabusu National Nature Reserve (Jilin)
大丰麋鹿国家自然保护区	Dafeng National Nature Reserve for Père David's Deer (Jiangsu)
大海陀国家自然保护区	Dahaituo National Nature Reserve (Hebei)
大黑山国家自然保护区	Dahei Mountain National Nature Reserve (Inner Mongolia)
大连斑海豹国家自然保护区	Dalian National Nature Reserve for Spotted Seal (Liaoning)
大明山国家自然保护区	Daming Mountain National Nature Reserve (Guangxi)
大盘山国家自然保护区	Dapan Mountain National Nature Reserve (Zhejiang)
大青沟国家自然保护区	Daqing Valley National Nature Reserve (Inner Mongolia)
大山包黑颈鹤国家自然保护区	Dashanbao National Nature Reserve for Black-Necked Crane (Yunnan)
大田坡鹿国家自然保护区	Datian National Nature Reserve for Eld's Deers (Hai'nan)

大围山国家自然保护区	Dawei Mountain National Nature Reserve (Yunnan)
大瑶山国家自然保护区	Dayao Mountain National Nature Reserve (Guangxi)
大洲岛海洋生态国家自然保护区	Dazhou Island National Nature Reserve for Marine Ecosystem (Hai'nan)
戴云山国家自然保护区	Daiyun Mountain National Nature Reserve (Fujian)
丹霞山国家自然保护区	Danxia Mountain National Nature Reserve (Guangdong)
鼎湖山国家自然保护区	Dinghu Mountain National Nature Reserve Guangdong)
东北黑蜂国家自然保护区	National Nature Reserve for Northeast Black Bees (Heilongjiang)
东洞庭湖国家自然保护区	National Nature Reserve for East Dongting Lake (Hu'nan)
东寨港国家自然保护区	East Harbour National Nature Reserve (Hai'nan)
董寨鸟类国家自然保护区	Dongzhai Bird National Nature Reserve (He'nan)
都庞岭国家自然保护区	Dupang Ridge National Nature Reserve (Hu'nan)
敦煌西湖国家自然保护区	West Lake National Nature Reserve in Dunhuang (Gansu)
额济纳胡杨林国家自然保护区	Ejina National Nature Reserve for Diversifolious Poplar Forest (Inner Mongolia)
鄂尔多斯遗鸥国家自然保护区	Ordos National Nature Reserve for Relict Gull (Inner Mongolia)
梵净山国家自然保护区	Fanjing Mountain National Nature Reserve (Guizhou)
防城上岳金花茶国家自然保护区	Fangcheng National Nature Reserve for Golden Camellia (Guangxi)
丰林国家自然保护区	Fenglin National Nature Reserve (Heilongjiang)
蜂桶寨国家自然保护区	Fengtongzhai National Nature Reserve (Sichuan)
凤阳山—百山祖国家自然保护区	Fengyang Mountain—Baishanzu National Nature Reserve (Zhejiang)
佛坪国家自然保护区	Foping National Nature Reserve (Shaanxi)

伏牛山国家自然保护区	Funiu Mountain National Nature Reserve (He'nan)
尕海—则岔国家自然保护区	Gahai Lake—Zecha National Nature Reserve (Gansu)
甘家湖梭梭林国家自然保护区	Ganjia Lake National Nature Reserve for Sacsaoul Forest (Xingjiangg)
高黎贡山国家自然保护区	Gaoligong Mountain National Nature Reserve (Yunnan)
贡嘎山国家自然保护区	Kanggar Mountains National Nature Reserve (Sichuan)
古海岸与湿地国家自然保护区	Palaeocoast and Wetland National Nature Reserve (Tianjin)
古田山国家自然保护区	Gutian Mountain National Nature Reserve (Zhejiang)
牯牛降国家自然保护区	Guniujiang National Nature Reserve (Anhui)
哈巴湖国家自然保护区	Haba Lake National Nature Reserve (Ningxia)
哈纳斯国家自然保护区	Hanas National Nature Reserve (Xingjiang)
哈腾套海国家自然保护区	Hatan Tohoi National Nature Reserve (Inner Mongolia)
汉中朱鹮国家自然保护区	Hanzhong National Nature Reserve for Crested Ibis (Shaanxi)
汗玛国家自然保护区	Hanma National Nature Reserve (Inner Mongolia)
合浦儒艮国家自然保护区	Hepu National Nature Reserve for Dugong (Guangxi)
贺兰山国家自然保护区	Helan Mountain National Nature Reserve (Ningxia, Inner Mongolia)
黑里河国家自然保护区	Heili River National Nature Reserve (Inner Mongolia)
黑龙江凤凰山国家自然保护区	Fenghuang (Phoenix) Mountain National Nature Reserve
衡水湖国家自然保护区	Hengshui Lake National Nature Reserve (Heibei)
红花尔基樟子松林国家自然保护区	Honghua'erji National Nature Reserve for Mongolian Pine (Inner Mongolia)

红松洼国家自然保护区	Hongsong Depression National Nature Reserve (Hebei)
洪河国家自然保护区	Honghe River National Nature Reserve (Heilongjiang)
洪泽湖湿地国家自然保护区	Wetland National Nature Reserve of Hongze Lake (Jiangsu)
后河国家自然保护区	Houhe River National Nature Reserve (Hubei)
呼中国家自然保护区	Huzhong National Nature Reserve (Heilongjiang)
虎伯寮国家自然保护区	Huboliao National Nature Reserve (Fujian)
花坪国家自然保护区	Huaping National Nature Reserve (Guangxi)
画稿溪国家自然保护区	Huagao Stream National Nature Reserve (Sichuan)
黄河三角洲国家自然保护区	National Nature Reserve for Yellow River Delta (Shandong)
黄河湿地国家自然保护区	Wetland National Nature Reserve of Yellow River (He'nan)
黄桑国家自然保护区	Huangsang National Nature Reserve (Hu'nan)
珲春东北虎国家自然保护区	Hunchun National Nature Reserve for Manchurian Tiger (Jilin)
辉河国家自然保护区	Huihe River National Nature Reserve (Inner Mongolia)
惠东港口海龟国家自然保护区	Sea Turtle National Nature Reserve at Huidong Harbor (Guangdong)
惠泽黑颈鹤国家自然保护区	Huize National Nature Reserve for Black-Necked Crane (Yunnan)
鸡公山国家自然保护区	Jigong Mountain National Nature Reserve (He'nan)
蓟县中上元古界国家自然保护区	Jixian National Nature Reserve for Middle-Upper Proterozoic Stratigraphic Section (Tianjin)
夹墙山自然风景区	Jiaqiang Mountain Natural Scenic Area (Hebei)
尖峰岭国家自然保护区	Jianfeng Ridge National Nature Reserve (Hai'nan)

江西武夷山国家自然保护区	Wuyi Mountain National Nature Reserve in Jiangxi (Jiangxi)
金佛山国家自然保护区	Jinfo Mountain National Nature Reserve (Chongqing)
金平分水岭国家自然保护区	Jinping Watershed National Nature Reserve (Yunnan)
金寨天马国家自然保护区	Jinzhai Tianma National Nature Reserve (Anhui)
缙云山国家自然保护区	Jinyun Mountain National Nature Reserve (Chongqing)
井冈山国家自然保护区	Jinggang Mountain National Nature Reserve (Jiangxi)
九段沙湿地国家自然保护区	Jiuduansha Wetland National Nature Reserve (Shanghai)
九连山国家自然保护区	Jiulian Mountain National Nature Reserve (Jiangxi)
九龙山国家自然保护区	Jiulong Mountain National Nature Reserve (Zhejiang)
九寨沟国家自然保护区	Jiuzhai Valley National Nature Reserve (Sichuan)
科尔沁国家自然保护区	Horqin National Nature Reserve (Inner Mongolia)
可可西里国家自然保护区	Hoh Xil National Nature Reserve (Qinghai)
宽阔水国家自然保护区	Kuankuoshui National Nature Reserve (Guizhou)
拉鲁湿地国家自然保护区	Lhalu Wetland National Nature Reserve (Tibet)
老秃顶子国家自然保护区	Laotu Dingzi National Nature Reserve (Liaoning)
雷公山国家自然保护区	Leigong Mountain National Nature Reserve (Guizhou)
类乌齐马鹿国家自然保护区	Riwoq/Leiwuqi National Nature Reserve for Red Deer (Tibet)
历山国家自然保护区	Lishan Mountain National Nature Reserve (Shanxi)
栗子坪国家自然保护区	Liziping National Nature Reserve (Sichuan)
连城国家自然保护区	Liancheng National Nature Reserve (Gansu)
连古城国家自然保护区	Liangucheng National Nature Reserve (Gansu)

连康山国家自然保护区	Liankang Mountain National Nature Reserve (He'nan)
莲花山国家自然保护区	Lianhua Mountain National Nature Reserve (Gansu)
凉水国家自然保护区	Liangshui National Nature Reserve (Heilongjiang)
梁野山国家自然保护区	Liangye Mountain National Nature Reserve (Fujian)
柳江盆地地质遗迹国家自然保护区	Liujiang Basin National Nature Reserve for Geologic Relic (Hebei)
六盘山国家自然保护区	Liupan Mountain National Nature Reserve (Ningxia)
龙栖山国家自然保护区	Longqishan National Nature Reserve (Fujian)
龙湾国家自然保护区	Longwan National Nature Reserve (Jilin)
龙溪—虹口国家自然保护区	Longxi—Hongkou National Nature Reserve (Sichuan)
隆宝国家自然保护区	Longbao National Nature Reserve (Qinghai)
芦芽山国家自然保护区	Luya Mountain National Nature Reserve (Shanxi)
罗布泊野骆驼国家自然保护区	Lop Nur National Nature Reserve for Bactrian Camel (Xinjiang)
罗山国家自然保护区	Luoshan Mountain National Nature Reserve (Ningxia)
绿春黄连山国家自然保护区	Huanglian Mountain National Nature Reserve (Yunnan)
麻阳河黑叶猴国家自然保护区	Mayang River National Nature Reserve (Guizhou)
马边大风顶国家自然保护区	Mabian Dafengding National Nature Reserve (Sichuan)
马山国家自然保护区	Mashan Mountain National Nature Reserve (Shandong)
芒康滇金丝猴国家自然保护区	Mangkam National Nature Reserve for Snub-Nosed Monkey (Tibet)

莽山国家自然保护区	Mangshan Mountain National Nature Reserve (Hu'nan)
猫儿山国家自然保护区	Mao'er Mountain National Nature Reserve (Guangxi)
茂兰国家自然保护区	Maolan National Nature Reserve (Guizhou)
梅花山国家自然保护区	Meihua Mountain National Nature Reserve (Fujian)
美姑大风顶国家自然保护区	Meigu Dafengding National Nature Reserve (Sichuan)
孟达国家自然保护区	Mengda National Nature Reserve (Qinghai)
孟达天池国家自然保护区	Mengda Tianchi National Nature Reserve (Qinghai)
米仓山国家自然保护区	Micang Mountain National Nature Reserve (Sichuan)
闽江源国家自然保护区	National Nature Reserve for Minjiang River Headwaters (Fujian)
莫莫格国家自然保护区	Melmeg National Nature Reserve (Jilin)
牡丹峰国家自然保护区	Mudan Peak National Nature Reserve (Heilongjiang)
木林子国家自然保护区	Mulinzi National Nature Reserve (Hubei)
木论国家自然保护区	Mulun National Nature Reserve (Guangxi)
纳板河国家自然保护区	Napan River National Nature Reserve (Yunnan)
南滚河国家自然保护区	Nangun River National Nature Reserve (Yunnan)
南麂列岛国家自然保护区	Marine National Nature Reserve of Nanji Islands (Zhejiang)
南岭国家自然保护区	Nanling Mountains National Nature Reserve (Guangdong)
南瓮河国家自然保护区	Nanweng River National Nature Reserve (Heilongjiang)
南阳恐龙蛋化石群国家自然保护区	Nanyang National Nature Reserve for Dinosaur-Egg Fossil Cluster (He'nan)
挠力河国家自然保护区	Raoli River National Nature Reserve (Heilongjiang)

内伶仃—福田国家自然保护区	Neilingding—Futian National Nature Reserve (Guangdong)
泥河湾国家自然保护区	Nihewan National Nature Reserve (Hebei)
牛背梁国家自然保护区	Niubeiliang National Nature Reserve (Shaanxi)
弄岗国家自然保护区	Nonggang National Nature Reserve (Guangxi)
努鲁儿虎山国家自然保护区	Nulu'erhu Mountain National Nature Reserve (Liaoning)
攀枝花苏铁国家自然保护区	Panzhihua National Nature Reserve for Cycas Revoluta (Sichuan)
庞泉沟国家自然保护区	Pangquan Valley National Nature Reserve (Shanxi)
鄱阳湖候鸟国家自然保护区	Poyang Lake National Nature Reserve for Migratory Birds (Jiangxi)
七星河国家自然保护区	Qixing River National Nature Reserve (Heilongjiang)
祁连山国家自然保护区	Qilian Mountain National Nature Reserve (Gansu)
千家洞国家自然保护区	Qianjia Cave National Nature Reserve (Guangxi)
羌塘国家自然保护区	Qiangtang National Nature Reserve (Tibet)
青海湖国家自然保护区	Qinghai Lake National Nature Reserve (Qinghai)
青龙山恐龙蛋化石群国家自然保护区	Qinglong Mountain National Nature Reserve for Dinosaur-Egg Fossil Cluster (Hubei)
清凉峰国家自然保护区	Qingliang Peak National Nature Reserve (Zhejiang)
若尔盖湿地国家自然保护区	Zoigê Marsh National Nature Reserve (Sichuan)
赛罕乌拉国家自然保护区	Saihan Ula National Nature Reserve (Inner Mongolia)
三江国家自然保护区	Sanjiang National Nature Reserve (Heilongjiang)
三江源国家自然保护区	Sanjiangyuan National Nature Reserve; Three-River-Source National Nature Reserve (Qinghai)
三亚珊瑚礁国家自然保护区	Sanya National Nature Reserve for Coral Reef (Hai'nan)

色林措国家自然保护区	Serling Lake National Nature Reserve (Tibet)
沙坡头国家自然保护区	Shapotou National Nature Reserve (Ningxia)
山口红树林国家自然保护区	Shankou National Nature Reserve for Mangrove Ecosystem (Guangxi)
山旺古生物化石国家自然保护区	Shanwang National Nature Reserve for Ancient-Life Fossil (Shandong)
蛇岛—老铁山国家自然保护区	Snake Island—Laotie Mountain National Nature Reserve (Liaoning)
深沪湾海底古森林国家自然保护区	Shenhu Bay National Nature Reserve for Ancient Submarine Forest Relic (Fujian)
神农架国家自然保护区	Shennongjia National Nature Reserve (Hubei)
升金湖国家自然保护区	Shengjin Lake National Nature Reserve (Anhui)
十万大山国家自然保护区	National Nature Reserve of Shiwan Grand Mountains (Guangxi)
石门壶瓶山国家自然保护区	Shimen National Nature Reserve of Huping Mountain (Hu'nan)
双台河口国家自然保护区	National Nature Reserve at Shuangtai River Estuary (Liaoning)
四姑娘山国家自然保护区	Siguniang (Four Girls) Mountain National Nature Reserve (Sichuan)
松山国家自然保护区	Songshan Mountain National Nature Reserve (Beijing)
塔里木胡杨保护区	Tarim National Nature Reserve for Euphrates Poplar (Xinjiang)
太白山国家自然保护区	Taibai Mountain National Nature Reserve (Shaanxi)
太行山猕猴国家自然保护区	Rhesus Monkey National Nature Reserve of Taihang Mountain in Jiaozuo (He'nan)
太统—崆峒山国家自然保护区	Taitong—Kongtong Mountain National Nature Reserve (Gansu)
唐家河国家自然保护区	Tangjia River National Nature Reserve (Sichuan)
桃红岭梅花鹿国家自然保护区	Taohong Ridge National Nature Reserve for Sika Deer (Jiangxi)

桃源洞国家自然保护区	National Nature Reserve for Peach Garden Cave (Hu'nan)
天宝岩国家自然保护区	Tianbaoyan National Nature Reserve (Fujian)
天鹅洲麋鹿国家自然保护区	Swan Islet National Nature Reserve for Père David's Deer/Elk (Hubei)
天佛指山国家自然保护区	Tianfozhi Mountain National Nature Reserve (Jilin)
天目山国家自然保护区	Tianmu Mountain National Nature Reserve (Zhejiang)
铜鼓岭自然保护	Tonggu Ridge National Nature Reserve (Hai'nan)
铜陵淡水豚国家自然保护区	Tongling National Nature Reserve for Freshwater Dolphin (Anhui)
图牧吉国家自然保护区	Tumuji National Nature Reserve (Inner Mongolia)
托木尔峰国家自然保护区	Tomur Peak National Nature Reserve (Xingjiang)
王朗国家自然保护区	Wanglang National Nature Reserve (Sichuan)
文山老君山国家自然保护区	Wenshan Mountain National Nature Reserve (Yunnan)
卧龙国家自然保护区	Wolong National Nature Reserve (Sichuan)
乌拉特梭梭林—蒙古野驴国家自然保护区	National Nature Reserve for Urad Sacsaoul Forest—Mongolian Wild Ass (Inner Mongolia)
乌日根国家自然保护区	Ergun National Nature Reserve (Inner Mongolia)
乌岩岭国家自然保护区	Wuyan Ridge National Nature Reserve (Zhejiang)
乌云界国家自然保护区	Wuyunjie National Nature Reserve (Hu'nan)
无量山国家自然保护区	Wuliang Mountain National Nature Reserve (Yunnan)
五大连池火山国家自然保护区	Wudalianchi (Five Lotus Ponds) National Nature Reserve (Heilongjiang)
五鹿山国家自然保护区	Wulushan Mountain National Nature Reserve (Shanxi)
五指山国家自然保护区	Wuzhi Mountain National Nature Reserve (Hai'nan)

武夷山国家自然保护区	Wuyi Mountain National Nature Reserve (Fujian)
雾灵山国家自然保护区	Wuling Mountain National Nature Reserve (Hebei)
西鄂尔多斯国家自然保护区	West Ordos National Nature Reserve (Inner Mongolia)
西双版纳国家自然保护区	Xishuangbanna National Nature Reserve (Yunnan)
西天山国家自然保护区	National Nature Reserve of West Tianshan Mountain (Xinjiang)
锡林郭勒草原国家自然保护区	Xilingol Grassland National Nature Reserve (Inner Mongolia)
习水中亚热带森林国家自然保护区	Xishui River National Nature Reserve of Midsubtropical Evergreen Broadleaved Forest (Guizhou)
厦门珍稀海洋物种国家自然保护区	Xiamen National Nature Reserve for Precious and Rare Marine Species (Fujian)
仙人洞国家自然保护区	Fairy Cave National Nature Reserve (Liaoning)
向海国家自然保护区	Xianghai National Nature Reserve (Jilin)
象头山国家自然保护区	Xiangtou Mountain National Nature Reserve (Guangdong)
小陇山国家自然保护区	Xiaolong Mountain National Nature Reserve (Gansu)
小秦岭国家自然保护区	Lesser Qinling National Nature Reserve (He'nan)
小五台山国家自然保护区	National Nature Reserve of Lesser Wutai Mountain (Hebei)
小溪国家自然保护区	Xiaoxi Streams National Nature Reserve (Hu'nan)
兴凯湖国家自然保护区	Xingkai Lake National Nature Reserve (Heilongjiang)
兴隆山国家自然保护区	Xinglong Mountain National Nature Reserve (Gansu)
星斗山国家自然保护区	Xingdou Mountain National Nature Reserve (Hubei)

宣城扬子鳄国家自然保护区	Xuancheng National Nature Reserve for Chinese Alligator (Anhui)
雪宝顶国家自然保护区	Xuebaoding National Nature Reserve (Sichuan)
鸭绿江口滨海湿地国家自然保护区	Coastal Marsh National Nature Reserve at Yalu River Estuary (Liaoning)
鸭绿江上游国家自然保护区	National Nature Reserve for Yalu River Upper-reaches (Jilin)
雅鲁藏布大峡谷国家自然保护区	Yarlung Zangbo National Nature Reserve of Grand Canyon (Tibet)
雅鲁藏布江中游黑颈鹤国家自然保护区	Black-Necked Crane National Nature Reserve at Midstream Valley of Yarlung Zangbo (Tibet)
亚丁国家自然保护区	Yading National Nature Reserve (Sichuan)
盐城沿海滩涂珍禽国家自然保护区	Yancheng National Nature Reserve for Coastal Mudflat and Precious Fowl (Jiangsu)
盐池湾国家自然保护区	Yanchi Bay National Nature Reserve (Gansu)
阳城莽河猕猴国家自然保护区	Manghe River National Nature Reserve for Rhesus Monkey in Yangcheng (Shanxi)
鹞落坪国家自然保护区	Yaoloping National Nature Reserve (Anhui)
伊通火山群国家自然保护区	Yitong National Nature Reserve for Volcano Cluster (Jilin)
医巫闾山国家自然保护区	Yiwulü Mountain National Nature Reserve (Liaoning)
鹰嘴界国家自然保护区	Yingzuijie National Nature Reserve (Hu'nan)
永德大雪山国家自然保护区	Yongde National Nature Reserve for Grand Snow Mountains) (Yunnan)
豫北黄河故道鸟类湿地国家自然保护区	National Nature Reserve for Birds and Wetland at the Old Course of Yellow River in Northern He'nan (He'nan)
扎尕那国家自然保护区	Gahai-Zecha National Nature Reserve (Gansu)
扎龙国家自然保护区	Zhalong National Nature Reserve (Heilongjiang)
湛江红树林国家自然保护区	Mangrove Forest National Nature Reserve in Zhanjiang (Guangdong)
张家界大鲵国家自然保护区	Zhangjiajie National Nature Reserve for Chinese Giant Salamander (Hu'nan)

漳江口红树林国家自然保护区	Mangrove Forest National Nature Reserve at Zhangjiang River Estuary (Fujian)
周至金丝猴国家自然保护区	Zhouzhi National Nature Reserve (Shaanxi)
珠江口中华白海豚国家自然保护区	National Nature Reserve for Chinese White Dolphin at Zhujiang River Estuary (Guangdong)
珠穆朗玛峰国家自然保护区	Qomolangma National Nature Reserve (Tibet)
子午岭国家自然保护区	Ziwuling National Nature Reserve (Shaanxi)

附录六　中国国家湿地公园

阿坝多美林卡国家湿地公园	Duomeilinka National Wetland Park of Aba County (Sichuan)
阿尔山哈拉哈河国家湿地公园	Halaha River National Wetland Park in Arxan (Inner Mongolia)
阿合奇托什干河国家湿地公园	Toshigan River National Wetland Park of Aheqi County (Xinjiang)
阿克苏多浪河国家湿地公园	Duolang River National Wetland Park in Aksu (Xinjiang)
阿拉善黄河国家湿地公园	Yellow River National Wetland Park in Alxa (Inner Mongolia)
阿里狮泉河国家湿地公园	Shiquan River National Wetland Park in Ali (Tibet)
阿蓬江国家湿地公园	A'peng River National Wetland Park (Chongqing)
爱辉刺尔滨河国家湿地公园	Ci'erbin River National Wetland Park in Aihui (Heilongjiang)
安邦河国家湿地公园	Anbang River National Wetland Park (Heilongjiang)
安达古大湖国家湿地公园	Guda Lake National Wetland Park in Anda (Heilongjiang)
安龙招堤国家湿地公园	Zhaodi National Wetland Park of Anlong County (Guizhou)
安陆府河国家湿地公园	Fuhe RiverNational Wetland Park in Anlu (Hubei)
安庆菜子湖国家湿地公园	Caizi Lake National Wetland Park in Anqing (Anhui)
安丘拥翠湖国家湿地公园	Yongcui Lake National Wetland Park in Anqiu (Shandong)

安仁永乐江国家湿地公园	Yongle River National Wetland Park of Anren County (Hunan)
安顺邢江河国家湿地公园	Xingjiang River National Wetland Park in Anshun (Guizhou)
安阳漳河峡谷国家湿地公园	Zhanghe Canyon National Wetland Park of Anyang County (Henan)
八家子古洞河国家湿地公园	Gudong River National Wetland Park of Bajiazi (Jilin)
八五八小穆棱河国家湿地公园	Bawuba National Wetland Park of Xiaomuling River (Heilongjiang)
巴楚邦克尔国家湿地公园	Bangkeer National Wetland Park of Bachu County (Xinjiang)
巴林雅鲁河国家湿地公园	Balinyalu River National Wetland Park (Inner Mongolia)
巴林左旗乌力吉沐沦河国家湿地公园	Uliji Mulong River National Wetland Park of Balinzuo Banner (Inner Mongolia)
巴美湖国家湿地公园	Bamei Lake National Wetland Park (Inner Mongolia)
巴青约雄措高山冰缘国家湿地公园	Alpine Periglacial National Wetland Park of Yuexiong Lake in Baqing (Tibet)
巴山湖国家湿地公园	Bashan Lake National Wetland Park (Chongqing)
巴塘姊妹湖国家湿地公园	Sister Lake National Wetland Park of Batang County (Sichuan)
巴彦江湾国家湿地公园	Jiangwan Bay National Wetland Park of Bayan County (Heilongjiang)
坝上闪电河国家湿地公园	National Wetland Park of Bashang Shandian River (Hebei)
白桦川国家湿地公园	Baihua Valley National Wetland Park (Heilongjiang)
白狼奥伦布坎国家湿地公园	Bailang Olenbukan National Wetland Park (Inner Mongolia)
白狼洮儿河国家湿地公园	Taoer River National Wetland Park in Bailang (Inner Mongolia)

白朗年楚河国家湿地公园	Nianchu River National Wetland Park of Bailang County (Tibet)
白山珠宝河国家湿地公园	Jewelry River National Wetland Park in Baishan (Jilin)
白水林皋湖国家湿地公园	Lingao Lake National Wetland Park of Baishui County (Shaanxi)
白玉拉龙措国家湿地公园	Lalongcuo National Wetland Park of Baiyu County (Sichuan)
百色福禄河国家湿地公园	Fulu River National Wetland Park in Baise (Guangxi)
柏林湖国家湿地公园	Bailin Lake National Wetland Park (Sichuan)
班戈江龙玛曲国家湿地公园	Jianglong Maqu National Wetland Park of Bange County (Tibet)
班玛玛可河国家湿地公园	Make River National Wetland Park of Banma County (Qinghai)
包头黄河国家湿地公园	Yellow River National Wetland Park in Baotou (Inner Mongolia)
包头昆都仑河国家湿地公园	Kundulun River National Wetland Park in Baotou (Inner Mongolia)
宝坻潮白河国家湿地公园	Chaobai River National Wetland Park in Baodi (Tianjin)
保靖酉水国家湿地公园	Youshui River National Wetland Park of Baojing County (Hunan)
保山青华海国家湿地公园	Qinghua Lake National Wetland Park in Baoshan (Yunnan)
北安乌裕尔河国家湿地公园	Wuyu'er River National Wetland Park in Bei'an (Heilongjiang)
北戴河国家湿地公园	Beidaihe National Wetland Park (Hebei)
北海滨海国家湿地公园	Seaside National Wetland Park in Beihai (Guangxi)
北盘江大峡谷国家湿地公园	National Wetland Park of North Panjiang Grand Canyon (Guizhou)
北镇新立湖国家湿地公园	Xinli Lake National Wetland Park in Beizhen (Liaoning)

比如娜若国家湿地公园	Biru Naruo National Wetland Park (Tibet)
碧江国家湿地公园	Bijiang National Wetland Park (Guizhou)
边坝炯拉措国家湿地公园	Jiongla Lake National Wetland Park of Bianba County (Tibet)
宾县二龙湖国家湿地公园	Erlong Lake National Wetland Park of Binxian County (Heilongjiang)
滨州秦皇河国家湿地公园	Qinhuang River National Wetland Park in Binzhou (Shandong)
滨州小开河国家湿地公园	Xiaokai River National Wetland Park in Binzhou (Shandong)
博乐博尔塔拉河国家湿地公园	Bortala River National Wetland Park in Bole (Xinjiang)
博山五阳湖国家湿地公园	Wuyang Lake National Wetland Park in Boshan (Shandong)
博斯腾湖国家湿地公园	Bosten Lake National Wetland Park (Xinjiang)
布尔津托库木特国家湿地公园	Tuokumute National Wetland Park of Buerjin County (Xinjiang)
彩云湖国家湿地公园	Caiyun Lake National Wetland Park (Chongqing)
曹县黄河故道国家湿地公园	National Wetland Park of the old course of the Yellow River in Caoxian (Shandong)
册亨北盘江国家湿地公园	National Wetland Park of North Panjiang River in Ceheng (Guizhou)
策勒达玛沟国家湿地公园	Damagou National Wetland Park of Cele County (Xinjiang)
茶陵东阳湖国家湿地公园	Dongyang Lake National Wetland Park of Chaling County (Hu'nan)
察布查尔伊犁河国家湿地公园	Ili River National Wetland Park of Chabuchar County (Xinjiang)
柴河固里国家湿地公园	Guli River National Wetland Park of Chaihe (Inner Mongolia)
昌江海尾国家湿地公园	Haiwei National Wetland Park of Changjiang County (Hainan)
昌图辽河国家湿地公园	Liaohe River National Wetland Park of Changtu County (Liaoning)

昌邑滨海国家湿地公园	Coastal National Wetland Park in Changyi (Shandong)
昌源河国家湿地公园	Changyuan River National Wetland Park (Shanxi)
长白泥粒河国家湿地公园	Nili River National Wetland Park of Changbai (Jilin)
长白山碱水河国家湿地公园	Jianshui River National Wetland Park at Changbai Mountain (Jilin)
长春北湖国家湿地公园	North Lake National Wetland Park in Changchun (Jilin)
长春新立湖国家湿地公园	Xinli Lake National Wetland Park in Changchun (Jilin)
长葛双洎河国家湿地公园	Shuangji River National Wetland Park in Changge (Henan)
长乐闽江河口国家湿地公园	Minjiang Estuary National Wetland Park in Changle (Fujian)
长沙洋湖国家湿地公园	Yanghu Lake National Wetland Park in Changsha (Hunan)
长寿岛国家湿地公园	Changshou Island National Wetland Park (Hubei)
长汀汀江国家湿地公园	Tingjiang River National Wetland Park of Changting County (Fujian)
长兴仙山湖国家湿地公园	Xianshan Lake National Wetland Park of Changxing County (Zhejiang)
长阳清江国家湿地公园	Qingjiang River National Wetland Park of Changyang County (Hubei)
常宁天湖国家湿地公园	Tianhu Lake National Wetland Park in Changning (Hu'nan)
绰尔雅多罗国家湿地公园	Chuer Yadoro National Wetland Park (Inner Mongolia)
绰源国家湿地公园	Chuoyuan National Wetland Park (Inner Mongolia)
巢湖半岛国家湿地公园	Peninsula National Wetland Park at Chaohu Lake (Anhui)
朝邑国家湿地公园	Chaoyi National Wetland Park (Shaanxi)

郴州西河国家湿地公园	Xihe River National Wetland Park in Chenzhou (Hunan)
陈巴尔虎陶海国家湿地公园	Taohai National Wetland Park in Chen Balhu (Inner Mongolia)
成武东鱼河国家湿地公园	Dongyu River National Wetland Park of Chengwu County (Shandong)
城步白云湖国家湿地公园	Baiyun Lake National Wetland Park of Chengbu County (Hu'nan)
茌平金牛湖国家湿地公园	Jinniu Lake National Wetland Park in Chiping (Shandong)
赤壁陆水湖国家湿地公园	Lushui Lake National Wetland Park in Chibi (Hubei)
崇明西沙国家湿地公园	Xisha National Wetland Park on Chongming Island (Shanghai)
崇阳青山国家湿地公园	Chongyang Qingshan National Wetland Park (Hubei)
崇义阳明湖国家湿地公园	Yangming Lake National Wetland Park of Chongyi County (Jiangxi)
淳化冶峪河国家湿地公园	Yeyue River National Wetland Park of Chunhua County (Shaanxi)
从江加榜梯田国家湿地公园	Jiabang Terrace National Wetland Park of Congjiang County (Guizhou)
错那拿日雍措国家湿地公园	Nariyong Lake National Wetland Park of Cuona County (Tibet)
达拉特旗乌兰淖尔国家湿地公园	Ulan Nur National Wetland Park of Dalat Banner (Inner Mongolia)
达日黄河国家湿地公园	Yellow River National Wetland Park of Dari County (Qinghai)
大安嫩江湾国家湿地公园	Nenjiang Bay National Wetland Park in Da'an (Jilin)
大昌湖国家湿地公园	Dachang Lake National Wetland Park (Chongqing)
大海林二浪河国家湿地公园	Erlang River National Wetland Park of Dahailin (Heilongjiang)

大伙房国家湿地公园	Dahuofang National Wetland Park (Liaoning)
大庆黑鱼湖国家湿地公园	National Wetland Park of Black Fish Lake in Daqing (Heilongjiang)
大石头亚光湖国家湿地公园	Yaguang Lake National Wetland Park of Dashitou (Jilin)
大汤河国家湿地公园	Datang River National Wetland Park (Liaoning)
大通湖国家湿地公园	Datong Lake National Wetland Park (Hunan)
大同桑干河国家湿地公园	Sanggan River National Wetland Park in Datong (Shanxi)
大瓦山国家湿地公园	Dawa Mountain National Wetland Park (Sichuan)
大新黑水河国家湿地公园	Heishui River National Wetland Park of Daxin County (Guangxi)
大兴安岭阿木尔国家湿地公园	Amur National Wetland Park in Greater Khingan Mountains (Heilongjiang)
大兴安岭古里河国家湿地公园	Guli River National Wetland Park in Greater Khingan Mountains (Heilongjiang)
大兴安岭砍都河国家湿地公园	Kandu River National Wetland Park in Greater Khingan Mountains (Heilongjiang)
大兴安岭漠河九曲十八湾国家湿地公园	Eighteen-Bend National Wetland Park of Mohe River in Greater Khingan Mountains (Heilongjiang)
大兴安岭双河源国家湿地公园	National Wetland Park of Shuanghe River Headwaters in Greater Khingan Mountains (Heilongjiang)
大杨树奎勒河国家湿地公园	Dayangshu Kuilehe National Wetland Park (Inner Mongolia)
大冶保安湖国家湿地公园	Bao'an Lake National Wetland Park in Daye (Hubei)
大余章水国家湿地公园	Zhangshui River National Wetland Park of Dayu County (Jiangxi)
丹凤丹江国家湿地公园	Danfeng River National Wetland Park of Danfeng County (Shaanxi)
丹江源国家湿地公园	National Wetland Park of Danjiang River Headwaters (Shaanxi)

当惹雍错国家湿地公园	Dangreyongcuo National Wetland Park (Tibet)
当阳青龙湖国家湿地公园	Qinglong Lake National Wetland Park in Dangyang (Hubei)
道源国家湿地公园	Daoyuan National Wetland Park (Anhui)
德江白果坨国家湿地公园	Baiguotuo National Wetland Park of Dejiang County (Guizhou)
德令哈尕海国家湿地公园	Gahai Lake National Wetland Park in Delingha (Qinghai)
德清下渚湖国家湿地公园	Xiazhu Lake National Wetland Park of Deqing County (Zhejiang)
德州减河国家湿地公园	Jianhe River National Wetland Park in Dezhou (Shandong)
邓州湍河国家湿地公园	Tuanhe River National Wetland Park in Dengzhou (Henan)
磴口奈伦湖国家湿地公园	Nailun Lake National Wetland Park of Dengkou County (Inner Mongolia)
迪沟国家湿地公园	Digou National Wetland Park (Anhui)
丁青布托湖国家湿地公园	Butuo Lake National Wetland Park of Dingqing County (Tibet)
鼎城鸟儿洲国家湿地公园	Niao'erzhou National Wetland Park in Dingcheng (Hu'nan)
东安紫水国家湿地公园	Zishui River National Wetland Park of Dong'an County (Hu'nan)
东阿洛神湖国家湿地公园	Luoshen Lake National Wetland Park of Dong'e County (Shandong)
东方红南岔湖国家湿地公园	Nancha Lake National Wetland Park of Dongfanghong (Heilongjiang)
东海西双湖国家湿地公园	Xishuang Lake National Wetland Park of Donghai County (Jiangsu)
东江国家湿地公园	Dongjiang River National Wetland Park (Guangdong)
东江湖国家湿地公园	Dongjiang Lake National Wetland Park (Hu'nan)
东江源国家湿地公园	National Wetland Park of Dongjiang River Headwaters (Jiangxi)

东京城镜泊湖源头国家湿地公园	Dongjing City National Wetland Park of Jingpo Lake Headwaters (Heilongjiang)
东兰坡豪湖国家湿地公园	Pohao Lake National Wetland Park of Donglan County (Guangxi)
东辽鴜鹭湖国家湿地公园	Cilu Lake National Wetland Park of Dongliao County (Jilin)
东明黄河国家湿地公园	Yellow River National Wetland Park of Dongming County (Shandong)
东宁绥芬河国家湿地公园	Suifen River National Wetland Park of Dongning County (Heilongjiang)
东平滨湖国家湿地公园	Lakeside National Wetland Park of Dongping County (Shandong)
东鄱阳湖国家湿地公园	East Poyang Lake National Wetland Park (Jiangxi)
洞口平溪江国家湿地公园	Pingxi River National Wetland Park of Dongkou County (Hu'nan)
都安澄江国家湿地公园	Chengjiang River National Wetland Park of Du'an County (Guangxi)
都兰阿拉克湖国家湿地公园	Alag Lake National Wetland Park of Dulan County (Qinghai)
都匀清水江国家湿地公园	Qingshui River National Wetland Park in Duyun (Guizhou)
独山九十九滩国家湿地公园	Jiushijiu Beach National Wetland Park of Dushan County (Guizhou)
杜尔伯特天湖国家湿地公园	Tianhu Lake National Wetland Park of Duerbote (Heilongjiang)
敦化秋梨沟国家湿地公园	Qiuligou National Wetland Park in Dunhua (Jilin)
多伦滦河源国家湿地公园	National Wetland Park of Luanhe River Headwaters in Duolun (Inner Mongolia)
多庆错国家湿地公园	Duoqingcuo National Wetland Park (Tibet)
额尔古纳国家湿地公园	Ergun National Wetland Park (Inner Mongolia)
额敏河国家湿地公园	E'min River National Wetland Park (Xinjiang)
洱源西湖国家湿地公园	West Lake National Wetland Park of Eryuan County (Yunnan)

法库獾子洞国家湿地公园	Badger Cave National Wetland Park of Faku County (Liaoning)
返湾湖国家湿地公园	FanwanLake National Wetland Park (Hubei)
方正湖国家湿地公园	Fangzheng Lake National Wetland Park (Heilongjiang)
房山长沟泉水国家湿地公园	Changgou Spring National Wetland Park in Fangshan (Beijing)
房县古南河国家湿地公园	GunanRiver National Wetland Park of Fangxian County (Hubei)
肥城康王河国家湿地公园	Kangwang River National Wetland Park in Feicheng (Shandong)
肥东管湾国家湿地公园	Guanwan National Wetland Park of Feidong County (Anhui)
肥西三河国家湿地公园	Sanhe National Wetland Park of Feixi County (Anhui)
丰宁海留图国家湿地公园	Fengning Hailiutu National Wetland Park (Hebei)
丰县黄河故道大沙河国家湿地公园	Fengxian National Wetland Park of Dasha River (the old course of the Yellow River) (Jiangsu)
峰峰滏阳河国家湿地公园	Fuyang River National Wetland Park in Fengfeng District (Hebei)
凤城草河国家湿地公园	Caohe River National Wetland Park in Fengcheng (Liaoning)
凤冈龙潭河国家湿地公园	Longtan River National Wetland Park of Fenggang County (Guizhou)
凤县嘉陵江国家湿地公园	Jialing River National Wetland Park of Fengxian County (Shaanxi)
凤翔雍城湖国家湿地公园	Yongcheng Lake National Wetland Park of Fengxiang County (Shaanxi)
扶余大金碑国家湿地公园	Fuyu Dajinbei National Wetland Park (Jilin)
浮桥河国家湿地公园	Fuqiao River National Wetland Park (Hubei)
涪江国家湿地公园	Fujiang River National Wetland Park (Chongqing)

福泉岔河国家湿地公园	Chahe National Wetland Park of Fuquan County (Guizhou)
抚顺社河国家湿地公园	Shehe River National Wetland Park of Fushun County (Liaoning)
抚州凤岗河国家湿地公园	Fenggang River National Wetland Park in Fuzhou (Jiangxi)
抚州廖坊国家湿地公园	Liaofang National Wetland Park in Fuzhou (Jiangxi)
阜康特纳格尔国家湿地公园	Tenager National Wetland Park in Fukang (Xinjiang)
阜南王家坝国家湿地公园	Wangjia Dam National Wetland Park of Funan County (Anhui)
富川龟石国家湿地公园	Guishi National Wetland Park of Fuchuan County (Guangxi)
富锦国家湿地公园	Fujin National Wetland Park (Heilongjiang)
富平石川河国家湿地公园	Shichuan River National Wetland Park of Fuping County (Shaanxi)
富裕龙安桥国家湿地公园	Fuyu Long'anqiao National Wetland Park (Heilongjiang)
富蕴可可托海国家湿地公园	Keketuohai National Wetland Park of Fuyun County (Xinjiang)
嘎朗国家湿地公园	Galang National Wetland Park (Tibet)
甘德班玛仁拓国家湿地公园	Bamarento National Wetland Park of Gande County (Qinghai)
甘河国家湿地公园	Ganhe River National Wetland Park (Inner Mongolia)
赣县大湖江国家湿地公园	Dahu River National Wetland Park in Ganxian (Jiangxi)
赣州章江国家湿地公园	Zhangjiang River National Wetland Park in Ganzhou (Jiangxi)
刚察沙柳河国家湿地公园	Shaliu River National Wetland Park of Gangcha County (Qinghai)
钢城大汶河国家湿地公园	Dawen River National Wetland Park in Gangcheng (Shandong)

高安锦江国家湿地公园	Jinjiang River National Wetland Park in Gao'an (Jiangxi)
高密胶河国家湿地公园	Jiaohe River National Wetland Park in Gaomi (Shandong)
根河源国家湿地公园	National Wetland Park of Genhe River Headwaters (Inner Mongolia)
公安崇湖国家湿地公园	Chonghu Lake National Wetland Park of Gong'an County (Hubei)
贡觉拉妥国家湿地公园	Latuo National Wetland Park of Gongjue County (Tibet)
构溪河国家湿地公园	Gouxi River National Wetland Park (Sichuan)
古城国家湿地公园	Gucheng National Wetland Park (Shanxi)
谷城汉江国家湿地公园	Hanjiang River National Wetland Park of Gucheng County (Hubei)
固原清水河国家湿地公园	Qingshui River National Wetland Park in Guyuan (Ningxia)
灌阳灌江国家湿地公园	Guanjiang River National Wetland Park of Guanyang County (Guangxi)
光山龙山湖国家湿地公园	Longshan Lake National Wetland Park of Guangshan County (Henan)
广安白云湖国家湿地公园	Baiyun Lake National Wetland Park in Guang'an (Sichuan)
广昌抚河源国家湿地公园	National Wetland Park of Fuhe River Headwaters in Guangchang (Jiangxi)
广水徐家河国家湿地公园	Xujia River National Wetland Park in Guangshui (Hubei)
广州海珠国家湿地公园	Haizhu National Wetland Park in Guangzhou (Guangdong)
贵德黄河清国家湿地公园	Huangheqing National Wetland Park of Guide County (Qinghai)
贵定摆龙河国家湿地公园	Bailong River National Wetland Park of Guiding County (Guizhou)
贵南茫曲国家湿地公园	Mangqu National Wetland Park of Guinan County (Qinghai)

贵阳阿哈湖国家湿地公园	A'ha Lake National Wetland Park in Guiyang (Guizhou)
贵阳百花湖国家湿地公园	Baihua Lake National Wetland Park in Guiyang (Guizhou)
桂林会仙喀斯特国家湿地公园	Huixian Karst National Wetland Park in Guilin (Guangxi)
桂阳春陵国家湿地公园	Guiyang Chongling National Wetland Park (Hu'nan)
哈巴河阿克齐国家湿地公园	Akqi National Wetland Park of Habahe County (Xinjiang)
哈尔滨阿勒锦岛国家湿地公园	Alejin Island National Wetland Park in Harbin (Heilongjiang)
哈尔滨阿什河国家湿地公园	Ashe River National Wetland Park in Harbin (Heilongjiang)
哈尔滨白渔泡国家湿地公园	Baiyu Lakelet National Wetland Park in Harbin (Heilongjiang)
哈尔滨松北国家湿地公园	Songbei National Wetland Park in Harbin (Heilongjiang)
哈尔滨太阳岛国家湿地公园	Sun Island National Wetland Park in Harbin (Heilongjiang)
哈密河国家湿地公园	Hami River National Wetland Park (Xinjiang)
哈素海国家湿地公园	Hasu Lake National Wetland Park (Inner Mongolia)
海口美舍河国家湿地公园	Meishe River National Wetland Park in Haikou (Hainan)
海口五源河国家湿地公园	Wuyuan River National Wetland Park in Haikou (Hainan)
海陵岛红树林国家湿地公园	Mangrove National Wetland Park on Hailing Island (Guangdong)
汉川汈汊湖国家湿地公园	Fucha Lake National Wetland Park in Hanchuan (Hubei)
汉丰湖国家湿地公园	Hanfeng Lake National Wetland Park (Chongqing)

汉寿息风湖国家湿地公园	Xifeng Lake National Wetland Park of Hanshou County (Hunan)
汉阴观音河国家湿地公园	Guanyin River National Wetland Park of Hanyin County (Shaanxi)
汉中葱滩国家湿地公园	Congtan Shallow National Wetland Park in Hanzhong (Shaanxi)
杭州湾国家湿地公园	Hangzhou Bay National Wetland Park (Zhejiang)
杭州西溪国家湿地公园	Xixi Stream National Wetland Park in Hangzhou (Zhejiang)
合川三江国家湿地公园	Three Rivers National Wetland Park in Hechuan (Chongqing)
合肥巢湖湖滨国家湿地公园	Chaohu Lakeside National Wetland Park in Hefei (Anhui)
合山洛灵湖国家湿地公园	Luoling Lake National Wetland Park in Heshan (Guangxi)
和布克赛尔国家湿地公园	Hoboksar National Wetland Park (Xinjiang)
和龙泉水河国家湿地公园	Quanshui River National Wetland Park in Helong (Jilin)
和硕塔什汗国家湿地公园	Tashihan National Wetland Park of Heshuo County (Xinjiang)
贺州合面狮湖国家湿地公园	Hemianshi Lake National Wetland Park in Hezhou (Guangxi)
赫山来仪湖国家湿地公园	Laiyi Lake National Wetland Park in Heshan (Hunan)
鹤壁淇河国家湿地公园	Qihe River National Wetland Park in Hebi (Henan)
鹤岗十里河国家湿地公园	Shili River National Wetland Park in Hegang (Heilongjiang)
鹤庆东草海国家湿地公园	National Wetland Park of Heqing Eastern Meadow Lake (Yunnan)
鹤泉湖国家湿地公园	Hequan Lake National Wetland Park (Ningxia)
黑河坤河国家湿地公园	Kunhe River National Wetland Park in Heihe (Heilongjiang)

黑瞎子岛国家湿地公园	Heixiazi Island National Wetland Park (Heilongjiang)
横峰岑港河国家湿地公园	Cengang River National Wetland Park of Hengfeng County (Jiangxi)
横县西津国家湿地公园	Xijin National Wetland Park of Hengxian County (Guangxi)
衡东洣水国家湿地公园	Mishui River National Wetland Park of Hengdong County (Hu'nan)
衡南莲湖湾国家湿地公园	Lianhu Bay National Wetland Park of Hengnan County (Hu'nan)
衡山萱洲国家湿地公园	Xuanzhou National Wetland Park in Hengshan (Hu'nan)
红河哈尼梯田国家湿地公园	National Wetland Park of Honghe Hani Terrace (Yunnan)
红花尔基伊敏河国家湿地公园	Yimin River National Wetland Park of Honghua'erji (Inner Mongolia)
红星霍吉河国家湿地公园	Huoji River National Wetland Park in Hongxing (Heilongjiang)
红原嘎曲国家湿地公园	Gaqu National Wetland Park of Hongyuan County (Sichuan)
洪江清江湖国家湿地公园	Qingjiang River National Wetland Park in Hongjiang (Hu'nan)
洪洞汾河国家湿地公园	Fenhe River National Wetland Park of Hongtong County (Shanxi)
呼兰河口国家湿地公园	Hulan Estuary National Wetland Park (Heilongjiang)
呼伦贝尔银岭河国家湿地公园	Yinling River National Wetland Park in Hulunbuir (Inner Mongolia)
呼图壁大海子国家湿地公园	Dahaizi Lake National Wetland Park of Hutubi County (Xinjiang)
呼中呼玛河源国家湿地公园	National Wetland Park of Huma River Headwaters in Huzhong (Heilongjiang)
葫芦岛龙兴国家湿地公园	Longxing National Wetland Park in Huludao (Liaoning)

虎林国家湿地公园	Hulin National Wetland Park (Heilongjiang)
互助南门峡国家湿地公园	National Wetland Park of South Gate Gorge of Huzhu County (Qinghai)
花都湖国家湿地公园	Huadu Lake National Wetland Park (Guangdong)
花垣古苗河国家湿地公园	Gumiao River National Wetland Park of Huayuan County (Hu'nan)
华容东湖国家湿地公园	East Lake National Wetland Park of Huarong County (Hu'nan)
华州少华湖国家湿地公园	Shaohua Lake National Wetland Park in Huazhou (Shaanxi)
华阴太华湖国家湿地公园	Taihua Lake National Wetland Park in Huayin (Shaanxi)
怀集燕都国家湿地公园	Yandu National Wetland Park of Huaiji County (Guangdong)
怀来官厅水库国家湿地公园	Guanting Reservoir National Wetland Park of Huailai County (Hebei)
怀宁观音湖国家湿地公园	Guanyin Lake National Wetland Park of Huaining County (Anhui)
怀仁口泉河国家湿地公园	Kouquan River National Wetland Park of Huairen County (Shanxi)
淮安白马湖国家湿地公园	White Horse Lake National Wetland Park in Huai'an (Jiangsu)
淮安古淮河国家湿地公园	Ancient Huaihe River National Wetland Park in Huai'an (Jiangsu)
淮北中湖国家湿地公园	Zhonghu Lake National Wetland Park in Huaibei (Anhui)
淮南焦岗湖国家湿地公园	Jiaogang Lake National Wetland Park in Huainan (Anhui)
淮阳龙湖国家湿地公园	Longhu Lake National Wetland Park of Huaiyang County (Henan)
环荆州古城国家湿地公园	Around-the-Ancient City National Wetland Park of Jingzhou (Hubei)
桓龙湖国家湿地公园	Huanlong Lake National Wetland Park (Liaoning)

皇华岛国家湿地公园	Huanghua Island National Wetland Park (Chongqing)
黄冈白莲河国家湿地公园	Bailian River National Wetland Park in Huanggang (Hubei)
黄冈遗爱湖国家湿地公园	Yi'ai Lake National Wetland Park in Huanggang (Hubei)
黄果树国家湿地公园	Huangguoshu National Wetland Park (Guizhou)
黄河岛国家湿地公园	Yellow River Island National Wetland Park (Shandong)
黄河玫瑰湖国家湿地公园	Rose Lake National Wetland Park at Yellow River (Shandong)
黄家湖国家湿地公园	Huangjia Lake National Wetland Park (Hu'nan)
黄沙古渡国家湿地公园	National Wetland Park of Yellow Sand Ancient Ferry (Ningxia)
汇川喇叭河国家湿地公园	Laba River National Wetland Park in Huichuan (Guizhou)
会昌湘江国家湿地公园	Xiangjiang River National Wetland Park of Huichang County (Jiangxi)
会同渠水国家湿地公园	Qushui River National Wetland Park of Huitong County (Hu'nan)
惠水鱼梁河国家湿地公园	Yuliang River National Wetland Park of Huishui County (Guizhou)
惠亭湖国家湿地公园	Huiting Lake National Wetland Park (Hubei)
惠州潼湖国家湿地公园	Tonghu National Wetland Park in Huizhou (Guangdong)
霍城伊犁河谷国家湿地公园	National Wetland Park of Ili River Valley of Huocheng County (Xinjiang)
霍林郭勒静湖国家湿地公园	Jinghu Lake National Wetland Park in Hollingol (Inner Mongolia)
吉木乃高山冰缘区国家湿地公园	National Wetland Park of Jimunai Alpine Periglacial Area (Xinjiang)
吉木萨尔北庭国家湿地公园	Beiting National Wetland Park of Jimusaer County (Xinjiang)

吉首峒河国家湿地公园	Donghe River National Wetland Park in Jishou (Hu'nan)
吉水吉湖国家湿地公园	Jihu Lake National Wetland Park of Jishui County (Jiangxi)
集安霸王潮国家湿地公园	Bawangchao National Wetland Park in Ji'an (Jilin)
集宁霸王河国家湿地公园	Bawang River National Wetland Park in Jining (Inner Mongolia)
济南白云湖国家湿地公园	Baiyun Lake National Wetland Park in Jinan (Shandong)
济西国家湿地公园	Jixi National Wetland Park (Shandong)
蓟县州河国家湿地公园	Zhouhe River National Wetland Park of Jixian County (Tianjin)
稷山汾河国家湿地公园	Jishan Fenhe National Wetland Park (Shanxi)
加格达奇甘河国家湿地公园	Ganhe River National Wetland Park in Jiagedaqi (Heilongjiang)
嘉禾钟水河国家湿地公园	Zhongshui River National Wetland Park of Jiahe County (Hunan)
嘉乃玉错国家湿地公园	Jianaiyucuo National Wetland Park (Tibet)
嘉兴运河湾国家湿地公园	Jiaxing Canal Bay National Wetland Park (Zhejiang)
嘉鱼珍湖国家湿地公园	Zhenhu Lake National Wetland Park of Jiayu County (Hubei)
嘉峪关草湖国家湿地公园	Caohu Lake National Wetland Park of Jiayu Pass (Gansu)
监利老江河故道国家湿地公园	Old River National Wetland Park of Jianli County (Hubei)
简泉湖国家湿地公园	Jianquanhu National Wetland Park (Ningxia)
建湖九龙口国家湿地公园	Jiulongkou National Wetland Park of Jianhu County (Jiangsu)
建宁闽江源国家湿地公园	National Wetland Park of Minjiang River Headwaters in Jianning (Fujian)
江川星云湖国家湿地公园	Xingyun Lake National Wetland Park in Jiangchuan (Yunnan)

江华涔天河国家湿地公园	Centian River National Wetland Park of Jianghua County (Hu'nan)
江口国家湿地公园	Jiangkou National Wetland Park (Guizhou)
江夏藏龙岛国家湿地公园	Canglong Island National Wetland Park in Jiangxia (Hubei)
江永永明河国家湿地公园	Yongming River National Wetland Park of Jiangyong County (Hunan)
江油让水河国家湿地公园	Rangshui River National Wetland Park in Jiangyou (Sichuan)
姜堰溱湖国家湿地公园	Qinhu Lake National Wetland Park in Jiangyan (Jiangsu)
介休汾河国家湿地公园	Fenhe River National Wetland Park in Jiexiu (Shanxi)
界首两湾国家湿地公园	Twin-Bay National Wetland Park in Jieshou (Anhui)
金川金水湖国家湿地公园	Jinshui Lake National Wetland Park in Jinchuan (Gansu)
金洞猛江河国家湿地公园	Mengjiang River National Wetland Park in Jindong (Hunan)
金沙湖国家湿地公园	Jinsha Lake National Wetland Park (Hubei)
金塔北海子国家湿地公园	Beihaizi Lake National Wetland Park of Jinta County (Gansu)
金坛长荡湖国家湿地公园	Changdang Lake National Wetland Park in Jintan (Jiangsu)
金乡金水湖国家湿地公园	Jinshui Lake National Wetland Park of Jinxiang County (Shandong)
晋宁南滇池国家湿地公园	National Wetland Park of South Dianchi Lake in Jinning (Yunnan)
泾阳泾河国家湿地公园	Jinghe River National Wetland Park of Jingyang County (Shaanxi)
荆门仙居河国家湿地公园	Xianju River National Wetland Park in Jingmen (Hubei)
荆门漳河国家湿地公园	Zhanghe River National Wetland Park in Jingmen (Hubei)

荆州菱角湖国家湿地公园	Lingjiao (Water Chestnut) Lake National Wetland Park in Jingzhou (Hubei)
景德镇玉田湖国家湿地公园	Yutian Lake National Wetland Park in Jingdezhen (Jiangxi)
景泰白墩子盐沼国家湿地公园	National Wetland Park of Baidunzi Salt Marsh of Jingtai County (Gansu)
靖西龙潭国家湿地公园	Longtan Lake National Wetland Park in Jingxi (Guangxi)
靖州五龙潭国家湿地公园	Wulong Lake National Wetland Park of Jinzhou County (Hu'nan)
静乐汾河川国家湿地公园	National Wetland Park of Fenhe River Plain in Jinle County (Shanxi)
九里湖国家湿地公园	Jiuli Lake National Wetland Park (Jiangsu)
九龙湾国家湿地公园	Jiulong Bay National Wetland Park (Shandong)
酒埠江国家湿地公园	Jiubu River National Wetland Park (Hu'nan)
酒泉花城湖国家湿地公园	Huacheng Lake National Wetland Park in Jiuquan (Gansu)
莒南鸡龙河国家湿地公园	Jilong River National Wetland Park of Junan County (Shandong)
莒县沭河国家湿地公园	Shuhe River National Wetland Park of Juxian County (Shandong)
句容赤山湖国家湿地公园	Chishan Lake National Wetland Park in Jurong (Jiangsu)
潏水国家湿地公园	Jushui River National Wetland Park (Shaanxi)
浚河国家湿地公园	Junhe River National Wetland Park (Shandong)
卡鲁奔国家湿地公园	Kaluben National Wetland Park (Inner Mongolia)
开平孔雀湖国家湿地公园	Peacock Lake National Wetland Park in Kaiping (Guangdong)
康保康巴诺尔国家湿地公园	Kangba Noel National Wetland Park of Kangbao County (Hebei)
康平辽河国家湿地公园	Liaohe River National Wetland Park of Kangping County (Liaoning)
康县梅园河国家湿地公园	Meiyuan River National Wetland Park of Kangxian County (Gansu)

科左后旗胡力斯台淖尔国家湿地公园	Hulistai Nur National Wetland Park of Kezuohou Banner (Inner Mongolia)
垦利天宁湖国家湿地公园	Tianning Lake National Wetland Park of Kenli County (Shandong)
孔江国家湿地公园	Kongjiang River National Wetland Park (Guangdong)
孔目江国家湿地公园	Kongmu River National Wetland Park (Jiangxi)
库都尔河国家湿地公园	Kudur River National Wetland Park (Inner Mongolia)
昆明捞渔河国家湿地公园	Laoyuhe National Wetland Park in Kunming (Yunnan)
昆山天福国家湿地公园	Tianfu National Wetland Park in Kunshan (Jiangsu)
拉里昆国家湿地公园	Lalikun National Wetland Park (Xinjiang)
拉姆拉错国家湿地公园	Ramlacuo National Wetland Park (Tibet)
来安池杉湖国家湿地公园	Chishan Lake National Wetland Park of Lai'an County (Anhui)
莱芜雪野湖国家湿地公园	Xueye Lake National Wetland Park in Laiwu (Shandong)
莱州湾金仓国家湿地公园	Jincang National Wetland Park at Laizhou Bay (Shandong)
濑溪河国家湿地公园	Laixi River National Wetland Park (Chongqing)
兰陵会宝湖国家湿地公园	Huibao Lake National Wetland Park of Lanling County (Shandong)
兰坪箐花甸国家湿地公园	Qinghua Meadow National Wetland Park in Lanping (Yunnan)
兰西呼兰河国家湿地公园	Hulan River National Wetland Park of Lanxi County (Heilongjiang)
兰州秦王川国家湿地公园	Qinwang Valley National Wetland Park in Lanzhou (Gansu)
老河口西排子湖国家湿地公园	Xipaizi Lake National Wetland Park in Laohekou (Hubei)
乐陵跃马河国家湿地公园	Yuema River National Wetland Park in Laoling (Shandong)

乐都大地湾国家湿地公园	Dadi Bend National Wetland Park in Ledu (Qinghai)
雷波马湖国家湿地公园	Leiboma Lake National Wetland Park (Sichuan)
雷州九龙山红树林国家湿地公园	Mangrove National Wetland Park of Jiulong Mountain in Leizhou (Guangdong)
耒水国家湿地公园	Leishui River National Wetland Park (Hu'nan)
类乌齐紫曲河国家湿地公园	Ziqu River National Wetland Park of Leiwuqi County (Tibet)
黎平八舟河国家湿地公园	Bazhou River National Wetland Park of Liping County (Guizhou)
礼泉甘河国家湿地公园	Ganhe River National Wetland Park of Liquan County (Shaanxi)
澧州涔槐国家湿地公园	Lizhou Cenhuai National Wetland Park (Hu'nan)
醴陵官庄湖国家湿地公园	Guanzhuang Lake National Wetland Park in Liling (Hu'nan)
丽水九龙国家湿地公园	Jiulong National Wetland Park in Lishui (Zhejiang)
利辛西淝河国家湿地公园	Xifei River National Wetland Park of Lixin County (Anhui)
荔波黄江河国家湿地公园	Huangjiang River National Wetland Park of Libo County (Guizhou)
荔浦荔江国家湿地公园	Lijiang River National Wetland Park in Lipu (Guangxi)
溧阳长荡湖国家湿地公园	Changdang Lake National Wetland Park in Liyang (Jiangsu)
溧阳天目湖国家湿地公园	Tianmu Lake National Wetland Park in Liyang (Jiangsu)
连南瑶排梯田国家湿地公园	Yaopai Terrace National Wetland Park of Liannan County (Guangdong)
莲花莲江国家湿地公园	Lianjiang River National Wetland Park of Lianhua County (Jiangxi)
涟源湄峰湖国家湿地公园	Meifeng Lake National Wetland Park in Lianyuan (Hunan)
濂江国家湿地公园	Lianjiang River National Wetland Park (Jiangxi)

梁河南底河国家湿地公园	Nandi River National Wetland Park of Lianghe County (Yunnan)
梁平双桂湖国家湿地公园	Shuanggui Lake National Wetland Park in Liangping (Chongqing)
梁山泊国家湿地公园	Liangshan Lake National Wetland Park (Shandong)
梁园黄河故道国家湿地公园	National Wetland Park of Yellow River Old Course in Liangyuan (Henan)
辽源凤鸣湖国家湿地公园	Fengming Lake National Wetland Park in Liaoyuan (Jilin)
辽中蒲河国家湿地公园	Puhe River National Wetland Park in Liaozhong (Liaoning)
聊城东昌湖国家湿地公园	Dongchang Lake National Wetland Park in Liaocheng (Shandong)
林州淇淅河国家湿地公园	Qixi River National Wetland Park in Linzhou (Henan)
临河黄河国家湿地公园	Yellow River National Wetland Park in Linhe (Inner Mongolia)
临江五道沟国家湿地公园	Wudaogou National Wetland Park in Linjiang (Jilin)
临澧道水河国家湿地公园	Daoshui River National Wetland Park of Linli County (Hunan)
临朐弥河国家湿地公园	Mihe River National Wetland Park of Linqu County (Shandong)
临洮洮河国家湿地公园	Taohe River National Wetland Park of Lintao County (Gansu)
临渭沋河国家湿地公园	Youhe River National Wetland Park in Linwei (Shaanxi)
凌源青龙河国家湿地公园	Qinglong River National Wetland Park in Lingyuan (Liaoning)
凌云浩坤湖国家湿地公园	Haokun Lake National Wetland Park of Lingyun County (Guangxi)
陵水红树林国家湿地公园	Lingshui Mangrove National Wetland Park (Hainan)

零陵潇水国家湿地公园	Xiaoshui River National Wetland Park in Lingling (Hunan)
浏阳河国家湿地公园	Liuyang River National Wetland Park (Hunan)
六安淠河国家湿地公园	Pihe River National Wetland Park in Lu'an (Anhui)
六盘水明湖国家湿地公园	Minghu Lake National Wetland Park in Liupanshui (Guizhou)
六盘水娘娘山国家湿地公园	Niangniang Mountain National Wetland Park in Liupanshui (Guizhou)
六盘水牂牁江国家湿地公园	Zangke River National Wetland Park in Liupanshui (Guizhou)
龙河国家湿地公园	Longhe River National Wetland Park (Chongqing)
龙胜龙脊梯田国家湿地公园	National Wetland Park of Longji Rice Terraces in Longsheng (Guangxi)
龙州左江国家湿地公园	Zuojiang River National Wetland Park of Longzhou County (Guangxi)
隆昌古宇湖国家湿地公园	Guyu Lake National Wetland Park of Longchang County (Sichuan)
隆化伊逊河国家湿地公园	Yixun River National Wetland Park of Longhua County (Hebei)
隆回魏源湖国家湿地公园	Weiyuan Lake National Wetland Park of Longhui County (Hu'nan)
卢龙一渠百库国家湿地公园	Yiqu Baiku National Wetland Park of Lulong County (Hebei)
芦溪山口岩国家湿地公园	Shankouyan National Wetland Park of Luxi County (Jiangxi)
庐陵赣江国家湿地公园	Ganjiang River National Wetland Park of Luling County (Jiangxi)
庐山西海国家湿地公园	Xihai Lake National Wetland Park in Lushan (Jiangxi)
庐阳董铺国家湿地公园	Dongpu National Wetland Park in Luyang (Anhui)

炉霍鲜水河国家湿地公园	Xianshui River National Wetland Park of Luhuo County (Sichuan)
泸西黄草洲国家湿地公园	Huangcaozhou National Wetland Park of Luxi County (Yunnan)
泸溪武水国家湿地公园	Wushui River National Wetland Park of Luxi County (Hu'nan)
陆浑湖国家湿地公园	Luhun Lake National Wetland Park (Henan)
鹿邑惠济河国家湿地公园	Huiji River National Wetland Park of Luyi County (Henan)
滦平潮河国家湿地公园	Chaohe River National Wetland Park of Luanping County (Hebei)
罗甸蒙江国家湿地公园	Mengjiang River National Wetland Park of Luodian County (Guizhou)
罗定金银湖国家湿地公园	Jinyin Lake National Wetland Park of Luoding County (Guangdong)
洛隆卓玛朗措国家湿地公园	Zhuomalang Lake National Wetland Park of Luolong County (Tibet)
洛南洛河源国家湿地公园	National Wetland Park of Luohe River Headwaters in Luonan (Shaanxi)
落星湾国家湿地公园	National Wetland Park of Luoxing River Bend (Shaanxi)
漯河市沙河国家湿地公园	Shahe River National Wetland Park in Luohe (Henan)
麻大湖国家湿地公园	Mada Lake National Wetland Park (Shandong)
麻阳锦江国家湿地公园	Jinjiang River National Wetland Park of Mayang County (Hunan)
麻涌华阳湖国家湿地公园	Huayang Lake National Wetland Park at Mayong Town (Guangdong)
马踏湖国家湿地公园	Mata Lake National Wetland Park (Shandong)
玛多冬格措纳湖国家湿地公园	Donggecuona Lake National Wetland Park of Maduo County (Qinghai)
玛纳斯国家湿地公园	Manas National Wetland Park (Xinjiang)
蚂蜒河国家湿地公园	Mayan River National Wetland Park (Heilongjiang)

麦盖提唐王湖国家湿地公园	Tangwang Lake National Wetland Park of Makit County (Xinjiang)
满归贝尔茨河国家湿地公园	Beltz River National Wetland Park of Mangui (Inner Mongolia)
满洲里二卡国家湿地公园	Erka National Wetland Park in Manzhouli (Inner Mongolia)
满洲里霍勒金布拉格国家湿地公园	Holekin Prague National Wetland Park in Manzhouli (Inner Mongolia)
毛里湖国家湿地公园	Maoli Lake National Wetland Park (Hu'nan)
湄潭湄江湖国家湿地公园	Meijiang Lake National Wetland Park of Meitan County (Guizhou)
蒙城北淝河国家湿地公园	North Feihe River National Wetland Park of Mengcheng County (Anhui)
蒙自长桥海国家湿地公园	Changqiao Lake National Wetland Park in Mengzi (Yunnan)
汨罗江国家湿地公园	Miluo River National Wetland Park (Hu'nan)
泌阳铜山湖国家湿地公园	Tongshan Lake National Wetland Park of Biyang County (Henan)
绵阳三江湖国家湿地公园	Sanjiang Lake National Wetland Park in Mianyang (Sichuan)
免渡河国家湿地公园	Miandu River National Wetland Park (Inner Mongolia)
民勤石羊河国家湿地公园	Shiyang River National Wetland Park of Minqin County (Gansu)
民权黄河故道国家湿地公园	National Wetland Park of Yellow River Old Course in Minquan (Henan)
莫愁湖国家湿地公园	Mochou Lake National Wetland Park (Hubei)
莫和尔图国家湿地公园	Mohertu National Wetland Park (Inner Mongolia)
莫力达瓦巴彦国家湿地公园	Bayan National Wetland Park in Molidawa (Inner Mongolia)
漠河大林河国家湿地公园	Dalin River National Wetland Park in Mohe (Heilongjiang)
磨盘湖国家湿地公园	Mopan Lake National Wetland Park (Jilin)

牟平沁水河口国家湿地公园	Qinshui Estuary National Wetland Park in Mouping (Shandong)
牡丹江沿江国家湿地公园	Mudanjiang Riverside National Wetland Park (Heilongjiang)
木兰松花江国家湿地公园	Songhua River National Wetland Park of Mulan County (Heilongjiang)
木兰围场小滦河国家湿地公园	Xiaoluan River National Wetland Park of Mulan Hunting Ground (Hebei)
牧马河国家湿地公园	Muma River National Wetland Park (Shaanxi)
穆棱雷锋河国家湿地公园	Leifeng River National Wetland Park in Muling (Heilongjiang)
那曲夯错国家湿地公园	Hangcuo Lake National Wetland Park in Nagqu (Tibet)
纳林湖国家湿地公园	Nalin Lake National Wetland Park (Inner Mongolia)
纳溪凤凰湖国家湿地公园	Phoenix Lake National Wetland Park in Naxi (Sichuan)
纳雍大坪箐国家湿地公园	Dapingqing National Wetland Park of Nayong County (Guizhou)
奈曼孟家段国家湿地公园	Mengjiaduan National Wetland Park in Naiman (Inner Mongolia)
南城洪门湖国家湿地公园	Hongmen Lake National Wetland Park of Nancheng County (Jiangxi)
南充升钟湖国家湿地公园	Shengzhong Lake National Wetland Park in Nanchong (Sichuan)
南川黎香湖国家湿地公园	Lixiang Lake National Wetland Park in Nanchuan (Chongqing)
南丹拉希国家湿地公园	Laxi National Wetland Park of Nandan County (Guangxi)
南丰傩湖国家湿地公园	Nuohu Lake National Wetland Parkof Nanfeng County (Jiangxi)
南丰潭湖国家湿地公园	Tanhu Lake National Wetland Park of Nanfeng County (Jiangxi)

南海金沙岛国家湿地公园	Jinsha Island National Wetland Park in Nanhai (Guangdong)
南河国家湿地公园	Nanhe River National Wetland Park (Sichuan)
南京长江新济洲国家湿地公园	Xinjizhou National Wetland Park at Yangtze River in Nanjing (Jiangsu)
南乐马颊河国家湿地公园	Majia River National Wetland Park of Nanle County (Henan)
南丽湖国家湿地公园	Nanli Lake National Wetland Park (Hainan)
南木雅克河国家湿地公园	Yake River National Wetland Park of Nanmu (Inner Mongolia)
南宁大王滩国家湿地公园	Dawang Rapids National Wetland Park in Nanning (Guangxi)
南阳白河国家湿地公园	Baihe River National Wetland Park in Nanyang (Henan)
南漳清凉河国家湿地公园	Qingliang River National Wetland Park of Nanzhang County (Hubei)
南洲国家湿地公园	Nanzhou National Wetland Park (Hu'nan)
内丘鹊山湖国家湿地公园	Queshan Lake National Wetland Park of Neiqiu County (Hebei)
尼勒克喀什河国家湿地公园	Kashi River National Wetland Park of Nilka County (Xinjiang)
尼雅国家湿地公园	Niya National Wetland Park (Xinjiang)
碾子山雅鲁河国家湿地公园	Yalu River National Wetland Park of Nianzi Mountain (Heilongjiang)
宁都梅江国家湿地公园	Meijiang River National Wetland Park of Ningdu County (Jiangxi)
宁强汉水源国家湿地公园	National Wetland Park of Hanshui River Headwaters in Ningqiang (Shaanxi)
宁乡金洲湖国家湿地公园	Jinzhou Lake National Wetland Park of Ningxiang County (Hu'nan)
宁远九嶷河国家湿地公园	Jiuyi River National Wetland Park of Ningyuan County (Hunan)
牛耳河国家湿地公园	Niuer River National Wetland Park (Inner Mongolia)

牛心套保国家湿地公园	Niuxin Taobao National Wetland Park (Jilin)
农安太平池国家湿地公园	Nong'an Taipingchi National Wetland Park (Jilin)
帕米尔高原阿拉尔国家湿地公园	National Wetland Park of Pamir Plateau Alaer (Xinjiang)
盘锦辽河国家湿地公园	Liaohe River National Wetland Park in Panjin (Liaoning)
盘山绕阳湾国家湿地公园	Raoyang Bay National Wetland Park of Panshan County (Liaoning)
蟠龙河国家湿地公园	Panlong River National Wetland Park (Shandong)
沛县安国湖国家湿地公园	Anguo Lake National Wetland Park in Peixian (Jiangsu)
蓬安相如湖国家湿地公园	Xiangru Lake National Wetland Park of Peng'an County (Sichuan)
平昌驷马河国家湿地公园	Sima River National Wetland Park of Pingchang County (Sichuan)
平顶山白龟湖国家湿地公园	Baigui Lake National Wetland Park in Pingdingshan (Henan)
平果芦仙湖国家湿地公园	Luxian Lake National Wetland Park in Pingguo (Guangxi)
平江黄金河国家湿地公园	Huangjin River National Wetland Park of Pingjiang County (Hu'nan)
平利古仙湖国家湿地公园	Guxian Lake National Wetland Park of Pingli County (Shaanxi)
平罗天河湾黄河国家湿地公园	National Wetland Park of Tianhe Bay Yellow River of Pingluo County (Ningxia)
平桥两河口国家湿地公园	Lianghe Estuary National Wetland Park in Pingqiao (Henan)
平塘平舟河国家湿地公园	Pingzhou River National Wetland Park of Pingtang County (Guizhou)
平天湖国家湿地公园	Pingtian Lake National Wetland Park (Anhui)
蒲城卤阳湖国家湿地公园	Luyang Lake National Wetland Park of Pucheng County (Shaanxi)

蒲城洛河国家湿地公园	Luohe River National Wetland Park of Pucheng County (Shaanxi)
濮阳金堤河国家湿地公园	Jindi River National Wetland Park in Puyang (Henan)
浦江浦阳江国家湿地公园	Puyang River National Wetland Park of Pujiang County (Zhejiang)
普洱五湖国家湿地公园	Five Lakes National Wetland Park in Pu'er (Yunnan)
普者黑喀斯特国家湿地公园	Puzhehei Karst National Wetland Park (Yunnan)
七台河桃山湖国家湿地公园	Taoshan Lake National Wetland Park in Qitaihe (Heilongjiang)
七星河国家湿地公园	Qixing River National Wetland Park (Shaanxi)
齐河黄河水乡国家湿地公园	Watery Region National Wetland Park of Yellow River in Qihe (Shandong)
齐齐哈尔江心岛国家湿地公园	River Island National Wetland Park in Qiqihar (Heilongjiang)
齐齐哈尔明星岛国家湿地公园	Mingxing Island National Wetland Park in Qiqihar (Heilongjiang)
祁连黑河源国家湿地公园	National Wetland Park of Heihe River Headwaters in Qilian (Qinghai)
祁阳浯溪国家湿地公园	Wuxi Stream National Wetland Park in Qiyang (Hunan)
綦江通惠河国家湿地公园	Tonghui River National Wetland Park in Qijiang (Chongqing)
蕲春赤龙湖国家湿地公园	Chilong Lake National Wetland Park of Qichun County (Hubei)
千层河国家湿地公园	Qianceng River National Wetland Park (Shaanxi)
千湖国家湿地公园	Qianhu Lake National Wetland Park (Shaanxi)
千龙湖国家湿地公园	Qianlong Lake National Wetland Park (Hu'nan)
千泉湖国家湿地公园	Qianquan Lake National Wetland Park (Shanxi)
千渭之会国家湿地公园	National Wetland Park at the Confluence of Qian-and-Wei Rivers (Shaanxi)

潜山潜水河国家湿地公园	Qianshui River National Wetland Park of Qianshan County (Anhui)
黔西水西柯海国家湿地公园	Shuixikehai Lake National Wetland Park in Qianxi County (Guizhou)
沁河源国家湿地公园	National Wetland Park of Qinhe River Headwaters (Shanxi)
青岛唐岛湾国家湿地公园	Tangdao Bay National Wetland Park in Qingdao (Shandong)
青冈靖河国家湿地公园	Jinghe River National Wetland Park of Qinggang County (Heilongjiang)
青河县乌伦古河国家湿地公园	Ulungur River National Wetland Park of Qinghe County (Xinjiang)
青龙湖国家湿地公园	Qinglong Lake National Wetland Park (Hebei)
青山湖国家湿地公园	Qingshan Lake National Wetland Park (Chongqing)
青铜峡鸟岛国家湿地公园	National Wetland Park of Bronze Gorge Bird Island (Ningxia)
青州弥河国家湿地公园	Mihe River National Wetland Park in Qingzhou (Shandong)
清水河县浑河国家湿地公园	Hunhe River National Wetland Park of Qingshuihe County (Inner Mongolia)
清镇红枫湖国家湿地公园	Hongfeng Lake National Wetland Park in Qingzhen of Wuchuan County (Guizhou)
晴隆光照湖国家湿地公园	Guangzhao Lake National Wetland Park in Qinglong (Guizhou)
邛海国家湿地公园	Qionghai Lake National Wetland Park (Sichuan)
琼湖国家湿地公园	Qionghu Lake National Wetland Park (Hu'nan)
琼结琼果河国家湿地公园	Qiongguo River National Wetland Park of Qiongjie County (Tibet)
秋浦河源国家湿地公园	National Wetland Park of Qiupu River Headwaters (Anhui)
渠县柏水湖国家湿地公园	Baishui Lake National Wetland Park of Quxian County (Sichuan)
衢州乌溪江国家湿地公园	Wuxi River National Wetland Park in Quzhou (Zhejiang)

曲阜孔子湖国家湿地公园	Confucius Lake National Wetland Park in Qufu (Shandong)
曲麻莱德曲源国家湿地公园	Dequyuan National Wetland Park of Qumalai County (Qinghai)
曲松下洛国家湿地公园	Qusong Xialuo National Wetland Park (Tibet)
全南桃江国家湿地公园	Taojiang River National Wetland Park of Quannan County (Jiangxi)
全州天湖国家湿地公园	Tianhu Lake National Wetland Park of Quanzhou County (Guangxi)
饶河乌苏里江国家湿地公园	Wusuli River National Wetland Park of Raohe County (Heilongjiang)
仁寿黑龙滩国家湿地公园	Heilong Beach National Wetland Park of Renshou County (Sichuan)
任县大陆泽国家湿地公园	Dalu Marsh National Wetland Park of Renxian County (Hebei)
日喀则江萨国家湿地公园	Jiangsa National Wetland Park in Xigaze/Shigatse (Tibet)
日照傅疃河口国家湿地公园	Futuan Estuary National Wetland Park in Rizhao (Shandong)
日照两城河口国家湿地公园	Liangcheng Estuary National Wetland Park in Rizhao (Shandong)
日照西湖国家湿地公园	West Lake National Wetland Park in Rizhao (Shandong)
汝州汝河国家湿地公园	Ruhe River National Wetland Park in Ruzhou (Henan)
乳源南水湖国家湿地公园	Nanshui Lake National Wetland Park of Ruyuan County (Guangdong)
瑞金绵江国家湿地公园	Mianjiang National Wetland Park in Ruijin (Jiangxi)
若尔盖国家湿地公园	Ruoergai National Wetland Park (Sichuan)
萨拉乌苏国家湿地公园	Salawusu National Wetland Park (Inner Mongolia)
赛里木湖国家湿地公园	Sailimu Lake National Wetland Park (Xinjiang)
三汊河国家湿地公园	Sancha River National Wetland Park (Anhui)

三清山信江源国家湿地公园	National Wetland Park of Xinjiang River Headwaters at Sanqing Mountain (Jiangxi)
三水云东海国家湿地公园	Yundonghai National Wetland Park in Sanshui (Guangdong)
三亚河国家湿地公园	Sanya River National Wetland Park (Hainan)
三原清峪河国家湿地公园	Qingyu River National Wetland Park of Sanyuan County (Shaanxi)
沙家浜国家湿地公园	Shajiabang National Wetland Park (Jiangsu)
沙湾大渡河国家湿地公园	Dadu River National Wetland Park in Shawan (Sichuan)
沙湾千泉湖国家湿地公园	Qianquan Lake National Wetland Park of Shawan County (Xinjiang)
沙洋潘集湖国家湿地公园	Panji Lake National Wetland Park of Shayang County (Hubei)
莎车叶尔羌国家湿地公园	Yeerqiang National Wetland Park of Shache County (Xinjiang)
单县浮龙湖国家湿地公园	Fulong Lake National Wetland Park of Shanxian County (Shandong)
上犹南湖国家湿地公园	Nanhu Lake National Wetland Park of Shangyou County (Jiangxi)
尚义察汗淖尔国家湿地公园	Chahan Nur National Wetland Park of Shangyi County (Hebei)
尚志蚂蚁河国家湿地公园	Ant River National Wetland Park in Shangzhi (Heilongjiang)
少海国家湿地公园	Shaohai National Wetland Park (Shandong)
邵阳天子湖国家湿地公园	Tianzi Lake National Wetland Park in Shaoyang (Hu'nan)
绍兴鉴湖国家湿地公园	Jianhu Lake National Wetland Park in Shaoxing (Zhejiang)
涉县清漳河国家湿地公园	Qingzhang River National Wetland Park of Shexian County (Hebei)
深圳华侨城国家湿地公园	National Wetland Park of Overseas Chinese Town in Shenzhen (Guangdong)

神农架大九湖国家湿地公园	Dajiu Lake National Wetland Park of Shennongjia (Hubei)
神溪国家湿地公园	Shenxi National Wetland Park (Shanxi)
沈北七星国家湿地公园	Qixing National Wetland Park in Shenbei (Liaoning)
十八站呼玛河国家湿地公园	Huma River National Wetland Park of Shibazhan (Heilongjiang)
十堰黄龙滩国家湿地公园	Huanglong Beach National Wetland Park in Shiyan (Hubei)
十堰泗河国家湿地公园	Sihe River National Wetland Park in Shiyan (Hubei)
十堰郧阳湖国家湿地公园	Yunyang Lake National Wetland Park in Shiyan (Hubei)
石城赣江源国家湿地公园	National Wetland Park of Ganjiang River Headwaters in Shicheng (Jiangxi)
石门仙阳湖国家湿地公园	Xianyang Lake National Wetland Park of Shimen County (Hu'nan)
石屏异龙湖国家湿地公园	Yilong Lake National Wetland Park of Shiping County (Yunnan)
石阡鸳鸯湖国家湿地公园	Yuanyang Lake National Wetland Park of Shiqian County (Guizhou)
石泉汉江莲花古渡国家湿地公园	National Wetland Park of Hanjiang River Lotus Ancient Ferry of Shiquan County (Shaanxi)
石首三菱湖国家湿地公园	Sanling Lake National Wetland Park in Shishou (Hubei)
石柱藤子沟国家湿地公园	Tengzigou National Wetland Park of Shizhu County (Chongqing)
石嘴山星海湖国家湿地公园	Xinghai Lake National Wetland Park in Shizuishan (Ningxia)
寿光滨海国家湿地公园	Coastal National Wetland Park in Shouguang (Shandong)
书院洲国家湿地公园	Shuyuanzhou National Wetland Park (Hu'nan)
疏勒香妃湖国家湿地公园	Xiangfei Lake National Wetland Park of in Shule (Xinjiang)

双龙湖国家湿地公园	Shuanglong Lake National Wetland Park (Shanxi)
双牌日月湖国家湿地公园	Riyue Lake National Wetland Park of Shuangpai County (Hu'nan)
双塔山滦河国家湿地公园	Luanhe River National Wetland Park at Shuangta Mountain (Hebei)
水府庙国家湿地公园	Shuifu Temple National Wetland Park (Hu'nan)
思南白鹭湖国家湿地公园	Bailu Lake National Wetland Park of Sinan County (Guizhou)
四会绥江国家湿地公园	Suijiang River National Wetland Park in Sihui (Guangdong)
四平架树台湖国家湿地公园	Jiashutai Lake National Wetland Park in Siping (Jilin)
泗河源国家湿地公园	National Wetland Park of Sihe River Headwaters (Shandong)
泗县石龙湖国家湿地公园	Shilong Lake National Wetland Park of Sixian County (Anhui)
松潘岷江源国家湿地公园	National Wetland Park of Minjiang River Headwaters in Songpan (Sichuan)
松雅湖国家湿地公园	Songya Lake National Wetland Park (Hu'nan)
松滋洈水国家湿地公园	Weishui National Wetland Park in Songzi (Hubei)
苏州太湖国家湿地公园	Taihu Lake National Wetland Park in Suzhou (Jiangsu)
睢县中原水城国家湿地公园	Zhongyuan Watertown National Wetland Park of Suixian County (Henan)
绥滨月牙湖国家湿地公园	Crescent Lake National Wetland Park of Suibin County (Heilongjiang)
绥宁花园阁国家湿地公园	Huayuange National Wetland Park of Suining County (Hu'nan)
绥阳国家湿地公园	Suiyang National Wetland Park (Heilongjiang)
随县封江口国家湿地公园	Fengjiang Estuary National Wetland Park of Suixian County (Hubei)
随州淮河国家湿地公园	Huaihe River National Wetland Park in Suizhou (Hubei)

遂川五斗江国家湿地公园	Wudou River National Wetland Park of Suichuan County (Jiangxi)
遂宁观音湖国家湿地公园	Guanyin Lake National Wetland Park in Suining (Sichuan)
桫椤湖国家湿地公园	Suoluo (Alsophila) Lake National Wetland Park (Sichuan)
索尔奇国家湿地公园	Suo'erqi National Wetland Park (Inner Mongolia)
塔城五弦河国家湿地公园	Wuxian River National Wetland Park in Tacheng (Xinjiang)
塔河固奇谷国家湿地公园	Guqi Valley National Wetland Park of Tahe County (Heilongjiang)
塔头湖河国家湿地公园	Tatouhu River National Wetland Park (Heilongjiang)
台儿庄运河国家湿地公园	Taierzhuang Canal National Wetland Park (Shandong)
台江翁你河国家湿地公园	Wengni River National Wetland Park of Taijiang County (Guizhou)
台前金水国家湿地公园	Jinshui River National Wetland Park of Taiqian County (Henan)
台山镇海湾红树林国家湿地公园	Haiwan Mangrove National Wetland Park of Taishan (Guangdong)
太白石头河国家湿地公园	Shitou River National Wetland Park of Taibai County (Shaanxi)
太和沙颍河国家湿地公园	Shaying River National Wetland Park of Taihe County (Anhui)
太湖花亭湖国家湿地公园	Huating Lake National Wetland Park of Taihu County (Anhui)
太湖三山岛国家湿地公园	Sanshan Island National Wetland Park in Taihu Lake (Jiangsu)
太平湖国家湿地公园	Taiping Lake National Wetland Park (Anhui)
太阳山国家湿地公园	Taiyangshan National Wetland Park (Ningxia)
泰安汶河国家湿地公园	Wenhe River National Wetland Park in Tai'an (Shandong)
泰湖国家湿地公园	Taihu River National Wetland Park (Heilongjiang)

汤河国家湿地公园	Tanghe River National Wetland Park (Shandong)
汤阴汤河国家湿地公园	Tanghe River National Wetland Park of Tangyin County (Henan)
汤峪龙源国家湿地公园	Tangyu Longyuan National Wetland Park (Shaanxi)
唐河国家湿地公园	Tanghe River National Wetland Park (Henan)
洮河源国家湿地公园	National Wetland Park of Taohe River Headwaters (Qinghai)
洮南四海湖国家湿地公园	Sihai Lake National Wetland Park in Taonan (Jilin)
桃江羞女湖国家湿地公园	Xiunǚ Lake National Wetland Park of Taojiang County (Hu'nan)
桃源沅水国家湿地公园	Yuanshui River National Wetland Park of Taoyuan County (Hu'nan)
特克斯国家湿地公园	Tekes National Wetland Park (Xinjiang)
滕州滨湖国家湿地公园	Lakeside National Wetland Park in Tengzhou (Shandong)
天湖国家湿地公园	Tianhu (Heavenly) Lake National Wetland Park (Ningxia)
天峻布哈河国家湿地公园	Buha River National Wetland Park of Tianjun County (Qinghai)
天门张家湖国家湿地公园	Zhangjia Lake National Wetland Park in Tianmen (Hubei)
天山阿合牙孜国家湿地公园	National Wetland Park of Tianshan Mountain Aheyazi (Xinjiang)
天山北坡头屯河国家湿地公园	Tunhe River National Wetland Park on the North Slope of Tianshan Mountain (Xinjiang)
天台始丰溪国家湿地公园	Shifeng Stream National Wetland Park of Tiantai County (Zhejiang)
天堂湖国家湿地公园	Paradise Lake National Wetland Park (Hubei)
铁岭莲花湖国家湿地公园	Lotus Lake National Wetland Park in Tieling (Liaoning)
通城大溪国家湿地公园	Daxi Stream National Wetland Park of Tongcheng County (Hubei)
通道玉带河国家湿地公园	Yudai River National Wetland Park of Tongdao County (Hunan)

通海杞麓湖国家湿地公园	Qilu Lake National Wetland Park of Tonghai County (Yunnan)
通河二龙潭国家湿地公园	Erlong Lake National Wetland Park of Tonghe County (Heilongjiang)
通化蝲蛄河国家湿地公园	Lagu (Squilla) River National Wetland Park of Tonghua County (Jilin)
通山富水湖国家湿地公园	Fushui Lake National Wetland Park of Tongshan County (Hubei)
同江三江口国家湿地公园	National Wetland Park of Three-River Confluence in Tongjiang (Heilongjiang)
桐城嬉子湖国家湿地公园	Xizi Lake National Wetland Park of Tongcheng County (Anhui)
铜川赵氏河国家湿地公园	Zhaoshi River National Wetland Park in Tongchuan (Shaanxi)
铜梁安居国家湿地公园	Anju National Wetland Park in Tongliang (Chongqing)
潼关黄河国家湿地公园	Yellow River National Wetland Park of Tongguan Pass (Shaanxi)
图里河国家湿地公园	Tuli River National Wetland Park (Inner Mongolia)
吐鲁番艾丁湖国家湿地公园	Aydingkol Lake National Wetland Park in Turpan (Xinjiang)
万安湖国家湿地公园	Wan'an Lake National Wetland Park (Jiangxi)
万绿湖国家湿地公园	Wanlü Lake National Wetland Park (Guangdong)
万年珠溪国家湿地公园	Zhuxi Stream National Wetland Park of Wannian County (Jiangxi)
万山长寿湖国家湿地公园	Changshou Lake National Wetland Park in Wanshan (Guizhou)
汪清嘎呀河国家湿地公园	Gaya River National Wetland Park of Wangqing County (Jilin)
王屋湖国家湿地公园	Wangwu Lake National Wetland Park (Shandong)
望谟北盘江国家湿地公园	National Wetland Park of North Panjiang River in Wangmo (Guizhou)

威海五垒岛湾国家湿地公园	National Wetland Park of Five-Island Bay in Weihai (Shandong)
威宁锁黄仓国家湿地公园	Suohuangcang National Wetland Park of Weining County (Guizhou)
微山湖国家湿地公园	Weishan Lake National Wetland Park (Shandong)
潍坊白浪河国家湿地公园	Bailang River National Wetland Park in Weifang (Shandong)
潍坊禹王国家湿地公园	Yuwang National Wetland Park in Weifang (Shandong)
尉犁罗布淖尔国家湿地公园	Luobunaoer National Wetland Park of Yuli County (Xinjiang)
蔚县壶流河国家湿地公园	Huliu River National Wetland Park of Yuxian County (Hebei)
温泉博尔塔拉河国家湿地公园	Bortala River National Wetland Park of Wenquan County (Xinjiang)
文圣太子河国家湿地公园	Taizi River National Wetland Park in Wensheng (Liaoning)
文县黄林沟国家湿地公园	Huanglin Gully National Wetland Park of Wenxian County (Gansu)
文峪河国家湿地公园	Wenyu River National Wetland Park (Shanxi)
翁源滃江源国家湿地公园	National Wetland Park of Wengjiang River Headwaters of Wengyuan County (Guangdong)
乌海龙游湾国家湿地公园	Longyou Bay National Wetland Park in Wuhai (Inner Mongolia)
乌兰都兰湖国家湿地公园	Dulan Lake National Wetland Park of Ulan County (Qinghai)
乌兰浩特洮儿河国家湿地公园	Tao'er River National Wetland Park in Ulanhot (Inner Mongolia)
乌鲁木齐柴窝堡湖国家湿地公园	Chaiwopu Lake National Wetland Park in Urumqi (Xinjiang)
乌伦古湖国家湿地公园	Ulungur Lake National Wetland Park (Xinjiang)
乌奴耳长寿湖国家湿地公园	Changshou Lake National Wetland Park of Wunu'er (Inner Mongolia)

乌齐里克国家湿地公园	Wuqilik National Wetland Park (Xinjiang)
乌什托什干河国家湿地公园	Taushgan Darya National Wetland Park of Wushi County (Xinjiang)
无锡长广溪国家湿地公园	Changguang Stream National Wetland Park in Wuxi (Jiangsu)
无锡蠡湖国家湿地公园	Lihu Lake National Wetland Park in Wuxi (Jiangsu)
无锡梁鸿国家湿地公园	Lianghong National Wetland Park in Wuxi (Jiangsu)
吴江同里国家湿地公园	Tongli National Wetland Park in Wujiang (Jiangsu)
吴淞炮台湾国家湿地公园	Paotai Bay National Wetland Park of Wusong (Shanghai)
吴忠黄河国家湿地公园	Yellow River National Wetland Park in Wuzhong (Ningxia)
梧州苍海国家湿地公园	Canghai Lake National Wetland Park in Wuzhou (Guangxi)
五峰百溪河国家湿地公园	Baixi River National Wetland Park of Wufeng County (Hubei)
五强溪国家湿地公园	Wuqiang Stream National Wetland Park (Hu'nan)
武汉安山国家湿地公园	Anshan National Wetland Park in Wuhan (Hubei)
武汉东湖国家湿地公园	East Lake National Wetland Park in Wuhan (Hubei)
武汉杜公湖国家湿地公园	Dugong Lake National Wetland Park in Wuhan (Hubei)
武汉后官湖国家湿地公园	Houguan Lake National Wetland Park in Wuhan (Hubei)
武河国家湿地公园	Wuhe River National Wetland Park (Shandong)
武隆芙蓉湖国家湿地公园	Furong Lake National Wetland Park in Wulong (Chongqing)
武平中山河国家湿地公园	Zhongshan River National Wetland Park of Wuping County (Fujian)
武清永定河故道国家湿地公园	Yongding River National Wetland Park in Wuqing (Tianjin)
武山湖国家湿地公园	Wushan Lake National Wetland Park (Hubei)

舞钢石漫滩国家湿地公园	Shiman Beach National Wetland Park in Wugang (Henan)
务川洪渡河国家湿地公园	Hongdu River National Wetland Park (Guizhou)
婺源饶河源国家湿地公园	National Wetland Park of Raohe River Headwaters in Wuyuan (Jiangxi)
西安浐灞国家湿地公园	Chan-Ba Rivers National Wetland Park in Xi'an (Shaanxi)
西安区海浪河国家湿地公园	Hailang River National Wetland Park in Xi'an (Heilongjiang)
西安田峪河国家湿地公园	Tianyu River National Wetland Park in Xi'an (Shaanxi)
西充青龙湖国家湿地公园	Qinglong Lake National Wetland Park of Xichong County (Sichuan)
西宁湟水国家湿地公园	Huangshui River National Wetland Park in Xining (Qinghai)
息县淮河国家湿地公园	Huaihe River National Wetland Park of Xixian County (Henan)
浠水策湖国家湿地公园	Cehu Lake National Wetland Park of Xishui County (Hubei)
淅川丹阳湖国家湿地公园	Danyang Lake National Wetland Park of Xichuan County (Henan)
锡林河国家湿地公园	Xilin River National Wetland Park (Inner Mongolia)
习水东风湖国家湿地公园	Dongfeng Lake National Wetland Park of Xishui County (Guizhou)
峡江玉峡湖国家湿地公园	Yuxia Lake National Wetland Park of Xiajiang County (Jiangxi)
峡山湖国家湿地公园	Xiashan Lake National Wetland Park (Shandong)
下营环秀湖国家湿地公园	Huanxiu Lake National Wetland Park in Xiaying (Tianjin)
夏津九龙口国家湿地公园	Xiajin Jiulongkou National Wetland Park (Shandong)
仙桃沙湖国家湿地公园	Shahu Lake National Wetland Park in Xiantao (Hubei)

咸宁向阳湖国家湿地公园	Xiangyang Lake National Wetland Park in Xianning (Hubei)
香河潮白河大运河国家湿地公园	Grand Canal National Wetland Park at Chaobai River of Xianghe County (Hebei)
湘阴洋沙湖—东湖国家湿地公园	Xiangyin National Wetland Park of Yangsha Lake and East Lake (Hu'nan)
襄城北汝河国家湿地公园	Beiru River National Wetland Park of Xiangcheng County (Henan)
襄阳汉江国家湿地公园	Hanjiang River National Wetland Park in Xiangyang (Hubei)
项城汾泉河国家湿地公园	Fenquan River National Wetland Park in Xiangcheng (Henan)
孝感老观湖国家湿地公园	Laoguan Lake National Wetland Park in Xiaogan (Hubei)
孝感朱湖国家湿地公园	Zhuhu Lake National Wetland Park in Xiaogan (Hubei)
孝河国家湿地公园	Xiaohe River National Wetland Park (Shanxi)
忻城乐滩国家湿地公园	Letan National Wetland Park of Xincheng County (Guangxi)
新丰鲁古河国家湿地公园	Lugu River National Wetland Park of Xinfeng County (Guangdong)
新化龙湾国家湿地公园	Longwan Bay National Wetland Park of Xinhua County (Hu'nan)
新会小鸟天堂国家湿地公园	Bird Paradise National Wetland Park in Xinhui (Guangdong)
新疆生产建设兵团第二师恰拉湖国家湿地公园	Qiala Lake National Wetland Park of the 2nd Division of Xinjiang Production and Construction Corps
新疆生产建设兵团第二师三十七团玉昆仑湖国家湿地公园	Yukunlun Lake National Wetland Park of the 37th Regiment of the 2nd Division of Xinjiang Production and Construction Corps
新疆生产建设兵团第七师胡杨河国家湿地公园	Huyanghe National Wetland Park of the 7th Division of Xinjiang Production and Construction Corps

新疆生产建设兵团第十师丰庆湖国家湿地公园	Fengqing Lake National Wetland Park of the 10th Division of Xinjiang Production and Construction Corps
新疆生产建设兵团第十四师昆玉胡木旦国家湿地公园	Kunyu Humudan National Wetland Park of the 14th Division of Xinjiang Production and Construction Corps
新疆生产建设兵团第四师木扎尔特国家湿地公园	Muzart National Wetland Park of the 4th Division of Xinjiang Production and Construction Corps
新津白鹤滩国家湿地公园	Baihe Beach National Wetland Park of Xinjin County (Sichuan)
新宁夫夷江国家湿地公园	Fuyi River National Wetland Park of Xinning County (Hunan)
新墙河国家湿地公园	Xinqiang River National Wetland Park (Hu'nan)
新青国家湿地公园	Xinqing National Wetland Park (Heilongjiang)
新邵筱溪国家湿地公园	Xiaoxi Stream National Wetland Park of Xinshao County (Hu'nan)
新县香山湖国家湿地公园	Xiangshan Lake National Wetland Park of Xinxian County (Henan)
新盈红树林国家湿地公园	Xinying Mangrove National Wetland Park (Hainan)
兴宾三利湖国家湿地公园	Sanli Lake National Wetland Park in Xingbin (Guangxi)
兴和察尔湖国家湿地公园	Cha'er Lake National Wetland Park of Xinghe County (Inner Mongolia)
兴化里下河国家湿地公园	Lixia River National Wetland Park of Xinghua County (Jiangsu)
兴隆白杨木河国家湿地公园	Poplar River National Wetland Park of Xinglong (Heilongjiang)
兴义万峰国家湿地公园	Wanfeng National Wetland Park in Xingyi (Guizhou)
星湖国家湿地公园	Xinghu Lake National Wetland Park (Guangdong)

休宁横江国家湿地公园	Hengjiang River National Wetland Park of Xiuning County (Anhui)
修河国家湿地公园	Xiuhe River National Wetland Park (Jiangxi)
修河源国家湿地公园	National Wetland Park of Xiuhe River Headwaters (Jiangxi)
修文岩鹰湖国家湿地公园	Yanying Lake National Wetland Park of Xiuwen County (Guizhou)
秀湖国家湿地公园	Xiuhu National Wetland Park (Chongqing)
秀山大溪国家湿地公园	Daxi National Wetland Park of Xiushan County (Chongqing)
徐水河国家湿地公园	Xushui River National Wetland Park (Shaanxi)
徐州潘安湖国家湿地公园	Pan'an Lake National Wetland Park in Xuzhou (Jiangsu)
溆浦思蒙国家湿地公园	Xupu Simeng National Wetland Park (Hu'nan)
宣恩贡水河国家湿地公园	Gongshui River National Wetland Park of Xuan'en County (Hubei)
雪峰湖国家湿地公园	Xuefeng Lake National Wetland Park (Hu'nan)
旬河源国家湿地公园	National Wetland Park of Xunhe River Headwaters (Shaanxi)
旬邑马栏河国家湿地公园	Malan River National Wetland Park of Xunyi County (Shaanxi)
寻乌东江源国家湿地公园	National Wetland Park of Dongjiang River Headwaters in Xunwu (Jiangxi)
雅尼国家湿地公园	Yani National Wetland Park (Tibet)
亚布力红星河国家湿地公园	Hongxing River National Wetland Park of Yabuli (Heilongjiang)
焉耆相思湖国家湿地公园	Xiangsi Lake National Wetland Park of Yanqi County (Xinjiang)
鄢陵鹤鸣湖国家湿地公园	Heming Lake National Wetland Park of Yanling County (Henan)
延安南泥湾国家湿地公园	Nanniwan National Wetland Park in Yan'an (Shaanxi)
沿河乌江国家湿地公园	Wujiang River National Wetland Park of Yanhe County (Guizhou)

盐城大纵湖国家湿地公园	Dazong Lake National Wetland Park in Yancheng (Jiangsu)
扬州宝应湖国家湿地公园	Baoying Lake National Wetland Park in Yangzhou (Jiangsu)
扬州凤凰岛国家湿地公园	Phoenix Island National Wetland Park in Yangzhou (Jiangsu)
阳东寿长河红树林国家湿地公园	Mangrove National Wetland Park by Shouchang River in Yangdong (Guangdong)
阳新莲花湖国家湿地公园	Lotus Lake National Wetland Park of Yangxin County (Hubei)
阳原桑干河国家湿地公园	Sanggan River National Wetland Park of Yangyuan County (Hebei)
药湖国家湿地公园	Yaohu Lake National Wetland Park (Jiangxi)
耀州沮河国家湿地公园	Juhe River National Wetland Park in Yaozhou (Shaanxi)
野鸭湖国家湿地公园	Yeyahu National Wetland Park (Beijing)
叶城宗朗国家湿地公园	Zonglang National Wetland Park of Yecheng County (Xinjiang)
伊川伊河国家湿地公园	Yihe River National Wetland Park of Yichuan County (Henan)
伊春茅兰河口国家湿地公园	National Wetland Park of Maolan Estuary in Yichun (Heilongjiang)
伊犁那拉提国家湿地公园	Ili Nalati National Wetland Park (Xinjiang)
伊犁雅玛图国家湿地公园	Ili Yamatu National Wetland Park (Xinjiang)
伊宁伊犁河国家湿地公园	Ili River National Wetland Park in Yining (Xinjiang)
伊图里河国家湿地公园	Yituli River National Wetland Park (Inner Mongolia)
夷陵圈椅淌国家湿地公园	Quanyitang National Wetland Park in Yiling (Hubei)
沂南汶河国家湿地公园	Wenhe River National Wetland Park of Yinan County (Shandong)
沂沭河国家湿地公园	Yishu River National Wetland Park (Shandong)
沂水国家湿地公园	Yishui National Wetland Park (Shandong)

宜城万洋洲国家湿地公园	Wanyangzhou National Wetland Park in Yicheng (Hubei)
宜都天龙湾国家湿地公园	Tianlong Bay National Wetland Park in Yidu (Hubei)
宜君福地湖国家湿地公园	Fudi Lake National Wetland Park of Yijun County (Shaanxi)
义县大凌河国家湿地公园	Daling River National Wetland Park of Yixian County (Liaoning)
银川国家湿地公园	Yinchuan National Wetland Park (Ningxia)
银川黄河外滩国家湿地公园	National Wetland Park of Yellow River Bund in Yinchuan (Ningxia)
印江车家河国家湿地公园	Chejia River National Wetland Park of Yinjiang County (Guizhou)
英吉沙国家湿地公园	Yingjisha National Wetland Park (Xinjiang)
英山张家咀国家湿地公园	Zhangjiazui National Wetland Park of Yingshan County (Hubei)
鹰潭信江国家湿地公园	Xinjiang River National Wetland Park in Yingtan (Jiangxi)
迎凤湖国家湿地公园	Yingfeng Lake National Wetland Park (Chongqing)
迎龙湖国家湿地公园	Yinglong Lake National Wetland Park (Chongqing)
盈江国家湿地公园	Yingjiang National Wetland Park (Yunnan)
营山清水湖国家湿地公园	Qingshui Lake National Wetland Park of Yingshan County (Sichuan)
颍泉泉水湾国家湿地公园	Quanshui Bay National Wetland Park in Yingquan (Anhui)
颍州西湖国家湿地公园	West Lake National Wetland Park in Yingzhou (Anhui)
永安龙头国家湿地公园	Yong'an Longtou National Wetland Park (Fujian)
永昌北海子国家湿地公园	Beihaizi Lake National Wetland Park of Yongchang County (Gansu)
永春桃溪国家湿地公园	Taoxi Stream National Wetland Park of Yongchun County (Fujian)

永年洼国家湿地公园	Yongnian Marsh National Wetland Park (Hebei)
永寿漆水河国家湿地公园	Qishui River National Wetland Park of Yongshou County (Shaanxi)
永顺猛洞河国家湿地公园	Mengdong River National Wetland Park of Yongshun County (Hunan)
西水河国家湿地公园	Youshui River National Wetland Park (Chongqing)
右玉苍头河国家湿地公园	Cangtou River National Wetland Park of Youyu County (Shanxi)
于田克里雅河国家湿地公园	Keriya River National Wetland Park of Yutian County (Xinjiang)
余庆飞龙湖国家湿地公园	Feilong Lake National Wetland Park of Yuqing County (Guizhou)
榆社漳河源国家湿地公园	yuan National Wetland Park of Zhanghe River Headwaters in Yushe (Shanxi)
虞城周商永运河国家湿地公园	Zhou-Shang-Yong Canal National Wetland Park of Yucheng County (Henan)
禹城徒骇河国家湿地公园	Tuhai River National Wetland Park in Yucheng (Shandong)
禹州颍河国家湿地公园	Yinghe River National Wetland Park in Yuzhou (Henan)
玉环漩门湾国家湿地公园	Xuanmen Bay National Wetland Park in Yuhuan (Zhejiang)
玉屏㵲阳河国家湿地公园	Wuyang River National Wetland Park of Yuping County (Guizhou)
玉树巴塘河国家湿地公园	Batang River National Wetland Park of Yushu County (Qinghai)
玉溪抚仙湖国家湿地公园	Fuxian Lake National Wetland Park in Yuxi (Yunnan)
郁南大河国家湿地公园	Dahe National Wetland Park of Yu'nan County (Guangdong)
远安沮河国家湿地公园	Juhe River National Wetland Park of Yuan'an County (Hubei)
月亮湾国家湿地公园	Moon Bay National Wetland Park (Shandong)
云和梯田国家湿地公园	Yunhe Terrace National Wetland Park (Zhejiang)

云蒙湖国家湿地公园	Yunmeng Lake National Wetland Park (Shandong)
云梦涢水国家湿地公园	Yunshui River National Wetland Park of Yunmeng County (Hubei)
云溪白泥湖国家湿地公园	Baini Lake National Wetland Park in Yunxi (Hunan)
泽库泽曲国家湿地公园	Zequ National Wetland Park of Zeku County (Qinghai)
泽普叶尔羌河国家湿地公园	Ye'erqiang River National Wetland Park of Zepu County (Xinjiang)
泽州丹河国家湿地公园	Zezhou Danhe National Wetland Park (Shanxi)
扎赉特绰尔托欣河国家湿地公园	Chuertuoxin River National Wetland Park of Zalait (Inner Mongolia)
扎兰屯秀水国家湿地公园	Xiushui River National Wetland Park in Zalantun (Inner Mongolia)
沾益西河国家湿地公园	West River National Wetland Park in Zhanyi (Yunnan)
张北黄盖淖国家湿地公园	Huanggainao National Wetland Park in Zhangbei (Hebei)
张掖国家湿地公园	Zhangye National Wetland Park (Gansu)
漳平南洋国家湿地公园	Nanyang National Wetland Park in Zhangping (Fujian)
长子精卫湖国家湿地公园	Jingwei Lake National Wetland Park of Zhangzi County (Shanxi)
昭平桂江国家湿地公园	Guijiang River National Wetland Park of Zhaoping County (Guangxi)
昭苏特克斯河国家湿地公园	National Wetland Park of Zhaosu Tekes River (Xinjiang)
照壁山国家湿地公园	Zhaobi Mountain National Wetland Park (Xinjiang)
肇源莲花湖国家湿地公园	Lotus Lake National Wetland Park of Zhaoyuan County (Heilongjiang)
肇岳山国家湿地公园	Zhaoyue Mountain National Wetland Park (Heilongjiang)

柘城容湖国家湿地公园	Ronghu Lake National Wetland Park of Zhecheng County (Henan)
镇赉环城国家湿地公园	Zhenlai Around-the-Cit National Wetland Park (Jilin)
镇坪曙河源国家湿地公园	Shuheyuan National Wetland Park of Zhenping County (Shaanxi)
镇朔湖国家湿地公园	Zhenshuo Lake National Wetland Park (Ningxia)
正蓝旗上都河国家湿地公园	Shangdu River National Wetland Park of Zhenglan Banner (Inner Mongolia)
正镶白旗骏马湖国家湿地公园	Junma Lake National Wetland Park of Zhengxiang White Banner (Inner Mongolia)
郑州黄河国家湿地公园	Yellow River National Wetland Park in Zhengzhou (Henan)
政和念山国家湿地公园	Nianshan National Wetland Park of Zhenghe County (Fujian)
枝江金湖国家湿地公园	Jinhu Lake National Wetland Park in Zhijiang (Hubei)
中方潕水国家湿地公园	Wushui River National Wetland Park of Zhongfang County (Hunan)
中山翠亨国家湿地公园	Cuiheng National Wetland Park in Zhongshan (Guangdong)
中卫香山湖国家湿地公园	Xiangshan Lake National Wetland Park in Zhongwei (Ningxia)
朱拉河国家湿地公园	Zhula River National Wetland Park (Tibet)
珠海横琴国家湿地公园	Hengqin National Wetland Park in Zhuhai (Guangdong)
诸城潍河国家湿地公园	Weihe River National Wetland Park in Zhucheng (Shandong)
诸暨白塔湖国家湿地公园	Baita Lake National Wetland Parkof Zhuji County (Zhejiang)
竹山圣水湖国家湿地公园	Shengshui Lake National Wetland Park of Zhushan County (Hubei)
竹溪龙湖国家湿地公园	Longhu Lake National Wetland Park of Zhuxi County (Hubei)

涿鹿桑干河国家湿地公园	Sanggan River National Wetland Park of Zhuolu County (Hebei)
资溪九龙湖国家湿地公园	Jiulong Lake National Wetland Park of Zixi County (Jiangxi)
秭归九畹溪国家湿地公园	Jiuwan Stream National Wetland Park of Zigui County (Hubei)
邹城太平国家湿地公园	Taiping National Wetland Park in Zoucheng (Shandong)
遵义乐民河国家湿地公园	Lemin River National Wetland Park in Zunyi (Guizhou)
左权清漳河国家湿地公园	Qingzhang River National Wetland Park of Zuoquan County (Shanxi)